CHILDREN EXPERIENCE LITERATURE

CHILDREN EXPERIENCE LITERATURE

Bernard J. Lonsdale and Helen K. Mackintosh

Random House, New York

First Edition

987654321

Library of Congress Cataloging in Publication Data

Lonsdale, Bernard J
Children experience literature.

Includes bibliographies.
1. Children's literature—History and criticism.
I. Title.
PN1009.A1L55   809'.89282   72-99450
ISBN 0-394-30368-7

Manufactured in the United States of America
by The Kingsport Press, Inc., Kingsport, Tenn.

Designed by Andrea Clark

Cover Sculpture by John Murello

Preface

Children Experience Literature is intended for several audiences: (1) as a textbook in college courses in children's literature, (2) as a source of information for educators involved in curriculum development programs in the field of children's literature, (3) as reference materials in schools and community libraries, and, (4) as an aid to parents in guiding their children's reading.

The authors of *Children Experience Literature* are convinced that literature experiences can make a significant contribution to personality development and the enrichment of children's lives. Through literature children can come to sense their roles in the life of the family, the school, the community, and the world. It is possible for them to grow in understanding the behavior of people and the many relationships people have with their social and physical environments. Through meaningful experiences in literature children begin to become acquainted with the principles underlying democratic living. Educators who are aware of the possibilities through experiences in literature for social and intellectual development give literature an important place in the daily program in the modern elementary school.

Teachers who sense the opportunities for guidance through literature recognize their responsibility as follows, (1) to know children—what they are like at three, at five, at nine, at thirteen years of age; what their reading interests are as they move from one year to the next; what reading skills they have acquired; what their attitudes are toward reading; (2) to know what literature is—what makes a book a good book; what authors and illustrators are contributing to a rich body of literature for boys and girls; how are the stories geared to the needs, interests, and abilities of children; and (3) to sense the proper time and the teachable moment for saying, "Tim, I think you will like this story because—"; and (4) to find ways of measuring the success of the literature program.

Children Experience Literature:

1. Shows the panorama of literature for children—dipping back into the past, calling to mind the classics but concentrating on the present.
2. Encourages teachers to read many children's books of a wide variety of

types with a broad spectrum of interests represented, covering the range of preschool through the elementary school.

3. Presents the principles involved in the selection of good literature for children today, but provides some contrasts with what was appropriate 25, 50, 75, and 100 years ago.
4. Provides many suggestions to teachers, librarians, and parents for making books and reading interesting to children at each stage in their development.
5. Presents *selected* lists of all types of books to which the child should be exposed.
6. Includes many sources of information about books for children, such as *The Horn Book, Bulletin of the Center for Children's Books,* and The Children's Book Council; and professional groups, such as The National Council of Teachers of English and the Association for Childhood Education, International.

The authors hope that *Children Experience Literature* will enrich the backgrounds of students, classroom teachers, librarians, and parents; that it will deepen their sensitivity to the values in literature, and that they will create conditions for children to experience literature in ways that will lead them to grow in appreciation and make literature a source of life-long enjoyment.

The objectives and the purposes stated imply a comprehensive program that involves all the various genre that constitute the content of literature. Background material is given related to each of the genre and extensive bibliographies are included to extend the readers experiences.

We express our deep appreciation to Maxine de Lappe Lonsdale for the extensive research she did related to the manuscript and to J. P. Lonsdale, who gave generously of his time reviewing and suggesting revisions in the manuscript. We would be amiss if we did not express our sincere appreciation to the staffs of the California State Library, the Sacramento County School Library, and the Sacramento City–County Library, who welcomed our use of their facilities and resources.

September 1972

B. J. L.
H. K. M.

Acknowledgments

Grateful acknowledgment is made to the following authors, illustrators, publishers, and agencies for permission to reprint selections from copyrighted material.

APPLETON-CENTURY-CROFTS "Why the Bear Is Stumpy-Tailed" from *Popular Tales from the Norse* by George W. Dasent. By courtesy of Appleton-Century-Crofts, Educational Division, Meredith Corporation.

ATHENEUM "Alligator on the Escalator!" by Eve Merriam. Copyright © 1966 by Eve Merriam. From *Catch a Little Rhyme*. Used by permission of Atheneum Publishers.

THOMAS Y. CROWELL Selection from *Land of the Free* by La Monte Meadowcraft. Copyright © 1961 by Thomas Y. Crowell Company, Publishers. Lines from . . . *And Now Miguel* by Joseph Krumgold. Copyright 1953 by Joseph Krumgold. Used by permission of Thomas Y. Crowell Company, Publishers.

CURTIS-BROWN, INC. "Take off with Books" by Ogden Nash. From *New Book of Knowledge Yearbook*. Copyright © 1968 by Curtis-Brown, Inc.

DODD, MEAD & COMPANY, INC. Lines from "The Table and the Chair." Reprinted by permission of Dodd, Mead & Company, Inc. from *The Complete Nonsense Book* by Edward Lear. Canadian rights for lines from "The Table and the Chair" by Edward Lear from *The Complete Nonsense Book*. For behalf of the Administration of Lady Strachey deceased.

DOUBLEDAY & COMPANY, INC. "Broadway: Twilight" by Tom Prideaux from *On City Streets; an Anthology of Poetry*, edited by Nancy Larrick. Copyright © 1968 by Tom Prideaux. Reprinted by permission of Doubleday & Company, Inc. "The Yak" by Theodore Roethke from *I Am! Says the Lamb*. Copyright 1952 by Theodore Roethke. Reprinted by permission of Doubleday & Company, Inc. "What Is Yellow?" from *Hailstones and Halibut Bones* by Mary O'Neill. Copyright © 1961 by Mary Le Duc O'Neill. Reprinted by permission of Doubleday & Company, Inc. Quotation from *The Door in the Wall* by Marguerite de Angeli. Copyright 1941 by Marguerite de Angeli. Reprinted by permission of Doubleday & Company, Inc.

E. P. DUTTON & CO., INC. "How Strange It Is" from the book *Poems of Earth and Sky* by Claudia Lewis. Text copyright © 1967 by Claudia Lewis. Reprinted by permission of E. P. Dutton & Co., Inc.

FOLLETT PUBLISHING COMPANY "Shell Castles" from *Songs from Around a Toadstool Table* by Rowena Bennett, copyright © 1930, 1937, by Follett Publishing Company. Copyright © 1967 by Rowena Bennett.

VIDA LINDA GUITERMAN "Strickly Germproof" by Arthur Guiterman from *The Laughing Muse.* As published by special permission of Vida Linda Guiterman.

HARCOURT BRACE JOVANOVICH, INC. Extract from *Always the Young Strangers* by Carl Sandburg. Copyright 1952, 1953 by Carl Sandburg. Reprinted by permission of Harcourt Brace Jovanovich. Quotation from *The Borrowers* by Mary Norton. Copyright 1953 by Mary Norton. Reprinted by permission of Harcourt Brace Jovanovich, Inc. "The Last Leaf" from *Windy Morning,* copyright 1953 by Harry Behn. Reprinted by permission of Harcourt Brace Jovanovich, Inc.

HARPER & ROW, PUBLISHERS Quotation from *In the Night Kitchen* by Maurice Sendak. Copyright © 1971 by Maurice Sendak. Reprinted with permission of Harper & Row, Publishers. "The Admiration of Willie" from *Bronzeville Boys and Girls* by Gwendolyn Brooks. Copyright © 1956 by Gwendolyn Brooks Blakely. Reprinted with permission of Harper & Row, Publishers. "Trucks" from *I Go A-Traveling* by James S. Tippett. Copyright © 1929 by Harper & Brothers; renewed 1957 by James S. Tippett. Reprinted with permission of Harper & Row, Publishers. Lines from *Sounder* by William H. Armstrong. Copyright © 1969 by William H. Armstrong. By permission of Harper & Row, Publishers. Quotations from *Where the Wild Things Are* by Maurice Sendak. Copyright © 1964 by Maurice Sendak. By permission of Harper & Row, Publishers.

DAVID HIGHAM ASSOCIATES, LTD. "Poetry" from *Poems for Children.* Copyright 1938 by Eleanor Farjeon. Reprinted by permission of David Higham Associates, Ltd.

HOLT, RINEHART AND WINSTON, INC. Quotation from *Sam, Bangs, and Moonshine* by Evaline Ness. Copyright © 1966 by Evaline Ness. Reprinted by permission of Holt, Rinehart and Winston, Inc. "Wishing" from *Is Somewhere Always Far Away?* by Leland B. Jacobs. Text copyright © 1967 by Leland B. Jacobs. Reprinted by permission of Holt, Rinehart and Winston, Inc. "The Last Word of a Bluebird." From *You Come Too* by Robert Frost. Copyright 1916 by Holt, Rinehart and Winston, Inc. Copyright 1944 by Robert Frost. Reprinted by permission of Holt, Rinehart and Winston, Inc.

HOUGHTON MIFFLIN COMPANY "How Glooskap Found the Summer" from *The Algonquin Legends of New England* by Charles Godfrey Leland. Used by permission of Houghton Mifflin Company. "Dolphins in Blue Water" from *The Complete Poetical Works of Amy Lowell* by Amy Lowell. Used by permission of Houghton Mifflin Company. "Grizzly Bear" from *Children Sing in the Far West* by Mary Austin. Copyright renewed in 1956 by Kenneth M. Chapman and Mary C. Wheelwright. Reprinted by permission of the publisher, Houghton Mifflin Company. "Sea Shell" from *The Complete Poetical*

Works of Amy Lowell by Amy Lowell. Copyright, 1955, by Houghton Mifflin Company. Reprinted by permission of the publisher. Quotation from *The Little Fishes* by Eric Christian Haugaard. Used by permission of Houghton Mifflin Company. Excerpt from *Johnny Tremain* by Esther Forbes. By permission of Houghton Mifflin Company. Quotation from *Sing Down the Moon* by Scott O'Dell. Used by permission of Houghton Mifflin Company.

INDIANA UNIVERSITY PRESS "The Pleiades" and "Porcupine and Beaver" from *Tales of the North American Indians* by Stith Thompson. Copyright © 1969 by Indiana University Press. By permission of Indiana University Press.

ALFRED A. KNOPF, INC. Excerpts from "Cinderella" by Walter de la Mare from *Tales Told Again.* Copyright © 1959 by Alfred A. Knopf, Inc. By permission of Alfred A. Knopf, Inc.

J. B. LIPPINCOTT COMPANY "The Pinwheel's Song" from *The Reason for the Pelican* by John Ciardi. Copyright © 1959 by John Ciardi. Reprinted by permission of J. B. Lippincott Company. Lines from "The Man Who Sang the Sillies." From the book *The Man Who Sang the Sillies* by John Ciardi. Copyright © 1961 by John Ciardi. Reprinted by permission of J. B. Lippincott Company. "Poetry" from *Poems for Children* by Eleanor Farjeon. Copyright 1938 by Eleanor Farjeon; copyright renewed © 1966 by Gervase Farjeon. Reprinted by permission of J. B. Lippincott Company. Excerpt from the book *All Around the Town* by Phyllis McGinley. Copyright, 1948, by Phyllis McGinley. Reprinted by permission of J. B. Lippincott Company.

LITTLE, BROWN AND COMPANY Excerpts from *Invincible Louisa* by Cornelia Meigs. Reprinted by permission of Little, Brown and Company. Quotation from *Favorite Fairy Tales Told in Greece* by Virginia Haviland. Adapted from *Modern Greek Folktales* by Richard McGillivray Dawkins, published by the Clarendon Press, Oxford, England. Copyright © 1970 by Virginia Haviland. Reprinted by permission of Little, Brown and Company. "Crickets." Copyright © 1961, 1962 by David McCord, from *Take Sky* by David McCord. Used by permission of Little, Brown and Company.

LUDLOW MUSIC, INC. THE KANSAS LINE. Collected, adapted and arranged by John A. Lomax and Alan Lomax. TRO Copyright 1938 and renewed 1966 LUDLOW MUSIC, INC. New York, New York. Used by permission.

McGRAW-HILL BOOK COMPANY. Stanza from *ABC* by Edward Lear. Copyright © 1965 by Theodore Besterman. Used with permission of McGraw-Hill Book Company. From *The Child in the Educative Process* by Daniel A. Prescott. Copyright © 1957 by McGraw-Hill Book Company. Used with permission of McGraw-Hill Book Company.

THE MACMILLAN COMPANY From *The Girl Who Sat by the Ashes* by Padraic Colum. Copyright © 1968 by Padraic Colum. Reprinted with permission of The Macmillan Company. Quotation from *Petidoe, the Colormaker* by Glen Dines. Copyright © 1959 by Glen Dines. Reprinted by permission of The Macmillan Company. Quotations from *The Useful Dragon of Sam Ling Toy* by Glen Dines. Copyright © 1956 by Glen Dines. Reprinted by permission of The Macmillan Company. "The Moon's the North Wind's Cooky" and "The Mysterious Cat." Reprinted with permission of The Macmillan

Company from *Collected Poems by Vachel Lindsay.* Copyright 1914 by The Macmillan Company, renewed 1942 by Elizabeth C. Lindsay. "Goody O' Grumpity" by Carol Ryrie Brink from *Poems Old and New,* edited by Helen Ferris. Copyright © 1957 by Carol Ryrie Brink. Used by permission of The Macmillan Company. Lines reprinted with permission of The Macmillan Company from *An American ABC* by Maud and Miska Petersham. Copyright 1941 by Maud Petersham and Miska Petersham, renewed © 1969 by Mrs. Maud Petersham and Miska Fuller Petersham.

THE MACMILLAN COMPANY OF CANADA LTD. Canadian rights for "The Prayer of the Little Ducks" from *Prayers from the Ark* by Carmen Bernos de Gasztold, translated by Rumer Godden. Reprinted by permission of The Macmillan Company of Canada Ltd., and Macmillan & Co. Ltd., London.

MACMILLAN & COMPANY LTD., LONDON Canadian rights for "The Prayer of the Little Ducks" from *Prayers from the Ark* by Carmen Bernos de Gasztold, translated by Rumer Godden. Reprinted by permission of The Macmillan Company of Canada Ltd., and Macmillan & Co. Ltd., London.

WILLIAM MORROW & COMPANY, INC. Line from *Little Eddie* by Carolyn Haywood. Copyright 1947 by Carolyn Haywood. Used by permission of William Morrow & Company, Inc.

PANTHEON BOOKS "Cinderella" and "Hans in Luck" from *Grimm's Fairy Tales,* translated by Margaret Hunt and James Stern. Copyright 1944 by Random House, Inc. Reprinted by permission of Pantheon Books, A Division of Random House, Inc. Lines from "Cinderella" in *Tales Told Again* by Walter de la Mare. Copyright © 1959 by Random House, Inc. Reprinted by permission of Random House, Inc.

PRENTICE-HALL, INC. Lines from *Hush Little Baby* by Aliki. Reprinted by permission of Prentice-Hall, Inc.

PUBLISHERS' WEEKLY Table used with the permission of *Publishers' Weekly* and Mrs. Marguerite Archer.

G. P. PUTNAM'S SONS "The Three Billy-Goats-Gruff" from *Popular Tales from the Norse* by Peter Christen Asbjorsen, trans. by G. W. Dasent. Reprinted by permission of G. P. Putnam's Sons. "The Pancake" from *Chimney Corner Stories* by Veronica Hutchinson. Reprinted by permission of G. P. Putnam's Sons.

RANDOM HOUSE, INC. Lines from *Dr. Seuss's ABC* by Dr. Seuss. Copyright © 1963 by Random House, Inc. Reprinted by permission of Beginner Books Division, Random House, Inc. Lines from *The Story of Babar, The Little Elephant* by Jean De Brunhoff. Copyright 1932, © 1958 by Random House, Inc. Reprinted by permission of Laurent De Brunhoff and Random House, Inc.

CHARLES SCRIBNER'S SONS Quotations from *The Wind in the Willows* by Kenneth Grahame. Copyright 1908; © 1968 by Charles Scribner's Sons. Reprinted by permission of Charles Scribner's Sons. "Zinderfoo" from *A Rumbudgin of Nonsense* by Arnold Spilka. Copyright © 1970 by Arnold Spilka. Reprinted by permission of Charles Scribner's Sons.

SIMON & SCHUSTER, INC. "What's Night to Me" by Sam Gilford and "When I Learned to Whistle" by Gordon Lea from *Miracles,* edited by Richard Lewis. Copyright © 1966 by Richard Lewis. Reprinted by permission

of Simon & Schuster, Inc. "Solomon Grundy" by Frederick Winsor and Marian Parry from *The Space Child's Mother Goose.* Copyright © 1956, 1957, 1958 by Frederick Winsor and Marian Parry. Reprinted by permission of Simon & Schuster, Inc.
SOCIETY OF AUTHORS "Silver" by Walter de la Mare from *The Complete Poems of Walter de la Mare.* Copyright © 1969. By permission of the Literary Trustees of Walter de la Mare and the Society of Authors as their representative.
TEACHERS COLLEGE PRESS Lines reprinted by permission of the publisher from Paul Leicester Ford (ed.), *The New England Primer.* (New York: Teachers College Press, 1962; copyright © 1962 by Teachers College, Columbia University), p. 47.
THE VIKING PRESS, INC. Excerpt from *Daniel Boone* by James Daugherty. Copyright 1939, © 1964 by James Daugherty. Reprinted by permission of The Viking Press, Inc. Quotation from *Fly High, Fly Low* by Don and Lydia Freeman. Copyright © 1957 by Don Freeman. Reprinted by permission of The Viking Press, Inc. Quotation from *Time of Wonder* by Robert McCloskey. Copyright © 1957 by Robert McCloskey. Reprinted by permission of The Viking Press, Inc. "The Prayer of the Little Ducks" from *Prayers from the Ark* by Carmen Bernos de Gasztold, translated by Rumer Godden. Copyright © 1962 by Rumer Godden. Reprinted by permission of The Viking Press, Inc.
FREDERICK WARNE & CO. Quotations from *Johnny Crow's Garden* by L. Leslie Brooke. Reproduced by kind permission of Frederick Warne & Co. Quotations from *Johnny Crow's Party* by L. Leslie Brooke. Reproduced by kind permission of Frederick Warne & Co.
FREDERICK WARNE & CO. LTD. Canadian rights for quotations from *Johnny Crow's Garden* by Leslie Brooke. Reproduced by kind permission of the Estate of L. Leslie Brooke and Frederick Warne & Co. Ltd. Quotations from *Johnny Crow's Party* by L. Leslie Brooke. Reproduced by kind permission of the Estate of L. Leslie Brooke and Frederick Warne & Co. Ltd.
WORLD PUBLISHING COMPANY Lines from *Bruno Munari's ABC* by Bruno Munari. Copyright © 1960 by Bruno Munari. Reprinted by permission of the World Publishing Company.

Grateful acknowledgment is made to the following authors, illustrators, publishers, and agencies for permission to reprint illustrations from copyrighted material.

BOBBS-MERRILL COMPANY, INC. From *The Legend of the Cid* by Robert Goldston. Illustrated by Stephani. Copyright © 1963 by the Bobbs-Merrill Company, Inc. Reprinted by permission of the Bobbs-Merrill Company, Inc.

THE BODLEY HEAD, LTD. Canadian rights for illustration from the book *Beowulf* by Rosemary Sutcliff. Illus. by Charles Keeping. Text copyright © 1962 by Rosemary Sutcliff. Illus. copyright © 1962 by The Bodley Head, Ltd. Reprinted by permission of The Bodley Head, Ltd. Canadian rights for illustration from *Flood Warning* by Paul Berna. Illus. by Charles Keeping. Copyright © 1962 by Random House, Inc. Reprinted by permission of The Bodley Head, Ltd.

THOMAS Y. CROWELL COMPANY From *Korolu, the Singing Bandit* by Barbara K. Walker. Illustration copyright © 1970 by Nickzad Nodjoumi. Reprinted by permission of the publisher, Thomas Y. Crowell Company, Inc., New York.

J. M. DENT AND SONS LTD. From the book *Treasure Island* by Robert Lewis Stevenson. Illus. by S. van Abbé. Text and illus. copyright © 1957 by J. M. Dent and Sons, Ltd. Reprinted by permission of J. M. Dent and Sons Ltd.

DODD, MEAD & COMPANY, INC. *From The Matchlock Gun* by Walter D. Edmonds. Illustrated by Paul Lantz. Reprinted by permission of the publisher, Dodd, Mead & Company, Inc.

DOUBLEDAY & COMPANY, INC. From *Just So Stories* by Rudyard Kipling. Illustrated by Rudyard Kipling. Copyright by Doubleday & Company, Inc. Reprinted by permission of Doubleday & Company, Inc.

E. P. DUTTON & CO., INC. From the book *Beowulf* by Rosemary Sutcliff. Illus. by Charles Keeping. Text copyright © 1962 by Rosemary Sutcliff. Illus. copyright © 1962 by The Bodley Head, Ltd. Published by E. P. Dutton & Co., Inc. and used with their permission. From the book *Treasure Island* by R. L. Stevenson. Illus. by S. Van Abbe. Children's Illustrated Classic. Published by E. P. Dutton & Co., Inc. and used with their permission.

HARCOURT BRACE JOVANOVICH, INC. From *The Borrowers* by Mary Norton, illustrated by Beth and Joe Krush, copyright © 1952, 1953, by Mary Norton. Reproduced by permission of Harcourt Brace Jovanovich, Inc. From *Mary Poppins Comes Back* by P. L. Travers, illustrated by Mary Shepard, copyright 1935, © 1963 by P. L. Travers. Reproduced by permission of Harcourt Brace Jovanovich, Inc.

HARPER & ROW, PUBLISHERS Illustrations by Garth Williams from *Charlotte's Web* by E. B. White. Copyright © 1952 by E. B. White. Reprinted by permission of Harper & Row, Publishers. Illustration by Garth Williams from *The First Four Years* by Laura Ingalls Wilder. Picture Copyright © 1971 by Garth Williams. Reprinted by permission of Harper & Row, Publishers. Illustration by Maurice Sendak from *The Moon Jumpers* by Janice May Udry. Picture Copyright © 1959 by Maurice Sendak. Reprinted by permission of Harper & Row, Publishers.

D. C. HEATH From *Goody Two Shoes* by Oliver Goldsmith. Illustrated by Marion L. Peabody. Copyright © by D. C. Heath and Company. Reprinted by permission of the publishers.

HOLIDAY HOUSE, INC. From *Hawaiian Legends of Tricksters and Riddlers* by Vivian L. Thompson. Illustrated by Vivian L. Thompson. Copyright © 1969 by Holiday House, Inc. All rights reserved. Reprinted by permission of Holiday House, Inc.

HOUGHTON MIFFLIN COMPANY From *The Biggest Bear* by Lynd Ward. Illustrated by Lynd Ward. Copyright © 1952 by Lynd Ward. Reprinted by permission of Houghton Mifflin Company. From *Johnny Tremain* by Esther Forbes. Illustrated by Lynd Ward. Copyright 1943 by Lynd Ward. Reprinted by permission of Houghton Mifflin Company. From *Lyle, Lyle, Crocodile* by Bernard Waber. Illustrated by Bernard Waber. Copyright © 1965 by Bernard Waber. Reprinted by permission of Houghton Mifflin Company. From *The Peterkin Papers* by Lucretia P. Hale. Reprinted by permission of Houghton Mifflin Company.

ALFRED A. KNOPF, INC. From *Amerigo Vespucci* by Nina Brown Baker. Illustrated by Paul Valentino. Copyright © 1959 by Alfred A. Knopf, Inc. Reprinted by permission of Alfred A. Knopf. From *Beauty and the Beast* by Mme. Leprince de Beaumont. Illustrated by Erica Ducornet. Copyright © 1968 by Alfred A. Knopf, Inc. Reprinted by permission of Alfred A. Knopf, Inc. From *Freddy the Detective* by Walter R. Brooks. Illustrated by Kurt Wiesel. Copyright 1932 by Alfred A. Knopf, Inc. Reprinted by permission of Alfred A. Knopf. From *The Greedy Goat* by Emma Brock. Illustrated by Emma Brock. Copyright 1931, renewed © 1959 by Alfred A. Knopf, Inc. Reprinted by permission of Alfred A. Knopf, Inc. From *Insect Summer* by James Kirkup. Illustrated by Naoko Matsubara. Copyright © 1970 by Alfred A. Knopf, Inc. Reprinted by permission of Alfred A. Knopf, Inc. From *John Henry and His Hammer* by Harold W. Felton. Illustrated by Alden A. Watson. Copyright © 1959 by Alfred A. Knopf, Inc. Reprinted by permission of Alfred A. Knopf, Inc. From *Legends of Paul Bunyan* by Harold W. Felton (comp. and ed.). Illustrated by Richard Bennett. Copyright © 1961 by Alfred A. Knopf, Inc. Reprinted by permission of Alfred A. Knopf, Inc. From *Petunia* by Roger Duvoisin. Illustrated by Roger Duvoisin. Copyright © 1950 by Alfred A. Knopf, Inc. Reprinted by permission of Alfred A. Knopf, Inc. From *A Small Piece of Paradise* by Geoffrey Morgan. Illustrated by David Knight. Copyright © 1967 by Alfred A. Knopf, Inc. Reprinted by permission of Alfred A. Knopf, Inc. From *The Smallest Elephant in the World* by Alvin Tresselt. Illustrated by Milton Glaser. Copyright © 1959 by Alfred A. Knopf, Inc. Reprinted by permission of Alfred A. Knopf, Inc. From *The Street Kids* by Herbert Danska. Illustrated by Herbert Danska. Copyright © 1970 by Alfred A. Knopf, Inc. Reprinted by permission of Alfred A. Knopf, Inc. From *Tales Told Again* by Walter de la Mare. Illustrated by Alan Howard. Copyright 1927 by Alfred A. Knopf, Inc. Reprinted by permission of Alfred A. Knopf, Inc. From *A Time for Watching* by Gunilla Norris. Illustrated by Paul Giovanopoulos. Copyright © 1969 by Alfred A. Knopf, Inc. Reprinted by permission of Alfred A. Knopf, Inc. From *Trail to Lone Canyon* by Gus Tavo. Illustrated by Gil Walker. Copyright © 1963 by Alfred A. Knopf, Inc. Reprinted by permission of Alfred A. Knopf, Inc. From *Veronica* by Roger Duvoisin. Illustrated by Roger Duvoisin. Copyright © 1961 by Alfred A. Knopf, Inc. Reprinted by permission of Alfred A. Knopf, Inc.

McGRAW-HILL BOOK COMPANY From *Anatole over Paris* by Eve Titus and Paul Galdone. Copyright © 1961 by Eve Titus and Paul Galdone. Used with permission of McGraw-Hill Book Co.

THE MACMILLAN COMPANY Reprinted with permission of The Macmillan Company from *The Children's Homer: The Adventure of Odysseus and the Tale of Troy* by Padraic Colum (reteller). Illustrated by Willy Pogany. Copyright 1918 by The Macmillan Company, renewed 1946 by Padraic Colum and Willy Pogany. Reprinted with permission of The Macmillan Company from *Gulliver's Travels* by Padraic Colum (reteller). Illustrated by Willy Pogany. Copyright 1917 by The Macmillan Company, renewed 1945 by Padraic Colum and Willy Pogany.

GEORGE MACY COMPANIES, INC. From *The Wind in the Willows* by Kenneth Grahame. Illustrated by Arthur Rackham. Copyright © 1940 by Arthur Rackham. Reprinted by permission of George Macy Companies,

PANTHEON BOOK, A DIVISION OF RANDOM HOUSE, INC. From *A Boy of Old Prague* by Sulamith Ish-Kishor. Illustrated by Ben Shahn. Copyright © 1963 by Random House, Inc. Reprinted by permission of Pantheon Books, A Division of Random House, Inc. From *Drusilla* by Sulamith Ish-Kishor. Illustrated by Thomas Morley. Copyright © 1970 by Random House, Inc. Reprinted by permission of Pantheon Books, A Division of Random House, Inc. From *Flood Warning* by Paul Berna. Illustrated by Charles Keeping. Copyright © 1962 by Random House, Inc. Reprinted by permission of Pantheon Books, A Division of Random House, Inc. From *Flowers of Delight* by Leonard de Vries (ed.). Copyright © 1965 by Random House, Inc. Reprinted by permission of Pantheon Books, A Division of Random House, Inc. From *A Hound, a Bay Horse, and a Turtle Dove* by James Playstead Wood. Illustrated by Douglas Gorsline. Reprinted by permission of Pantheon Books, A Division of Random House, Inc. From *The Leatherstocking Saga* by James Fenimore Cooper, Allan Nevins (ed.). Illustrated by Reginald Marsh. Copyright © 1954 by Random House, Inc. Reprinted by permission of Pantheon Books, A Division of Random House, Inc. From *Oté* by Pura Belpré. Illustrated by Paul Galdone. Copyright © 1969 by Random House, Inc. Reprinted by permission of Pantheon Books, A Division of Random House, Inc. From *The Restless Ghost* by Leon Garfield. Illustrated by Saul Lambert. Copyright © 1969 by Random House, Inc. Reprinted by permission of Pantheon Books, A Division of Random House, Inc. From *The Snow Party* by Beatrice Schenk de Regniers. Illustrated by Beatrice de Schenk Regniers. Copyright © 1959 by Random House, Inc. Reprinted by permission of Pantheon Books, A Division of Random House, Inc. From *The Story of a Bad Boy* by Thomas Aldrich. Illustrated by Reginald Marsh. Reprinted by permission of Pantheon Books, A Division of Random House, Inc. Fron *Vengeance of the Zulu King* by Jenny Seed. Illustrated by Jenny Seed. Copyright © 1971 by Random House,

Inc. Reprinted by permission of Pantheon Books, A Division of Random House, Inc.
G. P. PUTNAM'S SONS Reproduced by permission of G. P. Putnam's Sons from *Little Toot* by Hardie Gramatky. Copyright 1939 by Hardie Gramatky; renewed © 1967 by Hardie Gramatky.
RANDOM HOUSE, INC. From *Aesop's Fables* by Anne Terry White (reteller). Illustrated by Helen Siegl. Copyright © 1964 by Random House, Inc. Reprinted by permission of Random House, Inc. From *Andersen's Fairy Tales* by Rose Dobbs (reteller). Illustrated by Gustav Hjortlund. Copyright © 1959 by Random House, Inc. Reprinted by permission of Random House, Inc. From *The Blue Fairy Book* by Andrew Lang (ed.). Illustrated by Grace Dalles Clarke. Copyright © 1959 by Random House, Inc. Reprinted by permission of Random House, Inc. From *The Complete Works of Lewis Carroll* by Lewis Carroll. Illustrated by John Tenniel. Reprinted by permission of Random House, Inc. From *Ghosts and More Ghosts* by Robert Arthur. Illustrated by Irv Docktor. Copyright © by Random House, Inc. Reprinted by permission of Random House, Inc. From *Mrs. Poggi's Holiday* by Saul Lambert. Illustrated by Saul Lambert. Copyright © by Random House, Inc. Reprinted by permission of Random House, Inc. From *The Story of Babar, The Little Elephant* by Jean de Brunhoff. Illustrated by Jean de Brunhoff. Copyright 1933 by Random House, Inc. Reprinted by permission of Random House, Inc. From *Tino* by Marlene Fanta Shyer. Illustrated by Janet Palmer. Copyright © 1969 by Random House, Inc. Reprinted by permission of Random House, Inc. From *Two If by Sea* by Leonard Everett Fisher. Illustrated by Leonard Everett Fisher. Copyright © 1970 by Random House, Inc. Reprinted by permission of Random House, Inc. From *William Penn* by Hildegard Dolson. Illustrated by Leonard Fisher. Copyright © 1971 by Random House, Inc. Reprinted by permission of Random House, Inc. From *The Wizard of Oz* by L. Frank Baum. Reprinted by permission of Random House, Inc. From *Women of Courage* by Dorothy Nathan. Illustrated by Carolyn Cather. Copyright © 1964 by Random House, Inc. Reprinted by permission of Random House, Inc.
CHARLES SCRIBNER'S SONS From *The Merry Adventures of Robin Hood of Great Reknown in Nottinghamshire* by Howard Pyle. Illustrated by Howard Pyle. Reprinted by permission of Charles Scribner's Sons.
VANGUARD PRESS, INC. From *The 500 Hats of Bartholomew Cubbins* by Dr. Seuss. Illustrated by Dr. Seuss. Reprinted by permission of Vanguard Press, Inc.
THE VIKING PRESS, INC. From *Daniel Boone* by James Daugherty. Copyright 1939, © 1967 by James Daugherty. Reprinted by permission of The Viking Press, Inc. From *Madeline* by Ludwig Bemelmans. Copyright 1939 by Ludwig Bemelmans, renewed © 1967 by Mrs. Madeline Bemelmans and Mrs. Barbara Bemelmans Marciano. Reprinted by permission of The Viking Press. From *Mister Penny* by Marie Hall Ets. Copyright 1935, © 1963 by Marie Hall Ets. Reprinted by permission of The Viking Press, Inc.
HENRY Z. WALCK, INC. From *Little Tim and the Brave Sea Captain* by Edward Ardizzone. Used with permission of Henry Z. Walck, Inc. publishers.

FREDERICK WARNE & CO., LTD. From *Johnny Crow's Party* by L. Leslie Brooke. Illustrated by L. Leslie Brooke. Reproduced by kind permission of the publishers, Frederick Warne & Co., Ltd. From *The Jumblies and Other Nonsense Verse* by Edward Lear. Illustrated by Edward Lear. Reproduced by kind permission of the publishers, Frederick Warne & Co., Ltd. From *The Three Jovial Huntsmen* by Randolph Caldecott. Illustrated by Randolph Caldecott. Reproduced by kind permission of Frederick Warne & Co., Ltd.
ALBERT WHITMAN & COMPANY From *What Mary Jo Wanted* by Janice May Udry. Illustrated by Eleanor Hill. Copyright © 1968 by Albert Whitman & Company. Reprinted by permission of Albert Whitman & Company.

Contents

CHILDREN EXPERIENCE LITERATURE

From *The Complete Works of Lewis Carroll* by Lewis Carroll, illustrated by John Tenniel.

1

Experiencing Literature: listening, reading, sharing, and enjoying

Literature, like other art forms, is a manifestation of man's efforts to interpret, to enjoy, and to enrich his environment. These endeavors give evidence of a creative impulse that seems to be peculiar to human beings. The urge to creativity manifests itself in many ways. One way is through the medium of words. Some individuals recognize the power of words and use them to describe modes of living, to express their feelings about life, and to relate their reactions to their experiences. They are sensitive to life and its numerous dimensions. Their powers of perception, imagination, and control over the use of word symbols make it possible for them to present a meaningful picture of human experiences. They bring to life and make understandable the many ways in which man meets the unlimited opportunities awaiting him.

The writings of those who have succeeded in picturing man in relation to his social and physical world—his joys, hopes, aspirations, successes, and failures—constitute a body of literature made up of stories, poems, plays, essays, letters, biographies, and autobiographies. In its broadest sense, literature is everything that uses words to express ideas. As such, it includes even comic books, advertisements, and instructions on packages.

In a narrower sense, literature should be conceived of as written expression on such a level that it becomes one of the fine arts. It should offer something more than the writing found in a compilation of facts, a list of instructions, or a recipe. A pamphlet on how to hold a baseball bat, how to catch a fly ball, or how to run for home base is very different from a story about a boy who struggles to overcome a physical handicap so that he can earn a place on the school team.

In his superb manner Paul Hazard (4) emphasizes the artistic aspect of literature when he states, "I like books that remain faithful to the very essence of art . . . namely, those books that offer to children an intuitive and direct way of knowledge, a simple beauty capable of being perceived immediately, arousing in their souls a vibration which will endure all their lives" (p. 42).

Literature and Communication

There are two aspects to literary communication: (1) the expressing aspect and (2) the receiving aspect. For literature to be complete the ideas expressed by one individual must be received or taken in by other individuals. This receiving process involves skills, attitudes, and values by which individuals assign meanings to word symbols in order to understand what is written. When the ideas and feelings expressed by those who produce them evoke and release ideas and feelings in those who receive them, literature communicates—there is communion between the one who expresses and the one who receives through the medium of literature.

Manuel Barken in *A Foundation for Art Education* (1) emphasizes this aspect of the arts when he says, "The arts . . . may be viewed as a means of both communion and communication. Viewed as communion, the arts are a way of perceiving and a means for rediscovering things one has taken for granted. As communication, the arts are a form of language and a medium of expression" (p. 6).

Marcia Brown (2) also expresses the communion-communication idea of literature when she says, "A picture book really exists only when a child and a book come together; when the stream that formed in the artist's mind and heart flows through the book and into the mind and heart of the child" (p. 269). This idea could be applied to other types of literature as well.

The Role of Literature

Literature plays an important role in modern education. This role was clearly defined more than fifty years ago by J. F. Hosic in *Reorganization of English in Secondary Schools* (5), when he stated the current views of the objectives in teaching literature to be: to broaden, deepen, and enrich the imaginative life of the student; to arouse an admiration for great personalities, both of authors and of characters in literature; to raise enjoyment in reading to progressively higher levels; and to bring the student wide knowledge of the scope and content of literature.

Twenty years later, Louise M. Rosenblatt prepared a report entitled *Literature As Exploration* (11), in which she claimed that experience with literature is not passive but demands intensive personal activity and is therefore a medium of exploration for the reader; through books the reader may explore himself, other people, or the world. According to Rosenblatt, literature is not merely emotional and aesthetic; it is also intensely human. Therefore, the sciences that describe and explain human conduct can contribute much to the study of literature.

Ten years after the report cited above, Warren Taylor in *Literature and General Education* (13) concluded that literature contributes the following: a sense of the interdependence of men; an imaginative and concrete vivification and increase of what one sees, feels, thinks, and does; a sense of the creative means by which men triumph over destructive changes; and a perspective for judgment and decision.

In 1946 The National Council of Teachers of English set up a national commission to study the place of English in the total curriculum. The first report of this commission, entitled *The English Language Arts* (7), appeared in 1952. In this report the commission emphasized the following points of view as guides to the teaching of literature: The growth of the student in values derived from literature is far more important than his knowledge of certain books and authors; a single narrow curriculum must make way for a wide range of materials and methods to meet a wide range of abilities; individualized reading is strongly advocated, perhaps with some disregard of values gained from group study; various approaches to the organization of literature are tolerable, but the chronological course is frowned upon; wide use of mass media such as magazines, newspapers, radio, television, and movies is encouraged; and the end result sought is to develop values derived from aesthetic understandings and appreciations.

Until recently, experiences in literature appeared to be the prerogative of the secondary school, as evidenced by the large number of studies related to literature in the secondary school in comparison to the limited number related to literature in the elementary school, and by the overwhelming number of studies on reading (rather than literature) in the elementary grades. It seemed as if the elementary school were teaching reading for reading's sake alone.

In recent years more research has been directed toward literature experiences for young readers. These studies have reconfirmed the findings of earlier research regarding literature's role in education. The second publication of the Commission on the Curriculum, National Council of Teachers of English, *Language Arts for Today's Children* (8), states:

All the ferment in the world of children's reading grows from a conviction that books can enrich the lives of boys and girls. First of all, books bring enjoyment . . . Books can give boys and girls the information they need to satisfy their curiosity concerning the world about them . . . Books can expand the child's horizons in time and space . . . Books can help boys and girls understand themselves and others . . . Books of fantasy and invention delight children because of their own active imaginations and offer temporary release from the problems and tensions of real life . . . Finally, through books children relive the spiritual experiences of the human race. [Pp. 147–149]

In the modern school the study of literature is regarded as a means toward enriching life and developing human and aesthetic values; it performs an important role in furthering both the general and specific goals of education. The New York City Board of Education (9) states: "The subject area in the curriculum which deals most obviously with the inner life of man, since it is a direct reflection of that life, is literature" (p. 9).

David H. Russell (12), a well-known authority in the field of children's literature, has described the goals of literature study as follows:

. . . research gives no definite information about the effects of particular types of stories or activities on individual children . . . The teaching of literature, accordingly, is directed toward such goals as the following:

1. The Extension and Enrichment of the Child's Experience of the Complex Ways of Man's Living
2. Giving Opportunity to Relive and Re-experience the Adventures and Ideas of Others
3. Gaining Insight into One's Own Personality and Problems
4. Providing Materials Which Help to Create an Appreciation and Understanding of the Problems of Others
5. The Development of Love of Country and Democratic Ideals
6. The Discovery of Ethical Values Which Are Common to Different Creeds and Which Form a Foundation of Good Character in the Modern World
7. Providing Opportunities for Fun and for Escape
8. The Development of Worthwhile Tastes and Permanent Interests in Good Literature. [Pp. 415–417]

Out of her long experience with books for children, Josette Frank (3) describes goals to be realized through experiences in literature, stating:

. . . We [adults] have more than merely utilitarian reasons for wanting our children to read. We think of reading as one of the great pleasures of life, and we are eager that they [the children] shall not miss this enjoyment . . . books offer more than learning, more than pleasure . . . books serve special needs for boys and girls, unlocking a world of thought and emotion which cannot be reached in any other way. Reading is a close and intimate communication. The child immersed in a book is living with the people in it. He sits in with them, so to speak. They may be people like his own family and friends or they may be a strange sort such as he is not likely to meet face to face. To his great joy, he finds he can revisit them at will whenever he pleases. Thus, the places to which he journeys in a book may become familiar haunts, though they may be places he may never see or live in. Not only the present but the past become living realities. Books bring him the thoughts and feelings of people who lived long ago, or at the ends of the earth. He comes to understand new aspects of human beings and the forces that move them. He sees the world of man and nature in new dimensions through the eyes of great writers. He communes with the great minds of all time. Through books, it may literally be said he inherits the earth. [Pp. 14–15]

Experiencing Literature—Alone and with Others

Today, children have the opportunity to meet and enjoy literature through many different media and in various places. They may listen to stories told at home, at school, at the library, and at many social occasions. The most common source of children's literature is books and magazines. Some boys and girls can find these at home, and all can enjoy them at school. It is a rare supermarket, corner drugstore, bus terminal, or airport waiting room that does not have book racks loaded with a bewildering assortment of books and magazines for children. Literature may be enjoyed by listening to the radio, records, or tape recordings; it may come through headphones plugged into listening posts in a classroom or by way of television. With the varied media of mass communication making literature available, it should be a source of recreation and pleasure for all.

Members of a family frequently enjoy reading stories together in the friendly atmosphere of the home. Sometimes literature is most thoroughly appreciated when one listens with his classmates to a story or a poem being read by the teacher or on a good recording. Libraries often give children the opportunity of hearing a professional storyteller. But many boys and girls prefer to enjoy their books away from other people. A quiet reading room in the library may seem to be the ideal place to get inside a book. Whether they read alone or with others, countless children find that the most fun in reading a story comes from sharing their reactions to literature with the family at home and the friends at school.

Experiencing Vicariously

Children need not have their lives restricted by what they see, taste, touch, hear, and smell. They have a way of seeing that hurdles boundaries; it is the priceless gift of imagination. The vicarious experiences that children have through the various media of communication provide springboards to adventure anywhere imaginable. The quality of the reader's experiences will depend upon the meanings he brings to the reading materials, the nature of the materials, and the situation in which the materials are encountered.

Research has consistently shown that firsthand experiences are the most effective ways of bringing about learning. However, the realities of living limit the extent of one's firsthand experiences. These limitations can be compensated for in some measure through vicarious experiences in literature.

Fred T. Wilhelms in an article in *Educational Leadership* (14) speaks of vicarious experiences and the humanities in the following manner:

> . . . with reasonable fortune a young person may be close to a few adults who can lift him—a parent or relative of rare quality, a great teacher or two, a friend in his church or neighborhood. But even for those who are this fortunate, it is still too little. We simply cannot learn enough from those who happen to be nearby.
>
> Ultimately, to learn humanity at its higher levels, we must all lean heavily upon vicarious contacts, still learning from people, but reaching out to them —to the fine and the great in all times and places—through whatever media will bring us closest. To establish this contact is the function of the humanities.
>
> Interpreted thus, the humanities are not a body of subject matter. They are rather, a way of approach, a set of purposes. Some subject fields, notably literature and music and the arts, have obvious and direct opportunities to serve the purposes. For poems and songs, sculpture and paintings, and the novel and biography and drama have the capacity to move people enormously.

In *Human Development and Learning* (10) Hugh V. Perkins, Jr., writes:

> *Some learnings are enhanced through first-hand, concrete experiences, while others may be achieved as effectively through vicarious experiences.* Children learn most easily and readily those things that relate to their own concrete experiences and thus have personal meaning and significance for them. . . . To depend on first-hand or concrete experiences at all times, however, would be foolish or impossible. The accumulated wisdom of a culture is communicated to succeeding generations through established customs and traditions and through

literature and art forms. Students are able to identify themselves with people, events, and ideas beyond face-to-face contacts, and eventually to show concern for problems larger than those they can solve at first hand, problems they can learn about only through second- and third-hand sources, such as books and mass media. [P. 470]

How far can literature extend and enrich one's life space? Children whose lives are bounded by blocks of blistering concrete and rat-infested alleys, impoverished communities hidden behind magnolia curtains, houses made from makeshift materials salvaged from a dump, can for brief periods of time, at least, enjoy parks with cool grass, water fountains, and shade, highways that lead to faraway places, and homes that resemble castles in Spain. In like manner boys and girls in a middle-class suburb may better understand what it is like to be poor.

There is magic in literature. The experiences to be had through books are limitless. Books can stretch and break boundary lines that often hem in children. Ogden Nash expresses the power of books in his poem, "Take Off with Books" (6):

Take off with books;
Not with the rocket's roar,
Take off in silence
And in fancy soar
At rocket speed
To every land and time
And see, spread out beneath,
Past, present, future
as you higher climb.
Explore those worlds the
rocket cannot reach,
Troy, Camelot, and Crusoe's
lonely beach.
No path forbid, no darkling
secret hid;
Books reached the moon
before real rockets did.

Extending Experiences for the Reader

1. Read *A Foundation for Art Education* by Manuel Barken (1). What parallels can be drawn between literature and the other arts?
2. Read Marcia Brown's "Acceptance Paper, Caldecott Medal Books" (2). What qualities does Marcia Brown's work have that make it outstanding?

3. Read *Books, Children and Men* by Paul Hazard (4). Discuss his philosophy of literature with other teachers. Why is this book considered outstanding by many teachers of children's literature?
4. Interview a number of teachers to find out how extensively they think the guidelines for teaching literature established by the National Council of Teachers of English (7) have been put into practice. The following interview schedule is suggested:
   a. How is evidence of the growth of students' values through the study of literature secured?
   b. What provision is made for the use of a wide range of materials and methods to meet a wide range of reading abilities?
   c. How is provision made for individualized reading as well as group reading?
   d. What different organizational approaches are used?
   e. How do the mass media – magazines, newspapers, radio, television, and motion pictures – influence literature?

Extending Experiences for Children

1. Hold a discussion with four or five classmates on the subject "Why I Like to Read."
2. List several of your favorite books.
3. List some of the boys and girls you have met in books and would like to have for friends.
4. List several books in which people perform courageous actions.
5. Prepare a chart on which to keep a record such as the following:

Story	Author	Setting	Character I Liked Best

Chapter References

1. BARKEN, MANUEL. *A Foundation for Art Education.* New York: The Ronald Press, 1955.
2. BROWN, MARCIA. "Acceptance Paper, Caldecott Medal Books 1938–1957." Boston: The Horn Book.
3. FRANK, JOSETTE. *Your Child's Reading Today.* Rev. ed. Garden City, N. Y.: Doubleday, 1969.
4. HAZARD, PAUL. *Books, Children and Men.* Boston: The Horn Book, 1944.
5. HOSIC, J. F. *Reorganization of English in Secondary Schools.* U. S. Bureau of Education, Bulletin No. 2, Washington, D. C., 1917.
6. NASH, OGDEN. "Take Off with Books," in *New Book of Knowledge Yearbook.* New York: Grolier.
7. NATIONAL COUNCIL OF TEACHERS OF ENGLISH, COMMISSION ON THE ENGLISH CURRICULUM. *The English Language Arts.* N. C. T. E. Curriculum Series. New York: Appleton-Century-Crofts, 1952, Vol. I.
8. ______. *Language Arts for Today's Children.* N. C. T. E. Curriculum Series. New York: Appleton-Century-Crofts, 1954, Vol. II.
9. New York City Board of Education. *Curriculum and Materials,* 15, 3 (Spring 1961).
10. PERKINS, HUGH V., JR. *Human Development and Learning.* Belmont, Calif.: Wadsworth, 1969.
11. ROSENBLATT, LOUISE M. *Literature As Exploration.* New York: Appleton-Century-Crofts, 1938.
12. RUSSELL, DAVID H. *Children Learn to Read.* 2nd ed. Boston: Ginn, 1961.
13. TAYLOR, WARREN. *Literature and General Education.* Washington, D. C.: American Association of University Professors, B32–1946.
14. WILHELMS, FRED T. "The Unexpected Inch—We Learn Humanity from Humanity," *Educational Leadership,* Vol. 20, No. 4. Washington, D. C.: Association for Supervision and Curriculum Development, January 1963.

Further Reading for Teachers, Parents, and Librarians

ARBUTHNOT, MAY HILL. *Children and Books.* 3rd rev. ed. Glenview, Ill.: Scott, Foresman, 1964.

BECHTEL, LOUISE S. *Books in Search of Children.* New York: Macmillan, 1969.

CHILD STUDY ASSOCIATION. *The Children's Bookshelf: A Parents' Guide to Good Books for Boys and Girls.* New York: Bantam, 1965.

EAKIN, MARY K. *Good Books for Children.* Chicago: University of Chicago Press, 1962.

EATON, ANNE T. *Treasure for the Taking.* Rev. ed. New York: Viking, 1957.

EGOFF, SHEILA, *et al.* *Only Connect: Readings on Children's Literature.* New York: Oxford University Press, 1969.

FENNER, PHYLLIS (ed). *Something Shared: Children's Books.* New York: John Day, 1959.

FIELD, ELINOR. *Horn Book Reflections on Children's Books and Reading.* Boston: Horn Book, 1969.

FRANK, JOSETTE. *Your Child's Reading Today.* Rev. ed. New York: Doubleday, 1969.

HAZARD, PAUL. *Books, Children and Men.* Boston: The Horn Book, 1944.

HILDICK, WALLACE. *Children and Fiction. Critical Studies of the Artistic and Psychological Factors Involved in Writing Fiction for and About Children.* Cleveland and New York: World, 1972.

HUCK, CHARLOTTE, AND DORIS YOUNG KUHN. *Children's Literature in the Elementary School.* New York: Holt, Rinehart & Winston, 1968.

KARL, JEAN. *From Childhood to Childhood: Children's Books and Their Creators.* New York: John Day, 1970.

LANES, SELMA. *Down the Rabbit Hole.* New York: Atheneum, 1971.

LARRICK, NANCY. *A Teachers' Guide to Children's Books.* Columbus, Ohio: Merrill, 1960.

———. *A Parent's Guide to Children's Reading.* New York: Doubleday, 1964.

LEPMAN, JELLA. *A Bridge of Children's Books.* Chicago: American Library Association, 1969.

MEIGS, CORNELIA, *et al.* *A Critical History of Children's Literature.* Rev. ed. New York: Macmillan, 1969.

SAYERS, FRANCES CLARKE. *Summoned by Books.* New York: Viking, 1965.

SMITH, DORA V. *Fifty Years of Children's Books.* Champaign, Ill.: National Council of Teachers of English, 1963.

SMITH, LILLIAN H. *The Unreluctant Years: A Critical Approach to Children's Literature.* Chicago: American Library Association, 1953.

TOWNSEND, JOHN ROWE. *A Sense of Story. Essays on Contemporary Writers for Children.* Philadelphia: Lippincott, 1972.

WALSH, FRANCES (ed.). *That Eager Zest: First Discoveries in That Magic World of Books.* Philadelphia: Lippincott, 1961.

From *Gulliver's Travels* by
Jonathan Swift, retold by Padraic Colum,
illustrated by Willy Pogany.

2

Teachers Study Children

The trend in modern education is to plan experiences that will help children meet their physical, social, and intellectual needs. This demands that teachers study child and adolescent behavior. They must also know the individual boys and girls with whom they are working, since individuals mature at different rates physically, socially, and intellectually and each matures at a rate peculiar to himself.

Individuals Are Different but Alike

How is the five-year-old like the eight-year-old? How is he different? Why is one boy shy and retiring while another is bold and aggressive? What makes one teen-ager so antagonistic and his brother so cooperative? Why is one girl's vocabulary so limited at six years of age while another child at the same age speaks like an adult?

Research studies of children's growth over a period of years reveal that there are some similarities in human beings although each child appears to be so different. Most individuals go through the same pattern of growth and development, but each one goes through the different stages at a rate peculiar to himself. Although two infants may start to cut their teeth a full year apart, each one eventually develops a full set of teeth. Frequently boys and girls pass each other in the various areas of growth and development, yet eventually they all reach some degree of maturity with similar needs, interests, and values.

All human beings have basic physical, social, and emotional needs that must be met if they are to maintain and improve their physical and mental health and enjoy wholesome personality development.

The need for food, water, air, rest, and activity affects the behavior of all human beings. The extent or degree to which an individual either satisfies or fails to satisfy these needs is readily apparent. Less obvious, but just as impelling as determinants of behavior, are an individual's social and emotional needs.

What Every Child Needs

Perhaps the most important and all-encompassing need is love. Every child should feel that his parents love, want, and enjoy him. Maurice Sendak emphasizes this need for love in *Where the Wild Things Are* (15). In spite of all the successes the boy Max experiences, Mr. Sendak says, "Then Max the King of all wild things was lonely and wanted to be where someone loved him best of all" (unpaged).

The feeling of acceptance is also essential. Every child needs to believe that his parents like him for himself, just the way he is, and that they like him all the time, not only when he acts according to their ideas of good behavior. He must feel assured that he will be able to grow and develop in his own way.

Security is another necessity for every child. He should know that his home is a safe place and that his parents will always be on hand, especially in times of crisis when he needs them most. Knowing that he belongs to a family and that there is a niche reserved for him makes a child feel secure. This is as true for the child in school in relation to his teacher as it is at home with his parents.

Any descriptions of the characteristics of the growth and development of children are a help to teachers in understanding the behavior of children. Such descriptions indicate the needs that are basic to human beings as well as the situations in which children of different ages most frequently find themselves. They also describe behavior that indicates the extent to which these needs are met or thwarted and suggest problems likely to arise as boys and girls strive to meet their needs. With this background of information, the teacher is able to bring more insights to his observation of children. However, the teacher should know each boy and girl as an individual if he is to know what the individual likes to read, what he hopes to accomplish in reading, and how well he reads.

To guide an individual's reading, the teacher should be familiar with the child's personal likes and dislikes, aspirations, ideals, hobbies, fears, and wishes. To help a child find what he hopes to find in reading, the teacher may also seek to know how much pleasure the individual gets from reading, whether or not he is having undue tensions, what problems he is facing in adjusting to certain physical changes and personal-social relationships, what need he has for emotional escape or redirection of his emotions, and how his emotions are presently being released through motion pictures, television programs, physical activities, or art activities. As teachers grow in their understanding of children and deepen their insights into their needs, interests, and abilities, they begin to see each child as a unique individual, each with a different background of experience and his own set of attitudes and values.

Studies and Stories of Growth Patterns

Numerous scientific studies describe the growth patterns in various areas of development which provide insights into the needs, capacities, and interests of each particular age group. Countless books on psychology furnish a wealth of materials to help teachers learn about boys and girls. Henry W. Maier in *Three Theories of Child Development* (7) describes Erik H. Erikson's psychoanalytic theory, which is the basis of his conception of development; the cognitive theory of Jean Piaget; and the learning theory of Robert R. Sears. John H. Flavell's *The Developmental Psychology of Jean Piaget* (5) is a comprehensive treatment of Piaget's studies and their relation to development. Jerome S. Bruner in *The Process of Education* (1) and other writings, particularly those related to structure, has had an impact on methods and curriculum in recent years. The early writings of Daniel H. Prescott and Erik H. Erikson report research and describe growth and development in terms of the need theory.

In addition to the contributions of scientists and psychologists to the understanding of child growth and development, many novelists have described various stages of their hero's or heroine's development: In *The Bridal Wreath* (22), the first book of the trilogy *Kristin Lavransdatter,* Sigrid Undset describes the growing up of her heroine, Kristin, in medieval days in Norway. *A Tree Grows in Brooklyn* (17) by Betty Smith relates the plight of two children growing up in an impoverished area of Brooklyn. *A Day of Pleasure* (16) by Isaac Bashevis Singer is a collection of stories of a boy growing up in Warsaw. Countless novels, biographies, and autobiographies provide insight into the characteristics of growth and development of boys and girls.

Reading these books will help teachers and parents to understand and interpret the adventures, imaginings, and pretendings of children as well as their wishes, dreams, ambitions, ideals, rebellions, and sensitivities. Misunderstanding these characteristics often creates gaps between children and adults, leaving boys and girls groping for support and security, and leaving adults in a quandary.

Interests as Guides

Authorities in the field of reading and literature are aware of the importance of interests in building skill in reading and appreciation of literature. As interests are satisfied and new interests develop, boys and girls begin to look upon reading as an enjoyable and satisfying experience that can be used to attain knowledge and understanding as well as to entertain.

In the early 1920s, as the focus in curriculum planning shifted to the child, educators began to sense the importance of children's interests in the learning process. A number of studies were made in an effort to discover the interests of children at different age levels. Among the early studies were those by Fannie W. Dunn (4), Lewis M. Terman and Margaret Lima (20), Robert Thorndike (21), and Mary Wollnar (25).

Although these studies and others of the period made no attempt to study the causes of reading interests, they did provide the schools with abundant evidence concerning the choices children exercise in their reading. A common pattern runs through the different studies, and there is general agreement on a number of the factors involved. They reveal, for example, that intelligence is not a particularly significant factor affecting the reading preferences of a majority of children, whereas sex difference is highly significant. The age of the child is of greater importance during the elementary-school years than it is later. Reading preferences are also affected markedly by differences in socioeconomic backgrounds. The response patterns are different in relation to the content of the reading material; elements such as humor, surprise, and suspense-filled plots appeal to most young readers.

Loretta Byers (2) explored the interests of first-grade pupils and discovered that the topics of greatest interest were science and nature, possessions, personal experiences, family and home activity, and outdoor recreation. In analyzing the content of readers, especially at the first-grade level, it was suggested that they include stories about the familiar and near at hand and place more emphasis on science.

Jo M. Stanchfield (19) used personal interviews with 153 boys in grades four, five, and eight. The study confirmed the general findings reported in the earlier studies that were based on questionnaires, check lists, and similar techniques. The most comprehensive studies in terms of numbers were done by G. W. Norvell (8) in which children reacted to specific titles frequently included in school programs. Norvell's work has been particularly helpful in suggesting the particular books that should be made available in the curriculum. Norvell also found that Mother Goose rhymes were liked as late as grade six. Fables and fairy tales were especially interesting to grades three to five. Myths, legends, and folk tales were most popular in grades five to seven.

Bette J. Peltola (11) found that a significantly high number of picture books not in the prize category were chosen over prize books by children in grade one. She also discovered in a study of favorite characters that boys and girls in grade four named more characters from recommended titles than did those in grade six and that characters from realistic stories were preferred to those from fanciful writing. Children who tended to choose the unrecommended books had significantly higher reading achievement scores than others in the study.

In 1968 R. C. Ford and J. Koplyay (6) attempted to measure the story preferences of young children through the use of a nonverbal instrument. Kindergarten and first-grade pupils were asked to circle a picture indicating a story they would most like to read and to cross out the picture illustrating a story they would not like to read. The results, using both middle-class and lower-class children, showed a greater relationship of preferences to age and sex than to socioeconomic background. In describing the study Samuel Weintraub (24) states:

> A useful follow-up to their study would be some type of in-depth interview to note what children were reacting to in the illustrations used. The pictures identified as Negro heritage or children in inner-city environments may have been interpreted as something quite different by the subjects of the study. [P. 657]

Securing Information About Children's Interests

To guide an individual's reading, the teacher must be familiar with the child's personal likes and dislikes, aspirations, ideals, hobbies, fears, and wishes. The most practical interest study for the guidance of a teacher is the one he makes of the individuals with whom he is working by means of conversation with them about the books they are reading and observation of their reactions to stories, their eagerness to share stories they have heard or read, their selection of books on particular subjects, and their use of the school library.

Inventories and Questionnaires

A technique frequently used by teachers as a means of discovering the interests and activities of their pupils is an interest inventory. Illustrative of one type of interest inventory is the following:

TAKING A LOOK AT YOURSELF

A good way to know yourself better is to take a look at yourself—at the things you like to do and the way you feel about yourself and about other people. This is not a test. Number your paper from 1 to 30. After each number write the answer you think is best for each question. You might want to write, "Always," "Sometimes," or "Never." Or, for example, in question number five, you might want to write, "It depends on my partner." Try, if you can, to keep your answers to one word. After you finish, think about your answers. You might like to get together with three or four of your friends and compare your responses; perhaps many of your friends have interests and feelings like yours. You might want to discuss with them the reasons why you feel the way you do.

1. Do you like to be alone?
2. Do you like to be with a particular person most of the time?
3. Do you like to be with friends most of the time?
4. Do you like to go to parties?
5. Do you like to dance?
6. Do you like to read?
7. Do you like to belong to clubs?
8. Do you like to take part in games?
9. Do you like to take trips away from home?
10. Do you ever feel lonely?
11. Do you like clothes?
12. Do you think the other boys and girls in your class like you?
13. Do you like to serve on committees?
14. Do you like to take care of younger children?
15. Do you like to help with work at home?
16. Do you like to work with tools?
17. Do you like to take part in class programs?
18. Do you like to have your friends come to visit you?
19. Do you like to visit your friends?
20. Do you like to attend church?
21. Do you like to make dates with other boys and girls?
22. Do you like to cook?
23. Do you like to select and take care of your own clothes?
24. Do you like to take camping trips?
25. Do you like to sew?
26. Do you work on a hobby?
27. Do you like to talk to older people?
28. Do you like to become acquainted with new boys and girls?
29. Do you ever wish you were somebody else?
30. If you could be another person, who would you like to be?

Inventories will vary depending upon the purposes for which they are planned. Caution needs to be exercised in preparing items for inclusion to avoid embarrassing boys and girls from different socioeconomic groups. Frequently teachers like to get some idea of the recreational interests of their pupils, particularly in relation to reading. Illustrative of a type of questionnaire that might be used to get a picture of broader interests than those related to reading is the following:

LIKES AND DISLIKES

How much time do you spend a week listening to music? ______ hours.
Name your three favorite singers or rock groups.
1. ______. 2. ______. 3. ______.
How much time do you spend a week watching television? ______ hours.
Name your three favorite programs.
1. ______. 2. ______. 3. ______.
How many movies do you see a month? ______.
Name the three school subjects you like best in the order in which you like them.
1. ______. 2. ______. 3. ______.
Name the book you are reading now. ______.
What kind of stories do you like to read? ______.
Of all the books you have read, name the three you like the most.
1. ______. 2. ______. 3. ______.
Tell why you like them.

Other Techniques

As education becomes more individualized, teachers, administrators, and educational consultants use various techniques to secure information as a basis for understanding their students. The information is used as the basis for group and individual guidance. Children's feelings, interests, and attitudes can be elicited in many interesting and different ways. The suggestions that follow have proved to be effective in securing desired information.

Reaction sheets. Use blank, unsigned sheets for pupils to express their feelings about a problem, incident, or mood.

Picture story. Ask pupils to bring a picture, to draw a picture, or to use one already provided as a basis for a story.

Open-ended questions. Ask pupils to finish sentences such as, "I get angry when ______," or "I often worry about ______."

"Things I'd like to know." Ask pupils to hand in a list of topics or questions on which they want information or opinions. Names on papers are optional.

Interest inventory. Develop with pupils a list of possible interests and hobbies or desirable activities; then use the list for a survey, tally, and discussion.

Pro and con session. Discuss opinions for and against a certain problem, practice, or proposal that is significant to the group. A variety of schemes can be used for organizing the discussion, such as panels, a jury, or small discussion groups.

Three wishes. Ask pupils to list, draw, or write about their three greatest wishes.

"Mathematics and me." Ask pupils to write about and to discuss their feelings on arithmetic, music, art, physical education, or other school subjects in order to discover the climate for learning.

Pursuit of happiness. Ask pupils to bring in pictures of happy and unhappy people and to give their feelings about why such people are happy or unhappy.

"Best time I ever had." Ask pupils to write an essay about an exciting occasion.

Autobiography. Have pupils write a story about their lives, including significant influences, people, events, achievements, failures, successes, growth, and feelings. Use this as a basis for discussion.

Child Study and Literature

The fun that youngsters have with nursery and Mother Goose rhymes is soon transferred to stories heard and read. It is not unusual for them to have favorites that they ask to hear over and over again. Telling and reading stories is a ritual in many homes, especially at bedtime. As boys and girls move out of the milieu of the family, they often carry with them a feeling for literature that is nourished by experiences at school. Fortunate are the boy and girl whose teacher and parents have a love and enthusiasm for literature. Children who come from bookless homes where enthusiasm for literature is lacking should be encouraged by the teacher, who can, for example, schedule class visits to the library or suggest that they read to younger brothers and sisters. For such children the teacher holds the capability, and responsibility, of forming a love of books.

The pleasant aura that boys and girls begin to build around books in the early years should be maintained and strengthened. They sense the magic in words and are eager to learn to read so that they can unlock the pleasures waiting for them in books. Carl Sandburg (14) expressed this eagerness beautifully when he said, "I asked my mother to point out those words for me so my eyes would know how spoken words look when fastened down in black on white paper" (p. 59).

Parents, teachers, librarians, and producers of the mass media of communication share the responsibility of giving the guidance and making the kinds of materials available that will build in children an abiding interest in literature. If one is to guide children effectively in the enjoyment of literature to the extent that it becomes a lifelong way of experiencing, one must be aware of the growth patterns of boys and girls at different ages.

Effects of Literature on Development

Research gives little definite information about the effects of particular types of stories or activities on individual children. Because the teacher can never hope to affect positively every child in a class through one type of material or literature experience, he must attempt a varied program in the hope of influencing children with wide individual differences in interests, abilities, and personality adjustments. Some leads as to possible effects of literature on children can be given to guide such a program of varied activities. Literature contributes to an individual's development by:

- Providing opportunities for fun, relaxation, and recreation
- Helping the individual define his role in the home, school, and community
- Helping him to understand the interrelations of people in the society of which he is a part
- Acquainting him with the many ways of life throughout the world
- Helping him gain insight into his own personality problems and extend his understanding of the problems of others
- Developing pride in his cultural heritage
- Helping him develop his own set of values in harmony with those of his society
- Building his sensitivity to beauty and developing a permanent interest in literature

Evidence suggests that children learn what they practice directly, in reading as in other activities. Accordingly, if they are to interpret what they read and to apply their reading to their own problems, self-concepts, or social insights, they must be encouraged in such thinking by their teachers. What little research is available about the effects of reading on young people's lives suggests that this impact depends upon at least three factors: (a) the needs and attitudes of the reader himself, (b) the contents of the materials read, and (c) the circumstances or setting in which the reading takes place.

In much of the reading that goes on in school, the pupil works at the level of literal comprehension—to get the main idea, sequence, or conclusion as stated. In such circumstances his responses are fairly objective and can probably be classified as right, partly right, or wrong. But when the child or adolescent moves into the realm of imaginative literature in a literature lesson or at his leisure, his interpretations may vary much more widely, and the effects of this kind of reading on him are therefore much less predictable.

Despite the individual response to literature, some beginning research gives clues to the possible effects of reading on ideas, attitudes, and behavior. In one group of studies, Nila Banton Smith (18), Samuel Weingarten (23), and David H. Russell (13) had elementary pupils, adolescents, and elementary teachers each write about the effects of reading on their lives. Smith found that 60 percent of the elementary pupils reported changes in their attitudes and 30 percent changes in their concepts and ideas as a result of reading, but only 9 percent of the group indicated changes in behavior. Weingarten's survey of the responses of over 1200 adolescents demonstrated that through reading these young people could attain understanding of themselves, a worthy concept of self, recognition of an ideal person to emulate, understanding of others' motivations, and awareness of others' solutions to their problems. Elementary teachers indicated that in their childhood reading the most frequent effects were identification with character(s), enjoyment of humor and adventure, enrichment of everyday experiences, enjoyment of fantasy stimuli to dramatic play, and added knowledge.

Although the results of these studies may have been influenced by the respondents' desires to give favorable replies to direct questions, the findings show that the effects of reading may be widespread and profound. When the second-grade teacher reads a story to her class or the seventh-grade teacher encourages responses to a play or poem, he may be affecting the fundamental values of young people's lives. The responsibility is enormous. The teacher must realize that there is no guarantee that profound effects will take place, but he must do his best to match children and relevant literature. In a speech at the New York Public Library, Spring 1967, master storyteller Isaac B. Singer, recollecting the long-lasting effect of the stories his mother told, said: "The storyteller doesn't know what he does . . ." (16).

There is no final evidence that any one literature experience will help to satisfy the needs of a particular child. At best the teacher can hope to recognize the predominance of one or more of these needs in the child and then, from his knowledge of available literature, attempt to supply materials that will help to satisfy these needs. With Robin in *The Door in the Wall* (3) by Marguerite De Angeli the teacher may learn "that the measure of success is what one does with what he has" and that "each of us has his place in the world. If we cannot serve in one way there is always another. If we do what we are able, a door always opens to something else" (p. 71).

Extending Experiences for the Reader

1. Compile the data on children's records of their activities on several Saturdays (see "Extending Experiences for Children," No. 3). Analyze the data in terms of the interests of the group and of individuals in the group.
2. Select two boys of the same age to observe over a period of time and compare them according to their energy output, interests, attention span, and personality. What insights is it possible to gain through such observations and comparisons? What other characteristics might be compared?
3. Read and compare one of the early researches and one of the more recent researches on children's interests. What findings are similar, and what findings are different? How might one account for the differences?
4. Analyze the interest inventory, "Taking a Look at Yourself" (p. 21). How might it contribute to one's better understanding of an individual?
5. Keep a record of the techniques you have used in an effort to understand your students.
6. Observe several students for evidence of whether or not their needs are being met. To facilitate this study, secure information about the students observed in relation to:
   a. What they have been working on or trying to do.
   b. What they have been up against.
   c. What their assets are.
   d. What the school has done, and what it could do to bring about the healthiest development of these children.
7. Secure a copy of *A Process for In-School Screening of Children with Emotional Handicaps,* by Eli Bower and Nadine Lambert, Educational Testing Service, Princeton, New Jersey. How practical do you feel this method is for the average teacher? Can you think of other methods for early identification of problems?
8. Summarize and analyze the data from the "Likes and Dislikes" questionnaire. What are the implications from the data for planning the literature program?

Extending Experiences for Children

1. Write a description of your best friend. Tell what it is that you like about him.
2. Write a description of yourself. Tell about the things you like to do.
3. Keep a record by the half hour of your activities on several Saturdays.
4. Keep a record of your height and weight over a definite period of time.
5. Make a list of subjects about which you like to read.
6. Keep a diary of the books you read. Record the author and title of the book and a comment about it.
7. Take the interest inventory, "Taking a Look at Yourself."
8. Fill in the "Likes and Dislikes" questionnaire.
9. Pick two characters from the story you are reading. Make a list of the words that describe the two characters. Discuss the lists with others who have read the same story.
10. Hold a class discussion on "Stories That Make Me Feel Happy—Stories That Make Me Feel Unhappy."

Chapter References

1. BRUNER, JEROME S. *The Process of Education,* Cambridge, Mass.: Harvard University Press, 1960.
2. BYERS, LORETTA. "The Interests of Space-Age First-Graders," *Elementary School Journal,* 64 (1964), 237–241.
3. DE ANGELI, MARGUERITE. *The Door in the Wall.* Garden City, N. Y.: Doubleday, 1949.
4. DUNN, W. FANNIE. *Interest Factors in Primary Reading Materials.* Contributions to Education, No. 113. New York: Teachers College, Columbia University, 1921.
5. FLAVELL, JOHN H. *The Developmental Psychology of Jean Piaget.* Princeton, N. J.: Van Nostrand, 1963.
6. FORD, R. C., AND J. KOPLYAY. "Children's Story Preferences," *The Reading Teacher,* 22 (1968), 233–237.
7. MAIER, HENRY W. *Three Theories of Child Development.* New York: Harper & Row, 1965.
8. NORVELL, G. W. "Wide Individual Reading Compared with the Traditional Plan of Studying Literature," *School Review,* 49 (1941), 603–613.
9. ———. *The Reading Interests of Young People.* Boston: Heath, 1950.
10. ———. *What Boys and Girls Like to Read.* Morristown, N. J.: Silver-Burnett, 1958.

11. PELTOLA, BETTE J. "A Study of Children's Book Choices," *Elementary English,* 40 (1963), 690–695, 702.
12. ———. "A Study of the Indicated Literary Choices and Measured Literary Knowledge of Fourth and Sixth Grade Boys and Girls." Ph.D. dissertation. University of Minnesota, 1965.
13. RUSSELL, DAVID H. "Teachers' Memories and Opinions of Children's Literature," *Elementary English,* 26 (December 1949), 475–482.
14. SANDBURG, CARL. *Always the Young Strangers.* New York: Harcourt Brace Jovanovich, 1952.
15. SENDAK, MAURICE. *Where the Wild Things Are.* New York: Harper & Row, 1963.
16. SINGER, ISAAC BASHEVIS. *A Day of Pleasure.* New York: Farrar, Straus & Giroux, 1969.
17. SMITH, BETTY. *A Tree Grows in Brooklyn.* New York: Harper & Row, 1947.
18. SMITH, NILA BANTON. "Some Effects of Reading on Children," *Elementary English,* 25 (May 1948), 271–278.
19. STANCHFIELD, JO M. "Reading Interests of Eighth Grade Boys," *Reading Teacher,* 16 (1962), 41–44.
20. TERMAN, LEWIS M., AND MARGARET LIMA. *Children's Reading.* New York: Appleton-Century-Crofts, 1935.
21. THORNDIKE, ROBERT L. *Children's Reading Interests.* New York: Appleton-Century-Crofts, 1941.
22. UNDSET, SIGRID. *The Bridal Wreath,* from *Kristin Lavransdatter.* New York: Knopf, 1935.
23. WEINGARTEN, SAMUEL. "Developmental Values in Voluntary Reading," *School Review,* 62 (April 1954), 222–230.
24. WEINTRAUB, SAMUEL. "Children's Reading Interests," *The Reading Teacher,* 22, (April 1969), 657.
25. WOLLNAR, MARY H. *Children's Voluntary Reading as an Expression of Individuality.* New York: Teachers College, Columbia University, 1949.

Further Reading for Parents, Teachers, and Librarians

ALMY, MILLIE. *Ways of Studying Children.* New York: Teachers College, Columbia University: Horace Mann Lincoln Institute of School Experimentation, 1959.

ANDREWS, SIRI (ed.). *The Hewins Lectures, 1947–1962.* Boston: The Horn Book, 1963.

BAYLEY, NANCY. *Correlations of Maternal and Child Behaviors with the Development of Mental Abilities,* data from *The Berkeley Growth Study* by Nancy Bayley and Earl S. Schaefer. Chicago: Child Development Publications, Society for Research in Child Development, 1964.

CHURCH, JOSEPH. *Language and the Study of Reality: A Developmental Psychology of Cognition.* New York: Random House, 1966.

COHEN, DOROTHY H., AND VIRGINIA STERN. *Observing and Recording the Behavior of Young Children.* New York: Teachers College, Columbia University, 1968.

COMBS, ARTHUR W. *Individual Behavior: A Perceptual Approach to Behavior.* New York: Harper & Row, 1959.

CRILE, GEORGE. *A Naturalistic View of Man: The Importance of Early Training in Learning, Living, and the Organization of Society.* Cleveland and New York: World Publishing, 1969.

DAVIS, ALLISON, AND ROBERT HAVINGHURST. *Father of the Man.* Boston: Houghton Mifflin, 1947.

DINKMEYER, DON C. *Child Development: The Emerging Self.* Englewood Cliffs, N. J.: Prentice-Hall, 1965.

EMANS, ROBERT. "What Do Children in the Inner City Like to Read?" *Elementary School Journal,* 69 (December 1968), 118–122 1 B.

ERIKSON, ERIK H. *Childhood and Society.* 2nd ed. New York: Norton, 1963.

ESTVAN, FRANK J., AND ELIZABETH W. ESTVAN. *The Child's World: His Social Perception.* New York: Putnam, 1963.

GESELL, ARNOLD, AND FRANCES L. ILG. *Infant and Child in the Culture of Today.* New York: Harper & Row, 1943.

GINSBERG, HERBERT, AND SYLVIA OPPER. *Piaget's Theory of Intellectual Development: An Introduction.* Englewood Cliffs, N. J.: Prentice-Hall, 1969.

GORDON, IRA J. "New Conceptions of Children's Learning and Development," in *Learning and Mental Health in the School, 1966 Yearbook,* Association for Supervision and Curriculum Development. Washington, D. C.: National Education Association, 1966.

———. *Studying the Child in the School.* New York: Wiley, 1966.

HAVINGHURST, ROBERT J. *Developmental Tasks and Education.* New York: David McKay, 1955.

HOFFMAN, M. L., AND L. N. W. HOFFMAN. *Review of Child Development Research.* New York: Russell Sage Foundation, 1964.

HUUS, HELEN. "Interpreting Research in Children's Literature," in *Children, Books and Reading. Perspectives in Reading.* Newark, Del.: International Reading Association, 1964.

HYMES, JAMES L. *The Children Under Six.* Englewood Cliffs, N. J.: Prentice-Hall, 1963.

JERSILD, ARTHUR T. *Child Psychology.* 6th ed. Englewood Cliffs, N. J.: Prentice-Hall, 1968.

JORDAN, ALICE M. *Children's Classics.* Boston: The Horn Book, 1967.

LANE, HOWARD, AND MARY BEAUCHAMP. *Understanding Human Development.* Englewood Cliffs, N. J.: Prentice-Hall, 1959.

LE SHAN, EDA. *The Conspiracy Against Childhood.* New York: Atheneum, 1967.

MAIER, HENRY WILLIAMS. *Three Theories of Child Development: The Contributions of Erik H. Erikson, Jean Piaget, and Robert S. Sears, and Their Applications.* Rev. ed. New York: Harper & Row, 1969.

PECK, BERNARD, AND DANIEL A. PRESCOTT. "The Program at the Institute for Child Study, the University of Maryland," *Personnel and Guidance Journal,* 37 (October 1958), 115–122.

PERKINS, HUGH V. *Human Development and Learning.* Belmont, Calif.: Wadsworth, 1969.

PRESCOTT, DANIEL A. *Helping Teachers Understand Children.* Washington, D. C.: Commission on Teacher Education, American Council on Education 1945.

———. *The Child in the Education Process.* New York: McGraw-Hill, 1957.

REDL, FRITZ. *Understanding Children's Behavior.* New York: Teachers College, Columbia University, 1949.

ROGER, CARL R. *On Becoming a Person.* Boston: Houghton Mifflin, 1961.

ROHRBERGER, MARY, SAMUEL H. WOODS, JR., AND BERNARD F. DUKORE. *An Introduction to Literature.* New York: Random House, 1968, pp. 3–16.

RUSSELL, DAVID H. *Children's Thinking.* Boston: Ginn, 1956.

WAETJEN, WALTER B. (ed.). *Human Variability and Learning.* Washington, D. C.: Association for Supervision and Curriculum Development, 1961.

WANN, KENNETH D., *et al.* *Fostering Intellectual Development in Young Children.* New York: Teachers College, Columbia University, 1962.

From *The Wizard of Oz* and *The Land of Oz*
by L. Frank Baum

3

Teachers and Books

In addition to understanding children, the teacher must be well acquainted with children's books if he is to help boys and girls to find what they like to read in books that match their reading skills. He will need to know which books treat the subject matter that will satisfy the interests of individual children and which books describe problems that specific children can identify with. He will also need to know the style in which the subject matter is presented, because this determines to a large degree the ease or difficulty of the book.

The main sources to which teachers may go for information about books include both public and private agencies that prepare and distribute, usually at small cost, annotated bibliographies of books for children. The following are a few of the many sources available:

A Bibliography of Books for Children. Rev. ed. Association for Childhood Education International, 3615 Wisconsin Avenue N. W., Washington, D. C. 20016. 1968. An annotated bibliography of over 1,500 books for ages 2–12. Author and title indexed. Reference books section.

Books for Children. 1965–1966, 1966–1967, 1967–1968. American Library Association, 50 E. Huron Street, Chicago, Ill. 60611. Annotated, classified, and indexed bibliographies of books reviewed by the *Booklist and Subscription Books Bulletin* from September through August of the years indicated, ranging from preschool to grade nine.

Children's Books. Compiled by Virginia Haviland and Lois Watt. Supt. of Documents, Government Printing Office, Washington, D. C. 20402. An annual annotated bibliography arranged by subject and age group with reading level indication.

Children's Books for Schools and Libraries: 1968–1969. R. R. Bowker Co., 1180 Avenue of the Americas, New York, N. Y. 10036. 24,000 in-print juveniles arranged by author and title. Many are on recommended lists and are so coded.

Children's Books of the Year. Book Committee of Child Study Association of America. Child Study Association of America, 9 E. 89th Street, New

York, N. Y. 10028. An annual classified annotated bibliography of about 500 selected children's books arranged by ages and subject areas.

These listings give some idea of the subject matter of the books, the quality of the writing, and the reading level within a wide range. They will, however, only keep a teacher informed. To know books well, he will have to read and to evaluate them according to the particular needs of the children he is teaching.

Children's Tastes in Literature

Teachers may receive considerable help in choosing books by asking children what they look for when they read a story. Their answers are extremely enlightening in terms of the criteria boys and girls have evolved. Teachers come to realize that values in reading are of all grades, sizes, and qualities and that the supreme values that enrich life cost effort and are acquired slowly.

Children's comments indicate that they are interested chiefly in subject, plot, and characters. The treatment given these three factors will determine to a large extent the enjoyment boys and girls will receive from a book.

Subjects That Appeal

The subject should satisfy an interest that the reader has or open up a new one. A subject that appeals to one individual may have little or no appeal for another. Some prefer subjects based on the realities of living that face boys and girls in the process of growing up, for example, getting along with other members of the family and friends at school, finding one's self, establishing boy-girl relationships, finding one's place in the community, adjusting to adverse living conditions, participating in sports, enjoying pets, and other subjects within the range of the individual's experience as well as interest.

The realism in children's literature should be fair to life. It should emphasize the values people live by and the challenges these values have made upon them. Especially during adolescence, when boys and girls are having difficulty in establishing values, it seems unfair to heighten their uncertainties by depicting life as a futile struggle.

While some children prefer subjects of a realistic nature, others prefer subjects that appeal to their fancy, such as stories of people living in a pretend land, the exploits of an imaginary hero or heroine, strange adventures in foreign lands, exploration of distant planets, the solving of mysteries and the apprehending of criminals, the invention of time machines, and other subjects of a highly imaginative nature.

The subject should be a wholesome portrayal of life. Stories that excite disgust and depict contemptuous human relationships or stories that incite feelings of despair and futility have little place in children's literature.

Plots That Intrigue

To be satisfying to boys and girls the plot must be sharply defined. It should be built on a platform of action, since it is not what a character thinks, but what he does that interests children. The plot should strike a straight course with as few subplots as possible. With few exceptions, the story should have a hero or heroine who deserves success or good fortune. The hero or heroine should be headed for a clearly outlined goal. The ending must be crucial.

The plot must have allure. The romantic touch may be skillfully handled, but it must be there. For boys and girls the world of fiction is one of higher caliber than the real world. For them it is a world of things as they wish them to be rather than as they are. Even the grim realities of the hardships encountered by the pioneers crossing the country in covered wagons assume an alluring aspect because they are of another time.

One of the elements of the plot that might also be considered is the setting. The setting of a children's story can be anywhere and at any time if the subject is sufficiently simplified. Motion pictures and television have greatly increased the capacities of children to visualize unusual settings but too much descriptive detail of the setting is fatal to their enjoyment of a book. The ideal setting is one that enlarges the individual's mental horizon through a sparing use of detail.

Another element of the plot can be humor. Boys and girls especially enjoy humor of the broad type. They enjoy exaggeration and find the "tall tale" with its Paul Bunyan type of character hilariously funny. They also enjoy an amusing surprise or an unexpected turn of events, particularly if it is brought about by one character's outwitting another. They delight in finding characters in embarrassing situations. Amusing misconceptions such as those found in *The Blind Men and the Elephant* (6) delight them. Such nonsense tales as *The Peterkin Papers* (5) by Lucretia P. Hale, *The Enormous Egg* (1) by Oliver Butterworth, and numerous books by Scott Corbett including *Baseball Trick* (2), *Ever Ride a Dinosaur?* (4), and *Case of the Fugitive Firebug* (3).

If the story is built upon fancy or nonsense, it should keep the spirit throughout—children are quick to sense any infidelity to the spirit of the story.

Individual Choices

If the teacher expects to guide boys and girls into literature that will provide for emotional release and will help them to tighten their hold on reality instead of merely escaping from it, he will have to start by respecting the individual's choice of reading even if it is the exploits of a character in a comic strip. He will have to give such reading matter the same status as that of other books and let the children enjoy it openly. The teacher may use whatever material individuals seem to be enjoying to analyze their needs, capacities, and interests. It is up to the teacher to recommend materials of more permanent value that will lead to compensatory pleasures. By respecting the individual's choice of reading, the teacher takes the first step in gaining respect for his own choices.

Building Attitudes

Children's attitudes toward literature depend to a large extent upon the experiences they have had with it in the past. For many boys and girls reading is an enjoyable experience through which they realize some of their greatest satisfactions. Some are indifferent to it, and others are antagonistic. A number of factors in their backgrounds may contribute to and determine these attitudes. Too many times literature is imposed upon children by teachers who judge its value in terms of adult standards, regardless of the pleasure (or lack of pleasure) it affords the reader; too frequently little cognizance is taken of the individual's needs, capacities, and interests. Many children have had to overintellectualize their emotional experiences. This is apparent by the number and types of reports boys and girls have been required to fill in after reading a book and the ways in which poems are analyzed in detail. Boys and girls have often not been allowed simply to enjoy literature.

These various attitudes of children will influence the procedure that the teacher uses in working with individuals. For those who are already enjoying literature, the teacher may enrich their enjoyment by extending their interests and developing a sense of values by which they can evaluate the books they read. These will be the ultimate aims of the guidance of each individual. For those who are indifferent, the teacher may seek to find the factors underlying this attitude. It is not uncommon to hear a teacher say, "My pupils don't like to read," or "My class doesn't like poetry," yet she has made no effort to find out what past experiences have developed these attitudes.

Building and Reinforcing Reading Skills

The teacher should know how well an individual reads if he is to help him in his enjoyment of reading. One of the convenient tools that teachers use for determining reading abilities is the standardized test, but defining the individual's reading ability in terms of established norms will not be as valuable to the teacher as knowing each student individually.

Many schools emphasize the skills related to comprehension, word analysis, vocabulary meanings, location of materials, organization, and map and graph reading. These skills come into play in most types of reading. In addition there are those skills that are peculiar to the appreciation and enjoyment of literature. Acquisition of the following skills helps boys and girls to achieve breadth and depth of appreciation in literature:

Ability to follow a series of events in a story
Ability to recognize the high points in the plot
Ability to foretell what is going to happen next
Ability to differentiate between reality and fantasy
Ability to appreciate the beauty of words and phrases
Ability to give meaning to a figurative expression
Ability to identify with the characters in the story
Ability to associate situations in the story with one's own experiences
Ability to uncover hidden meanings

The acquisition of these skills can be accomplished only through a balanced reading program along with individual guidance.

Extending Experiences for the Reader

1. Serve on a local book evaluation committee.
2. Read new books to pupils to get their reactions to the stories.

3. Participate in regular meetings of teachers and librarians for the purpose of sharing and evaluating new books as they are published.
4. Help boys and girls evolve guidelines for evaluating a book.
5. Prepare bibliographies on subjects of interest to post on the bulletin board.
6. Arrange a display of book jackets on the bulletin board to attract the attention of boys and girls to certain books.

Extending Experiences for Children

1. Make a list of the subjects that you like to read about the most.
2. Keep a record of the books you read about your favorite subject.
3. Divide into groups on the basis of favorite subjects. Share the stories that have handled those subjects in the most satisfactory and interesting way.
4. Answer the following questions about a story you have read:
   a. What is the setting of the story?
   b. Who is the leading character in the story? What other characters are introduced?
   c. What is the conflict in which the leading character is involved?
   d. How do forces for and against the leading character line up?
   e. As one conflict is resolved, what new conflicts develop?
   f. When is the climax of the story reached?
   g. How does the story come to a satisfactory conclusion?
5. Form a group of children who have read the same story. Discuss the story and analyze it in terms of the seven points above.

Chapter References

1. BUTTERWORTH, OLIVER. *The Enormous Egg.* Boston: Atlantic Monthly Press, Little, Brown, 1956. Grades 4–6.
2. CORBETT, SCOTT. *Baseball Trick.* Boston: Atlantic Monthly Press, Little, Brown, 1965. Grades 4–6.
3. ———. *Case of the Fugitive Firebug.* Boston: Atlantic Monthly Press, Little, Brown, 1969. Grades 4–7.
4. ———. *Ever Ride a Dinosaur?* New York: Holt, Rinehart & Winston, 1969. Grades 4–7.
5. HALE, LUCRETIA. *The Peterkin Papers.* New York: Dover, 1960. Paperback. Grades 5–7.
6. SAXE, JOHN. *The Blind Men and the Elephant.* New York: McGraw-Hill, 1963. Kindergarten–grade 3.

Further Reading for Parents, Teachers, and Librarians

ARBUTHNOT, MAY HILL. *Children and Books.* Chicago: Scott, Foresman, 1964.

GEORGIOU, CONSTANTINE. *Children and Their Literature.* Englewood Cliffs, N.J.: Prentice-Hall, 1969.

HALL, MARY ANNE. *Teaching Reading as a Language Experience.* Columbus, Ohio: Merrill, 1970, Chapter 6.

HAVILAND, VIRGINIA. *Children's Literature: A Guide to Reference Sources.* Washington, D. C.: Library of Congress, 1966.

HUCK, CHARLOTTE S., AND DORIS YOUNG KUHN. *Children's Literature in the Elementary School.* 2nd ed. New York: Holt, Rinehart & Winston, 1968.

HYMES, JAMES. *Before the Child Reads.* Evanston, Ill.: Row, Peterson, 1958.

JACOBS, LELAND (ed.). *Using Literature with Young Children.* New York: Teachers College, Columbia University, 1965.

RUSSELL, DAVID H. *Children Learn to Read.* 2nd ed. Boston: Ginn, 1961, Chapter 13.

SMITH, JAMES STEEL. *A Critical Approach to Children's Literature.* New York: McGraw-Hill, 1967.

SOLOMON, DORIS (comp.). *Best Books for Children.* New York: Bowker, 1969.

TOOSE, RUTH. *Your Children Want to Read: A Guide for Teachers and Parents.* Englewood Cliffs, N.J.: Prentice-Hall, 1957.

WHITEHEAD, ROBERT. *Children's Literature: Strategies of Teaching.* Prentice-Hall, 1968.

From *Vengeance of the Zulu King* by Jenny Seed.

4

Meeting People Through Literature

Children's books keep alive a sense of nationality; but they also keep alive a sense of humanity. They describe their native land lovingly but they also describe faraway lands where unknown brothers live. They understand the essential quality of their own race but each of them is a messenger that goes beyond mountains and rivers, beyond the seas, to the very ends of the earth in search of new friendships. Every country gives and every country receives—innumerable are the exchanges—so that it comes about that in our impressionable years the universal republic of childhood is born. [P. 146]

In the above message, Paul Hazard (60), a man qualified to speak for children and for literature, expresses his conviction that boys and girls can become sensitive to the meaning of the brotherhood of man.

People in Life and in Literature

Literature tells the story of man by re-creating human experiences through the medium of words. It depicts how man relates to his world in his efforts to satisfy his basic needs and desires. As literature unfolds the story of living, the reader is brought into intimate relations with people. It reveals the ways in which human beings in different parts of the world carry on various social functions, such as conserving and improving human and natural resources; communicating ideas; producing, processing, and consuming goods; transporting goods and people; providing education; establishing governments; expressing aesthetic impulses; and participating in recreational activities.

The ways in which people carry on these social functions result in a variety of cultural patterns. As readers meet people engaging in human activities in various settings, they acquire certain knowledge and understanding of the physical environment in which people live, the extent to which scientific methods have affected man's way of living, important events in the story of civilization, and institutions, laws, and customs that men have developed to improve group living. Readers can also learn about events occurring in the world today and the necessity of world interdependence. Literature becomes the vehicle through which children can meet people throughout the world as they strive to maintain and improve their particular society.

Regardless of the differing conditions and circumstances under which men live, there is a thread that binds man to man — his struggle to control his environment and to reap the benefits of good human relations. Stories reveal man in the many facets of his living. The important thing for boys and girls to learn is that people throughout the world are more alike than they are different. Literature makes a significant contribution to the improvement of human relations when it helps boys and girls to attain this understanding.

Literature also makes it possible to live in the past, the present, and the future, to travel to both real and imagined places, and to meet people of every description. With Robinson Crusoe (34) one may carve out an existence on a lonely island, and with Phileas Fogg (133) one may circle the globe in eighty days, meeting people and having exciting adventures. Or one may join Kim (75) and the old lama as the lama searches for the Sacred River of the Arrow and Kim searches for the red bull on a green field.

Differences among children as to their learning objectives are as varied as in other areas of development. However, it is safe to say that most boys and girls are interested in the other people who make up their world; they want to build relations with them and observe the relations people have with each other. Through literature they come to sense that whether a child is living on a South Sea Island, within the Arctic Circle, or on the east side of New York City, he has similar needs and desires. The need for love and belonging and the need to face reality are universal, although the ways these needs are met in one ethnic or culture group may be diametrically opposed to the ways they are met in another. Along with television and travel, reading helps make the world a smaller place for today's children.

In the United States

Ours is a vast country made up of many scenes—crowded cities, farms, deserts, mountains, and prairies—and many cultures. Appreciation of the people who make up the way of life in present-day America may be enriched as understandings are deepened through literature, understandings of such factors as the influence of environment upon ways of living, the likenesses and differences in religious and ethnic groups, and the different values that govern people's behavior.

Among the values characteristic of American culture are the worth and uniqueness of each individual. In spite of hardships and tragedy individuals struggle to maintain their integrity.

The tragedy that often accompanies hardships is reflected in *Sounder* (4), a powerful story told by William H. Armstrong. *Sounder* is the story of a Black sharecropper's family who cherish their relations with each other and of a coon dog named "Sounder" who is "a mixture of Georgia redbone hound and a bulldog" (p. 4). In desperation the father steals food for his hungry family. He is arrested and taken away from home. In his attempt to protect his master, Sounder is shot and badly wounded. With determination but without success, the oldest son searches for his father in jails and chain gangs. On one of his trips the boy meets an elderly schoolmaster who offers to take him in to do chores in return for which he will teach him to read. The boy diligently returns home to help when he is needed. With dignity and courage the boy and his mother face the inevitable: the death of the father, who returns home broken in body and spirit, and the passing of the aged and crippled dog. Making the characters nameless gives universality to the story. Each character stands out as an individual and could be anybody who faces adversity with courage and an indomitable will. The artistry of the writing has a biblical quality. *Sounder* received the Newbery Award in 1970.

Boys and girls live under various conditions in different parts of our country. Some live with poverty, distress, and heartaches, while others live in affluence. The contrasts are often startling, and the reader finds good and bad human relations under both conditions. Through stories about boys and girls living in varied environments, readers may come to appreciate the many problems involved in growing up.

Set in Oklahoma in the 1940s, *Cactus Kevin* (61) by Bessie Holland Heck is a story of eleven-year-old Kevin, whose parents move from Tulsa to the country. The family's early misfortunes on the farm and the boy's adjustment and growth are told with warmth, humor, and understanding.

White Bird (22) by Clyde R. Bulla is a poignant story of a lonely orphaned boy in the 1800s who discovers a new and different world when he leaves his hermitage in an isolated valley to search for his stolen pet, a white crow. Black-and-white illustrations by Leonard Weisgard add to the story.

Twelve-year-old Reuben and his adored grandfather are the characters about whom Alice Christgau's story *Runaway to Glory* (28) revolves. Reuben is considered too young and irresponsible and the grandfather too old and cantankerous to be of any real help on the family's Minnesota farm. However, Reuben and his grandfather prove their courage and ingenuity by outwitting some bank robbers and thus win the respect they earnestly desire. The relationship between the old man and the boy is sympathetically portrayed in a lively, appealing story of a rural Swedish-American family at the turn of the century.

New York City's Chinatown is shown through the eyes of an orphan boy and his friend Mister Chu in Norma Keating's *Mister Chu* (74). The story is rich with warm human relations. Beautiful illustrations complement the descriptions of the celebrations common in Chinatown.

When the Mississippi River overflows its banks, the animals and people who are forced to seek safety on higher ground become the subjects of *Mississippi Possum* (90) by Miska Miles. A possum finds security with a human family living in an army tent. The unusual illustrations portray a family and convey the natural surroundings and the way of life along the Mississippi River.

Impressions of the neighborhoods of New York City are conveyed by the text and illustrations in Anne Rockwell's *Gypsy Girl's Best Shoes* (112). The main character is Maggi, a gypsy girl, and the story tells about her efforts to dance in the red patent leather shoes that her father finds.

A story of gang life in a city, *Durango Street* (14) by Frank Bonham points up the inadequacies of city life for some youths. The breakdown of supportive activities—schooling, stable family life, and communities—in relation to these young people is strongly drawn. The setting is in a Los Angeles area inhabited largely by Blacks. The story is highlighted with dramatic sequences and moments of suspense.

Behind the Magic Line (43) by Betty K. Erwin is an appealing story of eleven-year-old Dozie Western and her Black family. The story opens with Dozie's mother adding another member to an already overcrowded ghetto household. Trouble seems to come with the new baby: Dozie's father disappears, her brother is involved in a robbery, and there is very little money. Finally the luck of the Western family changes. The father returns and with a small amount of money the family leaves for the West Coast, looking forward to better times. The characters are well portrayed as they move through the story.

The Day of the Bear (122) by Nancy Spofford is a perceptive story about a boy's first hunting trip and his sense of values. The excitement of a bear hunt in the cattle lands of central Florida, as well as the hard work and the final opportunity for Andy to do a man's job, makes an exciting story. The dialogue and attitudes of the people of this region are convincingly portrayed.

The Empty Schoolhouse (23) by Natalie Savage Carlson is a story told by Emma, the oldest of three children in a Black family living in a Louisiana parish. Emma has dropped out of school but is proud of her small sister, Lullah, who is very bright. Lullah and her best friend, Oralee, a little white girl, are thrilled at the idea of going to the newly integrated St. Joseph's school together. There is trouble, partly fomented from outside the town, and St. Joseph's is opened without pupils. A new barrier between Oralee and Lullah is ended when Lullah is hurt in a racial incident. The violence makes some of the parents realize the shame of their situation, and most of the St. Joseph's parents—of both races—decide to send their children back to school. This is an honest, timely story with particularly good dialogue.

The problems of Black children who are attending a newly integrated junior high school are well described in *Mary Jane* (123) by Dorothy Sterling. In addition to the usual examples of how fear and ignorance skew judgment, the story is descriptive of the social problems of today. Mary Jane, the heroine, finds herself all alone until she meets Sally, a white girl who is rejected because of her physical underdevelopment. The two girls try to work out a system for friendship, but the climate and traditions of a Southern town block their efforts. The emphasis is on the way Mary Jane faces the realities related to her own potential.

Tino (118) by Marlene F. Shyer is a happy, carefree story built

From *Tino* by Marlene Fanta Shyer, illustrated by Janet Palmer.

around Tino's uncle Benedicto's motto, "Fun first, worry later." The story relates the humorous antics of a small Puerto Rican boy in New York and a chicken he has raised from an egg. Tino's mother and the landlord are not enthusiastic about having a live chicken in an apartment. Tino's dramatic solution to the chicken dilemma makes exciting reading.

When Arnold McWilliams comes home from the hospital after breaking his ankle, he is using old, wooden crutches loaned to him by the hospital. *Where the Good Luck Was* (92) by Osmond Molarsky relates how his chums, black and white, decide that he should have new aluminum crutches. They organize and engage in some enterprising schemes to raise the money. Appealing illustrations and lively dialogue tell much of the story.

Sixteen-year-old David, a Southern Black who moves to a city near Detroit, faces more than the usual problems of adjustment in *North Town* (52) by Lorenz B. Graham. Despite initial difficulties that include an innocent brush with the law and having to take a factory job during his father's illness, David succeeds in making a place for himself at an integrated high school and holds on to his dream of becoming a doctor. Racial and economic discrimination and the diverse attitudes of Northern Blacks and whites are depicted with realism and conviction in this timely story for younger teen-age readers.

The setting of *City Rhythms* (53) by Ann Grifalconi is an interracial neighborhood in the crowded inner city. Jimmy's father tells him that the city has a beat and a rhythm of its own. As Jimmy plays or lies in bed, he thinks about what his father has said. One day Jimmy experiments with a range of sounds made by thumping various objects. Other children join Jimmy, thumping happily away, and Jimmy suddenly realizes that the combination of a thousand sounds is the rhythm of the city.

I Wish I Had an Afro by John Shearer (115) is a documentary-style presentation of a Black family's day-to-day struggle to survive. The story is interestingly told in the form of soliloquies by John, an eleven-year-old boy, and his father and mother.

Advanced readers, particularly boys, will enjoy *The Long Green* (48) by William C. Gault. It is a well-written story of Don Shea, a quick-tempered, defensive, Mexican-American boy, from the time he begins to work on the driving range at the age of thirteen, through his amateur competition in high school and college, to his first year on the golf tournament trail. Don's character development makes interesting reading.

Advanced readers will find *Berries Goodman* (95) by Emily Neville an interesting and stimulating story. At sixteen years of age, Berries Goodman looks back to his ninth year when his family moved from a

New York City apartment to a house in a suburb, and Berries came face-to-face with anti-Semitism as it affected his relationship with his best friend, Sidney Fine, the only Jewish boy in Berries' new school. The theme of anti-Semitism is handled with an honesty and understanding seldom found in books for children. Events in the story are described with clarity, humor, and unusual perception.

The popular theme of finding a place of one's own is sympathetically told in *A Quiet Place* (12) by Rose Blue. Matthew, a foster child, longs for a permanent home. Life for him has been a constant change of people and places. Just when he derives some comfort from a large yellow chair in the local library, the library is replaced by a bookmobile. How Matthew finally finds a place of his own makes an appealing story.

It is not always easy for an Indian boy who has lived on a reservation to adjust to living in a city. *Indian Hill* (21) by Clyde R. Bulla is a warm and understanding story of a Navajo boy's adjustment. The boy's father wants to make life easier for his family by working as a carpenter in the city. The boy and his mother refuse to see the good things about the new ways of living and want only to return to the reservation. The boy finally understands the selfishness of this attitude and helps his mother to see it too. The author brings out in a believable style the gentle characteristics of these people.

When two orphaned Puerto Rican children in New York are threatened by welfare, they manage to survive all summer on their own by setting up housekeeping on the top floor of a partially abandoned building. Tomas, the eleven-year-old brother, provides for his older sister in Charlene J. Talbot's *Tomas Takes Charge* (127), a moving story.

In the Fiftieth State

After their farm is destroyed by lava from Kilauea Iki, Moke Moore and his family move to the Kona coast on the island of Hawaii to start a new life. *Pacific Blue* (86) by Steve Lomas tells how Moke had always longed to become part of the famous Kona fishing fleet but to his disappointment he was considered a "Joner" and was unable to find a berth on any of the boats. Moke's courage and determination lead to an unusual solution and a suspenseful story.

Lani, a young girl who lives in a quaint Hawaiian village, dreams of hearing about faraway places. As she meets incoming planes and supplies leis for the passengers, she hopes to find someone who can tell her about his travels. She befriends a girl about her own age who has always traveled with her father and mother and has never had a chance to stay in one place and make friends. How the friendship of these girls opens new horizons for them and provides a solution for both of their wishes offers entertaining reading in *Faraway Friends* (128) by Vivian L. Thompson.

In Canada, Iceland, Lapland, and Greenland

O Canada! (6) by Isabel Barclay brings Canada's exciting past to life with a fast-moving text tracing the development of the country from the life of its earliest settlers to its present status as a prosperous nation. The delightful color pictures tell the story of the coming of the white man, the conflicts among nations that resulted, the pioneering spirit of the explorers and early settlers, and the gradual settlement of Canada from the Atlantic to the Pacific.

Information about the Lapp culture is woven into Ingrid Pelletier's well-written story *Daughter of Lapland* (102). Ingre revisits the strange land where her father had drowned on the annual Lapp trek to the coast when she was very young. Ingre enjoys her vacation until she learns she will be going on the annual migration. She is horrified at the start but soon learns that she can cope with difficulties and responsibilities.

Boys who like outdoor adventure will revel in *Windigo* (3) by Jane and Paul Annixter. When his father dies Andy Cameron is left with the responsibility of running a trap line in the French Canadian woods. With the help of his Indian dog Chinook, Andy solves the mystery of what was robbing his traps and in so doing unexpectedly takes on a partner who teaches him a great deal about the fur industry.

Ice Falcon (108) by Rita Richie is an exciting adventure story taking place during the Viking age. Kurt, son of a lord's falconer in Saxony, journeys to the far north searching for a priceless white gyrfalcon that can be found only around Iceland. Kurt, whose family has been Christianized in Europe, has to make his hazardous way among the Norsemen who still worship the old gods of fire and thunder and believe in blood feuds. Advanced readers will enjoy the suspense in the story.

A fast-moving, interesting story, *Horned Helmet* (129) by Henry Treece is set at the beginning of the eleventh century. The plot revolves around an orphaned Icelandic boy who ships with a Viking crew. The writing style has strength, vitality, and simplicity that is particularly suitable for the historical period and the Viking theme.

Wild Swans at Suvanto (71) by Alan C. Jenkins depicts the customs and severity of life in Lapland. In the rugged life of the Laplanders, the coming of the wild swans announces the return of summer after eight months of dark and bitter winter. Fifteen-year-old Jouni finds himself in a difficult situation when Marjatta, the girl he wants to marry, requires him to kill one of the wild birds for her. The black-and-white drawings reflect the landscape of the story.

Tony Palazzo's *Jan and the Reindeer* (98) is built around Jan, a Lapp boy, and his pet, White Reindeer. How the reindeer herds in Lapland move with the food supply and how the Lapps depend upon the reindeer for their living provide a vivid picture of life in Lapland. The beautiful illustrations by the author add to the enjoyment of the story.

Translated from the Swedish by Annabelle MacMillan, *Children of the North Pole* (62) by Ralph Herrmann brings intimate glimpses of the way of life of the Eskimos of Greenland through color photographs with little text. During the brief summer months in Greenland, the food must be gathered to last through the long dark winter, but this summer Serkok's father is recovering from an injury and cannot hunt. The experiences of Serkok and his sister in trying to help their family and their concern for each other and for the family reflect the author's firsthand experience with the Eskimo people.

In Mexico and the Caribbean

In a setting in rural Mexico, Ester Wier depicts the home, food, clothing, religion, aspirations, work, and close family relationships of a father, mother, a seven-year-old blind girl, and her thirteen-year-old brother in *Gift of the Mountains* (136). The "gift of the mountains" is a long-buried treasure that the boy discovers on one of his wood-gathering trips to the mountains. How the treasure is found and how it is used make a story rich with happy human relations.

In the story *Juan* (126) Mary Slattery Stolz brings to life an unforgettable boy who lives in a Mexican orphanage although he insists he is not an orphan. The poignant story of Juan's adjustment to life in the orphanage, where he longs for love and recognition in an environment in which love is available only in limited measures, is ably told and well illustrated.

Although *Tuchin's Mayan Treasure* (47) by Mary Jane Foltz has a simple story line, the book gives a picture of family problems and of the pull between superstitions and everyday needs. Tuchin, a ten-year-old boy in Yucatan, is hired by an archaeologist to be his interpreter for the Mayan Indian workman assisting in the search for treasures from the past. During the exploration of the sacred well of the rain god, Tuchin is able to overcome his fears and superstitions and help dive for Mayan sacrificial artifacts.

Three Came Riding (96) by Ellsworth Newcomb is a touching story about ten-year-old José Perez, who lives in Puerto Rico. José is faced with the necessity of selling his beloved horse in order to provide food and clothing for his fatherless family. By good fortune José finds a job at the last moment and is able to earn enough money to keep his horse.

Wanda, a little Puerto Rican girl, writes a birthday letter to her Uncle Carlos. The brief text and colored photographs in *Dear Uncle Carlos* (107) by Seymour Reit should please preschool and kindergarten children.

Robert Barry's story *The Musical Palm Tree: A Story of Puerto Rico* (7) is concerned with a small boy, Pablito, and his efforts to make enough money to buy a mantilla for his mother. The boy acts as a guide and takes visitors on a tour of special places in San Juan, Puerto Rico. A much-traveled musician who claims to have seen better places than those suggested in the various guidebooks becomes intrigued by Pablito's offer to take him to a musical palm tree.

Monty, a motherless boy living with his grandmother in a rural, primitive section of Jamaica, is suddenly transferred to the new, modern, city home of his policeman father and young stepmother in *Monty of Montego* (40) by Virginia Gardiner Durstine. His adjustment from the old ways of life to the new provides a plot within which Monty has many exciting and fearful adventures.

To Catch a Mongoose: A Picture Story in English and French (110) by Barbara Ritchie has the island of Martinique as its setting. Henri, a young boy, has a wonderful idea to earn money: catching a mongoose in his chicken house and selling it to the man who would make it fight snakes! Beautiful illustrations accompany the text.

In Europe

Europe is the homeland of the ancestors of the majority of children in our country, who therefore feel a certain affinity for the different countries from which their ancestors came. Young readers will find pleasure in the historical and fictional literature that portrays life in the different European countries. Every country in Europe is rich in story material, and numerous writers and artists have provided children's books acquainting us with boys and girls living in Europe.

When the little English town of Peaceful builds a balloon, flight-minded Benjamin Buckley stows away and, with his cat, is the only one aboard when the balloon suddenly breaks loose during its launching and becomes airborne in *The Brave Balloon of Benjamin Buckley* (134) by Barbara Wersba. The story is unusual in its use of creative language, fanciful situations, and fun that are rarely found in books for older children.

A Proper Place for Chip (93) by Anne Molloy is a warm story of a boat trip through the English countryside. Chip had always wanted to make a trip on an English canal boat. His chance comes when his aunt and uncle, who own the *Meg and Kate,* agree to take him. Life on the boat opens up a new way of living to the young boy.

The story of a little boy and his search for a shoe box so that he may play the shoe-box game with the older children of the Jewish quarter of Manchester, England, is the essence of Leila Berg's *A Box for Benny* (9). The account of Benny's efforts to learn the old ragman's magic secret as he works to obtain the box provides a glimpse into the life of the Jewish community through the eyes of a sensitive little boy. The description of the games, special delicacies, and hardships of the people of this poor district in Manchester add to the meaning of the story.

Gray Dog from Galtymore (27) by Joseph E. Chipperfield is developed in an outdoor setting and gives full play to the senses. A little puppy, Silver, running away from an Irish farm to find his young master, accepts the overtures of the tinker's dog and is captured by the tinker. The reader is given a dramatic account of Silver's escape from the tinker, his meeting with an author who becomes his beloved master, and his final meeting with the tinker whom he is seeking to avenge the supposed death of his master. The book is written in a lyrical fashion with many Irish expressions.

Shaun is proud to be the son of the best boat builder in Ballymoran and to have a part in building the *Curragh* in which his father wins the race. The Irish lilt and turn of phrase are part of the charm of *Shaun and the Boat* (94) by Anne Molloy. Barbara Cooney's beautiful illustrations give a friendly picture of the Connemara coast.

Life in Ireland is interestingly portrayed in *A Family of Foxes* (38) by Eilis Dillon. The story centers around the people of the island of Inishownan and their superstition that all foxes are evil. Patsy and his three friends discover a pair of silver foxes that were washed ashore from a boat during a storm. Action arises when the boys take care of the two foxes and the four pups that were born to them while they wait for the real owner to be reached. Dillon shows his talent for creating mood and revealing character by using the rhythm of Irish speech.

The spirit of the Irish countryside and the people are well portrayed in Dillon's *A Herd of Deer* (39). Fifteen-year-old Peter Regan takes a job with a man who has imported a herd of deer from Scotland instead of trying to farm the poor land he has in Connemara. Peter's job becomes exciting when he sets out to find the deer that have been stolen from the herd.

In Emma Smith's *Out of Hand* (119) a family of four brothers and sisters spend a glorious summer with their elderly, happy-go-lucky cousin Polly, who lives alone in an untidy house on a run-down farm in Wales. The children thoroughly enjoy the semigypsy existence, but their idyll ends when Polly breaks her leg. Two stern, middle-aged relatives move in to care for the invalid. They take charge of the children, who they think are "quite out of hand." The story has a rich assortment of characters.

Foxes in the Valley (13) by Hilda Boden is the story of young people living on a farm in present-day Wales. The characters are well portrayed, and the description of Welsh farms and countryside provides pleasant reading.

Originally a short French film, *The Red Balloon* (79) by Albert Lamorisse is an appealing fantasy that follows Pascal, a little boy, through the streets of Paris. He catches a red balloon that accompanies him wherever he goes. Some cruel boys chase Pascal, seize his balloon, and burst it. As the balloon breaks, Pascal's spirits begin to die. At the same time, however, all over Paris the balloons revolt and sail up into the air.

Henri's walk to Paris, the great city about which he dreams, is interrupted by a bird who leads Henri safely home to Reboul in *Henri's Walk to Paris* (76) by Leonore Klein. The illustrations in this story are particularly rich in design.

The Emperor and the Drummer Boy (111) by Ruth Robbins is based on a true incident from Napoleon's life. In 1804, at Boulogne, Napoleon insisted on reviewing his fleet of vessels in spite of an approaching storm. The tragedy of the shipwrecks and drowned men is seen alternately through the eyes of the emperor and through those of the little drummer boy whose best friend was aboard one of the ships. The illustrations in this distinguished book add forcefully to the drama of the story.

A proud Parisian cat who owns a hotel, a bored and grouchy little American boy, and an undernourished rival alley cat combine to make *Fredou* (125) by Mary Slattery Stolz a humorous tale told with originality and perception. The atmosphere of Paris is vividly portrayed.

Pursuit in the French Alps (15) by Paul-Jacques Bonzon is an exciting story with elements of mystery and suspense woven into the plot. The story concerns the adventures of a French youth who is spending the summer in the French Alps above his village home. The youth crosses the mountain pass into Italy to help an Italian friend and is arrested by the Italians because he has no papers. In this strong story a boy's courage and loyalty are set against the danger of man and mountain.

The author's description of the strange land through which the Rhone River flows on its last few miles to the Mediterranean Sea helps the reader to understand the setting and experiences of *White Horses and Black Bulls* (70) by Alan C. Jenkins. In the area of France known as the Camargue roam great herds of black bulls and beautiful, courageous white horses. Young Paul Christophe also lives there and longs for the time when he will be big and strong enough to catch and train one of the wild horses and join his father's cowboys when they brand the bulls. How he comes to own a horse is the basis for a good story.

In Paul Berna's *Flood Warning* (10) five boys and a schoolmaster are cut off from the other students during an unexpected storm in southwestern France. The rising flood waters force them to seek refuge in an old mill tower. The descriptions of the beginnings of the disaster, of courage and desperation while the flood is at its height, and of the rescue are vivid and convincing. Each character in his own way changes for the better through the tension and trial of danger.

Captain Nuno (82) by L. N. Lavolle (translated from the French by James Kirkup) relates the story of Nuno, who has to work in a dry goods store to support his mother and sister when his Portuguese father is drowned. In spite of his dull job, Nuno persists in trying to find ways to continue his dream of becoming a famous fisherman like his father. The way in which Nuno's dream comes true makes interesting reading.

The Little Red Pony (18) by Mies Bouhuys is a humorous story about gypsies in the low country of The Netherlands and how they contrive to take anything they wish from the hard-working farmers. Farmer

From *Flood Warning* by Paul Berna, illustrated by Charles Keeping.

Klass is determined to get back his two beloved horses and return the little red pony to the gypsy girl. The amusing things that happen to Farmer Klass, his wife, and Policeman Klemp as they go about outwitting the gypsies make a fun-filled story.

An early story by Meindert De Jong is *The Wheel on the School* (37). With its setting in Holland, the story relates how six Dutch school children in the little town of Shora worry because the storks never come to their town to build their nests. Since there are no trees in the village, they realize that they must provide wheels on their roofs on which the storks can build their nests, as was the custom in other villages. With the encouragement of their amiable schoolmaster and the involvement of the adults in the community, they carry on a successful search that calls upon their physical endurance and courage. De Jong brings each character to life with his skill in painting word pictures. An unusual story that successfully uses the colloquial talk of children, *The Wheel on the School* won the Newbery Medal in 1955.

In 1969 Meindert De Jong was presented with the first National Book Award to be given in the field of children's literature for the novel *Journey from Peppermint Street* (36), a beautifully told story with its setting in Holland in the early 1900s. In the story, the boy Siebren goes with his grandfather from his home on Peppermint Street to visit his great-aunt on an inland farm—the longest journey of his life away from his mother and father and Knillis, his little brother. Siebren's journey is filled with wonders. He is fascinated by his dwarf-sized aunt and her deaf-mute husband. One exciting happening follows another, and the joyous ending for Siebren gives him reason to believe in miracles.

The Empty Moat (116) by Margaretha Shemin has its setting in Holland during the Nazi occupation. Sixteen-year-old Elizabeth is determined not to risk the loss of Swaenenburg Castle and her own safety by permitting the Dutch underground to hide Jewish refugees in the castle dungeon. Elizabeth changes in her attitude and becomes a courageous, active participant in the resistance movement. *The Empty Moat* is a fast-moving, suspense-filled story.

Told in the first person, *Friedrich* (109) by Hans Peter Richter is a documentary novel with its setting in Germany during the hectic days preceding and during World War II. The story relates the narrator's observations of what happens to Friedrich in a frenzied society because he is a Jew.

The cars, track, mechanics, and drivers are so carefully drawn in *Grand Prix Germany* (5) by Jeffrey Ashford that it is like being in the middle of the action. With Dick Knox at the wheel driving through sleet and rain in the Nurburgring auto race, the author provides excellent excitement for young racing enthusiasts.

In *Coming Home from the War: An Idyll* (77) James Kruess recalls his impressions of life in Germany between February and August of 1945. Writing in the first person, the author gives a grim account of war and its effects. The young German boy in the narration walks across his homeland following the demobilization of Nazi soldiers in 1945.

A Monkey's Uncle (58) by Wilhelm Hauff is a clever story with its setting in a small German town. The plot of the story revolves around a stranger who teaches the townspeople a lesson by taking advantage of their curiosity and false values. When the stranger keeps to himself, the townspeople become curious and angry. The stranger becomes irritated and secretly brings in a clever orangutan. He dresses him up like a man, trains him, and presents him as his nephew as a joke to all the townspeople.

The Hilbrand family move from a home in a small village to a large housing development in Stuttgart, Germany. New pets, new friends, new sights, small incidents of home life, family affection, and responsibility are introduced with natural and realistic details in *New Friends in Shepherd's Meadow* (67) by Franz Hutterer. Translated from the German, this is an excellent story about making friends and adaptability.

Young Niels Rasmussen of Denmark introduces readers to the legends, history, and customs of farm life in his country in *My Village in Denmark* (49) by Sonia and Tim Gidal.

May 17 is Norway's Independence Day. It is a day when no boy, especially one who beats a drum in a parade as Per does, wishes to break out with measles—a strong possibility, since Per's sister has just spent a miserable time in bed with the red spots peppering her face. *Great Day in Norway: The Seventeenth of May* (65) by Zinken Hopp is a short story that describes the interesting dress of the people and tells of their history.

A sensitive story *A Time for Watching* (97) by Gunilla Norris relates an in-between time in the life of a ten-year-old Swedish boy. It is a lonely summer for Joachim without his best friend. Everything he does seems to turn to trouble until he finds that by helping someone else he is able to do the thing he most desires.

Seacrow Island (85) by Astrid Lindgren is an amusing story sparked by humorous incidents about a motherless Swedish family who rent a cottage for the summer on a small island. The father, a writer, loves his four children but leaves it to the oldest daughter to hold the family together. Into this quiet atmosphere a villain enters and provides suspense by trying to take the cottage away from the Melkerson family.

Simon's Way (45) by Margery Evernden is an interesting story of a

From *A Time for Watching* by Gunilla Norris, illustrated by Paul Giouanopoulos.

boy's adventures that take him from France to Norway looking for his father. In Nidaros, Norway, Simon is befriended by young Haakon, a king's son, and because of his friendship becomes involved in the succession to the Norwegian throne. This adventure story is colorfully set in the thirteenth century.

Katie and Nan (69) by Nan Inger, with its setting in modern Sweden, is a quiet story that depicts the comfortable daily life of a close-knit family who move from the country to an apartment in the city. The two little girls are spirited and mischievous, and the troubles they get into are very lifelike.

Mature girls will find *Signpost to Switzerland* (1) by Mabel Esther Allan of particular interest. Camilla, a spoiled seventeen-year-old, is sent by her father to stay with an old acquaintance of his in Switzerland. The Swiss family are hotelkeepers. Camilla is determined not to like them or to cooperate with them in any way but a family crisis arises and Camilla pitches in to help. The more she helps, the happier she becomes, and in the end she finds love and happiness where she least expects them.

The Spinning Tops of Naples (135) by Tyler Whittle draws interesting characters from a real life situation. Human relationships are sympathetically portrayed and the story is compelling reading. Realizing that there will not be enough room in his family's apartment when the twelfth child arrives, fifteen-year-old Ferdinando decides to leave Rome and seek his fortune in Naples. His younger brother Orlando, who follows him, is slow to learn but adores his older brother, and Ferdinando does not have the heart to send him back. In Naples in order to survive, the brothers join up with three other boys who are known as *scugnizzi*—children with no families or homes, who go from place to place, job to job, and chance to chance. These "spinning tops" must live by their wits from day to day.

Mrs. Poggi's Holiday (78) by Saul Lambert is a light-hearted story about the citizens of Bonsi, a little Italian fishing village where the people think they are too busy to take a holiday. Mrs. Poggi, who is responsible for keeping the town hall clean, notices how dirty the holiday flags have become. She decides to wash them and hang them on the town hall to dry. The townspeople joyfully mistake the flying flags as the proclamation of a holiday—and what a holiday follows!

You Have a Friend, Pietro (54) by Josef C. Grund is a well-written story of the vendetta—the blood revenge practiced by families in Corsica. Young Pietro is the innocent victim of the superstition of

From *Mrs. Poggi's Holiday* by Saul Lambert.

the people in a lonely village who believe that he has "the evil eye." He is ignored and teased by the boys whose friendship he seeks, but his fate is suddenly changed by the appearance of a mysterious old stonecutter known as Emilio. Five curious boys decide to discover Emilio's secret, and what they finally learn involves a legendary feud spanning many generations.

Progress in the form of a new waterworks comes to a small, sunny Greek village, and everyone forgets about Mr. Nero, his old horse Cobra, and the pink water cart until something happens that makes the villagers remember and appreciate Mr. Nero in *The Story of Mister Nero* (99) by Theodore Papas.

Reneé Reggiani has written a lively tale of five Sicilian children whose association with the peasant Turi, their trusted mentor and beloved bandleader, takes them from their native Sicily to Milan, Italy, in *Five Children and a Dog* (105). The efforts of the children to be self-reliant involve them in a variety of humorous and pathetic escapades.

In another story by Reneé Reggiani a Sicilian girl and her family leave their home to escape the terror of the local baron and begin a new free life in Torino. *The Sun Train* (106) has as its background contemporary Italian social conditions.

The Little Fishes (59) by Erik Christian Haugaard is an eloquently written story that deals with such an eternal truth as the need for a human being to develop and to live by a code of ethics that involves responsibility to one's self and love and understanding of others. The story revolves around twelve-year-old Guido, one of the displaced children left to wander in the bombed city of Naples in 1943. After his mother's death, Guido follows her advice that the two worthwhile things one needs in life are love and strength. Guido proves that he has both. He becomes the sole support of Anna and Mario, fellow refugees. Guido with his companions joins the refugee lines moving toward Casino. They live in and out of caves, never free from danger and the threat of starvation. In spite of his harsh life, in his relations with people Guido explains that he finally accepts men as they are. "It is understanding that makes the difference between us and animals and when you understand, you can feel a kind of happiness in the worst misery" (p. 213).

Annuzza, A Girl of Romania (114) by Hertha Seuberlich is a first-person narrative of a sixteen-year-old Romanian peasant girl. Annuzza, who has always lived in a small village with her family, yearns for more education. Although discouraged from such pursuits by her family, she wins an opportunity to go to school in the city, where she is faced with the problem of how to remain loyal to her peasant background and family while finding a place for herself within a different class. The descriptions of family relationships in the Romanian culture are convincingly presented.

Insight into the Turkish-Greek trouble and descriptions of the Cyprian landscape are woven into *Operation Sippacik* (51) by Rumer Godden. The story revolves around Refat, a seven-year-old Turkish Cypriote whose grandfather sells Sippacik Refat's beloved donkey to the British soldiers. The donkey is so stubborn that Refat has to go to the British camp to manage her. As a result, he is instrumental in rescuing a wounded man who turns out to be his father, long absent as a Greek Cypriot prisoner.

Aunt America (11) by Marie H. Bloch is an interesting story of an eleven-year-old Ukranian girl who is visited by an American aunt. Lesya greatly admires her Uncle Vlodko, who has prospered more than her own father because he has fully complied with all regulations and has pleased the authorities, while Lesya's father is in disfavor for his independent thinking. The American aunt, on the other hand, recognizes integrity and courage where the child has seen only rashness. As Lesya's viewpoint changes, she grows in understanding and love for her father.

With its setting in Scotland in the early part of the eighteenth century, *The Lothian Run* (66) by Mollie Hunter abounds with spies, smugglers, and reprobates. Sandy Maxwell, a young lawyer's clerk, joins with an agent of his Majesty's Customs Service to track down a smuggler.

Once in a Lifetime (72), written by Lev Kassil and translated by Anne Terry White, is a glamour-tinted story about a thirteen-year-old Russian girl's experience as a movie "find." She is thrilled with the new world into which she moves where she meets with immediate success in her first role. The mediocre role she is offered for her second picture convinces her that it would be better to take the advice of her mentor and go back to school.

In Africa

Africa is no longer thought of as "the Dark Continent." In recent years a new Africa has emerged and come to life for boys and girls through movies, television, and books of fact and fiction. American children are becoming acquainted with their African counterparts in stories rich with humor, suspense, and likable characters living together in friendly relationships. As different countries in Africa emerge and take their place with the other countries of the world, they bring with them backgrounds rich in story material. They describe the different ways in which the Black people of Africa and their culture have contributed to American life.

Contemporary life in a remote North African oasis is portrayed through an eventful day with Maha, a young Arab girl, in *Maha and Her Donkey* (138) by Hed Wimmer. The sensitive photographic studies accompanying the text add to the reader's understanding and appreciation of customs and community life quite different from our own.

The Secret Elephants (89) by Catherine Marsden is the story of a friendship between Manuel, son of a Portuguese trader, and Bolamba, son of a Kosa chief in Mozambique. Together the boys protect a herd of sacred elephants. Many of the customs of the Kosa people and facts about African wildlife are threaded through the story.

Mogo's Flute (131) by Hilda Van Stockum is a story highlighting the values, beliefs, and customs of an East African village. Mogo, a frail Kikuyu boy living in Kenya, finds the answer to his problems through many strengthening experiences as he tries to live up to the expectations of Mundo-Mugo, the wise man who gave him this riddle to solve: "What is good to have, better to lose, and best to find again?"

Geraldine Kaye in *Great Day in Ghana: Kwasi Goes to Town* (73) relates the adventures of young Kwasi, a village boy, during his trip to Accra, capital of Ghana, on Independence Day (1957). Changes, customs, and the old along with the new are accurately described. The book gives a feeling for the life of a village boy in present-day Africa.

Mongo Homecoming (42) by Mary Elting and Robin McKown introduces readers to the Mongo Tribe living near the Congo River in Africa. The information related to the activities, customs, and traditions of the Mongo Tribe was obtained through interviews by one of the authors with a girl from Kinshasa.

Juma, The Little African (88) by John Mansfield is an unusual story with philosophical and psychological concepts simply stated in poetic terms. In the tall forest near his village, Juma walks alone and learns the ways of the wild animals around him. So he knows what to do when a blind bull elephant sweeps him up in his trunk "to be his eyes" and takes him on a journey to the secret place of the elephants. Life and death are presented in a way that helps the young reader to accept the fact that things and people live and die. The values of keen observation, courage, self-reliance, respect, and honor are accented.

Fifteen-year-old Calvi, an orphan and waterfront boy of Nantes, France, is trained by a kindly sea captain and then sent on a journey to Africa in command of a trading vessel in René Guillot's *Riders of the Wind* (55). Sailing up the Senegal River, Calvi is carried off by

Moorish raiders and remains a prisoner in their desert stronghold for two years before he finally finds his way back to the coast and home. The feelings of the people of North Africa are reflected in this exciting story.

The Lazy Little Zulu (63) by James Holding is a read-aloud picture book about a young African boy, Chaka, who would rather go off by himself and watch the animals than work. His knowledge of ant hills and tea seeds helps him to earn money to aid his sick mother. The color illustrations supplement the text in creating a feeling for life in Africa.

Strong family relationships and believable adventures make *Bemba: An African Adventure* (29) by Andree Clair a tale for young readers to enjoy. The story of village life in the Congo depicts the conflicts resulting from the rapid changes in ways of living in that area today.

More mature readers will find *Kalena and Sana* (16) by Esma R. Booth an interesting story. Set in the Belgian Congo, the story portrays the life of a young African woman who, after graduating from school, marries a medical student and goes to live in a large city. The problems of an emerging nation and the conflicts between old ways and new are realistically presented in this picture of the educated younger people of the Congo.

Children from many regions of Africa have ambitions and problems in common with boys and girls throughout the world as revealed in *Children of Africa* (124), a collection of stories by Louise A. Stinetorf.

Visit to a Chief's Son: An American Boy's Adventure in Africa (56) by Robert Halmi and Ann Kennedy is a pictorial record of a ten-year-old American boy's visit to a Masai tribe in Kenya. Black-and-white photographs and a brief, simple text describe the daily life of the people and country as the American makes friends with a young Masai. Contrasting customs are highlighted as the two boys engage in activities of interest to both. The story is based on a *Life* magazine picture story.

In three separate humorous stories of Morocco today, two boys and a girl present some interesting dilemmas in *Mechido, Aziza, and Ahmed* (83) by Giggy Lezra. Although the three had never met before, these two boys and a girl are all a trial to their parents. The black-and-white sketches with their Moroccan flavor add to the fun of the stories.

The ancient African kingdom of Abyssinia comes to life in *The Princess and the Lion* (31) by Elizabeth Coatsworth. Based on historical fact, the story tells of a princess who aids one of her brothers in becoming heir to the throne. The beautiful full-page illustrations in tones of brown, gray, black, and white flavor the story.

Abou's greatest wish was for a donkey of his own. Katherine Evans' lively story *A Donkey for Abou* (44) tells how he earns the money with which to buy the donkey. The setting in the Moroccan city of Fez adds interest to the story.

Life in a remote village in Ethiopia and in the surrounding region is portrayed in *Meeting with a Stranger* (19) by Duane Bradley, an American who comes to the village to teach the shepherds new ways of caring for their flocks. The difficulties that arise when the two cultures try to understand each other and the patience with which a technical assistance program needs to proceed are well brought out. The story utilizes suspense and character growth.

Zamani Goes to Market (46) by Muriel Feelings describes a day in the life of Zamani, a young boy from a village in East Africa. The excitement of his first trip to market with his father and brothers, the bustling marketplace, and the pleasure of choosing and giving his first gift make this a memorable day for Zamani. The sepia-and-white illustrations capture the life style of the locale.

In *Anna and Dula* (132) by Robert Vavra, Anna receives a baby gorilla to be her own pet to feed and care for. Anna lives in Central Africa where her father catches live birds and animals for zoos and circuses all over the world. The story is told with a simple text and beautiful color photographs.

Wacheera, Child of Africa (26) by Fay Childs is a sensitive story about the daily life of a twelve-year-old African girl and her family, who live with their tribal group in a village at the foot of Mt. Kenya. Native ways, occupations, family ties, and the desire of the younger generation for education and different ways of living are described.

Oasis of the Stars (41) by Olga Economakis revolves around Abu, a young boy who lives with his nomad family on the great desert. Abu is tired of moving from place to place in search of water; he wants an oasis with as many drops of water as stars in the sky which his family would never have to leave. Abu gets his wish in this well-written story.

In the Middle East

Each of the countries that make up the Middle East has its own distinguishing characteristics. One senses this when he leaves India, the largest country in the Middle East, and travels into the surrounding countries—Iran and Pakistan—and then into Israel and the Arab states.

The setting of *Langurni, Little Monkey of India* (33) by Louanna

Culp is in the hill country of India—the land of monkeys, jackals, and tigers—where a very little monkey named Langurni is spending her first day in the pine forest. Langurni's adventures were conceived by the author while she was living in that part of India at the foot of the Himalayan Mountains.

The blending of old superstitions with the reality of modern situations makes *Man-Eater* (24) by Arthur Catherall an interesting story of India today. A man-eating leopard terrorizes a village in India until the village is delivered from the leopard by land mines left in the ground from the days when soldiers used the area for special training.

The love story and adventure in Jean Bothwell's *The Emerald Clue* (17) will appeal particularly to older boys and girls. The vivid Indian setting enhances this story of a girl's rebellion against the cloistered life that has been imposed on Indian women for centuries.

The White Bungalow (120) by Aimee Sommerfelt realistically treats the problems that face people in India. The story of a fifteen-year-old boy, Lalu, brings to the surface those practical problems that the people of India need help in solving.

Kumar (142) by Charlotte C. Wyckoff is the story of eleven-year-old Kumar, who leaves Madras with his family after the death of his father and goes to live in a village. The story is set in India during the last days of colonialism and the first days of independence. Village and farm life, school for boys and even girls, changes in the thinking of young people and adults, and the role of Gandhi all figure prominently in the story.

Old Mali and the Boy (117) by D. R. Sherman is the story of a twelve-year-old English boy and the wise old Indian gardener, Mali, who loves and treats him as a son. Mali takes the boy on a three-day hunting trip into the forest and shows him how to shoot a bow and arrow. An accident that costs Mali's life projects the boy into manhood and teaches him the meaning of integrity and courage. The universality of the theme is conveyed in compelling, simple style by the young Rhodesian author.

In Pearl S. Buck's story *The Big Fight* (20) an Indian family struggles to make a living with an animal circus. The family is overjoyed when an American motion picture company asks to rent the circus. The tiger and the leopard almost spoil the whole plan, but a pet deer comes to appear more ferocious than either of them and saves the day.

The setting for *The Flying Cow* (32) by Ruth Philpott Collins is a village in the south of India. The village receives the gift of a cow from American friends to help improve the native breed of cattle. Because the breed is foreign and different, it is not accepted by all members of the community, but the vigilance and courage of ten-year-old Rama prevents the destruction of the cow.

Two stories that capture in varying degrees the atmosphere of life in Nepal are *Boy of Nepal* (80) by Peter Larsen and *Gurkhas and Ghosts* (91) by Luree Miller and Marilyn Silverstone. Each story is illustrated with photographs and revolves around a Nepalese boy who describes city and country life in Nepal.

Flight to the Promised Land (57) by Laszlo Hamori is a story of a thirteen-year-old boy reaching out for new ways and ideas. Based on the actual experiences of a real person, this Jewish boy, along with other Jews of Marib, makes the long trek from Yemen, one of the most backward countries in the world, to the new state of Israel. On their way to Israel they come into contact with jeeps, airplanes, and other marvels of technology that seem both miraculous and threatening to their deep religious convictions.

Advanced readers will find *Growing Up in Israel* (64), by Desider Holisher, an interesting story of the history and development of an ancient land into a modern nation. Through the description of the lives of two young Israelis, who are deeply affected by the biblical past and at the same time by a democratic society that has developed modern institutions, the author gives an interesting account of the culture of the people, and life in an Israeli city.

Shaer of Afghanistan (121) by Judith M. Spiegelman relates the every-day life of an eleven-year-old farm boy who attends two schools: the mosque for religious training and the government school for the study of academic subjects.

The Girl Without a Name (8) by Gunnel Beckman is the story of the friendship between a Swedish girl and a Persian girl who was orphaned in an Iranian earthquake. Although the relationship between the two is often strained, they resolve their differences in interesting ways.

Rich with suspense, *Red Sea Rescue* (25) by Arthur Catherall has its setting on an island in the Red Sea off the coast of Egypt. When fourteen-year-old Ibrahim and his sister return from a beachcombing expedition late at night, they find their lighthouse-keeper father missing and the signal lamp unlit. An exciting chain of events follows, and the strong characterizations of those involved makes a gripping story.

A picture of how oil and the airplane have changed the age-old ways of living in the desert is presented in *Bouboukar, Child of the Sahara* (139) by Marjorie Worthington. Bouboukar, the orphan around whom the story is built, is a pathetic little boy who was always "on the outside looking in" until the arrival of an American lady who tries to be kind to him. The impact made on his life by the American is the basis for this interesting and unusual story. Descriptions of life in the Sahara Desert are woven into the story.

Achmed, Boy of the Negev (113) by Margalit Russcol is illustrated with beautiful photographs of the day-to-day life of a young Arab boy whose father is the sheik of a nomadic Bedouin tribe. The story describes the various aspects of the culture that are reflected in Achmed's daily activities.

Isfendiar and the Wild Donkeys (104) by Bronson Potter is the story of the son of an Iranian charcoal burner whose family lives in a village at the edge of the great southern desert. Isfendiar's dreams have always been filled with wild donkeys, and his adventures are exciting as he sets across the desert to find them. The story catches and portrays the daily life of an Iranian village where boys are filled with dreams by the storytellers.

In the Far East

A glimpse of Chinese culture and an old-style Chinese peasant home is the background of *Old Wind and Liu Li-san* (50) by Aline Glasgow. By following the words of his mother, the young Chinese boy in the story befriends the Wind, who helps his father and mother find their way home.

The exciting, kite-flying New Year's Day in China is described from a young boy's point of view in *Great Day in China: The Holiday Moon* (87) by Peter Lum. The fun as well as the solemn meanings and ancient ceremonials of the day adds flavor to the story.

The modern yet age-old life in Taiwan is interestingly portrayed in *Hai Yin, the Dragon Girl* (2) by Joy Anderson and Jay Yang. Hai Yin, born in the Year of the Dragon in Taipei, longs to be famous. She reaches her goal through perseverance and hard work.

The setting of *The Bamboo School in Bali* (81) by Jef Last and U. P. Tisna is a small mountain village on the island of Bali in Indonesia. The quiet life of the village is changed considerably when the first school is built. The story highlights the adventures of two boys and their friends on the colorful island with its ancient folklore and customs.

Blue in the Seed (68) by Kim Yong Ik is a well-written story of a young boy who finds friends and school rewarding but not before he has many trials because he is not like others. Chun Bok's blue eyes, a rarity in Korea, are the source of his unhappiness. There is an entrancing quality to this story based on a universal theme.

The House of Sixty Fathers (35) by Meindert De Jong revolves around the adoption by an air force outfit of a homeless Chinese orphan, Tien Pao. The story takes place during World War II when the Japanese invaded China. Tien Pao and his family flee the advancing Japanese army and are living on the outskirts of the city of Hengyang. A storm breaks when Tien Pao is left alone on the sampan, and he is carried down the river into Japanese-occupied territory. One harrowing experience follows another and Tien Pao is near starvation before he is found by two air force men who carry him back to their base. He is nursed back to health and is adopted by the men; their barracks become his house and the men his sixty fathers. Meindert De Jong strips war of its glamour and presents a realistic picture of its horrors and suffering. *The House of Sixty Fathers* won the Newbery Award in 1956.

Taka-Chan and I: A Dog's Journey to Japan (84) by Runcible as told to Betty Jean Lifton takes place in contemporary Japan. Runcible, a Weimaraner, digs a hole in the shore at Cape Cod. He digs until he finds himself on the other side of the world—on a beach in Japan. Taka-chan finds Runcible. He follows her home to protect her from the Black Dragon of the Sea. Black Dragon catches them and releases them only when Runcible finds the most loyal person in Japan.

The old adage that one can find happiness in his own backyard is beautifully illustrated in Yoshiko Uchido's tenderly told story *In-Between Miya* (130). Twelve-year-old Miya Okamoto visits her wealthy relatives in Tokyo. Because of all the lavishness surrounding her, Miya begins to feel unhappy and discontented with the simplicity of her own family's village life. A number of unusual experiences make Miya realize that money and happiness are not synonymous.

From *Insect Summer* by James Kirkup, illustrated by Naoko Matsubara.

In Australia

Riverboat Family (137) by Elizabeth Wilton has its setting in the river boat country of South Australia during the Victorian era. Insisting upon their independence, a family raises a sunken paddlewheel steamer from the river bottom. They rebuild it into a trading boat on which they live and from which they deliver goods to riverside communities. The story exudes the pioneer flavor of the river country behind Adelaide.

The Min-Min by Mavis Clark (30) is set in an isolated area of Australia where young people face hardships and danger in a brave attempt to give meaning to their lives. The descriptions of the back country in Australia are excellent.

The summer adventures of an Australian family at the beach provide the plot for *The Feather Star* (140) by Patricia Wrightson. Fifteen-year-old Lindy discovers many unusual creatures at the shore. The account of the daily happenings of her friends will appeal to young people, as will the night fishing from the tidal wall, the bonfires of driftwood on the beach, the captured crabs in the paper sack that escape at the wrong time, and the entry of Queenie, the white cat with one blue eye and one green eye, who triggers unexplainable situations. This gentle, reflective story portrays unsophisticated adolescents enjoying themselves.

Also written by Patricia Wrightson, *An Older Kind of Magic* (141) relates the strange relationship among three children, a calculating businessman, an expert in the modern mystery of advertising, and the Pygmies of aboriginal Australia. The book is illustrated by Noela Young.

Four of the six children in the family living on a sheep station in New South Wales, Australia, band together to make enough money to pay for an operation for their mother. *The Family Conspiracy* (103) by Joan Phipson follows the efforts of each child to get jobs. Each member of the family comes alive as an individual, the sense of family loyalty is strong, and the Australian scene and way of life are vividly portrayed.

A sudden loss of both parents in an auto accident leaves the hero of the story stunned, lost, and desperately rejecting the idea of becoming a burden to anyone in Richard Parker's *Voyage to Tasmania* (101). On board ship bound for Tasmania—an Australian island south of the mainland—where Ray will live with his aunt, a boy from Finland who knows no English smiles his way into Ray's heart. The characters are sensitively drawn in this exceptionally well-written story.

A Valley Full of Pipers (100) by Richard Parker is the story of a feuding family in Tasmania. The slight plot is made interesting by the emphasis on family relationships, community life, and school incidents. In spite of a dramatic flood at the end, the story is made believable by lively writing and natural dialogue.

Extending Experiences for the Reader

1. Lead a class discussion on social functions. Select a social function and describe how it is carried on in each of three different stories.
2. Select descriptions of the countrysides from several stories with their settings in different countries.
3. Discuss with the class the meaning of Paul Hazard's (60) statement "Children's books keep alive a sense of nationality; but they also keep alive a sense of humanity."
4. Establish guidelines for evaluating a story about another country and discuss them with the class.
5. Plan a bulletin board using magazine articles of people from different African countries wearing both modern and native dress.
6. Plan a bulletin board featuring prints of paintings and sculpture by famous American and European artists.
7. Plan a bulletin board showing pictures of famous resort areas in Europe, for example, the Swiss Alps, the French and Italian Rivieras, the island of Majorca, and the Roman ruins.
8. Encourage boys and girls to bring to class people visiting their family or their friends from other countries. Have the visitors tell stories that are popular in their countries.
9. Teach the class folk songs and folk dances of several countries about which they are reading. Plan a pageant for an assembly program around these songs and dances.
10. Plan a program of recorded music around the works of several composers of nationalistic music, for example, Béla Bartók and Edvard Grieg.

Extending Experiences for Children

1. Invite adults who grew up in another country to come to school and share their experiences with the class.
2. Invite a person from another country who might be visiting your fam-

ily or friends to read and discuss a book written about his country. He should tell the class in what ways, according to his opinion, the story gives a true picture of his country and in what ways it does not.
3. Share with the class the ways in which people in the story you are reading meet their basic needs for food, clothing, and shelter.
4. Share with the class descriptions of the countrysides in books you are reading that are set in different lands.
5. Collect pictures of people engaged in various activities in a particular country and make a scrapbook to share with the class.
6. Read at least two stories with their settings in Ireland. Make a collection of expressions that are characteristic of the language of some of the Irish people. Select other countries with which to do the same thing.
7. Name at least three stories in which these values are characteristic of the leading hero: courage, self-reliance, respect for others, pride in achievement, and honor.
8. Read a story about a boy or girl growing up in a sparsely settled region of the world and a story about a young person growing up in a densely populated community. Prepare a report to show whether or not children raised in different environments have the same basic needs. Discuss with your classmates.
9. Read a story about a child living in an impoverished environment and a story about a child living in a privileged environment. Compare the basic needs of these children and decide whether they are similar or different. Discuss with the class.
10. Read and share with the class a story in which the environment of the leading character influences his behavior.

Chapter References

1. ALLAN, MABEL ESTHER. *Signpost to Switzerland.* New York: Criterion, 1964. Grades 7–11.
2. ANDERSON, JOY, AND JAY YANG. *Hai Yin, The Dragon Girl.* New York: Harcourt Brace Jovanovich, 1970. Grades 4–6.
3. ANNIXTER, JANE, AND PAUL ANNIXTER. *Windigo.* New York: Holiday House, 1963. Grades 7–9.
4. ARMSTRONG, WILLIAM H. *Sounder.* New York: Harper & Row, 1969. Grades 7–9.
5. ASHFORD, JEFFREY. *Grand Prix Germany.* New York: Putnam, 1970. Grade 6 and up.
6. BARCLAY, ISABEL. *O Canada!* Garden City, N.Y.: Doubleday, 1964. Grades 4–6.
7. BARRY, ROBERT. *The Musical Palm Tree: A Story of Puerto Rico.* New York: McGraw-Hill, 1965. Kindergarten–grade 3.
8. BECKMAN, GUNNEL. *The Girl Without a Name.* Anne Parker (tr.). New York: Harcourt Brace Jovanovich, 1970. Grades 4–6.
9. BERG, LEILA. *A Box for Benny.* Cleveland: World Publishing, 1966.

10. BERNA, PAUL. *Flood Warning.* New York: Pantheon, 1963. Grades 5–7.
11. BLOCH, MARIE H. *Aunt America.* New York: Atheneum, 1963. Grades 3–7.
12. BLUE, ROSE. *A Quiet Place.* New York: Watts, 1969. Grades 4–6.
13. BODEN, HILDA. *Foxes in the Valley.* New York: David McKay, 1963. Grades 7–9.
14. BONHAM, FRANK. *Durango Street.* New York: Dutton, 1965. Grade 7 and up.
15. BONZON, PAUL-JACQUES. *Pursuit in the French Alps.* New York: Lothrop, Lee & Shepard, n.d. Grades 5–9.
16. BOOTH, ESMA R. *Kalena and Sana.* New York: David McKay, 1962. Grade 9 and up.
17. BOTHWELL, JEAN. *The Emerald Clue.* New York: Harcourt Brace Jovanovich. Grade 10 and up.
18. BOUHUYS, MIES. *The Little Red Pony.* Eau Claire, Wis.: Hale, 1962. Grades 3–5.
19. BRADLEY, DUANE. *Meeting with a Stranger.* Philadelphia: Lippincott, 1964. Grades 4–6.
20. BUCK, PEARL S. *The Big Fight.* New York: John Day, 1965. Grades 4–6.
21. BULLA, CLYDE R. *Indian Hill.* New York: T. Y. Crowell, 1963. Grades 2–5.
22. ———. *White Bird.* New York: T. Y. Crowell, 1966. Grades 2–5.
23. CARLSON, NATALIE SAVAGE. *The Empty Schoolhouse.* New York: Dell, 1968. Paperback. Grades 2–8.
24. CATHERALL, ARTHUR. *Man-Eater.* New York: Criterion, 1964.
25. ———. *Red Sea Rescue.* New York: Lothrop, Lee & Shepard, 1970. Grades 5–9.
26. CHILDS, FAY. *Wacheera, Child of Africa.* New York: Criterion, 1965. Grades 5–7.
27. CHIPPERFIELD, JOSPEH E. *Gray Dog from Galtymore.* New York: David McKay, 1962. Grades 7–9.
28. CHRISTGAU, ALICE. *Runaway to Glory.* Reading, Mass.: Addison-Wesley, 1965. Grades 5–8.
29. CLAIR, ANDREE. *Bemba: An African Adventure.* Marie Ponsat (tr.). New York: Harcourt Brace Jovanovich, 1962. Paperback. Grades 4–6.
30. CLARK, MAVIS. *The Min-Min.* New York: Macmillan, 1969. Grades 5–9.
31. COATSWORTH, ELIZABETH. *The Princess and the Lion.* New York: Pantheon, 1963. Grades 3–7.
32. COLLINS, RUTH PHILPOTT. *The Flying Cow.* New York: Walck, 1963. Grades 4–6.
33. CULP, LOUANNA. *Langurni, Little Monkey of India.* San Carlos, Calif.: Golden Gate Junior Books, 1964. Grades 1–4.
34. DEFOE, DANIEL. *Robinson Crusoe.* New York: Dutton, 1954. Grades 5–9.
35. DE JONG, MEINDERT. *The House of Sixty Fathers.* New York: Harper & Row, 1969. Paperback. Grade 5 and up.
36. ———. *Journey from Peppermint Street.* New York: Harper, 1971. Paperback. Grade 5 and up.

37. ______. *The Wheel on the School.* New York: Harper & Row, 1954. Grade 5 and up.
38. DILLON, EILIS. *A Family of Foxes.* New York: Funk & Wagnalls, 1965. Grades 3–7.
39. ______. *A Herd of Deer.* New York: Funk & Wagnalls, 1970. Grades 7–11.
40. DURSTINE, VIRGINIA GARDINER. *Monty of Montego.* Indianapolis: Bobbs-Merrill, 1963. Grades 3–7.
41. ECONOMAKIS, OLGA. *Oasis of the Stars.* New York: Coward-McCann, 1965. Kindergarten–grade 3.
42. ELTING, MARY, AND ROBIN MCKOWN. *Mongo Homecoming.* New York: Evans, 1969. Grade 3 and up.
43. ERWIN, BETTY K. *Behind the Magic Line.* Boston: Little, Brown, 1969. Grades 3–7.
44. EVANS, KATHERINE. *A Donkey for Abou.* New York: Abelard-Schuman, 1964. Kindergarten–grade 3.
45. EVERNDEN, MARGERY. *Simon's Way.* New York: Walck, 1963. Grades 4–6.
46. FEELINGS, MURIEL. *Zamani Goes to Market.* New York: Seabury, 1970. Grades 1–4.
47. FOLTZ, MARY JANE. *Tuchin's Mayan Treasure.* New York: Morrow, 1963. Grades 4–6.
48. GAULT, WILLIAM C. *The Long Green.* New York: Dutton, 1965. Grade 7 and up.
49. GIDAL, SONIA, AND TIM GIDAL. *My Village in Denmark.* New York: Pantheon, 1963. Grades 2–5.
50. GLASGOW, ALINE. *Old Wind and Liu Li-san.* Irvington-on-Hudson, N. Y.: Harvey House, 1962. Grades 2–5.
51. GODDEN, RUMER. *Operation Sippacik.* New York: Viking, 1969. Grades 5–9.
52. GRAHAM, LORENZ B. *North Town.* New York: T. Y. Crowell, 1965. Grade 7 and up.
53. GRIFALCONI, ANN. *City Rhythms.* Indianapolis: Bobbs-Merrill, 1965. Kindergarten–grade 3.
54. GRUND, JOSEF C. *You Have a Friend, Pietro.* M. Mutch (tr.). Boston: Little, Brown, 1966. Grades 5–7.
55. GUILLOT, RENÉ. *Riders of the Wind.* Chicago: Rand McNally, 1961. Grades 4–6.
56. HALMI, ROBERT, AND ANN KENNEDY. *Visit to a Chief's Son: An American Boy's Adventure in Africa.* New York: Holt, Rinehart & Winston, 1963. Grades 4–6.
57. HAMORI, LASZLO. *Flight to the Promised Land.* Annabelle MacMillan (tr.). New York: Harcourt Brace Jovanovich, 1963. Grade 7 and up.
58. HAUFF, WILHELM, AND DORIS ORGEL (ed.). *A Monkey's Uncle.* New York: Farrar, Straus & Giroux, 1969. Grades 3–7.
59. HAUGAARD, ERIK CHRISTIAN. *The Little Fishes.* Boston: Houghton Mifflin, 1967. Grades 6–8.
60. HAZARD, PAUL. *Books, Children and Men.* Boston: The Horn Book, 1960. Paperback.

61. HECK, BESSIE H. *Cactus Kevin.* Cleveland: World Publishing, 1965. Grades 4–9.
62. HERRMANN, RALPH. *Children of the North Pole.* Annabelle MacMillan (tr.). New York: Harcourt Brace Jovanovich, 1964. Grades 2–5.
63. HOLDING, JAMES. *The Lazy Little Zulu.* New York: Morrow, 1962. Kindergarten–grade 3.
64. HOLISHER, DESIDER. *Growing Up in Israel.* Oceanside, N. Y.: Blue Star Book Club, 1971. Paperback. Grades 5–8.
65. HOPP, ZINKEN. *Great Day in Norway: The Seventeenth of May.* New York: Abelard-Schuman, 1962. Grades 1–4.
66. HUNTER, MOLLIE. *The Lothian Run.* New York: Funk & Wagnalls, 1970. Grade 7 and up.
67. HUTTERER, FRANZ. *New Friends in Shepherd's Meadow.* New York: Lothrop, Lee & Shepard, 1963. Grades 2–5.
68. IK, KIM YONG. *Blue in the Seed.* Boston: Little, Brown, 1964. Grades 4–6.
69. INGER, NAN. *Katie and Nan.* Annabelle MacMillan (tr.). New York: Harcourt Brace Jovanovich, 1965. Grades 2–4.
70. JENKINS, ALAN C. *White Horses and Black Bulls.* New York: Norton, 1963. Grades 4–7.
71. ———. *Wild Swans at Suvanto.* New York: Norton, 1965. Grades 4–6.
72. KASSIL, LEV. *Once in a Lifetime.* Anne Terry White (tr.). Garden City, N. Y.: Doubleday, 1970. Grades 3–7.
73. KAYE, GERALDINE. *Great Day in Ghana: Kwasi Goes to Town.* New York: 1962. Grades 2–4.
74. KEATING, NORMA. *Mister Chu.* New York: Macmillan, 1965. Kindergarten–grade 3.
75. KIPLING, RUDYARD. *Kim.* New York: Macmillan, 1962. Paperback. Grade 7 and up.
76. KLEIN, LEONORE. *Henri's Walk to Paris.* Reading, Mass.: Addison-Wesley, 1962. Preschool–grade 2.
77. KRUESS, JAMES. *Coming Home from the War: An Idyll.* Heidi Bruehl (tr.). Garden City, N. Y.: Doubleday, 1970. Grade 10 and up.
78. LAMBERT, SAUL. *Mrs. Poggi's Holiday.* New York: Random House, 1969. Kindergarten–grade 3.
79. LAMORISSE, ALBERT. *The Red Balloon.* Garden City, N. Y.: Doubleday, 1957. Grades 3–5.
80. LARSEN, PETER. *Boy of Nepal.* New York: Dodd, Mead, 1970. Grade 2 and up.
81. LAST, JEF, AND U. P. TISNA. *The Bamboo School in Bali.* Marietta Moskin (tr.). New York: John Day, 1969. Grades 3–5.
82. LAVOLLE, L. N. *Captain Nuno.* James Kirkup (tr.). New York: Lothrop, Lee & Shepard, n.d.
83. LEZRA, GIGGY. *Mechido, Aziza, and Ahmed.* New York: Atheneum, 1969. Grades 3–7.
84. LIFTON, BETTY JEAN. *Taka-Chan and I: A Dog's Journey to Japan.* New York: Norton, 1967. Kindergarten–grade 3.
85. LINDGREN, ASTRID. *Seacrow Island.* Evelyn Ramsden (tr.). New York: Viking, 1969. Grade 7 and up.

86. LOMAS, STEVE. *Pacific Blue.* New York: Washburn, 1962. Grades 7–9.
87. LUM PETER. *Great Day in China: The Holiday Moon.* New York: Abelard-Schuman, 1963. Grades 1–4.
88. MANSFIELD, JOHN. *Juma, The Little African.* New York: Nelson, 1965. Grades 1–3.
89. MARSDEN, CATHERINE. *The Secret Elephants.* New York: Dutton, 1966. Grades 4–6.
90. MILES, MISKA. *Mississippi Possum.* Boston: Atlantic Monthly Press, 1965. Grades 2–6.
91. MILLER, LUREE, AND MARILYN S. SILVERSTONE. *Gurkhas and Ghosts.* New York: Criterion, 1970. Grades 3–9.
92. MOLARSKY, OSMOND. *Where the Good Luck Was.* New York: Walck, 1970. Kindergarten–grade 3.
93. MOLLOY, ANNE. *A Proper Place for Chip.* New York: Hastings House, 1965. Grades 1–4.
94. ______. *Shaun and the Boat.* New York: Hastings House, 1965. Grades 1–4.
95. NEVILLE, EMILY. *Berries Goodman.* Eau Claire, Wis.: Hale, 1965. Grade 6 and up.
96. NEWCOMB, ELLSWORTH. *Three Came Riding.* New York: Norton, 1964. Grades 3–7.
97. NORRIS, GUNILLA. *A Time for Watching.* New York: Knopf, 1969. Grades 3–7.
98. PALAZZO, TONY. ELIZABETH M. GRAVES (ed.). *Jan and the Reindeer.* Champaign, Ill.: Garrard, 1963. Grades 1–3.
99. PAPAS, THEODORE. *The Story of Mister Nero.* New York: Coward-McCann, 1966. Kindergarten–grade 3.
100. PARKER, RICHARD. *A Valley Full of Pipers.* Indianapolis: Bobbs-Merrill, 1963. Grades 4–7.
101. ______. *Voyage to Tasmania.* Indianapolis: Bobbs-Merrill, 1963. Grades 4–7.
102. PELLETIER, INGRID. *Daughter of Lapland.* New York: Putnam, 1970. Grades 4–7.
103. PHIPSON, JOAN. *The Family Conspiracy.* New York: Harcourt Brace Jovanovich, 1964. Paperback. Grades 4–6.
104. POTTER, BRONSON. *Isfendiar and the Wild Donkeys.* New York: Atheneum, 1967. Grades 5–7.
105. REGGIANI, RENEÉ. *Five Children and a Dog.* New York: Coward-McCann, 1965. Grades 3–6.
106. ______. *The Sun Train.* New York: Coward-McCann, 1966. Grades 6–8.
107. REIT, SEYMOUR. *Dear Uncle Carlos.* New York: McGraw-Hill, 1969. Kindergarten–grade 3.
108. RICHIE, RITA. *Ice Falcon.* New York: Norton, 1963. Grades 5–8.
109. RICHTER, HANS PETER. *Friedrich.* Edite Kroll (tr.). New York: Holt, Rinehart & Winston, 1970. Grades 5–8.
110. RITCHIE, BARBARA. *To Catch a Mongoose: A Picture Story in English and French.* Berkeley, Cal.: Parnassus, 1963. Grades 3–6.

111. ROBBINS, RUTH. *The Emperor and the Drummer Boy.* Berkeley, Cal.: Parnassus, 1962. Grades 2–6.
112. ROCKWELL, ANNE. *Gypsy Girl's Best Shoes.* New York: Parents' Magazine, 1966. Kindergarten–grade 3.
113. RUSSCOL, MARGALIT. *Achmed, Boy of the Negev.* New York: Putnam, 1965. Grades 4–7.
114. SEUBERLICH, HERTHA. *Annuzza, A Girl of Romania.* Chicago: Rand McNally, 1962. Grades 7–9.
115. SHEARER, JOHN. *I Wish I Had an Afro.* New York: Cowles, 1970. Grades 5–9.
116. SHEMIN, MARGARETHA. *The Empty Moat.* New York: Coward-McCann, 1969. Grades 5–9.
117. SHERMAN, D. R. *Old Mali and the Boy.* New York: Pocket Books, n.d. Paperback. Grade 8 and up.
118. SHYER, MARLENE F. *Tino.* New York: Random House, 1969. Grades 4–6.
119. SMITH, EMMA. *Out of Hand.* New York: Harcourt Brace Jovanovich, 1964. Grades 4–6.
120. SOMMERFELT, AIMEE. *The White Bungalow.* Eau Claire, Wis.: Hale, 1963. Grades 3–7.
121. SPIEGELMAN, JUDITH M. *Shaer of Afghanistan.* New York: Messner, 1969. Grades 3–5.
122. SPOFFORD, NANCY. *The Day of the Bear.* Chicago: Follett, 1964. Grades 4–6.
123. STERLING, DOROTHY. *Mary Jane.* Garden City, N. Y.: Doubleday, 1959. Grades 4–6.
124. STINETORF, LOUISE A. *Children of Africa.* Philadelphia: Lippincott, 1964. Grades 4–6.
125. STOLZ, MARY SLATTERY. *Fredou.* New York: Harper & Row, 1962. Grades 2–6.
126. ———. *Juan.* New York: Harper & Row, 1970. Grades 3–7.
127. TALBOT, CHARLENE J. *Tomas Takes Charge.* New York: Lothrop, Lee & Shepard, 1966. Grades 3–6.
128. THOMPSON, VIVIAN L. *Faraway Friends.* New York: Holiday House, 1963. Grades 2–6.
129. TREECE, HENRY. *Horned Helmet.* New York: Criterion, 1963. Grades 6–10.
130. UCHIDO, YOSHIKO. *In-Between Miya.* New York: Scribner, 1967. Grades 3–7.
131. VAN STOCKUM, HILDA. *Mogo's Flute.* New York: Viking, 1966. Grades 4–6.
132. VAVRA, ROBERT. *Anna and Dula.* New York: Harcourt Brace Jovanovich, 1966. Grade 2 and up.
133. VERNE, JULES. *Around the World in Eighty Days.* Airmont, 1964. Paperback. Grade 8 and up.
134. WERSBA, BARBARA. *The Brave Balloon of Benjamin Buckley.* New York: Atheneum, 1963. Grades 2–7.
135. WHITTLE, TYLER. *The Spinning Tops of Naples.* Philadelphia: Chilton, 1965. Grades 6–7.

136. WIER, ESTER. *Gift of the Mountains.* New York: David McKay, 1963. Grades 6–8.
137. WILTON, ELIZABETH. *Riverboat Family.* New York: Farrar, Straus & Giroux, 1969. Grades 7–9.
138. WIMMER, HED. *Maha and Her Donkey.* Chicago: Rand McNally, 1965.
139. WORTHINGTON, MARJORIE. *Bouboukar, Child of the Sahara.* Boston: Little, Brown, 1962. Grades 4–6.
140. WRIGHTSON, PATRICIA. *The Feather Star.* New York: Harcourt Brace Jovanovich, 1963. Grade 7 and up.
141. ———. *An Older Kind of Magic.* New York: Harcourt Brace Jovanovich, 1972. Grades 3–7.
142. WYCKOFF, CHARLOTTE C. *Kumar.* New York: Norton, 1965. Grades 5–7.

More Stories for Children

Kindergarten–Grade 3

BULLA, CLYDE R. *New Boy in Dublin.* New York: T. Y. Crowell, 1969. An Irish country boy comes to Dublin to work in a big hotel to earn enough money to buy his mother a gold ring.

CRETAN, GLADYS Y. *A Gift from the Bride.* Boston: Little, Brown, 1964. Even though the Armenian village in which she lives has no school, Mari finds a way to attend classes.

HAYS, WILMA P. *The Goose That Was a Watchdog.* Boston: Little, Brown, 1967. A simple, friendly picture of a Black family's life in the rural South is portrayed in this story.

HIRSH, MARILYN. *Where is Yonkela?* New York: Crown, 1969. This very simple story about Baby Yonkela who is feared to be lost is set in an early twentieth-century Jewish village in Hungary.

HOFF, SYD. *Roberto and the Bull.* New York: McGraw-Hill, 1969. Syd Hoff's drawings heighten the nonsense of this book about Roberto and his family, who live on their poor farm in Spain.

LIFTON, BETTY J. *The One-Legged Ghost.* New York: Atheneum, 1968. This old Japanese legend tells of a strange, round, one-legged creature that Yoshi discovers can serve as an umbrella and keep people from getting wet.

MOLARSKY, OSMOND. *Song of the Empty Bottles.* New York: Walck, 1968. In this story a creative little Black boy earns enough money to purchase a guitar by composing a lovely song.

PARISH, PEGGY. *Little Indian.* New York: Simon & Schuster, 1968. Little Indian soon learns it is not easy to earn the name he will be known by.

PRIETO, MARIANA. *When the Monkeys Wore Sombreros.* New York: Harvey House, 1969. Two Mexican boys take their mother's woven sombreros to market on the family burros and discover a way to improve the product.

REIT, SEYMOUR. *A Week in Hagar's World.* New York: Macmillan, 1969. Life on an Israeli kibbutz is portrayed as a happy combination of work and play for Hagar and her family.

WEISS, HUGH. *A Week in Daniel's World.* New York: Macmillan, 1969. This simple, realistic story portrays life in a French suburban family.

Grades 3–6

BIALK, ELISA. *Tizz at the Stampede.* New York: Children's Press, 1968. A family takes a summer vacation in the Canadian Rocky Mountains.

CAMILLE, JOSEPHINE. *Carlos and the Brave Owl.* New York: Random House, 1968. Carlos acquires a most unusual pet—a little owl that becomes the village hero at the annual blessing of the animals.

CHURCH, RICHARD. *The White Doe.* New York: John Day, 1968. This story of the life on an English county estate in 1910 focuses on the personal relationships of three boys over the persecution of a white doe.

CREDLE, ELLIS. *Little Pest Pico.* New York: Nelson, 1969. This picture story relates little Chico's successful efforts to earn four pesos with which to buy Pico, a tame parrot that can whistle the Mexican national anthem.

FENNEMA, ILLONA. *Dirk's Wooden Shoes.* New York: Harcourt Brace Jovanovich, 1970. Two Dutch families become involved in the exchange of a pair of clogs and a pair of red shoes.

FENTON, EDWARD. *A Matter of Miracles.* New York: Holt, Rinehart & Winston, 1967. Gino, who lives in a small Sicilian village, watches his wish come true when he visits a puppet show and his excited dog jumps onto the puppet stage.

GARLAN, PATRICIA, AND M. DUNSTAN. *The Boy Who Played Tiger.* New York: Viking, 1968. This is an exciting story about a mischievous schoolboy in Burma.

GREENBERG, POLLY. *Oh Lord, I Wish I Was a Buzzard.* New York: Macmillan, 1968. A Black girl working in the fields with her father dreams of changing places with other creatures in the field. There is a poetic quality to the writing in this story.

HEADY, ELEANOR B. *Brave Johnny O'Hare.* New York: Parents' Magazine, 1969. The koala bear, the kangaroo, the dingo dog, and the kookaburra all have a part in this delightful story of brave Johnny O'Hare from Australia.

JACOB, HELEN P. *A Garland for Gandhi.* Berkeley, Calif.: Parnassus, 1968. An excellent picture of village life and the people's response to Gandhi's leadership is presented in this book.

LEWIS, MARY. *Joey and the Fawn.* New York: Washburn, 1967. This moving story with its soft illustrations depicts the life of a Black family living in the country.

LEXAU, JOAN M. *Striped Ice Cream.* Philadelphia: Lippincott, 1968. The everyday life of a poor, fatherless Black family is described in this story, which centers on Becky, who as the youngest of five children finds life very trying.

MILES, MISKA. *Gertrude's Pocket.* Boston: Little, Brown, 1970. This story portrays the life of a poor Appalachian family. Gertrude's new dress has been made from the skirt of Grammaw's old red dress.

SURANY, ANICO. *Malachy's Gold.* New York: Holiday House, 1968. In the California Sierras after the forty-niners have left, the old prospector Malachy is rescued from death by an orphaned Indian boy.

Grade 7 and Up

CLARK, MAVIS T. *Blue Above the Trees.* New York: Meredith, 1968. The wild, dense rain forest of Victoria, Australia, is converted into a dairyland by hardy pioneers of the late 1800s.

DUKE, MADELAINE. *The Secret People.* Garden City, N.Y.: Doubleday, 1969. This book portrays Australia as a land of contrast in which two different civilizations meet.

INNIS, PAULINE. *Wind of the Pampas.* New York: David McKay, 1967. This story recounts the adventures of sixteen-year-old Marco, who leaves an Argentine orphanage to seek his fortune with his friend Frasco. Together they succeed in starting their own tourist guide business.

SMITH, VIAN. *Come Down the Mountain.* Garden City, N. Y.: Doubleday, 1968. This story reveals insights into contemporary English village life and the relationships between generations and between peers.

Further Reading for Teachers, Parents, and Librarians

ANDERSON, MARION P. *Books to Grow On.* New York: American Jewish Committee, 1961.

BANKS, JAMES A. "A Content Analysis of the Black American in Text Books," *Social Education,* 33 (December 1969), 954–957, 963.

CROSBY, MURIEL. *Reading Ladders for Human Relationships.* Washington, D. C.: American Council on Education, 1963.

GOLDEN, LORETTA. "The Treatment of Minority Groups in Primary Social Studies Text Books," Ph. D. dissertation, Stanford University, 1964, *Dissertation Abstracts,* 25 (January 1965), 3912.

HARNEY, IRENE E., AND LUCILLE P. BURGDORF. "Urban Children Study Interaction Among People," *The Instructor,* 78 (December 1968), 92–94.

HUUS, HELEN. *Children's Books to Enrich the Social Studies.* Rev. ed. Washington, D. C.: National Council for the Social Studies, 1966.

KENNEDY, JOHN F. *Profiles in Courage.* New York: Harper & Row, 1956.

KENWORTHY, LEONARD. *Introducing Children to the World.* New York: Harper & Row, 1956.

MEAD, MARGARET. *People and Places.* Cleveland and New York: World Publishing, 1959.

MOTT, PAUL E. *The Organization of Society.* Englewood Cliffs, N. J.: Prentice-Hall, 1965.

From *Freddy the Detective* by Walter Brooks, illustrated by Kurt Wiese.

5

Laughter in Literature

> Laughter and jollity as a theme in literature strike a responsive chord in young children. The fun can involve pure nonsense, incongruities, surprises, silly antics, unusual manipulation of language patterns, peculiarities, or exploration of the impossible, the incredible, the implausible . . . The funny stories are best when they laugh *with* rather than *at* the characters, so that the sympathetic responses are evoked. They are most effective when the humor emerges effervescently from the character, the events, or the language patterns employed rather than from the conscious effort of an author to make children laugh. [(36), p. 198]

The primary purpose in reading is pleasure. Although one may read to find out something, the finding out is exhilarating, satisfying, and pleasurable. Children often find in books a joy that is somehow above and beyond the entertainment provided by radio, television, magazines, motion pictures, and other media of mass communication. They find that they can return time and again to the enjoyment they have discovered in a book. This pleasure contributes to a love of literature and helps to build lifelong enjoyment in reading.

Many authors have written stories for children with the sole purpose of recreation and pleasure. Indeed, it is difficult to find a person writing in the field of children's literature who does not stress the role of fun and laughter. It is the reactions of the characters in the situations and the way that the characters work their way out that children find funny: how Lazy Tommy Pumpkinhead manages to live in an all-electric house after the current is turned off, how Burt Dow the old fisherman gets his codfish hook out of the tail of a whale, how Sylvester gets out of the precarious position of being face to face with a lion.

However, Margery Fisher (24) makes these surprising statements about humor:

I doubt whether many small children really recognize humour as such at all. To do so, they need the experience to sort out the incongruous from the congruous, the likely from the unlikely; and, for them, the distinction hardly exists. They will almost always accept Alice in Wonderland, for instance, as serious fantasy. Alice's rapid changes in size, the behaviour of the sheep in the wool shop or the flutterings of the White Queen, seem to them exciting and odd rather than laughable.

Perhaps an appreciation of humour begins, most usually, at seven or eight, with practical jokes and the more innocent types of coarseness . . .

Children of later school age do not so often look for funny books. Humour in stories suits them better. Humour in school stories . . . ; humour in a sophisticated family idiom, as in Elizabeth Enright's stories about the Melendys, . . . humour in fairy-tales when the ordinary world is turned upside-down. All kinds of humour by the way, but not humour for its own sake. [P. 153]

Many authors of stories for young readers have created characters that are immediately identified with fun and laughter. The mention of such names as Tom Sawyer, Huckleberry Finn, Homer Price, and Henry Huggins brings broad smiles to the faces of boys and girls and chuckles from adults who have been fortunate enough to make their acquaintance. These and many other characters call to mind humorous situations that make reading fun.

Humor is always popular with children. Of all the recommendations young readers make of the books they read, one given most frequently and enthusiastically is that the story is funny. Ask a child to name his favorite character, and often he will name a humorous one, a character who gets into hazardous predicaments, whose escapades often provide extravagant nonsense, who furnishes fun, and who moves the reader to laughter.

It takes a master hand to write in a humorous vein and to create humorous characters and funny situations.

Tom Sawyer

The Adventures of Tom Sawyer (93) by Mark Twain (Samuel Langhorne Clemens) is an excellent illustration of a book written for the purpose of recreation and pleasure. The book is based on reminiscences of the author's boyhood in a small Mississippi River town in Missouri and tells the adventures of mischievous Tom and his pal, Huckleberry Finn, to whom he has sworn enduring friendship. Tom lives with his rigid Aunt Polly. His maneuvers to outwit her, his scheme for getting the fence whitewashed, and his romance with Becky Thatcher are only a few of the escapades that follow one after another. Along with a pal, Joe Harper, Tom and Huck hide out on

Jackson's Island and are given up for dead. A highlight of the story occurs when Tom and Huck appear at their own funeral. One of the outstanding features of the story that continues to make it a favorite over the years is its warm, friendly humor, it is full of fun and laughs. Tom has a lark with life: He loves the role he lives, plays it to the hilt, and is willing to share the fun with others. He becomes the hero of every boy the minute he outwits not only his Aunt Polly but every Aunt Polly around the world who stands in the way of a boy's good time.

Years later, Twain wrote *The Adventures of Huckleberry Finn* (92) in which he recounts the adventures of Huck, his dog, and his friend, Negro Jim, drifting down the Mississippi River.

Following the success of *Tom Sawyer, Huckleberry Finn,* and "The Celebrated Jumping Frog of Calaveras County" (96), Mark Twain lectured with tremendous success. His reputation as a lecturer was rivaled only by his reputation as a writer. And each was nurtured by his ability as a humorist. Enthusiastic audiences greeted him wherever he appeared, and he became somewhat of a world traveler.

After visiting the countries of Europe, Mark Twain wrote his first travel book, *Innocents Abroad* (95). In addition to *Innocents Abroad,* he wrote three more travel books that added to his popularity. *Roughing It* (98) relates his experiences traveling to the West. *A Tramp Abroad* (99) is a European travel book.

To add further to the reading pleasure of boys and girls, Mark Twain wrote *The Prince and the Pauper* (97) with its setting in England during the time of King Henry VIII and King Edward VI and *A Connecticut Yankee in King Arthur's Court* (94), which lampoons the legends of King Arthur and his knights. However, it is *Tom Sawyer* and *Huckleberry Finn* that will continue to be favorite reading as long as boys and girls delight in deviltry and are determined to make boyhood a happy adventure and a time to remember.

Tom Sawyer Leads the Parade

Tom Sawyer carved a niche for himself and immediately set the pace for sheer fun in other literature for young readers. Two other fun-loving, mischievous boys appeared on the literary scene and kept company with Tom for a while: the rascal in *Peck's Bad Boy and His Pa* and Tom Bailey in *The Story of a Bad Boy.*

Peck's Bad Boy and His Pa (67) by George W. Peck first appeared serially in Mr. Peck's own newspaper, the *Milwaukee Sun,* and then in a series of books from 1883 to 1907. They are episodic stories of the practical jokes that a mischievous boy plays on his father. The episodes were enlivened by a raw and boisterous kind of humor that is reminiscent of the pie-throwing, slapstick comedies of the early motion pictures. The author became so popular through his stories that he was elected governor of Wisconsin in 1890.

The Story of a Bad Boy (1) by Thomas Bailey Aldrich is largely autobiographical and relates the pranks and adventures of its hero, Tom Bailey, in the quaint New England town called Rivermouth, which in reality is Portsmouth, New Hampshire. Tom and his pals engage in the typical activities that make a boy's world exciting. There is a homey style to the writing that gives a nostalgic glow to boyhood and the portrayal of a New England town.

Popular for a time, and now literary memorabilia, the bad boys and Tom Bailey have given way to other boys who provide fun and laughter and continue to hold the stage with Tom Sawyer. Among them are Homer Price, Henry Reed, Henry Huggins, and Eddie Wilson, as well as many less popular characters.

Homer Price (61) by Robert McCloskey stands out as the speaker for boys from small American towns. Homer lives about two miles outside of Centerburg where Route 56 meets Route 56A, a typical country crossroads with its two-pump gas station, the combination garage, grocery store and hotel, its barber shop, doughnut shop, and movie, to say nothing of a staid group of citizens. Homer's father owns a tourist camp and runs the filling station, his mother cooks in the lunch room and takes care of the tourist cabins, and Homer does odd jobs.

One hilarious situation after another makes a laughter-packed story. With the help of his tame skunk Aroma, Homer apprehends a band of robbers and turns them over to the sheriff; he comes to the rescue of Super-Duper, a superman caught in a barbed-wire fence; he starts the doughnut machine in his uncle's doughnut shop and floods the restaurant with doughnuts; and he plays an active part in every civic and social activity in Centerburg. Bits of mystery and lots

From *The Story of a Bad Boy* by Thomas Aldrich, illustrated by Reginald Marsh.

of suspense are threaded through the different incidents, and the illustrations add a hometown quality to the story.

In *Henry Huggins* (16), Beverly Cleary created a boy who speaks for all boys who revel in collecting strange and sometimes unmanageable things, who succeed in coming out of difficult situations, and who make decisions with the wisdom of Solomon. The story opens with Henry collecting a dog that plays an important part in the story. The guppies he acquires multiply so rapidly that he has to trade them in for a catfish that seldom has babies. He also collects night crawlers to make money to pay for a football that had belonged to another boy and had been carried off by a man into whose car Henry had inadvertently thrown it. Regardless of the precariousness of the situations in which Henry becomes involved, he and his dog Ribsey always manage to come out on top.

Henry, his friend Beatrice (pronounced Beezus), and her interferring little sister Ramona received a hearty welcome from both boys and girls, and their popularity continued to grow with the stories that followed. *Henry and Beezus* (14) relates the many difficulties Henry experiences in his efforts to earn a bicycle. He is helped by Beezus but hindered by Ramona and Ribsey. *Henry and Ribsey* (15) is filled with humorous situations. Henry's father makes a deal with Henry: He promises to take Henry salmon fishing if he keeps Ribsey out of mischief for a month.

Eddie Wilson is another irrepressible boy who has joined Tom's procession of laugh provokers. *Little Eddie* (35) was introduced to young readers by Carolyn Haywood in 1947. Since then he has increased his popularity as new titles are published.

Like Henry Huggins, Eddie is a born collector. He "brought all of the stray animals home with him. Stray cats, stray dogs, birds that had fallen out of their nests, turtles, snails, garter snakes; anything that was alive, Eddie brought home with him" (p. 10). Eddie's other passion is for signs. When you open Eddie's door, you read, "Stop, Look, and Listen," "Silence, Man Working," "Slow," "Danger," and "Road Under Construction." What Eddie calls "valuable property," his father calls "junk."

After introducing Eddie, Carolyn Haywood continued to entertain young readers with his doings at regular intervals. When Eddie's father buys him an old fire engine as a birthday gift, hilarious situations follow in *Eddie and the Fire Engine* (31). More of Eddie's laugh-provoking escapades can be enjoyed in *Eddie and Gardenia* (29), *Eddie's Pay Dirt* (34), *Eddie Makes Music* (32), *Eddie and Louella* (30), and *Eddie's Green Thumb* (33).

Carolyn Haywood also wrote the Betsy series. The first in the series, *"B" Is for Betsy* (28), relates a little girl's experiences during her first year in school. The stories that follow take Betsy and her friends through the early grades. Although the Betsy stories started more than thirty years ago, they are still enjoyed by many little girls.

Dr. Seuss' Characters

Boys and girls quickly come to know the authors upon whom they can rely for a good laugh. A taste of the fun in any one of Dr. Seuss' books leads children to rush to every story into which this prolific writer has poured his inimitable and seemingly unlimited supply of humor. They are able to sense that he is kidding with his outlandish but euphonious names for the characters, his broad, often slapstick, brand of humor, and his clever way of twisting and turning plots, and they love it all.

Dr. Seuss captured a following of boys and girls, not to mention adults, with his first book, *And to Think That I Saw It on Mulberry Street* (81). There is a lilt to the text of *Mulberry Street* that dances its way through the story. The illustrations have a quality that has become the trademark of Dr. Seuss. Marco, the hero of the story, is admonished by his father, who says, "Marco, keep your eyelids up/ And see what you can see." Marco is challenged, and he rises to it gloriously in his imagination, which gallops ahead of him. After building the story of what he has seen on Mulberry Street to fantastic proportions, he lets it collapse in a heart-warming way when his father asks for a report.

The popularity of *And to Think That I Saw It on Mulberry Street* with its appeal to both children and adults has been the subject of numerous reviews. Some reviewers place it in the fantasy genre. Other reviewers have described it as a child's tragedy. Be that as it may, it is a pleasant story that entertains both young and old. Although adults may read it with sad feelings for Marco, most children laugh uproariously over Marco's skill in embroidering facts.

After the enthusiastic reception of his first contribution to children's literature, Dr. Seuss drew upon his brand of humor time and again for the entertainment of boys and girls. *And to Think That I Saw It on Mulberry Street* was followed by the captivating story *The Five Hundred Hats of Bartholomew Cubbins* (83). In this hilarious story, with its fairy-tale quality, Bartholomew Cubbins innocently starts to town one Saturday morning to sell cranberries. Upon reaching the town he is detained by the passing of the king. The captain of the king's own court shouts to the bystanders, "Hats off to the King." When Bartholomew takes off his hat a strange thing happens. Another hat

From *The 500 Hats of Bartholomew Cubbins* by Dr. Seuss.

appears on his head. Every time he takes off his hat there is another one in its place. There is no way of stopping the flow of hats. Excitement rises when the king's nephew suggests that the only way to get Bartholomew to take off his hat is to have his head cut off. There is nothing for Bartholomew to do but to go down to the dungeon to see the executioner, but the executioner refuses to decapitate anyone with a hat on. At last, after 499 hats have been taken from Bartholomew's head and the king has threatened all kinds of punishments, the 500th hat appears. What a beautiful creation it is! At the story's end Bartholomew is hatless but richer by 500 gold pieces and the king is wearing the beautiful hat.

Remembering the fun in Dr. Seuss' first two books, boys and girls received his next laughter-filled story, *The King's Stilts* (87), with delight. Again there is the kind of fanciful and nonsensical dialogue that young children enjoy.

With Dr. Seuss well established as a favorite author and illustrator of stories for children, one book after another followed at regular intervals; each one in varying degrees of quality continued to delight young children. *Horton Hatches the Egg* (85) followed *The King's Stilts* and then came such extravagantly nonsensical titles as *Thidwick: The Big-Hearted Moose* (88), *Bartholomew and the Oobleck* (82), *Horton Hears a Who* (86), and *Green Eggs and Ham* (84), all planned to provoke children's laughter for years to come.

Miss Pickerell

Ellen MacGregor capitalizes on a type of humor that appeals to boys and girls a bit older than those who find fun and entertainment in the Seuss stories. In each of the Seuss stories the plot revolves around a different leading character, whereas in the MacGregor stories, Miss Pickerell, a little old lady wearing a pink sweater, almost always plays the lead.

These stories are frequently referred to as The Miss Pickerell Series. In the first of the series, *Miss Pickerell Goes to Mars* (56), Miss Pickerell takes a trip against her wishes and the wishes of the crew of the rocket ship in which she travels.

Three more stories with the plot revolving around Miss Pickerell came in quick succession: *Miss Pickerell Goes Undersea* (58), *Miss Pickerell and the Geiger Counter* (55), and *Miss Pickerell Goes to the Arctic* (57). In *Miss Pickerell Goes Undersea* she tangles with the navy and an atomic-powered submarine in her efforts to salvage her collection of Mars rocks that were lost when the ship on which they were being returned sank. In *Miss Pickerell and the Geiger Counter* one humorous situation after another arises when Miss Pickerell attempts to take her cow to a circus veterinarian and her two nephews to an atomic exhibition. Through her interest in weather forecasting, Miss Pickerell, in *Miss Pickerell Goes to the Arctic,* goes to Alaska with a rescue mission and finds herself helping the crew of a ship that had been stranded in the Arctic.

Ellen MacGregor put aside Miss Pickerell to tell boys and girls about a turtle who remembers and forgets in such a way that he creates a funny story. *Theodore Turtle* (59), as well as the Miss Pickerell stories, is enhanced by the clever illustrations of the well-known artist Paul Galdone.

Whereas Dr. Seuss uses numerous ways of provoking laughter, Ellen MacGregor makes Miss Pickerell humorous in a quiet sort of way. It is often the incongruous things that Miss Pickerell does at her age that are funny.

The Peterkins

During the 1880s Lucretia P. Hale made her contribution to humorous characters in children's literature by introducing the young readers of our country to the Peterkin family. The Peterkins first ap-

From *The Peterkin Papers* by Lucretia Hale.

peared in serial form in *Our Young Folks,* a magazine published in Boston and edited by Lucy Larcom and J. T. Trowbridge. *The Peterkin Papers* (27) were continued afterward in the *St. Nicholas* magazine.

It is fun to read how the Peterkin family gets in and out of one hilarious predicament after another. The reader waits each time to find out what oracular decisions the Lady from Philadelphia will make when, for example, Mrs. Peterkin puts salt in her coffee, even though the reader has decided beforehand what Mrs. Peterkin should do. Sophistication does not dim the humor of Elizabeth Eliza's playing the piano through the porch window because the men who delivered it turned the piano the wrong way, or of Agamemnon preparing to write his book and then discovering he has nothing to say, or of the Christmas tree episode when Mr. Peterkin and the little boys in their India rubber boots bring home a Christmas tree so tall that a hole has to be cut in the ceiling of the parlor to accommodate it.

One can understand how reading *The Peterkin Papers* as they appeared serially would be a hilarious experience for a family as they waited for each installment to arrive and then shared it. Boys and girls today still enjoy having the doings of the Peterkins read to them in installments.

Dr. Dolittle

The lovable and humorous Dr. Dolittle, created by Hugh Lofting, arrived early on the literary scene and has stayed on for generation after generation for the pleasure of young readers. *The Story of Doctor Dolittle* (52) has the intriguing subtitle:

Being the
History of This Peculiar Life
At Home and Astonishing Adventures Abroad
In Foreign Parts Never Before Printed

Dr. Dolittle lives in a little town called Puddleby-on-the-Marsh where everyone loves him including the dogs, the children, and the crows who live in the church tower. He is fond of animals and keeps pets of every variety. But having his animals all over the place causes him to lose his practice. His savings are spent buying food for his animals, and he becomes poorer and poorer. His fortune takes a turn for the worse when he lets a crocodile, a circus refugee, live with him. His patients are afraid of the crocodile, and his practice comes to an end.

After the tremendous reception the first Doctor Dolittle story received from young readers, it is easy to understand why they welcomed each story that followed. Between 1920, when Dolittle made his entrance into the literary world, and 1952, eleven Doctor Dolittle stories were published. The next to follow *The Story of Doctor Dolittle* was *The Voyages of Doctor Dolittle* (53), in which he travels to Spidermonkey Island to learn the language of the shellfish. For this imaginative story, Hugh Lofting received the 1923 Newbery Award.

Story after story followed in quick succession. *Doctor Dolittle's Post Office* (50) is about the fastest mail service in the world, Swallow Mail, which is established through Doctor Dolittle's efforts. In *Doctor Dolittle's Circus* (49) the kind-hearted doctor and pushmipullyu, an animal the monkeys gave Dr. Dolittle to show their appreciation for what he had done for them when he went to Africa, join a circus in order to earn money to pay for the boat that Dr. Dolittle borrowed and wrecked on his trip to Africa. Because of his love for animals, Dr. Dolittle could not resist planning a zoo, which he eventually builds in the garden at Puddleby-on-the-Marsh. The zoo, its inhabitants, and their elaborate accommodations are described in *Doctor Dolittle's Zoo* (51).

Doctor Dolittle's Caravan (48) is somewhat of a departure from the preceding Dr. Dolittle stories. The story is built around a little hen canary that can sing, although only male canaries are supposed to have singing voices. The little hen's singing starts a movement called "Singing for Women," which the male and old-maid canaries oppose. It is easy to understand how each of Dr. Dolittle's stories is an invitation to laughter.

Two Characters from Abroad

Two mischievous, irresponsible, yet lovable characters have come from across the ocean to join the ranks of those characters who provide fun and entertainment for American boys and girls. A boy, Pinocchio, came from Italy; and a girl, Pippi Longstocking, came from Sweden.

Pinocchio (17) by Carlo Lorenzini, who wrote under the pseudonym of Carlo Collodi, is the story of a puppet who behaves like a rascal but finally becomes a good little boy.

Pinocchio first appeared in 1881 in the *Children's Journal,* published in Rome. The first installment immediately caught the fancy of boys and girls who demanded more, and Collodi wrote succeeding installments as the fancy struck him. When it came out in book form it was a best seller not only in Italy but around the world. It was translated into many languages including Gaelic and Japanese.

Pinocchio does the things many boys wish they dared to do. In spite of the fantastic nature of the story, the characters are realistically drawn and take on lifelike personalities. There is no letup in the action in which Pinocchio proceeds from bad to worse. And each time Pinocchio tells a lie, his nose gets longer and longer and longer. This kind of plot keeps youngsters reading, and Pinocchio continues to be a popular figure in children's literature.

If a devilish character ever cavorted through the pages of a book for the enjoyment of children, it is in *Pippi Longstocking* (47) by Astrid Lindgren. Pippi arrived on the literary scene with varied reactions from adults. For some, Pippi was too reckless to become a part of children's lives; for others, Pippi was a hoodlum of considerable dimensions—almost a delinquent—but one to know and to cherish.

Pippi arrives at Villa Villekulla with her monkey, Mr. Nelson, and a big suitcase full of gold pieces. One of the most remarkable things about Pippi is her physical strength. She buys a horse with one of her gold pieces, and she keeps him on the porch of the house; whenever she wants to have afternoon coffee on the porch, she just lifts up the horse and sets him down in the garden. Tommy and Annika, the boy and girl who live next door, are taken in wholeheartedly by Pippi and become a part of her absurd adventures. Pippi has a brief fling at schooling, in which she dismays the teacher while she entertains the boys and girls. It seems natural for Pippi to exaggerate, perhaps even lie. After ending her brief stay in school, Pippi goes on engaging in unexpected, daring, and devilish adventures—the kind that fascinate young readers and keep them reading on. Pippi Longstocking is destined to have a long career in children's literature.

Astrid Lindgren has not let her young readers down. Following *Pippi Longstocking* came *Pippi Goes on Board* (45) and *Pippi in the South Seas* (46). Each story has its own peculiar adventure and absurdity that continue to make Pippi a fascinating character.

Some New Humorous Characters

A runner-up for the 1970 Caldecott Award, *Pop Corn and Ma Goodness* (70) by Edna M. Preston is a humorous picture-story book that relates the meeting of Pop Corn and Ma Goodness, their wedding, and how they build a house, make a farm, and raise a family.

The solution to the sad plight of Quangle-Wangle Quee, who lives in an immense beaver hat on the top of Crumpetty Tree, is delightfully told in Edward Lear's highly imaginative picture-story book *The Quangle-Wangle's Hat* (44). The large colored illustrations by Lear add to the fun of the story.

Wilfred the Lion (37) by Syd Hoff relates the story of a lively boy who likes lions so much that he imagines he is one. He soon discovers that being king of the beasts can be fun but that it also can be lonely.

Duck in the Gun (18) by Joy Cowley is a lively and appealing story about a general who cannot make war on a town because a duck has made her nest in his one and only cannon. While waiting for the eggs to hatch, the general falls in love with the daughter of the captain of the enemy army, and the troops decide they want to go home. Humorous illustrations accentuate the fun.

Ollie's Team and the Football Computer (69) by Clem Philbrook is an exciting football story with a computer as an added attraction. IDIOT 50–50 is a computer—a computer in charge of Ollie Scrugg's father. Thirteen-year-old Ollie has access to IDIOT for football games. The result is excitement and action.

The Twenty-One Balloons (20) by William Pené Du Bois is a lively tale of a retired professor's balloon trip to the island of Krakatoa, where he discovers a wealthy communal society supported by a large diamond mine. The professor is induced to remain on the island—until disaster strikes. The laughter-packed story is narrated by the professor, who has been found floating in the Atlantic Ocean on the remains of the twenty-one balloons.

Homerhenry (3) by Cora Annett is a highly entertaining story. Mr. Homer, a tailor, and Mr. Henry, a shoemaker, decide to make their dream of being a horse come true. Their result, Homerhenry, is a dubious success. However, after unsuccessful attempts as a police and then a fire horse, they do make a hit at the circus, but not in the way they have hoped.

Humorous Animal Stories

Writers of children's literature are aware of how interested children are in animals. No animal is too large or too small to be included in the realm of a child's affection. It is difficult to find an animal regardless of its size, habitat, or manners that is not featured in a story.

The Big Ones

Just as little boys like to flex their muscles to show how strong they are, they enjoy projecting themselves into big, fierce animals such as bears, lions, and elephants. The projection makes them feel fierce and strong. For their satisfaction there are many stories about the prowess of big animals.

Bears are natural laugh provokers. Both children and adults enjoy their antics in spite of their sometimes ferocious behavior. There is always that cuddly Teddy Bear that gets into the baby's crib and remains as an important member of the family and a close companion of the child for a number of years. Then, often ragged and torn, the little bear is put away and kept as a remembrance of happy childhood days. Later comes the delightful experience of listening to that favorite of childhood stories, *The Three Bears.* Young children never seem to tire of listening to, telling, dramatizing, and then reading for themselves this story that holds such magic for them.

Authors of stories for children, sensitive to the cozy feeling that young children have for bears, have written stories built around their antics, placing the bears in humorous situations and having them perform in ways that provoke laughter.

In the early 1950s Lynd Ward added a bear and a boy to the parade of bear stories in his amusing *The Biggest Bear* (101). Johnny, the boy in the story, wants to own the biggest bearskin in the valley but succumbs to a baby bear he meets and takes for a pet. Johnny's bear grows bigger and bigger, until he becomes a nuisance to the people of the valley because of his ravenous appetite and his plunderous ways of getting food. Johnny finally must get rid of the bear. Although he is sincere in his efforts to do so, he is unsuccessful in all of his attempts. The bear is eventually trapped by the man from the zoo where he is taken to live in a cage with a sign on it that says, "Biggest Bear, gift of Mr. John Orchard."

Bears (41) by Ruth Krauss has little text but many illustrations of bears doing both believable and unbelievable things in a humorous style.

Buzzy Bear tries hard to help Father Bear in the garden, but everything he does is wrong. Father shows Buzzy how to be a real helper in Dorothy Marino's well-illustrated story *Buzzy Bear in the Garden* (60).

Little Bear's Christmas (10) by Janice Brustlein is a happy story about Little Bear who is awakened from his winter sleep by a dream in time to enjoy his first Christmas. Little Bear discovers the pleasure of giving and sharing as he accompanies Santa Claus on his rounds and then returns home to a surprise Christmas party.

Rhinoceroses, hippopotamuses, and elephants are huge members of the animal kingdom that provide laughs for boys and girls at the zoo, on television, and in story books. Their hugeness seems to intrigue children.

The wonderful world of animals from chimpanzee to rhinoceros is examined from the child's point of view in selecting a pet in *A Rhinoceros, Preposterous* (79) by Letta Schatz. Even though guppies and goldfish may be the parents' choice, they are not the kind of pets that a young outdoor man dreams about. A rhinoceros would be fun, but the parents' reaction would be "Preposterous!" The little boy settles on one little pup. The text is enlivened by Ed Emberley's small, humorous illustrations.

Just to look at the pictures of Harriet who does not want to be a hippopotamus anymore makes one feel sad. When Harriet leaves the river and goes to live in a house, she forgets how to smile. She makes a friend, Mouse, who tries his utmost to help her remember. The story, *The Unhappy Hippopotamus* (64), by Nancy Moore and Edward Leight and the illustrations by Ermintrude are done with such flair that Harriet and her friend Mouse have to evoke chuckles.

Baby Elephant and the Secret Wishes (39) by Sesyle Joslin and Leonard Weisgard is about a very happy and excited baby elephant who on Christmas Eve asks each member of his family, "Do you have a secret wish for something that you have always wanted?" When they respond, he describes each gift he has for them and asks if it is one of their secret wishes. The adults are struck with amazement at being asked about exactly the wished-for thing. Bubbling humor, tenderness, and the rare understanding of the family make a delightful story.

Thai, Kao, and Tone are three curious, playful, young elephants living in Thailand in Tony Palazzo's humorous tale *Thai, Kao and Tone: An Elephant Story* (66). Thai's love for bananas gets the elephant trio into trouble in the forest. The older elephants rescue the frightened youngsters when they meet a tiger.

In a zoo the elephants get keen competition from the monkeys for the attention of boys and girls. From the huge gorilla to the little spider monkey there are numerous kinds, each with his own characteristics to observe.

A number of children's authors have a favorite animal around whom they build their stories. The animal often seems to be human. The laughter-filled reception these heroes receive from young readers encourages the authors to try a second story. Thus a series is often born. One series that features a monkey has delighted readers for several generations.

In *Curious George* (71) by Hans A. Rey a lovable little monkey swung his way into the affection of young readers over thirty years ago. George's curiosity leads to his capture. Brought to this country, George has difficulty adjusting to city life. When he unintentionally puts in a fire alarm, he is put in prison. He escapes only to get into trouble with the balloon man. Finally, the man who brought George from Africa rescues him from his unexpected balloon flight. The man puts George in a zoo where he thoroughly enjoys his new home.

Curious George's creator, Hans A. Rey, combines text and illustrations to make George a lively and likable little monkey. The illustrations in strong, dark colors, full of action, on white paper mirror the agility of Curious George. The text and the illustrations move at a breathless pace.

Young readers have looked forward to more Curious George stories. The pattern remains much the same throughout the series. George's curiosity gets him into one precarious situation after another. He manages to escape in ways that add more hilarity to the stories. Some of the titles that follow reveal the humorous situations in which George performs: *Curious George Rides a Bike* (74), *Curious George Gets a Medal* (72), *Curious George Flies a Kite* (75) written by Margaret Rey, *Curious George Learns the Alphabet* (73), and *Curious George Goes to the Hospital* (76) coauthored with Margaret Rey. Some thirty titles follow the first Curious George story.

The antics of monkeys come to life in the illustrations of Jane Rietveld's story *Monkey Island* (77). Zippo is an unhappy little monkey. He wants to know how the boys and girls who come to the zoo live. He manages to escape from the zoo and after a series of adventures returns to the zoo wiser for his travels.

In Ida Chittum's *Farmer Hoo and the Baboons* (13) a mix-up in names brings a huge crate filled with rare ringtailed baboons destined for Happleton Zoo to the farm of Appleton Hoo, operated by a man not given to making adjustments whenever emergencies arise. Of course, this is not a usual emergency! Suspense and excitement flavored with slapstick follow when Farmer Hoo attempts to keep his curious wife, son, and hired man at their jobs while he copes with the 41 baboons that get loose. Glen Rounds' action drawings are a perfect accompaniment to the hilarious happenings in this picture-story book.

Dogs and Cats Galore!

Ghost Dog of Killicut (22) by Mel Ellis is a well-written suspense story of outdoor adventure. Eighteen-year-old Guy Hardin braves the dangerous fog and battles the sea to search for a dog most people believe to be a ghost.

By the Sea (2) is an amusing and well-illustrated textless storybook by Berthe Amoss. A small boy carried into a cloud by a kite is rescued by his dog.

Animal lovers will be pleased with *Little Dog Lost* (26) by René Guillot. When a Welsh Corgi puppy is lost, he is adopted by a fox. For a time he is a little girl's Tiny and then a boy's Domino. Having fun in each situation, he finally brings all of his families together.

An unhappy farm dog meets up with a witch who transforms him into a whingdingdilly in Bill Peet's story *The Whingdingdilly* (68). After some harrowing experiences, he is happy to go back to being a dog.

The age-old theme of a boy's longing for a dog is well related in Liesel M. Skorpen's story *All the Lassies* (89). The small boy in the story wants a dog; instead he gets first a fish, then a bird, a turtle, and a kitten. He names each one of them Lassie. When he finally gets a dog, he names him Walter.

Too Many Bozos (63) by Lilian Moore is an appealing story about a boy's desire to have a dog. When Danny's mother says "no" to a dog, he acquires a frog, pet mouse, and ants. His mother finally decides that a dog would be the best pet.

Jan M. Robinson's *The December Dog* (78) tells of a dog who was mistreated early in life. She avoids people until she must seek help from the Martin family to protect her puppies. A pleasant relationship soon develops between the Martins and the dog.

Illustrations full of action and rich with color enhance *The Sky Dog* (91) by Brinton Turkle. A boy who imagines a shaggy, white dog in a cloud formation has his fantasy become a reality when he is able to keep a real shaggy white dog for his own.

Big Ben (100) by David Walker is the story of an amiable St. Bernard who becomes part of a farming family in Maine as a result of a near tragic accident. Big Ben endears himself to the family when he chases a savage bear away from the children and saves them from an attack by the neighbor's vicious dog. The characterizations in the story are excellent.

When Junket, the dog who likes everything, returns from a romp in the woods, he finds that his former owners have distributed the farm animals throughout the community and have moved away. The new owner of the farm is not interested in animals. How Junket succeeds in convincing him that animals are important, and how he eventually manages their return, makes *Junket* (102) by Anne H. White a story rich with laughter-provoking incidents.

Kittens and cats are popular subjects for stories. Some of their unbelievable antics provide fun and suspense as they come to life on the pages of well-written stories. Gay illustrations enhance the story of the adventures of a little lost kitten trying to find his way home in *Little Lost Kitten* (54) by Lois Lovett.

Dolly Moses (12) by Mary Ellen Chase is a well-written story about a strange, absurd, fantastic, and unbelievably funny cat that comes to live with the Chase family.

When a cat boasts as to what can be done with a fine tail and four legs, other animals relate their outstanding accomplishments in *Four Legs and a Tail* (38) by Aurora Dias Jorgenson. A boy reports what he can do and tops them all. The amusing illustrations add to the fun.

A fragment of ancient lore is imaginatively presented by Jerzy Laskowski in *Master of the Royal Cats* (43), a tale of ancient Egypt which describes how the boy Anput, with the help of a sacred crocodile, finds the perfect animals to protect the precious grain from the rats and is thereby given the title Master of the Royal Cats. The story is enriched by beautiful color illustrations.

When the cross-eyed cat in a story by Margaret Embry, *Mister Blue* (23), invites himself to a third-grade classroom, things begin to happen—humorous events take place in and out of the classroom. The experiences, expressions, and feelings of the children are portrayed realistically.

How small Kate finally acquires her own cat and kittens is a charming story by Phyllis La Farge titled *Kate and the Wild Kittens* (42).

Color cartoon-type illustrations complement Crosby Bonsall's humorous story *The Case of the Cat's Meow* (5) about the disappearance of Snitch's beloved cat, Mildred. Wizard, Tubby, and Skinny, three of Snitch's friends, help him investigate the case. When Mildred finally turns up for food, the four boys trail her back to her basket where they happily discover her family of kittens.

A cat, a rabbit, a bird, and a bullfrog meet a perplexing problem in *The Big Green Thing* (80) by M. Schlein, a simple story with a slight plot that provides fun through word repetition.

The Little Ones

There is something about mice that seems to send shivers up and down people's spines and makes them scream and run. Mice in stories are quite different; they can delight the reader with their mischievous ways.

John Burningham's outstanding book *Trublhoff: The Mouse Who Wanted to Play the Balalaika* (11) is about a musical mouse who leaves his comfortable home in a little village inn in Central Europe to follow the gypsies in order to learn to play the balalaika. By good fortune, he returns to his family in time to save them from eviction by convincing the innkeeper of the usefulness of his unusual musical talent. Trublhoff and the other members of his family organize a balalaika band that becomes famous in the country. Imaginative illustrations add to the story.

Punky: Mouse for a Day (65) by John Moreton is a mystery story for young readers. Punky is a mouse who, from day to day, changes into all kinds of wonderful animals—each one larger than the one before. Punky soon becomes so big that no one knows what to do with him.

Mousekin's Golden House (62) by Edna Miller is all about a little mouse who escapes from an owl by hiding in a deserted jack-o'-lantern. He enjoys his hideout so much that he refuses all suggestions that he seek a warmer place for the winter. The pumpkin begins to shrivel—the eyes, nose, and mouth close—while inside the mouse sleeps serenely on the bed of down he has gathered for himself. The fanciful tale is enriched by beautiful illustrations.

A little yellow field mouse finds that life has many exciting and terrifying experiences in *Peek, the Piper* (4) by Vitali Bianki. He also learns by experience that he has many natural enemies but that nature has given him ways to escape from them.

Gregory, a mouse, provides fun and nonsense in *The Tail of Gregory* (19) by Polly Curren. Gregory would never have been noticed as he carefully crept upstairs to watch his favorite television program, if he did not have such a long tail. He escapes being caught and finally solves his entertainment problem in a most ingenious way.

In a simple style with black-and-white illustrations, Mary Stolz in *Siri the Conquistador* (90) tells about a well-stocked delicatessen storeroom that is the home of two small, brave mice. Siri, the resident cat, and the mice are upset by a fierce dog who visits the delicatessen. They manage to endure him until he leaves, but when the shop owner decides to get a huge dog of his own, which he names Maximilian, the story takes a surprising turn.

Irmengarde Eberle's story *Pete and the Mouse* (21) tells how a lasting friendship develops between Pete the farm horse and a determined field mouse who visits Pete's barn at night. The story has a suspenseful climax. The bold color illustrations by Gerald Rose add to the pleasure of the story.

Too many mice in a family create a housing problem in Rumer Godden's *Mouse House* (25), but the adventures of one little mouse result in a new house for the whole family.

In *Mouse at Sea* (40) by Robert Kraus a real mouse meets a mechanical mouse on a trip to Europe. Together they enjoy all the pleasures of sea travel and, in addition, save the ship from disaster.

And Finally . . .

It is difficult to find an animal that has not been made the hero of a story or a series of stories. Without question the most long-lived pig in children's literature is Freddy, a very knowing pig, created by Walter R. Brooks. As a child Brooks had enjoyed stories about talking animals—picking animals to carry his stories seemed only natural. In his first book, all the animals shared equally in the adventures, but by the end of the third story, Freddy the pig, because of his resourcefulness, had assumed leadership and became the hero of what seemed to be an inexhaustible list of Freddy stories. Some twenty-five books have appeared with such intriguing titles as *Freddy the Detective* (7), *Freddy the Magician* (8), *Freddy the Pilot* (9), and *Freddy and the Space Ship* (6).

From *Freddy the Detective* by Walter Brooks, illustrated by Kurt Wiese.

Extending Experiences for the Reader

1. Reread several humorous stories written for the enjoyment of boys and girls, such as *The Adventures of Tom Sawyer* (93) by Mark Twain, *The Five Hundred Hats of Bartholomew Cubbins* (83) by Dr. Seuss, *Miss Pickerell and the Geiger Counter* (55) by Ellen MacGregor, *Homer Price* (61) by Robert McCloskey, and *Henry Huggins* (16) by Beverly Cleary. Analyze the types of humor found in these stories. Select parts to read to the class that you think boys and girls will consider humorous. Observe their reactions.
2. Prepare a bibliography of humorous stories about animals to read to the class.
3. Read a number of short humorous stories to the class.
4. Encourage the class to write a humorous poem about an animal. Give them a couple of lines to start, such as:

    As I was walking down the road,
    I met a hippity-hoppity toad.

5. If possible, take a group of children on a visit to the zoo. Have them discuss the animals they see.

Extending Experiences for Children

1. Select humorous parts of a story to share with the class. Discuss what makes you laugh in the book you are reading.
2. Compare the humor of different writers, such as Mark Twain in *The Adventures of Tom Sawyer* (93), Robert McCloskey in *Homer Price* (61), and Ellen MacGregor in *Miss Pickerell Goes to Mars* (56).
3. Choose two or three children in the class who have read the same story. Prepare a skit based on a situation in the story to present to the class.
4. Draw a picture to illustrate a dramatic incident in a humorous story.
5. Compare the humor in *And to Think That I Saw It on Mulberry Street* (81) by Dr. Seuss with the humor in his story *Horton Hatches the Egg* (85).
6. Read one of Dr. Seuss' stories. Make a list of the words in the story that are made up by Dr. Seuss.
7. Write a word portrait of your favorite character in a humorous story to share with the class.
8. Share an episode from *The Peterkin Papers* (27) with the class.
9. Make a list of characters you have met in stories who are similar to Tom Sawyer. How are they alike?

10. Make a puppet of Pinocchio. Write and produce a play based on Collodi's *Pinocchio* (17).
11. Make a puppet of Pippi Longstocking. Have the puppet tell the story of Pippi Longstocking's life.
12. Make a paper-bag puppet of the head of your favorite animal. Have him describe himself to the class.

Chapter References

1. ALDRICH, THOMAS BAILEY. *The Story of a Bad Boy.* New York: Pantheon, 1951. Grade 7 and up.
2. AMOSS, BERTHE. *By the Sea.* New York: Parents' Magazine, 1969. Kindergarten–grade 3.
3. ANNETT, CORA. *Homerhenry.* Reading, Mass.: Addison-Wesley, 1969. Grades 3–6.
4. BIANKI, VITALI. *Peek, the Piper.* New York: Braziller, 1964. Grades 2–6.
5. BONSALL, CROSBY. *The Case of the Cat's Meow.* New York: Harper & Row, 1965. Kindergarten–grade 3.
6. BROOKS, WALTER R. *Freddy and the Spaceship.* New York: Knopf, 1953. Grades 3–7.
7. ———. *Freddy the Detective.* New York: Knopf, 1932. Grades 3–7.
8. ———. *Freddy the Magician.* New York: Knopf, 1947. Grades 3–7.
9. ———. *Freddy the Pilot.* New York: Knopf, 1952. Grades 3–7.
10. BRUSTLEIN, JANICE. *Little Bear's Christmas.* New York: Lothrop, Lee & Shepard, 1964. Preschool–grade 1.
11. BURNINGHAM, JOHN. *Trublhoff: The Mouse Who Wanted to Play the Balalaika.* New York: Random House, 1965.
12. CHASE, MARY ELLEN. *Dolly Moses.* New York: Norton, 1964.
13. CHITTUM, IDA. *Farmer Hoo and the Baboons.* New York: Delacorte, 1971. Kindergarten–grade 2.
14. CLEARY, BEVERLY. *Henry and Beezus.* New York: Morrow, 1952. Grades 4–6.
15. ———. *Henry and Ribsey.* New York: Morrow, 1954. Grades 4–6.
16. ———. *Henry Huggins.* New York: Morrow, 1950. Grades 4–6.
17. COLLODI, CHARLES (LORENZINI, CARLO). *Pinocchio.* New York: Macmillan, 1951. Grade 4 and up.
18. COWLEY, JOY. *Duck in the Gun.* Garden City; N. Y.: Doubleday, 1969. Kindergarten–grade 3.
19. CURREN, POLLY. *The Tail of Gregory.* San Carlos, Cal.: Golden Gate, 1964.
20. DU BOIS, WILLIAM PENÉ. *The Twenty-One Balloons.* New York: Dell. Paperback. Grades 4–8.
21. EBERLE, IRMENGARDE. *Pete and the Mouse.* New York: Abelard-Schuman, 1964. Preschool–grade 3.

22. ELLIS, MEL. *Ghost Dog of Killicut.* New York: Four Winds Press, 1969. Grades 5–10.
23. EMBRY, MARGARET. *Mister Blue.* New York: Holiday House, 1963. Kindergarten–grade 3.
24. FISHER, MARGERY. *Intent upon Reading.* New York: Watts, 1962.
25. GODDEN, RUMER. *Mouse House.* New York: Viking, 1968. Grades 2–5.
26. GUILLOT, RENÉ. *Little Dog Lost.* John Selby-Lownes (tr.). New York: Lothrop, Lee & Shepard, 1970. Grades 2–6.
27. HALE, LUCRETIA P. *The Peterkin Papers.* New York: Dover, 1960. Paperback. Grades 5–7.
28. HAYWOOD, CAROLYN. *"B" Is for Betsy.* New York: Harcourt Brace Jovanovich, 1968. Paperback. Grades 1–5.
29. ———. *Eddie and Gardenia.* New York: Morrow, 1951. Grades 4–6.
30. ———. *Eddie and Louella.* New York: Morrow, 1959. Grades 4–6.
31. ———. *Eddie and the Fire Engine.* New York: Morrow, 1949. Grades 4–6.
32. ———. *Eddie Makes Music.* New York: Morrow, 1957. Grades 4–6.
33. ———. *Eddie's Green Thumb.* New York: Morrow, 1964. Grades 4–6.
34. ———. *Eddie's Pay Dirt.* New York: Morrow, 1953. Grades 4–6.
35. ———. *Little Eddie.* New York: Morrow, 1947. Kindergarten–grade 3.
36. HERRICK, VIRGIL E., AND LELAND JACOBS (eds.). *Children and the Language Arts.* Englewood Cliffs, N. J.: Prentice-Hall, 1955.
37. HOFF, SYD. *Wilfred the Lion.* New York: Putnam, 1969. Kindergarten–grade 3.
38. JORGENSON, AURORA DIAS. *Four Legs and a Tail.* New York: Lothrop, Lee & Shepard, 1962.
39. JOSLIN, SESYLE, AND LEONARD WEISGARD. *Baby Elephant and the Secret Wishes.* New York: Harcourt Brace Jovanovich, 1962. Preschool–grade 3.
40. KRAUS, ROBERT. *Mouse at Sea.* New York: Harper & Row, 1959. Preschool–grade 1.
41. KRAUSS, RUTH. *Bears.* New York: Harper & Row, 1948. Kindergarten–grade 2.
42. LA FARGE, PHYLLIS. *Kate and the Wild Kittens.* New York: Knopf, 1965. Kindergarten–grade 3.
43. LASKOWSKI, JERZY. *Master of the Royal Cats.* New York: Seabury, 1965. Kindergarten–grade 3.
44. LEAR, EDWARD. *The Quangle-Wangle's Hat.* New York: Watts, 1969. Preschool–grade 3.
45. LINDGREN, ASTRID. *Pippi Goes on Board.* New York: Viking, 1970. Paperback. Grades 4–6.
46. ———. *Pippi in the South Seas.* New York: Viking, 1970. Paperback. Grades 3–7.
47. ———. *Pippi Longstocking.* New York: Viking, 1969. Paperback. Grades 4–6.
48. LOFTING, HUGH. *Doctor Dolittle's Caravan.* Philadelphia, 1926. Grades 4–6.

49. ______. *Doctor Dolittle's Circus.* New York: Dell, 1967. Paperback. Grades 4 and up.
50. ______. *Doctor Dolittle's Post Office.* New York: Dell, n.d. Paperback. Grade 5 and up.
51. ______. *Doctor Dolittle's Zoo.* New York: Dell, 1967. Paperback. Grade 4 and up.
52. ______. *The Story of Doctor Dolittle.* New York: Dell, 1967. Paperback. Grade 4 and up.
53. ______. *The Voyages of Doctor Dolittle.* New York: Dell, 1967. Paperback. Grade 4 and up.
54. LOVETT, LOIS. *Little Lost Kitten.* New York: Random House, 1962. n.g.l.
55. MACGREGOR, ELLEN. *Miss Pickerell and the Geiger Counter.* New York: McGraw-Hill, 1953. Grades 4–6.
56. ______. *Miss Pickerell Goes to Mars.* New York: McGraw-Hill, 1951. Grades 4–6.
57. ______. *Miss Pickerell Goes to the Arctic.* New York: McGraw-Hill, 1954. Grades 4–6.
58. ______. *Miss Pickerell Goes Undersea.* New York: McGraw-Hill, 1953. Grades 4–6.
59. ______. *Theodore Turtle.* New York: McGraw-Hill, n.d. Kindergarten–grade 3.
60. MARINO, DOROTHY. *Buzzy Bear in the Garden.* New York: Watts, 1963. Kindergarten–grade 3.
61. MCCLOSKEY, ROBERT. *Homer Price.* New York: Viking, 1943. Grades 4–6.
62. MILLER, EDNA. *Mousekin's Golden House.* Englewood Cliffs, N. J.: Prentice-Hall, 1971. Paperback. Kindergarten–grade 3.
63. MOORE, LILIAN. *Too Many Bozos.* New York: Golden Press, 1969. Kindergarten–grade 2.
64. MOORE, NANCY, AND EDWARD LEIGHT. *The Unhappy Hippopotamus.* New York: Vanguard, 1957. Preschool–grade 3.
65. MORETON, JOHN. *Punky: Mouse for a Day.* New York: Putnam, 1964. Grades 2–5.
66. PALAZZO, TONY. *Thai, Kao and Tone: An Elephant Story.* New York: Abelard-Schuman, 1966. Kindergarten–grade 3.
67. PECK, GEORGE W. E. F. BLEILER (ed.). *Peck's Bad Boy and His Pa.* New York: Dover, 1959. Paperback. Grades 3–7.
68. PEET, BILL. *The Whingdingdilly.* Boston: Houghton Mifflin, 1970. Kindergarten–grade 3.
69. PHILBROOK, CLEM. *Ollie's Team and the Football Computer.* New York: Hastings House, 1968. Grades 4–6.
70. PRESTON, EDNA M. *Pop Corn and Ma Goodness.* New York: Viking, 1969. Kindergarten–grade 3.
71. REY, HANS A. *Curious George.* Boston: Houghton Mifflin, 1941. Kindergarten–grade 3.
72. ______. *Curious George Gets a Medal.* Boston: Houghton Mifflin, 1957. Kindergarten–grade 3.

73. ———. *Curious George Learns the Alphabet.* Boston: Houghton Mifflin, 1963. Kindergarten–grade 3.
74. ———. *Curious George Rides a Bike.* Boston: Houghton Mifflin, 1952. Kindergarten–grade 3.
75. REY, MARGARET. *Curious George Flies a Kite.* Boston: Houghton Mifflin, 1958. Kindergarten–grade 3.
76. ———, AND H. A. REY. *Curious George Goes to the Hospital.* Englewood Cliffs, N. J.: Prentice-Hall, 1970. Paperback. Kindergarten–grade 3.
77. RIETVELD, JANE. *Monkey Island.* New York: Viking, 1963. Kindergarten–grade 3.
78. ROBINSON, JAN M. *The December Dog.* Philadelphia: Lippincott, 1969. Grades 4–6.
79. SCHATZ, LETTA. *A Rhinoceros, Preposterous.* Austin, Tex.: Steck-Vaughn, 1965. Kindergarten–grade 3.
80. SCHLEIN, M. *The Big Green Thing.* New York: Grosset & Dunlap, 1963. n.g.l.
81. SEUSS, DR. *And to Think That I Saw It on Mulberry Street.* Eau Claire, Wis.: Hale, 1937. Grades 1–3.
82. ———. *Bartholomew and the Oobleck.* New York: Random House, 1949. Kindergarten–grade 3.
83. ———. *The Five Hundred Hats of Bartholomew Cubbins.* New York: Vanguard, 1938. Kindergarten–grade 3.
84. ———. *Green Eggs and Ham.* New York: Beginner Books, 1960. Grades 1–2.
85. ———. *Horton Hatches the Egg.* New York: Random House, 1938. Kindergarten–grade 3.
86. ———. *Horton Hears a Who.* New York: Random House, 1954. Kindergarten–grade 3.
87. ———. *The King's Stilts.* New York: Random House, n.d. Kindergarten–grade 3.
88. ———. *Thidwick, the Big-Hearted Moose.* New York: Random House, 1948. Kindergarten–grade 3.
89. SKORPEN, LIESEL M. *All the Lassies.* New York: Dial, 1970. Preschool–grade 2.
90. STOLZ, MARY. *Siri the Conquistador.* New York: Harper & Row, 1963. Grades 1–5.
91. TURKLE, BRINTON. *The Sky Dog.* New York: Viking, 1971. Grades 4–7.
92. TWAIN, MARK (SAMUEL CLEMENS). *The Adventures of Huckleberry Finn.* New York: Crowell Collier & Macmillan, 1962. Paperback. Grade 7 and up.
93. ———. *The Adventures of Tom Sawyer.* New York: Crowell Collier & Macmillan, 1962. Paperback. Grade 7 and up.
94. ———. *A Connecticut Yankee in King Arthur's Court.* New York: New American Library, n.d. Paperback. Grade 5 and up.
95. ———. *Innocents Abroad.* New York: New American Library, n.d. Paperback. Grade 9 and up.
96. ———. *The Jumping Frog.* New York: Dover, 1971. Paperback.

97. ______. *The Prince and the Pauper.* New York: Crowell Collier & Macmillan, 1962. Paperback.
98. ______. *Roughing It.* New York: New American Library, n.d. Paperback.
99. ______. *A Tramp Abroad.* St. Clair Shores, Mich.: Scholarly Press, 1968. Paperback.
100. WALKER, DAVID. *Big Ben.* Boston: Houghton Mifflin, 1969. Grades 3–5.
101. WARD, LYND. *The Biggest Bear.* Boston: Houghton Mifflin, 1952. Kindergarten–grade 3.
102. WHITE, ANNE H. *Junket.* New York: Viking, 1969. Paperback. Grades 4–6.

More Laughter in Literature About People

Kindergarten–Grade 3

BROWN, JEFF. *Flat Stanley.* New York: Harper & Row, 1964. Stanley is flattened to a half-inch in thickness when a bulletin board pins him down.

FENTON, EDWARD. *The Big Yellow Balloon.* Garden City, N. Y.: Doubleday, 1967. When Roger walks down the street with his big yellow balloon, Tom the cat thinks it is the sun and prowls after it to put it out. The dog, the dogcatcher, a lady, and others follow the cat, and in the end Roger becomes a hero.

FLORA, JAMES. *My Friend Charlie.* New York: Harcourt Brace Jovanovich, 1964. Talking to fish, skating on his head while eating noodles, and finding a submarine caught in a wad of bubble gum are some of the hilarious escapades Charlie experiences.

MERRIAM, EVE. *Miss Tibbett's Typewriter.* New York: Knopf, 1966. Hilarious consequences result whenever the E key sticks on Miss Tibbett's typewriter.

PARRISH, PEGGY. *Amelia Bedelia.* New York: Harper & Row, 1963. Amelia Bedelia's intentions are good when she starts to do housework for Mrs. Rogers, but her interpretation of Mrs. Rogers' written orders make rare comedy.

______. *Amelia Bedelia and the Surprise Shower.* New York: Harper & Row, 1966. To Bedelia a shower is a downpour of rain.

______. *Thank You, Amelia Bedelia.* New York: Harper & Row, 1964. In spite of Amelia's many misinterpretations, her hot apple pie crowns her with glory.

PIATTI, CELESTINO, AND URSULA HUBER. *The Nock Family Circus.* Barbara Kowal Gollab (trans.). New York: Atheneum, 1968. The text and illustrations of this fascinating story convey the spirit and fun of the Nock family, who for generations have entertained the people of small European towns with their family circus.

TREZ, DENISE, AND ALAIN TREZ. *The Royal Hiccups.* New York: Viking, 1965.

This story, told in cartoon pictures and with little text, relates the adventures of a rajah's son who goes looking for a tiger to frighten away his hiccups.

WILSON, CHRISTOPHER B. *Oliver at Sea.* New York: Norton, 1969. A highly imaginative boy creates a story with his rollicking drawings.

Grades 4–6

BUTTERWORTH, OLIVER. *The Enormous Egg.* Boston: Little, Brown, 1956. The hatching of a dinosaur egg creates problems for a boy and his family in a New England town.

GARLAN, PATRICIA, AND M. DUNSTAN. *The Boy Who Played Tiger.* New York: Viking, 1968. This exciting story is about a mischievous schoolboy in Burma.

More Laughter in Literature About Animals

Kindergarten–Grade 3

BERENSTAIN, STAN, AND JAN BERENSTAIN. *The Bears' Picnic.* New York: Random House, 1966. A wild cross-country marathon develops when Papa bear keeps searching for the "perfect picnic spot" for his family.

BOWEN, ELIZABETH. *The Good Tiger.* New York: Knopf, 1965. This story combines outstanding illustrations with exercises for beginning readers.

BURNINGHAM, JOHN. *Borka: The Adventures of a Goose with No Feathers.* New York: Random House, 1964. Borka lives in misery until she meets a friend who takes her to Kew Gardens. This story was awarded the Kate Greenaway Medal.

COATSWORTH, ELIZABETH. *Pika and the Roses.* New York: Pantheon, 1959. The little rock rabbits manage to tire and fool the weasel. Illustrations tell the story as beautifully as does the text.

DEJONG, DAVID C. *Alexander the Monkey-Sitter.* Boston: Little, Brown, 1965. This amusing story concerns a monkey and a cat.

EASTMAN, P. D. *Everything Happens to Aaron All Year Long.* New York: Random House, 1967. The happenings of a lovable alligator named Aaron are described in a hilarious and charming book.

EBERLE, IRMENGARDE. *Evie and Cookie.* New York: Knopf, n.d. The smart, mannerly kangaroo Cookie becomes so homesick that she is given a kangaroo party.

ERICKSON, PHOEBE. *Who's in the Mirror?* New York: Knopf, 1965. Few words and simple illustrations provide fine irony as the animals try to find the answer to this question.

HOYLAND, ROSEMARY. *Ethelbert: A Tale of a Tiger.* New York: Knopf, 1955. This tiger is fond of swimming and has many adventures.

JOHNSTON, JOHANNA. *Great Gravity the Cat.* New York: Knopf, 1958. There is a good deal of fun in observing Gravity's reaction to the change a baby makes in a household.

JONAS, NITA. *The Wild and Woolly Animal Book.* New York: Random House, 1961. This picture book for the very youngest of zoogoers is a riot of bright colors with a page devoted to each animal.

LATHAM, BARBARA. *Perrito's Pup.* New York: Knopf, n.d. A young puppy tries to make friends with an older dog.

LOBEL, ARNOLD. *Martha the Movie Mouse.* New York: Harper & Row, 1966. This picture-story book written in verse will appeal to little children who like mice.

POTTER, MIRIAM C. *Mrs. Goose and Her Funny Friends.* Philadelphia: Lippincott, 1964. Animal Town is the home of Mrs. Goose and her friends, who enjoy eleven humorous experiences.

SHULMAN, MILTON. *Preep: The Little Pigeon of Trafalgar Square.* New York: Random House, 1964. Preep is adored by his family despite his odd color and his ridiculous beak.

VILLAREJO, MARY. *The Famous Blue Gnu of Colonel Kachoo.* New York: Knopf, 1964. A little man collects animals for a zoo and for himself until his home is crowded.

WEBB, CLIFFORD. *The Thirteenth Pig.* New York: Warner, 1966. Matl the pig comes home after trying a number of other pigstys, is greeted happily by his family, and decides that home is really best.

WHITE, DAVID OMAR. *I Know a Giraffe.* New York: Knopf, 1965. A child responds nonsensically to the "What if . . ." question.

Grades 4–6

CAMILLE, JOSEPHINE. *Carlos and the Brave Owl.* New York: Random House, 1968. A little owl turns out to be the hero of a Mexican village.

FEAGLES, ANITA. *Twenty-Seven Cats Next Door.* New York: Scott, 1965. A woman with twenty-seven cats is considered a public nuisance by her neighbors. Humor and seriousness are combined in this story.

MANNIX, DANIEL. *The Outcasts.* New York: Dutton, 1965. An eleven-year-old city boy makes good in the country when he tames a family of skunks who later rout the local bully.

PLENN, DORIS T. *The Violet Tree.* New York: Farrar, Straus & Giroux, 1962. Tico, the fighting rooster, does not really like fighting. He would much rather crow and announce the hours like most other roosters.

SMITH, EMMA. *Emily's Voyage.* New York: Harcourt Brace Jovanovich, 1966. An engaging cast of animal characters includes a guinea pig, a water rat, and monkeys who participate in a sea voyage, a shipwreck, and a visit to a tropical island.

STOLZ, MARY. *Maximilian's World.* New York: Harper & Row, 1966. Maximilian, a tiny Chihuahua, describes his adventures to the cat Siri.

WILLIAMS, ELMA M. BUMBLE. *Pig in Paradise.* New York: John Day, 1965. The runt of a litter of pedigreed pigs is taken to live in a girl's animal paradise in a Welsh valley.

Further Reading for Teachers, Parents, and Librarians

BRUMBAUGH, FLORENCE N. "Laughter and Teachers," *Educational Method*, 20 (1940), pp. 69–70.

DING, GLADYS F., AND A. T. JERSILD. "A Study of the Laughing and Smiling of Pre-School Children," *Journal of Genetic Psychology*, 40 (1932), pp. 452–472.

EASTMAN, MAX. *Enjoyment of Laughter.* New York: Simon & Schuster, 1937.

FISHER, MARGERY. *Intent upon Reading.* Market Place, Leicester, England: Brockhampton Press, 1961.

GARRISON, WEBB. "Laughter the Elusive Wonder Drug," *Today's Health*, March 1971, pp. 27–32.

KAPPAS, KATHERINE H. "A Developmental Analysis of Children's Responses to Humor," *Library Quarterly*, 37 (January 1967), pp. 67–77.

LEACOCK, STEPHEN. *Humor: Its Theory and Technique.* New York: Dodd, Mead, 1935.

MONSON, DIANNE LYNN. "Children's Responses to Humorous Situations in Literature." Unpublished Ph.D. dissertation, University of Minnesota, 1966.

RUSSELL, DAVID H. *Children's Thinking.* Boston: Ginn, 1956, pp. 150–152.

SMITH, JAMES STEEL. *A Critical Approach to Children's Literature.* New York: McGraw-Hill, 1967, chap. 9.

From *A Small Piece of Paradise* by Geoffrey Morgan, illustrated by David Knight.

6

Literature and Personal Growth

For years teachers, librarians, parents, and authors have used stories for the purpose of helping children come to grips with their personal problems and as guides to personality development. As one reviews the development of children's literature he becomes aware of the extent to which reading materials have been used with the hope of building desirable character traits and high moral values in the reader. The emphasis has been different from time to time. In the past didacticism reigned supreme. *The New England Primer* (111) was saturated with admonitions such as the following:

> He who ne'er learns his A.B.C.
> Forever will a blockhead be;
> But he who learns his letters fair
> Shall have a coach to take the air. [P. 47]

To some extent the McGuffey Readers continued in the tradition of *The New England Primer.* The purpose of these readers was to teach children how to read. They played an important role in the reading lives of boys and girls during the last half of the nineteenth and the beginning of the twentieth centuries. They were written by William Holmes McGuffey, an American educator and clergyman, for the first six grades of the elementary school. The Preface to McGuffey's *Fifth Eclectic Reader* (105) states:

> The plan of the revision of *McGuffey's Fifth Reader* is the same as that pursued in the other books of the *Revised Series.* The book has been considerably enlarged, but the new pieces have been added or substituted only after the most careful consideration, and where the advantages to be derived were assured.
>
> It has been the object to obtain as wide a range of leading authors as possible, to present the best specimens of style, to insure interest in the subjects,

to impart valuable information, and to exert a decided and healthful moral influence. Thus, the essential characteristics of *McGuffey's Readers* have been carefully kept intact. [P. iii]

Apparently American literature did not play an important role in the curriculum during the nineteenth century, since the Preface also states:

Particular attention is invited to the actions of authors. Comparatively few pupils have the opportunity of making a separate study of English and American literature and the carefully prepared notices in the *Revised Series* are designed, therefore, to supply as much information in regard to the leading authors as is possible in the necessarily limited space assigned. [P. iv]

The various objectives described in the Preface are illustrated in the reader itself in a story by John Greenleaf Whittier entitled "The Fish I Didn't Catch."

THE FISH I DIDN'T CATCH

John Greenleaf Whittier (b 1807) was born in East Haverhill, Mass. His boyhood was passed on a farm, and he never received a classical education. In 1829 he edited a newspaper in Boston. In the following year he moved to Hartford, Conn., to assume a similar position. In 1836 he edited an anti-slavery paper in Philadelphia. Since 1840 he has resided in Amesbury, Mass. Mr. Whittier's parents were Friends, and he has always held to the same faith. He has written extensively both in prose and verse. As a poet, he ranks among those most highly esteemed and honored by his countrymen. "Snow-Bound," published in 1865, is one of the longest and best of his poems.

1. Our bachelor uncle who lived with us was a quiet, genial man, much given to hunting and fishing; and it was one of the pleasures of our young life to accompany him on his expeditions to Great Hill, Brandy-brow Woods, the Pond, and, best of all, to the Country Brook. We were quite willing to work hard in the corn-field or the haying-lot to finish the necessary day's labor in season for an afternoon stroll through the woods and along the brookside.

2. I remember my first fishing excursion as if it were but yesterday. I have been happy many times in my life, but never more intensely so than when I received that first fishing-pole from my uncle's hand, and trudged off with him through the woods and meadows. It was a still, sweet day of early summer; the long afternoon shadows of the trees lay cool across our path; the leaves seemed greener, the flowers brighter, the birds merrier, than ever before.

3. My uncle, who knew by long experience where were the best haunts of pickerel, considerately placed me at the most favorable point. I threw out

my line as I had so often seen others, and waited anxiously for a bite, moving the bait in rapid jerks on the surface of the water in imitation of a frog. Nothing came of it. "Try again," said my uncle. Suddenly the bait sank out of sight. "Now for it," thought I: "Here is a fish at last."

4. I made a strong pull, and brought up a tangle of weeds. Again and again I cast out my line with aching arms, and drew it back empty. I looked at my uncle appealingly. "Try once more," he said; "we fishermen must have patience."

5. Suddenly something tugged at my line, and swept off with it into deep water. Jerking it up, I saw a fine pickerel wriggling in the sun. "Uncle!" I cried, looking back in uncontrollable excitement, "I've got a fish!" "Not yet," said my uncle. As he spoke there was a splash in the water; I caught the arrowy gleam of a scared fish shooting into the middle of the stream, my hook hung empty from the line. I had lost my prize.

6. We are apt to speak of the sorrows of childhood as trifles in comparison with those of grown-up people; but we may depend upon it the young folks don't agree with us. Our griefs, modified and restrained by reason, experience, and self-respect, keep the proprieties, and, if possible avoid a scene; but the sorrow of childhood, unreasoning and all-absorbing, is a complete abandonment to the passion. The doll's nose is broken, and the world breaks up with it; the marble rolls out of sight, and the solid globe rolls off with the marble.

7. So, overcome with my great and bitter disappointment, I sat down on the nearest hassock, and for a time refused to be comforted, even by my uncle's assurance that there were more fish in the brook. He refitted my bait, and, putting the pole again in my hands, told me to try my luck once more.

8. "But remember, boy," he said, with his shrewd smile, "never brag of catching a fish until he is on dry ground. I've seen older folks doing that in more ways than one, and so making fools of themselves. It's no use to boast of any thing until it's done, nor then, either, for it speaks for itself."

9. How often since I have been reminded of the fish that I did not catch. When I hear people boasting of a work as yet undone, and trying to anticipate the credit which belongs only to actual achievement, I call to mind that scene by the brookside, and the wise caution of my uncle in that particular instance takes the form of a proverb of universal application: "NEVER BRAG OF YOUR FISH BEFORE YOU CATCH HIM."

Definitions. — 1. Ge ni-al, *cheerful.* 3. Haunts, *places frequently visited.* Consid er-ate-ly, *with due regard to others, kindly, thoughtful.* 4. Ap-peal ing-ly, *as though asking for aid.* 6. Mod i-fied, *qualified, lessened.* Pro-pri e-ties, *fixed customs or rules of conduct.* Ab-sorb-ing, *engaging the attention entirely.* 7. Hassock, *a raised mound of turf.* 9. An tic i-pate, *to take before the proper time.* A-chieve ment, *performance, deed.* [Pp. 63–66]

A brief biographical sketch of John Greenleaf Whittier is given to acquaint the student with this prominent American author. The paragraphs in the story are numbered presumably for ready reference. The author interrupts the story to compare the reaction of children to sorrow with the reaction of adults; this technique illustrates the didactic approach. The last three paragraphs of the story are devoted to pointing up the moral, "Never Brag of Your Fish Before You Catch Him." At the end of the story definitions are given for a selected number of words.

It is interesting to compare, both in format and content, didactic children's literature as presented in *McGuffey's Eclectic Readers* and such literature for children as published today.

Literature and Identification

Educators, librarians, and parents are sensitive to the influence literature plays in changing and directing behavior and personality development. The degree of influence is determined largely by the extent to which the reader identifies with the characters and situations and becomes emotionally involved with them.

Identification plays an important role in the acculturation of an individual into the society of which he is a member. Social psychologists describe identification as the process by which a person develops an integrated set of roles and aspirations that direct his life. According to Robert J. Havinghurst (73) these roles and aspirations are taken "from parents, siblings, playmates, teachers, preachers and others, from present, historical and fictional characters and are worked into his own thought and action" (p. 242).

Robert Peck (114) described identification as "largely an unconscious process of coming to 'feel like' the model person with whom he identifies and to perceive situations, in the same way the 'model' perceives them" (p. 147). This process of identification may be observed in children at an early age as one sees them identify with their fathers and mothers: "I talk like Daddy." "I have my mother's curly hair." Hugh V. Perkins (116) states:

> One of the most important and most effective ways one learns his culture is through identification. Identification is the process through which the individual incorporates into his own feeling, doing, and thinking the behavior, attitudes, and characteristics of another person whom he wishes to be like. It involves more than imitation, although the tendency of the child or adolescent to model himself after another is a frequently observed characteristic

> of identification. Identification appears to be largely an unconscious process wherein one comes to feel like and to perceive the world like the model with whom he identifies. [P. 153]

The young child's identification is not limited to people; it is common, too, for him to identify so closely with his toys and pets that he becomes in his imagination a particular toy or pet. He expresses sympathy for a fallen tree, a dead bird, a crushed flower. Observed in his play he may be found identifying with any of the people, places, and things that make up his world.

Bibliotherapy

Bibliotherapy, using books for therapy, has been defined by David H. Russell and Caroline Shrodes (129) as a dynamic interaction between the personality of the reader and literature. Bibliotherapy may help the individual to know himself better, to deepen his insights into human behavior, to understand better the relations of people to one another, and to find interests outside himself. This kind of therapy may also contribute to an individual's socialization: the process of developing the skills necessary for effective human relations. It may promote empathy in the reader and thus increase his ability to shed himself of stereotyped or negative attitudes that stand in the way of healthy and happy human relations.

The summary of an article by Barbara Lindeman and Martin Kling (96) states:

> Bibliotherapy is defined as an interaction between the reader and certain literature which is useful in aiding personal adjustment. A review of the literature includes a discussion of its uses in mental hospitals, with maladjusted individuals; and in the classroom, with retarded, gifted and average students. . . . It is concluded that bibliotherapy can help meet the developmental needs not only of young people in the classroom, but also of some maladjusted individuals. [P. 36]

The article later states:

> Differences in definition depend upon whether one is talking about bibliotherapy for the mentally ill, as treatment for the maladjusted, or as a natural part of the classroom curriculum used in meeting the developmental needs of children. Differences also depend upon who does the defining: the physician, the counsellor, or the teacher. [P. 36]

Every boy and girl grows up with deep concerns, some of which become problems of varying degrees of intensity. Through books they can meet other boys and girls who are beset with the same real or imagined problems. A character in a story tends to become real to the reader, who is interested in finding out how the character with whom he has identified copes with his problems and adjusts to certain situations. The story becomes a vehicle that helps the reader to face reality rather than escape from it. The problem of the character in the story and the problem of the reader need not have a one-to-one relationship; for example, a boy or girl who is having difficulty accepting a physical handicap may meet a fictional child with a physical handicap of a different type. The important thing is how the character in the story copes with the handicap and deals with his concern over it.

Individuals with handicaps may find characters with whom they can identify in such stories as *Danny Goes to the Hospital* (29) by James Collier, *Porko Von Popbutton* (52) by William Pené DuBois, *The Very Little Girl* (82) by Phyllis Krasilovsky, and *Hideout at Winter House* (126) by Eric Rhodin.

Many individuals find it difficult to cope with peers, jealousies, disappointments, and extended imaginations. Characters in the following stories have similar difficulties: *Ellen Grae* (25) by Vera and Bill Cleaver, *Marius* (49) by Rolf Docker, *Two and Me Makes Three* (70) by Roberta Greene, *The Shy Little Girl* (81) by Phyllis Krasilovsky, *Dance in the Desert* (87) by Madeleine L'Engle, *Joey and the Fawn* (93) by Mary Lewis, *One to Grow On* (100) by Jean Little, *The Twenty-five Cent Friend* (106) by Peggy Mann, *The Noonday Friends* (136) by Mary Stolz, *A Sound of Crying* (138) by Rodie Sudbury, *I'll Fix Anthony* (146) by Judith Viorst, and *The Hating Book* (156) by Charlotte Zolotow.

Coping with prejudice, environment, family problems, and death is especially difficult for many individuals. The following stories have characters with similar difficulties: *Turn the Next Corner* (1) by Gudrun Alcock, *The Girl Without a Name* (5) by Gunnel Beckman, *Escape* (11) by Ben Bova, *Benjie on his Own* (94) by Joan M. Lexau, *Can't You Pretend?* (155) by Miriam Young, *With Dad Alone* (6) by Jerrold Beim, and *Man of the Family* (109) by Ralph Moody.

Individuals coping with the difficulty of discovering themselves may find help in identifying with fictional characters with the same difficulty who find themselves by helping others in such stories as *Matthew, Mark, Luke and John* (16) by Pearl S. Buck, *Rosanna the Goat* (27) by Mary Cockett, *Hugo* (71) by Maria Gripe, *Next Door* (72) by Ruth Harnden, *Look Through My Window* (99) by Jean Little, *Frog and Toad Are Friends* (103) by Arnold Lobel, and *Where the Good Luck Was* (108) by Osmond Molarsky.

Being a member of a minority group frequently poses difficulties for individuals. There are a number of stories with Black characters who face the same difficulties: *Two Is a Team* (7) by Lorraine and Jerrold Beim, *Lonesome Boy* (9) by Arna Bontemps, and *Bright April* (39) by Marguerite De Angeli.

Of course, no one story or character that a boy or girl with similar problems meets in reading is going to work a miracle. To a large extent, the effectiveness of bibliotherapy will depend on the depth of the problem and the degree to which the emotions of the reader are aroused.

Principles of Identification

Although there may be some question about the effectiveness of bibliotherapy, we can pose a number of principles for some degree of therapy through identification with the characters and situations in stories.

A child often identifies most easily with a character like himself. It appears that identification depends partly upon the story calling forth a situation, a relationship, or an attitude that the child himself has experienced. The boy who lives in the city and plays baseball with other boys his age will identify more easily with Mark in *Boy at Bat* (124) by Marion Renick than with Ivik in *Eskimo Boy* (62) by Pipaluk Freuchen. A girl who is a tomboy will identify with *Pippi Longstocking* (97) by Astrid Lindgren more easily than with a very proper lady.

Identification is an active process for the child, not a passive matter of looking at himself in the person of a fictional character. The young reader who has heard or read a cowboy story often will pretend that he is a cowboy. If he has read *The Biggest Bear* (148) by Lynd Ward, he too has captured a bear. Or if he is reading *Treasure Island* (135) by Robert Louis Stevenson he, too, is hiding in the apple barrel. The child who follows the trials of Robin in *Batman* on television often feels the same emotions as the character with whom he has identified.

The socialization of the child may be helped through identification. Identification is one way in which a child develops desirable social characteristics. At first, identification is with the parents but it later spreads to other persons as well. In assuming the identity of another person, the boy or girl often adopts the speech and manners of that individual. At times it is difficult to get a child out of the character he is emulating. The identification process may operate at a level deeper than imitation in developing techniques for group living; reading about a boy from a lower-class home, for example, may extend the social sympathies of a boy from a more prestigious socioeconomic background.

From *The Biggest Bear* by Lynd Ward.

Identification may contribute to good mental health. It is perfectly normal for children to have aggressions, but conventions and the process of socialization frequently make the direct discharge of these aggressions difficult, if not impossible. When the individual's energies are blocked or threatened, unpleasant emotions are experienced. On the other hand, when barriers are broken down and the individual is able to act freely toward the accomplishment of his goals, pleasant emotions are experienced.

In the past, emotions were regarded by many as undesirable, even dangerous. Today emotions are recognized as a natural part of all behavior and experience. Emotions are invigorating to mental and physical processes alike; they make living more exciting and do no harm. Through identification with characters and situations in literature, children may become emotionally aroused. Thus the medium of books provides a channel for the wholesome release of emotions.

Identification with a group has a value for the individual. Conditions of living in our country have changed immeasurably in recent years. Smaller families, the mobility of the population, and the increased tendency for people to live anonymously point up the importance of children's gaining the security of some sort of group membership. Although there are many opportunities for boys and girls to identify with some individual in children's literature, the opportunities for identification with a group are more limited. One finds exceptions, for example, in Leo Politi's beautifully illustrated stories that depict the customs and festivals of the Mexican-Americans in California: *Juanita* (119), *Pedro, the Angel of Olvera Street* (121), and *The Song of the Swallows* (122). He has also written *A Boat for Peppe* (118), which is set in the Sicilian section of Monterey, California, and *Moy Moy* (120), which is about a little girl living in the Chinese section of Los Angeles.

Other foremost authors have written stories about groups of people living in different regions of our country. Lois Lenski has made a significant contribution to regional literature for children with such stories as *Bayou Suzette* (89), with its setting in the Louisiana Bayou country; *Strawberry Girl* (91), a story about a little girl in Florida, her family, and their neighbors; and *Judy's Journey* (90), which portrays a family of migrant workers who pick vegetables and fruit from Florida to New Jersey.

Marguerite De Angeli has acquainted boys and girls with regional groups. Such fascinating stories as *Henner's Lydia* (42), *Bright April* (39), *Thee Hannah* (45), *Yonie Wondernose* (46), and *Skippack School* (44), as well as *Empty Barn* (38), written with her son Arthur, have their settings in the Pennsylvania Dutch country, which the author knows well and for which she expresses sensitive feelings. *Copper-Toed Boots* (40) has its setting in central Michigan; *Jared's Island* (43) describes life in Colonial days along the New Jersey coast; and *Elin's Amerika* (41) has the settlements along the Delaware River for its locale.

Outstanding authors have contributed stories that make it possible for boys and girls to identify with groups of people not only in our own country but around the world (see Chapter 4). When children do not have opportunities for group identification through other areas of living, literature may give them feelings of belonging and group identification that they can hold onto in a rather chaotic world.

Identification with causes may contribute to wholesome personality development. Boys and girls, particularly early adolescents, are eager to subscribe to causes. Many of them join organizations with the worthy purpose of doing good. Selling Girl Scout cookies, selling tickets for a Boy Scout jamboree, bundling newspapers, and collecting recyclable cans and bottles are only a few of the many causes for which early adolescents ring doorbells and state their causes. Something within them seems to be urging them to do something for somebody else. It is a part of that feeling of self-sufficiency that they are beginning to feel about themselves: "I am capable; someone else isn't; he needs help; I can help him." The causes with which they identify are not always limited to their own self-interests. They often throw themselves into civic and political movements with force and vigor.

Growth in Concepts of Self

In psychological literature the term "self" is described as the mental processes that characterize the person and the meanings that the individual derives from these ongoing processes. Each individual has his own private store of ideas about himself: "I am somebody." "I am nobody." "People like me." "Nobody likes me." "I can." "I can't." "I will." "I won't." These ideas are powerful factors in determining the individual's perceptions, his levels of aspiration, his techniques for defending himself from loss of self-respect, and his behavior in many situations.

When Nikko's teacher suggested that he write something about himself, Nikko, though only ten years old, expressed a concept of self with a sound psychological basis. He wrote:

> I am I, and that's what I
>   have to be.
> If I am not, I don't know
>   who I am.
> I am me, and who can stop me from being
>   what I am.
> If anyone can stop me from
>   being me,
> I'm Foof, I'm gone.
>   What am I?
> I'm me.
>
> Nikko, grade 4

Concepts of self emerge through our relations with others. The individual thus comes to know himself not only by introspection but also by exploring his culture and his world. The ways in which an individual engages in certain processes determines the meanings, feelings, attitudes, and values he will hold about himself. They will make him a unique personality and develop his selfhood. The processes are common to all, but each individual goes through them in a way that is peculiar to himself: (a) The individual interacts with his physical world. (b) He learns what his body can do. (c) He acquires meanings for the world of symbols in which he lives and communicates through symbols with others. (d) He assimilates himself to the culture of which he is a part. (e) He imitates social roles and builds belongingness. (f) He develops a code of ethics, a set of values, standards of conduct—a philosophy of life—which guides his behavior. (g) He identifies with his family and friends.

Daniel A. Prescott (123) says:

> . . . The concept of self is many-sided and any aspect of it may be vulnerable to damage or distortion. If we study psychiatric and psychoanalytic literature to find out what has happened to the self-concepts of persons who are mentally ill, we can see quite clearly the essential facets which, together, determine the form of each individual's self-concept. For example, we find such persons variously described as feeling: threatened, insecure, rejected, inferior, inadequate, frustrated, or in conflict with themselves. Logically, *a healthy self-concept should involve* feelings which are the obverse of these, namely, *feelings of safety, security, belonging, adequacy, self-realization, and integrity.* These, then, are the feelings which a child or youth needs to have about himself to maintain full and vigorous mental and emotional health. [Pp. 403–404]

The most important person with whom one has to live is oneself. Yet living comfortably with oneself is one of the most difficult tasks an individual has to accomplish in his life, particularly in our country where there are fewer rituals connected with coming of age than there are in many other countries. At a very young age, boys and girls begin to ask questions about themselves. "Who am I?" "Am I somebody?" "Do the people who know me care whether or not I am here?" This is a common refrain with many boys and girls as they struggle to find themselves, and it is also a common theme in literature.

Miguel, in the story . . . *And Now Miguel* (83) by Joseph Krumgold, belongs to the Chavez family—a family that has raised sheep in New Mexico for many years. Miguel expresses his feelings about himself as follows:

> I am Miguel. For most people it does not make so much difference that I am Miguel but for me, often, it is very great trouble.
>
> . . .
>
> It would be different if I were Pedro. He is my younger brother, only seven years old. For Pedro everything is simple. Almost all the things that Pedro wants, he has—without much worry. . . . It would be good to be Pedro. But how long can you stay seven years old? The trouble with me is that I am Miguel.
>
> . . .
>
> It would be good to be Gabriel. He is also my brother, and he is nineteen years old. Next to my Grandfather, and my Uncle Bonifacio, and my Uncle Eli, and next to my father who is Old Blas, and my biggest brother who is called Young Blas and who wears a badge and drives the school bus, Gabriel is the greatest man in the world.
>
> . . .
>
> Everything that Gabriel wants he can get. [Pp. 1–4]

Miguel's dream of happiness is to be able to go with Gabriel and Young Blas and all the men of the family when they take the sheep to summer pasture high in the beautiful mountain meadows of the Sangre de Cristo Mountains. He is not consoled by the kind but disappointing answers he gets from his elders when he begs to do a man's work. His mother tries to comfort him by saying:

> . . . You already have become one whole man, Miguel. But even a whole man must learn to wait until his time comes. He can work, and he can prepare. But he must know how to wait, too. [P. 30]

Growing boys and girls often have such difficulty finding themselves in their eagerness to grow up.

Stories About Personal Growth

A number of distinguished authors have written stories that show their familiarity with the growth and development patterns characteristic of particular age groups. They are sensitive to children's needs and interests. Knowing the ingredients that make a good story as well as knowing children and having an interest in them has resulted in a large body of literature for young listeners and readers.

Stories for the Young Reader

Very young readers will enjoy listening to *Too Many Crackers* (17) by Helen E. Buckley. It is the story of a little boy who is suddenly lonesome and wants his mother and father to return from their vacation. The device his mother thinks of to help him keep track of the days is intriguing, and a misunderstanding of the connection between what he does and his parents' return will delight the listeners as well as the readers.

When I Am Big (133) by Robert P. Smith tells about a small boy who looks forward to the time when he will be able to do all the responsible things that grownups do, such as picking up pieces of broken glass, plugging plugs into sockets, and changing tires.

Quiet Story (92) by Rhoda Levine is a book that will help children to become aware of themselves, their friends, and the world around them. This sensitive book conveys a quiet mood as two children take hands and go for a walk. As they silently stroll along, they wonder about what they see. Rosalie Richards sustains the mood of the story throughout with her beautiful illustrations.

Katie, an active five-year-old who is found to need glasses, is the center of a delightful story in prose and verse, *Katie's Magic Glasses* (66) by Jane Goodsell. The changes in Katie's world and her feelings about wearing glasses plus illustrations by Barbara Cooney make this an enjoyable book.

The Girl Who Was a Cowboy (80) by Phyllis Krasilovsky is an appealing, humorous story about a young girl who is as attached to her red cowboy hat as some small children are to a piece of old blanket. The problem is solved when Grandmother sends Margaret a very feminine, flowered straw hat, and Margaret realizes that her cowboy playmate admires it.

The text of *The Little Girl and Her Mother* (48) by Beatrice Schenk De Regniers and Esther Gilman describes the ways in which a small girl imitates her mother and points out that a little girl cannot do everything her mother does and vice versa. The expressive etchings in pink, black, and white are admirably suited to the quiet text.

Cathy wants the sun to shine because it is her birthday and she is six years old. Her teacher and classmates have a secret that Cathy does not share until a surprise birthday party turns the day into a very special one in Betty Katzoff's happy story *Cathy's First School* (79).

In *Thy Friend, Obadiah* (142) by Brinton Turkle Obadiah, a young Quaker boy of long ago, is irritated by a sea gull that follows him everywhere. Obadiah's feelings change when he removes something entangled in the bird's back and discovers that one way to feel good is to do something for someone else. The Nantucket background is beautifully portrayed in the outdoor scenes, and the indoor scenes reflect the warmth of home and family.

Free as a Frog (74) by Elizabeth J. Hodges is the story of a shy black boy who finds freedom in his own way. Six-year-old Johnnie admires his outgoing and spirited sister and wishes he could talk as easily as she does. One day he catches a frog and takes it home in a jar. To his great joy, he finds that he has something to tell people and, when he takes the frog to school, all the children are eager to listen to the story.

A child's first experience with death is sensitively told in *Growing Time* (147) by Sandol S. Warburg. Jamie is desolate when his old dog, which has been his companion since babyhood, dies. The different concepts of death held by the different adult members of the family confuse Jamie more than they console him. Jamie refuses the gift of a new puppy until he is won over by the puppy's helplessness.

Someone Small (10) by Barbara Borack relates interesting happenings during several growing years in the life of a little girl who has everything she could ask for. The little girl is quite indifferent to a baby sister who joins the family. For a time she seems to enjoy

Fluffy, a pet bird, more than her sister. As time passes, she begins to find that a sister is much more company and much more fun than a bird. A touch of humor is threaded through the story.

Your Hand in Mine (34) by Sam Cornish is the story of Sam, a small boy who spends most of his time alone. It exemplifies the lives of many Black children in the city, and more important it offers acquaintance with one well-adjusted Black boy. Hungering for both food and friendship on a day when he has forgot to bring his lunch to school, Sam—who makes up poems to sustain him in his fear and loneliness—leaves a poem on his teacher's desk and is rewarded with an apple and his teacher's hand in friendship. The story is complemented by appealing drawings.

Stories for the Middle Reader

An eleven-year-old orphan boy with no education and with a sense of bitterness is sent to live on a small, lonely river island with his curt recluse great-uncle in *Big Blue Island* (63) by Wilson Gage. At first he is bored, resentful, and unresourceful, but he gradually falls under the spell of the wilderness. Through his new interest in conservation, the boy begins to feel that he has a place of his own and a role to play.

The Boy Who Wasn't Lonely (113) by Richard Parker is a perceptive story of Cricket, a self-sufficient only child who adroitly manages to elude adult schemes to encourage his friendship with other children. It is Rain, a quiet Pakistani girl he meets while visiting his grandmother, who finally succeeds in changing his attitude and in helping him to appreciate the companionship of his peers. The story is well told; the incidents and characters are real. Young readers will understand and identify with the problems of this shy, inhibited boy.

A well-written story, showing a basic understanding of disappointments experienced by young people, is Arthur D. Stapp's *Too Steep for Baseball* (134). Dave Knight, the hero of the story, whose chief interest is baseball, must spend the summer with his family at an isolated mountain cabin, where it is too steep to play his favorite sport. Deprived of radio broadcasts of baseball, David is bored and resentful. Later he discovers some books on meteorology and becomes interested in spite of himself. Later in the summer, Dave is able to put his newly acquired knowledge to use when a destructive hurricane approaches the area.

Coming from an impersonal life in a large city, Virgilia has a hard time adjusting to the small community where people know each other well. *What Happened to Virgilia?* (127) by Ruth Rolberg tells how

Virgilia comes to stay with her Aunt Emma in Rockport while her college professor parents go to Europe to do research. Shy Virgilia makes friends, takes part in neighborhood activities, acquires a healthy appetite, spends time out-of-doors, helps other people, and most of all develops real self-confidence. When her mother and father return, they are delighted with Virgilia. She faces going back to the city without sadness, knowing that she can return to her Rockport friends in the summer and that she can make friends in the city by being a friend herself.

Told with simplicity and without sentimentality, *Cousin Tryg* (4) by Laura N. Baker is a well-written story about a boy's adjustment after the death of his father. Eleven-year-old Norris has plans to run the farm himself. When his cousin Tryg arrives to help the family, Norris is determined not to like him or to accept him. This is the story of a boy moving into adolescence and gaining awareness of his own problems as well as of the problems of others.

Rim of the Ridge (51) by Cena C. Draper is the story of Punk, a young orphan boy who has been raised by his step-grandmother and is desperately lonesome for the company of men. When the woodsman, Hummy, who was once his granny's beau, takes him for a trip to learn about the wilds and tells him about his family, the boy is able to go home again and be happy and gentle with his granny. Punk's life becomes full as Hummy and Granny become friends again.

Best Friends (115) by Jessie C. Pegis is a perceptively drawn story of the relationship between two girls, with a nice balance between home and school episodes. Living with her widowed mother at the edge of a Canadian forest, Helen Brewster is a lonely and prim child who devotes much of her time to animals. Mary, a new sixth-grade classmate, becomes Helen's first close friend. Mary and Helen complement each other. By the time Mary must leave Canada, both she and Helen have benefited from their relationship and have grown as individuals.

The "Roaring Twenties" are the background for *That Barbara!* (140) by Wilma Thompson. Barbara Berry is not concerned with the excitement of the times but rather with the problems she is facing in the process of growing up. Her life during that somewhat bewildering period is a series of misadventures along with her new adventures. Her insistence upon proving herself to be a young lady not only embarrasses but also endangers nearly everyone in her home town of Tumpelo, Oregon. Early adolescents will find her story full of laughter as well as of tears.

Two Are Better Than One (15) by Carol R. Brink is set in Idaho in the early 1900s. The story relates episodes from the lives of two small-town girls as they begin to face the usual fears, privileges, and responsibilities of growing up.

A Girl Called Al (69) by Constance Greene is a sympathetic treatment of the grim realities that Al, short for Alexandra, has to face. Al, a brilliant nonconformist whose divorced mother leaves her alone in their apartment most of the time, develops a friendship with a girl in a nearby apartment who narrates the story. As their friendship develops, Al's insecurity and loneliness are revealed in contrast to her friend's happy, normal life.

A Rainbow for Robin (145) by Marguerite Vance is the story of a year in the life of a thirteen-year-old, musically talented girl, blind since birth. This book is an inspiring fictional diary as well as an informative account of the adjustment of an individual to a physical handicap and the positive approach of members of a warm and understanding family. Delicate line drawings in black and white add to the emotional appeal of the story.

In *The Summer Birds* (56) Penelope Farmer has caught the delicate mood of a boy who must make a difficult decision and seeks solace on a wild and lonely hill. The boy, Stephen, on a visit to his grandmother's, finds an injured seagull and decides to make it his pet. The gull does become tamer, but it is not a comfortable tameness. Stephen knows that his grandmother feels that the bird must go free, but he clings to his plan to possess the bird and take it home to London.

Jean Little has written a thoughtful story, *One to Grow On* (100), that reveals the inside feeling of Janie, a twelve-year-old girl. Janie, unsure about her friends and family, continually justifies herself by lying. A vacation with her grandmother gives Janie a new outlook on life as she becomes able to enjoy her freedom and her friends for what they are, and her lying becomes a thing of the past.

In *Peter and Butch* (117) by Joan Phipson a boy grows up in a small Australian country town. Peter is a boy without a father who is often unsuccessful in satisfying his need for male images. He starts out with what he considers to be handicaps: a pretty face, a slight build, and a mother who hovers over him. He gets the idea that masculinity and toughness go together. His ideas change as he starts going through the adolescent growing process; with the help of adults, a different boy emerges at the end of the story from the one the reader met at the beginning.

A Dog for Joey (65) by Nan Gilbert is the story of a thirteen-year-old boy's trouble in adjusting to a new situation when his family, the Van Oolbekinks, move from Iowa to Oregon. To help him make his adjustment, he is allowed to raise and train a seeing-eye dog, Eric, as his 4-H project. At first Joey regards Eric as an object to show off until he comes to love the pup for its own sake. When he comes to a full realization that the dog is not his, he attempts unsuccessfully to untrain him. In the end, Joey shows a new-found maturity when Eric graduates a full-fledged guide dog.

Stampede North (60) by Ruth Franchere is an unusual story told in the first person by a fourteen-year-old boy, who recounts the hardships of Klondike gold seekers. Charlie, who accompanies his photographer father as an assistant on a picture-taking assignment in the mining camps, is soon disenchanted by the grim realities in the gold fields, but the experience gives him an opportunity to develop a better relationship with his father.

Sasha, My Friend (33) by Barbara Corcoran tells a story of adventure, courage, adaptation to a wilderness life, and love for a pet white wolf. After her mother is killed in an automobile accident, Hallie goes with her convalescing father to his Christmas tree farm in Montana. In spite of the loss of her Los Angeles home, friends, and way of life, Hallie makes a new life for herself in a small house trailer.

Portrait of Ivan (59) by Paula Fox is a sensitively told story about a motherless boy who lives with his busy father and a Haitian housekeeper. While he sits for his portrait, he comes to know and enjoy Matt Mustazza, the artist, and Miss Manderby, the lady who reads to him while he is having his portrait painted. It is through his friendship with the artist and Miss Manderby and a trip he takes with them that he comes to know himself as a person.

The Half Sisters (23) by Natalie S. Carlson expresses the longing of a little girl, Luvena, to be one of "The Girls," as her three older half-sisters were called, instead of being referred to as one of "The Children" along with her two younger sisters. The plot revolves around an eventful summer full of mixed times—some happy, some sad. Before the story ends, Luvena has won the respect of The Girls.

In *Ride the Wild Storm* (125) by Marjorie Reynolds David Long is sent off to be a summer boarder with the Macys, a family living on Nantucket Island. The Macys and their son, who is David's age, are a warm, loving family who help David to grow into self-confidence.

Emily, an only child, is happy when her parents move from an apartment to an eighteen-room house, in Jean Little's story *Look Through My Window* (99). To add to her happiness, her parents take into the family four young cousins whose mother has become ill. Emily enjoys the skylight room where she can go when she wants to dream and write. Life for Emily is further enriched when she meets another girl her own age who also writes poetry. They become special friends as the story continues in a happy vein.

The Cheerful Quiet (76) by Betty Horvath is a highly amusing story about Patrick O'Brien's quest for a little cheerful quiet. Mr. O'Brien's house with seven children, an Irish setter, a cat, two goldfish, a turtle, and a canary is certain to be filled with noise. Even though it is a cheerful noise, Mr. O'Brien would prefer some cheerful quiet. His search for that cheerful quiet is full of amusing happenings.

The Mimosa Tree (26) by Vera and Bill Cleaver describes the harsh life of a family who leave their home in the Great Smokies to settle in a Chicago tenement. Deserted by their stepmother, fourteen-year-old Marvella and her ten-year-old brother Hugh take over the responsibility of caring for their blind father, who is helpless in the situation, and their three little brothers. How the determination of Marvella and Hugh succeeds in keeping the family together and eventually in getting them back to Goose Elk in the Smokies is a story of faith and courage.

Hoagie's Rifle Gun (107) by Miska Miles relates a family incident in Appalachia. Times are bad: There are only potatoes left in the garden and Pa is out of work. Hoagie usually does not miss a shot with his rifle gun. How he misses Old Bob, a mountain lion, makes a suspense-filled story. The staunch, spiritual strength of the people is reflected in their language and in the bold black-and-white drawings.

A Small Piece of Paradise (110) by Geoffrey Morgan is a story about values, understanding, and growing up. Joe and Mr. Penny work hard to make a garden at the back of the junkyard. It turns into a refuge from the dirty streets and dilapidated buildings and becomes a home for their animals, as well as a place of peace and friendship. Suddenly, all this is threatened by a redevelopment project.

Stories for the Older Child

The problem of anti-Semitism is presented to the unsophisticated reader in *The Wind Dies at Sunrise* (130) by Lois Santalo. The story revolves around two intelligent modern girls seeking to find themselves and at the same time trying to reconcile their differences and to achieve tolerance and understanding.

In Beverly Butler's story *Light a Single Candle* (20), Cathy Wheeler finds that she must face a very difficult and different way of living when she loses her sight at fourteen. Her training with a guide dog and her entrance into a public high school take place during the difficult eighteen-month adjustment that follows.

The problems of the migrant worker are realistically portrayed in *Migrant Girl* (85) by Carli Laklan. No chance for schooling, unbearable working conditions, cruel bosses, and escape. Sixteen-year-old Dacey and the other members of the Carter family from six-year-old

Gaither to Grandma, all field workers, are caught in this seemingly hopeless situation. Juan, a twenty-year-old field worker with ideas of unionization, dares to stand up to the unscrupulous crew boss. Dacey's meeting with Juan helps her to grow as a person and to see a promise of better living in the future.

A Horse Came Running (47) by Meindert De Jong is a penetrating story of a boy's character development. Mark becomes a wise boy when a chain of events follows a tornado's destruction to his farm and the surrounding countryside. Although the tornado brings Mark a new horse, it hastens the death of a horse with whom Mark had had a long friendship. The disastrous results of the tornado force Mark to a realization of the value of self-sacrifice and cooperation. What might appear to be didacticism at times is forestalled by De Jong's great gift as a storyteller.

Julie, a shy and insecure girl of fifteen, describes a year at boarding school in *A Year to Grow* (75) by Felice Holman. Nothing that seems important happens to Julie during the year, but there are important changes in her reactions and attitudes to the people around her. She comes to understand the insecurity of her roommate, Nora, and at the death of the school president's retarded son, Julie mourns deeply though his life barely touched her own.

Set in present-day rural Georgia, *The Skating Rink* (86) by Mildred Lee quietly portrays pain, love, conflict, and growth. Tuck, a fifteen-year-old boy, lives at home with a bitter father and a sympathetic but overprotective stepmother. Pete Degley, who is building a skating rink, senses Tuck's loneliness and teaches him to skate. As Tuck begins to find himself, he stars on opening night at the skating rink.

The 1967 winner of the Newbery Award, *Up a Road Slowly* (77) by Irene Hunt is a moving story of a girl's growing up. The heroine, Julie Trelling, describes her life from the time her mother dies until her high-school graduation, ten years later. Julie goes to live with her Aunt Cordelia, whose ramrod nature seems hard to take. But when Julie's father remarries, Julie finds to her surprise that she has become used to Aunt Cordelia and loves her dearly. The problems of growing up—first love, jealousy, parental relations, and snobbishness—are handled realistically.

Older boys in particular will find *The Big Road* (24) by Tom E. Clarke an interesting and revealing story. Young Vic Martin runs away from home because of trouble with his stepfather, hoping to get a job even though it is the middle of the 1930 depression. After he tries to join the Navy and the Civilian Conservation Corps but is rejected by both, he resorts to riding the rails. After a series of experiences, Vic finally returns home.

Mature readers will find *Who Is Erika?* (55) by Ann M. Falk an interesting first-person recounting of a year of changes in the life of a girl of fifteen. Erika, living in Stockholm with her widowed mother and younger brother, is disappointed and unhappy when her mother remarries. She is scornful about her stepfather, dislikes the new town and school, and is emotionally upset when she learns that her mother is going to have a baby. The story has integrity and presents the reflections of adolescent thought, changing attitudes, and shifting relationships.

Pitcher is a scrawny, clumsy, new boy at a boarding school in *Pitcher and I* (28) by Stephen Cole. Robby, the story's narrator and Pitcher's roommate, takes a protective interest in him. He likes Pitcher's ability to laugh at his shortcomings. As the story develops, it presents a realistic picture of growing boys facing problems of honesty and fair play.

Madeleine L'Engle provides provocative reading for older children in *The Moon by Night* (88). On a vacation trip from Connecticut to California fourteen-year-old Vicky is confronted with some ideas and experiences that many teenagers have to face in growing up. The author portrays Vicky's self-image with sympathy and understanding.

One year in the life of a girl in New York City is told in Karen Rose's *Brooklyn Girl* (128). Kay's summer spent on a farm in Virginia is rewarding and at the same time painful. Kay learns to love a puppy and grieves when she leaves knowing well that her home in Brooklyn is no place for a dog. She comes to the realization that she is growing up when it dawns on her that she is walking down a flight of stairs, not taking the steps three or four at a time. The story is enlivened with home, school, and neighborhood experiences.

Window on the Sea (137) by Adrien Stoutenburg is built around the way a high-school girl has her outlook on life changed by her friendship with a boy whom her family considers a freak because he is more interested in ecology and glaucous-winged sea gulls than in baseball and cars and he intends to go on to college. The pull between the girl's family background and her discovery of her own intellectual curiosity makes an interesting story.

Pamela Travers has contributed an interesting and realistic story for young adolescent girls, *I Go by Sea, I Go by Land!* (141). The book is written as a diary by an eleven-year-old English girl during World War II. When their town is bombed by Germans, Sabrina and her eight-year-old brother are sent to America. She records her impressions of her boat trip across the Atlantic and of the first months of her life in America with relatives and friends.

The Loner (149) by Ester Wier was a runner-up for the Newbery Medal in 1964. An orphaned, nameless boy is given a home and a name by a woman he befriends. The boy develops loyalties, skills, and goals. He learns to love and trust people. The story reaches high drama when the boy kills a bear that has killed the only son of his benefactor.

Mature readers will find *Liza* (22) by Hope Campbell a romance that does not follow the usual pattern. Liza is short, slightly plump, and somewhat bored by the beach vacation to which she has looked forward. Her mother arranges a job for her in a restaurant-theater which delights her. She immediately falls in love with Michael, whose interest in her is half-hearted. He promptly falls in love with Rosalind who takes Liza's place when Liza is fired. A deviation from the usual—Michael does not discover that Rosalind is heartless, but he turns back to Liza when Rosalind leaves. Another unusual twist is that Liza does not discover that Michael is superficial, but realizes that he was swept off his feet by Rosalind and she might as well swallow her pride and admit it.

In her junior year in high school, Sue Morgan learns that it is possible to be happy without conforming, and she also manages to face squarely a problem of integrity—cheating. *The Losing Game* (53) by Anne Emery is an honest book about a common problem. The style of writing is simple; the characterizations are varied and convincing. Warm family relationships and realistic problems are ably portrayed.

Vivid characterization and fine writing make *A Kingdom in a Horse* (152) by Maia Wojciechowska an outstanding story. David's bitterness toward his father and toward life stems from his father's decision to leave his work as a rodeo clown. How the chestnut mare, Gypsy, and her elderly owner, Mrs. Tierney, change his resentment to love and appreciation makes interesting reading.

The Amethyst Summer (12) by Bianca Bradbury is a well-written story without melodrama and contrived successes. Sixteen-year-old Bayley must cope with keeping house for her father and three brothers when her mother leaves to stay with a relative who is ill. Bayley also becomes concerned about the new family next door: The Sudak twins are slow to become friendly; their mother who had been in a concentration camp is still afraid of strangers. Bayley learns to organize her work, to appear calm for her father's sake, and to be more thoughtful of other people. Mature readers faced with responsibilities similar to Bayley's will find *The Amethyst Summer* most interesting.

Boys beginning to think of careers will find *Deadline for Jim* (37) by Graham M. Dean interesting and unusual. The story is an account of a summer night spent by a high-school boy as a cub reporter on his uncle's newspaper. Wars between rival newspapers, honest reporting deterred by ambitious politicians, and the difficulties encountered in being a responsible publisher serving a cause add up to a good plot.

Two teen-age boys gain a new respect for policemen and sane driving in *The Wheel of a Fast Car* (21) by William E. Butterworth. When seventeen-year-old Greg attempts to outrun some police cars, he ends up with a revoked driver's license. A summer spent with his uncle, a veteran Nascar driver, and a teen-age cousin who is a rookie racing car driver proves eventful for Greg and his friend.

In *Whose Town?* (68) by Lorenz Graham a Black family moves from the South to the North in the hope of finding freedom from discrimination and prejudice. The story relates the experiences of David Williams, a high-school senior who finds his family faced with the same social problems they had hoped to leave behind: Father loses his job, Mother must work as a domestic, a principal lacks understanding, and an unfair murder charge is placed against David. It is difficult to believe that after all his unhappy experiences David has faith that their new town can become everyone's town.

The Street Kids (36) by Herbert Danska is a heart-warming story of an elderly man, Hannibal Servatious Serendipity, a watchman for a building on which construction has been stopped due to a strike. Mr. Serendipity makes friends with "the Street Kids," who are mostly

From *The Street Kids* by Herbert Danska.

Black and Puerto Rican. Together they plant a flower garden, and in a short time the iron girders of the nine-story building are alive with blooming flowers, much to the dismay of the police and the vice-president of the company whose building is being erected. Mr. Serendipity is happy when he finds a new home where his talents will be appreciated.

Growth in Enjoying One's Role—In the Home, the School, and the Community

Boys and girls frequently find it difficult to define their roles at home, at school, and in the community. Family life—with its happy times and sad times, problems of adjustment, misunderstandings, and strained relations—is a popular subject in stories for children. The plots of many stories also revolve around school life and community activities. Children are able to understand and sympathize with the situations in the stories because of their own experiences, and they are helped to solve problems confronting them as they meet fictional characters with similar problems who work them out satisfactorily.

In the past, children's stories of family life were of a didactic nature. The plots were sentimental and designed to bring forth a shower of tears. Near the middle of the present century, stories of family life began to move away from tear-jerking plots to more realistic portrayals of boys and girls living in wholesome natural family situations. Previous to this trend boys were portrayed as Little Lord Fauntleroys or the valiant heroes of Horatio Alger stories, charged with the responsibility of supporting a widowed mother and a number of brothers and sisters, one of whom, usually a sister, was often crippled. The girls were portrayed as sweet and demure, and those who were crippled suffered in patience.

For a long time it was almost impossible to find a father in children's literature. Even in *Little Women* (2) by Louisa May Alcott, still one of America's most beloved stories of family life, Mr. March is missing; he has left for war before the story opens. With the publication of *Caddie Woodlawn* (14) by Carol R. Brink in 1935, a new image was created for fathers in children's literature by Caddie's father, Mr. Woodlawn. The story realistically portrays life in a pioneer community in Wisconsin in the early 1860s.

Today countless stories of family, school, and community life are available for the enjoyment of children of all ages.

Stories for the Young Reader

True-to-life family situations can be humorously portrayed in the form of animal stories. Patricia Coombs has presented a situation of sibling rivalry in a racoon family in *Waddy and His Brother* (31). Through the responsibility of taking care of the baby when his mother needs to be away, Waddy comes to realize that he is appreciated by the baby and particularly by his mother.

Zoo, Where Are You? (104) by Ann McGovern tells of a little boy's adventure in searching for wild animals for a zoo. Instead of wild animals, the boy finds some junk that becomes precious to him. This quiet story with handsome and sensitive illustrations portrays an understanding mother who gives the little boy apples, cookies, and a kiss and sends him on his way; when he returns, she agrees that his junk is beautiful.

Certain experiences are familiar to all children living in a family—a fight or rejection one moment, a game and fun together the next. *Willy Is My Brother* (112) by Peggy Parish presents an amusing description of a brother-sister relationship seen through the eyes of a little sister.

There is magic in every child's very own day—his birthday. *Happy Birthday!* (102) by Myra C. Livingston describes the highlights of a little girl's special day from waking with the realization that it is her birthday to the moment when she has been kissed goodnight at the end of a lovely and completely satisfactory day.

In *Alexander* (101) by Harold Littledale, Chris confesses all his misdeeds of the day to his father. He recounts these actions as being performed by Alexander, a red-and-green-striped imaginary horse. Father listens patiently and then sums up the situation by saying, "Alexander had a bad day and will be a wonderful little horse tomorrow," knowing full well that Chris was talking about himself. There is warmth in the illustrations which add amusement to the story.

Janice M. Udry's *End of the Line* (144) is a story about a little girl and her grandfather who enjoy each other's companionship. They fish together and take trips by streetcar just for the fun of it. The two are therefore unhappy when the city decides to scrap the streetcars and install buses instead. Finally they hit upon a clever plan to give the old cars a new usefulness and at the same time increase the fish population.

Big Cowboy Western (131) by Ann H. Scott is a story of family life in an urban housing development. Martin's imaginative play with his cowboy hat, holster, and two toy guns is a little noisy for adults, but Martin and his parents become perfectly satisfied when an understanding fruit peddler gives him the job of watching his horse. The simple text and realistic illustrations portray a Black family and a small boy's imagination in a pleasant way.

Miki Takino was born in Japan but came to a new home in New York so young that he does not remember life in Japan. He is pleased when the teacher and children choose him to be the Japanese boy in the program, but is sad and confused when he learns that grandparents are to be honored guests. Miki has no grandparents. How young Miki solves his problem through his friendly relationships makes *Meet Miki Takino* (32) by Helen Copeland a warm and pleasant story for young children.

Peter hated the old brownstone house in New York where he lived with his great-grandfather; he wanted to live across the street in the tall, new apartment building that had an elevator and a doorman. Why Peter decides he wants to stay in the old house makes *Peter's Brownstone House* (30) by Hila Colman a warm and surprising story.

For the Middle Reader

Meg lived with her brother on a small harbor boat after the death of their parents. She is unhappy and resentful and rebels against her new life when she is taken to live with her aunt and uncle on a chicken ranch. Finally she comes to appreciate the love and care given her in her new home as portrayed in *Meg of Heron's Neck* (84) by Elizabeth Ladd.

In Neta M. Frazier's story *The Magic Ring* (61) boys and girls meet a resourceful family living during the early 1900s without the present-day comforts of electricity, central heating, automobiles, radio, and television. Becky, a ten-year-old girl with a vivid imagination, helps the reader to appreciate the realities of those times.

Young readers will enjoy *Jenny* (78) by Gene Inyart in which Jenny finally gets a long-awaited baby brother, a puppy of her own, and a new family next door. While the mother next door writes novels, the four friendly boys efficiently run the house. All this means happy times for Jenny. Jenny's lack of jealousy and realistic attitude toward her baby brother add significance to the story.

When a stray dog appears on the island where Becky and her family are living, Becky tries in every way to persuade her family to let her keep her new friend. During the week before the mailboat arrives that would have taken the dog away, the dog convinces the family that she should be allowed to stay. Family relationships are realistic and the pictures of the island community and the shore atmosphere are vividly portrayed in *Visitor from the Sea* (132) by Dorothy Simpson.

D. J.'s Worst Enemy (19) by Robert Burch is a story of the meanness of one boy who finally realizes that he is his own worst enemy. The remorse he experiences changes his attitude, and he makes the effort to take his place as a cooperating member of his own family. The plot emphasizes contrasts in behavior and develops appreciation of desirable family relationships.

Boston at the beginning of the 1900s makes an interesting background for the story of Sarah Ann McCarty and her adopted family. Girls particularly will find *A Family for Sarah Ann* (35) by Polly Curren a satisfying story.

Clyde Downer, the hero of *A Dash of Pepper* (8) by Thelma H. Bell, feels that his parents are unreasonable not to let him have a horse he so dearly wants. Doc Wilkins, a friend of the family, convinces Clyde's parents that they should change their minds. Events happen in rapid succession: Clyde becomes a hero, his parents return to the country, and a friend's health is restored.

There is a blend of realism and fantasy in *George* (143) by Agnes S. Turnbull. A beguiling imaginary rabbit, named George, becomes the friend and adviser of two children and their mother. He improves their manners and helps them with their homework until Father Weaver puts a stop to the pretending when the family departs for a vacation.

Keefer's Landing (151) by Robert J. Willis is a well-written story about the Keefer family whose home and place of business is Keefer's Landing. The family sells fuel, fishing supplies, and groceries until a new highway cuts off their property and leaves them without any business. Randy Keefer, fifteen, wants to be treated as an equal by his brother and grandfather, but his desire for status and recognition makes him rebellious at times. Particularly well portrayed are the relationships within the family.

The Noonday Friends (136) by Mary Stolz was one of the runners-up for the 1966 Newbery Award. The story centers around the Davis family. Franny Davis' father is the nicest, dearest, smartest man in the world but he cannot keep a job; as a result, Franny's mother has to work. Franny and Jim must have free lunch passes, and Franny has no time to be with her best friend because she has to go straight home after school to take care of four-year-old Marshall and do housework. The story reveals the family's problems and pleasures, and the humor, natural dialogue, and vivid characterizations make enjoyable reading.

Doctor's Boy (3) by Karin Anckarsvard is a warm story of a country doctor in Sweden in the early part of the century and of the way in which the doctor and his son were able to help another boy. Slum areas and the people living in them are described with understanding and feeling. The emphasis in the simple plot is on the development of the friendship between the two boys and on good family relationships.

In *Home from Far* (98) by Jean Little a family adjusts to the accidental death of one of their two oldest children, the boy of a pair of twins. Trying to help the adjustment, the parents bring home a foster sister for Jenny, the remaining twin. The foster sister has a brother who is also brought into the MacGregor home. The boy not only is the same age as Jenny but also has the same name as her twin brother. This results in additional problems for Jenny. The split loyalties, the rejections, and the gradual acceptance of the children as a part of Jenny's life make an understanding, insightful, and appealing story.

Healthy family relationships and a pleasant background of farm life are portrayed in *The Wild One* (58) by Henry R. Fea. Twelve-year-old Bruce is led into many ingenious attempts to capture and win the friendship of a wild dog by his persistent sense of ownership. His trial-and-error beginnings change to knowledgeable plans as he gains in self-discipline and learns how to work with the dog.

Number 5 Hackberry Street (67) by Christine Govan is set in a small town in Tennessee in the early 1900s. The story centers around the three children of the family, their growing pains, their triumphs, and their joys. The homes, food, recreation, and way of life of this period are described in a style that uses the vernacular of the times and region.

A different pattern of family life is portrayed in a story about an eight-year-old Black girl, *Melindy's Medal* (57) by Georgene Faulkner and John Becker. Life is very exciting for Melindy, whose father plays the saxophone and whose grandmother tells marvelous stories about the medals that belong in Melindy's family. There is a happy ending with Melindy winning her medal for "just pure bravery."

William, Andy, and Ramon (18) by P. Buckley and H. Jones centers around three families of different racial backgrounds who live in the same apartment house and whose children attend the same school. The emphasis is on how people of different cultural backgrounds live together in family groups.

For the Older Reader

Against many odds a young girl persists in her training to become a champion skier. A realistic picture of wholesome family life and interesting peer relationships with a bit of romance thrown in will make *Flying Skis* (154) by Josephine M. Wunsch exciting reading for girls, particularly those interested in sports.

Frequently girls feel that they are not understood by their families and friends. *The Trouble with Terry* (95) by Joan M. Lexau tells of Terry's troubles and how she works through them with the help of good relationships with family and friends.

In *Shoes in September* (13) by Bianca Bradbury sixteen-year-old Meg is the mainstay in a family of casual ten-year-old twins and a charming but irresponsible artist father. Meg longs to live where people know all about you, help you get out of trouble, and expect you to do the same for them. The summer comes to have real meaning for each member of the family as their stay in a weather-beaten house on Block Island off the Rhode Island coast comes to an end.

Family relationships, particularly those between a father and a son, are sympathetically drawn in *Gull Number Seven Thirty Seven* (64) by Jean C. George. The story revolves around Luke's father, Dr. Rivers, who is doing research in herring gulls. The family lives on a bleak island, and Luke wishes he could get a job instead of having to work with his father. Luke's father becomes discouraged because of a lack of interest in his work and is about to give up his project when the government asks his help in clearing Logan Airport of birds, since birds have caused a plane crash. Still wishing to break away, Luke is obedient and goes along with his father. Finally Luke makes a declaration of independence and, encouraged by another older biologist, goes off to do his own research on gulls.

Extending Experiences for the Reader

1. Read to the class "The Fish I Didn't Catch" by John Greenleaf Whittier. Discuss didactic writing with the class.
2. Bring to class illustrations of didactic writing.
3. Read to the class several stories that were written recently with the purpose of teaching a lesson. Evaluate these stories with the group in terms of their literary quality.
4. In what ways do you agree or disagree with the following statement by Ruth M. Tews (139):

   > Bibliotherapy is a process of selected activity involving reading materials, planned, conducted, and controlled as a treatment under the guidance of a physician for emotional and other problems. It must be administered by a skilled professionally trained librarian within the prescribed purpose and goals.

5. Observe a group of children at work and at play and record the opportunities for therapy in the curriculum.

6. Observe young children in dramatic play situations. Record evidences of their interests and goals. What provisions are made to help them satisfy their interests and needs?
7. Observe children in dramatic play situations. Record behaviors that reveal correct and incorrect concepts that might have their bases in the nature of their environment.
8. Read . . . *And Now Miguel* (83) and then present the 16-mm. film made from the book. Discuss them with your class. How might the story and the film contribute to one's personal development?
9. Read excerpts from *Up a Road Slowly* (77) by Irene Hunt, *Shadow of a Bull* (153) by Maia Wojciechowska, and *Doctor's Boy* (3) by Karin Anckarsvard. Discuss with the class the contributions that these stories might make to a young person's social development.

Extending Experience for Children

1. Select a story written for the purpose of teaching a lesson. Discuss with the class the lesson the story aims to teach.

Chapter References

1. ALCOCK, GUDRUN. *Turn the Next Corner.* New York: Lothrop, Lee & Shepard, 1969. Grades 4–7.
2. ALCOTT, LOUISA MAY. *Little Women.* New York: Macmillan, 1962. Paperback. Grades 6–8.
3. ANCKARSVARD, KARIN. *Doctor's Boy.* Annabelle MacMillan (tr.). New York: Harcourt Brace Jovanovich, 1965. Grades 4–7.
4. BAKER, LAURAN. *Cousin Tryg.* Philadelphia: Lippincott, 1966. Grades 4–6.
5. BECKMAN, GUNNEL. *The Girl Without a Name.* Anne Parker (tr.). New York: Harcourt Brace Jovanovich, 1970. Grades 4–6.
6. BEIM, JERROLD. *With Dad Alone.* New York: Harcourt Brace Jovanovich, 1954. Grades 4–7.
7. BEIM, LORRAINE, AND JERROLD BEIM. *Two Is a Team.* New York: Harcourt Brace Jovanovich, 1945. Kindergarten–grade 3.
8. BELL, THELMA H. *A Dash of Pepper.* New York: Viking, 1965. Grades 4–6.
9. BONTEMPS, ARNA. *Lonesome Boy.* Boston: Houghton Mifflin, 1967. Grade 7 and up.
10. BORACK, BARBARA. *Someone Small.* New York: Harper & Row, 1969. Preschool–grade 3.
11. BOVA, BEN. *Escape.* New York: Holt, Rinehart & Winston, 1970. Grades 7–12.

12. BRADBURY, BIANCA. *The Amethyst Summer.* New York: Washburn, 1963. Grades 6–8.
13. ———. *Shoes in September.* New York: Washburn, 1964. Grades 6–8.
14. BRINK, CAROL R. *Caddie Woodlawn.* Rev. ed. New York: Macmillan, 1970. Paperback. Grades 4–6.
15. ———. *Two Are Better Than One.* New York: Macmillan, 1968. Grades 4–6.
16. BUCK, PEARL S. *Matthew, Mark, Luke and John.* New York: John Day, 1967. Grades 4–6.
17. BUCKLEY, HELEN E. *Too Many Crackers.* New York: Lothrop, Lee & Shepard, 1966. Preschool–grade 2.
18. BUCKLEY, PETER, AND H. JONES. *William, Andy, and Ramon.* New York: Holt, Rinehart & Winston, 1966. Grade 1.
19. BURCH, ROBERT. *D. J.'s Worst Enemy.* New York: Viking, 1965. Grades 4–7.
20. BUTLER, BEVERLY. *Light a Single Candle.* New York: Simon & Schuster, 1970. Paperback. Grade 7 and up.
21. BUTTERWORTH, WILLIAM E. *The Wheel of a Fast Car.* New York: Norton, 1969. Grades 7–10.
22. CAMPBELL, HOPE. *Liza.* New York: Norton, 1965. Grades 5–9.
23. CARLSON, NATALIE S. *The Half Sisters.* New York: Harper & Row, 1970. Grades 4–8.
24. CLARKE, TOM E. *The Big Road.* New York: Lothrop, Lee & Shepard, 1963. Grade 7 and up.
25. CLEAVER, VERA, AND BILL CLEAVER. *Ellen Crae.* New York: Dell, 1969. Paperback. Grades 4–6.
26. ———. *The Mimosa Tree.* Philadelphia: Lippincott, 1970. Grades 5–7.
27. COCKETT, MARY. *Rosanna the Goat.* Indianapolis: Bobbs-Merrill, 1970. Grades 1–4.
28. COLE, STEPHEN. *Pitcher and I.* New York: Farrar, Straus & Giroux, 1963. Grades 7–11.
29. COLLIER, JAMES. *Danny Goes to the Hospital.* New York: Grosset & Dunlap, n.d. Kindergarten–grade 3.
30. COLMAN, HILA. *Peter's Brownstone House.* New York: Morrow, 1963. Kindergarten–grade 3.
31. COOMBS, PATRICIA. *Waddy and His Brother.* New York: Lothrop, Lee & Shepard, 1963. Preschool–grade 1.
32. COPELAND, HELEN. *Meet Miki Takino.* New York: Lothrop, Lee & Shepard, 1963. Preschool–grade 3.
33. CORCORAN, BARBARA. *Sasha, My Friend.* New York: Atheneum, 1969. Grades 5–9.
34. CORNISH, SAM. *Your Hand in Mine.* New York: Harcourt Brace Jovanovich, 1970. Grades 2–4.
35. CURREN, POLLY. *A Family for Sarah Ann.* Indianapolis: Bobbs-Merrill, 1962. Grades 2–5.
36. DANSKA, HERBERT. *The Street Kids.* New York: Knopf, 1970. Grade 7 and up.

37. DEAN, GRAHAM M. *Deadline for Jim.* New York: Criterion, 1961. Grades 7–10.
38. DE ANGELI, ARTHUR, AND MARGUERITE DE ANGELI. *Empty Barn.* Philadelphia: Westminster, 1966. Kindergarten–grade 3.
39. DE ANGELI MARGUERITE. *Bright April.* Garden City, N. Y.: Doubleday, 1946. Grades 3–5.
40. ———. *Copper-Toed Boots.* Garden City, N. Y.: Doubleday, 1938. Kindergarten–grade 4.
41. ———. *Elin's Amerika.* Garden City, N. Y.: Doubleday, 1941. Grades 4–6.
42. ———. *Henner's Lydia.* Garden City, N.Y.: Doubleday, 1936. Grades 3–5.
43. ———. *Jared's Island.* Garden City, N. Y.: Doubleday, 1947. Grades 3–5.
44. ———. *Skippack School.* Garden City, N. Y.: Doubleday, 1939. Grades 4–6.
45. ———. *Thee Hannah.* Garden City, N. Y.: Doubleday, 1949. Grades 1–5.
46. ———. *Yonie Wondernose.* Garden City, N. Y.: Doubleday, 1944. Grades 1–4.
47. DE JONG, MEINDERT. *A Horse Came Running.* New York: Macmillan, 1970. Grade 4 and up.
48. DE REGNIERS, BEATRICE SCHENK, AND ESTHER GILMAN. *The Little Girl and Her Mother.* New York: Vanguard, 1963.
49. DOCKER, ROLF. *Marius.* Oliver Stallybrass (tr.). New York: Harcourt Brace Jovanovich, 1970. Grades 4–6.
50. DODGE, ELIZABETH MAPES. *Hans Brinker or the Silver Skates.* Garden City, N. Y.: Doubleday, 1956. Grades 3–7.
51. DRAPER, CENA C. *Rim of the Ridge.* New York: Criterion, 1965. Grades 3–7.
52. DUBOIS, WILLIAM PENÉ. *Porko Von Popbutton.* New York: Harper & Row, 1969. Grade 5 and up.
53. EMERY, ANNE. *The Losing Game.* Philadelphia: Westminster, 1965. Grades 7–10.
54. ENRIGHT, ELIZABETH. *Thimble Summer.* New York: Harcourt Brace Jovanovich, 1938. Grades 4–6.
55. FALK, ANN M. *Who Is Ericka?* Annabelle MacMillan (tr.). New York: Harcourt Brace Jovanovich, 1963. Grade 7 and up.
56. FARMER, PENELOPE. *The Summer Birds.* New York: Harcourt Brace Jovanovich, 1962. Grades 4–6.
57. FAULKNER, GEORGENE, AND JOHN BECKER. *Melindy's Medal.* New York: Messner, 1945. Grades 3–6.
58. FEA, HENRY R. *The Wild One.* New York: Washburn, 1964. Grades 4–6.
59. FOX, PAULA. DICK JACKSON (ed.). *Portrait of Ivan.* Englewood Cliffs, N. J.: Bradbury, 1969. Grades 5–7.
60. FRANCHERE, RUTH. *Stampede North.* New York: Macmillan, 1969. Grades 5–8.

61. FRAZIER, NETA M. *The Magic Ring.* New York: David McKay, 1959. Grades 3–7.
62. FREUCHEN, PIPALUK. *Eskimo Boy.* New York: Lothrop, Lee & Shepard, 1951. Grades 4–6.
63. GAGE, WILSON. *Big Blue Island.* New York: Simon & Schuster, 1969. Paperback. Grades 4–6.
64. GEORGE, JEAN. *Gull Number Seven Thirty Seven.* New York: T. Y. Crowell, 1964. Grades 7–11.
65. GILBERT, NAN. *A Dog for Joey.* New York: Harper & Row, 1967. Grade 5 and up.
66. GOODSELL, JANE. *Katie's Magic Glasses.* Boston: Houghton Mifflin, 1965. Kindergarten–grade 3.
67. GOVAN, CHRISTINE. *Number 5 Hackberry Street.* Cleveland: World, 1964. Grades 4–6.
68. GRAHAM, LORENZ. *Whose Town?* New York: T. Y. Crowell, 1969. Grade 5 and up.
69. GREENE, CONSTANCE. *A Girl Called Al.* New York: Viking, 1970. Paperback. Grades 3–7.
70. GREENE, ROBERTA. *Two and Me Makes Three.* New York: Coward-McCann, 1970. Grades 1–3.
71. GRIPE, MARIA. *Hugo.* New York: Delacorte, 1970. Grades 3–7.
72. HARNDEN, RUTH. *Next Door.* Boston: Houghton Mifflin, 1970. Grades 4–8.
73. HAVINGHURST, ROBERT J., *et al.* "The Development of the Ideal Self," *Journal of Educational Research*, 40 (1946), 242.
74. HODGES, ELIZABETH J. *Free as a Frog.* Reading, Mass.: Addison-Wesley, 1969. Kindergarten–grade 3.
75. HOLMAN, FELICE. *A Year to Grow.* New York: Norton, 1968. Grades 5–9.
76. HORVATH, BETTY. *The Cheerful Quiet.* New York: Watts, 1969. Kindergarten–grade 3.
77. HUNT, IRENE. *Up a Road Slowly.* New York: Grosset & Dunlap, 1968. Paperback. Grade 7 and up.
78. INYART, GENE. *Jenny.* New York: Simon & Schuster, 1970. Paperback. Grades 3–6.
79. KATZOFF, BETTY. *Cathy's First School.* New York: Knopf, 1964. Kindergarten–grade 2.
80. KRASILOVSKY, PHYLLIS. *The Girl Who Was a Cowboy.* Garden City, N. Y.: Doubleday, n.d. Kindergarten–grade 3.
81. ———. *The Shy Little Girl.* Boston: Houghton Mifflin, 1970. Kindergarten–grade 3.
82. ———. *The Very Little Girl.* Garden City, N. Y.: Doubleday, 1953. Paperback. Kindergarten–grade 3.
83. KRUMGOLD, JOSEPH. *. . . And Now Miguel.* New York: T. Y. Crowell, 1953. Grade 6 and up.
84. LADD, ELIZABETH. *Meg of Heron's Neck.* New York: Morrow, 1961. Grades 3–6.
85. LAKLAN, CARLI. *Migrant Girl.* New York: McGraw-Hill, 1970. Grades 7–9.

86. LEE, MILDRED. *The Skating Rink.* New York: Dell, 1970. Paperback. Grade 5 and up.
87. L'ENGLE, MADELEINE. *Dance in the Desert.* New York: Farrar, Straus & Giroux, 1969. Grade 7 and up.
88. ______. *The Moon by Night.* New York: Farrar, Straus & Giroux, 1963. Grades 7–11.
89. LENSKI, LOIS. *Bayou Suzette.* Philadelphia: Lippincott, 1943. Grades 4–6.
90. ______. *Judy's Journey.* New York: Dell, 1966. Paperback. Grades 3–7.
91. ______. *Strawberry Girl.* New York: Dell, 1967. Paperback. Preschool–grade 7.
92. LEVINE, RHODA. *Quiet Story.* New York: Atheneum, 1963. Preschool–grade 2.
93. LEWIS, MARY. *Joey and the Fawn.* New York: Washburn, 1967. Grades 1–3.
94. LEXAU, JOAN M. *Benjie on His Own.* New York: Dial, 1970. Preschool–grade 3.
95. ______. *The Trouble with Terry.* New York: Dial, 1962. Grades 3–7.
96. LINDEMAN, BARBARA, AND MARTIN KLING. "Bibliotherapy: Definitions, Uses, and Studies," *Journal of School Psychology,* 7 (1968–1969), 36–41.
97. LINDGREN, ASTRID. *Pippi Longstocking.* Florence Lambort (tr.). New York: Viking, 1969. Paperback. Grades 4–6.
98. LITTLE, JEAN. *Home from Far.* Boston: Little, Brown, 1965. Grade 5 and up.
99. ______. *Look Through My Window.* New York: Harper & Row, 1971. Paperback. Grades 4–6.
100. ______. *One to Grow On.* Boston: Little, Brown, 1969. Grades 3–7.
101. LITTLEDALE, HAROLD. *Alexander.* New York: Parents' Magazine Press, 1964. Kindergarten–grade 3.
102. LIVINGSTON, MYRA C. *Happy Birthday!* New York: Harcourt Brace Jovanovich, 1964.
103. LOBEL, ARNOLD. *Frog and Toad Are Friends.* New York: Harper & Row, 1970. Kindergarten–grade 3.
104. MCGOVERN, ANN. *Zoo, Where Are You?* New York: Harper & Row, 1964. Kindergarten–grade 3.
105. MCGUFFEY, WILLIAM HOLMES. *Fifth Eclectic Reader.* Cincinnati and New York: Van Antwerp, Bragg. Grade 5.
106. MANN, PEGGY. *The Twenty-Five Cent Friend.* New York: Coward-McCann, 1970. Grades 2–6.
107. MILES, MISKA. *Hoagie's Rifle Gun.* Boston: Atlantic Monthly Press, 1970. Grades 1–3.
108. MOLARSKY, OSMOND. *Where the Good Luck Was.* New York: Walck, 1970. Kindergarten–grade 3.
109. MOODY, RALPH. *Man of the Family.* New York: Norton, 1951. Grades 5–11.
110. MORGAN, GEOFFREY. *A Small Piece of Paradise.* New York: Knopf, 1968. Grades 5–7.

111. *New England Primer, The.* Paul L. Ford (ed.). New York: Teachers College Press, 1962. Paperback.
112. PARISH, PEGGY. *Willy Is My Brother.* New York: Scott, 1963. n.g.l.
113. PARKER, RICHARD. *The Boy Who Wasn't Lonely.* Indianapolis: Bobbs-Merrill, 1964. Grades 2–6.
114. PECK, ROBERT. "The Child Models Himself After His Favorite Model," *Fostering Mental Health in Our Schools,* 1950 Yearbook, ASCD.
115. PEGIS, JESSIE C. *Best Friends.* New York: Hastings House, 1964. Grades 4–6.
116. PERKINS, HUGH V. *Human Development and Learning.* Belmont, Cal.: Wadsworth, 1969.
117. PHIPSON, JOAN. *Peter and Butch.* New York: Harcourt Brace Jovanovich, 1969. Grade 7 and up.
118. POLITI, LEO. *A Boat for Peppe.* New York: Scribner, 1950. Preschool–grade 3.
119. ———. *Juanita.* New York: Scribner, 1948. Preschool–grade 3.
120. ———. *Moy Moy.* New York: Scribner, 1960. Preschool–grade 3.
121. ———. *Pedro, the Angel of Olvera Street.* New York: Scribner, 1946. Preschool–grade 2.
122. ———. *The Song of the Swallows.* New York: Scribner, 1949. Kindergarten–grade 3.
123. PRESCOTT, DANIEL A. *The Child in the Educative Process.* New York: McGraw-Hill, 1957.
124. RENICK, MARION. *Boy at Bat.* New York: Scribner, 1949. Kindergarten–grade 4.
125. REYNOLDS, MARJORIE. *Ride the Wild Storm.* New York: Macmillan, 1969. Grades 4–6.
126. RHODIN, ERIC. *Hideout at Winter House.* Philadelphia: Westminster, 1970. n.g.l.
127. ROLBERG, RUTH. *What Happened to Virgilia?* Eau Claire, Wis.: Hale, 1963. Grades 5–7.
128. ROSE, KAREN. *Brooklyn Girl.* Chicago: Follett, 1963. Grade 5 and up.
129. RUSSELL, DAVID H., AND CAROLINE SHRODES. "Contributions of Research in Bibliotherapy to the Language-Arts Program," *The School Review,* 58 (September 1950), 335.
130. SANTALO, LOIS. *The Wind Dies at Sunrise.* Indianapolis: Bobbs-Merrill, 1965. Grades 6–9.
131. SCOTT, ANN H. *Big Cowboy Western.* New York: Lothrop, Lee & Shepard, 1965. Preschool–grade 2.
132. SIMPSON, DOROTHY. *Visitor from the Sea.* Philadelphia: Lippincott, 1965. Grades 4–6.
133. SMITH, ROBERT P. *When I Am Big.* New York: Harper & Row, 1965. Kindergarten–grade 3.
134. STAPP, ARTHUR D. *Too Steep for Baseball.* New York: Harper & Row, 1964. Grades 3–7.
135. STEVENSON, ROBERT LOUIS. *Treasure Island.* New York: Macmillan, 1962. Paperback. Grade 7 and up.
136. STOLZ, MARY. *The Noonday Friends.* New York: Harper & Row, 1971. Paperback. Grades 3–7.

137. STOUTENBURG, ADRIEN. *Window on the Sea.* Philadelphia: Westminster, 1962. Grades 7–10.

138. SUDBURY, RODIE. *A Sound of Crying.* New York: McCall Books, 1970. Grades 5–8.

139. TEWS, RUTH M. (ed.). "Bibliotherapy," *Library Trends,* 11 (October 1962), "Introduction," 99.

140. THOMPSON, WILMA. *That Barbara!* New York: Dell, 1970. Paperback. Grades 4–7.

141. TRAVERS, PAMELA. *I Go by Sea, I Go by Land!* New York: Dell, n.d. Paperback. Grades 3–7.

142. TURKLE, BRINTON. *Thy Friend, Obadiah.* New York: Viking, 1969. Kindergarten–grade 3.

143. TURNBULL, AGNES S. *George.* Boston: Houghton Mifflin, 1965. n.g.l.

144. UDRY, JANICE M. *End of the Line.* Chicago: Whitman, 1962. Grades 1–3.

145. VANCE, MARGUERITE. *A Rainbow for Robin.* New York: Dutton, 1966. Grades 3–7.

146. VIORST, JUDITH. *I'll Fix Anthony.* New York: Harper & Row, 1969. Preschool–grade 3.

147. WARBURG, SANDOL S. *Growing Time.* Boston: Houghton Mifflin, 1969. Kindergarten–grade 3.

148. WARD, LYND. *The Biggest Bear.* Boston: Houghton Mifflin, 1952. Kindergarten–grade 3.

149. WIER, ESTER. *The Loner.* New York: David McKay, 1963. Grades 7–9.

150. WIGGIN, KATE DOUGLAS. *Rebecca of Sunnybrook Farm.* New York: Grosset & Dunlap, n.d. Paperback. Grades 7–9.

151. WILLIS, ROBERT J. *Keefer's Landing.* Chicago: Follett, 1964. Grades 4–6.

152. WOJCIECHOWSKA, MAIA. *A Kingdom in a Horse.* New York: Harper & Row, 1965. Grade 7 and up.

153. ———. *Shadow of a Bull.* New York: Atheneum, 1964. Grade 5 and up.

154. WUNSCH, JOSEPHINE M. *Flying Skis.* New York: David McKay, 1962. Grade 8 and up.

155. YOUNG, MIRIAM. *Can't You Pretend?* New York: Putnam, 1970. Preschool–grade 1.

156. ZOLOTOW, CHARLOTTE. *The Hating Book.* New York: Harper & Row, 1969. Preschool–grade 3.

More Stories About Personal Growth

Kindergarten–Grade 3

BROWN, MYRA B. *Pip Moves Away.* San Carlos, Calif.: Golden Gate Junior Books, 1967. Pip does not want to move but soon adjusts when he finds a new friend.

BUDD, LILLIAN. *Larry.* New York: David McKay, 1966. A small backwoods boy feels abandoned when his brother gets married, but, with love, he begins to grow up.

COHEN, MIRIAM. *Will I Have a Friend?* New York: Macmillan, 1967. The concerns of a small child entering school are portrayed in this story.

DUNCAN, LOIS. *Giving Away Suzanne.* New York: Dodd, Mead, 1963. Mary Kay finds out that a goldfish is no substitute for a real little sister.

EMBERLEY, BARBARA. *Night's Nice.* Garden City, N. Y.: Doubleday, 1963. To counteract fear of the dark and difficulties associated with going to bed, the things that make night nice are described.

FELT, SUE. *Hello-Goodbye.* Garden City, N. Y.: Doubleday, 1960. After a lonesome week in their new home, Lucy and Candice realize that they have not really tried to make friends.

FISHER, AILEEN L. *My Mother and I.* New York: T. Y. Crowell, 1967. A little girl learns to appreciate her mother.

GUILLAUME, JEANETTE, AND MARY LEE BACHMAN. *Amat and the Water Buffalo.* New York: Coward-McCann, 1962. Amat's long wait is rewarded when his family realizes that he is big enough to ride the water buffalo and to go to school as his older brothers do.

HALL, NATALIE. *The World in a City Block.* New York: Viking, 1960. What Nick finds out about the world as he visits the shops on his city block is vividly described in this story.

HAWKINS, QUAIL. *Who Wants an Apple?* New York: Holiday House, 1957. Although she feels strange about moving from the city to the country, Quail realizes that wherever her parents are is home.

HEILBRONER, JOAN. *The Happy Birthday Present.* New York: Harper & Row, 1961. Pet and Davey shop around for the "just right" gift for their mother's birthday.

HORVATH, BETTY. *Hooray for Jasper.* New York: Watts, 1966. This is a good story to help little boys with their growing up problems.

HUNTER, EDITH. *Child of the Silent Night.* Boston: Houghton, Mifflin, 1963. Deaf and blind, Laura comes to love the world around her about which she learns through her sense of touch.

JOHNSTON, JOHANNA. *Edie Changes Her Mind.* New York: Putnam, 1964. Having her own way about going to bed one night convinces Edie that her parents do know best.

KLEIN, LEONORE. *Runaway John.* New York: Knopf, 1963. John wants to take along the essentials—his parents, friend, and dog—when he runs away from home.

LEVINE, RHODA. *Harrison Loved His Umbrella.* New York: Atheneum, 1964. One day, when all the other children have umbrellas, Harrison shows up with a yo-yo. Quiet style, nonsense humor, a sly message, and some interesting long words for the young folks to tackle make this a good story for children.

LEXAU, JOAN M. *I Should Have Stayed in Bed!* New York: Harper & Row, 1965. Sam, a Black, feels that his best friend Albert, a white boy, has deserted him; but the two boys stay after school together and Sam feels for sure that they are still friends.

MCNEER, MAY Y. *My Friend Mac.* Boston: Houghton Mifflin, 1960. A new friend at school replaces Little Baptiste's pet moose.

MEMLING, CARL. *Happy-Go-Lucky Skipper.* New York: Random House, 1965. A little girl tries to become involved in the activities going on around her.

NORDSTROM, URSULA. *The Secret Language.* New York: Harper & Row, 1960. Two eight-year-old girls have a difficult year at boarding school, but adapt to it.

ORGEL, DORIS. *Sarah's Room.* New York: Harper & Row, 1963. Sister's room is never messy, and Little Jenny proves that she is big enough to play there.

SANDBURG, HELGA. *Bo and the Old Donkey.* New York: Dial Press, 1965. This appealing story of a family living on a farm portrays some of the realities of life and death for a young boy.

SCHLEIN, MIRIAM. *Laurie's New Brother.* New York: Abelard-Schuman, 1961. Laurie's parents help him accept the new baby.

SCOTT, SALLY. *Jenny and the Wonderful Jeep.* New York: Harcourt, Brace Jovanovich, 1963. A girl offers her friendship to a younger child after the older children have rejected her.

SMARIDGE, NORAH. *Impatient Jonathan.* Nashville: Abingdon, 1964. Being impatient causes Jonathan to lose friends and the right to have a pet of his own.

SNAVELY, ELLEN. *Shoes for Angela.* Chicago: Follett, 1962. Angela has a windfall of colored shoes when she puts out the request for her birthday and learns that sometimes a person can have too much of even a good thing.

TAMBURINE, JEAN. *How Now Brown Cow.* Nashville: Abingdon, 1967. A second-grader learns to like the part she is given in the play she wrote.

THOMPSON, VIVIAN. *Sad Day, Glad Day.* New York: Holiday House, 1962. The nice park near her new home turns moving day into a happy one for Kathy.

VREEKEN, ELIZABETH. *The Boy Who Would Not Say His Name.* Chicago: Follett, 1959. This story relates Bobby Brown's experiences when he is lost and a policeman asks him his name.

WARBURG, SANDOL S. *Growing Time.* Boston: Houghton Mifflin, 1969. The members of his family try to help Jamie through his first experience with death.

Grades 4–6

ARMER, ALBERTA. *Screwball.* Cleveland: World Publishing, 1963. Crippled by polio at three years of age, Mike, nicknamed Screwball, still makes a name for himself by winning the Soap Box Derby.

ARTHUR, RUTH. *Requiem for a Princess.* New York: Atheneum, 1967. This is an unusual story of how a girl's deep absorption in another girl's problems helps her gain perspective on her own.

BOND, GLADYS B. *A Head on Her Shoulders.* New York: Abelard-Schuman, 1963. Traveling to the Northwest by boxcar, Brita finds that she can responsibly take care of her younger brothers and sisters.

BRADBURY, BIANCA. *Two on an Island.* Boston: Houghton Mifflin, 1965. This is a well-told story about two children marooned on an island.

BROTHERTON, R. O. *Me 'n' Steve.* New York: Macmillan, 1965. The story of two twentieth-century Tom Sawyers.

CHRISTOPHER, MATTHEW F. *Baseball Flyhawk.* Boston: Little, Brown, 1963. When Chico stops trying so hard, he finds that being a Puerto Rican is no bar to winning his teammates' friendship.

DARINGER, HELEN F. *The Turnabout Twins.* New York: Harcourt Brace Jovanovich, 1960. Identical twins are separated during vacation time and come to appreciate each other's individual personality.

DUNCOMBE, FRANCES R. *Cassie's Village.* New York: Lothrop, Lee & Shepard, 1965. Community life in a New York village and a young girl's determination to save the family house when it is threatened by a new dam make this an interesting story.

ENRIGHT, ELIZABETH. *Gone-Away Lake.* New York: Harcourt Brace Jovanovich, 1957. This story demonstrates how older-younger friendships can be fun and describes how the Melendy children find a new home in the swamp.

FARLEY, CAROL. *Sergeant Finney's Family.* New York: Watts, 1969. A family adjusts to the father's absence in Vietnam and their new life in a rural Michigan community.

FURMAN, VICTORIA. *Five in a Tent.* New York: Parents' Magazine, 1966. An anecdotal account of the adventures of a group of girls in a summer camp.

HARMON, LYN. *Clyde's Clam Farm.* Philadelphia: Lippincott, 1966. A story about an orphan boy who develops an interest in oyster farming when he goes to live with his hermit-like uncle.

HAYES, WILLIAM. *Project: Genius.* New York: Atheneum, 1962. The school prize—a trip to the state science fair—is won through perseverance.

HOFFINE, LYLA. *Jennie's Mandan Bowl.* New York: David McKay, 1960. Jennie is no longer ashamed of her Indian ancestry when she recognizes things of which she can be proud.

KONTTINEN, AILI. *Kirsti Comes Home.* New York: Coward-McCann, 1961. Kirsti has to choose between the material advantages offered by wealthy foster parents and her parents' love.

LANSING, ELIZABETH H. *Liza of the Hundredfold.* New York: T. Y. Crowell, 1960. Retaining some of her tomboy characteristics, Liza still finds it pleasant to be a girl when she shelters a flooded-out family in her home.

LEWITON, MINA. *That Bad Carlos.* New York: Harper & Row, 1964. Carlos finds it necessary to learn respect for others' property and to make his own decisions when he moves to New York with his family.

MILES, BETTY. *Feast on Sullivan Street.* New York: Knopf, 1963. Michael is assured that he can help his parents next year after he gets a job on his own during the fiesta of St. Anthony and does well.

ROBINSON, BARBARA. *Across from Indian Shore.* New York: Lothrop, Lee & Shepard, 1962. Daydreaming and irresponsibility are over when Luke undertakes a trip to bring help for his desperate mother.

ROBINSON, JACKIE, AND A. DUCKETT. *Breakthrough to the Big League.* New York:

Harper & Row, 1965. The first Black major league baseball player relates the efforts he had to make to overcome the anger or discouragement he felt when attacked or insulted.

RYDBERG, ERNIE. *The Dark of the Cave.* New York: David McKay, 1965. Intercultural understanding, racial prejudice, adjustment to a handicap, and friendship combine in the story of Ronnie and his Black friend.

SEREDY, KATE. *The Good Master.* New York: Viking, 1935. Kate gets over the spoiled, headstrong ways she had in Budapest after a year on her uncle's farm.

SHEEHAN, ARTHUR, AND ELIZABETH SHEEHAN. *Rose Hawthorne.* New York: Farrar, Straus & Giroux, 1959. Rose Hawthorne overcomes her rather unhappy childhood by learning how one can find fulfillment in helping others.

SHIELDS, RITA. *Cecila's Locket.* New York: David McKay, 1961. Despite setbacks and with the help of her friends the Luchettes, Cecilia and her stepmother finally develop a good relationship.

———. *Mary Kate.* New York: David McKay, 1963. Katie takes a special interest in little Robbie, who is taken in at the orphanage, and finds it hard to let him go back to his parents when that time comes.

SHUMSKY, LOU, AND ZENA SHUMSKY. *Shutterbug.* New York: Funk & Wagnalls, 1963. A handicap changes Shep Riley's ideas about "W.W.'s" (Wak Willies) and shows him the danger of name calling.

STAPP, ARTHUR D. *Polliwog.* New York: Harper & Row, 1962. After the first year in a new neighborhood, a boy takes his experiences in stride and continues to ask questions about everything he does not understand.

STEELE, WILLIAM O. *The Far Frontier.* New York: Harcourt Brace Jovanovich, 1959. Tobe finds a different kind of courage while working as an apprentice to a naturalist.

STERLING, DOROTHY. *Mary Jane.* Garden City, N. Y.: Doubleday, 1959. Friendly Mary Jane has many problems at first in an integrated junior high school, but she does make a start toward solving them when she makes her first friend.

STOLZ, MARY. *A Wonderful, Terrible Time.* New York: Harper & Row, 1967. Two thoroughly believable, winsome girls grow in experience and understanding by spending two weeks away at camp.

TIBBETS, ALBERT B. *A Boy and His Dad.* Boston: Little, Brown, 1964. These seven short stories present experiences of a boy and his dad that make their relationship a richer one.

WIER, ESTER. *The Rumptydoolers.* New York: Vanguard, 1964. A long trek to summer pasture lands changes Whit's ideas about the ranch hands on his uncle's ranch, as he learns the value of cooperation and hard work.

Grades 7–9

BRAGDON, ELSPETH. *There Is a Tide.* New York: Viking, 1964. Nat begins to think of others, rather than himself, after spending a summer with his father.

BRODERICK, DOROTHY M. *Hank.* New York: Harper & Row, 1966. A resentful boy decides that he must identify himself with society rather than fight against it.

CHIPPERFIELD, JOSEPH. *A Dog to Trust.* New York: David McKay, 1964. How Ralph is helped by his friends to accept his loss of sight and comes to find help in his constant companion, his guide dog, is the subject of this story.

CONE, MOLLY. *Only Jane.* New York: Nelson & Sons, 1962. An awkward fifteen-year-old dreads being a wallflower and never having a date.

DEJONG, DOLA. *One Summer's Secret.* New York: David McKay, 1963. Seventeen-year-old Laurie helps a Black girl who has run away from a foster home make a new start.

FIFE, DALE. *Walk a Narrow Bridge.* New York: Coward-McCann, 1966. A family of Alsatian immigrants with a sixteen-year-old daughter find it difficult to give up their old ways when they move to Ohio.

FRANCHERE, RUTH. *The Travels of Colin O'Dae.* New York: T. Y. Crowell, 1966. Fourteen-year-old Colin has some hazardous experiences when he joins a traveling show.

FRICK, C. H. *The Comeback Guy.* New York: Harcourt Brace Jovanovich, 1961. Jeff changes his arrogant ways and is no longer resented by his classmates.

FRITZ, JEAN. *Brady.* New York: Coward-McCann, 1960. Helping a runaway slave reach freedom develops a sense of responsibility in talkative Brady.

HALL, MARJORY. *Bright Red Ribbon.* New York: Funk & Wagnalls, 1961. A boy's interest jolts Beverly into taking a new look at herself and discovering what is really important in life.

HARTWELL, NANCY. *Something for Laurie.* New York: Holt, Rinehart & Winston, 1962. Laurie finds a place for herself despite her feelings of being unable to compete with her more gifted family members.

HENTOFF, NAT. *Jazz Country.* New York: Harper & Row, 1965. This is a story about a sixteen-year-old boy who learns all he can about jazz.

HEUMAN, WILLIAM. *Tall Team.* New York: Dodd, Mead, 1966. Three high-school boys and their struggles on and off the basketball court are the subjects of this story.

LAWRENCE, MILDRED. *The Treasure and the Song.* New York: Harcourt Brace Jovanovich, 1966. Binnie changes from a bitter, confused girl to a girl with a new perspective on life.

MEYNIER, YVONNE. *The School with a Difference.* New York: Abelard-Schuman, 1965. This books consists of letters exchanged between two young sisters and their parents during the time of the German occupation of France during World War II.

MILLER, MARTHA. *Timberline Hound.* New York: Knopf, 1963. Teddy, nicknamed Fatso, has a rewarding year with his aunt in the Colorado Mountains after his parents' death.

NELSON, MARG. *Mystery of the Missing Dowry.* New York: Farrar, Straus & Giroux, 1965. A girl who wants to be a beautician faces surprises.

NOBLE, IRIS. *Megan.* New York: Messner, 1965. This story presents a realistic picture of immigrant life and the blending of nationalities in becoming Canadians as a sixteen-year-old orphan girl from Wales shares the labor and hardships of homesteading.

PILGRIM, ANNE. *The First Time I Saw Paris.* New York: Abelard-Schuman, 1961. The death of her father causes Roberta to come to an awareness of the meaning of loss and change in life and to share this awareness with others.

RAWLINGS, MARJORIE K. *The Yearling.* New York: Scribner, 1961. Jody takes a big step toward maturity when he agrees to return his pet fawn to freedom even though he is aware of the loneliness he will carry with him all his life.

SIMPSON, DOROTHY. *New Horizons.* Philadelphia: Lippincott, 1961. After being away at school where she felt alone and strange, Janie finds that it is different at home too and is therefore better able to adjust when she goes back to school.

SWIFT, HELEN M. *Second Semester.* New York: David McKay, 1961. Through helping each other and heeding what they have learned in a psychology class, two unpopular girls change their ways.

WALDEN, AMELIA E. *My World's the Stage.* New York: McGraw-Hill, 1964. Romantic and professional difficulties are resolved by a young actress, when she is given the chance to step into the leading part of a play.

WERSBA, BARBARA. *The Dream Watcher.* New York: Atheneum, 1968. The son of an unhappily married couple is influenced by an old woman's tale of her career.

YOUNG, BOB. *Across the Tracks.* New York: Messner, 1958. Bettina finds much to be proud of in her Mexican heritage, and she tries to encourage other Mexican-American students to participate in school activities.

Further Reading for Teachers, Parents, and Librarians

BROCKI, A. C. "New Literature for Inner-City Students," *English Journal,* Vol. 58, No. 69, pp. 1151–1161.

CAHOE, E. "Bibliotherapy for Handicapped Children," *National Education Association Journal,* 49 (May 1960), 34–36.

CROSBY, MURIEL (ed.). *Reading Ladders for Human Relations.* 4th ed. Washington, D. C.: The American Council on Education, 1936.

DINKMEYER, DON C. *Child Development—The Emerging Self.* Englewood Cliffs, N. J.: Prentice-Hall, 1965.

GLASSER, WILLIAM. *Reality Therapy.* New York: Harper & Row, 1965.

HANNA, GENEVA R., AND MARIANA K. MCALLISTER. *Books, Young People, and Reading Guidance.* New York: Harper & Row, 1960.

JOSEPH, SISTER FRANCIS, OSF. "Guidance Through Books," *Elementary English,* 46 (February 1969), 147–150.

KIRCHER, CLARA J. *Behavior Patterns in Children's Books.* Washington, D. C.: The Catholic University of America Press, 1966.

LARRICK, NANCY. *A Parent's Guide to Children's Reading.* Garden City, N. Y.: Doubleday, 1964.

MCCANDLESS, BOYD. *Children and Adolescents: Behavior and Development.* New York: Holt, Rinehart & Winston, 1961.

MARTIN, WILLIAM E., AND CELIA STENDLER. *Child Development and Behavior.* Rev. ed. New York: Harcourt Brace Jovanovich, 1959.

PRESCOTT, DANIEL A. *The Child in the Educative Process.* New York: McGraw-Hill, 1957.

ROGERS, CARL R. *On Becoming a Person: A Therapist's View of Psychotherapy.* Boston: Houghton Mifflin, 1961.

From *Flowers of Delight*,
edited by Leonard de Vries.

7

A Historical View of Children's Literature

Books for boys and girls are relatively new in the publishing world. Before the year 1700 it would have been quite beneath the dignity of an author to write consciously for children.

The Earliest Books for Children—From the Seventh Through the Seventeenth Century

The earliest books for children showed little concern for the nature and interests of those who were going to use them. Most were Latin texts on grammar, rhetoric, and music for use in the instruction of pupils in the monastery schools. The names of certain monks and scholars associated with the beginnings of children's literature have come down to us through the years.

Monks and Scholars

One of the first names to live on as a precursor of children's literature is that of ALDHELM, the abbot of Malmesbury and bishop of Sherborn, who lived during the last half of the seventh century and the first half of the eighth. Aldhelm is thought to be one of the first scholars to write lesson books for the instruction of children. One of his contributions to the literature of his times bore the title *De Septenario, de Metris, Enigmatibus ac Pedum Regielis,* which was translated as *Concerning the Number Seven, Meter, Enigmas, and the Rules of Feet.* A long essay on the meaning and use of the number seven in the Bible was included. Probably the most interesting contribution of Aldhelm to children's literature was his use of the question-and-answer form that set the pattern in children's literature until about 1500.

About the same time that Aldhelm was writing, the VENERABLE BEDE (673–735), a teacher at the monastery school of Jarrow in Durham County, England, was also writing books for the purpose of instruction. He wrote in Latin in a clear, understandable style and is remembered most for his *De Natura Rerum,* which contained all the knowledge then known on natural science, natural history, and botany, and which for years was recognized as an authoritative source. He produced some forty books, many of which were interpretations and commentaries on the Scriptures. His arithmetic materials were used for several hundred years by succeeding generations of English schoolboys.

Following close upon the works of Aldhelm and the Venerable Bede came those of ALCUIN (735–804), who spent his life furthering the cause of education. Alcuin studied at the famous school founded by Egbert of York, one of the famous scholars of his day. Egbert had collected for his library the works of Aldhelm and the Venerable Bede as well as the writing of Orosius, an authority on history, and books by outstanding Greek and Roman authors. Alcuin used the question-and-answer form in writing a wide variety of lesson books, many of which were on the subject of grammar. He became famous as the tutor of the sons of Charlemagne as well as of several girls of the court in Aachen.

During the last half of the tenth century, AELFRIC (955–1020), a teacher in the monastic school in Winchester, carried on the tradition of the scholars who had preceded him. He is remembered most for his *Vocabulary,* the oldest Latin-English dictionary extant. He also wrote a *Colloquy* in the form of questions and answers on subjects related to everyday life.

Another event of importance in children's literature occurred during the last half of the eleventh century when ANSELM, the archbishop of Canterbury, produced the first encyclopedia for children. It bore the title *Educidarium.*

A New Art Arrives

A significant milestone in the history of literature took place in 1496 when WILLIAM CAXTON opened his printing business in London near Westminster Abbey. His most significant contribution to literature was the publication of his version of Malory's *Story of King Arthur,* thereby preserving this story for posterity. Sensitive to the thinking of his times that the young should read only what would instruct and improve them, Caxton published in the second year of his printing career *The Book of Curtesye or Lytyll John.* The maxims and instructions were in rough and homely rhyme in the hope that they would help boys to mind their manners in the households of royalty. Detailed directions are given regarding rising, dressing, behaving at table, serving a superior, and walking in the street. Of more importance to children's literature was Caxton's publishing of *Reynard the Fox* in 1481 and *Aesop's Fables* in 1484. The story of sly Reynard and Aesop's Fables continue to be read today. Many of the fables have been used separately as entire picture books.

Following Caxton's death his printing enterprises were carried on by WYNKYN DE WORDE. De Worde's first publication was *The Wyse Child of Thre Yere Old,* an encyclopedia first printed in Cologne in 1470 and then translated into English from the original Latin.

When by spectators I am told
What beauty doth adorn me,
Or in a glass when I behold
How sweetly God did form me
Hath God such comeliness bestowed
And on me made to dwell,
What pity such a pretty maid
As I should go to Hell!

Titles of other books of the period indicate the concern of adults for the welfare of children and youth: *Divine Prospect* and *Looking Glass for Youth* and *Youth's Divine Pastime.*

JOHN BUNYAN, an English minister in a nonconformist church, held deep religious convictions for which he spent much time in jail where he wrote many religious works, including *Pilgrim's Progress.* The book was written as a religious message with a moral purpose for adults, but its clear style and fast-moving actions began to appeal to children and youth. Many schools used it as a text in the 1700s. Although much of it is allegorical in nature, children and youth who read it must have skipped the heavy discourses and looked for the parts that move along in dramatic style. The long theological dialogues are omitted in modern editions for young readers, and in many editions beautiful illustrations by well-known artists enliven the text. It is a simple story into which fundamental truths within the understanding of children are imbedded. Although a host of characters move in and out of the story, the principal characters are clearly portrayed. It is the display of heroism that holds the interest of the young reader. John Bunyan showed further concern for the moral and social welfare of boys and girls by writing *Divine Emblems or Temporal Things Spiritualized.*

CHARLES PERRAULT (1628–1703), a gifted man, a teller of tales, and a lover of children, gave not only to the children of France but to children everywhere those favorite stories of childhood that continue to remain in a class of their own—*Sleeping Beauty, Cinderella, Little Red Riding Hood, Blue Beard, Puss-in-Boots,* and *Hop-o-my Thumb.* These stories, called *The Fairies* by Perrault, are few in number but make a rich literary heritage for children.

Also credited to the genius of Charles Perrault and his love for children was his creation of that famous mysterious character beloved through the years—Mother Goose. She made her debut into the world of children's literature in a picture on the title page of Perrault's *Contes du Temps Passe,* where she is spinning and telling a story to several little children.

Gathering Momentum—The Eighteenth Century

The interest in children's literature that had been growing from century to century began to gain momentum and to take on different dimensions during the eighteenth century. The religious emphasis declined and entertainment as well as instruction became a purpose in writing for children.

A number of writers in both France and England wrote vigorously to instruct and entertain children. The emphasis on instruction still persists today and in many instances divides writers into two camps, if not three: those who write to instruct, those who write to entertain, and those who are able to do both. The result is a body of literature that provides glimpses into the social, political, and economic life of the time in which the literature was produced.

The Early Literary Scene in France

The following thumbnail sketches are of some of the outstanding writers in France who contributed to the field of children's literature from the turn of the eighteenth century into the nineteenth century.

JEAN DE LA FONTAINE (1621–1695), a contemporary of Charles Perrault, published his first collection of *Fables* in verse. He dedicated the collection to the Dauphine of France, who was then just past six years of age. The fables were not all original, but were collected from many sources including Aesop, Phaedrus, and the Indian fables of Bidpai. The popularity of Fontaine's fables in verse has continued. Recent publications of his fables, beautifully illustrated, attest to their popularity with children.

MADAME LE PRINCE DE BEAUMONT (1711–1780) created a historical market in children's literature with the publication in 1757 of a remarkable journal, *Magasin des Enfants.* The full title, which is really a summary of the contents, is *The Children's Magazine or Conversation of a Wise Governess with Her Most Distinguished Pupils, in Which Young People Are Made to Think, Speak and Act According to the Talent, Temperament and Inclinations of Each. The Faults of Their Age Are Set Forth, a Way Is Shown to Correct Them: as Much Attention Is Paid to Molding the Heart as to Guiding the Spirit. Included is a Summary of Sacred History, of Fable, of Geography, etc., The Whole Filled with Useful Reflections.* Of the seventy volumes written by Madame Le Prince de Beaumont, the story that gained fame for this prolific writer was *Beauty and the Beast.* It has been a source of enjoyment since its publication and its later translations into different languages.

MADAME DE GENLIS (1746–1830) enjoyed a popular and colorful career in the literary world. She had two consuming passions, writing and teaching—and she experienced success in both. Although she expressed opposition to children's reading fairy tales, her

From *Beauty and the Beast*
by Mme. Leprince de Beaumont

Evenings at Home follows the pattern of *The Arabian Nights.* The Marquis de Clemire is the storyteller in *Evenings at Home,* who entertains his family each evening with a series of stories, most of them lacking in literary quality. Previous to *Evenings at Home* Madame de Genlis had written *Adele et Theodore, Lettres sur L'Education,* and *Les Veillées du Chateau.* Altogether Madame de Genlis wrote ninety books for children, a number of which were translated into English, and for a time she was popular both in France and in England.

ARNAUD BERQUIN (1749–1791), like Madame de Genlis, was a popular figure in literary circles in France and England during the last half of the eighteenth century, but his popularity was short lived since he died at the age of forty-two. In 1782 Berquin published *L'Ami des Enfants,* a small-sized journal that came out once a month. It contained comedies, dialogues, tales, and letters and was distributed in Paris and in the nearby provinces. When *L'Ami des Enfants* proved to be a success, he published another journal, *L'Ami des Adolescents,* which enjoyed the same success as the earlier journal. Berquin is described by Paul Hazard as a vain, mawkish, and pathetic little man. He was born in Bordeaux, but at an early age he left his home to go to Paris, where he quickly identified himself with the literati of the day. His writing reflected the conditions and aspirations of his own life. The heroes in his stories and plays wept copious tears—usually because of the sad things happening to other people. Most of the characters were noblemen, symbolic of his desire to move in the aristocratic circles of the day. His writings portrayed his effort to persuade children that everything in this world is for the best. He pointed out that the seasons—summer, autumn, winter, and spring—are all delicious and waiting for one to enjoy. He tried desperately to impose upon children his strange idea that it is far better to love poverty and to scorn riches than to be an owner of property and to have the bother of keeping up castles, parks, crops, and vineyards. He even said that it is useless as well as unpleasant to own a gold watch and a child should be just as happy with an old silver one. The things he urged children to discard and to stop striving for are the very things that he wanted for himself. Ironically, his great desire in living was to be in the circle of the royalty.

The Early Literary Scene in England

It is only natural that literature flowed freely between England and France. The works of French writers were translated, and vice versa. The influence of French philosophers such as Rousseau and others could readily be traced in the works of the English as well as in those of the French. Many writers were popular in both countries. The following thumbnail sketches describe some of the outstanding English writers who contributed to the field of children's literature during the eighteenth and nineteenth centuries.

JOHN NEWBERY (1713–1767), referred to by many scholars of children's literature as "the first genuine children's publisher," left farming to become the assistant and partner of William Carnan, a printer and bookseller of Reading. When Carnan died, Newbery took over the business. An astute businessman with unlimited energy, Newbery traveled extensively, observing business conditions and opportunities.

He quickly established himself as a publisher when he moved to London in 1744 and soon became well known in the literary circles of the day. Among the outstanding authors whose acquaintance he made were Dr. Samuel Johnson, Tobias Smollett, and Oliver Goldsmith. Newbery recognized Oliver Goldsmith's talent and employed him to write for his periodicals and later for his children's library. Among the writings for children attributed to Oliver Goldsmith are *Mother Goose* (1760), *The History of Little Goody Two-Shoes* (around 1765), and *Tom Thumb's Folio* (1768).

John Newbery demonstrated his own understanding and love of children by publishing attractive books with pleasing stories for them to read. Among them were *The History of Giles Gingerbread, Pretty Poems for Children Three Foot High,* and *Tom Trip's History of Birds and Beasts.*

MRS. SARAH KIRBY TRIMMER (1741–1810) was influenced by the writings of Madame de Genlis and also of Jean Jacques Rousseau. Mrs. Trimmer maintained individuality in her writing, which emphasized the importance of moral teaching. Like so many of the other writers of her day, she showed an awareness of Rousseau's philosophy but in many instances misinterpreted it. Rousseau's influence is shown in Mrs. Trimmer's *Easy Introduction to the Knowledge of Nature,* which was published in 1782 and ran into eleven editions. However, Rousseau's idea of living close to nature was that nature provides the basis for character and personality development, whereas Mrs. Trimmer's idea of living close to nature was having her characters take a walk through a meadow. She did, however, teach the moral lessons through the children's own experiences, the principle of which was in harmony with Rousseau's. She opened a number of Sunday Schools at Brentwood, where she had her home, and many of the books she wrote were intended for use in Sunday Schools.

From *Goody Two Shoes* by Oliver Goldsmith, illustrated by Marion Peabody.

MRS. ANNA LETITIA BARBAULD (1743–1825) and her brother DR. JOHN AIKIN (1747–1822) were identified with the teaching-preaching school of writers. In 1780 Mrs. Barbauld's *Easy Lessons for Children from Two to Three Years Old* was published. This was followed the next year by *Hymns in Prose for Children.* Both books carried a step further Rousseau's philosophy that children should live close to nature. Mrs. Barbauld was concerned with religious training as well as the moral teaching of children, and she expressed the idea that when children live close to nature they come to know God. This idea was not acceptable to Rousseau.

Before Anna Laetitia Aikin married Reverend Rochemont Barbauld, her brother John Aikin was instrumental in publishing her book of poems and later her *Miscellaneous Pieces in Prose.* These publications catapulted her into London literary society where she was considered one of the significant authors of her day. She married Reverend Barbauld and with him established a boarding school for boys at Palgrave, Suffolk. When Reverend Barbauld's failing health made it necessary for them to give up the school, they moved to Stoke Newington, where Mrs. Barbauld would be near her brother with whom she was collaborating on *Evenings at Home.*

Mrs. Barbauld's popularity continued in spite of Charles Lamb's criticism of her and Mrs. Trimmer. In a letter to Samuel Taylor Coleridge in 1802, Charles Lamb said that these "idiotic women," referring to Mrs. Barbauld and Mrs. Trimmer, "and their crew have brought rust and pestilence to everything human in men and children." In spite of some antagonism and negative criticism toward the writings of these two women, they have made their marks in the field of children's literature.

HANNAH MORE (1745–1833) enjoyed popularity in the London literary circles at the same time as Mrs. Barbauld; but after twelve years in London the glamour of the literary circle began to dim, and Miss More decided to take up the cause of the poor and illiterate. Returning to Bristol, she joined her two sisters, who had retired from the successful operation of a school for girls near Bristol, in furthering the Sunday School movement started by Robert Raikes and expanded by Mrs. Trimmer. Miss More and her sisters opened the first school at Cheddar. Together they laid out the instructional program, did some of the teaching, and often drove great distances to speak to parents, likely patrons, and potential teachers.

Because of her ability as a writer and her awareness of the need for suitable reading material for children, she started writing what were known as *Cheap Repository Tracts.* Three tracts a month were published from 1792 to 1795. Each tract contained a story, a brief set of verses, and a short sermon to be read in the schools. The stories carried such titles as "Black Giles the Poacher," "Tawny Rachel the Fortuneteller," "The Happy Waterman," and "The Two Wealthy Farmers." The titles give broad clues to the subjects of the stories. In all of them the "rags were as velvet, when worn for virtue's sake," the bad were punished and the good were rewarded. The tracts met with tremendous success, became best sellers of the day, and were published by the millions.

THOMAS DAY (1748–1789) was one of the best known didactic writers of his day. He is remembered for *The History of Sandford and Merton,* the primary purpose of which was instruction. It was encyclopedic in its scope of information, which ranged from religious instruction to moralistic fables like "Androcles and the Lion" and bits of history featuring Leonidas, Cyrus, and other heroes of ancient times. He used the Socratic method to instruct in astronomy, biology, geography, ethnology, political economy, and cardinal virtues. It is also interesting that he attempted—in the eighteenth century—to give insight into the temperament of Blacks and American Indians.

CHARLES LAMB (1776–1834) and his sister MARY LAMB (1764–1847) wrote to entertain rather than to instruct. Their writings show a keen understanding of the needs and interests of children. In 1807 the Lambs published *Tales from Shakespeare,* which put some of Shakespeare's plays into a form that could be read by children and would familiarize them with the plays of this great writer. Charles interpreted the tragedies and Mary interpreted the comedies. A year later Charles published *The Adventures of Ulysses,* which was his simplified version of the great Greek epic poem. These books have outlived the writings of most of the authors who wrote at the same time as Charles and Mary Lamb.

The Early Literary Scene in America

The literary scene in our country during colonial days was anything but bright. The founding fathers had determination and set purposes in living both for themselves and for their children—they wanted their descendants to be staunch Puritans and to perpetuate the Puritan beliefs. The elders demanded that the children live according to Puritan rules as children of God. Family worship, admonitions from the elders, home instruction, strict attendance at school, and close attention to lessons all were aimed at perpetuating those ideals and values for which the parents themselves had sacrificed so much. To the elders, the important part of education was learning to read, write, and figure. Only literature that would instruct and warn was tolerated.

It is possible that the Puritans brought books with them to their new life. Since literature in the homeland was directed toward the admonition and improvement of children, it is to be expected that literature in the new land would be even more didactic and severe. This didacticism and severity strengthened the determination of the elders to render growing minds and bodies so strong that they could withstand all temptations and worldly attractions.

JOHN COTTON, the grandfather of Cotton Mather, wrote a book with the awesome title, *Spiritual Milk for Boston Babes in Either England, Drawn from the Breasts of Both Testaments for Their Souls' Nourishment.* In 1646, when this book was published, John Cotton was a clergyman and occupied a pulpit in Boston.

From *Flowers of Delight,* edited by Leonard de Vries.

Typical of the literature of that time, *Spiritual Milk for Boston Babes . . .* was written in question-and-answer form. For example, "What hath God done for you? God hath made me, He Keepeth me, and He can save me . . . . How did God make you? I was conceived in sin and born in iniquity." The questions about the nature of sin which followed became deeper and more theological and philosophical in nature. A typical question of this sort was, "What is the bond of the Covenant in which the Church is joined together?" One is not surprised when the book ends on the dire note: "The righteous shall go into life eternal and the wicked shall be sent into everlasting fire with the devil and his angels."

Previous to the importation of *Spiritual Milk for Boston Babes . . .*, J. Foxe's *Book of Martyrs* (1563) and Bunyan's *Pilgrim's Progress* (1678) were available. Both of these books became required reading for boys and girls coming to maturity under the rigors of colonial life.

The question-and-answer style of *Spiritual Milk for Boston Babes . . .*, which dates back to Aldhelm, continued to be the model of books for children and came to its fullest fruition in *The New England Primer.*

BENJAMIN HARRIS (1660?–1720) is best known for his publication of *The New England Primer,* which occupies a unique position in children's literature. There is no doubt that it had tremendous influence upon children's thinking and children's literature during the many years of its popularity.

The *Primer* had its origins in an English publication, but it soon took on characteristics of its own that set it off from other publications. Harris, a London printer, published *The Protestant Tutor for Youth,* which he probably had written. A later publication, *A Protestant Petition,* landed him in the pillory. He left London and arrived in Massachusetts in 1686, where he entered the publishing business and opened a shop which was known as "The Sign of the Bible over Against the Blew Anchor." It was in this shop between 1687 and 1690 that *The New England Primer* came into being. It was patterned closely after *The Protestant Tutor for Youth,* which contained upper- and lower-case alphabets, pages of syllables to be memorized, the Lord's Prayer, the Creed, and the Ten Commandments. As a literary feature it contained the story of the burning of the Reverend John Rogers. Following the account of the burning, there was a poem supposedly written by John Rogers just before his death and addressed to his nine children:

I leave to you a little book
For you to look upon
That you may see your father's face,
When I am dead and gone.

The New England Primer suited the elders, since it combined a prayer book and school text, and its definite purpose was to encourage children to read the Bible. It proved, for the times, to be a most successful instrument for religious instruction. It reinforced the elders' determination to teach their children the Bible, Protestantism, the possibility of the good dying young, and the need to store up treasures in heaven.

One innovative feature of *The New England Primer* was the rhyming alphabet, which went through many changes in content over a period of years. "In Adam's Fall, we sinned all" remained standard from the beginning, but the more secular sentiments, such as "The Dog Will Bite a Thief at Night" and "An Eagle's Flight is Out of Sight" were changed in a few years to comments that were more scriptural in nature. One hundred years later the primer was still in use and this scriptural influence at its height. Changes continued to be made in the writing and contents. An edition in 1781 included for the first time "Now I Lay Me Down to Sleep." Even with its ominous line "If I should die before I wake," it has endured as a bedtime prayer for children in many families.

The New England Primer was probably the first work of American literature to be popular abroad. One can sense its impact when one realizes that Puritan children in England and Scotland were required to use it as a textbook. Its powerful influence on behavior lasted for more than a hundred years while it went through dozens of editions.

ISAIAH THOMAS (1749–1831) is often referred to as the American John Newbery. A printer, publisher, and bookseller of Boston and Worcester, Massachusetts, Thomas did in his own way for American children what John Newbery had done somewhat earlier for children everywhere. With Newbery he shared an understanding of what children wanted and should have in literature. Thomas became known as the most outstanding printer and publisher of his time.

It has never been ascertained how Isaiah Thomas obtained a large number of John Newbery's little books; but it is possible that *The Renowned History of Little Goody Two-Shoes, Mother Goose,* and *Robinson Crusoe* were smuggled in during the Revolutionary War. During that same time Thomas succeeded in importing and selling other books for children published in England. When the war ended he began publishing them on his own. The works of John Newbery continued to be Thomas' chief source, from which he chose the best books to publish. Among them were *Mother Goose* (the one often attributed to Oliver Goldsmith); *Be Merry and Wise; A Little, Pretty Pocketbook; Nurse Truelove's New Years Gift;* and a number of others. In addition he published the works of Newbery's widow and the two nephews who continued operating Newbery's business after his death as well as books of other writers who followed Newbery. It is also interesting that in 1785 Thomas published *The Beauty and the Monster,* a play for children by Madame de Genlis.

Isaiah Thomas was unique in his selection of books and stories to publish. Apparently he was not enthusiastic about *The New England Primer.* In spite of the popularity and the many editions through which the primer went, only one was printed by him. He seemed to prefer Noah Webster's *Blue Back Speller,* which was first published in 1783 at Hartford. There was less theology in the speller than in the primer, but it emphasized moral tales such as that of the boy who stole apples and brought a rain of turf and stones upon himself. The speller had the distinction of standing unrivaled among American textbooks in circulation and length of life during the nineteenth century and even into the twentieth.

Isaiah Thomas continued the tradition of John Newbery in a number of ways. He made his books small and beautiful. He could not secure the flowered paper from Holland that Newbery had used so effectively on his covers, but he did use marbled or embossed paper for the bindings. He patterned his advertising after Newbery's style, and the good children in his stories always, as in Newbery's stories, receive a reward for their goodness. The children in Thomas' books —with such names as Miss Betsy Allgood, Miss Nancy Careful, and Miss Amelia Lovebook—overdo their goodness and are often too good to be true. A typical example of the fate of bad children is shown by that of Tommy Careless: Within a week he falls into the water, loses his kite, falls out of an apple tree, burns himself, kills his bird by neglecting to give it water, pulls hairs out of Dobbin's tail until the horse kicks him, and at last gets his finger caught in a mouse trap.

Coming of Age in Children's Literature—The Nineteenth Century in America

The nineteenth century had its highlights in children's literature in America. During the previous century, except for the few writers and publishers mentioned earlier, very little literature was published that was indigenous to the New World. For the most part the tendency was to reprint English books exactly as they were published in England. A few attempts were made to localize the literature, but in general the stories for children remained in English settings.

One of the persons who held the spotlight in children's literature in America in the nineteenth century was SAMUEL GOODRICH (1793–1860). A prolific writer, he authored nearly 175 books under the pseudonym of Peter Parley. Starting with the *Tales of Peter Parley About America* (1827), Goodrich carried on in series style for the following thirty years. Titles such as *Tales of Peter Parley About Europe* (1828), *Peter Parley's Evening Tales* (1829), and *Juvenile Tales* (1830) followed one after another in rapid succession. Production continued with *Tales of Peter Parley* as well as numerous books on a variety of subjects including natural science, astronomy, biography, history, and travel with special reference to America. Goodrich's simple, matter-of-fact style made for easy reading. As a result his books became popular abroad as well as at home. In fact, they were so popular that a number of unscrupulous writers not only pirated his works, but had the audacity to use the name of Peter Parley as the author of their own works.

Samuel Goodrich enjoyed a successful but quiet role in the literary circles of his time. He had nothing but contempt for such stories as "Little Red Riding Hood," "Jack the Giant Killer," and "Puss in Boots." He labeled such stories atrocious, claiming that they belonged to a barbarous age. He was convinced that these stories would lead children to vice and crime, and he felt that Christian parents were doing an injustice to their children by letting them read such nonsense. With these convictions Samuel Goodrich naturally continued in the tradition of the didactic writers of the preceding century.

Another American writer who contributed to children's literature about the same time as Samuel Goodrich was JACOB ABBOTT (1803–1879), a scholarly teacher and preacher whose life spanned most of the nineteenth century. Abbott was one of the first mass producers of literature for children. In a number of ways his life and writing bore close resemblance to those of his contemporary Goodrich. Each published countless books that covered a variety of subjects and sold extensively. Both Abbott and Goodrich opposed the fairy tale and fanciful type of literature for children. In his writings Goodrich strove to emphasize truth, which he claimed children loved. Abbott believed that literature for children should teach but not necessarily preach. He continued in the tradition of Pestalozzi, who believed that a pupil learns best by using his senses and discovering for himself. In *Leonard and Gertrude* a mother teaches her children through object lessons related to daily living. While the mother prepares and cooks foods, she teaches chemistry. Learning where their food and household objects come from, the children learn geography. This philosophy is not far removed from the philosophy underlying the curricula in modern schools.

Jacob Abbott was remembered by many for his Rollo, Lucy, Jonas and Franconia books of which countless volumes were published. The successes that his series enjoyed were the impetus for a deluge of series of varying quality by other writers. The boys and girls in Abbott's series maintained a close resemblance to average boys and girls. Many of them were too good to be true, but they went sleighing, popped corn, roasted apples, and at the same time used their eyes to good purpose so that opportunities to instruct the reader were not lost. This natural behavior of children was not always as successfully portrayed by the writers who followed Abbott.

In addition to contributing popular characters to children's literature, Jacob Abbott started a trend that has continued through the years in the introduction of history into children's literature. Abbott, with considerable insight into the interests and needs of boys and girls, sensed the necessity of knowledge of the past for children and felt that there was a general lack of this knowledge. This motivated him to produce between 1849 and 1861 *Abbott's Illustrated Histories* (1849–1861), which told the stories of *Cyrus the Great, Darius the Great, Xerxes the Great,* and *Alexander.* A number of writers followed his lead, among the best known of whom were Elbridge Brooks and Edward Everett Hale.

A creative person sensitive to the needs and interests of children, MARY ELIZABETH MAPES DODGE (1831–1905) carved for herself a brilliant literary career, not only through her own writing and editing, but also through the encouragement she gave to other writers.

Her first effort, "George the Drummer Boy," pleased her father, an editor as well as a publisher, who issued it as one of the eight stories in her first book, *Irvington Stories.* After *Irvington Stories* was printed, a publisher suggested to Mrs. Dodge that she do another story with the Civil War background. But to the good fortune of boys and girls for years to come, Mrs. Dodge had another idea in mind.

Instead of a Civil War story, she began to write *Hans Brinker or the Silver Skates* (16). Working assiduously, Mrs. Dodge completed *Hans Brinker* in 1865 when she was thirty-four years of age. By 1900 the book had been printed in more than one hundred editions, was translated into half a dozen languages, and became the recipient of the coveted Montyon Literary Prize awarded by the French Academy. *Hans Brinker* is read as often today as when it came into being.

Following the popular reception of *Hans Brinker,* Mrs. Dodge continued her writing with regularity. In 1869 *A Few Friends and How They Amused Themselves* was published. *Rhymes and Jingles* followed in 1874, *Theophilus and Others* in 1876, and *Along the Way* in 1879.

When the board of directors of Charles Scribner and Sons decided to publish a high-quality magazine for children, they made the happy choice of Mary Mapes Dodge as editor of the new publication. The idea of such a publication intrigued her, and with her limitless enthusiasm she entered upon the editorship of a magazine that was destined to make literary history not only for children in the United States but for boys and girls around the world. Upon accepting the editorship, Mrs. Dodge gave the magazine the title *St. Nicholas: A Magazine for Boys and Girls.*

The content of *St. Nicholas* was not limited to stories for pleasure reading. The magazine also contained articles on science, history, and biography written in a style that appealed to boys and girls. The quality of *St. Nicholas* and possibly the charm of the editor attracted such distinguished writers as Howard Pyle, Sarah Orne Jewett, Mark Twain, Edward Everett Hale, and Jack London. Louisa May Alcott's *Jo's Boys* (3), *An Old-Fashioned Girl* (6), and *Eight Cousins* (1) appeared as serials in *St. Nicholas.* Kipling's Indian stories, which appeared first in *St. Nicholas,* were published later as *The Jungle Book* (27) and *The Second Jungle Book* (28).

From *Just So Stories* by Rudyard Kipling.

Mrs. Dodge communicated with numerous writers who held the same dream as she had for children's literature. As soon as she became the editor of *St. Nicholas*, Mrs. Dodge expressed her philosophy in the following editorial policy:

> To give clean, genuine fun to children of all ages
> To give them examples of the finest types of boyhood and girlhood
> To inspire them with a fine appreciation of pictorial art
> To cultivate the imagination in profitable directions
> To foster a love of country, home, nature, truth, beauty, and sincerity
> To prepare boys and girls for life as it is
> To stimulate their ambitions along normally progressive lines
> To keep pace with the activities of a fast-moving world
> To provide reading matter that every parent may pass to his children unhesitatingly [P. 257]

The Century Publishing Company bought *St. Nicholas* in 1898, and established the *St. Nicholas* League. The motto of the league was "Learn to live, and live to learn." Gold and silver badges were awarded for good writing in prose and verse that was published in *St. Nicholas*. The roster of those who received either gold or silver badges includes such well-known names as: Ring Lardner, Richard Bentley, Deems Taylor, Cory Ford, Stephen Vincent Benet and his wife Rosemary, Alan Seeger, Cornelia Otis Skinner, Babette Deutsch, Peggy Bacon, Elinor Wylie, Norman Bel Geddes, Bennett Cerf, Sigmund Spaeth, and Edmund Wilson. It is easily seen that for some time the literary world revolved around *St. Nicholas*.

An Illustrious Procession—Bridging the Nineteenth and Twentieth Centuries

Literature for children flourished during the last half of the nineteenth century. A number of authors following the growing trend of writing children's stories began to contribute their talents to this field. Many of those who started to write in the last half of the nineteenth century continued their writing into the early part of the twentieth century, and some of their stories have continued to be as popular today as when they were first published.

One of the most illustrious of the writers of children's literature during the latter half of the nineteenth century was LOUISA MAY ALCOTT (1832–1888). In 1868 she published *Little Women* (5), which has since become one of the best-loved stories in children's literature. The story of *Little Women* is based on the girlhood experiences of Louisa May Alcott; Jo March in the book is Louisa herself. The first part of *Little Women* appeared in an early issue of *St. Nicholas.* Its readers both juvenile and adult demanded a sequel, which was published in 1869.

Family life in Alcott novels was filled with happiness in spite of the material hardships that had to be endured. She followed *Little Women* with such enjoyable stories as *An Old-Fashioned Girl* (6), which tells about some of the experiences Miss Alcott had in earning her own living; and *Little Men* (4), which is also built around the experiences of the March family. As aunts and uncles and cousins joined the March family Louisa May portrayed them in *Eight Cousins* (1) and *Rose in Bloom* (7). *Under the Lilacs* (8) and *Jack and Jill* (2) came out serially in *St. Nicholas.* These and everything else Louisa May Alcott wrote had a flair that predicted well for the future of children's literature.

How fortunate for boys of yesterday, today, and for years to come that Samuel Langhorne Clemens, more popularly known as MARK TWAIN (1835–1910), spent his boyhood in the sleepy little river town of Hannibal, Missouri, where he was free to live the kind of adventurous life every boy dreams of: He led a gang of boys who fished and swam at their leisure in the Mississippi River; they borrowed boats without getting permission from the owners and explored the mysteries of that temperamental river; they made expeditions to Turtle's Island, which they could turn into a make-believe land; they raided melon patches and rolled stones down Holliday's Hill just to scare people as they were driving by; and, what would be the envy of every boy, they used a cave south of town as a rendezvous for planning the kinds of deviltry dear to the hearts of boys. Best of all, Clemens had the knack for writing in such a way that his experiences as a boy come to life for other children to relive and enjoy.

Samuel Clemens stands at the head of the procession of those writers who wrote for the fun and entertainment of children. His characters—Tom Sawyer, Aunt Polly, Becky Thatcher, Huckleberry Finn, and Injun Joe—provide pleasure for boys and girls and conjure up pleasant memories for adults year after year. His many novels and short stories are discussed in detail in Chapter 4, "Fun with Literature."

Shortly after Mark Twain, JOEL CHANDLER HARRIS (1848–1908) made his contribution—of quite a different nature—to the literature of our country. He created Uncle Remus, who holds a special place in the affections of both young and old readers. Harris was born in Putnam County, Georgia. His mother was deserted by his father shortly after Joel's birth. After attending the local school, Joel was apprenticed, when he was fourteen years of age, as a printer for a weekly newspaper that was published at a country plantation near Eatonton, Georgia. Joel became familiar with the people on the plantation and was particularly interested in the speech and stories told by the old. Following the Civil War, he worked at various newspaper jobs in Macon, Georgia; New Orleans, Louisiana; and Atlanta, Georgia.

Harris' Uncle Remus stories first appeared in the newspapers for which he worked. Uncle Remus told old stories about clever Br'er Rabbit who always outwitted Br'er Fox. Harris' first book, *Uncle Remus: His Songs and His Sayings* (25), was followed by *Nights with Uncle Remus* (22). Then at regular intervals followed *Uncle Remus and His Friends* (24), *On the Plantation* (23), and *Told by Uncle Remus* (1904). Joel Chandler Harris rounded out his unusual journalistic and literary career by publishing an Uncle Remus magazine with his son Julian.

LAURA E. HOWE RICHARDS (1850–1943) first became recognized as a literary figure for her nonsense verse, which appeared in early volumes of *St. Nicholas* and was later published under such titles as *In My Nursery*, *The Hurdy Gurdy Man*, written in 1902, and *Tirra Lirra* (34). The pleasant flow of coined words, rhythmic melody, and joyous moods in her verse delight children today as they did in the latter part of the nineteenth century.

Laura E. Richards' happy childhood is reflected in the seventy books she wrote for boys and girls. *Captain January and Little Colonel* (33), which has been made into a motion picture at two different times, is the most widely read of Laura E. Richards' books today.

Born near Wilmington, Delaware, HOWARD PYLE (1853–1911) expressed his ambition to become an artist at an early age, and his mother encouraged him in realizing his ambition. In spite of the hard times following the Civil War, he took drawing lessons and later attended the Art Students League in New York. Pyle was known as a hard worker with a lively imagination. His sense of pictorial design, his strong style of drawing, and his creativity made him popular as an illustrator. For years he drew illustrations for *Harper's Monthly* and for books written by other authors. In the early 1930s he turned to writing and illustrating his own stories. His versions of *The Merry Adventures of Robin Hood* (31) and *The Story of King Arthur and His Knights* (32) were written with vigor and still appeal to young readers. As a teacher Howard Pyle helped develop the talents of such well-known artists as Maxfield Parrish, Edward A. Nelson, and N. C.

Wyeth. Children's books have been enriched immeasurably by the beautiful illustrations he did for other authors' books as well as for his own.

KATE DOUGLAS WIGGIN (1856–1923), writer and educator, was born in Philadelphia in 1856. At the age of seventeen she went to Santa Barbara, California, to teach school. Her first story, *The Birds' Christmas Carol* (47), a tender, heart-rending story, is still read at Christmas time in classrooms across the nation. *Rebecca of Sunnybrook Farm* (49) appeared in 1903 and proved to be one of the most popular children's books at the turn of the century. Many young readers, especially young girls and nostalgic adults, find pleasure in reading it.

Kate Douglas Wiggin and her sister, Nora A. Smith, made a collection of fairy stories, folk tales, and fables. These appeared as *Magic Casements* (52), *The Fairy Ring* (50), *Tales of Wonder* (55), and *Tales of Laughter* (54). The sisters also compiled two books of poetry, *Golden Numbers* (51) and *The Posy Ring* (53). In 1898 Kate Douglas Wiggin organized the first free kindergarten in the United States west of the Rocky Mountains. Several years later she founded the California Kindergarten Training School for educating kindergarten teachers. Her autobiography, *My Garden of Memory* (48), written in 1923, the year of her death, is a sentimental journey into the literary world at the turn of the century.

LAURA INGALLS WILDER (1867–1957) was born in a log cabin in Pepin, Wisconsin, where her pioneer parents were carving out a rugged existence. When she was fifteen years old, she started teaching school. For seventeen years she and her husband lived in frontier communities. When she was twenty-seven years old, the Wilders moved to Mansfield, Missouri, to make their home in the Ozarks, which held a fascination for them. For twelve years she was editor of the *Missouri Ruralist.* She also contributed articles to the *Country Gentleman* and *McCall's.*

It was not until Laura Ingalls Wilder was sixty-five years of age that she started to write the "Little House" books for which she has received such wide acclaim. They are tender, humorous stories that show the importance of close-knit family life. They are of historical importance because of their authentic portrayal of closely knit family life both in the woods and on the prairie.

The first book in the "Little House" series, *The Little House in the Big Woods* (59), describes her early childhood. How the family moved to what is now Kansas is the subject of *The Little House on the Prairie* (60). Life in Minnesota, the move the Wilder family made in a covered wagon to Dakota Territory, and life on the frontier are told in *On the Banks of Plum Creek* (63), *By the Shores of Silver Lake* (56), *The Long Winter* (62), and *The Little Town on the Prairie* (61). *These Happy Golden Years* (64) is about their married life. The only book not in the series is *Farmer Boy* (57), which is about the boyhood of Alonzo Wilder, the husband. A new posthumous book, *The First Four Years* (58), has recently been published. Discovered among Mrs. Wilder's papers, the ninth Little House book ends where *These Happy Golden Years* begins. It tells of the newly married Wilders and their struggle to prove their claim on a Dakota homestead.

The Children's Library Association established the Laura Ingalls Wilder Award in 1954. It is given every five years to an author or artist for his lasting contribution to children's literature. Laura Ingalls Wilder was the first to receive this award.

Another author who wrote both for children and adults is CAROLINE DALE SNEDEKER (1871–1956). She was born in New Harmony, Indiana, a town that became famous as an educational and cultural center during the 1820s. Three of Caroline Dale Snedeker's books are set in New Harmony. Early in life she became interested in ancient Greece, and a number of her books have their setting in this period of history. She married Rev. Charles H. Snedeker, Dean of the Cathedral in Cincinnati, at which she had studied music. The Snedekers moved to Long Island, where Mrs. Snedeker continued with her writing. Young readers enjoy her stories of ancient Greece, but most of all they seem to like *Downright Dency* (42), the story of a live, lovable girl with its setting in Nantucket a hundred years ago.

From *The First Four Years* by Laura Ingalls Wilder, illustrated by Garth Williams.

An array of books that fascinate young readers was contributed by CHARLES JOSEPH FINGER (1871–1941). *Tales from Silver Lands* (19), which won the Newbery Medal in 1942, is an outstanding contribution to folk literature. Born in Willesden, England, Finger attended King's College and later studied music at Frankfort-on-Main. At an early age he left England in search of adventure and had little trouble finding it. He sailed the Straits of Magellan, went around Cape Horn twice, and experienced a shipwreck in Patagonia. Ten years were spent roaming through South America where he herded sheep, hunted for gold, and listened to the old tales and legends the Indians were glad to tell him. He kept traveling—from Africa to the Klondike gold fields, through Mexico and a large part of the United States. At the age of fifty he bought a farm in the Ozark Hills in Arkansas where he settled down with his wife and five children and started to write. His travels provided him with a tremendous backlog of material upon which to draw for his stories. Among his thirty books for children and adults are *Tales Worth Telling* (20), *Courageous Companions* (18), *A Dog at His Heels,* written in 1936, and *Give a Man a Horse,* written in 1938.

A genius at storytelling and writing for children, RUTH SAWYER (1880–) was born in Boston and grew up in New York City. She completed her education at Columbia University, where she studied folklore and storytelling. As a little girl, Ruth Sawyer was fortunate to have an Irish nurse who was a fabulous storyteller, and her storytelling instilled in her little charge a love of Irish folklore. Ruth Sawyer went to work for the New York *Sun,* which sent her to Ireland twice to gather material for a series of articles on Irish folklore, Gaelic festivals, and Irish cottage industries. Her travels to Ireland, as well as to Spain, other European countries, and Mexico, provided her with rich materials for her writing. Among her stories popular with young readers are *The Voyage of the Wee Red Cap, Picture Tales from Spain* (37), *Tono Antonio, The Least One* (35), *The Long Christmas* (36), and *Roller Skates* (38), which remains the most popular of Miss Sawyer's pleasant stories for young readers. In *Roller Skates* readers enjoy a happy, carefree year in New York City with parent-free Lucinda, who returns four years later to entertain older readers in *The Year of Jubilo* (40). *The Way of the Storyteller* (39), one of the most creative books on storytelling, is also written by Ruth Sawyer.

Born in Leipsic, Ohio, JAMES CLOUD BOWMAN became interested in American folklore when he did graduate work at Columbia University. He decided to retell the tall tales. His first book was *The Adventures of Paul Bunyan.* He turned to the legends of cowboys and wrote *Pecos Bill* (10). He studied the legends of the American Indians and then wrote *Winahogo: Master of Life* (11). From his pen also came such delightful tales as *John Henry the Rambling Black Ulysses*, *Mike Fink* (9), and *The Snag of the Mas-sas-sip*. One of his most delightful books was the one he wrote with Margery Williams Bianco on a collection of folk tales and fables from Finland, *Tales from a Finnish Tupa* (12).

These are only a few of the brilliant writers of children's literature who bridged the nineteenth and twentieth centuries. Their success indicates that books for children had come to occupy a place of prominence in the field of literature. With highly creative writers and illustrators turning their talents to writing and illustrating for the enjoyment of children, a rich heritage of children's literature has accumulated. These early writers built a platform for those who were to follow.

The Procession Moves Along—The Twentieth Century

Quantity vs. Quality

The publishing of books is big business in the United States. There has been a steady increase since 1930 which has reached phenomenal proportions since 1960.

Year	New Books Published	Juvenile Only	New Editions Published	New Juvenile Editions
1960	12,069	1,628	2,943	97
1961	14,238	1,513	3,822	113
1962	16,448	2,328	5,456	256
1963	19,057	2,605	6,727	371
1964	20,542	2,533	7,909	275
1965	20,234	2,473	8,361	422
1966	21,819	2,375	8,231	338
1967	21,877	2,390	6,885	321
1968	23,321	2,318	7,066	164
1969	21,787	1,321	7,792	85
1970	24,288	2,472	11,783	168*

*The statistics above tabulate the publication of juvenile titles as compared with total of fiction books published since 1960. These statistics have appeared as annual reports on American book production in *Publishers' Weekly*, but were collected in this form for the years 1960–1965 by Mrs. Marguerite Archer, librarian of the Mamaroneck Avenue School, Mamaroneck, New York. Statistics for the years 1966 through 1970 were compiled directly from *Publishers' Weekly*.

It is interesting to observe how long this growth has continued and what the implications are for parents, teachers, and librarians. The increase in population and in school enrollments are major factors affecting this increase in book publishing. Various government-subsidized projects provide funds for the purchase of books that school districts previously could not afford. Methods of teaching reading have improved, and more children are experiencing success in reading. Probably the most important factor is the wealth of beautiful books written to satisfy every age group.

The avalanche of books that floods the market each year has led to the presence of reading racks for children in drugstores, supermarkets, and bus and airline terminals. One has only to observe the concentration of the youngsters as they pick and choose the books available to them on these reading racks to ascertain their interests. The important questions are: What is the quality of these books, and what tastes are being developed?

With the tremendous volume of books published each year for children, it is natural to raise a question regarding the quality of the books. At one counter in a shop where books are for sale, it is possible to pick up a book with an attractive format, by an outstanding author, illustrated by a well-known artist—a true work of art. Another counter in the same shop may be stacked with scores of cheaply bound, glossily covered, drably illustrated books without a single feature to recommend them as literature. One may often find more boys and girls fingering and selecting the books on the latter counter. Publishers have a serious responsibility in selecting the books they offer for the enjoyment of boys and girls.

Adaptations for Children—Arguments Pro and Con

The question of adapting has been rearing its head since publishers, authors, teachers, librarians, and others dealing with children's literature have gotten together. Those who are for adapting, retelling, or rewording say that many stories are too wordy and cumbersome for children to handle. The action is delayed to the point where interest is lost. Stevenson's *Treasure Island* (43), Defoe's *Robinson Crusoe* (15), Bunyan's *Pilgrim's Progress* (13), and Shakespeare's plays are most frequently used to support the argument for adapting.

Educators opposed to adapting feel that these and similar stories were never intended for children's reading in the first place. Children usurped them because of the paucity of material available to them at the time they were published. As a result these stories have been kept in the field of children's literature when they belong instead in the literature for young adults and adults. The opponents of adaptations say that whenever stories are stripped down and retold they lose the literary qualities that made these stories live through the years. Reading *Tales of Shakespeare* (29) by Charles and Mary Lamb, one is not reading Shakespeare, one is reading Charles and Mary Lamb. Paul Hazard (26) argues against adapting as follows:

> We needn't worry; children do not let themselves be oppressed without resistance. We wish to dominate, but they wish to be free; the result is a grand battle. In vain we offer them a book designed to make them more knowing than Pico della Mirandola and wiser than Solomon. Just as they used to turn away from the watch when its tick-tick no longer interested them, so they turn with an air of disgust from the book offered to them. . . . What precocious skill they have for skipping paragraphs, pages, whole chapters! A glance of the eye, a thrust of the thumb, is all they need. They sense the coming of a sermon and skip it dexterously. [Pp. 47–48]

Easy-to-Read Books

An issue as sharp as that of adaptations is the proliferation of easy-to-read books intended for teaching reading to beginners. The proponents of easy-to-read books hold that one of the early developmental tasks of five-, six-, and seven-year-olds is success in learning to read. They maintain that the vocabularies in many books used for teaching beginning reading are too difficult and discourage learners in their first efforts to read. They believe, too, that by using a limited number of words, a story that will be of interest can be told. In spite of the vocabulary studies that place the oral understanding vocabularies around 25,000 words, the question the proponents ask is how many of the words in the child's oral understanding can the child bring to the written symbol.

A number of educators are not in agreement with the proponents of easy-to-read books. They agree that reading is one of the developmental tasks of early childhood and that success in accomplishing this task is important. However, they hold that the developmental task does not spell out what the learner should read or by which method he should be taught. They maintain that the easy-to-read books with their limited vocabularies talk down to children, as do many preprimers, primers, and first-grade readers.

Assembly-Line Stories

Not all the writers of books for children at the turn of the century held the same philosophy as did Mary Mapes Dodge. Although she and her followers fought bravely to provide enjoyment for young readers, there was another group who, like Jacob Abbott in his Rollo Series, rapidly turned out didactic books. Parents, happy to have someone preach to their children for them, bought these books in quantity.

It was when Edward Stratemeyer appeared on the literary horizon that literature for children went into a decline. Early in the 1900s he formed a syndicate whose basic purpose in writing for young readers was to make a profit. No consideration was given to the needs of children and their different interests at different stages of development. Stratemeyer wrote about fifty books under his own name before he began using pseudonyms. As "Arthur Winfield" he authored the best-selling series *The Rover Boys* (1899). Hardly a boy in the early 1920s did not wait eagerly for the next Rover Boy book. Inspired by his success with *The Rover Boys* he put out the *Motor Boys* under the name of "Clarence Young." He organized a syndicate that produced the *Tom Swift* (45) stories by "Victor Appleton" and *The Bobbsey Twins* (44) by "Laura Lee Hope." Stratemeyer also plotted over 800 other books for anonymous writers to complete. Thus an assembly line was set up to produce books for children.

Unfortunately assembly-line stories still flood the market. No one person like Stratemeyer is writing under his own name or other names today; however, that does not mean that all publishing houses refute Stratemeyer's philosophy of quantity rather than quality. But today the purpose of a series is generally to give information that will enrich the social studies. Some books are outstanding in quality, and often each book in the series is by an outstanding author and an authority in his field.

Extending Experiences for the Reader

1. Arrange a bulletin board with prints reproduced from illustrations in early books. Encourage the group to set up a file of similar illustrations.
2. If possible take the group to see a collection of the earliest literature books for children.
3. Plan a bulletin board around facsimiles of *The New England Primer*, Horn Books, and *Battledoors*.
4. Read a story to the group by one of the early writers of stories for children, such as Armand Berquin, John Aikin, and Mrs. Barbauld.
5. Read excerpts to the group from *The Renowned History of Little Goody Two-Shoes* ascribed to Oliver Goldsmith.
6. Plan an exhibit of copies of the now out-of-print *St. Nicholas* magazine. Read several stories from that magazine to the group.

7. Read *Little Women* (5) by Louisa May Alcott, *Anne of Green Gables* (30) by L. M. Montgomery, and *Rebecca of Sunnybrook Farm* (49) by Kate Douglas Wiggin. How do their themes and story lines compare in terms of the interests of young people today, particularly girls?
8. Read Mark Twain's story of "The Jumping Frog of Calaveras County" (46). What kind of a picture of frontier life does it give young readers?
9. Read excerpts from one story by Laura E. Richards to the group. Compare the story read with a modern story having a similar theme.
10. Read *The Birds' Christmas Carol* (47) to the group. Note their reactions to it. What character seems to impress them the most?
11. Read several books in the *Rover Boys* series and several in the *Motor Boys* series. Analyze the plots. In what way are they similar, and in what way are they different?
12. Make a list of modern books that you think have a theme of social significance.

Extending Experiences for Children

1. Locate book collectors in the community. Invite them to talk to the class and show some of their collections.
2. Invite the owner of a bookstore in the community to talk to the class on a subject related to books.
3. Design a page for a Horn Book or *The New England Primer.*
4. Divide into groups. Have each group select one of the stories of Charles Perrault and prepare a skit to present to the class.
5. Plan a skit with its setting in John Newbery's shop "The Bible and the Sun." Have individuals describe the books that are for sale.
6. After four or five have read one or more stories by Laura Ingalls Wilder, plan a way to introduce these stories to the class.
7. After four or five have read *Hans Brinker or the Silver Skates* (16) by Mary Mapes Dodge, plan a way of presenting the highlights of the story to the rest of the class.
8. Hold a clothesline art show of pictures drawn to illustrate several of Louisa May Alcott's stories.
9. Read a story written at the beginning of the twentieth century to share with the class. Read a later story by the same author. Compare the two stories as to theme, plot development, character delineation, and climax.

Chapter References

1. ALCOTT, LOUISA MAY. *Eight Cousins.* Cleveland: World Publishing, 1948. Grades 4–6.

2. ______. *Jack and Jill.* Cleveland: World Publishing, 1948. Grades 4–6.
3. ______. *Jo's Boys.* New York: Macmillan, 1962. Paperback. n.g.l.
4. ______. *Little Men.* New York: Macmillan, 1962. Paperback. Grades 6–8.
5. ______. *Little Women.* New York: Macmillan, 1962. Paperback. Grades 6–8.
6. ______. *An Old-Fashioned Girl.* Cleveland: World Publishing, 1947. Grades 4–6.
7. ______. *Rose in Bloom.* Boston: Little, Brown, 1876. Grade 7 and up.
8. ______. *Under the Lilacs.* New York: Macmillan, 1962. Paperback. Grade 7 and up.
9. BOWMAN, JAMES CLOUD. *Mike Fink.* Boston: Little, Brown, 1957. Grade 7 and up.
10. ______. *Pecos Bill.* Chicago: Albert Whitman, 1937. Grades 5–8.
11. ______. *Winahogo: Master of Life.* Chicago: Albert Whitman, 1941. n.g.l.
12. ______, AND MARGERY WILLIAMS BIANCO. *Tales from a Finnish Tupa.* Chicago: Albert Whitman, 1936. Grades 5–8.
13. BUNYAN, JOHN. *Pilgrim's Progress.* New York: Holt, Rinehart & Winston, n.d. Paperback. Grade 10 and up.
14. CARLSON, NATALIE SAVAGE. *The Empty Schoolhouse.* New York: Dell, 1968. Paperback. Grades 2–8.
15. DEFOE, DANIEL. JAMES SUTHERLAND (ed.). *Robinson Crusoe.* Boston: Houghton Mifflin, 1968. Paperback. Grade 7 and up.
16. DODGE, MARY MAPES. *Hans Brinker or the Silver Skates.* Garden City, N. Y.: Doubleday, 1956. Paperback. Grades 3–7.
17. ESTES, ELEANOR. *The Hundred Dresses.* New York: Harcourt Brace Jovanovich, 1944. Kindergarten–grade 3.
18. FINGER, CHARLES JOSEPH. *Courageous Companions.* New York: David McKay, 1929. Grades 7–9.
19. ______. *Tales from Silver Lands.* Garden City, N. Y.: Doubleday, 1924. Grades 7 and up.
20. ______. *Tales Worth Telling.* New York: Appleton-Century-Crofts, 1927. n.g.l.
21. GATES, DORIS. *The Blue Willow.* New York: Viking, 1969. Paperback. Grades 4–6.
22. HARRIS, JOEL CHANDLER. *Nights with Uncle Remus.* Boston: Houghton Mifflin, 1883. n.g.l.
23. ______. *On the Plantation.* Boston: Houghton Mifflin, 1892. n.g.l.
24. ______. *Uncle Remus and His Friends.* Boston: Houghton Mifflin, 1892. n.g.l.
25. ______. M. ALINE BRIGHT (ed.). *Uncle Remus: His Songs and His Sayings.* Rev. ed. New York: Hawthorn, 1921. Preschool–grade 3.
26. HAZARD, PAUL. *Books, Children and Men.* Boston: The Horn Book, 1969. Paperback.
27. KIPLING, RUDYARD. *The Jungle Book.* New York: Grosset & Dunlap, 1950. Paperback. Grades 2–6.
28. ______. *The Second Jungle Book.* Garden City, N. Y.: Doubleday, 1923. Grades 5–7.

29. LAMB, CHARLES, AND MARY LAMB. *Tales from Shakespeare.* Garden City, N. Y.: Doubleday, 1807. Grades 7–9.
30. MONTGOMERY, L. M. *Anne of Green Gables.* New York: Grosset & Dunlap, 1969. Paperback. Grade 7 and up.
31. PYLE, HOWARD. *The Merry Adventures of Robin Hood.* New York: Dover, 1968. Grades 3–6.
32. ——. *The Story of King Arthur and His Knights.* New York: Dover, 1971. Paperback. Grade 7 and up.
33. RICHARDS, LAURA E. HOWE. *Captain January and Little Colonel.* New York: Random House, 1959. n.g.l.
34. ——. *Tirra Lirra.* Boston: Little, Brown, 1955. Grades 1–3.
35. SAWYER, RUTH. *The Least One.* New York: Viking, 1941. n.g.l.
36. —— (ed.). *The Long Christmas.* New York: Viking, 1941. Grade 7 and up.
37. ——. *Picture Tales from Spain.* Philadelphia: Lippincott, 1936.
38. ——. *Roller Skates.* New York: Dell, 1969. Paperback. Grades 3–7.
39. ——. *The Way of the Storyteller.* New York: Viking, 1965. Paperback. Grade 7.
40. ——. *The Year of Jubilo.* New York: Viking, 1970. Paperback. Grades 4–7.
41. SHOTWELL, LOUISA R. *Roosevelt Grady.* New York: Grosset & Dunlap, 1964. Paperback. Grades 7–11.
42. SNEDEKER, CAROLINE DALE. *Downright Dency.* Garden City, N. Y.: Doubleday, 1927. Grade 8 and up.
43. STEVENSON, ROBERT LOUIS. *Treasure Island.* New York: Macmillan, 1962. Paperback. Grade 7 and up.
44. STRATEMEYER, EDWARD (Laura Lee Hope). *The Bobbsey Twins.* New York: Grosset & Dunlap, 1968.
45. —— (Victor Appleton). *Tom Swift.* New York: Grosset & Dunlap, 1916.
46. TWAIN, MARK. *Jumping Frog.* New York: Dover, 1971. Paperback.
47. WIGGIN, KATE. *The Birds' Christmas Carol.* Eau Claire, Wis.: Hale, 1941. Grades 3–6.
48. ——. *My Garden of Memory.* Boston: Houghton Mifflin, 1923.
49. ——. *Rebecca of Sunnybrook Farm.* New York: Grosset & Dunlap, n.d. Paperback. Grades 7–9.
50. ——, AND NORA A. SMITH (eds.). *The Fairy Ring.* Rev. ed. Garden City, N. Y.: Doubleday, 1967. Grades 2–5.
51. ——. *Golden Numbers.* Freeport, N. Y.: Books for Libraries, 1902.
52. ——. *Magic Casements.* Garden City, N. Y.: Doubleday, n.d.
53. ——. *The Posy Ring.* Freeport, N. Y.: Books for Libraries, 1903.
54. ——. *Tales of Laughter.* Garden City, N. Y.: Doubleday, 1926.
55. ——. *Tales of Wonder.* Garden City, N. Y.: Doubleday, 1909.
56. WILDER, LAURA INGALLS. *By the Shores of Silver Lake.* Garth Williams (ill.). New York: Harper & Row, 1971. Paperback. Grades 4–8.
57. ——. *Farmer Boy.* Garth Williams (ill.). New York: Harper & Row, 1971. Paperback. Grades 3–7.

58. ———. *The First Four Years.* Garth Williams (ill.). New York: Harper & Row, 1971. Paperback. Grades 4–8.
59. ———. *The Little House in the Big Woods.* Garth Williams (ill.). New York: Harper & Row, 1971. Paperback. Grades 3–7.
60. ———. *The Little House on the Prairie.* Garth Williams (ill.). New York: Harper & Row, 1971. Paperback. Grades 3–7.
61. ———. *The Little Town on the Prairie.* Garth Willims (ill.). New York: Harper & Row, 1971. Paperback. Grades 4–8.
62. ———. *The Long Winter.* Garth Williams (ill.). New York: Harper & Row, 1971. Paperback. Grades 4–8.
63. ———. *On the Banks of Plum Creek.* Garth Williams (ill.). New York: Harper & Row, 1971. Paperback. Grades 3–7.
64. ———. *These Happy Golden Years.* Garth Williams (ill.). New York: Harper & Row, 1971. Paperback. Grade 5 and up.
65. YATES, ELIZABETH. *Amos Fortune, Free Man.* New York: Dutton, 1950. Grade 7 and up.

Further Reading for Teachers, Parents, and Librarians

ANDREWS, SIRI (ed.). *The Hewins Lectures, 1947–1962.* Boston: The Horn Book, 1963.

BARRY, FLORENCE. *A Century of Children's Books.* New York: Doran, 1923.

CROUCH, MARCUS. *Treasure Seekers and Borrowers: Children's Books in Britain 1900–1960.* London: Library Association, 1962.

DARLING, RICHARD L. *The Rise of Children's Book Reviewing in America, 1865–1881.* New York: Bowker, 1967.

DARTON, F. J. HARVEY. *Children's Books in England, Five Centuries of Social Life.* 2nd ed. Cambridge, England: Cambridge University Press, 1966.

FENWICK, SARA INNIS (ed.). *A Critical Approach to Children's Literature.* Chicago: University of Chicago Press, 1967.

FISHER, MARGERY. *Intent upon Reading: A Critical Appraisal of Modern Fiction for Children.* New York: Watts, 1962.

FOLMSBEE, BEULAH. *A Little History of the Horn Book.* Boston: The Horn Book, 1942.

FRYATT, NORMA R. (ed.). *A Horn Book Sampler.* Boston: The Horn Book, 1959.

KIEFER, MONICA M. *American Children Through Their Books, 1700–1835.* Philadelphia: University of Pennsylvania Press, 1948.

MEIGS, CORNELIA, *et al.* (eds.). *A Critical History of Children's Literature: A Survey of Children's Books in English.* Rev. ed. New York: Macmillan, 1969.

ROBINSON, EVELYN R. (ed.). *Reading About Children's Literature.* New York: David McKay, 1966.

SMITH, DORA V. *Fifty Years of Children's Books, 1910–1960: Trends, Backgrounds, Influences.* Champaign, Ill.: National Council of Teachers of English, 1963.

ST. JOHN, JUDITH. *The Osborne Collection of Early Children's Books, 1566–1910: A Catalogue.* Toronto, Canada: Toronto Public Library, 1958.

TARG, WILLIAM. *Bibliophile in the Nursery: A Bookman's Treasury of Collectors Lore on Old and Rare Children's Books.* Metuchen, N. J.: Scarecrow, 1969.

From *Flowers of Delight,* edited by Leonard de Vries.

A a

B b

C c

8

Children Experience Poetry

Nursery Rhymes and Mother Goose

Experiences with literature come early in the lives of many children. Lullabies, nursery rhymes, and word games are built into their sleeping, eating, and play. At an early age they take over from the persons who make up their world the pleasant sounds that accompany their activities. Soon the early sounds make words, words make phrases and sentences, and sentences tell them stories. Little children delight in hearing adults count off their toes while saying:

This little pig went to market;
This little pig stayed home;
This little pig had roast beef;
This little pig had none;
This little pig said "wee, wee, wee!"
All the way home.

Long before they can say the words, the little ones make their own sounds as they go through the motions of

Pat-a-cake, pat-a-cake, baker's man!
Bake me a cake as fast as you can;
Roll it and pat it and mark it with "B"
And put it in the oven for baby and me.

And many a child has tried to change the weather with

Rain, rain, go away.
Come again another day;
Little Tommy wants to play.

Mother Goose has worked her way into the hearts of children everywhere. Long before any rhymes attributed to Mother Goose found their way into print, they were handed down from generation to generation by word of mouth. It is easy to understand why it is possible to find a number of different versions of a particular rhyme since the transmitting was done from memory.

The niche that Mother Goose has made for herself is attested to by the large number of books of nursery and Mother Goose rhymes now available. There is scarcely a publisher of children's books who has not published a book of Mother Goose rhymes. Most editions are profusely and beautifully illustrated by outstanding artists, and they come in all shapes and sizes with such titles as *The Tall Book of Mother Goose* (64), *Jessie Wilcox Smith's Little Mother Goose* (59), and *The Real Mother Goose* (51). A number of collections are identified by the name of the artist who selected the rhymes and did the illustrations. For example, there are Marguerite de Angeli's *Book of Nursery and Mother Goose Rhymes* (12), Brian Wildsmith's *Mother Goose: A Collection of Nursery Rhymes* (68), Hilary Knight's *Mother Goose* (25), and L. Leslie Brooke's *Ring O' Roses* (53).

Who is this Mother Goose who has such a following not only with children and parents but with authors, artists, and publishers as well? Years of study and research have been devoted to tracing the origin and background of Mother Goose and Mother Goose rhymes.

It is certain that some credit for the creation of Mother Goose must go to Charles Perrault. On the title page of his *Histoires ou Contes du Temps Passé: des Moralites* (49), published about 1697, there is a picture of an old woman spinning. A girl, a boy, a man, and a cat are listening attentively to the tale the old lady is telling. Printed on the background of the title page is the inscription "Contes de Ma Mere l'Oye," meaning "Tales of My Mother Goose." This was the debut of that fabulous character into the world of enchantment enjoyed by children. The artist who created Mother Goose is unknown, but most artists who have pictured her since have continued in the same tradition—an old lady with a hawkish nose and chin, a somewhat mischievous smile, a broad-brimmed hat with a pointed crown, and a goose on which to fly through the air.

Some thirty years later, John Newbery used her name for the first time in connection with poetry. Translated, the book carried this title:

Mother Goose's Melody, or Sonnets for the Cradle. In Two Parts. Part I Contains the Most Celebrated Songs and Lullabies of the Old British Nurses, Calculated to Amuse Children and to Excite Them to Sleep. Part II. Those of the Sweet Songster and Muse of Wit and Humour, Master William Shakespeare. Embellished with Notes and Maxims, Historical, Philosophical, and Critical.

It is believed that John Newbery published the above, with the assistance of Oliver Goldsmith, between 1760 and 1765 although there are no extant copies. The book was well received and went through a number of editions.

To this day there is a tombstone in an old graveyard in Boston with the name Goose inscribed on it which is supposed to be the tombstone of Mother Goose. As the story goes, Thomas Fleet, a Boston printer, published a book of songs and rhymes in 1719 titled *Songs for the Nursery,* which were the rhymes his mother-in-law sang and recited to his children. Just as there seems to be no extant copy of John Newbery's *Mother Goose's Melody,* there is no copy available of Mr. Fleet's publication. There seems to be more fiction than fact surrounding these episodes in children's literature.

In 1785 Isaiah Thomas, printer, publisher, and dealer in books, published Newbery's *Original Mother Goose's Melody* (42), the first American edition of Mother Goose. Although there is no extant copy of Newbery's original book, it appears that Thomas pirated Newbery's plates and printed from them. It is a delightful book done in miniature as were most of the books for children at that time. The illustrations were woodcuts, small in size but rich in detail.

About the same time that Isaiah Thomas republished Newbery's *Original Mother Goose's Melody* in America, Joseph Ritson published *Gammer Gurton's Garland* (54) in England. Twenty-five years later a four-part edition of the *Garland* made its appearance in the bookshops in London. This edition contained over a hundred rhymes—some old, some new, and many still popular today.

In 1824 Munroe and Francis of Boston published *Mother Goose's Quarto: or Melodies Complete* (39). This publication contained nearly 200 rhymes. Many of them were taken from Newbery's *Mother Goose's Melody* and Ritson's *Garland.* Nine years later a second edition of this book was published, containing a foreword by Edward Everett Hale, which has served as a valuable reference through the years. In 1905 Lothrop, Lee & Shepard of New York published *The Only True Mother Goose,* a faithful reproduction in text and illustrations of the volume that Munroe and Francis had published in 1833.

Nursery and Mother Goose rhymes have caught the fancy and interest of a number of scholars in the field of children's literature. One of these is James Orchard Halliwell-Phillipps, whose research on rhymes of English origin made a significant contribution to Mother Goose material. His collection *Nursery Rhymes of England* (23) was published in 1842, followed by *Nursery Rhymes and Nursery Tales of England.*

The most comprehensive collections of nursery and Mother Goose rhymes available today are the scholarly works of Iona and Peter

Opie, who are recognized as leading authorities on eighteenth-century children's literature. *The Oxford Dictionary of Nursery Rhymes* (46), which they edited, was published by the Oxford University Press in 1952. The dictionary is often referred to as an essential tool for all who are engaged in the study and teaching of children's literature. In 1955 the Opies edited *The Oxford Nursery Rhyme Book* (47), a collection of 800 rhymes and ditties. The Opies describe the contents as "the infant jingles, riddles, catches, tongue trippers, baby games, toe names, maxims, alphabets, counting rhymes, prayers, and lullabies, with which generation after generation of mothers and nurses have attempted to please the youngest and have, somehow, usually succeeded" (p. V).

A is for Apple

Along with the introduction of nursery and Mother Goose rhymes into children's literature came the ABC books, which originated as features of the *Hornbook* and the *Primer.* The *Hornbook* and *Primer* with their emphasis on prayer and instruction served the purposes for which they were intended and then became a part of the history of children's literature. ABC books, however, become more beautiful and more clever each year and continue to play an important role in the field of children's literature.

Alphabet books made their appearance on the literary scene in England toward the middle of the sixteenth century. The license to print them was given to various printers by the king in accordance with how orthodox the printer was: The king desired that things be done in harmony with the wishes of the Church. Between the middle of the sixteenth century and the middle of the next century at least eight editions of the ABC books appeared.

In the early ABC books the alphabet appeared mainly in three forms. The first of these three forms was the *Hornbook;* the second was the small *ABC Tracts;* and the third appeared on a leaf inserted in the primer of the *Layman's Prayer Book,* which was also known as the *Book of Hours and Prayers.* Following the Reformation, alphabet books were printed to further the cause of Protestantism.

The first rhymed alphabet books were published in Boston in 1690. They preceded *The New England Primer* and were called *Royal Primers.* They were used as textbooks, and over 5 million were sold during the years they were in use.

For a period of time after that there seems to have been a moratorium on the writing and publishing of such books. Not until 1923, with the publication of *ABC Book* (16) by C. B. Falls, was much interest aroused among well-known writers and artists. The woodcuts by Falls, in rich contrasting colors, give an elegant tone to his book. Each letter of the alphabet is represented by an animal beginning with that letter. Most of them are well known, such as antelope, bear, cat, and duck; others, such as ibis, newt, unicorn, and xiphius, are not as familiar, but young readers delight in hearing and saying their names.

Ten years later Wanda Gag's *ABC Bunny* (20) was published. It is easily understood why this book made a happy addition to children's literature and stimulated an interest in ABC books. The letters of the alphabet lead Bunny into a series of fascinating experiences. The expressions on his face and on the faces of the little creatures he meets complement the catchy rhymes with their lilting rhythm. The book is illustrated by the author with hand lettering and lithographs.

Many modern ABC books continue this tradition of employing a varied assortment of animals to represent the alphabet. Fritz Eichenberg not only used animals in his book *Ape in a Cape: An Alphabet of Odd Animals* (15), but selected odd animals, placed them in funny situations, and accompanied them by humorous rhymes, such as "carp with a harp" and "dove in love."

The letters of the alphabet stand for sounds and actions that have to do with night and sleep in Margaret Wise Brown's *Sleepy ABC* (9). The illustrations by Esphyr Slobodkin carry out the sleepy child motif with a paper-cutting and pasting effect.

A nonsense alphabet book that has recently become popular is Edward Lear's *ABC* (27), penned and illustrated by Lear himself. The pages of Lear's original are reproduced exactly as they appeared in his manuscript. The things chosen to illustrate the letters provide few surprises—A for Ants, B for Bat, C for Cat, D for Duck—but the verses have that Lear touch, a combination of nonsense and fantasy.

> N were some nuts
>   which hung on a tree,
> So shiny and brown,
> One, two, and three
>   N!
> Nice little nuts! [unpaged]

One wishes that Clare T. Newberry's kittens could leave the pages of *The Kittens' ABC* (41) and come to life. They are the purring, appealing kind that Clare Newberry does with such distinction. One kitten is more irresistible than the other.

Bruno Munari's *Bruno Munari's ABC* (40) has double-page illustrations in striking colors and bold strokes that combine charm and humor. In Munari's book each letter stands for many things, and the incongruous combination makes for humor; for example, *S* is for:

A Sack
of Stars
and Snow
    for
Santa Claus

Stop
and a Sign

All kinds of Shells [unpaged]

In his inimitable style of illustrating and rhyming Dr. Seuss makes his contribution to the field of ABC books. His illustrations are laugh provokers, and his rhymes are the kind that young children like to repeat, such as those found in *Dr. Seuss's ABC* (58):

Big A
    little a
What begins with A?
Aunt Annie's alligator . . . A . . . a . . . A [Pp. 3–5]

And then there are always Seuss' made-up words (58) like:

Four fluffy feathers
on a
Fiffer-feffer-feff. [P. 16]

Young children delight in mouthing such made-up words over and over again and then making up some of their own.

Most alphabet books that appear on the market attempt to relate the ABCs to some part of the world of children. Certainly the cars and trucks depicted in Anne Alexander's *ABC of Cars and Trucks* (1) are right out of the lives of boys and girls.

The Petershams rose to the challenge of doing an ABC book that would be different from others with their *An American ABC* (50). Appealing full-page illustrations accompany the text. Each letter introduces an event in American life or history, and there is also an accompanying story that really turns this alphabet book into a history book. The book opens with

A is for America
    The land I love, [P. 6]

and ends with

Z is for Zeal
    An American trait. [P. 54]

Phyllis McGinley's *All Around the Town* (35) is full of chuckles and laughs. The rhymes are lively and the illustrations are in bright colors. There are many things around town to make the alphabet interesting and exciting, such as:

E
E is the Escalator
    That gives an elegant ride
You step on the stair
With an easy air
    And up and up you glide.
It's nicer than scaling ladders
    or scrambling 'round a hill,
For you climb and climb
But all the time
    You're really standing still. [P. 16]

There is an unsophisticated quality about the rhymes that has immediate appeal to little children.

There is an element of instruction in the ABC books, but it is presented pleasantly without the admonitions, threats, and gloom that accompanied the instruction in the *Hornbook* and *Primer.* Little children see the ABC books as sources of fun.

The World of Poetry

Ideally poetry begins with the first rock of the cradle when Mother lulls the child to sleep with a song. *The Annotated Mother Goose* (4) says:

The lullaby is a simple form, yet of all the "Mother Goose" rhymes, it is lullabies which come the closest to being true poetry . . . but the child grows older. At first he is delighted by such simple infant fare as "This little Pig went to Market." He does not suspect that from them he is learning to count to five. . . . When he is free to do as he wants to do the child is likely to turn to such solitary pleasures as riding a hobbyhorse, swinging, or simply marching up and down—and often each of these has a rhyme to go with it. . . . Next comes a game with a companion of the child's own age—teeter-tottering, perhaps?—and here too, there are "trivial verses" to accompany the amusement.

Then comes group play. Who of all these children is to be "It?" We meet with the counting out rhyme . . . [Pp. 223–224]

Thus poetry begins at the earliest age and continues through life as an integral part of everyday living.

Experiencing the World Through Poetry

POETRY

What is Poetry? Who knows?
Not a rose, but the scent of the rose;
Not the sky, but the light in the sky;
Not the fly, but the gleam of the fly;
Not the sea, but the sound of the sea;
Not myself, but what makes me
See, hear, and feel something that prose
Cannot: and what it is, who knows? [P. 58]

In her poem, Eleanor Farjeon (17) sets the stage for enjoying a wide range of poems that appeal not only to the young in years, but also to the young in heart. Her poem extends the experience of the listener or the reader above and beyond the ability to see and to comprehend.

What makes a poem? Not so much what the poet puts into it specifically as what he implies, what he leaves to the imagination. The poet expresses his reactions to living. Through the medium of words he finds release for the feelings that have been stirred by his contact with life. Individuals know the world about them through their five senses. They come to know a thing by the way it looks, sounds, feels, tastes, or smells, or some combination of these. The poet has all these ways of experiencing, and, in addition, he has the power to express these feelings in language that stirs the same emotions in the listener or the reader as he himself has felt.

The poet not only sees accurately, but he sees things in their many relationships. Objects conjure up images in his mind, and he converts this imagery into words. When individuals read of the things the poet saw, they are amazed that they have not seen these same things themselves, but, at the same time, they are convinced of their truth. Sometimes individuals recognize that they have had the same experience, but they have never been able to express it in words. After reading the poem, they may return to the world as they knew it, but now they see it through the eyes of the poet.

The moon that we see nightly in the sky takes on a different meaning after we hear or read Vachel Lindsay's "The Moon's the North Wind's Cooky" (31). The moon assumes a sort of magic combined with witchery when one reads Walter de la Mare's "Silver" (14).

SILVER

Slowly, silently, now the moon
Walks the night in her silver shoon;
This way, and that, she peers, and sees
Silver fruit upon silver trees;
One by one the casements catch
Her beams beneath the silvery thatch;
Couched in his kennel, like a log,
With paws of silver sleeps the dog;
From their shadowy cote the white
    breasts peep
Of doves in a silver-feathered sleep;
A harvest mouse goes scampering by,
With silver claws, and silver eye;
And moveless fish in the water gleam,
By silver reeds in a silver stream. [P. 181]

Adults and children as well may hunt for other moon poems such as "Moon Folly" in which Conn the Fool sets off for the mountain planning to bring the moon back in his sack. This poem helps stretch the imagination and is an example of fantasy expressed in graphic word pictures in language only the poet would use. Through acquaintance with poetry children become more keenly aware of the sights and sounds about them and find enjoyment and satisfaction in the sense impressions expressed through imagery.

Color

Color has a special appeal to all persons, young and old. This is an age of color—color television has spoiled this generation for black and white. The world itself is full of color. In her book *Sing-Song* (56) Christina Rossetti included "What Is Pink?" a long-time favorite with children and teachers. It has often served as a springboard for children to create similar couplets, using the same or other colors.

A modern-day poet, Mary O'Neill, has produced a delightful book with the intriguing title *Hailstones and Halibut Bones* (45). From that volume and from a whole spectrum of colors comes:

WHAT IS YELLOW?

Yellow is the color of the sun
The feeling of fun
The yoke of an egg

A duck's bill
A canary bird
And a daffodil.
Yellow's sweet corn
Ripe oats
Hummingbirds'
Little throats
Summer squash and
Chinese silk
The cream on top
Of Jersey milk
Dandelions and
Daisy hearts
Custard pies and
Lemon tarts.
Yellow blinks
On summer nights
In the off-and-on of
Firefly lights.
Yellow's a topaz,
A candle flame.
Felicity's a
Yellow name.
Yellow's mimosa,
And I guess,
Yellow's the color of
Happiness. [Pp. 55–56]

Perhaps a child who thinks that he does not like poetry because the poems he has heard do not appeal to him will be lured by Mary O'Neill's book into exploring the hundreds of things in the everyday world that possess color.

Sound

Another life experience to which poets are sensitive is sound. To some people sound is recognized only as noise. But the poet's ear is tuned to the myriad sounds even in what are thought of as everyday places. To these sounds he attaches significance and meaning as he expresses them in his poems.

A group of teachers who were working cooperatively to discover ways of making children more aware of sounds spent five minutes listening with no one speaking, and then in small groups they produced some free verse based on what they had heard. One of these might suggest the many aspects of sound that are often overlooked but are discovered when a group attempts to develop a "listening ear."

SOUNDS

Grating of chairs
Voices—hum
Crackling paper
Tap, tap upon steps
Rumble of cars
Tick of a watch
Tires—hum
Dangling of a bracelet on a desk
Shuffling of feet
Rustle of silk
Mixed voices
Clear voices
Silence—thinking
Pencil on paper
Confusion
Soft voices
Laughter
Closing of a door
Snapping sound—purse
Click of a door
Elevator door!

The poet not only has a sensitive ear for sound, but by the very words he uses and by repetition and alliteration he causes the reader or listener to share his experience, or perhaps, even to create his own personal experience. Anyone who has read Amy Lowell's "Sea Shell" (33) can scarcely have failed to experience this feeling of participation.

SEA SHELL

Sea Shell, Sea Shell,
    Sing me a song, O please!
A song of ships, and sailor men,
And parrots, and tropical trees.
Of islands lost in the Spanish Main
    Which no man ever may find again,
Of fishes and corals under the waves,
    And sea-horses stabled in great green caves.

Sea Shell, Sea Shell,
Sing of the things you know so well. [P. 23]

These lines re-create for a child the experience of holding a sea shell to one's ear and imagining that he hears the sound of the sea, even though he may live far inland and may have never seen the ocean.

Other Senses the Poet Cultivates

Although less used in poetry, touch, taste, and smell also heighten the effect of poetry when they are used. In many instances these appeals are woven into poems that have some other major emphasis. Carol Ryrie Brink's "Goody O'Grumpity" (18) would appeal to children for the delicious smells as well as the mouth-watering tastes described.

GOODY O'GRUMPITY

When Goody O'Grumpity baked a cake
The tall reeds danced by the mournful lake,
The pigs came nuzzling out of their pens,
The dogs ran sniffing and so did the hens,
And the children flocked by dozens and tens.
They came from the north, the east and the south
With wishful eyes and watering mouth,
And stood in a crowd about Goody's door,
Their muddy feet on her sanded floor.
And what do you s'pose they came to do!
Why, to lick the dish when Goody was through!
And throughout the land went such a smell
Of citron and spice—no words can tell
How cinnamon bark and lemon rind,
And round, brown nutmegs grated fine
A wonderful haunting perfume wove,
Together with allspice, ginger and clove,
When Goody but opened the door of her stove.
The children moved close in a narrowing ring,
They were hungry—as hungry as bears in the spring;
They said not a word, just breathed in the spice,
And at last when the cake was all golden and nice,
Goody took a great knife and cut each a slice. [P. 312]

One poem that emphasizes touch by its very title is "Fuzzy Wuzzy Creepy Crawly" (2) by Lillian Schultz. Children can be helped to become "detectives" in finding words or phrases that appeal to any of the senses as they are encouraged to read widely on their own.

Poetry for Different Interests and Needs

There are many ways to categorize poems. Whatever plan is used should make it possible for the teacher to locate quickly and easily the right poem for a particular moment. It is important for prospective and practicing teachers to be guided by children's interests, which are many and varied.

Poetry Just for Fun

It would be difficult to find a child or a group that does not enjoy humor. Some is broad humor; some is more sophisticated. Some has been in print for a long time; some is modern indeed. Some is in story form. There is a wide range of choice, and a few examples can be suggested for each of these types.

One modern author, Eve Merriam, well understands the children of today and frequently uses a familiar situation as a setting for the action. A good example of her poetry is "Alligator on the Escalator" (36):

ALLIGATOR ON THE ESCALATOR

Through the revolving door
Of a department store
There slithered an alligator.
When he came to the escalator,
He stepped upon the track with great dexterity;
His tail draped over the railing,
And he clicked his teeth in glee:
"Yo, I'm off on the escalator,
Excited as I can be!
It's a *moving* experience,
As you can plainly see.
On the moving stair I go anywhere,
I rise to the top
Past outerwear, innerwear,
Dinnerware, thinnerwear—
Then down to the basement with bargains galore,
Then back on the track to the top once more!
Oh, I may ride the escalator
Until closing time or later,
So tell the telephone operator
To call Mrs. Albert Q. Alligator
And tell her to take a hot mud bath
And not to wait up for me!" [Pp. 28–29]

Children will enjoy choosing the most amusing lines and giving reasons for their choices. If they have had previous experience with an amusing poem, they will be able to make some comparisons. This poem may encourage children to look through collections of poems such as *Favorite Poems Old and New* (18) compiled by Helen Ferris, *This Singing World* (67) edited by Louis Untermeyer, or Carl Sandburg's *Complete Poems* (57).

A more sophisticated poem is Mary Austin's "Grizzly Bear" (3), published in 1928. Children's response with laughter or the failure to laugh will tell the teacher whether they need to examine the poem further.

GRIZZLY BEAR

If you ever, ever, ever meet a grizzly bear,
You must never, never, never ask him *where*
He is going,
Or what he is doing;
For if you ever, ever dare
To stop a grizzly bear,
You will never meet *another* grizzly bear.

A more recent author—unknown—wrote these lines, perhaps to explain the original:

Algy saw a bear,
The bear saw Algy,
The bear was bulgy,
The bulge was Algy.

Activities that can lead to further exploration by children themselves are highly desirable. Children may even try to write some lines themselves in the same style as a poet they admire. Ogden Nash, Lewis Carroll, Edward Lear, Laura E. Richards, and Charles Edward Carryl all employ interesting patterns in verse that children might try to emulate.

Nonsense Poems

Although it is difficult to distinguish between humor and nonsense, one might say that in humor the real is absurd, whereas in nonsense the absurd is real. Humor most often deals with real characters in an amusing manner.

The nonsense poems of Edward Lear are often able to intrigue children into reading poetry, even though they say that they do not like it. Perhaps the reason is that children enjoy the humor of the ridiculous. Lear's *The Complete Nonsense Book* (28) includes long and short poems, poems of people, and poems of birds and animals both real and imaginary, as well as his famous limericks. He possessed a real understanding of children that enabled him to make them laugh with him. "The Table and the Chair" is an example of the way in which he encourages children to use their imaginations as he creates persons out of inanimate objects such as an ordinary table and a chair.

THE TABLE AND THE CHAIR

Said the Table to the Chair,
"You can hardly be aware
How I suffer from the heat
And from chilblains on my feet.
If we took a little walk,
We might have a little talk;
Pray let us take the air,"
Said the Table to the Chair.

Said the Chair unto the Table,
"Now, you know we are not able:
How foolishly you talk,
When you know we cannot walk!"
Said the Table with a sigh,
"It can do no harm to try.
I've as many legs as you:
Why can't we walk on two?"

So they both went slowly down,
And walked about the town
With a cheerful bumpy sound
As they toddled round and round;
And everybody cried,
As they hastened to their side,
"See! the Table and the Chair
Have come out to take the air!"

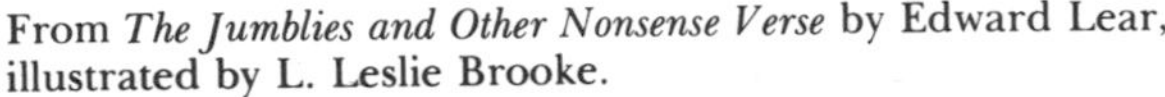

From *The Jumblies and Other Nonsense Verse* by Edward Lear, illustrated by L. Leslie Brooke.

But in going down an alley
To a castle in a valley,
They completely lost their way,
And wandered all the day;
Till, to see them safely back,
They paid a Ducky-quack,
And a Beetle, and a Mouse,
Who took them to their house.

Then they whispered to each other,
"O delightful little brother,
What a lovely walk we've taken!
Let us dine on beans and bacon."
So the Ducky and the leetle
Browny-Mousy and the Beetle
Dined, and danced upon their heads
Till they toddled to their beds.

Following Edward Lear and Lewis Carroll came Laura E. Richards, W. S. Gilbert, and Hilaire Belloc. Mrs. Richards' "Eletelphony" appears in many anthologies as well as in her own volume *Tirra Lirra* (52). Among the more recent writers of nonsense are John Ciardi, Theodore Roethke, and Arnold Spilka.

John Ciardi is well known to adult readers of poetry. For children he writes lyrical nonsense about dancing creatures who are curiously like themselves. A favorite is *The Man Who Sang the Sillies* (10):

THE MAN WHO SANG THE SILLIES

Oh, the Sillies are the sweetest that i know;
They have grins as big as tickles,
They have titters up their sleeves,
They make faces dill as pickles,
And they spin like autumn leaves,
They have cheeks as red as cherry,
And they're always losing shoes,
    But they're very very very
        Easy to amuse.
            . . . [P. 9]

A later nonsense book by Ciardi is *Someone Could Win a Polar Bear* (11).

Theodore Roethke, who won the Pulitzer Prize for poetry in 1953, also wrote for children in *I Am! Says the Lamb* (55). Among his strange and hilarious creatures is:

THE YAK

There was a most odious Yak
Who took only toads on his Back:

If you asked for a ride,
He would act very snide,
And go humping off, yicketty-yak. [P. 178]

Arnold Spilka is the artist and poet of *Once Upon a Horse* (61), *A Lion I Can Do Without* (60), and other nonsense poetry. His *A Rumbudgin of Nonsense* (62) is a celebration of the ridiculous that combines the absurd with the real in humor. One of its more whimsical poems is

A Zinzerfoo
Upon a fan
Sat thimbing of three other am.

Said Zinzerfoo,
"If I bidee,
Can Snufflefalls
So vender me?"

"They surely can,
Of Zinzerfoo,"
Said three am then
"Because it's true!"

So thue it was
And fump it is
That all of em
Are happy is.

Poems of Rhyme, Rhythm, and Repetition

Poems of rhyme, rhythm, and repetition appeal to children especially when they are read aloud. The first two examples given here especially lend themselves to verse speaking or choral reading. But in any case, a child should not meet these poems first of all on the printed page. Rather, he should hear them well read, either by the teacher or on a recording.

Vachel Lindsay once said that poems should be danced as they were chanted. This idea would apply to his own poem "The Mysterious Cat" (31), which lends itself also to dramatization as the group chants the lines.

THE MYSTERIOUS CAT

I saw a proud, mysterious cat,
I saw a proud, mysterious cat
Too proud to catch a mouse or rat—
Mew, mew, mew.

But catnip she would eat, and purr,
But catnip she would eat, and purr.
And goldfish she did much prefer—
Mew, mew, mew.

I saw a cat—'twas but a dream.
I saw a cat—'twas but a dream
Who scorned the slave that brought her cream—
Mew, mew, mew.

Unless the slave were dressed in style,
Unless the slave were dressed in style
And knelt before her all the while—
Mew, mew, mew.

Did you ever hear of a thing like that?
Did you ever hear of a thing like that?
Did you ever hear of a thing like that?
Oh, what a proud, mysterious cat.
Oh, what a proud, mysterious cat.
Oh, what a proud, mysterious cat.
Mew. . . mew . . . mew. [Pp. 38–39]

Although children are thought to be wary of long polysyllabic words, it makes a difference if they are tongue tickling and laugh provoking. Arthur Guiterman in both his *The Laughing Muse* (21) and *The Mirthful Lyre* (22) uses words that are unexpected and help to make a situation amusing. In the poem "Strictly Germproof" there are long technical words, but the reader is not too disturbed if he does not know their exact meaning. It is possible that children will be intrigued into using a dictionary to discover what some of the words mean. The situation is clear, and there is no doubt about the action and the outcome, since the Bunny, the Baby, and the Prophylactic Pup all live happily together ever after.

STRICTLY GERMPROOF

The Antiseptic Baby and the Prophylactic Pup
Were playing in the garden when the Bunny gamboled up;
They looked upon the Creature with a loathing undisguised;—
It wasn't Disinfected and it wasn't Sterilized.

. . .

There's not a Micrococcus in the garden where they play;
They bathe in pure iodoform a dozen times a day;
And each imbibes his rations from a Hygienic Cup—
The Bunny and the Baby and the Prophylactic Pup. [Pp. 11–12]

Another quite different type of poem seems to belong in this category because of its musical qualities. This type of poem can be used for choral reading or speaking because it has antiphonal lines. For those who already know and love the sea, "Shell Castles" (7) may bring back memories. For those who have never seen or heard the sea, it creates some of the sensuous feeling of both the sound and sight of the seashore. It might inspire children to create music that would be appropriate for it. With a skillful music teacher children can broaden their experience to combine music and poetry. Rowena Bastin Bennett is the author of this imaginative poem.

SHELL CASTLES

A sea shell is a castle
Where a million echoes roam,
    A wee castle,
    Sea castle,
Tossed up by the foam;
    A wee creature's.
    Sea creature's,
Long deserted home.

. . .

But my ears cannot distinguish
    The words it sings to me,
        The sea shell,
        The wee shell,
    I hold so reverently,
And I only hear a whisper
Like the ghost voice of the sea. [Pp. 26, 29]

Nature and the Out-of-Doors

Robert Frost's "The Last Word of a Bluebird" (19) describes in a different way the passage of summer and fall with the arrival of winter not far away.

THE LAST WORD OF A BLUEBIRD

As I went out a Crow
In a low voice said "Oh,
I was looking for you.
How do you do?
I just came to tell you
To tell Lesley (will you?)
That her little Bluebird
Wanted me to bring word
That the north wind last night
That made the stars bright

And made ice on the trough
Almost made him cough
His tail feathers off.
He just had to fly!
But he sent her Good-by,
And said to be good,
And wear her red hood,
And look for skunk tracks
In the snow with an ax—
And do everything!
And perhaps in the spring
He would come back and sing!" [P. 160]

Found not too long ago by accident in an old cupboard in England was a book of poems written in France—each one the prayer of an animal. The author's name is Carmen Bernos de Gasztold. Rumer Godden, the well-known English author who found the book of poems, has translated them in a book called *Prayers from the Ark* (13). Here is the poem about the ducks:

THE PRAYER OF THE LITTLE DUCKS

Dear God,
Give us a flood of water.
Let it rain tomorrow and always.
Give us plenty of little slugs
and other luscious things to eat.
Protect all folk who quack
and everyone who knows how to swim.
Amen [P. 25]

There are twenty-seven prayers in all. Children will especially enjoy those about animals they know. These might include the dog, the goldfish, the little pig, the donkey, the bee, the monkey, the butterfly, the giraffe, the cat, the mouse, the elephant, the ant, and the old horse. With a younger group of children it would be interesting after reading several of the poems to let them suggest what they think the animal's wish might be before the poem is read. If there are children in the group who are studying French, they will be interested in reading the French captions under the pictures.

In strong contrast to "The Prayer of the Little Ducks" is the poem "Crickets" (34) by David T. McCord. Anyone who has ever heard a cricket will chuckle to think of this insect as a ticket taker. But then he may feel a bit sorry for the cricket and for all other insects and living creatures when the summer is over. Children might make an insect menagerie of poems about the ant, the grasshopper, the bee, the firefly—and others that are to be found where they live.

CRICKETS

all busy punching tickets,
clicking their little punches.
The tickets come in bunches,
good for a brief excursion,
good for a cricket's version
of travel (before it snows) to
the places a cricket goes to.
Alas! the crickets sing alas
in the dry September grass.
Alas, alas, in every acre,
every one a ticket-taker. [P. 99]

Harry Behn, who wrote "The Last Leaf" (5), is thinking about other things that happen in autumn. The best time to read this poem would be when the last leaf is about to fall. From the window or walking home from school, each child may have his own special spot to report on.

THE LAST LEAF

A few leaves stay for a while on the trees
After their color begins to turn,
And no other leaves seem as gold as these
Not even the ones our bonfires burn
With golden flames in piles on the ground.

A few leaves stay so long that I found
The one last leaf on a tree in the snow,
And when a galloping wind came round
The edge of our house and started to blow
Snow dust to sparkles floating free,

When the wind ran away, almost with me,
And sunshine settled quiet and cold,
There, like a bird, still on the tree
Was that lonesome leaf, no longer gold
But curly and brown and dry and old. [P. 53]

If children live in Florida, California, the Hawaiian Islands, or in some of the larger cities of the United States, they may find performing dolphins. "Dolphins in Blue Water" (33) by Amy Lowell uses just the right words to give an exact picture of the movements of the dolphin. This poem creates an experience as exciting as if we were watching the dolphin ourselves.

DOLPHINS IN BLUE WATER

Hey! Crackerjack—jump!
Blue water,
Pink water,
Swirl, flick, flitter;
Snout into a wave-trough,
Plunge, curl.
Bow over,
Under,
Razor-cut and tumble.
Roll, turn—
Straight—and shoot at the sky,
All rose-flame drippings.
Down ring,
Drop,
Nose under,
Hoop,
Tail,
Dive,
And gone;
With smooth over-swirlings of blue water,
Oil-smooth cobalt.
Slipping, liquid lapis lazuli,
Emerald shadings,
Tintings of pink and ochre.
Prismatic slidings
Underneath a windy sky. [P. 224]

Storytelling Poems

Ballads are the earliest forms of poetry still in use in schools today. Many of the early ballads told the sad story of someone who was killed in battle, lost his true love, or was overcome by some great misfortune. "Sir Patrick Spence" (70) drowned with all his men when their ship went down. The treachery of a sister against sister is told in "The Twa Sisters" (70). Unusual in its humor is the well-known ballad, "Get up and Bar the Door" (70), with its argument between husband and wife. Sir Walter Scott's ballad "Lochinvar" (70) has a happy ending, after the exciting theft of the bride. It is a good example of the ballad in relatively modern times. Alfred Noyes has more recently used the ballad form with success in such poems as "A Song of Sherwood" (43) and the famous tragic tale of "The Highwayman" (44).

The United States owes a debt of gratitude to John A. Lomax and his son Allan, who roamed the United States to collect folk songs and ballads of the people in the Appalachian Mountains, of the workers on the railroads and in the lumber camps, and especially of the cowboys in the cattle country. Many of these are now available in the Library of Congress. In 1925 John A. Lomax and Allan Lomax published a volume entitled *Cowboy Songs, and Other Frontier Ballads* (32). The music for the most widely known ballads was frequently included. Typical is the ballad entitled "The Kansas Line" (32).

THE KANSAS LINE

. . .

The cowboy's life is a dreadful life,
He's driven through heat and cold;
I'm almost froze with the water on my clothes,
A-ridin' through heat and cold.

I've been where the lightnin', the lightnin'
tangled in my eyes,
The cattle I could scarcely hold;
Think I heard my boss man say:
"I want all brave-hearted men who ain't afraid to
die
To whoop up the cattle from morning till night,
Way up on the Kansas line."
. . . [P. 22]

Poetry for Children of the Space Age

A poem, in fact, is very much like you, and that is quite natural, since there is a rhythm in your own body: in your pulse, in your heart beat, in the way you breathe, laugh, or cry; in the very way you speak . . . . Many kinds of rhythms surround us every day of our lives, although we go on our way unaware of them until a poem comes along to bring the hidden music out into the open . . . [37]

Children of today belong to the next century, but poetry is ageless. It has come down to this generation as to all preceding generations from the beginnings of history. Singing and chanting developed into ballads that provide both literary and historical records of our early ancestors.

Poetry can do things for children and young people, and even for older people who never learned to like it as children. It can re-create, refresh, and relax. It can provide for personal choice and for sharing, and can help the listener or reader to recall a special feeling, a situation, an experience, or it may offer an entirely new way of looking at a familiar happening.

Every teacher who is trying to bring children and poetry together needs to know about the child as a person. The child moves, uses his hands, sees, tastes, smells, hears, listens, wonders, imitates, evaluates, using every possible avenue of learning. Each child chooses those roads to learning that are best for him. It is the teacher's responsibility to find the kind of poetry that will interest each child.

Little children respond to poetry as they respond to music. Four-year-old David was riding with his parents and a family friend up Franklin Mountain one summer evening. A brand new moon was lying on the curving shoulder of the mountain. Then from one of the grownups came this poem by Vachel Lindsay (31):

THE MOON'S THE NORTH WIND'S COOKY

The Moon's the North Wind's cooky.
He bites it day by day,
Until there's but a rim of scraps
That crumble all away.

The South Wind is a baker.
He kneads clouds in his den,
And bakes a crisp new moon *that . . . greedy*
North . . . Wind . . . eats . . . again! [Pp. 25–26]

David commanded, "Say it again." Out came the poem a second time. "Say it again." David's friend turned toward him and repeated the lines again. The poem was recited nine times in all, sometimes as a duet, enjoying the ideas, the pictures, and the pauses, as they experimented with various ways of sharing it.

When they reached home, David's father carried the sleepy little boy upstairs and put him to bed in his own room where the moon was shining in. His father and mother heard David saying some of the poem's words as he dropped off to sleep.

In the morning when David wakened, he fairly shouted to his father, "Daddy, come here!" When his father came, David exclaimed, "Daddy, I know that poem!" And he said it word for word.

Several weeks later when David's father returned from a trip, the little boy confided, "Daddy, I made up my own poem. Do you want to hear it?" This is the poem:

I must hurry, hurry, hurry
I must hurry,
The great big sea is calling me.

Little Golden Duck is floating down the stream
I hope he takes me to the sea
And the sea takes me to the ocean.

The great big sea is too much for me
The great big sea is playing with me
It bites me and throws me into the air.

A week later when David's friend came to have dinner with the family, David climbed into a big chair with her and remarked, "I can say that poem." And say it he did.

A modern-day poet called Frederick Winsor has rewritten Mother Goose rhymes as science fiction in *The Space Child's Mother Goose* (69). The author has bridged the centuries, using an old well-known rhyme as a pattern for telescoping time and space.

Solomon Grundy
Walked on Monday
Rode on Tuesday
Motored Wednesday
Planed on Thursday
Rocketed Friday
Spaceship Saturday
Time Machine Sunday
Where is the end for
Solomon Grundy? [No. 22]

Children want to be where the action is, and today's action is out in space with the astronauts. Children of these later years of the twentieth century are children of the earth, sky, sea, air, sun, moon, stars, constellations—of outer space itself. Largely because of television, they are more knowledgeable, science minded, resourceful, and world oriented than children were in the past. They are characterized by curiosity and are unafraid of the century ahead, which some adults look forward to with dread. At the same time, they can be fascinated with the past or be interested in the real people of today. They may also enjoy both fantasy and reality and may take humor or sadness in their stride when they find these qualities in poetry.

Modern children interested in flying may read in that biographical volume, *A Book of Americans* (6) by Rosemary and Stephen Vincent Benét, a poem about the Wright brothers entitled "Wilbur Wright and Orville Wright." It tells the story of a conversation between the two brothers as they made their historic flight. Or they could read John Ciardi's space poem, "The Pinwheel's Song" (10), which leaves much to the imagination as the varicolored pinwheels are launched and finally fall short of the moon.

THE PINWHEEL'S SONG

Seven around the moon go up
    (Light the fuse and away we go)
Two in silver and two in red
And two in blue, and one went dead.
    Six around the moon.

. . .

Two around the moon, well, well.
    Two to reach the moon.
But Silver turned left, and Red turned right,
And CRASH! they splattered all over the night
    Falling away from the moon.

None of them going as far as the moon?
    None of them going that far?
Quick! Somebody light me another fuse.
But I'm all burned out . . . it's just no use. . . .
    It's really
        too far
            to
                the
                    moo. . . . [Pp. 22–23]

A recent poem, "How Strange It Is" (29) by Claudia Lewis, expresses the feelings not only of children, but of adults as well, as they read, listen to television, or talk with friends about the happenings in the world above and around the earth.

HOW STRANGE IT IS

In the sky
Soft clouds are blowing by.
Nothing more can I see
In the blue air over me.

Yet I know that planetoids and rocket cones,
Telstars studded with blue stones,
And many hundred bits of fins
And other man-made odds and ends
Are wheeling round me out in space
At a breathless astronautic pace.

How strange it is to know
That while I watch the soft clouds blow
So many things I cannot see
Are passing by right over me. [P. 9]

Poems of Travel

Children of today have seen more of the United States and of foreign lands than those who lived ten years ago. Nevertheless there are some values and some experiences that do not change with time. A good many years ago Robert Louis Stevenson wrote for children who had seldom visited other countries of the world. His description of many of the sights and sounds are still realistic, although some of the places have changed with the years. The poem "Travel" (63) tells what he would have liked to see.

For the vast majority of contemporary children, the automobile and the truck have the most meaningful travel experiences to offer. In his poem "Trucks" (65) James S. Tippett wrote down-to-earth lines that enable children to have a vicarious experience.

TRUCKS

Big trucks for the steel beams,
Big trucks for coal,
Rumbling down the broad streets,
Heavily they roll.

Little trucks for groceries,
Little trucks for bread,
Turning into every street,
Rushing on ahead.

Big trucks, little trucks,
In never ending lines,
Rumble on and rush ahead
While I read their signs. [P. 18]

And Tom Prideaux, in *On City Streets; an Anthology of Poetry* (26), describes city sounds:

BROADWAY: TWILIGHT

Roaring, clanking,
Sirens screaming
In confusion;
Pink and yellow,
Shifting, gleaming
In profusion.

Above the deepening blue
The stars blink calmly through.

Children as the Poet Sees Them

Leland B. Jacobs, a professor of children's literature turned poet in the past few years, has the insight to express what children feel but may not be able to put into their own words. The poem "Wishing" (24) speaks for itself:

WISHING

I wish I had a kitten,
    I wish I had a dog,
I wish I had a crocodile,
    Or a pollywog.

I wish I had a magic hat,
    A magic cloak and stick,
I wish I had an uncle
    Who could do a magic trick.

I wish I had a sailing ship
    That had a jolly crew—
I wish I had a wish, for once,
    That really would come true. [P. 29]

Gwendolyn Brooks writes not only for Black children, but for all children growing up in the world today. She has a keen understanding of what children are like and what they like. Her poems in *Bronzeville Boys and Girls* (8) enable children to find verse about other children appropriate for any place or any hour of the day.

THE ADMIRATION OF WILLIE

Grown folks are wise
About tying ties
And baking cakes
And chasing aches,
Building walls
And finding balls
And making planes
And cars and trains—
And kissing children into bed
After their prayers are said. [P. 40]

How Children See Their World

Children have written and are writing today about their own experiences. Other children have seen their poems in magazines or in collections made and published by individual schools or school systems.

One of the most recent books of poems written for children is that by Richard Lewis, entitled *Miracles* (30). Included are poems that the author collected in many parts of the world. Such a volume gives a feeling of accomplishment to any boy or girl whose writing is included. Some well-known poet of the future may be getting his start by seeing his name and poem in print. Many poems represent the United States in this collection, two of which appear below. Each one is quite different. And each one is highly personalized. They do not have rhyme, but they have rhythm and a poetic use of language to convey their feelings.

WHAT'S NIGHT TO ME

Sam Gilford Age 8 United States

Night is a beautiful thing,
One big black ball
As the clouds push it around.
Sometimes I think I am being rolled over by it.
Sometimes I think it's smiling at me.
The moon is the nose
The stars are the mouth.
And it is drinking the Milky Way.
Sometimes I dream that it will swallow me.
Night is the time for dreams.
Not day dreams but night dreams. [P. 210]

WHEN I LEARNED TO WHISTLE

Gordon Lea Age 11 United States

I remember the day when I learned to whistle,
It was in Spring and new sounds were all around.
I was five or six and my front teeth were missing,
But I blew until my cheeks stuck out.

I remember walking up and down the block,
Trying to impress those who heard me
With the tunes and sounds that came from my mouth,
For I sounded much better than the birds in the trees.

I remember being hurt, for nobody seemed to care,
And then I met an old man who stopped and smiled.
He too blew until his cheeks stuck out.
He sounded just like me, for his front teeth were missing. [P. 67]

Capturing Children's Interest in Poetry

Sarah Teasdale once said that children should enjoy poetry just as they might enjoy going for a ride in a car: In order to take pleasure in it they do not need to know the mechanism behind it or what the inventor had in mind when he made it. Children need to be exposed to many poems, to hear them read well, and to be able to hear them again and again. For younger children, the poem especially enjoyed may be written on a large chart. For older children a collection of anthologies and books of individual authors should be available for browsing or for locating a poem already enjoyed. Experiences with poetry should be pleasurable and should never be associated with work. Teachers defeat their own purpose if they attempt to analyze the structure or form of the poem other than to show whether it rhymes; what the verse pattern is; and whether it is a ballad, a limerick, a lyric poem, or perhaps a haiku. Children in elementary schools should be asked questions of preference and of feeling rather than of knowing.

From the enjoyment of poetry may come the desire to create one's own poems. One teacher made it possible for any child in his group to drop a copy of what he had written into a special box, knowing that only his understanding teacher would see it. Teachers should accept what children have to offer and then help them to move on in new directions. Children may be stimulated to write poetry by hearing and then by reading poems written by other children, as in *Miracles: Poems by Children of the English Speaking World* (30).

The teacher should be the judge of where and when a poem can best be read, depending upon the experiences children have had with poetry in previous school years. Children should be encouraged to share poems they have come to know in various ways, and they should be encouraged to use a tape recorder and to hear themselves as they sound to others.

Choral speaking is one way of stimulating children's interest in poetry. The aim in the elementary school is not to help children to present a finished production, but rather to get pleasure through joining with other voices to give pleasure to others. Choral speaking provides an opportunity to use the voice like a musical instrument. Boys and girls should understand that this form of expression is a cooperative effort—they speak as one voice by blending voices together.

Poems chosen to be read chorally should be the proper length for the age and the experience of the child. All poems should be rhythmic and should include many words that emphasize sound as in music. In beginning with any group, especially with younger children, the reading should be done in unison. Gradually, children can be divided into groups depending on whether their voices are high, medium, or low.

The teaching of poetry can follow no set pattern. Unless the teacher himself likes and enjoys it, the children will not respond enthusiastically. The teacher's own choice of poetry guides children in building their own individual yardsticks. The good teacher will expand his acquaintance with poems to meet the needs of each child. It is important to build on what experiences children bring with them as they enter school at the beginning of a new school year. Children's own ideas and suggestions must have an important place in planning and carrying out experiences with poetry. Each teacher's own definition of poetry will determine how far he will carry children into the realm of poetry.

Extending Experiences for the Reader

Mother Goose and ABCs

1. Read several versions of the origin of Mother Goose.
2. Plan an exhibit of Mother Goose books. Have the class choose the edition they like the best giving their reasons for their choice.
3. Select four or five Mother Goose rhymes. Find as many variants of each as possible.
4. Find the political significance of a number of rhymes.
5. Use Mother Goose rhymes for speech exercises with the class.
6. Evolve criteria with the group for a good ABC book.
7. Arrange a display of ABC books. Have the group select the book in the display that meets their criteria.

Poetry

1. Select a poem that you feel children would enjoy. Read it several times and memorize it. Try it with a child of the age to enjoy it. Add to your repertoire of memorized poems so that you can share them at any time and at any place with someone who would enjoy them.
2. Choose a poet whom you have never read before, one of the new generation of poets who are writing for themselves, for children, and for adults

as well. Check out the book from the library. Skim through it to find the poems that appeal to you. Give *those* a second chance by rereading them. Choose one to share with the group.

3. Try to remember a poem you especially liked as a child. Do you still enjoy it as much as when you were a child? Less? More? Can you discover a good reason for your reaction?
4. Read the poem "Darius Green and His Flying Machine" (66) by John T. Trowbridge and possibly *Old Greek Folk Stories* (48) by Josephine P. Peabody or any other book of Greek myths that tells the story of Daedalus and Icarus. Does this exploration of the past give you a different feeling about the present? In what way?
5. As individuals or as a group, experiment with listing sounds and putting them together in some meaningful and unique way.
6. Read Edna St. Vincent Millay's poem entitled "The Ballad of the Harp Weaver" (38). The relationship between the mother and the child and the problem they face should remind any reader, especially those interested in children, in a poignant way of the thoughts and feelings of a child. How does the poem make you feel? Does it affect in any way your point of view about children? You might divide into small groups to discuss these questions and others aroused by reading this poem.
7. As a class group, collect as many of the volumes of poetry as are available. Make these books available on a portable library cart, for use during class periods.
8. Collect from the past five years of the magazine *Elementary English* (official publication of the National Council of Teachers of English) new titles of volumes of poetry for children, as they are listed in the section, "Books for Children."
9. Check the magazine *Elementary English* (listed in 8 above) for articles on the teaching of poetry, published in the past five years.
10. Experiment in several small groups within the class in developing ability in choral reading that can be shared with the whole group.
11. Reread the poem "Sounds," on page 194. It was written by a group of teachers sitting in a room, with doors closed, and listening for any audible sound. Encourage each of several small groups to create a comparable poem.

Extending Experiences for Children

Mother Goose and ABCs

1. Divide into groups of four or five and plan dramatizations of Mother Goose rhymes.
2. Select a Mother Goose rhyme to pantomime. Have the class guess what rhyme you represent.
3. Pretend to be a Mother Goose character. Describe yourself without telling who you are and have the class guess what character you are.

4. Dress as Mother Goose characters and have a Mother Goose party. Invite another class to the party. Plan the decor for the party around Mother Goose rhymes.
5. Make shadow boxes of scenes from Mother Goose rhymes.
6. Paint a mural of Mother Goose characters in a procession.
7. Learn to sing some of the Mother Goose rhymes that have been put to music.
8. Decide on a subject—for example, animals, names of automobiles, names of characters in story books, or names of persons in the class—and write an ABC book about it as a class enterprise.

Poetry

1. Compile in list form the suggestions made in this chapter, for children's activities with poetry. Choose several to try out with children in the classroom. Encourage children to suggest other activities they would enjoy, and make a catalogue of them.
2. Dramatize A. A. Milne's *The King's Breakfast.* One child takes the part of the book and reads the narrative. Other children take the parts of the King, the Queen, the Dairymaid, and the Cow and read their respective lines. Children will find that they need practice to do such cooperative reading smoothly. Those who are not reading are the audience.
3. Select a favorite short poem to read to a tape recorder. Does the reader sound like *you* when it is played back? Each child can practice reading aloud to a partner until he is satisfied with the result. Then he reads again to the tape recorder. The whole group will want to listen in when the final taping is played; the class group will try to identify each reader.
4. On a piece of yellow paper, for each child, the teacher, with a medicine dropper, leaves one drop of green ink. Each child folds his paper in the middle; presses it together in all directions; opens the paper; and looks at what he has made. He is encouraged to write a four-line verse about what he imagines the figure to be.
5. Suggest that each child write a verse about something he has seen, heard, felt, touched, tasted, smelled. Encourage each child to share what he has written with the class.
6. After hearing Christina Rossetti's "What is Pink?" (56) read aloud by the teacher, children are invited to use the couplet form to make a rhyme about one of the colors mentioned, or another which the poem did not use.

Chapter References

1. ALEXANDER, ANNE. *ABC of Cars and Trucks.* Garden City, N. Y.: Doubleday, 1956. Paperback. Kindergarten–grade 2.
2. Association for Childhood Education International (comps.). *Sung*

Under the Silver Umbrella. New York: Macmillan, 1935. Kindergarten–grade 6.

3. AUSTIN, MARY. *Children Sing in the Far West.* Boston: Houghton Mifflin, 1928.
4. BARING-GOULD, WILLIAM S., AND CEIL BARING-GOULD (eds.). *The Annotated Mother Goose.* New York: Bramhall House, 1962; New York: Meridan Books, 1967. Paperback.
5. BEHN, HARRY. *Windy Morning.* New York: Harcourt Brace Jovanovich, 1953. Kindergarten–grade 3.
6. BENÉT, ROSEMARY, AND STEPHEN VINCENT BENÉT. *A Book of Americans.* Holt, Rinehart & Winston, 1933. Grade 7 and up.
7. BENNETT, ROWENA BASTIN. *Songs from Around a Toadstool Table.* Chicago: Follett, 1937. Grades 3–4.
8. BROOKS, GWENDOLYN. *Bronzeville Boys and Girls.* New York: Harper & Row, 1956. Grades 3–6.
9. BROWN, MARGARET WISE. *Sleepy ABC.* Esphyr Slobodkin (ill.). New York: Lothrop, Lee & Shepard.
10. CIARDI, JOHN. *The Reason for the Pelican.* Philadelphia: Lippincott, 1959. Grades 4–6.
11. ______. *Someone Could Win a Polar Bear.* E. Gorey (ill.). Philadelphia: Lippincott, 1970. Kindergarten–grade 3.
12. DE ANGELI, MARGUERITE (ed.). *Book of Nursery and Mother Goose Rhymes.* Garden City, N. Y.: Doubleday, 1954. Kindergarten–grade 3.
13. DE GASZTOLD, CARMEN BERNOS. *Prayers from the Ark.* Rumer Godden (tr.). New York: Viking, 1962. n.g.l.
14. DE LA MARE, WALTER. *Complete Poems of Walter de la Mare.* New York: Knopf, 1969. Kindergarten–grade 6.
15. EICHENBERG, FRITZ. *Ape in a Cape: An Alphabet of Odd Animals.* New York: Harcourt Brace Jovanovich, 1952. Preschool–grade 3.
16. FALLS, C. B. *ABC Book.* Garden City, N. Y.: Doubleday, 1957. Preschool.
17. FARJEON, ELEANOR. *Poems for Children.* Philadelphia: Lippincott, 1926.
18. FERRIS, HELEN (comp.). *Favorite Poems Old and New.* Garden City, N. Y.: Doubleday, 1957. Grades 4–8.
19. FROST, ROBERT. *Complete Poems of Robert Frost.* New York: Holt, Rinehart & Winston, 1958.
20. GAG, WANDA. *ABC Bunny.* New York: Coward-McCann, 1933. Kindergarten–grade 2.
21. GUITERMAN, ARTHUR. *The Laughing Muse.* New York: Harper & Row, 1915. Grades 4–8.
22. ______. *The Mirthful Lyre.* New York: Harper & Row.
23. HALLIWELL-PHILLIPPS, JAMES ORCHARD. *Nursery Rhymes of England.* Detroit, Mich.: Singing Tree, 1969.
24. JACOBS, LELAND B. *Is Somewhere Always Far Away?* New York: Holt, Rinehart & Winston, 1967. Kindergarten–grade 3.
25. KNIGHT, HILARY (ed.). *Mother Goose.* New York: Golden Press, 1962.
26. LARRICK, NANCY (ed.). *On City Streets; an Anthology of Poetry.* Philadelphia: Lippincott, 1968. Grades 1–8.

27. LEAR, EDWARD. *ABC.* New York: McGraw-Hill, 1965. Kindergarten–grade 3.

28. ———. *The Complete Nonsense Book.* New York: Dodd, Mead, 1946. Grades 4–6.

29. LEWIS, CLAUDIA. *Poems of Earth and Space.* New York: Dutton, 1967. Grades 3–7.

30. LEWIS, RICHARD. *Miracles: Poems by Children of the English Speaking World.* New York: Simon & Schuster, 1966. Grades 2–6.

31. LINDSAY, VACHEL. *The Congo and Other Poems.* New York: Macmillan, 1914.

32. LOMAX, JOHN A., AND ALLAN LOMAX. *Cowboy Songs, and Other Frontier Ballads.* New York: Macmillan, 1925. Grades 5–8.

33. LOWELL, AMY. *Complete Poems.* Boston: Houghton Mifflin, 1958.

34. MCCORD, DAVID T. *Take Sky.* Boston: Little, Brown, 1961–1962. Grade 4 and up.

35. MCGINLEY, PHYLLIS. *All Around the Town.* Philadelphia: Lippincott, 1948. Kindergarten–grade 3.

36. MERRIAM, EVE. *Catch a Little Rhyme.* New York: Atheneum, 1966. Grades 1–4.

37. ———. *There Is No Rhyme for Silver.* New York: Atheneum, 1962. Grades 3–6.

38. MILLAY, EDNA ST. VINCENT. *The Harp Weaver and Other Poems.* New York: Harper & Row, 1923.

39. *Mother Goose's Quarto: or Melodies Complete.* Boston: Munroe and Francis, 1824, 1833. Reprinted as *Mother Goose's Melodies: Facsimile of the Original Munroe and Francis.* New York: Dover, 1971. Paperback.

40. MUNARI, BRUNO. *Bruno Munari's ABC.* Cleveland and New York: World, 1960. Kindergarten–grade 2.

41. NEWBERRY, CLARE T. *The Kittens' ABC.* New York: Harper & Row, 1964. Preschool–grade 2.

42. NEWBERY, JOHN, *et al.* (eds.). *Original Mother Goose's Melody.* Detroit, Mich.: Singing Tree, 1969; reprint of 1892 ed.

43. NOYES, ALFRED. *Collected Poems.* 2nd ed. Port Washington, N. Y.: McCutcheon, 1966.

44. ———. *The Highwayman.* Young Collectors Series. Englewood Cliffs, N. J.: Prentice-Hall, 1969. Grades 4–9.

45. O'NEILL, MARY. *Hailstones and Halibut Bones.* Garden City, N. Y.: Doubleday, 1961. Kindergarten–grade 5.

46. OPIE, IONA, AND PETER OPIE (eds.). *The Oxford Dictionary of Nursery Rhymes.* New York and Oxford, England: Oxford University Press, 1951. Preschool–grade 3.

47. ———. *The Oxford Nursery Rhyme Book.* New York and Oxford, England: Oxford University Press, 1955. Preschool–grade 3.

48. PEABODY, JOSEPHINE P. *Old Greek Folk Stories.* Boston: Houghton Mifflin, 1897.

49. PERRAULT, CHARLES. *Histoires ou Contes du Temps Passé: des Moralites.* 1697. Reprinted as *Perrault's Fairy Tales.* A. E. Johnson and S. R. Littlewood (trs.). Gustave Doré (ill.). New York: Dover, 1971. Paperback.

50. PETERSHAM, MAUD, AND MISKA PETERSHAM. *An American ABC.* New York: Macmillan, 1941. Kindergarten–grade 3.
51. *The Real Mother Goose.* Blanche Fisher Wright (ill.). Chicago: Rand McNally, 1916. Preschool–grade 1.
52. RICHARDS, LAURA E. *Tirra Lirra.* Boston: Little, Brown, 1955. Kindergarten–grade 3.
53. *Ring o' Roses.* L. Leslie Brooke (ill.). New York: Frederick Warne, 1922. Grades 1–4.
54. RITSON, JOSEPH. *Gammer Gurton's Garland.* New York: AMS Press, n.d. Reprint of 1910 ed.
55. ROETHKE, THEODORE. *The Collected Poems of Theodore Roethke.* New York: Doubleday.
56. ROSSETTI, CHRISTINA. "What Is Pink?" in *Sing-Song.* New York: Macmillan, 1925.
57. SANDBURG, CARL. *Complete Poems.* New York: Harcourt Brace Jovanovich, 1950.
58. SEUSS, DR. *Dr. Seuss's ABC.* New York: Random House, 1963. Kindergarten–grade 3.
59. SMITH, JESSIE WILCOX. *Jessie Wilcox Smith's Little Mother Goose.* New York: Dodd, Mead, 1954, 1971. Grades 1–3.
60. SPILKA, ARNOLD. *A Lion I Can Do Without.* New York: Walck, 1964. Kindergarten–grade 3.
61. ———. *Once Upon a Horse.* New York: Walck, 1966. Kindergarten–grade 3.
62. ———. *A Rumbudgin of Nonsense.* New York: Scribner, 1970. Kindergarten–grade 3.
63. STEVENSON, ROBERT LOUIS. *A Child's Garden of Verses.* New York: Macmillan. Preschool–grade 3.
64. *The Tall Book of Mother Goose.* Feodor Rojankovsky (ill.). New York: Harper & Row, 1942. Preschool–grade 1.
65. TIPPETT, JAMES S. *I Go A-Traveling.* New York: Harper & Row, 1929.
66. TROWBRIDGE, JOHN T. "Darius Green and His Flying Machine," in Curry and Clippenger, *Children's Literature.* Chicago: Rand McNally, 1923.
67. UNTERMEYER, LOUIS (ed.). *This Singing World.* New York: Harcourt Brace Jovanovich, 1923.
68. WILDSMITH, BRIAN (ed.). *Mother Goose: A Collection of Nursery Rhymes.* New York: Watts, 1964.
69. WINSOR, FREDERICK. *The Space Child's Mother Goose.* New York: Simon & Schuster, 1958. Paperback. n.g.l.
70. WITHAM, R. ADELAIDE. *English and Scottish Popular Ballads.* Boston: Houghton Mifflin, 1909.

More Books for Children

More Nursery Rhymes, Mother Goose, and ABCs

ANGLUND, JOAN WALSH. *In a Pumpkin Shell: A Mother Goose ABC.* New York: Harcourt Brace Jovanovich, 1960.

BECKER, MAY LAMBERTON. *The Rainbow Mother Goose.* Lili Cassel (ill.). Cleveland: World Publishing, 1947.

BISHOP, ANN. *Riddle-culous Ridalphabet Book.* Chicago: Whitman, 1971.

The Boyd Smith Mother Goose. Collated and verified by Laurence Elmendorf. E. Boyd Smith (ill.). New York: Putnam, 1919.

CHARDIET, BERNICE. *C Is For Circus.* New York: Walker, 1971.

CHWAST, SEYMOUR. *Still Another Alphabet Book.* Seymour Chwast and Martin Stephen Moskof (ills.). New York: McGraw-Hill, 1969.

DOMANSKA, JANINA (reteller). *If All the Seas Were One Sea.* New York: Macmillan, 1971.

FALLON, ROBERT. *Zoophabet.* Indianapolis: Bobbs-Merrill, 1971.

FYLEMAN, ROSE (tr.). *Picture Rhymes from Foreign Lands.* Valery Carrick (ill.). Philadelphia: Lippincott, 1935.

GALDONE, PAUL. *The Life of Jack Sprat, His Wife and His Cat.* New York: McGraw-Hill, 1969.

The Gay Mother Goose. Françoise (ill.). New York: Scribner, 1938.

HOLL, ADELAIDE. *Hide and Seek ABC.* New York: Platt & Munk, 1971.

LANG, ANDREW (ed.). *Nursery Rhyme Book.* L. Leslie Brooke (ill.). New York: Frederick Warne, 1947.

LEACH, MARIA. *Riddle Me, Riddle Me, Ree.* New York: Viking, 1970.

LINES, KATHLEEN. *Lavender's Blue.* Harold Jones (ill.). New York: Watts, 1954.

MENDOZA, GEORGE. *The Christmas Tree Alphabet Book.* Cleveland: World Publishing, 1971.

MILES, MISKA. *The Apricot ABC.* Boston: Little, Brown, 1969.

MONTRESOR, BENI. *A for Angel Beni Montresor's A.B.C. Picture Stories.* New York: Knopf, 1969.

MOORE, MARGARET, AND JOHN TRAVERS. *Certainly Carrie, Cut the Cake: Poems A to Z.* Indianapolis: Bobbs-Merrill, 1971.

Mother Goose: Seventy-Seven Verses. Tasha Tudor (ill.). New York: Walck, 1944.

OPIE, IONA (ed.). *Ditties for the Nursery.* Monica Walters (ill.). New York: Oxford University Press, 1954.

PARSON, VIRGINIA. *Animal Parade.* Garden City, N. Y.: Doubleday, 1970.

PEPPE, RODNEY (comp.). *Hey Riddle Diddle.* Rodney Peppe (ill.). New York: Holt, Rinehart & Winston, 1971.

REED, PHILLIP. *Mother Goose and Nursery Rhymes.* New York: Atheneum, 1963.

SCHMIDERER, DOROTHY. *The Alphabeast Book: An Abccedarium.* New York: Holt, Rinehart & Winston, 1971.

WELSH, CHARLES. *Rhymes from Mother Goose.* Boston: Heath.

WERNER, JANE (ed.). *The Golden Mother Goose.* Alice Provensen and Martin Provensen (ills.). New York: Simon & Schuster, 1948.

WITHERS, CARL (comp.). *A Rocket in My Pocket: The Rhymes and Chants of Young Americans.* Susanne Suba (ill.). New York: Holt, Rinehart & Winston.

WYNDHAM, ROBERT (ed.). *Chinese Mother Goose Rhymes.* Ed Young (ill.). Cleveland: World Publishing, 1968.

More Poetry for Children

ALDIS, DOROTHY. *All Together: A Child's Treasury of Verse.* New York: Putnam, 1925; 1952. Grades 1–4.

ARBUTHNOT, MAY HILL (ed.). *Time for Poetry.* Glenview, Ill.: Scott, Foresman, 1952. n.g.l.

BARUCH, DOROTHY W. *I Would Like to Be a Pony and Other Wishes.* New York: Harper & Row, 1959. Kindergarten–grade 5.

BREWTON, JOHN E. (ed.). *Under the Tent of the Sky.* New York: Macmillan, 1937. Grades 4–6.

BROWN, MARGARET WISE. *Nibble, Nibble.* New York: Addison-Wesley, 1959. Kindergarten–grade 5.

BROWNING, ROBERT. HAROLD JONES (ed.). *The Pied Piper of Hamelin.* Harold Jones (ill.). New York: Watts, 1962. Kindergarten–grade 3.

COATSWORTH, ELIZABETH. *Poems.* New York: Macmillan, 1957. Grades 4–6.

DE REGNIERS, BEATRICE SCHENK, AND IRENE HAAS. *Something Special.* New York: Harcourt Brace Jovanovich, 1958. Kindergarten–grade 3.

DUNNING, STEPHEN, *et al.* (eds.). *Reflections on a Gift of Watermelon Pickle and Other Modern Verse.* New York: Lothrop, Lee & Shepard, 1967. Grade 7 and up.

ELKIN, R. H. (tr.). *Old Dutch Nursery Rhymes.* Harold Jones (ill.). New York: Watts, 1954. n.g.l.

FIELD, RACHEL. *Taxis and Toadstools.* Garden City, N. Y.: Doubleday, 1926. Grades 3–6.

FISHER, AILEEN. *Cricket in a Thicket.* New York: Scribner, 1963. Kindergarten–grade 3.

FYLEMAN, ROSE. *Fairies and Chimneys.* Garden City, N. Y.: Doubleday, 1929; 1944. Grades 4–5.

KOCH, KENNETH. *Wishes, Lies, and Dreams.* New York: Random House, n.d. Paperback. n.g.l.

LARRICK, NANCY (ed.). *Green Is Like a Meadow of Grass.* Champaign, Ill.: Garrard, 1968. Grades 1–7.

———. *Piping Down the Valleys Wild.* New York: Delacorte, 1968. Grades 3–6.

LEWIS, C. S. (ed.). *There Are Two Lives: Poems by Children of Japan.* New York: Simon and Flynn, 1970. n.g.l.

MARY-ROUSSELIERE, GUY. *Beyond the High Hills: A Book of Eskimo Poems.* Cleveland: World Publishing, 1971. Grades 3–7.

MILNE, A. A. *When We Were Very Young.* New York: Dell, 1970. Paperback. Grades 1–6.

NASH, OGDEN (ed.). *Everybody Ought to Know.* Philadelphia: Lippincott, 1961. Grades 7–11.

REEVES, JAMES. *Prefabulous Animiles.* New York: Dutton, 1960. n.g.l.

SMITH, WILLIAM JAY. *Typewriter Town.* New York: Dutton, 1960. n.g.l.

STARBIRD, KAY. *Don't Ever Cross a Crocodile.* Philadelphia: Lippincott, 1936; 1963. Kindergarten–grade 3.

WELLES, WINIFRED. *Skipping Along Alone.* New York: Macmillan, 1931. n.g.l.

WERTHEIM, B. (ed.). *Talkin' About Us.* New York: Hawthorn, n.d. n.g.l.

From *The Story of Babar* by Jean de Brunhoff.

9

Picture-Story Books

Picture-story books are a happy combination of the pictorial arts and the writing arts which when properly combined produce a distinctive kind of literature. The art and the writing are so closely integrated that together they tell a story that holds to the criteria of good literature.

The age range for the picture-story books begins with the child just old enough to hear a story or to hold a book and usually extends to the third or fourth grade. Many older children and adults still enjoy a good picture-story book. Often the book intended to be read to the younger child [for example, *Pantaloni* (110) by Bettina Ehrlich] may be too difficult for him to read to himself until much later. Others use a simple vocabulary or a small amount of text that can be read by beginning readers.

Young listeners and readers want action. If it is not there they make it up. Their concern is what is going to happen next and how the story is going to end. In the best of picture-story books young children can often "read" the action through the art.

The young listener or reader also wants the story to take him beyond himself into an imaginary world where he can identify with the hero around whom the story revolves. There is no limit to who might be the hero of a picture-story book. The hero is a Scottie in Marjorie Flack's *Angus and the Ducks* (132), a little house in Virginia Lee Burton's *The Little House* (57), and a Japanese boy in Taro Yashima's *Crow Boy* (322). Frequently the more unusual the hero and the place, the more enjoyable the story. At the same time the more familiar the hero, the more inclined the young listeners and readers are to identify with him.

Young children also enjoy having picture-story books read to them. They begin to have favorite stories that they like to hear again and again. Soon they repeat with the reader certain favorite words, phrases, and rhymes. Many children memorize and dramatize these stories.

Today, publishers of children's books make available a large collection of picture-story books for young children to enjoy. Imaginative literary style, artistic illustrations, and beautiful bookmaking combine to make joyful experiences for children of all ages.

Early Beginnings

Previous to the twentieth century, the few picture-story books available of outstanding quality were imported from Europe. At the end of the nineteenth and into the twentieth century L. Leslie Brooke kept alive the tradition of the great English book artists of the nineteenth century—Walter Crane, Randolph Caldecott, and Kate Greenaway. It was during the last half of the century and the beginning of the twentieth century that these great artists made their significant contributions to children's literature.

WALTER CRANE (1845–1915), son of an artist, reared in an artistic environment, showed an interest in drawing at an early age. As a young man he was apprenticed to an engraver. After his apprenticeship he joined evening classes at a well-known art school in London. His first independent art work was designing the paper covers of cheap railway novels published by Edmund Evans, the English color printer who violently opposed the crude illustrations in children's books. The prominent London publisher Frederick Warne also recognized the need for improved illustrations, and Walter Crane's first nursery books were published by Frederick Warne's firm. Crane especially enjoyed drawing animals and outdoor scenes and frequently decorated the pages with elaborate borders. In his first picture-story book he used flat, bright colors and bold lines. He planned his text and illustrations with great care to ensure a harmony between them. Crane's *The Fairy Ship* (1869), *The Baby's Opera* (1877), *The Baby's Bouquet* (1879), *The Baby's Aesop* (1886), and *Flora's Feast* are rare treats of decorative book production.

RANDOLPH CALDECOTT (1846–1886), an outstanding English illustrator, was born in Chester. As a young boy, he liked to draw animals, model in clay, and carve wooden figures. At fifteen he went to work in a bank in Shropshire. The English countryside fascinated him, and he spent all of his spare time in the out-of-doors sketching

From *The Three Jovial Huntsmen* by Randolph Caldecott.

animals, people, and landscapes. He was then transferred to a bank in Manchester where he attended the Manchester School of Art. Although he missed the Shropshire countryside he continued with his sketching, modeling, and wood carving.

In 1870, determined to pursue a career in art, Caldecott went to London where he had already made connections with publishers through his illustrations. He soon made the acquaintance of people in art and publishing circles in London and began to contribute to the *London Graphic, Punch, Harper's Monthly Magazine,* and *The Daily Graphic of New York.*

While spending three summers at the cottage of his close friend and editor Henry Blackburn, he worked on illustrations for Washington Irving's *Christmas at Bracebridge Hall* (189). In partnership with the engraver Edmund Evans, he produced such beautiful picture books as *John Gilpin* (62), *The House That Jack Built* (61), *The Three Jovial Huntsmen* (64), *A Frog He Would a-Wooing Go* (59), *Sing a Song for Sixpence* (63), and "The Great Panjandrum Himself" (60).

The aura of rural living with its action, humor, robust characters, and English landscapes is captured in Caldecott's illustrations.

Caldecott and his wife made a trip to Florida desperately hoping to improve his ill health but he died in St. Augustine at the age of 40. The Caldecott Medal is named in honor of this outstanding English illustrator of children's literature.

KATE GREENAWAY (1846–1901) was the third member of the illustrious trio of English illustrators. Miss Greenaway was born in London in the same year as was Randolph Caldecott. Her interest in drawing gardens and flowers and happy children started early in life. When she was twelve years old she began to take art lessons: she later studied at the Slade Art School in London. She painted in watercolors and drew Christmas cards, valentines, and magazine sketches before illustrating books for children. There is delicacy about Kate Greenaway's drawing of flowers and gardens and flower-like children dressed in the style of a previous period. Miss Greenaway often wrote verses to accompany her pictures. Her first book, published in 1879, was *Under the Window* (165). Among her other books were *The Language of Flowers, with Value Guide* (163) in 1884, *Marigold Garden* (164) in 1885, and *A—Apple Pie* (162) in 1886.

An English portrait painter and water colorist, L. LESLIE BROOKE began his career by illustrating the works of other writers. His illustrations in George MacDonald's *The Light Princess* (232), in Mary Louisa Molesworth's numerous stories, and in *The Nursery Rhyme Book* (210), edited by Andrew Lang, hold a place of their own among the illustrations to be found in children's books at the turn of the century.

In 1903 Brooke wrote and illustrated his own *Johnny Crow's Garden* (40). His skill in portraying the personalities and feelings of animals and his artistic use of line and color have made a distinguished place for him as both a storyteller and illustrator.

In *Johnny Crow's Garden*, the reader has only to follow the sign that says,

> This way to
> Johnny Crow's
> Garden [unpaged]

to arrive at the gate with the welcome sign over it. Each animal takes on a distinct personality through his facial expression. The lion thinks he is the head of the party until the bear "who had nothing to wear" is measured for an outfit. At the right time with the right expression, Johnny Crow appears and gives the story a happy ending

From *Johnny Crow's Party* by L. Leslie Brooke.

by letting his guests out of the stocks into which the wily fox had locked them all.

Because Johnny Crow had a garden, it is only natural that he should have a garden party, which is described in *Johnny Crow's Party* (42). A delightful time is had by all the guests except for the cock, who "Had a very nasty knock" (unpaged) when the rake fell on him. "So the Hen said: 'We'll never come again to Johnny Crow's Garden!'" (unpaged). The expressions on the faces of the hen and the cock are the epitomy of Brooke's skill in showing the feelings of his characters.

In 1935 L. Leslie Brooke added *Johnny Crow's New Garden* (41) to his delightful Johnny Crow stories. All the old friends who were at *Johnny Crow's Party* return and a few more are added. Following a series of mishaps, wounds and feelings are healed, sicknesses are cured, and the visit ends with everyone in a happy mood.

Except for C. B. Falls' *ABC Book* (122) in 1923, the twenties had almost passed before another worthwhile picture-story book appeared. It was *Clever Bill* (245) by WILLIAM NICHOLSON, a story written in England but published in America in 1927. The text has a slightly English flavor. The plot of *Clever Bill* has a universal appeal. Mary, a little girl, is invited to visit her aunt. She has trouble deciding what to take with her and how to pack the things she needs. In her hurry and confusion she forgets to pack Bill Davis, a toy soldier. He provides suspense by running after her and finally catching up with her. On the last page Bill is addressed by Mary as "Clever Bill." The illustrations are rich with color.

Author-Illustrators of the Thirties and Forties

In the year following the publication of *Clever Bill* a significant event occurred in literary fare for boys and girls with the publication of WANDA GAG's *Millions of Cats* (145). This delightful tale is as popular today as when it was published over forty years ago. Young listeners and readers enjoy the story of a very old man and very old woman who want a cat to end their loneliness. How the old man goes out to find a cat and returns with "hundreds of cats, thousands of cats, millions and billions and trillions of cats" is told in a fascinating text enhanced by the unusual illustrations that were destined to be Wanda Gag's trademark in the years to come. Many of her illustrations have decorative borders and other details that children enjoy.

Her characters appear in somewhat comic style. The rhythm and movement in her drawings carry them beyond the page.

The Funny Thing (143) has the same charm in the text and illustrations as *Millions of Cats.* Bobo is the kind little man of the mountains who has many good things for the birds and animals to eat at the door of his cave. How Bobo diverts the Funny Thing from eating dolls makes a delightful tale.

Wanda Gag's parents migrated from Germany to this country and settled in New Ulm, Minnesota, a community populated entirely by German people who had carried the traditions of the Old World with them to the New World. Wanda Gag grew up steeped in European tradition and customs. Thus it is natural that her stories have a folk quality and her drawings have an Old World flavor. It is natural, too, that Wanda Gag has turned to adapting folk tales and retelling fairy stories. *Gone Is Gone* (144) is her rendering of the old folk tale of the man and woman who decide to change places for a day. Struggling with the housework and the care of the cow, the old man has a very strenuous day and is glad to go back to his own work. The story is enhanced by Miss Gag's quaint pictures.

Tales from Grimm (147), *Snow White and the Seven Dwarfs* (146), and *Three Gay Tales from Grimm* (148) followed *Gone Is Gone.* The stories are enriched by illustrations that have an earthy Old World quality.

The same year that Wanda Gag's *The Funny Thing* was published EMMA L. BROCK's first picture-story book, *The Runaway Sardine* (37), appeared on the literary scene. Miss Brock traveled extensively in Europe and wherever she went she found in the atmosphere ideas for her writing. In her stories is a folksy human quality with an overlay of humor.

Set in France *The Runaway Sardine* relates through words and pictures the narrow escapes of Zacharias, a sardine, as he tries to make his way to the sea. He eventually decides that the sea is not as good a place as his tub. Following the hearty reception that *The Runaway Sardine* received, Emma Brock continued to write story after story for young listeners and readers.

A number of her stories, including *Here Comes Kristie!* (35), are built around Kristie, a wonderful white horse belonging to two Minnesota farm boys. Other favorite stories by Emma L. Brock still being read and enjoyed by countless boys and girls are her Mary series and such favorites as *Greedy Goat* (34), *To Market, to Market* (38), and *Plaid Cow* (36). In *Topsy-Turvey Family* (39) the Wiggens family faces one amusing incident after another in a tale of early pioneer days in

From *The Greedy Goat* by Emma Brock.

Minnesota. Miss Brock's characters are as diversified as her travels and reflect the pleasure she experienced wherever she lived.

In the years that followed the earliest beginnings in the field of picture-story books, a group of outstanding author-illustrators wrote and illustrated books for young boys and girls. Stories were illustrated with individuality by such talented artists as Clare T. Newberry, Helen Sewell, Marjorie Flack, and Lois Lenski.

One of the early stories by CLARE T. NEWBERRY was *Marshmallow* (241), in which a cuddly bunny named Marshmallow and a bachelor cat named Oliver become housemates in a Manhattan apartment. Oliver's behavior causes tension at the beginning of the story, but with a change of behavior on Oliver's part, the story ends on a happy note.

Among some of the other early stories by Clare Newberry that still delight young listeners and readers are *Pandora* (242) and *Smudge* (243). One of Miss Newberry's more recent stories that is considered by many to be her best from the standpoint of both content and illustrations is *T-Bone, the Baby Sitter* (244).

HELEN SEWELL was an early contributor to the field of children's literature, both through the illustrations she did for the stories of other authors and through the stories she herself wrote and illustrated. After illustrating such popular stories as *The Bears of Hemlock Mountain* (75) by Alice Dalgliesh, *Five Bushel Farm* (73) by Elizabeth Coatsworth, and *Bluebonnets for Lucinda* (265) by Frances Clark Sayers, Helen Sewell produced her own stories, *A Head for Happy* (282), *Blue Barns* (281), *Ming and Mehitable* (283), and *Peggy and the Pony* (284). Each of these was well received.

BORIS ARTZYBASHEFF, son of a famous Russian novelist and editor, was born in the Soviet Union where he spent most of his boyhood. He joined the Ukranian Army at the start of the Revolution. When it was defeated, he made his escape by sea and traveled around the world. Determined to have a career in art, he later moved to New York.

Artzybasheff was one of the first young artists in the early twenties to turn to illustrating books for children. In 1928 he made a collection of poems that he illustrated with a technique that produced the effect of wood blocks. He gave the book the inviting title *The Fairy Shoemaker and Other Poems* (24).

Artzybasheff is usually thought of as an illustrator rather than an author because of the numerous books by other authors he has illustrated, including Viking's 1933 edition of *Aesop's Fables* (1), which he also edited, Margery Bianco's *Apple Tree* (33), and *Gay-Neck: The Story of a Pigeon* (236) by Dhan Gopal Mukerji. His illustrations are masterpieces of design, imagination, and skillful techniques. In 1937 Artzybasheff made a significant contribution to literature by retelling and illustrating the old Russian folk tale *The Seven Simeons: A Russian Tale* (25), the story of Douda, a king who, though he had riches, wisdom, power, and good looks, was very unhappy. Its publication started a trend toward the translating, retelling, and illustrating of folk tales.

MARJORIE FLACK created Angus, a very fetching Scottie with expressive eyes and an insatiable curiosity. All the cuteness that makes a Scottie so appealing is found in the Angus stories. Angus' curiosity leads him out into the world where he narrowly escapes disaster in *Angus Lost* (133). He learns rapidly about most things but not about a cat's skill in escaping him in *Angus and the Cat* (131). Angus' bravery is short-lived when two ducks he thinks he has frightened turn on him in *Angus and the Ducks* (132).

Following *Angus and the Ducks* came one of Miss Flack's most popular books—*The Story About Ping* (134), written after much research about the ancestry and habits of ducks and life on the Yangtze River. Miss Flack had the happy thought of having Kurt Wiese illustrate her story, since he had lived in China for years. The result has remained a favorite with preschoolers.

LOIS LENSKI has also devoted her talents to writing and illustrating stories of high quality for young listeners and readers. Her first two stories, *Skipping Village* (216) and *A Little Girl of 1900* (214), came out of her own childhood experiences in Ohio. In 1938 Miss Lenski started her series of little picture books—*The Little Airplane* (212), *The Little Train* (215), and *The Little Farm* (213)—which were warmly received by young children, who found something in them that was just right for their inquiring minds. With simple illustrations in black and white and backgrounds occasionally colored, the stories give accurate information in a straightforward style about airplanes, trains, farms, cowboys, and a host of other subjects that fascinate young listeners and readers.

The little picture-book series was followed by the Mr. Small stories. The exploits of Mr. Small, whether he appears as Pilot Small, Engineer Small, or Farmer Small, provide the thread that ties the stories together.

Contemporary Author-Illustrators

JOAN WALSH ANGLUND's most popular works are a group of small books bearing such sentimental titles as *A Friend Is Someone Who Likes You* (12), *Love Is a Special Way of Feeling* (13), and *Childhood Is a Time of Innocence* (9). As the titles suggest, the text and pictures are intended to develop concepts, but the text often does not meet this heavy responsibility. Children enjoy Miss Anglund's cowboy stories: *Brave Cowboy* (8), *Cowboy and His Friend* (10), and *Cowboy's Secret Life* (11). Her *Nibble, Nibble Mousekin: A Tale of Hansel and Gretel* (14) is a playful retelling of the favorite fairy tale. Miss Anglund's delicate drawings appear in black ink and rich colors.

An outstanding contributor to the field of children's literature is EDWARD ARDIZZONE. Because he came from a long line of sea-

From *Little Tim and the Brave Sea Captain* by Edward Ardizzone.

men and spent his childhood in Ipswich, England, a small seacoast port, it is natural that the sea should provide the background for his delightful stories.

Ardizzone's most beloved stories are those in which fearless Tim is the hero. The first of these was *Little Tim and the Brave Sea Captain* (15). Little Tim, who lives in a house by the sea, longs to be a sailor, much to the dismay of his mother and father, but Tim's parents finally agree. The story is loaded with fun and thrills, and Tim starts on his way to become a popular storybook hero.

Lucy Brown and Mr. Grimes (16) followed *Little Tim and the Brave Sea Captain.* Published in 1937 the book introduced Lucy Brown as a character in the Tim stories. An orphan girl, Lucy was adopted by Mr. Grimes, a rich old man. A 1970 revision has been published with a number of changes. Originally a tall book with hand-lettered text, it has been reduced in size and printed with large, clear type. The illustrations have been redrawn and the story has been made slightly longer. Children will continue to enjoy this action-packed, old-fashioned story.

Another of Ardizzone's exciting Tim stories is *Tim and Lucy Go to Sea* (19). Seven-year-old Lucy Brown, her old friend Mr. Grimes, and his housekeeper go to sea with Tim. They have a wonderful time on Mr. Grimes' beautiful steam yacht until they are threatened with being hijacked by a villainous crew they have rescued from the sea.

Some of the other Tim stories that provide fun and excitement are *Tim to the Rescue* (22), *Tim in Danger* (20), *Tim All Alone* (17), *Tim's Friend Towser* (23), *Tim and Ginger* (18), and *Tim to the Lighthouse* (21). In each of the stories Tim moves from one precarious position into another. The illustrations, some in black and white and some in sparkling watercolors, add to the fun of the stories. Mr. Ardizzone frequently uses balloons with hand-lettering as part of the illustrations.

Mr. Ardizzone has also illustrated numerous books by other authors. Eleanor Farjeon's *The Little Bookroom* (123), which he illustrated, received both the Carnegie Medal and the Hans Christian Andersen Medal. Published in 1956, *Tim All Alone* was the first winner of the Kate Greenaway Medal.

An Austrian by birth, LUDWIG BEMELMANS spent most of his life after his sixteenth year in the United States, with occasional trips to Paris. His first book for children was *Hansi* (27), which relates the adventures of a little boy of Innsbruck who spends his Christmas holiday with his uncle in an old house in the Austrian Tyrol.

For the pleasure of young listeners and readers Bemelmans created *Madeline* (28), a precocious little girl with irresistible charm who gets

From *Madeline* by Ludwig Bemelmans.

in and out of difficulties in hilarious ways. She is the smallest of twelve little girls living in an old vine-covered house in Paris under the watchful eye of Miss Clave. The same gay quality found in the first Madeline story enlivens those that followed: *Madeline's Rescue* (32), *Madeline and the Bad Hat* (29), *Madeline and the Gypsies* (30), and *Madeline in London* (31).

ALIKI BRANDENBURG's (pseudonym ALIKI) first book for children was *The Story of William Penn* (6), which she both wrote and illustrated. She works in an amazing variety of media—clay, silver, enamel, papier-mâché, mosaic, and collage—using the medium that she feels best fits the mood and style of each story.

Mrs. Brandenburg shows her versatility both in text and illustrations in *Keep Your Mouth Closed, Dear* (4). Charles is a young crocodile whose parents are dismayed by the problems that result every time he opens his mouth.

With illustrations in pastel colors resembling Greek friezes and simple text, Mrs. Brandenburg has written a picture biography for young children. *Diogenes: The Story of the Greek Philosopher* (2) relates the dramatic events in the life of a great man. Even with the slight text, young listeners and readers catch a glimpse of life in ancient Athens and Corinth, while making the acquaintance of Diogenes.

Mrs. Brandenburg has made a beautiful lullaby *Hush Little Baby*

(3) even more beautiful with her illustrations—richly colored wood blocks done in an eighteenth-century style.

> Hush, little baby, don't say a word,
> Papa's gonna buy you a mockingbird.
> If that mockingbird don't sing,
> Papa's gonna buy you a
> diamond ring. . . . [Unpaged]

The lullaby, which came to America from England, was a great favorite in the Appalachian Mountain region and then spread throughout the country, where it has soothed its listeners for years.

In *The Story of Johnny Appleseed* (5) Mrs. Brandenburg gives readers a glimpse of pioneer life in our country and the efforts of one man, John Chapman, later to be known as Johnny Appleseed, to make life richer not only for the pioneers but for future generations.

A well-known author-illustrator and adapter of stories, MARCIA BROWN attended the State College for Teachers in Albany where she designed and painted stage sets. A scholarship made it possible for her to study under Judson Smith for two summers at Woodstock School of Painting. She taught English for a few years before going to New York, where she worked part-time as a storyteller in the New York Public Library. At the same time she studied painting at the New School for Social Research and later worked on color woodblock prints under the eminent artist Louis Shanker.

Miss Brown's first picture-story book was *Little Carousel* (46), in which young Anthony has the time of his life when a merry-go-round comes to the crowded tenement district where he lives. The following books were runners-up for the Caldecott Medal: *Stone Soup* (51), 1947; *Henry Fisherman* (45), 1950; *Dick Whittington and His Cat* (44), 1951; *Skipper John's Cook* (49), 1952; *Puss in Boots* (48), 1953; and *The Steadfast Tin Soldier* (50), 1954. In 1955 Marcia Brown received the Caldecott Medal for *Cinderella, or the Little Glass Slipper* (43), and in 1961 she again received the Caldecott Medal for *Once a Mouse* (47), in which a hermit changes a mouse into a royal tiger and then changes him back again when the tiger behaves ungratefully.

Stone Soup is the retelling of an old French tale about three soldiers who convince a village of selfish people that they can make a delicious soup out of stones. *Henry Fisherman* is about a little boy living in the Virgin Islands whose greatest wish is to become a fisherman like his father. *Dick Whittington and His Cat* is the familiar story of the poor boy who thrice became Lord Mayor of London. In *Skipper John's Cook* a small boy signs on as a cook on a fishing boat. *Puss in Boots* tells how Puss takes charge of his master's affairs with such cleverness that his master comes to fame and fortune. In the beloved *The Steadfast Tin Soldier* the little tin soldier with only one leg falls in love with the dancer in the crepe-paper dress standing in front of a paper castle. The dancer follows him when he is thrown into the fireplace, and they die together. *Cinderella, or the Little Glass Slipper* is the perennial favorite about Cinderella and her handsome prince.

Miss Brown suits her style to the particular mood and tone of what she is illustrating. *Cinderella* is delicately done in pastels; *Once a Mouse* is carved in bold woodcuts with strong colors. She is unsurpassed in her skill in the use of a variety of media.

VIRGINIA LEE BURTON's creativity has embraced a number of areas: art, dancing, drama, and textile designing. Reared in a culturally rich environment, Miss Burton was encouraged to pursue her various artistic interests. In her junior year in high school, she won a scholarship to the California School of Fine Arts in San Francisco. After a year at art school, she returned East to live with her father in Boston where she worked as a sketcher for the music and drama critic of the Boston *Transcript* and took drawing lessons at the Boston Museum School. She married George Demetrious, a famous sculptor and painter who was teaching at the school, and together they established the Folly Cove Designers. There, George Demetrious continued with his sculpturing, and Virginia Lee Burton continued writing and illustrating books as well as designing textiles.

Virginia Burton's stories have inviting plots. The text and illustrations blend as one. The author's love of the dance has carried over into her illustrations, which have a dancing quality to them.

Her first book *Choo Choo* (56) took its place in a growing procession of picture-story books of high quality in 1937. With an engineer, a fireman, and a conductor to run her, Choo Choo, a fabulous little engine, does some remarkable things—some good, some bad. When Choo Choo runs away, one hilarious happening follows another.

Virginia Lee Burton's second book was *Mike Mulligan and His Steam Engine* (58) in 1939. Mike Mulligan's faithful steam shovel, Mary Anne, is outdated when the new models come along, but Mike takes her to Pepperville, where the people want a new town hall, and boasts that Mary Anne can dig as much in a day as a hundred men can dig in a week. People come from far and wide to see the thrilling race. Mike Mulligan and Mary Anne are successful, but the glory of success is almost lost because there is no exit left by which Mary Anne can get out of the deep excavation she has dug. Virginia Lee Burton's genius comes to the rescue, and Mike Mulligan and Mary Anne succeed.

Two years later came *Calico, the Wonder Horse* (55), an exciting story that Virginia Lee Burton wrote for her boys "in an attempt to wean them away from comic books." A horse named Calico shares in the adventures of Cowboy Hank. Cattle rustling and a runaway stage coach add to the suspense of the story.

The following year, 1942, came that appealing story with a sociological impact, *The Little House* (57), which received the Caldecott Medal. *The Little House* reflects a variety of moods—happiness, sadness, worry, relief, and nostalgia. Once in a quiet, pastoral setting, the house becomes surrounded by skyscrapers that look down on it, and people and trains that hurry by without taking notice except to think of it as an obstruction to progress. The happy day comes when the Little House is moved back to the country where it can watch the seasons come and go. The illustrations express perfectly the moods and feelings of the Little House.

JAMES DAUGHERTY started out in the art field by painting murals and illustrating other people's stories but soon moved on to writing and illustrating his own books. In 1938 his first picture-story book *Andy and the Lion* (76) was published. Daugherty subtitled it "A Tale of Kindness Remembered or the Power of Gratitude." Andy goes to the library to get a book on lions that he reads avidly through the evening and into the night. To add to Andy's pleasure his grandfather tells him tall tales about hunting lions in Africa. The next day Andy can think only of lions. On his way to school he runs into a lion. Frightened, Andy runs around a rock with the lion after him. Finally, exhausted, they both stop for breath. The lion shows Andy the cause of his trouble. He has a big thorn in his paw. With great effort, Andy removes the thorn. The lion shows his gratitude by licking Andy's face. In the spring the circus comes to town and Andy and the lion are reunited. The illustrations are rich with humor and excitement.

James Daugherty calls his book *The Picnic* (77) "A Frolic in Two Colors and Three Parts." He says that "so many people are getting so sore at each other all over the world everywhere that something ought to be done about it. That is why this book is dedicated to the promotion of good will and friendship among animals, people, and nations." Part I tells about the delightful picnic taken by Mr. Moses Merryman Mouse and his family. In Part II a lion is captured for the circus in a great strong net. As is to be expected Part III is "The Rescue," in which Mr. Moses Merryman Mouse and his family gnaw the lion free. The humorous illustrations, done in black and tan, provoke hearty laughs.

Early in the thirties, JEAN DE BRUNHOFF, a young French artist, created a lovable elephant destined to win a place in the hearts of young listeners and readers for years to come. It was really his wife who invented this amiable elephant as she told stories to entertain their three boys and their young friends. De Brunhoff himself became fascinated by the elephant and started writing stories down and illustrating them. The elephants were endowed with such engrossing personalities that there was no stopping the stories.

In 1931 *The Story of Babar, the Little Elephant* (88) arrived on the literary scene. After receiving a warm welcome in France, Babar went to England where he received a hearty reception and then came to the United States where he is still held in high favor. *The Story of Babar, the Little Elephant* has a tender beginning:

> In the great forest
> a little elephant is born.
> His name is Babar.
> His mother loves him very much.
> She rocks him to sleep
> with her trunk
> while singing softly to him. [P. 3]

Thus starts a delightful procession of stories about Babar, his family, his wife Celeste, his relatives, and his friends.

It takes the genius of Jean de Brunhoff to dream up the happenings that befall Babar and his wife in *The Travels of Babar* (89). Babar's unlimited ingenuity helps him to overcome every obstacle that would have spelled misfortune and sadness on their wedding trip. Their reunion with Babar's friend, the Old Lady, provides a happy ending.

In *Babar and His Children* (85) King Babar becomes the father of

From *The Story of Babar, the Little Elephant* by Jean de Brunhoff.

three baby elephants. What a celebration follows! Alexander is the most mischievous of the little elephants, and at times it appears as if he might go too far with disastrous results.

When the elephants' school at Celesteville is closed for the summer, Zephir returns home to visit his family. His adventures and his engagement to Princess Isabella are related in *Babar and Zephir* (86). Pictures exciting as Zephir's adventures complement the story.

A Babar story arrived on the literary scene each year until Jean de Brunhoff's death at the age of thirty-seven; the stories were continued thereafter by his son Laurent. Among the other Babar stories written by Jean de Brunhoff are *Babar the King* (87), *ABC Babar* (83), and *Babar and Father Christmas* (84).

GLEN DINES attended the University of Washington in Seattle and Sacramento State College in Sacramento, California, where he received his B.A. and M.A. degrees. He also studied for a time at the Art Center School in Los Angeles. He has done magazine illustrations and murals, as well as layout and advertising in commercial art. As general editor of Macmillan's *Frontier West Series* (99), Mr. Dines has written and illustrated many of the titles in the series.

Dines' first picture-story book, *The Useful Dragon of Sam Ling Toy* (96), captures the atmosphere and spirit of San Francisco's Chinatown. The little lizard to whom Sam Ling Toy gives a home becomes "a large dragon with horns of silver and whiskers of silk and a long and wiggly tail" (unpaged). The dragon tries hard to be useful and finally comes to glory as the leader of the Chinese New Year's parade. The vital, colorful illustrations add humor to the text.

Petidoe, and Colormaker (98) is another of Mr. Dines' picture-story books. It is a fanciful tale told in prose and rhyme about a skillful colormaker named Resk and his helper Petidoe. Although Petidoe has many jobs to do, he spends much of his time dreaming of the day he will become a master colormaker. One day Resk leaves on a journey to a faraway land to get "copper rust, silvery mist and crystal dust" (unpaged) and gives Petidoe instructions to follow while he is gone. Ignoring all the instructions, Petidoe raises havoc with the spring colors in the land. Fortunately Petidoe learns the secret of colormaking from a tear that rolls down his cheek, and he is able to restore the spring colors to the land before his master returns. The rainbow-like pastel-colored illustrations are as fantastic as the tale.

Glen Dines dipped back into colonial days for his prankish story *Gilly and the Whicharoo* (97). The story opens in a particularly quiet little village beside a river where many skillful goldsmiths live. When huge tracks appear in the streets and loud thumping noises are heard, the people of the village become frightened. Gilly Woodwill, the rag boy in the village, eventually solves the mystery. The mischievous illustrations add to the humor of the story.

WILLIAM PENÉ DU BOIS had his first book for young listeners and readers published when he was nineteen years old. Three interests made deep imprints upon his writing and painting. At an early age Jules Verne's stories had a keen fascination for him. He had a passion for the circus to such an extent that he attended the French Cirque d'Hiver once a week, and he knew the acts by heart. His third love was France—its unique sights, sounds, and atmosphere.

The Animal Factory located high up in the sky is the setting for Mr. Du Bois' amusing picture-story book *Lion* (101). One day the foreman of the Animal Factory makes up a new name for an animal—"lion." It takes some clever thinking and real imagination to make an animal to fit the name. Experiments with feathers, fur, and a rainbow of colors are tried before a satisfactory lion is produced.

The Bear Party (100), with its setting in Koala Park in Australia, is one of Du Bois' most delightful stories. The color illustrations give a light, fanciful touch to the story, which was a runner-up for the Caldecott Award in 1952.

According to Du Bois, *Otto in Africa* (103) "is the story of Otto's first medal, earned years ago when he was just a giant puppy." The book relates the hilarious adventures of this giant otterhound.

In *Otto and the Magic Potatoes* (102) William P. Du Bois relates how Otto, the giant dog of previous stories, is kidnapped by Baron Backgammon, who wants to learn how to make giant potatoes and a giant rose.

Austrian-born BETTINA EHRLICH is an author-illustrator whose books make a pleasing contribution to children's literature. At an early age Mrs. Ehrlich began to develop an interest in art. Later she attended art schools in Paris and London. She introduced children to Italy in her picture-story books *Cocolo* (108), *Cocolo's Home* (109), *Pantaloni* (110), and *Trovato* (111).

Cocolo is a dear little donkey who cannot stand a life of luxury given him when he is bought by a rich man as a pet for his daughter. He returns to his old home on an island in the Adriatic, the setting for the story.

Cocolo was followed by *Cocolo's Home.* Cocolo, his wife Carmen, and master Lucio are living quietly in Lobsterbay, an American village on the Atlantic coast, when Cocolo contracts a bad case of homesickness for Italy. They return to Italy, and their stay there is filled with the kind of excitement that young readers enjoy.

Pantaloni is a heart-warming story about a boy, Beppolino, and his dog, Pantaloni. The story includes one of the most exciting cases of mistaken identity and of a dog hunt in dog history! Color and black-and-white illustrations add luster to this story.

Unusual happenings in *Trovato* provide a suspense-filled story built around Miss Pattison, an old lady with rheumatism, and a little boy with a beautiful singing voice.

There seems to be no limit to the techniques Mrs. Ehrlich uses in illustrating her stories. She is proficient in the use of lithograph, etching, oils, water colors, and wood and linoleum cuts. Whatever medium is used, the illustrations reflect the atmosphere of the story.

In 1935 MARIE HALL ETS introduced *Mister Penny* (117) to young listeners and readers. Mister Penny's home is a tumbledown shed on a stony field by a path that leads to the village of Wuddle. He lives with his fabulous family made up of Limpy the horse, Mooloo the cow, Slop the goat, Pugwug the pig, Minkin the lamb, Chukluk a fat hen, and Doody the rooster. In 1956 Mister Penny came back for more laughs in *Mister Penny's Race Horse* (119) and once again in 1961 to the delight of young boys and girls in *Mister Penny's Circus* (118).

Among the other stories by Marie Hall Ets enjoyed by young listeners and readers are *Just Me* (115), in which a little boy leaves his world of make-believe and joins his father in a boat, and *Another Day* (113), which portrays a little boy having make-believe adventures in the forest.

Mister T. W. Anthony Woo (120), *Little Old Automobile* (116), and *Gilberto and the Wind* (114) are other stories by Marie Hall Ets. *Nine Days to Christmas* (121), coauthored with Aurora Labastida, received the Caldecott Award in 1960.

Marie Hall Ets succeeds in portraying the feelings, desires, and

From *Mister Penny* by Marie Hall Ets.

From *Oté* by Pura Belpre, illustrated by Paul Galdone.

dreams of children. There is an overtone of humor in her illustrations, and her characters are presented from a child's viewpoint. Her stories move smoothly from reality into fantasy.

Before becoming an illustrator and author of children's books, PAUL GALDONE studied at the Art Student's League, worked in the art department of Doubleday and Company, and designed book jackets and illustrated books on a free-lance basis.

His illustrations of *The Three Wishes* (155), a tale that dates back to Greek mythology and has appeared in many languages, give the story vitality, newness, and a decidedly humorous twist. Tom is treated in an hysterically funny way in Mr. Galdone's illustrations for *Tom, Tom the Piper's Son* (156).

Mr. Galdone followed the style of the chap books for his version of *History of Simple Simon* (153). Each blunder that Simon makes is illustrated with a delightful picture against the background of the times.

The expressive faces on the characters in the illustrations of *The Horse, the Fox, and the Lion* (149) give color and life to Galdone's adaptation of one of the popular tales by the Brothers Grimm. The text and illustrations carry the reader rapidly through the story which opens with a horse who is sad and forlorn and a farmer who is nervous and distraught. The brightly colored illustrations complement the text from its sad beginning to its happy ending.

Mr. Galdone has done a masterful job of retelling and illustrating the popular tale of the monkey who outwits the crocodile in *The*

Monkey and the Crocodile (151), a Jataka tale from India. Mr. Galdone is skilled in combining humor with touches of excitement in animal stories.

The old Scandinavian nursery tale *Little Tuppen* (150) is told with charm and illustrated with vigor and humor. The tale tells how an old hen Cluck-cluck and her little chick Tuppen go into the woods to find seeds to eat. In spite of her mother's warning, Little Tuppen tries to eat a big seed that starts her coughing. Cluck-cluck becomes frightened and runs to the spring to fetch Little Tuppen some water. The springs says, "I will give you some water if you will bring me a cup." Thus begins one of the most delightful cumulative tales to be found in children's literature.

In *Three Aesop Fox Fables* (154), adapted from Aesop by Galdone, the fox is outwitted in the first two tales but has his moment of triumph in the last one.

HARDIE GRAMATKY's first jobs included ghost writing a comic strip and working as an animator for the Disney studio. His education beyond high school was at Stanford University and Chouinard Art School in Los Angeles. Gramatky then moved to New York where he worked as a free-lancer for *Fortune* magazine. It was between his assignments on this job that he got his idea for *Little Toot* (160), a tugboat with a lot of personality and little ambition. After a slow start this book became a tremendous success and was featured in the movie "Melody Time" by Walt Disney. It has been adapted for radio and television and continues to hold its popularity with young listeners and readers.

From *Little Toot* by Hardie Gramatky.

Following *Little Toot*, Gramatky wrote *Hercules* (159), the story of an old-fashioned fire engine who comes out of retirement to put out a fire in City Hall.

The setting of *Bolivar* (158) is the city of Quito, the capital of Ecuador, high in the Andes Mountains. Trouble starts when Pepito tries to convince his father that he should keep Bolivar the donkey in spite of his friskiness and undependability. One misfortune after another happens to Bolivar on his way to the fiesta.

Young readers meet Little Toot again in *Little Toot on the Thames* (161). In this exciting tale the friendly but not always dependable little tugboat is pulled across the ocean by a tramp steamer. The strange traffic on the Thames in London befuddles him for a while, but in the end Little Toot shows that he has the potential to be a hero, though he is still a frivolous little tugboat trying to reform his ways.

DAHLOV IPCAR has had several one-man shows in New York City, and her work is to be found in a number of museums including the Whitney and the Metropolitan museums in New York City. Her love of farm life surrounded by the beauty of fields, woods, and animals is reflected in her realistic stories and paintings.

Mrs. Ipcar's *One Horse Farm* (187) portrays the work of the farmer through the seasons of the year. *Deep Sea Farm* (185) is a highly imaginative story portraying life as it might be on a farm at the bottom of the sea. The story is so well told that one begins to believe that there really are farms at the bottom of the sea. The exaggerations are the kind that stimulate the imaginations of young listeners and readers.

Dahlov Ipcar has given readers an unusual book—*Song of the Day Birds and the Night Birds* (188). Beautiful illustrations in strong colors and lyrical text introduce the birds that adorn the day and the night. The reader meets birds arrayed in their most gorgeous colors. The backgrounds and the borders of the pages against which the birds are portrayed add to the imaginative quality of the story.

The Marvelous Merry Go Round (186) is a recent story by Dahlov Ipcar about an old wood-carver who creates galloping merry-go-round horses. Of all the colors he paints the horses the children prefer the one that is dapple gray.

The Cat Came Back (184), Ipcar's latest book, is an adaptation of a favorite folk song, in which a cat lives far more than her allotted nine lives.

VIRGINIA KAHL was born and grew up in Milwaukee, Wisconsin. After graduating from college with a major in art, Miss Kahl worked as a librarian as well as a commercial artist. During World War I, she was sent as a librarian for the army first to Berlin and then to Salzburg, Austria, where she fell in love with its friendly people and beautiful country. She particularly enjoyed the music festival for which Salzburg is world famous. It was in this atmosphere that Virginia Kahl began to write and to illustrate books for children.

Away Went Wolfgang (196) is an amusing picture-story book about a small village in Austria where everyone, even the dogs, has a job to do. Everyone, that is, except Wolfgang, a large dog who is not very smart and is much too exuberant. After many disastrous attempts at being useful, he and the old lady who lives with him discover that as he drags the milk cart three times over the cobblestones around the church the milk in the cans is churned into excellent butter. This pleases the women of the town because they now do not have to do their own churning; it pleases the old lady because she is really very fond of Wolfgang; and it pleases Wolfgang because he can now be as exuberant as he wishes and still hold a job. Colorful and humorous illustrations accompany the text.

The Duchess Bakes a Cake (197) is a rollicking tale in rhyme. The Duchess lives happily with her Duke and thirteen daughters until one day she decides to bake "a lovely, light, luscious, delectable cake." It is light, all right—so light that it rises to the sky and takes the Duchess up with it. After trying to bring her down with cannon shot and arrows, the people give up and decide that she will simply have to remain on top of the cake. Then the baby Gunhilde begins to cry for her supper—and there is a solution! Everyone begins to eat cake until finally the Duchess is down again. Her husband and the King see to it that cooking is thereafter left to the cooks. The red and green illustrations add humor and appeal to the story.

Virginia Kahl's *How Do You Hide a Monster?* (198) is the story about Phinney, a happy lake-dwelling Loch Ness-type creature. Loved by the people living in a nearby village, Phinney is suddenly threatened by outsiders who consider him a fierce monster. The people of the town try to protect him from the outsiders, but Phinney has his own ideas about his welfare.

After service in World War II, EZRA JACK KEATS decided to become an illustrator. He was assigned by *Collier's* to do a number of full-color illustrations that paid him enough to make possible a year in Europe where he spent his time traveling and painting. Returning home he exhibited his work in the Associated American Artists Galleries in New York.

Warm human relations shine through the pages of his *Snowy Day* (205), which received the Caldecott Medal in 1963. Peter, the main character of *Snowy Day,* continues to endear himself to readers in *Whistle for Willie* (206). A boy does not amount to much, at least in his own estimation, unless he can whistle. Keats gets inside the feelings of a boy whose wish is fulfilled.

Jennie has the most beautiful hat that ever adorned a charming young lady's head when the story *Jennie's Hat* (202) ends, but the hat was not always so pretty. As she is walking home one day, wearing the plain hat her aunt had sent her, she notices that the birds she used to feed are dropping beautiful decorations on her hat and people are staring in amazement. Jennie's hat lends itself to richly colored illustrations making it a hat long to be remembered.

That special quality that Ezra Jack Keats has for telling and illustrating a story comes through with beauty and vigor in *Peter's Chair* (204). The old theme of a little boy displaced by a younger sister is told realistically with tenderness and feeling.

Young listeners and readers are taken into the grim realities of the world of young Black children in an underprivileged section of a big city in Keats' fast-moving story *Goggles* (200). With an economy of words the brief text moves quickly into the very marrow of children's feelings.

Other recent books by Ezra Jack Keats are *Hi, Cat* (201), *The Little Drummer Boy* (203), and *Apt. Three* (199). Peter, who plays the lead in several of the picture stories by Mr. Keats, steps back and allows his good friend Archie to play the lead in *Hi, Cat,* set in the inner city. A cat attaches himself to Archie and in so doing brings disaster to the show Archie and Peter are producing. The lavishly colored illustrations add to the story.

LEO LIONNI was born in Amsterdam, Holland. He came to the United States in 1939 and became art director of a large Philadelphia advertising agency. Eleven years later he became art director of *Fortune* magazine. He has had a brilliant career in the field of graphic arts as Chairman of the Graphic Design Department of the Parsons School of Design, President of the American Institute of Graphic Arts, managing editor of *Panorama,* a Time-Life publication in Italy, and a graphic arts consultant to various publications.

One of Mr. Lionni's masterpieces is *Swimmy* (219), in which the text and illustrations move together to an imaginative climax. Swimmy is a black fish born into a happy school of little red fish. One day when a tuna fish swallows all the little red fish, Swimmy is left alone to swim from place to place scared and sad. Swimming about he comes upon a school of little fish just like himself. The little fish are afraid the big fish will eat them if they leave the dark shade of the rocks and weeds. Swimmy gets an idea. He teaches them to swim close together in the form of a giant fish. Swimmy, as the eye of the giant fish, leads the school of little fish out to chase the big fish away and to enjoy the marvels of the sea.

Frederick (218), a little field mouse, does not prepare for winter in the same way as the other field mice do. While the other little mice work day and night storing food for the winter, Frederick gathers sun rays, colors, and words for the cold, dark winter days. *Swimmy* and *Frederick* were runners-up for the Caldecott Medal.

Tico and the Golden Wings (221) is a most unusual picture-story book from the standpoint of both story line and illustrations. Tico, a beautiful little bird, tells his own story.

Leo Lionni has added two new beautifully illustrated books to his contribution to literature for the young picture-book age. With an economy of words, Mr. Lionni relates the tender story of the friendship between a minnow and a tadpole in *Fish Is Fish* (217). The large, full-color illustrations bring to life the beauties of the sea. And *Theodore and the Talking Mushroom* (220) is a modern fable about a tiny mouse who insists that a talking mushroom has proclaimed him king of the animals.

ROBERT McCLOSKEY has created a place for himself in children's literature with such stories as *Make Way for Ducklings* (229), *Blueberries for Sal* (228), *One Morning in Maine* (230), and *Time of Wonder* (231).

Thirty years have not lessened the popularity of McCloskey's *Make Way for Ducklings,* winner of the 1941 Caldecott Medal. Mr. and Mrs. Mallard are in a dilemma looking for a place to rear their family. They finally find an island in the Charles River where they settle down to build their nest. There, eight little ducklings are hatched. When Mrs. Mallard is satisfied with the training of the little ones, she takes them across the river where they waddle along until they come to the highway. Mrs. Mallard and her eight children stop traffic with the help of friendly policemen. They win the hearts of Boston people. The illustrations are true to the Boston landscape, and each character including the eight little ducklings is given a distinct personality.

In *Blueberries for Sal* suspense rises when Little Sal goes with her mother up one side of Blueberry Hill to pick blueberries, and Little Bear comes with his mother up the other side of the hill. *One Morning in Maine* is a warm story of a family having a pleasant morning going about the everyday tasks of living.

The charm of Robert McCloskey's *Time of Wonder* starts in the very first sentence: "Out on the islands that poke their rocky shores above the waters of Penobscot Bay, you can watch the time of the world go by, from minute to minute, hour to hour, from day to day, season to season" (p. 6). Beautiful word pictures enriched by the use of the vernacular follow one after the other. Some are quiet; others are boisterous.

McCloskey has illustrated a number of stories by other authors, among which are Ruth Sawyer's *Journey Cake, Ho!* (264), *Junket* (321) by Anne H. White, Anne Malcolmson's *Yankee Doodle's Cousins* (233), and Keith Robertson's *Henry Reed, Inc.* (263).

EVALINE NESS has written and illustrated a number of outstanding books for young children. She studied at the Chicago Art Institute, the Corcoran Gallery in Washington, D. C., and the Accademia di Belle Arti in Rome. She has had several one-man shows.

Miss Ness, a resident of New York City, travels extensively. She lived for a year in Haiti where she found the inspiration for her first story for young readers, *Josefina February* (238), which the American Library Association chose as a Notable Children's Book in 1963. It was selected as a New York *Herald Tribune* Honor Book the same year.

Miki, a pelican who is neither intelligent nor handsome, and Sula Sula, a beautiful bird with tangerine-colored feathers, pink legs, and beak, are the hero and heroine of *A Gift for Sula Sula* (237). Its setting is a little rocky island in the Aegean Sea.

Pavo and the Princess (239) is a once-upon-a-time story set in a land of fantastic trees and exotic flowers where a beautiful princess named Phoebe lives with her father. The elegance and affluence of the court are caught in illustrations done in rich and varied colors.

Sam, Bangs, and Moonshine (240) is a tribute to the writing and illustrating genius of Evaline Ness. The story may appear humorous and flighty on the surface, but in reality it penetrates deeply into the behavior of many children. Sam, a nickname for Samantha, is a fisherman's orphaned daughter who "had the reckless habit of lying." The character of Sam is so convincingly drawn that although one does not believe her, one is able to understand her and identify with her. The illustrations are done in a style that contributes to the Moonshine that Sam talks and the fantasies she creates. *Sam, Bangs, and Moonshine* received the Caldecott Medal in 1967.

As well as illustrating her own stories Evaline Ness has illustrated other outstanding authors' stories such as *Thistle and Thyme* (211) by Sorche Nic Leodhas, *Favorite Fairy Tales Told in Italy* (172) retold by Virginia Haviland, and *The Princess and the Lion* (74) by Elizabeth Coatsworth.

TONY PALAZZO's first illustrations for children's books were for Al Graham's *Timothy Turtle* (157), which was published in 1949. Since then he has written and illustrated a number of stories and has had several one-man shows in New York and Chicago. His work has been included in the New York Museum of Modern Art, the Pennsylvania Academy of the Fine Arts, and the Chicago Art Institute.

Bianco and the New World (246) is an appealing story about Marco and his white burro who grow tired of working hard in the fields in Sicily and decide to go to New York. For a time misfortune seems to be their lot. Fortune changes, however, when Marco takes Bianco to the blacksmith shop to get new shoes.

Among some of the other early stories by Mr. Palazzo are *Jan and the Reindeer* (248), the favorite folk tale *The Little Red Hen* (249), *Mr. Whistle's Secret* (250), and *Charley the Horse* (247). The setting of *Mr. Whistle's Secret* is a toy shop where magic takes place. *Charley the Horse* starts out when Charley leaves his milk cart to become a race horse and win a race.

LEO POLITI was born of Italian parents in Fresno, California. His parents took him to Italy when he was seven years old. When he was fifteen, he received a scholarship to study at the Art Institute at the Royal Palace of Monza near Milan. At the age of twenty-three Politi returned to California and settled in Los Angeles. He lived on Olvera Street, the oldest street in Los Angeles, which had been restored to keep the history and flavor of the early Spanish days. There Politi wrote and illustrated his first story, *Pedro, the Little Angel of Olvera Street* (261). So began Politi's stories, which artfully preserve the traditions and spirit of early California.

With his gay pictures that portray real people, Politi wrote *Juanita* (259), set on Politi's favorite street in Los Angeles. The blessing of the animals at Easter time is described, and the joyousness of the occasion is caught in the illustrations.

The Song of the Swallows (262) is a beautifully told and sensitively illustrated story of the mystery that surrounds the coming and going of the swallows at San Juan Capistrano Mission, one of the twenty-one missions founded by Father Junipero Serra along the El Camino Real in California. The story describes the tender relationship between the little boy Juan and the bell-ringer Julian.

With words and pictures Leo Politi created a beautiful book that tells the story of the founding of the Franciscan missions in California under the valiant leadership of Father Junipero Serra. *The Mission Bell* (260) highlights the perils of travel in a new land—the vast desert to cross, the rugged mountains to climb, the unfriendly Indians to win. The faith, courage, and sacrifices of the founders of the missions are well described. The beauty of Father Junipero Serra's character is revealed to the reader through the eyes of an Indian boy.

Leo Politi brings the pleasures and loves of his own background to his stories and illustrations. The touch of his brush and his turn of a phrase breathe life into the characters. The primitive style of his illustrations gives depth to the characters and quality to the story. Romance and sentimentality ring true as he shares his joy in little things and depicts the happiness in simple living.

Pedro, The Little Angel of Olvera Street and *Juanita* were runners-up for the Caldecott Award in 1947 and 1949, respectively, and *Song of the Swallows* received the award in 1950.

MAURICE SENDAK set his goal to write and illustrate stories at an early age. Before realizing his goal he drew background illustrations for Mutt and Jeff comics, illustrated a book written by one of his high school teachers, and did the elaborate window displays for a well-known New York toy store. His only formal art study was two years of evening classes at the Art Students' League.

The first book he illustrated was Marcel Aymé's *Wonderful Farm* (26). Next came books by Ruth Krauss: *A Hole Is to Dig: A First Book of First Definitions* (208), *A Very Special House* (209), and *The Birthday Party* (207). He both wrote and illustrated first *Kenny's Window* (275) and then *Very Far Away* (276). He continued writing and illustrating his own stories as well as the stories of others. Before Sendak received his own Caldecott Medal, five books that he only illustrated were runners-up: *A Very Special House* by Ruth Krauss, *What Do You Say, Dear?* (192) by Sesyle Joslin, *The Moon Jumpers* (305) by Janice May Udry, *Little Bear's Visit* (235) by Else Holmelund Minarik, and

From *The Moon Jumpers* by Maurice Sendak.

Mr. Rabbit and the Lovely Present (324) by Charlotte Zolotow. In 1964 he received the medal for *Where the Wild Things Are* (277), which he both wrote and illustrated.

In his superb and often unpredictable style, Maurice Sendak takes an excursion into the realm of fantasy in *Higglety Pigglety Pop: Or, There Must Be More to Life* (273). Jennie who has everything leaves her affluent setting and starts down the road of experience. Her most perilous adventures come about when she takes on the job of nursemaid to a baby whose tantrums are frightening. One narrow escape follows another. Jennie finally comes into her own as the star of the World Mother Goose Theatre. The illustrations, rich in detail and emotional appeal, highlight the humor of the story.

In *Chicken Soup with Rice: A Book of Months* (272) the text sings its way from page to page. Each month gets the touch of humor that makes Sendak's writing so entertaining. And the devilish expressions on the faces of his children show Sendak's artistic wit.

Written and illustrated by Sendak, *Where the Wild Things Are* (277) stands as a significant contribution to literature. In this story Sendak shows his keen perception of the imaginative powers of early childhood. Max "made mischief of one kind or another"—perhaps because he has put on his wolf suit. His mother sends him to bed when he threatens to eat her up. In his room a forest starts to grow. The dense forest becomes an ocean with a boat for Max in which he sails off "through night and day and in and out of weeks and almost over a year to where the wild things are." When the wild things make an uproar, Max tells them to be quiet. He tames them with a magic trick, and the wild things make him king. Even a king can be lonely, so, in spite of the pleadings of the wild things, Max gives up being king. With a righteous expression on his face, Max sails back to his room, where his supper, still hot, is waiting for him.

A noise keeps Mickey awake in Maurice Sendak's story *In the Night Kitchen* (274). As Mickey protests he finds himself falling through the ceiling into adventure in the night kitchen where the jolly bakers are making a cake. They gleefully mix Mickey into the batter. Mickey escapes and secures the milk the bakers need. "Mission accomplished Mickey lets out a triumphant Cock-a-Doodle-Doo!" (unpaged). Again Sendak has written and illustrated a distinguished book for children to laugh over and for adults to enjoy and even to analyze. The illustrations use Mickey and the bakers as the centers of interest. The size of the characters gives emphasis to the action, and the details of the background are told in colors that do not detract from the happenings. Sendak has opened up more freedom for illustrators of children's stories through the drawings in *In the Night Kitchen.*

An author-illustrator who has won international fame for his unusual style in writing and his laughter-packed illustrations is THEODORE SEUSS GEISEL, more affectionately known to both children and adults alike as DR. SEUSS, whose stories and illustrations are discussed at length in Chapter 5.

Mr. Brown Can Moo! Can You? (280) is a recent one of Dr. Seuss' fun books for youngsters which involves all kinds of noises. There is a warning against despoiling natural resources in *The Lorax* (279). The story in verse tells about the useless destruction of the Truffula.

LOUIS SLOBODKIN left his hometown of Albany before finishing high school to attend the Beaux Arts Institute of Design in New York City where he studied sculpturing and drawing. He worked diligently for five years during which time he was awarded twenty-two medals as well as the Tiffany Foundation Scholarship. Following his studies at the Beaux Arts he worked for ten years as a sculptor. He occasionally did ghost work in addition to receiving commissions of his own. In 1941 he did his first drawings for a book for children, *The Moffats* (112) by Eleanor Estes. In the same year *Magic Michael* (287), which he wrote and illustrated, was published. Since then he has written and illustrated nearly fifty books by other authors. In 1944 he received the Caldecott Medal for his illustrations for James Thurber's *Many Moons* (292).

One of Slobodkin's early books that is filled with funny nonsense is *Hustle and Bustle* (286), a story about two hippopotamuses. Slobodkin's *The Amiable Giant* (285) is an excursion out of reality into fantasy. An amiable giant lives in a big, black, granite castle on the top of a tremendous mountain. When he gets lonely, he comes down the mountain to visit the little people living in a pretty village in the valley. Slobodkin's illustrations reflect the humor of the story.

Each page of Slobodkin's *Yasu and the Strangers* (288) is a delight to see and a pleasure to hear or read. Little Yasu is the smallest boy on a bus load of schoolchildren who are going to visit the great temple at Nara. Suspense begins when Yasu gets lost, but the story ends happily after Yasu finds a policeman.

Among the many stories Slobodkin has written, there is some unevenness in quality, but the illustrations are consistently excellent. From his background as a sculptor he gives the characters strong lines and a rather ephemeral make-up that he allows the reader's imagination to complete.

Born in the Siberian town of Cheliabinsk, ESPHYR SLOBODKINA spent her childhood in Siberia and Manchuria. She attended a Russian school in Manchuria and studied art privately before attending the National Academy of Design in New York for five years. Interested in abstract art, she joined in organizing the American Abstract Artist Group. Miss Slobodkina has had a number of one-man shows, and her work has been shown in several large museums as well as in many private collections throughout the country.

Pezzo the Peddler and the Circus Elephant (289) is a gay story about a peddler who sells caps, a circus parade, and a mischievous elephant. Pezzo watches the circus parade pass by in all its splendor. When Jumbo, the elephant, sees the stack of hats on Pezzo's head, he reaches for the top one, and they all tumble to the ground. What seems to be a calamity at first turns into good fortune for Pezzo when he is invited to join the circus.

Pinky and the Petunias (290) is the story of a soft little gray-and-white kitten with a weakness for petunias. Every morning right after breakfast Pinky walks out to see what is new in the neighborhood. To his delight he always finds a petunia bed waiting for "his dessert of tender young petunia buds" (unpaged). Neighbors try to stop Pinky in every way possible from eating their petunias but without success. Finally a bee in a petunia bud makes an impression upon Pinky.

FRANÇOISE SEIGNOSBOSC is a French author-illustrator who has created a number of picture-story books. FRANÇOISE, which is her pen name, was born in Lodeve, France. At an early age she drew soldiers, horses, and large families of children. Following her studies in various art academies and schools in the United States, she went to work with a publisher of children's books. In 1951 she received the New York *Herald Tribune* prize for her picture-story book *Jeanne-Marie Counts Her Sheep* (269). Most of Françoise's stories revolve around this charming lady named Jeanne-Marie.

In *Jeanne-Marie Counts Her Sheep* Jeanne-Marie and her precious white sheep, Patapon, talk about all the things they will buy and do if Patapon has seven little lambs. Jeanne-Marie is not too unhappy and Patapon is pleased when she has only one precious little lamb.

Jeanne-Marie tells Patapon about Christmas and all the lovely things Father Noel might bring her in *Noel for Jeanne-Marie* (271). Patapon is sad because he has no shoe for Father Noel to fill with presents. Jeanne-Marie goes to the little old man who makes wooden shoes and buys a pair for Patapon so that he, too, can have a happy Christmas.

Jeanne-Marie at the Fair (268) tells about the good time Jeanne-Marie has at the village fair to which her father takes her on his scooter. Patapon is unhappy because he cannot go. He tires of being alone and sets out to find Jeanne-Marie. Frightened, Patapon finally discovers Jeanne-Marie, and they return home together.

Françoise's story lines are simple and move along quickly. There is a naïvety about her drawing that is attractive to children.

JANICE MAY UDRY attended Northwestern University, where she received her B.S. degree, majoring in creative writing. With lyrical prose Miss Udry tells the story of *The Moon Jumpers* (305). The imagination of boys and girls in their nighttime play is described with sensitivity. Maurice Sendak in his superb style furthers the story by catching the moods, the magic, and the mystery of night as felt by children.

The text of *A Tree Is Nice* (307) has a friendly heart-warming quality that captures the niceness of trees. The things that trees do for people are related in such a way that the trees take on personalities. The illustrations by Marc Simont are striking in color and rich in detail. *A Tree Is Nice* received the Caldecott Medal in 1957.

Janice Udry makes an interesting story out of an everyday situation. Little children can easily identify with her characters. Among her delightful stories are *What Mary Jo Wanted* (309), *What Mary Jo Shared* (308), and *Next Door to Laura Linda* (306). *What Mary Jo Shared* is a realistic portrayal of a Black child who shares her father with her kindergarten.

The relationships in a friendly middle-class, Black family are

From *What Mary Jo Wanted* by Janice May Udry.

From *Lyle, Lyle, Crocodile* by Bernard Waber.

pleasantly told in *Mary Jo's Grandmother* (304). When Mary Jo is alone, her grandmother has an accident, and Mary Jo finds her lying on the kitchen floor. Mary Jo makes her as comfortable as possible and then goes for help in a snowstorm. The emphasis in the story is on the good family relationships in this Black family.

BERNARD WABER was born and grew up in Philadelphia. He attended the Museum of Fine Arts from 1946 to 1950, and from 1950 to 1951 he attended the Pennsylvania Academy of Fine Arts.

Mr. Waber chose a crocodile named Lyle as the hero for a number of his stories. The reader meets Lyle in a most unusual situation in Mr. Waber's hilarious story *The House on East 88th Street* (312). He also appears in *Lyle, Lyle, Crocodile* (314) and in *Lyle and the Birthday Party* (313).

Bernard Waber's delight in portraying animals is also illustrated in *"You Look Ridiculous" Said the Rhinoceros to the Hippopotamus* (315). *An Anteater Named Arthur* (310) is another of Bernard Waber's downright funny picture-story books. The story is related by Arthur's mother who, after exhausting all the adjectives possible in telling how wonderful Arthur is, finally admits that "sometimes Arthur is a problem." The illustrations make real characters out of Arthur and his mother.

Bernard Waber's versatility is shown both in his selection of subjects and in his illustrations. His recent story *A Firefly Named Torchy* (311) is about a firefly that is different. The illustrations are in a lighter vein and more capricious than the cartoon-like drawings in his earlier books. Torchy does not glow softly like the other fireflies. His light is so bright that he frightens them. After a night of cavorting with the bright lights of Broadway, Torchy is pleased to return home to twinkle and glow like the other fireflies.

Outstanding among author-illustrators is LEONARD WEISGARD, whose stories take unpredictable turns and whose illustrations glow with color. It was the art courses in high school that convinced Weisgard that he should study art at Pratt Institute in New York.

Weisgard's amiability, sense of humor, and imagination give an unsurpassed quality to both his writing and his illustrations. These qualities are well illustrated in his story *Silly Willy Nilly* (319), which opens with a mother elephant scolding her baby, Willy Nilly. Taking his mother's scolding to heart Willy Nilly decides to run away. He gets into difficulty when a lion decides to eat him. Fortunately Willy Nilly remembers the things his mother has warned him not to forget and escapes what would have been a dreadful fate. The reader leaves Willy Nilly as he is rocked to sleep in his mother's arms.

In lilting prose and striking double-page spreads Weisgard draws upon the imagination of young listeners and readers in *Who Dreams of Cheese?* (320) Different kinds of dreams are mentioned, and questions follow that stimulate creativity.

Leonard Weisgard made a significant contribution to Americana for children when he wrote *Mr. Peaceable Paints* (317). The setting is a little town on a hill beside the sea called Eagle's Landing; the time is the colonial period in our country. The story and illustrations are full of the romance of ships, the sea, and cargo from far-off lands.

Down Huckleberry Hill (316) is a cumulative tale full of fun and frolic. The dogcatcher leaves his wagon loaded with dogs of every breed and description at the top of a hill while he goes into the barber shop for a haircut. The wind is to blame for starting the commotion. As the wagon rolls down the hill, it upsets everything in its path—the laundryman's cart, the grocery boy's bicycle, the scissor-grinder's cart, to mention a few—until the wagon goes Bump! Bang! Crash! in the farmer's pumpkin patch. The illustrations vividly portray the confusion.

Little Island, written by Margaret Wise Brown and illustrated by Weisgard, won the Caldecott Medal in 1946.

Contemporary Authors

Many of the early authors and author-illustrators who came on the literary scene in the forties and fifties continue to make outstanding contributions to the field of children's literature. They have also set the pace for the many new contributors to the field of picture-story books. New art materials, as well as innovations in art styles, are being introduced.

REBECCA CAUDILL has a friendly, heart-warming quality to her stories. Her characters are realistic, and she reveals a sympathetic understanding of the behavior of children.

In *The Best-Loved Doll* (66) Betsy enters her plain, shabby doll in a contest. How Betsy's doll wins a prize for a most unusual reason makes a very pleasant story.

The setting for *A Pocketful of Cricket* (67) is a rural area in Kentucky, and the main characters are a farm boy and a cricket. Through the story the author presents a realistic portrayal of regional children. Miss Caudill's rich imagery and her sensitivity to the feelings of young listeners give quality to her writing that enriches literature for readers of all ages. *A Pocketful of Cricket* is enhanced by Evaline Ness' appealing color illustrations.

ANN NOLAN CLARK was born in New Mexico. At an early age she became interested in the Indians of the region and their culture. Her desire to know the Indians better prompted her to travel and live in Indian country for years. When she taught in an Indian school, she found that the textbooks being used were unsuitable for non-English-speaking children. She wrote new books for them with decided success. In order to broaden her background in Indian culture, she followed the suggestion of the Director of Indian Education and spent a year with various tribes and wrote books from the Indian point of view.

In My Mother's House (68) was written with the help of the Tewa Indian children of the Tesque pueblo near Santa Fe. Its short sentences read like free verse. This beautiful story, which served as a geography book for the Indian children, has significance for all children.

Her second book of a similar nature was *Little Navajo Bluebird* (69), the story of a Navajo family as they live through the seasons of the year. Their devotion to each other, to their home, and to their relatives is told in lyric prose. Ann Nolan Clark's perceptions of the problems that face the Indians and their relationships with the white man deepen the significance of the story.

Mrs. Clark then spent five years on a program of training teachers to work with underprivileged children for the Inter-American Educational Foundation. Her work took her to Mexico, Guatemala, Costa Rica, Ecuador, Peru, and Brazil. She gathered materials on her travels which she used in her stories.

Tia Maria's Garden (72) is a tenderly told story in which a little boy tells of his early-morning walks with his aunt in her enchanting, fenceless, limitless garden—the desert. The text has Ann Nolan Clark's usual poetic quality, and Ezra Jack Keats' beautiful illustrations complement the moods created.

Ann Nolan Clark departs from the serious tone and purposes of her earlier stories to write in a more humorous vein. The mischievous style of *This for That* (71) and *Third Monkey* (70) provide fun for the reader. Don Freeman's illustrations for both of the stories are perfect backdrops for the actions of the characters.

Born in Lafayette, Indiana, BEATRICE SCHENK DE REGNIERS attended the University of Illinois, was graduated from the University of Chicago, did graduate work, and then studied in France for a time.

The need that every little child feels to have a little place all his own is told with charming text and lovable illustrations in *A Little House of Your Own* (93), which is coauthored with Irene Haas. The little house may be under the dining room table or a doll house in the backyard or even a big umbrella or a big box. The important thing is that each child has a special place to call his very own and that each one respects each other's "little house."

The Little Girl and Her Mother (92), written along with Esther Gilman, describes the ways in which a small girl imitates her mother, pointing out that there are some things that each of them can do that the other cannot.

A happy addition to the illustrious list of Caldecott Medal winners is Beatrice Schenk de Regniers' *May I Bring a Friend?* (90), illustrated by Beni Montresor. The detailed illustrations resemble stage sets. In addition to the full-color pages there are prankish drawings in black and white showing the king and queen in informal activities.

Other stories by Beatrice Schenk de Regniers are *A Child's Book of*

The Snow Party by Beatrice Schenk de Regniers.

Dreams (95), which is written with Bill Sokol, *Snow Party* (91), and *Something Special* (94), which is coauthored with Irene Haas.

SESYLE JOSLIN has written a number of appealing stories around Baby Elephant. Young listeners and readers have a hilarious time listening to and reading *Baby Elephant's Trunk* (195), which is coauthored with Leonard Weisgard. They are intrigued with the French words as well as the clever story line in which Baby Elephant and his mother prepare for a trip to France. While Baby Elephant packs his trunk, eats his supper, and prepares for bed, his mother teaches him the French expressions that will make the visit fun. The glossary of French expressions helps young children to feel as if they have learned to speak French.

Sesyle Joslin wrote a number of clever stories from a game she invented to teach some manners to her daughters. In *What Do You Say, Dear?* (192) clever illustrations and text present the fundamentals of manners for young children. This simple book about etiquette is sparked by humorous pictures by Maurice Sendak. The author presents absurd situations, answered by polite refrains that are hilarious under such situations.

With the success of *What Do You Say, Dear?* she wrote "A Second Handbook of Etiquette for Young Ladies and Gentlemen to Be Used as a Guide for Everyday Social Behavior." *What Do You Do, Dear?* (191) has the same style of delightful humor and clever illustrations as its predecessor. The elegance with which courtesies are extended gives boys and girls both a laugh and a lesson.

Other stories by Sesyle Joslin enjoyed by young readers are *Spaghetti for Breakfast: and Other Useful Phrases in Italian and English* (193), created with Katherina Barry, *There Is a Bull on My Balcony* (190), and *There Is a Dragon in My Bed* (194), written with Irene Haas.

WILLIAM LIPKIND (whose pseudonym is WILL) has written a number of amusing stories for the pleasure of young readers. The sixteen children's books by Mr. Lipkind have been illustrated by Nicolas Mordvinoff (pseudonym NICOLAS) with the exception of one illustrated by Roger Duvoisin.

The Two Reds (227) was the first book on which Mr. Lipkind and Mr. Mordvinoff collaborated as author and artist. The two Reds in the story are a red-headed boy and a red cat who live on St. Marks Place in New York City. The boy and the cat become friends when the cat saves the boy from the attacks of the unfriendly Seventh Street Gang. The story and its illustrations present a boy's-eye view of the rushing, bustling life of a big city.

In *Finders Keepers* (225) Nap and Winkle, two shaggy dogs, dig for a bone. How they first lose and then retrieve the bone they uncover and enjoy it together makes an unbelievably funny story. This book received the Caldecott Medal in 1952.

Nubber Bear (222) is an amusing story about a running, jumping, rolling little bear who could not be still. Other stories written by Mr. Lipkind and illustrated by Mr. Mordvinoff that young readers enjoy are *Circus Ruckus* (224), *Four-Leaf Clover* (226), and *Chaga* (223). Mr. Lipkind intends his stories to be funny, and Mr. Mordvinoff furthers the fun with his vigorous illustrations.

Born in New York City, EVE TITUS is the author of the popular Anatole stories. In *Anatole* (293), a book that is very popular with preschool children, Mrs. Titus created "a mouse of action, a mouse of honor, a mouse magnifique."

The same delightful kind of humor permeates the Anatole stories that followed. Anatole is very proud of his job and enjoys his work as a cheese taster at the factory of M'sieur Duval. However, the job becomes both exciting and dangerous in *Anatole and the Cat* (294). In *Anatole and the Robot* (296), when the owner of the cheese factory has the measles, his cousin takes over the work at the factory. To Anatole's dismay the cousin establishes a robot to do his work. A smashing climax establishes Anatole as a hero, ends the robot's life, and puts

Anatole over Paris by Eve Titus.

the cousin in his humble place. Other entertaining Anatole stories are *Anatole over Paris* (298), jointly written with Paul Galdone, and *Anatole and the Poodle* (295).

Eve Titus left Anatole to relate the adventures of a mouse and a lion who set out to see the people of the world in *The Mouse and the Lion* (297).

ALVIN R. TRESSELT's first book was *Rain Drop Splash* (300). In lyrical prose the sounds, movements, and magic of rain move through the story. Roger Duvoisin's illustrations done in vivid colors complement the varying moods of the text.

White Snow, Bright Snow (303) portraying the fun of the first snowfall for children and its effect on adults followed *Rain Drop Splash.* The natural quality of the text and the beautiful illustrations by Roger Duvoisin capture the out-of-doors in all its snowy splendor. *White Snow, Bright Snow* received the Caldecott Medal in 1948.

Among the many titles that portray the wonders of nature are *Follow the Wind* (299), *A Thousand Lights and Fireflies* (301), and *Under the Trees and Through the Grass* (302). The magic and the power of the wind are beautifully described through rhythmic text and colorful illustrations that sweep across the pages and give strength to the story in *Follow the Wind.* The lyrical text of *A Thousand Lights and Fireflies* and the color illustrations catch the moods of the city and country. Prose glows under Tresselt's pen, and what he does not say with words, Roger Duvoisin says beautifully with pictures in *Under the Trees and Through the Grass.*

The excellence of Tresselt's stories comes across in the way he portrays the out of doors. No mood of nature escapes his pen. His feelings for the wonders of nature are beautifully expressed in rhythmic prose that captures the beauty, excitement, and drama of the natural world. Such outstanding illustrators as Roger Duvoisin, Leonard Weisgard, and Yaroslava have extended and enriched Tresselt's writing.

CHARLOTTE ZOLOTOW went to the University of Wisconsin on a writing scholarship. After that she worked for a time in New York as an editorial assistant in Harper and Row's juvenile book department. Her first book for children, *The Park Book* (325), was published in 1944.

The Storm Book (327) was published in 1952, the beginning of a succession of picture-story books that have come at the rate of two and three a year. *The Storm Book* is rich with the sights and sounds that accompany a storm.

In *Do You Know What I'll Do?* (323) a little girl in her dream tells her small brother with tenderness and love all the things that she will do when the flowers grow, when it snows, when it rains, and when the wind blows.

Mr. Rabbit helps a little girl to think of a birthday present for her mother. The little girl knows that her mother likes red, yellow, green, and blue. Mr. Rabbit suggests such things as a red roof, a yellow taxicab, a green caterpillar, and a blue lake, but the little girl selects apples, bananas, pears, and grapes. When they are artistically arranged, they make a lovely present. This amusing story is told entirely in dialogue. The full-color illustrations by Maurice Sendak catch the mood of *Mr. Rabbit and the Lovely Present* (324).

When Thomas and his family move into a new house on a new street in *A Tiger Called Thomas* (329), Thomas is afraid that the people in the new neighborhood will not like him. In spite of his mother's coaxing, he refuses to go off the porch. When Halloween comes his mother buys him a tiger suit to wear when he goes out to trick or treat. He is sure that no one will recognize him, but to his surprise wherever he goes people call him by his first name, and the boys and girls he meets invite him to come and play with them. Thomas returns home feeling that everyone likes him, and he likes them, too.

Other stories from the prolific pen of Charlotte Zolotow which young children enjoy are *The Three Funny Friends* (328) and *The Sky Was Blue* (326).

Author-Illustrator Teams

One is inclined to associate certain authors with certain illustrators, for example, William Lipkind and Nicolas Mordvinoff, Roger Duvoisin and Louise Fatio. The author and the illustrator are a team. The illustrators sense the feeling and the moods the authors wish to express and through their illustrations add another dimension to the story. The following author-illustrator teams have contributed significantly to the enrichment of children's literature.

CONRAD and MARY BUFF are a husband-and-wife pair who have made children's literature richer with their stories and illustrations. Conrad and Mary both write, and Conrad illustrates both his own and his wife's books.

The first story on which Conrad and Mary Buff collaborated was *Kobi: A Boy of Switzerland* (54), published in 1936. It is natural that the Buffs should have a Swiss setting for their first story, since Conrad Buff was born and grew up there. The book gives a beautiful picture of Swiss life as it still is today in many of the cantons. When Kobi goes into the high Alpine meadows to herd his sheep, the music from the cowbells and the singing and yodeling of the herders blend into a picture of pastoral beauty and joyous living. The strength and rugged beauty of the lithographs give a distinctive quality to the book.

The Buff's next story was set in the Navajo country. In *Dancing Cloud* (52) the reader becomes acquainted with the history, customs, and social functions of the Navajo Indians through the activities of two Navajo children, Dancing Cloud and his younger sister Lost Tooth. This story catches the full flavor of desert living. The beautiful lithographs emphasize both the beauty and starkness of the desert and the rigors of Navajo life.

Following *Dancing Cloud*, the Buffs presented one of their animal stories for young listeners and readers. There is a tender, poetic quality to the text, and the illustrations sustain the various moods of the animals and the seasons in *Dash and Dart* (53), a story of the first year in the life of twin fawns. The double-page illustrations, rich in colors, show the grandeur of the far western homeland of the twin fawns.

With their varied subjects, well told and beautifully illustrated, the Buffs have made a significant contribution to the enrichment of literature for boys and girls.

EDGAR PARIN and INGRI D'AULAIRE are a husband-and-wife team who by pooling their talents have added immeasurably to the riches in children's literature.

When the d'Aulaires turned to writing for children, their first book was *The Magic Rug* (80), a story built around the sketches they had made on a trip to Northern Africa. *The Magic Rug* was illustrated with prints made by lithography, a process that the d'Aulaires have continued to use in their illustrations.

Their stories fall into three groups. There are those that draw upon Ingri's happy childhood in Norway. Another group is rich with the flavor of the history and spirit of America, and a third group seems to reveal some of the d'Aulaire's personal interests.

Ola (81), a picture book of a boy's winter-time adventures in Norway, appeared in 1932. *Ola and Blankken and Line, Sine, Trine* (82), a sequel to *Ola*, followed. It tells how Ola and the three little girls, Line, Sine, and Trine, with the help of the farm animals save Blankken, the horse, from the great troll cock that threatened to take him.

The d'Aulaires showed their love of America, their adopted country, by writing biographies of a number of our heroes. The first one selected was Abraham Lincoln. His life is followed from the time he was a toddler in a log cabin in Kentucky to the time he served as President of the United States in *Abraham Lincoln* (78).

The d'Aulaires left historical subjects to do an enjoyable picture-story book about animals. In *Animals Everywhere* (79) no animal is left out, and just the right word is chosen to describe each animal and his behavior—"the lively monkey," "the sly zebra," "the swift little antelope," and so on. The lithographs provide humor and give personalities to the animals.

ROGER DUVOISIN and LOUISE FATIO are a husband-and-wife team who were both born in Switzerland but have made the United States their permanent home.

Lions fascinated Miss Fatio, and she chose one to be the leading character in a number of her stories, all of which were illustrated by her husband. Lions are not always fierce; they can be friendly, as is shown in *The Happy Lion* (124). *The Happy Lion's Quest* (126) relates further adventures of the Happy Lion. What could be more exciting than a vacation with a lion? *The Happy Lion's Vacation* (128) is heavy on unusual happenings filled with suspense and excitement. Other laughter-filled stories about the Happy Lion followed: *The Happy Lion Roars* (125), *The Three Happy Lions* (129), *The Happy Lion and the Bear* (130), coauthored with her husband, and *The Happy Lion's Treasure* (127). Roger Duvoisin's illustrations extend the fun of his wife's Happy Lion stories.

Mr. Duvoisin chose unusual characters around which to build and illustrate his stories. A number of his stories feature Petunia, a

Veronica by Roger Duvoisin.

Petunia by Roger Duvoisin.

unique goose, and Veronica, an aggressive hippopotamus. One of Duvoisin's early stories introduces *Petunia* (104) to young listeners and readers. Her silliness and haughtiness bring her close to disaster. Petunia is not so silly in *Petunia and the Song* (105). In fact, her song brings about the capture of an apple thief. Racoon certainly was not sincere when he said, "Petunia I Love You." It soon becomes obvious that his motives are questionable, and the extent of his insincerity and the depth of his evil desires become apparent. Roger Duvoisin spins a tale in which the innocent Petunia outwits the wiley Racoon at every turn. Illustrations in splotches of black and white and bold colors provide just the right comedy relief to *Petunia I Love You* (106).

Veronica (107) is the story of an unhappy hippopotamus whose great desire is to be different and famous. But instead of finding fame and fortune in the city, Veronica almost finds herself in jail.

DON and LYDIA FREEMAN have collaborated on such books as *Chuggy and the Blue Caboose* (141) and *Pet of the Met* (142), which was a *Herald Tribune* Spring Festival Award winner.

Pet of the Met is a fanciful tale set in the New York Metropolitan Opera House. Maestro Petrini, a white mouse, lives with his wife and their three little Petrinis in a forgotten harp case in the attic of the house. Maestro Petrini works as a page turner for the prompter. The protagonist of the story is Mefisto, the cat, who "hated music more than anything else in the world except mice." In the end Maestro Petrini and Mefisto become fast friends, and it is said that between them they have the run of the entire Metropolitan Opera House.

Don Freeman's *The Turtle and the Dove* (140) is a sweet, little love story about a beautiful white dove and a friendly turtle. His *Fly High,*

Fly Low (137) goes beyond the usual picture-story book with its imaginative text and illustrations. The story is set "In the beautiful city of San Francisco, a city famous for its fogs and flowers, cable cars and towers" (p. 6).

Stories that Don Freeman has both written and illustrated are *Come Again, Pelican* (135), *Cyrano the Crow* (136), *Norman the Doorman* (138), and *A Rainbow of My Own* (139). The last is considered by many to be Mr. Freeman's best, especially from the standpoint of the drawings. With poetic text and rainbow-like illustrations he imaginatively expresses the thoughts and feelings of a host of little children.

BERTA and ELMER HADER are a husband-and-wife team whose *joie de vivre* shines through in the stories they write and illustrate for children. Their books give pleasure as well as an awareness of the life of animals and the beauty of nature. Their artfully illustrated books were written primarily to provide information on different subjects, rather than to tell a story.

An early book, *Pancho* (169), is one of the Haders' exciting contributions to picture-story books. Beautiful color and black-and-white drawings enhance the tale of Pancho, who unwittingly captures the bull with the crooked tail and is rewarded with a purse filled with gold.

In *Reindeer Trail* (170) a report by Sheldon Jackson, General Agent of Education in Alaska, relates his trip to Lapland to bring Lapp herders and their reindeer to Alaska. The Haders' story centers around Ahlook, a little Eskimo boy living long ago in Alaska, his father, his mother, and his little sisters. *Reindeer Trail* is useful as an enrichment book for the social studies. It is particularly interesting in light of today's awakening concern of the government over the present-day living conditions of the Eskimos in Alaska.

The Big Snow (166) opens with a warning to the animals of the woods that winter is coming—the geese are flying south. How the various animals react to this warning makes an interesting story. The illustrations of the wild creatures are realistic. *The Big Snow* received the Caldecott Medal in 1949.

Among the other children's stories by the Haders are: *Little Appaloosa* (168), a story of horses whose ancestry can be traced back to the ancient kingdoms of Asia; *Little Antelope: An Indian for a Day* (167), about a little boy who dreams he is an Indian; and *Two Is Company, Three's a Crowd* (171), the story of bird migration.

RUSSELL and LILLIAN HOBAN met as young art students at the Graphic Sketch Club in Philadelphia and both studied at the Philadelphia Museum School.

A number of the most delightful stories by the Hobans are about a lovable little badger, Frances, and her family. The first of the Frances stories, *Bedtime for Frances* (175), was published in 1960 and was illustrated by Garth Williams. Frances puts on an act that is typical of many little children. The other Frances stories are illustrated by Lillian Hoban in either pencil or pen-and-ink wash.

A Baby Sister for Frances (173) is a humorous tale about the badger family. Frances feels neglected because of the arrival of a new baby. After providing herself with plenty of food, she "runs away from home" under the dining room table. Quiet comments from Mother and Father about how they will miss her and how little babies should really have a big sister gradually bring Frances out from under the table and into the family once more.

In *Bread and Jam for Frances* (176) Mother cures Frances of eating bread and jam by restricting her diet entirely to bread and jam. Frances soon changes her taste and demands the same kind of food the family is eating.

The animals in the Hoban stories have distinct personalities. Charlie, a young beaver, acts like any youngster desiring a little independence in *Charlie the Tramp* (177). The tone of this little tale is light and charming, and the green-and-white pictures are a happy complement to a story that is not offensive in spite of its fatalistic message about staying home and being content with a predestined lot.

A Bargain for Frances (174) is a recent story by the Hobans. The story relates further experiences of the little badger Frances. Although her mother warns her to be careful when she goes to play with her friend Thelma, who always seems to be getting the better of her, it appears as if she is going to be fooled again. Instead of getting the tea set she wants, she is coerced into taking an old one from Thelma. By using her head, Frances brings the story to a happy ending.

CLEMENT HURD and EDITH THATCHER each wrote and illustrated children's books before they were married. Clement Hurd's first break came when he was chosen by Gertrude Stein to illustrate her only published book for children, *The World Is Round* (291). It was while Edith Thatcher was studying in New York City that her first book was accepted by a publisher. It was then that she decided to write realistic stories for children—stories about streamlined trains, bulldozers, and fire engines.

Benny the Bulldozer (178) was one of the first stories that the Hurds collaborated on. Another early story by the Hurds was *Willy's Farm*, which describes the different work done and the equipment used for doing the work on a farm.

The Hurds also did a series of stories built around Mr. Charlie, including *Mr. Charlie's Chicken House* (180), *Mr. Charlie's Gas Station*, *Mr. Charlie's Camping Trip* (179), and *Mr. Charlie's Farm* (181).

MISKA and MAUD PETERSHAM first illustrated school books and books of other authors. *Miki* (256), the first book they did together, pictures life in Hungary, where Miska was born.

A three-month trip to Palestine inspired them to write *The Christ Child* (254), one of their best-known books. They used the text from St. Matthew and St. Luke as their source for this beautiful story of the Nativity.

The Petersham's love of the United States is reflected in their writing. *The Silver Mace* (257) describes Williamsburg. The historical background is well portrayed through text and illustrations. In *Story of the Presidents of the United States of America* (258) the qualities and personalities of each president are realistically portrayed.

Other stories by the Petershams are *The Box with Red Wheels* (253), *Circus Baby* (255), and *A Bird in the Hand* (252). In the last, Benjamin Franklin's sayings are given a humorous twist by the use of little details in the brightly colored illustrations.

Extending Experiences for the Reader

1. Read the acceptance speeches of the following recipients of the Caldecott Medal (see "Further Reading," pages 285 and 286): Maurice Sendak, Robert McCloskey, and Leonard Weisgard. Compare the philosophies they express.
2. Collect pictures for a file of authors and illustrators of picture-story books.
3. Analyze the story line in *Angus and the Ducks* (132) by Marjorie Flack. Read to the class this and three other stories with the same story line.
4. Make an exhibit of books that have received the Caldecott Medal.
5. While reading a picture-story book, have the class pantomime the actions of the characters.
6. Analyze *Sam, Bangs, and Moonshine* (240) by Evaline Ness, *Higglety Pigglety Pop: Or, There Must Be More to Life* (273) by Maurice Sendak, and *Horton Hatches the Egg* (278) by Dr. Seuss in terms of themes, story lines, characterizations, and illustrations. What similarities do you find? What differences?
7. Compare and contrast the illustrations of L. Leslie Brooke, Randolph Caldecott, and Kate Greenaway. Share the illustrations of these artists with the class.
8. Prepare a picture bibliography of picture-story books about the following subjects: people, animals, nature, machinery.

9. Analyze the following picture-story books in terms of ecology: *The Little House* (57) by Virginia Lee Burton, *Farewell to Shady Glade* (251) by Bill Peet, and *Swamp Spring* (65) by Carol and Don Carrick. Share the analysis with the class.

Extending Experiences for Children

1. From an exhibit of picture-story books arranged by the teacher select the one you like the best and tell why.
2. Plan a mural depicting scenes from picture-story books. Divide into groups of three or four and paint one scene from a book to add to the mural.
3. In groups of three or four take turns acting out a picture-story book for the class.
4. Listen to a reading of *The Egg Tree* (234) by Katherine Milhous. Plant an egg tree in your school room.
5. Cut out pictures from magazines and newspapers. Bring them to school and make up a story about them to read to the class.
6. Make a mobile using characters you have drawn from your favorite picture-story books.

Chapter References

1. *Aesop's Fables.* Boris Artzybasheff (ed. and ill.). New York: Viking, 1933. Grades 4–6.
2. ALIKI (Aliki Brandenburg). *Diogenes: The Story of the Greek Philosopher.* Englewood Cliffs, N. J.: Prentice-Hall, 1968. Preschool–grade 3.
3. ———. *Hush Little Baby.* Englewood Cliffs, N. J.: Prentice-Hall, 1968. Preschool–grade 1.
4. ———. *Keep Your Mouth Closed, Dear.* New York: Dial, 1966. Kindergarten–grade 3.
5. ———. *The Story of Johnny Appleseed.* Englewood Cliffs, N. J.: Prentice-Hall, 1963. Kindergarten–grade 2.
6. ———. *The Story of William Penn.* Englewood Cliffs, N. J.: Prentice-Hall, 1964. Kindergarten–grade 3.
7. ———. *The Wish Workers.* New York: Dial, 1966. Kindergarten–grade 3.
8. ANGLUND, JOAN WALSH. *Brave Cowboy.* New York: Harcourt Brace Jovanovich, 1959. Preschool–grade 2.
9. ———. *Childhood Is a Time of Innocence.* New York: Harcourt Brace Jovanovich, 1964. Grades 3–6.
10. ———. *Cowboy and His Friend.* New York: Harcourt Brace Jovanovich, 1961. Preschool–grade 2.

11. ———. *Cowboy's Secret Life.* New York: Harcourt Brace Jovanovich, 1963. Preschool–grade 2.
12. ———. *A Friend Is Someone Who Likes You.* New York: Harcourt Brace Jovanovich, 1958. Kindergarten–grade 3.
13. ———. *Love Is a Special Way of Feeling.* New York: Harcourt Brace Jovanovich, 1960. Grade 1 and up.
14. ———. *Nibble, Nibble, Mousekin: A Tale of Hansel and Gretel.* New York: Harcourt Brace Jovanovich, 1962. Kindergarten–grade 3.
15. ARDIZZONE, EDWARD. *Little Tim and the Brave Sea Captain.* New York: Walck, 1955. Kindergarten–grade 3.
16. ———. *Lucy Brown and Mr. Grimes.* New York: Walck, 1971. Grades 1–4.
17. ———. *Tim All Alone.* New York: Walck, 1957. Grades 1–5.
18. ———. *Tim and Ginger.* New York: Walck, 1965. Kindergarten–grade 3.
19. ———. *Tim and Lucy Go to Sea.* New York: Walck, 1958. Grades 1–5.
20. ———. *Tim in Danger.* New York: Walck, 1953. Grades 1–5.
21. ———. *Tim to the Lighthouse.* New York: Walck, 1968. Kindergarten–grade 3.
22. ———. *Tim to the Rescue.* New York: Walck, 1949. Grades 1–5.
23. ———. *Tim's Friend Towser.* New York: Walck, 1962. Kindergarten–grade 3.
24. ARTZYBASHEFF, BORIS. *The Fairy Shoemaker and Other Poems.* New York: Macmillan, 1928. n.g.l.
25. ———. *The Seven Simeons: A Russian Tale.* New York: Viking, 1961. Grades 4–8.
26. AYME, MARCEL. *Wonderful Farm.* Maurice Sendak (ill.). New York: Harper & Row, 1951. Kindergarten–grade 3.
27. BEMELMANS, LUDWIG. *Hansi.* New York: Viking, 1934. Grades 3–7.
28. ———. *Madeline.* New York: Viking, 1969. Paperback. Kindergarten–grade 3.
29. ———. *Madeline and the Bad Hat.* New York: Viking, 1969. Paperback. Kindergarten–grade 3.
30. ———. *Madeline and the Gypsies.* New York: Viking, 1959. Kindergarten–grade 3.
31. ———. *Madeline in London.* New York: Viking, 1961. Kindergarten–grade 3.
32. ———. *Madeline's Rescue.* New York: Viking, 1953. Kindergarten–grade 3.
33. BIANCO, MARGERY WILLIAMS. *Apple Tree.* Boris Artzybasheff (ill.). New York: Doran, 1926. n.g.l.
34. BROCK, EMMA L. *Greedy Goat.* New York: Knopf, 1931. Kindergarten–grade 3.
35. ———. *Here Comes Kristie!* New York: Knopf, 1942. Kindergarten–grade 3.
36. ———. *Plaid Cow.* New York: Knopf, 1961. Kindergarten–grade 3.
37. ———. *The Runaway Sardine.* New York: Knopf, 1929. Kindergarten–grade 3.

38. ______. *To Market, to Market.* New York: Knopf, 1930. Kindergarten–grade 3.
39. ______. *Topsy-Turvey Family.* New York: Knopf, 1944. Kindergarten–grade 3.
40. BROOKE, L. LESLIE. *Johnny Crow's Garden.* New York: Warne, 1903. Kindergarten–grade 2.
41. ______. *Johnny Crow's New Garden.* New York: Warne, 1935. Kindergarten–grade 3.
42. ______. *Johnny Crow's Party.* New York: Warne, 1907. Kindergarten–grade 3.
43. BROWN, MARCIA. *Cinderella, or the Little Glass Slipper.* New York: Scribner, 1954. Kindergarten–grade 3.
44. ______. *Dick Whittington and His Cat.* New York: Scribner, 1950. Kindergarten–grade 4.
45. ______. *Henry Fisherman.* New York: Scribner, 1949. Kindergarten–grade 3.
46. ______. *Little Carousel.* New York: Scribner, 1946. Kindergarten–grade 2.
47. ______. *Once a Mouse.* New York: Scribner, 1961. Kindergarten–grade 2.
48. ______. *Puss in Boots.* New York: Scribner, 1952. Kindergarten–grade 4.
49. ______. *Skipper John's Cook.* New York: Scribner, 1951.
50. ______ (ed.). *The Steadfast Tin Soldier.* New York: Scribner, 1953. Kindergarten–grade 5.
51. ______. *Stone Soup.* New York: Scribner, 1947. Kindergarten–grade 3.
52. BUFF, CONRAD, AND MARY BUFF. *Dancing Cloud.* Rev. ed. New York: Viking, 1957. Grades 2–5.
53. ______. *Dash and Dart.* New York: Viking, 1942. Kindergarten–grade 3.
54. ______. *Kobi: A Boy of Switzerland.* New York: Viking, 1965. n.g.l.
55. BURTON, VIRGINIA LEE. *Calico, The Wonder Horse.* Boston: Houghton Mifflin, 1941. Kindergarten–grade 3.
56. ______. *Choo Choo.* Boston: Houghton Mifflin, 1937. Kindergarten–grade 3.
57. ______. *The Little House.* Boston: Houghton Mifflin, 1942. Kindergarten–grade 3.
58. ______. *Mike Mulligan and His Steam Engine.* Boston: Houghton Mifflin, 1939. Kindergarten–grade 3.
59. CALDECOTT, RANDOLPH. *A Frog He Would A-Wooing Go.* New York: Warne, 1883. Kindergarten–grade 3.
60. ______. "The Great Panjandrum Himself," from *Picture Book No. 4.* New York: Warne, 1885. Kindergarten–grade 2.
61. ______. *The House That Jack Built.* New York: Warne, 1878. Kindergarten–grade 3.
62. ______. *John Gilpin.* New York: Warne, 1878. Kindergarten–grade 3.

63. ———. *Sing a Song for Sixpence.* New York: Warne, 1880. Kindergarten–grade 3.
64. ———. *The Three Jovial Huntsmen.* New York: Warne, 1880. Kindergarten–grade 3.
65. CARRICK, CAROL, AND DON CARRICK. *Swamp Spring.* New York: Macmillan, 1969. Kindergarten–grade 2.
66. CAUDILL, REBECCA. *The Best Loved Doll.* New York: Holt, Rinehart & Winston, 1962. Kindergarten–grade 4.
67. ———. *A Pocketful of Cricket.* New York: Holt, Rinehart & Winston, 1964. Paperback. Kindergarten–grade 3.
68. CLARK, ANN NOLAN. *In My Mother's House.* New York: Viking, 1941. Kindergarten–3.
69. ———. *Little Navajo Bluebird.* New York: Viking, 1943. Grades 2–5.
70. ———. *Third Monkey.* Don Freeman (ill.). New York: Viking, 1956. n.g.l.
71. ———. *This for That.* Don Freeman (ill.). San Carlos, Cal.: Golden Gate, 1965. Kindergarten–grade 3.
72. ———. *Tia Maria's Garden.* Ezra Jack Keats (ill.). New York: Viking, 1963. Grades 1–5.
73. COATSWORTH, ELIZABETH. *Five Bushel Farm.* Helen Sewell (ill.). New York: Macmillan, 1939. Grades 4–6.
74. ———. *The Princess and the Lion.* Evaline Ness (ill.). New York: Pantheon, 1963. Grades 3–7.
75. DALGLIESH, ALICE. *The Bears of Hemlock Mountain.* Helen Sewell (ill.). New York: Scribner, 1952. Grades 3–4.
76. DAUGHERTY, JAMES. *Andy and the Lion.* New York: Viking, 1970. Paperback. Preschool–grade 3.
77. ———. *The Picnic.* New York: Viking, 1958. Preschool–grade 3.
78. D'AULAIRE, EDGAR PARIN, AND INGRI D'AULAIRE. *Abraham Lincoln.* Rev. ed. Garden City, N. Y.: Doubleday, 1957. Grades 3–5.
79. ———. *Animals Everywhere.* Garden City, N. Y.: Doubleday, 1954. Kindergarten–grade 3.
80. ———. *The Magic Rug.* Garden City, N. Y.: Doubleday, 1931.
81. ———. *Ola.* Garden City, N. Y.: Doubleday, 1939. Kindergarten–grade 3.
82. ———. *Ola and Blankken and Line, Sine, and Trine.* Garden City, N. Y.: Doubleday, 1933.
83. DE BRUNHOFF, JEAN. *ABC Babar.* New York: Random House, n.d.
84. ———. *Babar and Father Christmas.* New York: Random House, 1940. Preschool.
85. ———. *Babar and His Children.* Merle Haas (tr.). New York: Random House, 1954. Preschool.
86. ———. *Babar and Zephir.* Merle Haas (tr.). New York: Random House, 1942. Preschool.
87. ———. *Babar the King.* New York: Random House, 1942. Preschool.
88. ———. *The Story of Babar, the Little Elephant.* New York: Random House, 1937. Preschool.
89. ———. *The Travels of Babar.* New York: Random House, 1934. Preschool.

90. DE REGNIERS, BEATRICE SCHENK. *May I Bring a Friend?* Beni Montresor (ill.). New York: Atheneum, 1964. Preschool–grade 2.
91. ———. *The Snow Party.* New York: Pantheon, 1959. Kindergarten–grade 3.
92. ———, AND ESTHER GILMAN. *The Little Girl and Her Mother.* New York: Vanguard, 1963.
93. ———, AND IRENE HAAS. *A Little House of Your Own.* New York: Harcourt Brace Jovanovich, 1955. Kindergarten–grade 3.
94. ———. *Something Special.* New York: Harcourt Brace Jovanovich, 1958. Kindergarten–grade 3.
95. ———, AND BILL SOKOL. *A Child's Book of Dreams.* New York: Harcourt Brace Jovanovich, 1957. Kindergarten–grade 3.
96. DINES, GLEN (ed.). *Frontier West Series.* New York: Macmillan, 1962. n.g.l.
97. ———. *Gilly and the Whicharoo.* New York: Lothrop, Lee & Shepard, 1968. Kindergarten–grade 4.
98. ———. *Pitidoe, the Colormaker.* New York: Macmillan, 1959. n.g.l.
99. ———. *The Useful Dragon of Sam Ling Toy.* New York: Macmillan, 1956. n.g.l.
100. DU BOIS, WILLIAM PENÉ. *The Bear Party.* New York: Viking, 1969. Paperback. Preschool–grade 2.
101. ———. *Lion.* New York: Viking, 1956. Kindergarten–grade 3.
102. ———. *Otto and the Magic Potatoes.* New York: Viking, 1970. Grades 3–5.
103. ———. *Otto in Africa.* New York: Viking, 1961. Kindergarten–grade 3.
104. DUVOISIN, ROGER. *Petunia.* New York: Knopf, 1950. Kindergarten–grade 3.
105. ———. *Petunia and the Song.* New York: Knopf, 1951. Kindergarten–grade 3.
106. ———. *Petunia I Love You.* New York: Knopf, 1965. Kindergarten–grade 3.
107. ———. *Veronica.* New York: Knopf, 1961. Kindergarten–grade 3.
108. EHRLICH, BETTINA. *Cocolo.* New York: Harper & Row, 1948. n.g.l.
109. ———. *Cocolo's Home.* New York: Harper & Row, 1950. n.g.l.
110. ———. *Pantaloni.* New York: Harper & Row, 1957. n.g.l.
111. ———. *Trovato.* New York: Ariel, 1959. n.g.l.
112. ESTES, ELEANOR. *The Moffats.* Louis Slobodkin (ill.). New York: Harcourt Brace Jovanovich, n.d. Paperback. Grades 4–6.
113. ETS, MARIE HALL. *Another Day.* New York: Viking, 1953. Preschool–grade 1.
114. ———. *Gilberto and the Wind.* New York: Viking, 1969. Paperback. Kindergarten–grade 3.
115. ———. *Just Me.* New York: Viking, 1970. Paperback. Kindergarten–grade 3.
116. ———. *Little Old Automobile.* New York: Viking, 1948. Preschool–grade 1.
117. ———. *Mister Penny.* New York: Viking, 1935. Preschool–grade 3.

118. ———. *Mister Penny's Circus.* New York: Viking, 1961. Preschool–grade 2.
119. ———. *Mister Penny's Race Horse.* New York: Viking, 1956. Preschool–grade 2.
120. ———. *Mister T. W. Anthony Woo.* New York: Viking, 1951. Preschool–grade 3.
121. ———, AND AURORA LABASTIDA. *Nine Days to Christmas.* New York: Viking, 1959. Preschool–grade 2.
122. FALLS, C. B. *ABC Book.* Garden City, N. Y.: Doubleday, 1957. Preschool.
123. FARJEON, ELEANOR. *The Little Bookroom.* Edward Ardizzone (ill.). New York: Walck, 1956. Grades 4–6.
124. FATIO, LOUISE. *The Happy Lion.* New York: McGraw-Hill, 1954. Kindergarten–grade 3.
125. ———. *The Happy Lion Roars.* New York: McGraw-Hill, 1957. Kindergarten–grade 3.
126. ———. *The Happy Lion's Quest.* New York: McGraw-Hill, 1961. Kindergarten–grade 3.
127. ———. *The Happy Lion's Treasure.* New York: McGraw-Hill, 1970. Kindergarten–grade 3.
128. ———. *The Happy Lion's Vacation.* New York: McGraw-Hill, 1967. Kindergarten–grade 3.
129. ———. *The Three Happy Lions.* New York: McGraw-Hill, 1959. Kindergarten–grade 3.
130. ———, AND ROGER DUVOISIN. *The Happy Lion and the Bear.* New York: McGraw-Hill, 1954. Kindergarten–grade 3.
131. FLACK, MARJORIE. *Angus and the Cat.* Garden City, N. Y.: Doubleday, 1971. Paperback. Preschool–grade 1.
132. ———. *Angus and the Ducks.* Garden City, N. Y.: Doubleday, 1939. Kindergarten–grade 2.
133. ———. *Angus Lost.* Garden City, N. Y.: Doubleday, 1941. Kindergarten–grade 2.
134. ———. *The Story About Ping.* Kurt Wiers (ill.). New York: Viking, 1933.
135. FREEMAN, DON. *Come Again, Pelican.* New York: Viking, 1961. Preschool–grade 3.
136. ———. *Cyrano the Crow.* New York: Viking, 1960. Preschool–grade 3.
137. ———. *Fly High, Fly Low.* New York: Viking, 1957. Kindergarten–grade 3.
138. ———. *Norman the Doorman.* New York: Viking, 1969. Paperback. Kindergarten–grade 3.
139. ———. *A Rainbow of My Own.* New York: Viking, 1966. Kindergarten–grade 3.
140. ———. *The Turtle and the Dove.* New York: Viking, 1964. Preschool–grade 1.
141. ———, AND LYDIA FREEMAN. *Chuggy and the Blue Caboose.* New York: Viking, 1951. n.g.l.

142. ______. *Pet of the Met.* New York: Viking, 1953. Preschool–grade 2.
143. GAG, WANDA. *The Funny Thing.* New York: Coward-McCann, 1920. Grades 1–3.
144. ______. *Gone Is Gone.* New York: Coward-McCann, 1935. Kindergarten–grade 3.
145. ______. *Millions of Cats.* New York: Coward-McCann, 1938. Kindergarten–grade 3.
146. ______ (adapter). *Snow White and the Seven Dwarfs.* New York: Coward–McCann, 1938. Grades 2–4.
147. ______ (adapter). *Tales from Grimm.* New York: Coward-McCann, 1936. Grades 3–5.
148. ______ (adapter). *Three Gay Tales from Grimm.* New York: Coward-McCann, 1943. Kindergarten–grade 4.
149. GALDONE, PAUL. *The Horse, the Fox, and the Lion.* New York: Seabury, 1968. Preschool–grade 1.
150. ______. *Little Tuppen.* New York: Seabury, 1967. Preschool–grade 2.
151. ______. *The Monkey and the Crocodile.* New York: Seabury, 1969. Preschool–grade 2.
152. ______. *Paddy the Penguin.* New York: T. Y. Crowell. n.g.l.
153. ______. *History of Simple Simon.* New York: McGraw-Hill, 1966. Kindergarten–grade 6.
154. ______. *Three Aesop Fox Fables.* New York: Seabury, 1971. Preschool–grade 2.
155. ______. *The Three Wishes.* New York: McGraw-Hill, 1961. Kindergarten–grade 3.
156. ______. *Tom, Tom the Piper's Son.* New York: McGraw-Hill, 1964. Kindergarten–grade 3.
157. GRAHAM, AL. *Timothy Turtle.* Tony Palazzo (ill.). New York: Viking, 1970. Paperback. Preschool–grade 2.
158. GRAMATKY, HARDIE. *Bolivar.* New York: Putnam, 1961. Kindergarten–grade 3.
159. ______. *Hercules.* New York: Putnam, 1971. Kindergarten–grade 3.
160. ______. *Little Toot.* New York: Putnam, 1939. Kindergarten–grade 3.
161. ______. *Little Toot on the Thames.* New York: Putnam, 1964. Kindergarten–grade 3.
162. GREENAWAY, KATE. *A—Apple Pie.* Rev. ed. New York: Warne, 1886. Kindergarten–grade 2.
163. ______. *The Language of Flowers, with Value Guide.* Watkins Glen, N. Y.: Century House, n.d.
164. ______. *Marigold Garden.* New York: Warne, 1885. Grades 2–5.
165. ______. *Under the Window.* New York: Warne, 1879. Grades 2–5.
166. HADER, ELMER, AND BERTA HADER. *The Big Snow.* New York: Macmillan, 1948. Kindergarten–grade 3.
167. ______. *Little Antelope: An Indian for a Day.* New York: Macmillan, 1962. Grades 1–2.
168. ______. *Little Appaloosa.* New York: Macmillan, 1949. Grade 7 and up.
169. ______. *Pancho.* New York: Macmillan, 1942. Kindergarten–grade 3.

170. ——. *Reindeer Trail.* New York: Macmillan, 1959. Grades 1–3.
171. ——. *Two Is Company, Three's a Crowd.* New York: Macmillan, 1965. Kindergarten–grade 3.
172. HAVILAND, VIRGINIA (ed.). *Favorite Fairy Tales Told in Italy.* Evaline Ness (ill.). Boston: Little, Brown, 1965. Grade 3 and up.
173. HOBAN, RUSSELL. *A Baby Sister for Frances.* Lillian Hoban (ill.). New York: Harper & Row, 1964. Kindergarten–grade 3.
174. ——. *A Bargain for Frances.* Lillian Hoban (ill.). New York: Harper & Row, 1970. Grades 1–4.
175. ——. *Bedtime for Frances.* Garth Williams (ill.). New York: Harper & Row, 1960. Kindergarten–grade 3.
176. ——. *Bread and Jam for Frances.* Lillian Hoban (ill.). New York: Harper & Row, 1964. Paperback. Kindergarten–grade 3.
177. ——, AND LILLIAN HOBAN. *Charlie the Tramp.* New York: Four Winds, 1967. Grades 2–3.
178. HURD, CLEMENT, AND EDITH THATCHER HURD. *Benny the Bulldozer.* New York: Lothrop, Lee & Shepard, 1957.
179. ——. *Mr. Charlie's Camping Trip.* Eau Claire, Wis.: Hale, 1957. Kindergarten–grade 2.
180. ——. *Mr. Charlie's Chicken House.* Philadelphia: Lippincott, 1955. n.g.l.
181. ——. *Mr. Charlie's Farm.* Eau Claire, Wis.: 1960. Kindergarten–grade 2.
182. IPCAR, DAHLOV. *Animals Hide and Seek.* New York: Scott, 1947. n.g.l.
183. ——. *Brown Cow Farm.* Garden City, N. Y.: Doubleday, 1959. Kindergarten–grade 3.
184. ——. *The Cat Came Back.* New York: Knopf, 1971. Kindergarten–grade 3.
185. ——. *Deep Sea Farm.* New York: Knopf, 1961. Kindergarten–grade 3.
186. ——. *The Marvelous Merry Go Round.* Garden City, N. Y.: Doubleday, 1970. Grade 7 and up.
187. ——. *One Horse Farm.* Garden City, N. Y.: Doubleday, 1950. Kindergarten–grade 2.
188. ——. *Song of the Day Birds and the Night Birds.* Garden City, N. Y.: Doubleday, 1967. Kindergarten–grade 3.
189. IRVING, WASHINGTON. *Christmas at Bracebridge Hall.* Rev. ed. New York: David McKay, 1962.
190. JOSLIN, SESYLE. *There Is a Bull on My Balcony.* New York: Harcourt Brace Jovanovich, 1966. Grades 1–6.
191. ——. *What Do You Do, Dear?* Maurice Sendak (ill.). Reading, Mass.: Addison-Wesley, 1961. Kindergarten–grade 4.
192. ——. *What Do You Say, Dear?* Reading, Mass.: Addison-Wesley, 1958. Grades 1–3.
193. ——, AND KATHERINA BARRY. *Spaghetti for Breakfast: And Other Useful Phrases in Italian and English.* New York: Harcourt Brace Jovanovich, 1965. Grades 1–6.

194. ———, AND IRENE HAAS. *There Is a Dragon in My Bed.* New York: Harcourt Brace Jovanovich, 1966. Kindergarten–grade 3.
195. ———, AND LEONARD WEISGARD. *Baby Elephant's Trunk.* New York: Harcourt Brace Jovanovich, 1961. Preschool–grade 3.
196. KAHL, VIRGINIA. *Away Went Wolfgang.* New York: Scribner, 1954. Kindergarten–grade 3.
197. ———. *The Duchess Bakes a Cake.* New York: Scribner, 1955. Kindergarten–grade 3.
198. ———. *How Do You Hide a Monster?* New York: Scribner, 1971. Kindergarten–grade 3.
199. KEATS, EZRA JACK. *Apt. Three.* New York: Macmillan, 1971. Kindergarten–grade 4.
200. ———. *Goggles.* New York: Macmillan, 1969. Kindergarten–grade 3.
201. ———. *Hi, Cat.* New York: Macmillan, 1970. Kindergarten–grade 3.
202. ———. *Jennie's Hat.* New York: Harper & Row, 1966. Kindergarten–grade 3.
203. ———. *The Little Drummer Boy.* New York: Macmillan, 1968. Kindergarten–grade 3.
204. ———. *Peter's Chair.* New York: Harper & Row, 1967. Kindergarten–grade 3.
205. ———. *Snowy Day.* New York: Viking, 1962. Preschool–grade 1.
206. ———. *Whistle for Willie.* New York: Viking, 1964. Preschool–grade 1.
207. KRAUSS, RUTH. *The Birthday Party.* Maurice Sendak (ill.). New York: Harper & Row, 1957. Kindergarten–grade 3.
208. ———. *A Hole Is to Dig: A First Book of First Definitions.* Maurice Sendak (ill.). New York: Harper & Row, 1952. Preschool–grade 1.
209. ———. *A Very Special House.* Maurice Sendak (ill.). New York: Harper & Row, 1953. Preschool–grade 1.
210. LANG, ANDREW (ed.). *The Nursery Rhyme Book.* L. Leslie Brooke (ill.). Rev. ed. New York: Warne, 1897. Grades 1–3.
211. LEODHAS, SORCHE NIC. *Thistle and Thyme.* Evaline Ness (ill.). New York: Holt, Rinehart & Winston, 1962. Grades 4–6.
212. LENSKI, LOIS. *The Little Airplane.* New York: Walck, 1938. Kindergarten–grade 3.
213. ———. *The Little Farm.* New York: Walck, 1942. Kindergarten–grade 3.
214. ———. *A Little Girl of 1900.* Philadelphia: Stokes, 1928.
215. ———. *The Little Train.* New York: Walck, 1940. Kindergarten–grade 3.
216. ———. *Skipping Village.* Philadelphia: Stokes, 1927.
217. LIONNI, LEO. *Fish Is Fish.* New York: Pantheon, 1970. Kindergarten–grade 3.
218. ———. *Frederick.* New York: Pantheon, 1966. Kindergarten–grade 3.
219. ———. *Swimmy.* New York: Pantheon, 1963. Preschool–grade 2.
220. ———. *Theodore and the Talking Mushroom.* New York: Pantheon, 1971. Kindergarten–grade 3.

221. ______. *Tico and the Golden Wings.* New York: Pantheon, 1964. Kindergarten–grade 4.
222. LIPKIND, WILLIAM, AND ROGER DUVOISIN. *Nubber Bear.* New York: Harcourt Brace Jovanovich, 1966. Kindergarten–grade 3.
223. LIPKIND, WILLIAM, AND NICOLAS MORDVINOFF. *Chaga.* New York: Harcourt Brace Jovanovich, 1945. Kindergarten–grade 3.
224. ______. *Circus Ruckus.* New York: Harcourt Brace Jovanovich, 1954. Kindergarten–grade 3.
225. ______. *Finders Keepers.* New York: Harcourt Brace Jovanovich, 1951. Kindergarten–grade 3.
226. ______. *Four-Leaf Clover.* New York: Harcourt Brace Jovanovich, 1959.
227. ______. *The Two Reds.* New York: Harcourt Brace Jovanovich, 1950. Kindergarten–grade 3.
228. MCCLOSKEY, ROBERT. *Blueberries for Sal.* New York: Viking, 1968. Paperback. Preschool–grade 1.
229. ______. *Make Way for Ducklings.* New York: Viking, 1969. Paperback. Kindergarten–grade 3.
230. ______. *One Morning in Maine.* New York: Viking, 1952. Kindergarten–grade 3.
231. ______. *Time of Wonder.* New York: Viking, 1957. Kindergarten–grade 3.
232. MACDONALD, GEORGE. *The Light Princess.* L. Leslie Brooke (ill.). New York: Farrar, Straus & Giroux, 1969. Grade 7 and up.
233. MALCOLMSON, ANNE. *Yankee Doodle's Cousins.* Robert McCloskey (ill.). Boston: Houghton Mifflin, 1941. Grades 4–8.
234. MILHOUS, KATHERINE. *The Egg Tree.* New York: Scribner, 1950. Kindergarten–grade 3.
235. MINARIK, ELSE HOLMELUND. *Little Bear's Visit.* Maurice Sendak (ill.). New York: Harper & Row, 1961. Kindergarten–grade 3.
236. MUKERJI, DHAN GOPAL. *Gay-Neck: The Story of a Pigeon.* Boris Artzybasheff (ill.). New York: Dutton, n.d. Grade 7 and up.
237. NESS, EVALINE. *A Gift for Sula Sula.* New York: Scribner, 1963. Kindergarten–grade 3.
238. ______. *Josefina February.* New York: Scribner, 1963. Kindergarten–grade 3.
239. ______. *Pavo and the Princess.* New York: Scribner, 1964. Kindergarten–grade 3.
240. ______. *Sam, Bangs, and Moonshine.* New York: Holt, Rinehart & Winston, 1966. Paperback. Preschool–grade 2.
241. NEWBERRY, CLARE T. *Marshmallow.* New York: Harper & Row, 1942. Kindergarten–grade 3.
242. ______. *Pandora.* New York: Harper & Row, 1944. n.g.l.
243. ______. *Smudge.* New York: Harper & Row, 1948. Preschool–grade 1.
244. ______. *T-Bone, the Baby Sitter.* New York: Harper & Row, 1950. Kindergarten–grade 3.

245. NICHOLSON, WILLIAM. *Clever Bill.* Garden City, N. Y.: Doubleday, 1961. n.g.l.
246. PALAZZO, TONY. *Bianco and the New World.* Eau Claire, Wis.: Hale, 1957. Kindergarten–grade 3.
247. ———. *Charley the Horse.* New York: Abelard-Schuman, 1966. Kindergarten–grade 3.
248. ———. *Jan and the Reindeer.* Champaign, Ill.: Garrard, 1963. Grades 1–3.
249. ——— (reteller). *The Little Red Hen.* Garden City, N. Y.: Doubleday, 1958. n.g.l.
250. ———. *Mr. Whistle's Secret.* New York: Viking, 1953. n.g.l.
251. PEET, BILL. *Farewell to Shady Glade.* Boston: Houghton Mifflin, 1966. Kindergarten–grade 3.
252. PETERSHAM, MISKA, AND MAUD PETERSHAM. *A Bird in the Hand.* New York: Macmillan, 1949. Kindergarten–grade 3.
253. ———. *The Box with Red Wheels.* New York: Macmillan, 1949. Kindergarten–grade 3.
254. ———. *The Christ Child.* Garden City, N. Y.: Doubleday, 1931. Grades 1–6.
255. ———. *Circus Baby.* New York: Macmillan, 1950. Kindergarten–grade 3.
256. ———. *Miki.* Garden City, N. Y.: Doubleday, 1929. n.g.l.
257. ———. *The Silver Mace.* New York: Macmillan, 1964. Grades 4–6.
258. ———. *Story of the Presidents of the United States of America.* Rev. ed. New York: Macmillan, 1966. Grades 4–6.
259. POLITI, LEO. *Juanita.* New York: Scribner, 1948. Preschool–grade 3.
260. ———. *The Mission Bell.* New York: Scribner, 1953. Grades 2–5.
261. ———. *Pedro, the Little Angel of Olvera Street.* New York: Scribner, 1946. Preschool–grade 2.
262. ———. *The Song of the Swallows.* New York: Scribner, 1949. Kindergarten–grade 3.
263. ROBERTSON, KEITH. *Henry Reed, Inc.* Robert McCloskey (ill.). New York: Grosset & Dunlap, n.d. Paperback.
264. SAWYER, RUTH. *Journey Cake, Ho!* Robert McCloskey (ill.). New York: Viking, 1970. Paperback. Preschool–grade 3.
265. SAYERS, FRANCES CLARK. *Bluebonnets for Lucinda.* Helen Sewell (ill.). New York: Viking, 1934. Kindergarten–grade 3.
266. SEIGNOSBOSC, FRANÇOISE. *The Big Rain.* New York: Scribner, 1961. Kindergarten–grade 2.
267. ———. *Biquette, the White Goat.* New York: Scribner, 1953. Kindergarten–grade 2.
268. ———. *Jeanne-Marie at the Fair.* New York: Scribner, 1959. Kindergarten–grade 2.
269. ———. *Jeanne-Marie Counts Her Sheep.* New York: Scribner, 1957. Preschool–grade 1.
270. ———. *Jeanne-Marie in Gay Paris.* New York: Scribner, 1956. Kindergarten–grade 2.

271. ———. *Noel for Jeanne-Marie.* New York: Scribner, 1953. Kindergarten–grade 2.
272. SENDAK, MAURICE. *Chicken Soup with Rice: A Book of Months.* New York: Harper & Row, 1962. Kindergarten–grade 3.
273. ———. *Higglety Pigglety Pop: Or, There Must Be More to Life.* New York: Harper & Row, 1967. Kindergarten–grade 3.
274. ———. *In the Night Kitchen.* New York: Harper & Row, 1971. Kindergarten–grade 3.
275. ———. *Kenny's Window.* New York: Harper & Row, 1956. Kindergarten–grade 3.
276. ———. *Very Far Away.* New York: Harper & Row, 1957. Kindergarten–grade 3.
277. ———. *Where the Wild Things Are.* New York: Harper & Row, 1963. Kindergarten–grade 3.
278. SEUSS, DR. (Theodore Seuss Geisel). *Horton Hatches the Egg.* New York: Random House, 1940. Kindergarten–grade 3.
279. ———. *The Lorax.* New York: Random House, 1971.
280. ———. *Mr. Brown Can Moo! Can You?* New York: Random House, 1970. Preschool–grade 1.
281. SEWELL, HELEN. *Blue Barns.* New York: Macmillan, 1964. Kindergarten–grade 3.
282. ———. *A Head for Happy.* New York: Macmillan, 1931. n.g.l.
283. ———. *Ming and Mehitable.* New York: Macmillan, 1936. n.g.l.
284. ———. *Peggy and the Pony.* New York: Oxford, 1937. n.g.l.
285. SLOBODKIN, LOUIS. *The Amiable Giant.* New York: Vanguard, n.d. Grades 1–3.
286. ———. *Hustle and Bustle.* New York: 1948. Kindergarten–grade 3.
287. ———. *Magic Michael.* New York: Macmillan, 1944. Kindergarten–grade 3.
288. ———. *Yasu and the Strangers.* New York: Macmillan, 1965. Kindergarten–grade 3.
289. SLOBODKINA, ESPHYR. *Pezzo the Peddler and the Circus Elephant.* New York: Abelard-Schuman, 1967. Kindergarten–grade 3.
290. ———. *Pinky and the Petunias.* Eau Claire, Wis.: Hale, 1959. Kindergarten–grade 3.
291. STEIN, GERTRUDE. *The World Is Round.* Clement Hurd (ill.). Scott, 1966. Grade 6 and up.
292. THURBER, JAMES. *Many Moons.* Louis Slobodkin (ill.). New York: Harcourt Brace Jovanovich, 1943. Grades 3–7.
293. TITUS, EVE. *Anatole.* New York: McGraw-Hill, 1956. Kindergarten–grade 3.
294. ———. *Anatole and the Cat.* New York: McGraw-Hill, 1957. Kindergarten–grade 3.
295. ———. *Anatole and the Poodle.* New York: McGraw-Hill, 1965. Kindergarten–grade 3.
296. ———. *Anatole and the Robot.* New York: McGraw-Hill, 1960. Kindergarten–grade 3.

297. ______. *The Mouse and the Lion.* New York: Parents' Magazine, 1965. Kindergarten–grade 3.
298. ______, AND PAUL GALDONE. *Anatole over Paris.* New York: McGraw-Hill, 1961. Kindergarten–grade 3.
299. TRESSELT, ALVIN R. *Follow the Wind.* Roger Duvoisin (ill.). New York: Lothrop, Lee & Shepard, 1950. Preschool–grade 3.
300. ______. *Rain Drop Splash.* Roger Duvoisin (ill.). New York: Lothrop, Lee & Shepard, 1946. Preschool–grade 3.
301. ______. *A Thousand Lights and Fireflies.* New York: Parents' Magazine, 1947. Preschool–grade 3.
302. ______. *Under the Trees and Through the Grass.* New York: Lothrop, Lee & Shepard, 1962. Preschool–grade 3.
303. ______. *White Snow, Bright Snow.* Roger Duvoisin (ill.). New York: Lothrop, Lee & Shepard, 1947. Preschool–grade 1.
304. UDRY, JANICE MAY. *Mary Jo's Grandmother.* Chicago: Albert Whitman, 1970. Preschool–grade 3.
305. ______. *The Moon Jumpers.* Maurice Sendak (ill.). New York: Harper & Row, 1959. Kindergarten–grade 2.
306. ______. *Next Door to Laura Linda.* Chicago: Albert Whitman, 1965. Preschool–grade 2.
307. ______. *A Tree Is Nice.* Marc Simont (ill.). New York: Harper & Row, 1956. Preschool–grade 1.
308. ______. *What Mary Jo Shared.* Chicago: Albert Whitman, 1966. Kindergarten–grade 3.
309. ______. *What Mary Jo Wanted.* Chicago: Albert Whitman, 1968. Kindergarten–grade 3.
310. WABER, BERNARD. *An Anteater Named Arthur.* Boston: Houghton Mifflin, 1967. Kindergarten–grade 3.
311. ______. *A Firefly Named Torchy.* Boston: Houghton Mifflin, 1967. Kindergarten–grade 3.
312. ______. *The House on East 88th Street.* Boston: Houghton Mifflin, 1962. Kindergarten–grade 3.
313. ______. *Lyle and the Birthday Party.* Boston: Houghton Mifflin, 1966.
314. ______. *Lyle, Lyle, Crocodile.* Boston: Houghton Mifflin, 1965. Kindergarten–grade 3.
315. ______. *"You Look Ridiculous" Said the Rhinoceros to the Hippopotamus.* Boston: Houghton Mifflin, 1966. Kindergarten–grade 3.
316. WEISGARD, LEONARD. *Down Huckleberry Hill.* New York: Scribner, 1947. n.g.l.
317. ______. *Mr. Peaceable Paints.* New York: Scribner, 1956. n.g.l.
318. ______. *The Plymouth Thanksgiving.* Garden City, N. Y.: Doubleday, 1967. Grades 3–4.
319. ______. *Silly Willy Nilly.* New York: Scribner, 1950. n.g.l.
320. ______. *Who Dreams of Cheese?* New York: Scribner, 1950. n.g.l.
321. WHITE, ANNE H. *Junket.* Robert McCloskey (ill.). New York: Viking, 1955. Grades 4–6.
322. YASHIMA, TARO. *Crow Boy.* New York: Viking, 1955. Kindergarten–grade 2.

323. ZOLOTOW, CHARLOTTE. *Do You Know What I'll Do?* New York: Harper & Row, 1958. Preschool–grade 1.
324. ———. *Mr. Rabbit and the Lovely Present.* Maurice Sendak (ill.). New York: Harper & Row, 1962. Kindergarten–grade 3.
325. ———. *The Park Book.* New York: Harper & Row, 1944. Preschool–grade 1.
326. ———. *The Sky Was Blue.* New York: Harper & Row, 1963. Kindergarten–grade 3.
327. ———. *The Storm Book.* New York: Harper & Row, 1952. Kindergarten–grade 3.
328. ———. *The Three Funny Friends.* New York: Harper & Row, 1961. Preschool–grade 1.
329. ———. *A Tiger Called Thomas.* New York: Lothrop, Lee & Shepard, 1963. Preschool–grade 3.

More Picture-Story Books

ADAMS, RUTH. *Mr. Picklepaw's Popcorn.* New York: Lothrop, Lee & Shepard, 1965. Kindergarten–grade 4. Popping popcorn creates a highly improbable situation.

ALBERTI, TRUDE (adapter). *The Animals' Lullaby.* Cleveland: World Publishing, 1967. n.g.l. This Icelandic song was inspired by the appealing tenderness of all small sleeping creatures.

ALDRIDGE, JOSEPHINE. *Fisherman's Luck.* Berkeley, Calif.: Parnassus, 1966. Grade 3 and up. A Maine fisherman loses his wharf and house in a storm but is helped to get a better house by some of the other fishermen.

AMOSS, BERTHE. *It's Not Your Birthday.* New York: Harper & Row, 1966. Kindergarten–grade 1. This simple picture-story book is about big brother's birthday.

AUERBACH, MARJORIE. *Seven Uncles Come to Dinner.* New York: Knopf, 1963. Grade 5 and up. When all of Emile's uncles from the south of France are invited to dinner, great-aunt Louise gives faithful Emile the grocery list in rhyme to remember.

BAUM, ARLINE, AND JOSEPH BAUM. *One Bright Monday Morning.* New York: Random House, 1962. Preschool. Preschoolers learn the days of the week as well as their numbers.

BEHRENS, JUNE. *Soo Ling Finds a Way.* San Carlos, Calif.: Golden Gate, 1965. Kindergarten–grade 3. The problems of the small businessman are presented with simple realism in this story of a little girl and her grandfather.

BELL, GINA. *Who Wants Willy Wells?* Nashville, Tenn.: Abingdon, 1965. Kindergarten–grade 3. When little time is spent with Willy after the new baby brother comes home, he goes away only to find on his return that he has been missed.

COLETTE. *The Boy and the Magic.* Christopher Fry (tr.). New York: Putnam,

1965. Kindergarten and up. A selfish, lazy, and cruel boy falls under a magic spell that is broken when he makes a kind gesture to a squirrel.

DUVOISIN, ROGER. *What Is Right for Tulip.* New York: Knopf, 1969. Kindergarten–grade 2. Expressive and colorful drawings introduce animals and people to make the point that animals and people are very much alike as well as being very different. The things that are right for Tulip, a polar bear, are not right for other animals or for people.

FISHER, AILEEN L. *Best Little House.* New York: Crowell, 1966. Kindergarten–grade 3. Moving to a new home in the country is the subject of this picture-story book.

GARELICK, MAY. *Where Does the Butterfly Go When It Rains?* New York: Addison-Wesley, 1961. Preschool–grade 1. The child is challenged to exercise his own powers of observation to answer the question in the title.

GEORGIOU, CONSTANTINE. *The Clock.* Irvington-on-Hudson, N. Y.: Harvey House, 1966. Kindergarten–grade 3. A little mouse helps a grandfather clock to continue ticking.

HEATHERS, ANNE, AND FRANCES ESTEBAN. *The Thread Soldier.* New York: Harcourt Brace Jovanovich, 1960. n.g.l. A little mouse and his friends indulge in their artistic fancy.

HOLDING, JAMES. *The Three Wishes of Hu.* New York: Putnam, 1965. Grades 1–3. Four impoverished and orphaned children who live in Hong Kong drum up business from the tourists for a local restaurant and tailor to earn their New Year's wishes.

KUMIN, MAXINE W. *The Beach Before Breakfast.* New York: Putnam, 1964. Grades 2–4. A little boy and an adult go out for an early morning walk along the shore, exploring everything on the beach at this magic hour and watching the sun come up.

LEXAU, JOAN. *I Should Have Stayed in Bed.* New York: Harper & Row, 1965. Kindergarten–grade 3. Sam tells how he went back to bed because his day had a bad start.

LIFTON, BETTY JEAN. *Joji and the Fog.* Eau Claire, Wis.: Hale, 1959. Kindergarten–grade 2. The gentle scarecrow protects his father's rice fields by kindness instead of fear.

MCNEILL, JANET. *The Giant's Birthday.* New York: Walck, 1964. Kindergarten–grade 3. Villagers celebrate and bring the Giant presents that turn out to be too small.

MARTIN, PATRICIA M. *The Pumpkin Patch.* New York: Putnam, 1966. Grades 2–5. This is the humorous story about the little mouse who lives in Kate's pumpkin.

MATSUNO, MASAKO. *Chie and the Sports Day.* Cleveland: World Publishing, 1965. Kindergarten–grade 3. When an older brother starts school, his small sister feels deserted.

MILES, BETTY. *A Day of Summer.* New York: Knopf, 1960. Kindergarten–grade 2. In carefully measured poetic prose the author evokes the delights of summer hours under the sun and stars.

______. *A Day of Winter.* New York: Knopf, 1961. Kindergarten–grade 3.

The excitement of snow and the snug comfort of a blanket, plus the look, sound, feel, and smell of a winter's day, are described in this story.

MILES, MISKA. *Rabbit Garden.* Boston: Atlantic Monthly Press, 1967. Kindergarten–grade 3. A young rabbit, his garden, and all the creatures he meets and sees make an interesting story.

MILLER, EDNA. *Mousekin Finds a Friend.* Englewood Cliffs, N. J.: Prentice-Hall, 1967. Preschool–grade 3. A tiny wood mouse searches for a fellow creature in this tender story.

NODSET, JOAN L. *Who Took the Farmer's Hat?* New York: Harper & Row, 1963. Kindergarten–grade 3. Brightly colored drawings tell the story of the farmer's search for his lost hat.

ORMONDROYD, EDWARD. *Theodore.* Berkeley, Calif.: Parnassus, 1966. Preschool–grade 3. Theodore, a somewhat soiled bear, is accidently included in the family laundry. He is unrecognizable until he becomes his rumpled self again.

PALAZZO, TONY. *Federico, the Flying Squirrel.* New York: Viking, 1951. Kindergarten–grade 3. Federico, a flying squirrel who can do many things an ordinary squirrel cannot, and Billy, the boy who lives in the house next to the tree in which Federico has his nest, become close friends.

PEET, BILL. *Chester the Worldly Pig.* Boston: Houghton Mifflin, 1965. Kindergarten–grade 3. Chester wants to go places, so he trains himself to stand on his nose and joins a circus.

———. *Jennifer and Josephine.* Boston: Houghton Mifflin, 1967. Kindergarten–grade 3. A cat and an old touring car have many adventures and are rescued by a farm boy who loves them both.

SANDBERG, INGER. *What Little Anna Saved.* New York: Lothrop, Lee & Shepard, 1965. Preschool–grade 2. What Mama calls rubbish, Anna makes into wonderful things.

SANDBURG, CARL. "The Wedding Procession of the Rag Doll and the Broom Handle Who Was in It," in *Rootabaga Stories.* New York: Harcourt Brace Jovanovich, 1967. Grades 4–6.

SCHEER, JULIAN. *Rain Makes Applesauce.* New York: Holiday House, 1964. Kindergarten–grade 2. The repetitive absurdities that children adore are coupled with finely etched pastel drawings in this picture-story book.

SCHLEIN, MIRIAM. *Billy, the Littlest One.* Chicago: Albert Whitman, 1966. Preschool–grade 1. Billy tackles the problem of size with the assurance that he will not always be the littlest.

SCOTT, SALLY. *Bobby and His Band.* New York: Harcourt Brace Jovanovich, 1954. n.g.l. The neighborhood children play on pans, pan covers, dinner bells, and the like and are ably assisted by an odd character who plays a comb.

SOULE, JEAN CONDER. *Never Tease a Weasel.* New York: Parents' Magazine Press, 1964. Kindergarten–grade 3. This humorous nonsense text has appealing rhythm and rhyme.

STANDON, ANNA. *Little Duck Lost.* New York: Delacorte, 1965. Kindergarten–grade 3. A newly hatched duck searches throughout Paris for his mother.

TREZ, DENISE, AND ALAIN TREZ. *The Little Knight's Dragon.* Cleveland: World Publishing, 1963. Kindergarten–grade 3. A little knight rescues a princess from a dragon.

UNGERER, TOMI. *Beast of Monsieur Racine.* New York: Farrar, Straus & Giroux, 1971. Kindergarten–grade 3.

———. *I Am Papa Snap and These Are My Favorite No Such Stories.* New York: Harper & Row, 1971. Kindergarten–grade 3.

VICTOR, JOAN B. *My Friend the Squirrel.* Indianapolis: Bobbs-Merrill, 1966. Grades 1–3. A little girl enjoys the squirrels in the park.

WATTS, MABEL. *The Light Across Piney Valley.* New York: Abelard-Schuman, 1965. Preschool–grade 3. A boy and a procession of various animals trail the early morning golden light.

WEIL, LISL. *Eyes-SO-O Big.* Boston: Houghton Mifflin, 1964. Kindergarten–grade 3. Two little Portuguese sisters push their luck trying to sell the salted fish from their father's catch.

WILDSMITH, BRIAN. *Brian Wildsmith's Circus.* New York: Watts, 1970. Kindergarten–grade 3. The excitement and pleasure that belong only to the circus are brought to life.

WRIGHT, DARE. *Edith and Mr. Bear: A Lonely Doll Story.* New York: Random House, 1964. Kindergarten–grade 3. A "lonely doll" climbs the staircase of books to see the pendulum clock.

YORK, CAROL B. *The Christmas Dolls.* New York: Watts, 1967. Grades 4–6. Two leftover dolls find a loving owner in one of the twenty-eight girls living in an orphanage.

Further Reading

COLBY, JEAN POINDEXTER. *Writing, Illustrating and Editing Children's Books.* New York: Hastings House, 1967.

FOSTER, JOANNA. *Pages, Pictures and Print.* New York: Harcourt Brace Jovanovich, 1958.

GORDON, STEPHEN F. *Making Picture-Books: A Method of Learning Graphic Sequence.* New York: Van Nostrand, 1970.

HEFFERNAN, HELEN, AND VIVIAN E. TODD. *The Kindergarten Teacher.* Boston: D.C. Heath, 1960, chap. 12.

HURLIMANN, BETTINA. *Picture-book World.* Brian W. Alderson, trans. and ed. Cleveland: World, 1969.

KLEMIN, DIANA. *The Art of Art for Children's Books.* New York: Potter, 1966.

KLINGMAN, LEE, *et al.* (comps.). *Illustrators of Children's Books, 1957–1966.* Boston: The Horn Book, n.d.

KLINGMAN, LEE, comp. *Newbery and Caldecott Medal Books, 1956–1965.* Boston: The Horn Book, 1965.

MAHONEY, BERTHA E., *et al.*, comps. *Illustrators of Children's Books, 1744–1945.* Boston: The Horn Book, n.d.

MEIGS, CORNELIA, *et al.* *A Critical History of Children's Literature.* New York: Macmillan, 1969. Rev. ed.

MILLER, BERTHA MAHONEY, AND ELINOR WHITNEY FIELD, eds. *Caldecott Medal Books, 1938–1957.* Boston: The Horn Book, n.d.

———. eds. *Newbery Medal Books, 1922–1955.* Boston: The Horn Book, n.d.

PITZ, HENRY C. *Illustrating Children's Books.* New York: Watson Guptill, 1963.

SIMON, IRVING B. *The Story of Printing.* Irvington-on-Hudson, N. Y.: Harvey House, 1965.

SMITH, IRENE. *A History of the Newbery and Caldecott Medals.* New York: Viking, 1957.

SMITH, LILLIAN H. *The Unreluctant Years.* New York: Viking, 1967, chap. 8.

TOWNSEND, JOHN ROWE. "Children's Books in Britain: Aiming Hard for a New Golden Age," *Publishers' Weekly,* July 19, 1971, pp. 67–69.

VIQUERS, RUTH HILL, *et al.* *Illustrators of Children's Books, 1946–1956.* Boston: The Horn Book, n.d.

The Children's Homer: The Adventures of Odysseus and the Tale of Troy retold by Padraic Colum, illustrated by Willy Pogany.

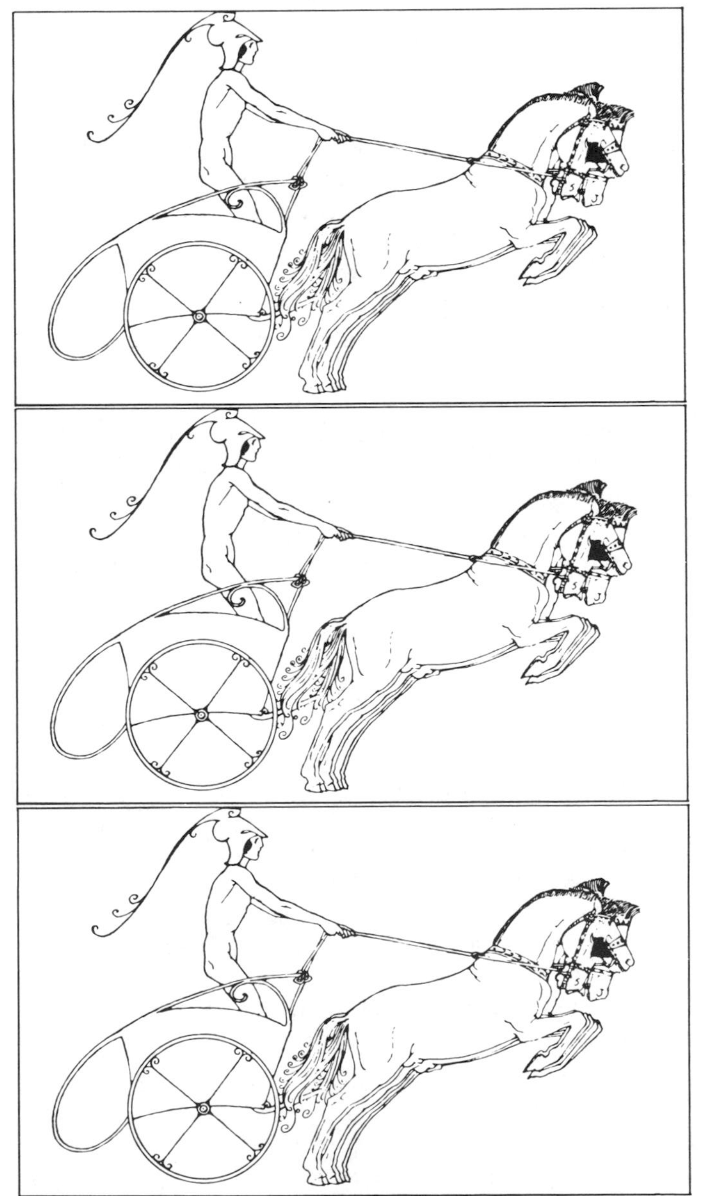

10

Folk Literature

Folk literature is as old as language. The different types of folk literature—myths and legends, fables and hero tales, folk and fairy tales—originated as soon as men began to communicate with each other. Its roots are deeply embedded in the past, and its long oral tradition is a matter of history. Tales were preserved through the ages by storytellers who were held in respect not only in the marketplaces and by the firesides of the peasants but in the courts of kings as well.

Definite purposes were served by the various types of folklore. Myths and legends were created to explain natural phenomena. Folk and fairy tales, created by the highly imaginative and embroidered by storytellers, served not only to entertain but to express a philosophy of life. Fables were made up by wise men to teach a lesson, and hero tales served to record and to glorify the deeds of heroes and forefathers.

Myths and Legends

Some of the finest literature man has today are the myths created by ancient man in his efforts to understand, explain, and enjoy his world. Like folk and fairy tales, myths are the products of the early stages of human thought and living. They date back to the time when the world was fresh and new and man toiled and struggled to survive and to become one with his world. As man moved from place to place, he took his myths and legends with him. Storytellers handed them down from generation to generation until they were caught and held in print. Even then changes were made by translators. Scholars of folklore have found variants of the same story among people as far apart as North America and India, Finland and South Africa. The variants of these stories are related to the different environments in which they flourished.

As primitive man observed the sun, the stars, the changes of seasons, and the varied forms of plant and animal life, he was unable without the aid of science to use any sound philosophical or scientific theories to explain their genesis and character. He had to create explanations. Without them he probably would have lived in fear and never ventured far from his cave. To explain everything around him, he therefore invented gods, giants, and heroes who were made in the likeness of men and beasts and had the weaknesses of man as well as his strengths. Each god or goddess had his or her responsibility and some power that was above that of man. Myths became primitive man's religion—they told what the gods did and what man could do to please them.

Myths of Creation

One of the greatest mysteries that faced early man was the creation of his world, and he turned to the gods he had invented for answers. The explanations that arose were as varied as the differences in the regions that gave birth to them.

A Primitive Concept of Creation

One explanation of the beginning of the world goes as follows:

A long time ago, more years than anyone can count, there was no earth, no sky, sun, moon or stars. There was only space. And, in this space, a huge shapeless mass hung suspended. It was without color, and it was neither hard nor soft. There was no water on it and no land, not even a blade of grass or the tiniest of living things.

No one knows how long this mass hung, motionless and barren, in the vastness of time. It might have stayed there forever–and there would have been no world for us to live in—had it not been for an invisible force that existed in the midst of chaos. The force was Nature, who discovered that millions of seeds lay hidden in the hot, thick bulk. Years passed while Nature, appalled by the dreadful waste, wondered how she could give life to still form. She finally appealed to a God who was so far away that he was scarcely aware of the tremendous mass which seemed no more than a tiny speck to him. He listened to Nature and agreed to help her, and with a word, he separated the earth from the sea and the heavens from both. There was a deafening clap of thunder as he spoke the word. Flames leapt high in the

> air and formed the skies. Beneath them the air arose, while the earth, being the heaviest, sank to the bottom. The seas boiled and swirled around it, and enormous hot waves, higher than mountains, washed over it. The air would not settle and the din it made as it rushed madly about was deafening. The heavens were jet black, shot with streaks of fire. Only the earth lay quiet, barren and dead. [(9), pp. 15–16]

Early man's concept of the structure of the universe seems strange but fascinating to us. Explorations and discoveries have changed our concept of the world. Man is no longer afraid of falling off the edge of the world, and changes in transportation and communication have brought its four corners closer together. Men feel a kinship with other men wherever they live. The physical, social, and political sciences helped man to understand and appreciate his world.

Other Versions of the Beginning of the World

Wherever primitive man lived, he sought to find an explanation for the beginning of the world. He relied upon some supernatural power to bring order out of chaos. He frequently started with an underworld and eventually built the world inhabited by man.

In Egypt the most important god was Ra, the god of the sun. He was believed to be the one ancestor of all the gods, of man, and of heaven and earth. He was pictured either in human form or with a human body and the head of a falcon. His symbol was the sun disk, and his main place of worship was Heliopolis, the Sun City. In his eagerness to have children, he married his own shadow. By this marriage a god of the dry air and a goddess of the waters were born. This god and goddess gave birth to a god of the earth and a goddess of the heavens. In due time the heavens were filled with gods and the earth with human beings. The pharaohs who ruled Egypt considered themselves sons of Ra.

The people who lived in the cold lands of northern Europe had quite a different belief about the way the world began. They thought that at one time there had been only a dark empty space holding water. The rain fell, and as the space filled, the water ran out forming twelve rivers that flowed downward until they made a huge block of ice. A great fire came from the south which melted some of the ice and changed the water into a cloud. The first giant came out of the cloud, and the first god came out of the ice. In a struggle between the giant and the god, the giant was killed. The god made the earth out of the giant's body, the sea out of his blood, the mountains out of his bones, and the trees out of his hair.

The San Gabriel Indians of California had a simple yet dramatic explanation of how the world came to be. Since the Indians lived close to nature, it is logical that insects and animals played an important role in their explanation.

THE PLEIADES

Long ago a party of Indians traveled several days toward good hunting ground which they had long known. When they reached Kan-ya-ti-yo "the beautiful lake," the chief of the band halted his party on the lakeshore. After giving thanks to the Great Spirit he said, "Here will we build our lodges for the winter."

As the pleasant autumn days passed, the children took a fancy to meet daily in a quiet spot by the lake to dance. One day a very old man with white hair that shone like silver, dressed in white feathers, came to them. He told the children they must stop their dancing or evil things would happen to them. The children paid little heed to the old man and continued to meet and dance.

One day a little boy suggested that they have a feast the next day. Their parents refused to give them food for the feast. They went to dance anyway. As they danced their heads became so light with hunger they found themselves rising little by little into the air. As they continued to rise, one said, "Do not look back for something strange is taking place."

One woman who saw them rising ran to the camp and everyone came rushing out with food of every kind, calling to the children to come back. One child looked back and he became a falling star. The others reached the sky and are now what we call the Pleiades, and the Onondagas call Oot-kiwa-tah. Every falling or shooting star recalls the story, and the seven stars shine on, a band of children dancing eternally in the sky. [(89), pp. 46–47]

Myths of the Seasons

The coming and going of the seasons must have been one of the most baffling natural phenomena that primitive man had to explain. He was aware of a time of growing and a time of dying, and much of his life was governed by it.

Pluto and Proserpina

The Romans believed that the change in seasons was caused by Pluto's kidnapping of Proserpina (38, 79), the daughter of Ceres, goddess of the harvest.

One day while Proserpina was picking flowers, Pluto, King of the

Underworld, kidnapped her and took her to his underground castle. Proserpina cried out for her mother and begged Pluto to take her home. Pluto tried to console her by telling her that his home is a palace, made of gold, with crystal windows and diamond lamps instead of sunshine and a throne on which she might sit and be his little queen. In spite of all the riches of the underworld and Pluto's kindness, Proserpina remained unhappy. She vowed she would not eat anything or drink a single drop even if Pluto kept her in his palace forever.

Ceres' despair reached a high pitch as she wandered far and wide over the earth trying to get a clue as to the whereabouts of her daughter. Finally, Phoebus, God of the Sun, gave her the news for which she was searching. In desperation Ceres made up her mind that not a stalk of grain, nor blade of grass, nor a potato, nor a turnip, nor any vegetable that is good for man or beast should be allowed to grow until her daughter was sent back. She was so unhappy that she even forbade the flowers to bloom. She proclaimed that if the earth were ever to be green again the grass would grow along the path by which her daughter returned to her.

For six months the earth was miserable. Not until Proserpina returned from the underworld to live with her mother for six months of each year did the earth again rejoice and spring to life with beauty, bloom, and fruit.

The Story of Baldur

While the Romans explained the seasons with the coming and going of Proserpina, the ancient Norsemen far to the north of Rome had a different family of gods who conditioned their lives. Their explanations had some likenesses to and some differences from those of the Romans. Norsemen associated the phenomenon of seasonal changes with the death of Baldur (13, 55), who was a son of Odin and Frigga. He was god of goodness, beauty, and wisdom. Baldur represented the summer which is all too short in the land of the Norsemen. Hodur, Baldur's blind and foreboding twin brother, was the winter with its cruel cold. Hodur's killing of Baldur is interpreted as the slaying of the summer by winter.

Porcupine and Beaver

Once Porcupine and Beaver quarreled about the seasons. Porcupine wanted five winter months. He held up one hand and showed his five fingers. He said, "Let the winter months be the same in number as the fingers on my hand." Beaver said, "No," and held up his tail, which had many cracks or scratches on it. He said, "Let the winter months be the same in number as the scratches on my tail." Now they quarreled and argued. Porcupine got angry and bit off his thumb. Then, holding up his hand with the four fingers, he said emphatically, "There must be only four winter months." Beaver became a little afraid, and gave in. *For this reason porcupines have four claws on each foot now.*

Since Porcupine won, the winter remained four months in length, until later Raven changed it a little. Raven considered what Porcupine and Beaver had said about the winters, and decided that Porcupine had done right. He said, "Porcupine was right. If the winters were made too long, people could not live. *Henceforth the winters will be about this length, but they will be variable.* I will tell you of the gaxewisa month, when people will meet together and talk. At that time of the year people will ask questions (or propound riddles), and others will answer. If the riddle is answered correctly, then the person who propounded it must answer, 'Fool-Hen.' " Raven chose this word because the fool-hen has a shorter beak than any other game-bird. "If people guess riddles correctly at this time of year, then the winter will be short, and the spring come early." [(89), pp. 38–39]

How Glooskap Found the Summer

One of the six chief divisions of Indians in North America was the Algonquin. A tribe in this division called themselves the Wabanski, which meant white or light, meaning that they lived nearest the rising sun or the east.

The Wabanski had in common the traditions of a great mythology, the central figure of which was a demigod or hero who presented traits much like Odin and Thor. The name of this hero was Glooskap, which strangely meant liar. He was given that name because it was said that when he left earth, he promised to return and never did.

Attributed to Glooskap are many brave deeds, and many stories telling of the contributions he made to the welfare of his people. One fascinating story is "How Glooskap Found the Summer" (62).

In the long ago time when people lived always in the early red morning, before sunrise, before the *Squid to neck* [world] was peopled as to-day, Glooskap went very far north, where all was ice.

He came to a wigwam. Therein he found a giant, a great giant, for he was Winter. Glooskap entered; he sat down. Then Winter gave him a pipe; he smoked, and the giant told tales of the old times.

The charm was on him; it was the Frost. The giant talked on and froze, and Glooskap fell asleep. He slept for six months, like a toad. Then the charm fled, and he awoke. He went his way home; he went to the south, and at every step it grew warmer, and the flowers began to come up and talk to him.

He came to where there were many little ones dancing in the forest; their queen was Summer. I am singing the truth: it was Summer, the most beautiful one ever born. He caught her up; he kept her by a crafty trick. The Master cut a moose-hide into a long cord; as he ran away with Summer he let the end trail behind him.

They, the fairies of Light, pulled at the cord, but as Glooskap ran, the cord ran out, and though they pulled he left them far away. So he came to the lodge of Winter, but now he had Summer in his bosom; and Winter welcomed him, for he hoped to freeze him again to sleep. I am singing the song of Summer.

But this time the Master did the talking. This time his *m'téoulin* [every thing] was the strongest. And ere long the sweat ran down Winter's face, and then he melted more and quite away, as did the wigwam. Then every thing awoke; the grass grew, the fairies came out, and the snow ran down the rivers, carrying away the dead leaves. Then Glooskap left Summer with them and went home. [Pp. 134–135]

Mythological Epics

The epic is a long poem about one hero or a group of heroes whose righteousness and deeds of valor were the subjects of the stories preserved by storytellers until they were written down for posterity. The dates and writers of the epics are unknown in most instances. They are characterized by beautiful, inspired writing and suspenseful narrative style.

The *Iliad* and the *Odyssey*

The *Iliad* (46), the earliest written record of Greek mythology, ranks in literary importance with the Bible and Shakespeare. This epic must have had a long oral tradition before it was put into writing by Homer. The exact dates of Homer's life and his writings are uncertain. However, the incidents of the Trojan War that the *Iliad* describes appear, from archeological discoveries of the last century, to have taken place in the twelfth century B.C.

The story related by the *Iliad* is an incident of about seven weeks

The Children's Homer: The Adventures of Odysseus and the Tale of Troy retold by Padraic Colum, illustrated by Willy Pogany.

in the tenth year of the Trojan War. The unifying theme throughout the twenty-four books of the poem is the wrath of the Greek hero Achilles. Other Greek heroes—Agamemnon, Patroclus, Hector, and Priam—move majestically and dramatically through the story.

Whereas the *Iliad* is devoted to martial maneuvering, Homer's *Odyssey* (47) is more concerned with romance and adventure. The story relates the events that befall Odysseus on his return to Ithaca after the capture of Troy. During his absence from Ithaca his beautiful, faithful wife, Penelope, is besieged by a host of aggressive suitors who hope that Odysseus is dead. The last four books of the *Odyssey* tell of Odysseus' vengeance in slaying the suitors and reestablishing his relationship with Penelope. Many of the adventures of Odysseus have the ring of tall tales. He is a cunning man who succeeds in overcoming numerous misfortunes.

Metamorphoses

What Homer did for Greek mythology, Ovid did for Roman mythology in his masterpiece of storytelling, *Metamorphoses* (72). The fifteenth book of the poem relates in epic style all the remarkable changes of mythology, from the creation to Caesar's appearance as a star after his death. The myths, drawn largely from Greek sources, are not told with the reverence for the Olympian gods that is found in Homer's writing. The Romans were beginning to discard the belief held by the Greeks that the gods played important roles in their personal lives. Ovid chose his stories for the opportunity they afforded to display narrative art. Among the best known are the stories of Deucalion and Pyrrha, Apollo and Daphne, Arachne, Midas, and Pyramus and Thisbe. Ovid retells these stories without any great depth of feeling but with a brilliant sophistication. Each story has its dramatic highlight, and the connecting principle between the stories is that each involves some metamorphosis, or change, such as shapeless water's changing into the world or Julius Caesar into a star. It is Ovid's clever style that gives continuity to the stories.

Just as the Greeks and the Romans had their great myths preserved for them, so did the Norsemen in *Poetica Edda* and the Germanic people in *Nibelungenlied.*

The *Poetica Edda*

In the latter part of the twelfth century and the beginning of the thirteenth century came the *Poetica Edda* (25), an anonymous collection of thirty-four ancient poems in old Norse or old Icelandic. According to H. A. Bellows (8), the brilliant translator for the American-Scandinavian Foundation, they constitute the original storehouse of German mythology. He considers them to be in many ways "the greatest literary monument preserved to us out of the antiquity of the kindred races which we call Germanic" (p. xii). When, where, or by whom these poems were composed is unknown. It is believed that some originated in Norway among learned emigrants to foreign parts, and some probably originated among Norse settlers on the islands of the North Atlantic and several in Greenland. However, they were collected and written down in Iceland. It is possible that there were written copies of an earlier date. For generations, the subject matter had been transmitted orally and part of it is of ancient origin.

The poems may be divided into two large groups: mythological and heroic. The mythological deal with the creation and final destruction of the world, a collection of precepts and proverbs, and the recovery of Thor's hammer. The heroic group is built around the great Germanic idol Siegfried. The verse forms are extremely involved. Only in a limited sense are they folk poetry. It is evident that their authors were brilliant artists who knew the details of their subject as well as the art of verse making. The material of the *Poetica Edda* gave rise in Germany in the thirteenth century to the *Nibelungenlied* and in the nineteenth century to the operas of Richard Wagner.

The *Nibelungenlied*

The *Nibelungenlied* (71), supposedly written by a monk in the twelfth century, is a combination of questionable historical facts and pure legend. As with the epics that have come out of other cultures, the *Nibelungenlied* had its foundation in oral tradition, and as it passed through the several phases of Germanic history it took on various changes until it was recorded in its epic form. The themes running through the epic are persistent personal loyalty and unyielding revenge. Brunhild plans for the murder of Siegfried when she discovers that it was he and not her husband Gunther who had overcome her Amazon powers upon which her strength depended. However, Gunther had arranged for Siegfried to overcome Brunhild with his magical cape and to defeat her at various games of chivalry. Brunhild therefore arranges for Siegfried to be murdered by Hagen, who had been made invulnerable by a bath in dragon's blood except for one spot between his shoulder blades. Siegfried's wife Kriemhild broods over the heinous deed and plans for revenge. Hagen incites Kriemhild further by robbing her of Siegfried's treasure—the gold of the Rhineland Nibelungen elf men. Kriemhild marries Etzel, who is historically based on Attila of the Huns. She invites her relatives to the Burgundian Royal House. Hagen, who is among them, provokes a conflict in which all are slain except Etzel, who is confused and unaware of the treacherous plans.

The *Nibelungenlied* preserves the characteristics of the pre-Christian age with a thin overlay of chivalry and Christian elements. It has become the national epic of the German people. Richard Wagner found in it his inspiration for some of his greatest operas. The *Ring of the Nibelungs* is a four-evening cycle of music dramas. Its parts are "The Rhinegold," "The Valkyries," "Siegfried," and "The Twilight of the Gods." Hundreds of thousands of music lovers around the world have thrilled to the drama and music of the Wagnerian operas.

Legendary Heroes

Every nation has its heroes—men of fabulous strength, indomitable daring, and unlimited courage, men who face dangers that seem insurmountable, rescue people who are in distress, and fight the enemies who attempt to invade their country and take over the throne. Often a birthmark is a symbol of royalty and proves a man's lawful right to a throne. It is not unusual for the hero to possess some magic power that protects him from assault and aids him in performing unusual feats.

Before history was recorded, historical events and the heroes who played important roles in them were honored in song and story by the storytellers who kept the memories of the events and heroes alive. These legends were handed down from generation to generation until they were finally written down and became the traditional backgrounds of the country.

The names of such heroes as Beowulf, Havelok, The Cid, Roland, King Arthur, Robin Hood, Sohrab, and Rustum are familiar names in the countries of their origin.

Beowulf

The Anglo-Saxon epic *Beowulf* (49) recounts the deeds and daring of that great hero. A nephew of the Geatish king Hygslac, Beowulf lived in the land of the Geats in the southern part of the Scandinavian peninsula. As the story goes, Hrothgar, King of the Danes, built a palace that Grendel, a monster, visited nightly for twelve years devouring the king's thanes. Beowulf had heard the story of how Grendel would come up from the low marshy land and carry off and devour men who sat in the great feasting hall of the palace. King Hrothgar and his men were plunged in gloom and despair.

King Hrothgar had at one time befriended Beowulf's father.

Beowulf retold by Rosemary Sutcliff, illustrated by Charles Keeping.

Beowulf decided to go, with fourteen companions, to the aid of King Hrothgar. There was great rejoicing when Hrothgar and his people heard the reason for Beowulf's coming.

As the men slept in the great hall of the palace, Grendel broke in and devoured one of Hrothgar's men. Beowulf struggled with Grendel. In the struggle Grendel lost an arm and returned to his cave beneath the lake to die. There was great rejoicing and celebrating among Hrothgar and his men. At the height of the celebration Grendel's mother entered the hall to avenge her son's death. She carried off one of Hrothgar's men. Beowulf pursued her to her den. With his enchanted sword he cut off her head and her son's head and returned to Hrothgar with his prizes. Beowulf was honored, and after the death of Hrothgar and his son he succeeded to the throne where he reigned for fifty years until a dragon ravaged the land.

With eleven of his men, Beowulf set out to search for the dragon. A fierce struggle ensued, and all but one of Beowulf's men deserted him. Beowulf killed the dragon but he was mortally wounded. His body was burned on a funeral pyre along with his armor and the dragon's treasure.

The author of this great epic is unknown. It is believed to have been written in the eighth century in England by a descendant of the Scandinavian settlers of Britain who brought with them the legends of their homeland.

Havelok

Havelok is one of the great Scandinavian heroes who has been perpetuated in romantic verse. Two stories run parallel in this verse. One centers around Goldborough, the daughter of Athelwold, King of England. Before Athelwold died, he chose Earl Godrich of Cornwall to rule the land if he would serve as guardian to Goldborough and give the crown over to her when she was grown. The earl became infatuated with the crown and betrayed his oath. He shut Goldborough up in a castle where she was dressed in poor clothes and fed scanty fare.

While Earl Godrich was ruling in England, Birkabeyn was king of Denmark. Birkabeyn was the father of two daughters and a son. At his death he called Godard, whom he thought to be his truest friend, and commended his children to him with the agreement that Godard should rule until Havelok, Birkabeyn's son, was grown and would be made king of Denmark. Godard soon forgot his promise and placed the children in a castle where they lived under dire circumstances. Fearing that his family would lose the crown, Godard went to the castle to kill the children. He murdered the two girls but lost heart when it came to murdering Havelok. Instead, he charged Grim, one of his bondsmen, to drown Havelok. However, when the bondsman's wife found a king's mark on Havelok's right shoulder, the bondsman decided to keep Havelok in hiding.

Fearing discovery and reprisal from Godard, Grim fled to England taking Havelok with him. Havelok found work as a scullion in Earl Godrich's kitchen where he gained a reputation for his good looks and tremendous strength. In a contest of strength, he succeeded in moving a huge stone farther than had anyone else. This feat prompted the Earl of Godrich to plan a marriage between Goldborough and Havelok. Goldborough resented her marriage to a bondsman until she saw the signs of a king about him; a light from his mouth and a mark on his shoulder. Both Goldborough and Havelok had a dream that prompted them to leave England and go to Denmark where after several trials, Havelok was recognized as the rightful heir to the throne. Leaving his scepter in the hands of Earl Uffe, who had welcomed him back to Denmark, Havelok left Denmark. Upon arriving in England, Havelok reminded Godrich of the promise he had sworn to Athelwold that Goldborough should be queen.

After fierce combat between Havelok and Godrich Havelok was victorious. When the English discovered that Goldborough was the rightful heir to the throne, they put up their swords and asked pardon of the queen. Havelok was crowned king in London, and he and Goldborough ruled England for sixty years.

The Cid

The deeds of Spain's national hero, Ruy Diaz de Vivar, are told in *Poem of the Cid* (76), which marks the beginning of Spanish literature. As with many of the stories of other great national heroes the author of *Poem of the Cid* is unknown.

The historical background of the epic is the period of Reconquesta, when the Spaniards were trying to regain their peninsula from the Moors who had held it since the early eighteenth century. Ruy Diaz, who became known as The Cid, played a leading role in these operations of reconquest. He captured town after town leading his warriors down to the Mediterranean coast and capturing Valencia. The Moors admired his bravery, and many quickly joined forces with him.

As the epic opens, Ruy Diaz has been sent by the king to collect

The Legend of the Cid
retold by Robert C. Goldston,
illustrated by Stephane.

tributes owed to him by the Moors. Intriguing courtiers accuse Ruy Diaz of withholding some of the money, and as a result he is sent into exile by the king. He places his wife Ximena and his two daughters Elvira and Sol in the monastery of Cardena.

Gathering together a little band of sixty lancers, Ruy Diaz raids the Moorish territories where he finds great riches. As his fame spreads, adventurers flock to his banner, and one victory after another follows until The Cid captures the city of Valencia, where he establishes himself with his wife and daughters.

Near tragedy enters the epic when The Cid gives his two daughters to two scoundrels who are eager to marry them for their wealth. The Cid seeks redress from the king for the abuse of his daughters by the scoundrels. The demands made by The Cid are granted. This triumph proves that the sons-in-law are traitors and that The Cid is a man of honor. One of The Cid's daughters marries the king of Navarre and the other marries the king of Aragon. Through these marriages The Cid becomes connected with the royal houses of Spain.

The Cid, also called *El Campeador*, is hailed as the national hero of Spain and champion of Christianity against the Moors. His exploits, real and imaginary, form the basis of many Spanish romances and chronicles.

King Arthur

King Arthur (29, 60, 81), the hero of a great cycle of medieval romances, is one of the most exciting of the legendary heroes whose lives and deeds have come down to us through literature. Historically he was a shadowy British chieftain of the sixteenth century, who fought many battles. He is said to have been a king of the Silures, a tribe of ancient Britons. According to legends he was wounded in the battle of Camlon in Cornwall and was taken to Glastonbury, where he died.

The first Arthur stories were written in French, since that was the language of the court during the Norman days. In the fifteenth century Sir Thomas Malory set out to write the story of King Arthur and his court using as his source the French writings. He gave permanent shape to the Arthurian legends in *Morte d'Arthur* (66), which means the death of Arthur, although the story starts with Arthur's birth and recounts his whole life. Many readers are more familiar with King Arthur through Alfred, Lord Tennyson's beautiful retelling of the Arthur stories in the *Idylls of the King* (87) based upon Sir Thomas Malory's work.

The *Idylls* are composed of twelve allegorical, narrative poems written in blank verse. They relate the story of the legendary Arthur from his supernatural birth to his supernatural death and tell of Arthur's ideals in the establishment of a "Round Table" to which he gathered a group of knights whose deeds of daring and chivalry won his court a high renown. The knights pledged their loyalty to Arthur and took the oath of knighthood.

The twelve poems relate the noble deeds of Arthur and his knights, the many colorful events of his reign, the gradual decline of his noble plan through the corruption of the court, and the destruction of the kingdom.

Robin Hood

Another popular legendary hero of Great Britain is Robin Hood (24, 80). In the Robin Hood cycle, which was written anonymously, the reader makes the acquaintance of such fascinating characters as Little John, Will Scarlet, Friar Tuck, Allan-a-Dale, George-a-Greene, and Maid Marian.

Robin Hood is the romantic outlaw and hero of English ballads. It is doubtful whether Robin Hood ever lived, but legend has it that he was born in 1160 at Locksley, Notts., or that he was the outlawed Earl of Huntington, Robert Fitzooth, in disguise. Sherwood Forest in Nottinghamshire was his chief haunt. There are numerous anecdotes of his personal courage, his skill in archery, his generosity, and his great popularity. Tradition has it that he robbed the rich to give to the poor and protected women and children with chivalrous magnanimity.

The Merry Adventures of Robin Hood of Great Reknown in Nottinghamshire by Howard Pyle.

Robin Hood lives not only in the delightful stories that feature him but in the songs and sayings that have become a part of the English language: for example, "a Robin Hood wind" is a cold thaw-wind, since Robin Hood supposedly said that he could bear any cold except that which a thaw-wind brought with it. "To go round Robin Hood's barn" is to arrive at the right conclusion by very roundabout methods. "To sell Robin Hood's pennyworth" is to sell things at half their value. As Robin Hood stole his wares, he sold them under intrinsic value, for just what he could get immediately.

Roland

Roland was the most famous of the twelve legendary champions in attendance upon Charlemagne. His mother was Charlemagne's sister. Charlemagne was proud of his nephew, who was often called "The Christian Theseus" and "The Achilles of the West." Legend has it that he was eight feet tall and handsome of face. He is the hero of the *Song of Roland* (33).

Roland had a wonderful ivory horn that he had won from the giant Jutmundus. He also wrested from the giant a sword that was supposed to have once belonged to Hector.

When Charlemagne had been in Spain for six years he sent Ganelon, one of his men, on an embassy to Marsilius, the pagan king of Saragossa. Out of jealousy, Ganelon revealed to Marsilius the route that the Christian army planned to take on its way home. The pagan king arrived at Roncesvalles just as Roland was conducting a rear guard of 20,000 men through the pass.

Roland fought until 100,000 Saracens were slain and only 50 of his 20,000 men survived. At that critical moment another pagan army of 50,000 poured down upon him from the mountains. When he was set upon, he sounded his ivory horn to give Charlemagne notice of his danger. At the third blast his horn cracked in two, but it was so loud that birds fell dead and the Saracen army was panic-stricken. Charlemagne heard the sound at St. Jean Pied de Port and rushed to Roland's aid, but he was too late. Legend relates that Roland took his sword, which had in its hilt a thread from the Virgin Mary's cloak, a tooth of St. Peter, one of St. Denis' hairs, and a drop of St. Basil's blood, and rather than let it fall into the hands of the Saracens tried to break it on a rock. As it was unbreakable, he hurled it into a poisoned stream where it still remains.

Rustum

Persian romances are full of the deeds of Rustum, chief of the Persian mythical heroes. The story of Rustum is told in the Persian epic *Shah Namah.* Rustum, according to legend, saved King Caicaus from prison but later fell into disgrace because he refused to follow the religious system of Zoroaster. The king sent his son, Asfendiar, to convert Rustum. Since he was unsuccessful in his attempt to do so, the two resorted to combat. They fought for two days before Rustum discovered that Asfendiar bore a charmed life and could not be wounded. The deeds of these two men are told in song and story. Rustum was famous, also, for his victory over the white dragon, Asdeev. In Matthew Arnold's poem *Sohrab and Rustum* (5), Rustum fights with Sohrab, overcomes him, and finds too late that he has slain his own son.

More Myths and Legends

Pegasus (91), retold by Krystyna Turska, is an attractive picture book that describes the daring adventures of the brave youth Bellerophon and Pegasus, his wonderful winged horse of Greek mythology fame.

Baldur, the god of innocence and goodness, is the main character in Cynthia King's *In the Morning of Time: The Story of the Norse God Baldur* (55), which describes the creation of the world as told by the early Norsemen. The various myths, first written by the Icelandic poets about the years A.D. 800–1000, relate the world in which the Norsemen lived. A glossary of names and terms is included and the illustrations make an interesting contribution to the text. This book is an excellent addition to the elementary school library.

Stories Told by the Aztecs: Before the Spaniards Came (7) is a collection of twenty-eight stories from Aztec mythology based upon original Aztec and early Spanish sources and retold by Carleton Beals. The collection presents the mythological system of a highly developed, distinguished civilization. Material on Indians, Mexico, and mythology make this book an excellent reference for the elementary school library.

Sundiata: The Epic of the Lion King (10) by Roland Bertol is an outstanding addition to the history of the highly developed empires of ancient Africa. The author has drawn upon ancient and modern sources as the basis for his retold version of the legendary Sundiata, ruler of thirteenth-century Mali. The retelling of the story is replete with sorcery, prophecies, taboos, and valiant deeds, all the qualities of ancient African storytelling.

Robust stories of seven giants are retold by Adrien Stoutenburg in the fabulous collection *Fee, Fi, Fo, Fum* (86). Included are the Irish Fingal, the American Indian Manabozho, Hurtali who rode Noah's ark, the Slavic Reygok, the Scottish Strong Man of the Wood, the Cornish Brown Willy, and the African giant Antaeua from Greek mythology. Outstanding woodcuts strengthen the characters. Sources for the stories are listed in the back of the book.

Among the pleasant legends of Hawaii is *Hawaiian Legends of Tricksters and Riddlers* (90) by Vivian L. Thompson. Twelve of the Hawaiian legends emphasize the primitive Hawaiians' courage and wit in overcoming evil spirits; the riddling tales relate the later, more cultured Hawaiians' skill in quick-witted debates. The illustrations add amusement to the legends.

According to Kermit Krueger, the stories in *The Serpent Prince: Folk Tales from Northeastern Thailand* (59) were collected during his two years as a Peace Corps volunteer in Thailand. The stories are well written and attractively illustrated in black and white by a Jap-

Hawaiian Legends of Tricksters and Riddlers by Vivian L. Thompson.

Korolu, the Singing Bandit by Barbara K. Walker, illustrated by Nickzad Nodjoumi.

anese artist. In an introduction, Krueger states that these stories are both the history and mythology of the people of the Mekhong plateau.

The moon is the villain in the imaginative Indian legend *The Angry Moon* (84), retold by William Sleator. An Indian girl who dares to laugh at the moon's face is spirited away and made a prisoner. The beautiful color illustrations incorporate Tlingit Indian designs portraying Indian characters and Alaskan settings.

Barbara Walker retells the legends of the Turkish folk-hero Korolu in *Korolu, the Singing Bandit* (96). The story relates how Korolu becomes a bandit to avenge the blinding of his father by the Bey of Bolu. The black-and-white illustrations portray the Turkish setting.

Another excellent reference for the elementary school library is *Gilgamesh and Other Babylonian Tales* (97) by Jennifer Westwood. The author's prefatory explanation and background notes provide a meaningful introduction to Sumerian and Babylonian mythology.

In *Tales of a Chinese Grandmother* by Frances Carpenter, Chinese folk lore is presented against the background of the Ling Household. An aged grandmother tells tales sometimes to only her two grandchildren and sometimes to the entire family.

Romanticism Takes Over

Baffled by the natural phenomena surrounding him, early man recognized a power beyond himself that controlled his world. He found satisfaction and security in creating myths and legends by which he guided his living. As groups grew and moved from place to place they carried with them the myths and legends they had inherited; to these they added folk and fairy tales for entertainment, building traditions, describing conduct, and expressing beliefs.

During the Middle Ages some folk and fairy tales found their way into crude chapbooks and into basic material for such great storytellers as Boccaccio and Chaucer, but they did not come into full flowering until the middle of the eighteenth and the beginning of the nineteenth centuries. Rationalism dominated European literature from the second half of the 1700s through the mid-1800s, at which time a wave of reaction began to rise and romanticism began to take over. Leadership in the romantic movement came from political philosophers, writers, and social leaders throughout Europe and the United States. Jean Jacques Rousseau, more than any other writer, represented the rebellion against the neoclassicism that had been dominating man's thinking during the Age of Reason. Robert Burns, William Wordsworth, Samuel Taylor Coleridge, Johann Wolfgang von Goethe, Alphonse de Lamartine, William Cullen Bryant, Vi-

Aesop's Fables by Anne Terry White. Illustrated by Helen Siegl.

comte de Châteaubriand, and Lord Byron were among the poets who furthered the romantic movement. The works of George Sand, Victor Hugo, and Sir Walter Scott also flourished during this period. It was the romantic movement that provided the fertile soil in which the writings of the Brothers Grimm, Jakob and Wilhelm, developed.

Early Folk and Fairy Tales

The Brothers Grimm

The Brothers Grimm, Jakob (1785–1863) and Wilhelm (1786–1859), were born in Hanau, Germany. . Both were well educated. Jakob made the acquaintance of *Des Knaben Wunderhorn* (*The Boy's Wonderhorn*), a collection of folk songs edited by Ludwig von Arnim and Clemens Brentano. Jakob was interested and excited by this collection, and his enthusiasm was caught by Wilhelm. Together the brothers saw the possibilities, not in collecting folk songs, but in collecting folk tales. The first volume of *Kinder und Hausmärchen* (36) was published in 1812; revised editions followed through the years. All of their writings were signed "The Brothers Grimm."

The Brothers Grimm can be credited with opening up a large body of literature that continues to delight listeners and readers. Interest and enthusiasm for folk tales spread rapidly. Elias Lonnrot in Finland; Peter Asbjornsen and his collaborator Jorgen Moe in Norway; and George Dasent, Andrew Lang, and Joseph Jacobs in England were among the leaders in the folk literature movement.

Hans Christian Andersen

Just as the Grimm brothers are closely identified with folk tales, Hans Christian Andersen is closely identified with fairy tales.

Hans Christian Andersen was born April 2, 1805, in the town of Odense on the island of Funen, off the coast of Denmark. At fourteen years of age he left home and went to Copenhagen determined to become famous.

Andersen's first book appeared in 1829 when he was twenty-four-years old. It was a fantasy entitled *A Walking Trip from Holmen's Canal to the East Point of Amger.* The critics and people of Copenhagen received it with considerable praise. His *Collected Poems* followed the next year. Then came a little book *Travel Silhouettes,* which was not

Andersen's Fairy Tales retold by Rose Dobbs, illustrated by Gustav Hjortland.

as well received as his first book. But in 1835, when Andersen was thirty years of age, his fortune changed with the publication and hearty reception of his novel *The Improvisator.*

The same year that *The Improvisator* was published, Andersen started to write the fairy tales that were to bring him fame and fortune. His first four stories were "The Tinder Box" (1), "Big Claus and Little Claus" (1), "The Princess and the Pea" (1), and "Little Ida's Flowers" (1). They were published in a pamphlet, and Hans called them "trifles." He found that wherever he went, children enjoyed these tales. This prompted him to write more, and the first four were followed by "Thumbelina" (1) and "The Traveling Companion" (1).

The king endowed Hans with a pension in 1838. This provided him with time for writing and for travel, which he thoroughly enjoyed. He made friends wherever he went and was in constant demand as a storyteller. From his pen flowed those stories that were to delight children everywhere—"The Dauntless Tin Soldier" (1), "The Ugly Duckling" (1), "The Nightingale" (1), "The Wild Swans" (1), and "The Snow Queen" (1). His stories were written in everyday speech full of vigor and strength.

Before Hans Christian Andersen's death in 1875, at the age of seventy, he had left a rich literary heritage to satisfy and challenge the imaginations of adults as well as to entertain boys and girls.

Fairy Tales—Pro and Con

Edna Johnson, Evelyn R. Sickels, and Frances Clarke Sayers in *Anthology of Children's Literature* (52) give reasons for the popularity of fairy tales with children.

> Everything is clear in the fairy tale. One knows exactly where to place one's sympathy. The issues are soon stated, with no unnecessary subtleties of emotion, no bewildering waivering between cause and effect. Everyone acts according to his nature, and the stories move in strong, direct action to the always expected end, where the good come to glory and joy, and evil is punished as befits it, with primitive symbols of suffering. The structure and style of the tales accustom the reader to the art of writing at its best, for there is economy of language, nothing that does not move to the ultimate finish, and yet there is imagery, there are flashes of poetic insight and the clear echoes of spoken words and individual ways of saying things. [Pp. 134–135]

Hans Christian Andersen (31) himself once explained what a fairy tale could mean.

> In the whole realm of poetry no domain is so boundless. It reaches from the blood-drenched graves of antiquity to the pious legends of a child's picture book; it takes the poetry of the people and the poetry of the artist. To me it represents all poetry, and he who masters it must be able to put into it tragedy, comedy, naïve simplicity, irony and humor. [P. 181]

Of the choice and content of fairy tales Lillian Smith (85) says:

> No advocate of fairy tales as a rich and essential part of children's literature denies the need for a reasonable and wise selection among the large and often unwieldy mass of folk material. But such selections have been made and are readily available—selections which keep in mind the wide variety in taste and temperament between individual children.
>
> From time to time criticisms have been leveled at incidents found in fairy tales which are termed "brutal" without giving consideration either to a child's attitude toward such incidents, or to the manner in which they are presented. Both the child's attitude and the characteristic narrative methods of the folk tale have an impersonal quality important to remember. [P. 59]

An even more potent statement is made by Meigs (69):

> Surely no type of literature has suffered such persecution as have the folk and fairy tale, nor has any other shown such indomitable and irrepressible vitality. Considered worldly and immoral in the Puritan period, impractical and frivolous in the didactic age, it has lived from generation to generation in the memories of the common people. [P. 288]

Aside from the question of here and now, as opposed to the never-never-land in children's literature, there are other problems involved in fairy tales. There are brutality and cruelty in some of the tales, and many people have strong feelings against giving children any knowledge of these.

Josette Frank offers a happy solution to this problem in her new and revised edition of *Your Child's Reading Today* (28). She says:

Shall we eliminate from our children's reading stories of this kind [folk and fairy tales]? It would be better, perhaps, to include them and to make use of the questions they raise as springboards for discussion, opportunities for the child to explore with his parent the moral issues involved. They represent folkways in thinking and behavior that need to be clarified for our children. . . .

. . .

Not all children can take the violence of fairy tales however. To some the fantasy is too real, or perhaps comes too close to their own fears and anxieties. For example a child who is vaguely troubled about something may be deeply upset by the story about the Big Bad Wolf and his huffing and puffing—a tale of threat that mirrors his own deepest fears. For others the story may represent only the delight of triumph over the wily tormentor. . . .

We tend in any case to read these traditional folk tales too early, perhaps to pick the wrong ones. The height of fairy tale interest comes at eight or perhaps nine. Nor is there any need to accept *all* the traditional tales. Not all are suited to young readers. Some are better at nine or ten or eleven, and some we may skip altogether, despite their hoary tradition—they are not really for children at all. [Pp. 83–84]

Types of Fairy Tales

Certain types of stories continually recur in folk and fairy tales. Laura F. Kready (57) lists the motifs that commonly occur in fairy tales as follows:

Child wandering into a home, as in "The Three Bears"

Transformation: simple as in "Puss in Boots," by love as in "Beauty and the Beast," by bathing as in "Catskin," or by violence as in "Frog Prince" and "White Cat"

Tasks as marriage tests as in "Cinderella"

Riddle test as in "Peter, Paul and Espen"

Magic sleep as in "Sleeping Beauty"

Magic touch as in "Golden Goose"

Stupid person causing royalty to laugh as in "Lazy Jack"

Exchange as in "Jack and the Beanstalk"

Curiosity punished as in "Bluebeard" and "The Three Bears"

Kindness to persons rewarded as in "Cinderella," "Little Two-Eyes," and "The House in the Wood"

Kindness to animals repaid as in "Thumbelina," "Cinderella," and "White Cat"

Industry rewarded as in "The Elves and the Shoemaker"

Hospitality rewarded as in "Tom Thumb"

Success of a venture as in "Dick Whittington" [P. 98]

Märchen

Different scholars have different groupings for folk and fairy tales. A grouping frequently used is the *Märchen,* a term borrowed from the studies of the Grimm brothers. Stith Thompson (88), the well-known American folklorist, describes the *Märchen* as stories that move "in an unreal world without definite locality or definite characters and [are] filled with the marvelous. In this never-never-land humble heroes kill adversaries, succeed to kingdoms, and marry princesses" (p. 8). "Märchen" is sometimes translated as "household stories" or "folk tales." In such tales the time and place are vaguely suggested as "Once upon a time," "long, long ago," "east of the Sun and west of the Moon," or "far, far away." Each opening is a stimulant to the reader's or listener's imagination.

One of the most popular and most beloved of the *Märchen* is "Cinderella," versions of which may be found in almost every country of the world. In some versions the prince runs an obstacle course that seems insurmountable; in other versions the course runs smoothly. The most popular version is that by the Brothers Grimm (35). All variations share a common core: Cinderella is abused by her stepmother and stepsisters. She has a fairy godmother who arranges for her to go to a place of her desire disguised in radiant splendor. A prince sees her, falls in love, and pursues her until he finds her and takes her as his bride. Perhaps the story of Cinderella was originally told and then written to teach a lesson: Accept hardships, have patience, be kind and cheerful, and you will have a prince for a husband!

Cinderellas have come out of cultures without any relationship to the tale by the Brothers Grimm. Adaptations to the Grimm story are usually made indigenous to the country of the writers who do the adaptations. Padraic Colum (16), for example, tells an Irish variation of this tale.

The Girl Who Sat by the Ashes

Now when Girl-go-with-the-Goats came back from the steppingstones with a shining star on her forehead (and how that star came to be there will be told to you afterward), when she came back to the house of her stepmother, lo and behold! a surprising thing was coming to happen.

For the King's son, no less! had come as far as the garden fornenst that house, and sitting upon his white jennet, he was looking across the ditch into the garden.

And there were Buttercup and Berry-bright standing on the doorstep and making curtsies to him. Girl-go-with-the-Goats stood one side of the garden ditch, letting a bush hide her from the King's son and from her two step-sisters.

"Give me berries out of your garden, fair maids," said the King's son to Berry-bright and to Buttercup. One came toward him and one went back into the house. To the one who came to him he handed a cup of silver.

"Take it into your hand, damsel," he said, "and fill it with berries."

It was Buttercup who had come toward him. She took the silver cup from the King's son and went into the garden. Berry-bright had gone into the house for a vessel, and she came back with an earthenware cup in her hands. When she saw her sister holding the silver cup in her hands she bit her lips in rage.

Buttercup went into the garden. She went to the raspberry bush to pick the berries. But as soon as she came near it, a flock of birds flew at her: sparrows and starlings they were, and they pecked at her eyes and her arms and drove her back to the door of the house.

"Unlucky wench," cried the King's son. "Let the other maid come now and gather me berries in her earthenware cup."

Berry-bright ran toward the red currant bush to pick from it the full of her earthenware cup of berries. But the swallows of the air darted down upon her. With their fierce eyes and wicked mouths they drove Berry-bright out of the garden.

"Unlucky wenches, both," cried the King's son. "Will I not be able to get from your garden a cup full of berries?"

Then Girl-go-with-the-Goats slipped from behind the bush and darted into the garden. She took up an old shoe that lay on the ground. She went toward the black currant bush, and no bird darted in anger at her. Instead two starlings flew down and lighting, one on each shoulder, sang to her. Then Girl-go-with-the-Goats gathered the black currants into the old shoe and took them to the King's son.

"Oh, to be served with black currants out of an old shoe and by a girl as ragged as this wench," cried the King's son. "Out of my sight," he cried when he ate the berries. He took up the old shoe and he struck Girl-go-with-the-Goats on the arm with it.

Still she did not move, but stood looking up at him, her mouth trembling but her eyes steady, and the two starlings resting, one on each shoulder.

"Gawk of a girl, out of my way," cried the King's son. Saying this, he rode his jennet forward and pushed Girl-go-with-the-Goats against the garden ditch.

Then he rode down the road, and the birds that had pecked at Berry-bright and Buttercup flew up into the air.

And there stood Buttercup on the step of the house with the silver cup in her hands, and there stood Berry-bright inside the garden gate with the earthenware cup in her hands, and each one saying to herself, "Who was it that put bad luck on me today?"

And there was Girl-go-with-the-Goats crouching against the garden ditch with the two starlings upon her shoulders, thinking that the very trees around her were singing and that their songs were like the light and like the darkness.

And there was her stepmother, Dame Dale, coming up the path from the steppingstones.

But now we have to tell you how it was that Girl-go-with-the-Goats came to get that shining star upon her forehead:

A shining star
Like a lonely blossom.

It was the Old Woman in the Crow-feather Cloak who had placed it there for her. They had come together to the steppingstones, the Old Woman holding under her arm the cake that Girl-go-with-the-Goats had kneaded and made and given her. "There is not much I can do for you, Maid-alone," said the Old Woman (for the girl had not called herself Girl-go-with-the-Goats but Maid-alone). "There is not much I can do for you," she said, "except let the world see what I see in you." And saying that, she took water from the stream and splashed it on the girl's forehead. And then came out the shining star. She told the girl to bend down and look at herself in the water of the stream. Girl-go-with-the-Goats bent down and saw the shining star on her forehead. Oh, long and in wonder did she look at it. And when she lifted her face from the flowing stream the Old Woman in the Crowfeather Cloak was not to be seen.

. . . [An] Old Woman came up to the house. Her dress was the queerest that anyone ever saw, a Cloak of Crow-feathers and nothing else.

"My, my, my," said the Old Woman as she came into the house. "My, my, my, what became of the big tree that used to grow fornenst your little house?"

"The big tree!" said Berry-bright. "I have heard my mother speak of that big tree. But she never saw it herself. They say that the gypsies once lighted their fires around that big tree, and that the leaves withered and the branches and the root, and the tree died away. But my mother never remembers to have seen it."

"My, my, my," said the Old Woman. "It must be a long time since I was round this way. And where is the well that used to be on my right-hand side as I came into the house?"

"I used to hear my grandmother speak of that well," said Buttercup. "But it was dried up before her time."

"My, my, my," said the Old Woman. "It's a long time since I was round this way. But now that I'm here, maidens dear, put the griddle on the fire and knead and bake a cake for me."

"There's no fire on the hearthstone as you see," said Berry-bright, "and we are not going to put down a fire for you now."

The differences between the Brothers Grimm version and the Padraic Colum version are typical of the marked variations in the Cinderella story as it appears in the different countries. The characters in the Grimm version are clear-cut; the stepmother and stepsisters are selfish and cruel, and there is no effort to soften their cruelty. Each move they make emphasizes their wickedness. The heaviness of the Grimm telling casts a sadness over the story which evokes pity for Cinderella and hatred for her stepsisters. However, the Colum version with its lilting style and poetic prose is overlaid with fun and laughter. The fight at the end is quickly dismissed.

Walter de la Mare (21) has still another version of "Cinderella" that is different from either the Brothers Grimm's tale as translated by Margaret Hunt or that of Padraic Colum. Like Padraic Colum's rendition de la Mare's is strung together in such style as to sing the story. He uses trilogies, similes, and metaphors to create such word pictures as the following:

> She [Cinderella] would jump out of bed, say her prayers, wash her bright face under the pump, comb her dark hair; then, singing too, not like the birds but softly under her breath, would begin her work. [P. 45]

> This little bunched-up old woman [Cinderella's fairy godmother] had a hump on her back, was dressed in outlandish clothes, and a high steeple hat. . . . The two impudent trollops [Cinderella's stepsisters] . . . had called her "Old Stump-Stump," had put out their tongues at her and laughed at every word she said. [Pp. 45–46]

> Shawls and silks of all the colours of the rainbow dangled from sill and balcony. [P. 48]

> The whole city under the tent of the starry night flared bright as a peep-show. [P. 48]

> . . . All was so hushed at last in the vacant kitchen that the ashes, like pygmy bells in a belfry, tinkled as they fell. [P. 49]

Droll Stories

According to the dictionary (82), droll is defined as "amusing in an odd way, whimsically humorous; waggish." This definition fits droll stories perfectly, since they are intended to be funny and to provoke laughter. They are realistic stories that emphasize comedy.

A plot that appears frequently in droll stories is built around three sons, often the sons of a poor man, the youngest of whom is considered to be a simpleton. Usually the simpleton proves to be smarter than his brothers and wins the hand of the princess or inherits what his father has to will. A good illustration of this plot is "The Golden Goose." "The Three Brothers" typifies a frequent variation of this plot in which no son is considered to be a simpleton, but each brother acquires a particular skill in order to compete for an inheritance.

In many of the droll stories the leading character goes it alone. He creates humorous situations by letting other people outwit him and by letting fortunes slip through his hands by doing absurd things. "Hans in Luck" (35) is that kind of story. After serving his master well for seven years, Hans decides to go home to his mother. His master agrees that Hans has served him well and gives him a piece of gold as big as his head. As Hans travels along the road he finds the piece of gold heavy and decides to trade it for a horse. He continues to trade one thing after another: He trades the horse for a cow, the cow for a pig, and the pig for a goose, thinking that each trade was to his benefit. As Hans passes through the last village, a scissors-grinder with his barrow sings as his wheel whirs:

"I sharpen scissors and quickly grind,
My coat blows out in the wind behind."

Hans stood still and looked at him; at last he spoke to him and said: "All's well with you, as you are so merry with your grinding." "Yes," answered the scissors-grinder, "the trade has a golden foundation. A real grinder is a man who as often as he puts his hand into his pocket finds gold in it. But where did you buy that fine goose?"

"I did not buy it, but exchanged my pig for it."

"And the pig?"

"That I got for a cow."

"And the cow?"

"I took that instead of a horse."

"And the horse?"

"For that I gave a lump of gold as big as my head."

"And the gold?"

"Well, that was my wages for seven years' service."

"You have known how to look after yourself each time," said the grinder. "If you can only get on so far as to hear the money jingle in your pocket whenever you stand up, you will have made your fortune."

"How shall I manage that?" said Hans. "You must be a grinder, as I am; nothing particular is wanted for it but a grindstone, the rest finds itself. I have one here; it is certainly a little worn, but you need not give me anything for it but your goose; will you do it?"

"How can you ask?" answered Hans. "I shall be the luckiest fellow on earth; if I have money whenever I put my hand in my pocket, why should I ever worry again?" and he handed him the goose and received the grindstone in exchange. "Now," said the grinder, as he took up an ordinary heavy stone that lay by him, "here is a strong stone for you into the bargain; you can hammer well upon it, and straighten your old nails. Take it with you and keep it carefully."

Hans loaded himself with the stones, and went on with a contented heart, his eyes shining with joy. "I must have been born with a caul," he cried; "everything I want happens to me just as if I were a Sunday-child."

Meanwhile, as he had been on his legs since daybreak, he began to feel tired. Hunger also tormented him, for in his joy at the bargain by which he got the cow he had eaten up all his store of food at once. At last he could only go on with great trouble, and was forced to stop every minute; the stones, too, weighted him down dreadfully. Then he could not help thinking how nice it would be if he had not to carry them just then.

He crept like a snail to a well in a field, and there he thought that he would rest and refresh himself with a cool draught of water, but in order that he might not injure the stones in sitting down, he laid them carefully by his side on the edge of the well. Then he sat down on it, and was to stoop and drink, when he made a slip, pushed against the stones, and both of them fell into the water. When Hans saw them with his own eyes sinking to the bottom, he jumped for joy, and then knelt down, and with tears in his eyes thanked God for having shown him this favor also, and delivered him in so good a way, and without his having any need to reproach himself, from those heavy stones which had been the only things that troubled him.

"There is no man under the sun so fortunate as I," he cried out. With a light heart and free from every burden he now ran on until he was with his mother at home. [Pp. 325–330]

Among the Charles Perrault *Tales of Mother Goose* (75), first collected in 1696, that have entertained boys and girls through the years is *The Master Cat,* or *Puss in Boots* (74). It is full of unexpected, hilarious happenings. One forgets about the two older sons and is not concerned with what happened to them. It is too exciting to follow the adventures of the youngest son and his wily cat. As the story goes:

PUSS IN BOOTS

Once upon a time there was a miller who died and left no more riches to his three sons than his mill, his ass and his cat.

There was no need for a lawyer to divide the property. The eldest son took the mill, the second the ass, and the youngest was left nothing but the cat.

The young fellow was wretched at having so small a share. "My brothers," said he, "can make a living well enough by joining fortunes. As for me, when I have eaten my cat and made me a muff of its skin, I shall die of hunger."

The cat pretended not to hear all this. He spoke up seriously, "Do not fret, master. Just get me a sack and have a pair of boots made for me so that I can run in the brambles. You'll see that you are not so badly off as you

The Blue Fairy Book edited by Andrew Lang, illustrated by Reisie Lonette.

think." The cat's master did not put much stock in what he said. But he had seen how clever Puss was at catching rats and mice—hanging by his heels or hiding in the meal playing dead. So he did not altogether give up hope. [Unpaged]

. . .

One's appreciation of droll stories would not be complete without making the acquaintance of the type in which husbands learn the realities of a woman's life as in "The Husband Who Was to Mind the House" (20).

Beast Tales

Many folk and fairy tales fall into a group that is usually described as animals who act and speak like human beings. These tales resemble fables to some extent, but they are longer than fables and are not strained to point up a moral. They have good story lines with overtones of humor and unexpected climaxes. "The Bremen Town-Musicians" (35), "The Three Billy-Goats-Gruff" (6), and "Chicken-Licken" illustrate the qualities that have kept beast tales alive. "Puss in Boots" is also an example of a beast story.

The ability to make the best of a situation is aptly portrayed in "The Three Billy-Goats-Gruff" (6).

THE THREE BILLY-GOATS-GRUFF

Once on a time there were three Billy-Goats who were to go up to the hill-side to make themselves fat, and the family name of the three goats was "Gruff."

On the way up was a bridge, over a burn they had to cross; and under the bridge lived a great ugly Troll, with eyes as big as saucers and a nose as long as a poker.

First of all came the youngest Billy-Goat-Gruff to cross the bridge.

"Trip, trap; trip, trap!" went the bridge.

"Who's that tripping over my bridge?" roared the Troll.

"Oh! it is only I, the tiniest Billy-Goat-Gruff; and I'm going up to the hill-side to make myself fat," said the Billy-Goat, with such a small voice.

"Now I'm coming to gobble you up," said the Troll.

"Oh, no! pray don't take me. I'm too little, that I am," said the Billy-Goat. "Wait a bit till the second Billy-Goat-Gruff comes; he's much bigger.

"Well! be off with you," said the Troll.

A little while after came the second Billy-Goat-Gruff to cross the bridge.

"Trip, trap! trip, trap! trip, trap!" went the bridge.

"Who's that tripping over my bridge?" roared the Troll.

"Oh! it's the second Billy-Goat-Gruff, and I'm going up to the hillside to make myself fat," said the Billy-Goat, who hadn't such a small voice.

"Now, I'm coming to gobble you up," said the Troll.

"Oh, no! don't take me. Wait a little till the big Billy-Goat-Gruff comes; he's much bigger."

"Very well; be off with you," said the Troll.

But just then up came the big Billy-Goat-Gruff.

"TRIP, TRAP! TRIP, TRAP! TRIP, TRAP!" went the bridge, for the Billy-Goat was so heavy that the bridge creaked and groaned under him.

"Who's that tramping over my bridge?" roared the Troll.

Tales Told Again by Walter de la Mare,
illustrated by Alan Howard.

"It's I! The Big Billy-Goat-Gruff," said the Billy-Goat, who had a big hoarse voice of his own.

"Now, I'm coming to gobble you up," roared the Troll.

"Well, come along! I've got two spears,
And I'll poke your eyeballs out at your ears,
I've got besides two curling-stones,
And I'll crush you to bits, body and bones."

That was what the big Billy-Goat said; so he flew at the Troll and poked his eyes out with his horns, and crushed him to bits, body and bones, and tossed him out into the burn, and after that he went up to the hillside. There the Billy-Goats got so fat they were scarcely able to walk home again; and if the fat hasn't fallen off them, why they're still fat; and so—

Snip, snap, snout,
This tale's told out. [Pp. 259–261]

There are other beast tales that are not of a humorous nature. In this type of beast tale, a human being, usually a prince, is living under a spell that has changed him into some kind of an animal. The animal is finally changed back to a human being through the kindness of a beautiful maiden whom he marries. "The Frog Prince" (36) is an excellent illustration of this type of tale.

Pourquoi Stories

Pourquoi or "why" stories often feature animals and explain how they acquired certain physical characteristics as shown by "Why the Bear Is Stumpy-Tailed" (20).

WHY THE BEAR IS STUMPY-TAILED

One day the Bear met the Fox, who came slinking along with a string of fish he had stolen.

"Whence did you get those from?" asked the Bear.

"Oh! my Lord Bruin, I've been out fishing and caught them," said the Fox.

So the Bear had a mind to learn to fish too, and bade the Fox tell him how he was to set about it.

"Oh! it's an easy craft for you," answered the Fox, "and soon learnt. You've only got to go upon the ice, and cut a hole and stick your tail down into it; and so you must go on holding it there as long as you can. You're not to mind if your tail smarts a little; that's when the fish bite. The longer you hold it there the more fish you'll get; and then all at once out with it, with a cross pull sideways, and with a strong pull too."

Yes; the Bear did as the Fox had said, and held his tail a long, long time down in the hole, till it was fast frozen in. Then he pulled it out with a cross pull, and it snapped short off. That's why Bruin goes about with a stumpy tail this very day. [P. 155]

Pourquoi stories may also explain natural phenomena not involving animals as in "Why the Sea Is Salt" (20).

Accumulative Stories

Some of the most delightful folk tales are the accumulative stories. Very young children are fascinated by them. The subject matter is not of as much importance as the form. The events in these stories build up to a climax; after the climax is reached there is often a recapitulation of the entire story in which the events unwind backward to the beginning. This provides a satisfactory conclusion, particularly from a child's point of view. Many children love to hear the stories again and again so that they can memorize the sequence of events.

"The Old Woman and Her Pig" (50) and "The House That Jack Built" (3) have been favorites through the years. Another accumulative story that will delight children with its combination of repetition and suspense is "The Pancake" (50).

The Blue Fairy Book edited by Andrew Lang, illustrated by Grace Dulles Clarke.

THE PANCAKE

Once upon a time there was a mother who had seven hungry children. She was making a milk Pancake for supper. There it was, a sizzling and a frying and a sizzling and a frying, and oh, it looked so good! The seven hungry children stood around watching it, and the father sat down and looked on.

The first child said, "Oh, dear mother, give me a bite."

The second said, "Oh dear good mother, give me a bite."

The third said, "Oh, dear sweet mother, give me a bite."

The fourth said, "Oh, dear sweet darling mother, give me a bite."

The fifth one said, "Oh, dear sweet darling best mother, give me a bite."

The sixth one said, "Oh, dear sweet darling dearest mother, give me a bite."

The seventh one said, "Oh, dear sweet darling loveliest mother, give me a bite."

"Now, children," said the mother; "just wait a moment until the Pancake turns itself." She should have said, "Now, children, wait a moment until I turn the Pancake," because as soon as she said, "Wait until the Pancake turns itself," the Pancake heard and was so frightened it flopped over on one side and fried nice and brown, then flopped over on the other side and fried nice and brown, then jumped right out of the frying pan, rolled out of the kitchen door, down the garden walk, through the garden gate, and down the road.

The seven hungry children, the Mother, and the Father ran after it, all of them calling, "Oh, Pancake, stop a moment. We want a bite of you."

But the Pancake rolled on and on and on.

Bye and bye it met a man.

"Good day!" said the man.

"Good day!" said the Pancake.

"Oh, wait a moment," said the man. "I want a bite of you."

"Oh, no," said the Pancake. "I've just rolled away from seven hungry children, a Mother, a Father, and I'll roll away from you, Manny-Panny." It rolled on and on and on.

Then it met a Hen.

"Good day!" said the Hen.

"Good day!" said the Pancake.

"Wait a moment," said the Hen. "I want a bite of you."

"Oh, no," said the Pancake. "I've rolled away from seven hungry children, a Mother, a Father, Manny-Panny, and I'll roll away from you, Henny-Penny," and it rolled on and on and on until it met a Cock.

"Good day!" said the Cock.

"Good day!" said the Pancake.

"Oh! wait a moment," said the Cock. "I want a bite of you."

"Oh, no," said the Pancake, "I've just rolled away from seven hungry children, a Mother, a Father, Manny-Panny, Henny-Penny, and I'll roll away from you, Cocky-Locky." And it rolled on and on and on until it met a Duck.

"Good day!" said the Duck.

"Good day!" said the Pancake.

"Oh, wait a moment," said the Duck. "I want a bite of you."

"Oh, no," said the Pancake. "I've just rolled away from seven hungry children, a Mother, a Father, Manny-Panny, Henny-Penny, Cocky-Locky, and I'll roll away from you, Ducky-Lucky." And it rolled on and on and on until it met a Goose.

"Good day!" said the Goose.

"Good day!" said the Pancake.

"Oh, wait a moment," said the Goose. "I want a bite of you."

"Oh, no," said the Pancake. "I've rolled away from seven hungry children, a Mother, a Father, Manny-Panny, Henny-Penny, Cocky-Locky, Ducky-Lucky, and I'll roll away from you, Goosey-Poosey." And it rolled on and on and on until it met a Gander.

"Good day!" said the Gander.

"Good day!" said the Pancake.

"Oh! wait a moment," said the Gander, "I want a bite of you."

"Oh, no," said the Pancake. "I've rolled away from seven hungry children, a Mother, a Father, Manny-Panny, Henny-Penny, Cocky-Locky, Ducky-Lucky, Goosey-Poosey, and I'll roll away from you, Gander-Pander," and it rolled on and on and on.

After it rolled a very long way it met a Pig.

"Good day!" said the Pig.

"Good day!" said the Pancake.

"Oh," said the Pig, "you need not hurry along so fast, as we are going the same way, we may just as well travel along together. "Besides," said the Pig, "it is not very safe in this wood, someone might eat you."

All went well until they came to a stream flowing through the wood. It was all very well for the Pig because he was so fat that he could swim across. But poor Pancake could not get over.

"I know what you can do," said the Pig, "just roll upon my snout and I will carry you across."

The Pancake rolled up on the Pig's snout.

"Ouf! Ouf!" went the Pig and down went the Pancake. [Pp. 19–24]

Folklore U.S.A.

The folklore of the United States is perhaps the most complex of any country in the world. As immigrants came from many lands to settle in America, they brought with them the folklore of their homeland which revealed the people themselves: their beliefs, their feelings, and their ways of life. Holding onto the folklore of their homeland gave them a feeling of security, and they therefore handed it down from generation to generation. After the first immigrants settled in a particular region, those who followed from the same country joined them, and national and cultural islands developed in different parts of the country. Many of these islands exist today, for example, the large sections in New York populated by Italians and Puerto Ricans, the large German, Czech, and Polish settlements in Wisconsin and Illinois, and the Scandinavian communities in Minnesota and the Dakotas. By living in groups with people of similar backgrounds it was easier for these people to hold onto the folklore that was such an integral part of their lives. It is possible to go into countless communities across the nation today where the folklore of the great-great-grandfathers still influences the way of living.

Indian Folklore

The early settlers in our country also came in contact with the folklore of the Indians, which varied according to the tribe and locale. It is natural that an important part of their folklore would take the form of myths and legends that served as the basis for their religious beliefs. It was not long before bits of folklore were taken over by the settlers from the Indians and by the Indians from the settlers.

In the first half of the nineteenth century, James Fenimore Cooper wrote *Leatherstocking Saga* (18), which consists of five novels of frontier life built around Natty Bumppo, a brave woodsman who lived and fought among Indians and early settlers of America. In relating the exploits of Natty Bumppo, Cooper acquaints the reader with the lives of Indians and preserves as a part of the country's literary heritage the folklore of certain tribes of American Indians.

African Folklore

The slaves who were brought to our country also brought their folklore with them. Just as exchanges of folklore occurred between the white man and the red man, exchanges also took place between the white man and the Black. As with the Indians, it was natural that much of the Black man's folklore was related to his religion, since it is estimated that more than half the people of Africa have their own tribal religions. Most of these religions teach that everything in nature has spirits that have good or bad influence upon people. Many of the Africans brought in as slaves to this country believed that the spirits of their dead ancestors could affect the lives of the living, as could the witch doctors. Their religious ceremonies expressed the wish that these spirits would bless the people with more children, food, protection, and health. The religious beliefs of the Africans were only a part of the folklore that came with them. Their beliefs found expression in the arts, particularly music and dance. Living under segregated conditions, there was little cross-fertilization between Black folklore and the folklore of the white man until after the Civil War.

Tall Tales of the West

As mobility became an outstanding characteristic of the peoples of our country, a mixture of folklore moved westward with them. The courage and bravery of the early settlers along the eastern seaboard lived on in the pioneers. The earliest settlers had come in fear, not sure what lay ahead of them. They met the challenges head-on and overcame obstacles that faced them. They were not afraid to meet new challenges. The spirit that had brought them to America still prevailed. The next generation and the generations that followed were ready to face more hardships and dangers in their determination to carve a new nation out of the wilderness. From the beginning the movement took on a rough-and-ready atmosphere. There were trails to break, settlements to establish, deserts to cross, mountains to conquer, wild animals and unfriendly Indians to face. It was extremely hard work calling for men, women, and children of strength and courage.

It was out of this background that a new layer of American folklore was born. As the settlers moved westward they returned to the oral tradition. After a long, strenuous day on the trail, songs, stories, and games revived their spirits. After riding the range all day, cowboys got together around the campfire or in the bunkhouse to brag unashamedly about their achievements of the day. Miners got together to swap stories to while away the time. Mark Twain's famous *Jumping Frog* (92) came out of such a situation. Lumberjacks spending the winter months practically in isolation from the outside world relied on stories, puzzles, riddles, and games for entertainment to break the monotony. When their personal experiences and backlog of folklore dulled, the cowboys, miners, and lumberjacks began to manufacture heroes who were capable of tremendous feats of strength and bravery. These men were not adverse to exaggeration. It was in this kind of climate that tall tales came into favor and lived on as a delightful bit of Americana.

Paul Bunyan—A Tall Tale Hero

One of the first invented heroes to come into being was Paul Bunyan (95). He lived in the lumber camps that stretched from Canada into the New England states, to the Middle West, and on to the Pacific Coast. Whenever a person told a story about Paul Bunyan, he authenticated it by saying something like this, "My cousin had a friend who knew a fellow who followed shortly after Paul Bunyan when he went through Wisconsin." The first story was a challenge to every listener to come through with a bigger story and so the story of Paul Bunyan grew, and his name became familiar in all the lumbering regions of our country.

The story of Bunyan's (26) breaking the log jam is one of the most famous about him. It happened up on the Wisconsin River one spring. The jam was so bad that the logs were piled 200 feet high and were backed up a whole mile upriver. No one could budge a stick of it. But when Paul and Babe the Blue Ox arrived, Paul just said, "Stand back." He put the big ox in the river in front of the jam and then began to pepper him with rifle shot. It felt like a lot of pesky flies to Babe, and he began to switch his tail. The tail went round and round and made such a churning in the water that the river began to flow upstream. Of course, gradually the logs floated upstream with it, and the jam was broken. Then Paul called the big ox out of the river and logs flowed down again as they should.

Davy Crockett

Not all of the heroes born during the building of our country were manufactured. Real live heroes kept pace with the imaginary ones. Many of their deeds were so fantastic that they were taken for tall

Legends of Paul Bunyan compiled by Harold W. Felton, illustrated by Richard Bennett.

John Henry and His Hammer compiled by Harold W. Felton, illustrated by Aldren A. Watson.

tales. One of those who holds the spotlight for his adventures on the frontier is Davy Crockett.

Crockett gained fame as a hunter, scout, soldier, and congressman. He also enjoyed a career as an author and was credited with having written the rare Nashville edition of *Crockett Almanac* (1839), containing such stories of his exploits as "Adventure with a Grizzly Bear." Davy Crockett's coonskin cap became a symbol of the frontier. His racy backwoods humor was a delight. His dress, his language, and his adventures—some fact, some fiction—have won him a place in history as one of the greatest heroes of American folklore.

John Henry

It seems that the heroes of our tall tales begin to show their potential at a very early age. When John Henry (22, 53) was still a baby, he showed his proclivity for swinging a hammer. When he grew up, he became the best spike driver in the whole country. To prove his strength, he tried to compete with a steam drill. He was the victor, but as his body slumped to the ground, he murmured, "A man ain't nothin' but a man," and died.

Mike Fink

Mike Fink (61) was a river boatman; in fact, he was known as King of the Keelboatmen on the Ohio and Mississippi rivers. One great achievement after another demonstrated his strength and bravado as he went up and down the Mississippi. His undoing finally came when he defied the steamboats and tried to make one get out of his way. Sensing that the glamour of the keelboat days was over, Mike joined the fur traders of the West. He carried on his tradition while hunting, trapping, and trading in the Rockies where he could, until the end, meet and outdo his adversaries.

Pecos Bill

A name revered in cowboy country is that of Pecos Bill (12, 27). His long list of achievements includes the invention of the lasso, the art of roping, and the six-shooter. He also reputedly taught broncos how to buck and then taught cowboys how to ride the bucking broncos. Perhaps the greatest achievement credited to Pecos Bill was his riding a cyclone until it rained out under him.

Casey Jones

Casey Jones was the engineer of the *Cannonball,* the crack train of Illinois Central Railroad, which ran between Memphis, Tennessee, and Canton, Mississippi. He prided himself on his feat of bringing the *Cannonball* in on time. He also prided himself on his skill at blowing the whistle, from a soft beginning to a shrill shriek that then died away. People would turn in their beds as the *Cannonball* whistled through and say, "There goes Casey." Casey Jones has been immortalized by his devoted Negro engine wiper, Wallace Saunders, in a ballad that has been translated into countless languages. In the archives of American folk song in the Library of Congress itself there are fourteen recorded versions of this song. The version below is attributed to T. Lawrence Seibert [*The Family Book of Verse,* Lewis Gannest (comp.) (New York: Harper & Row, 1961)].

CASEY JONES

Come, all you rounders, if you want to hear
A story 'bout a brave engineer.
Casey Jones was the rounder's name
On a six-eight wheeler, boys, he won his fame.
The caller called Casey at half past four,
Kissed his wife at the station door,
Mounted to the cabin with his orders in his hand
And he took his farewell trip to the promised land:
Casey Jones, mounted to the cabin,
Casey Jones, with his orders in his hand,
Casey Jones, mounted to the cabin,
And he took his farewell trip to the promised land.
"Put in your water and shovel in your coal
Put your head out the window, watch them drivers roll,
I'll run her 'till she leaves the rail
'Cause I'm eight hours late with the western mail."
He looked at his watch and his watch was slow,

He looked at the water and the water was low,
He turned to the fireman and then he said,
"We're going to reach Frisco but we'll all be dead":
Casey Jones, goin' to reach Frisco
Casey Jones, but we'll all be dead,
Casey Jones, goin' to reach Frisco,
"We're goin' to reach Frisco, but we'll all be dead." [Pp. 268–269]

. . .

Other American Folk Heroes

With every state in the country having its famous folk heroes, the list grows long. Some are honored more than others, but each is remembered in a way fitting to his particular achievement. Jean La Fitte earned a lasting position in history, song, and story, when he and his privateers helped Andrew Jackson defeat the British in the Battle of New Orleans. Barney Beal, Maine lobsterman, was a man of marvelous strength. Bowleg Bill, the bronco-buster, never learned the seaman's trade or talk although he spent years at sea. John Chapman left home in Massachusetts and for forty years wandered through Ohio and Indiana planting apple seeds and earning for himself the name "Johnny Appleseed." Wild Bill Hickok was a frontier marshal of magnificent physique, great strength, and superb marksmanship. William F. Cody earned the name of Buffalo Bill by killing over 4,000 buffaloes in eighteen months to supply meàt for railroad construction gangs. Annie Oakley, sharpshooter, traveled with Buffalo Bill and his Wild West Show. Calamity Jane, who was a scout with Custer, rode the Pony Express, and boasted of her marksmanship. Annie Christmas was a keelboat pilot on the lower Mississippi famous for her bully-killing.

Folk and Fairy Tales from Other Countries

Little Hans: The Devoted Friend (100) is an example of Oscar Wilde's beautiful fairy tales. The unforgettable story about two friends, honest little Hans the gardner, and big Hugh the selfish miller, it is told by the green linnet, a wise bird, to the water-rat, a bachelor. Published in large format, this book is illustrated with gray and yellow decorations on each page.

The Gypsy Fiddle (41) by John Hampden is a collection of twenty-three stories about gypsies that chiefly fall into the classification of familiar folk-tale variants. Eight are credited to Eastern Europe, four to the Middle East, and the rest are credited to England or Wales. The tales are written in smooth, lively style and the familiarity of the motifs proves that the tales were carried from land to land. Notes by the author on story sources form an appendix.

Tomi Ungerer's lively, colorful illustrations re-create with vigor the magician and his lazy apprentice in the large-format picture book in which the familiar folk tale *The Sorcerer's Apprentice* (43) is retold by Barbara Hazen.

Amusing black-and-white illustrations add to the fun of the fourteen humorous Hungarian tales told by Peggy Hoffmann and Gyuri Biro in *The Money Hat and Other Hungarian Folk Tales* (44). Justice is the dominant theme running throughout the tales.

In the poor-boy-wins-rich-girl tradition, an old-fashioned fairy tale *The Baker and the Basilisk* (65) is retold in pleasant style by Georgess McHargue. Based on an old Viennese tale, the book, with its happy illustrations, re-creates the spirit of the time and place.

The Wishing Pearl and Other Tales of Vietnam (72) by Kay and Jon Nielson is a beautifully illustrated collection of Vietnamese fairy tales rich with magic, wishes granted, luck, and love.

In *Ivan and the Witch: A Russian Tale* (19) by Mischa Damjan a small boy is kidnapped by a witch but manages to escape with the help of a wild goose. Beautiful illustrations help to make the book a pleasant reading, listening, and visual experience.

A number of old, famous tales from Russian folklore have been woven together about the high adventures of Prince Ivan in his search for the vanished Princess Vasilissa. Michel Fokine used the story in his famous ballet for which Igor Stravinsky wrote the music. *The Firebird* (11) is a large-format book magnificently illustrated in color by Toma Bogdanovic. No elementary school library should miss having the book on its shelves.

The Adventures of Strong Vanya (78) by Otfried Preussler weaves Russian folk-tale themes into an original story about the youngest son of a peasant farmer who learns that he is destined to become a czar. Although his older brother laughs at him and often threatens him, Vanya persists in strengthening himself, through hardships, for the tasks ahead.

In *Vasilisa, the Beautiful* (98) Thomas P. Whitney provides a new translation of the Russian Cinderella story from N. A. Afanasier's collection. The book is enriched by full-color, crayon-like drawings.

An old Russian folk tale, *The Fox and the Hare* (30), retold by Mirra Ginsburg, relates the way in which a hare is driven from his home by a fox. Bright illustrations, rhythmic text, and repetition add to the fun of the story.

Janko, a very lazy Hungarian farmer, helps out a Gypsy Queen and in return for his kindness is allowed one wish. How that wish changes his life makes *Janko's Wish* (93) by Judy Varga a breezy, fast-moving story.

Bright color illustrates the William Wiesner version of *Happy-Go-Lucky* (99), the Norwegian Gudbrand-of-the-Hillside story in which the negligent farmer bets that he can tell his wife the history of his losses without raising her wrath.

Large print and attractive black-and-white sketches enhance the eight representative Greek folk tales in Virginia Haviland's *Favorite Fairy Tales Told in Greece* (42). Included is the story about the king's daughter who "loved her father like salt" (pp. 21–27), a variant of "The Three Sillies," and other fairy stories.

The Magic Wall (94) by Judy Varga is a well-done adaptation of an old folk tale set in medieval Austria. As the story goes, good King Frederick is happy in a castle without walls, where he enjoys the fellowship of all of his people. However, he is convinced by a few that he should build walls for protection. He builds the walls and finds to his sorrow that his people no longer trust him.

The Little Horse of Seven Colors and Other Portuguese Folk Tales (64), retold by Patricia Tracy Lowe from translations from the Portuguese by Anne Marie Jauss, relates 28 stories taken from authentic nineteenth-century collections of Portuguese folk tales. Similar in theme and plot to many familiar European folk tales, they have a distinct flavor of their own. The book makes a significant contribution to national folk literature.

The Fairy Thorn Tree (4) by Gerry and George Armstrong, an Irish story written in folk-tale style, tells how Finvarra, King of the Fairies, comes to the aid of Owen and his family when a miserly man threatens to take away their farm and Owen's beloved violin.

Although not authentic African stories, *Tales from an African Drum* (14) by Helen Chetin have a folklore quality. The series of stories revolves around an African chief who trains his grandson to be a wise leader of the tribe.

Handsome woodcuts reflect the Congo world in *Bantu Tales* (45) by Virginia Holladay. Nineteen folk stories from the Bantu tribes handed down from one generation to another reflect the wisdom, humor, values, and way of life of the Baluba and Luala tribes of the Congo as they were four decades ago.

And the Jackal Played the Masinko (48) by Marjorie Hopkins is a traditional tale from Ethiopia that tells how young Haptu outwits the animals who will not obey him.

Princess of the Full Moon (39) by Frederic Guirma, from the folk lore of the Masai people who live in the Upper Volta, is the story of a beautiful but vain princess who is saved from the disastrous results of her foolish pride by an old shepherd who turns out to be a prince. The dynamic illustrations by the author complement the mood of the story.

A Story, a Story (40) is an African folk tale retold in rich prose and illustrated with woodcuts by Gail E. Haley. The story tells how Anansi is able to meet the Prince Myama, the Sky God, and how he demands all the stories that he keeps in the golden box. Recipient of the 1970 Caldecott Medal, *A Story, a Story* makes a significant contribution to children's literature.

Beautiful watercolor illustrations using motifs and themes from the Indonesian shadow theater enrich *The Princess of the Rice Fields: An Indonesian Folk Tale* (54) by Hisako Kimishima. This rendition tells why the rice plant is considered a sacred grain in many countries.

Ghost story fans will find *Ghosts and Spirits of Many Lands* (63) edited by Freya Littledale a pleasing collection of strange incidents from the substance of 21 tales from the folklore of many countries. The book is illustrated with handsome woodcuts.

Bold watercolor and collage silhouettes heighten *The Golden Swans: A Picture Story from Thailand* (58), a folk legend from a remote province in Thailand. The tale is retold by a Peace Corps teacher, Kermit Krueger, and explains how a swan statue is built by a remorseful hunter and how the Lake of Swans comes to be filled with pure, clear water.

Descriptive text and beautiful watercolors are combined in the Japanese folk tale *The Witch's Magic Cloth* (68), transcribed by Miyoko Matsutani and translated by Alvin Tresselt. In the story an old woman has the courage to help the witch of the mountains.

Japanese-style illustrations enhance *Gengoroh and the Thunder God* (67), a translation also by Miyoko Matsutani of a Japanese folk tale about a young man's magical powers that gain him wealth and adventure as a helper of the Thunder God in heaven.

In *The Boastful Fisherman* (56) by William Knowlton, a Hawaiian story with a folk-tale quality, three boastful fishermen must live up to their boasting.

The Rescue of the Sun and Other Tales from the Far North (70) by Edythe W. Newell is a collection of eleven folk tales that reflect the life of the people of the Far North. Background information on the customs and beliefs of the Stone Age Eskimos is included.

The Big Book of Stories from Many Lands (77), retold by Rhoda Power, is a collection of animal stories and folk and fairy tales from Ireland, Austria, ancient China, Spain, the United States, Russia, Algeria, and other countries.

Extending Experiences for the Reader

1. Read selections from *Heroes of the Kalevala* (23) by Babette Deutsch to the class.
2. Analyze with the class the characteristics of myths and legends.
3. Discuss with the class ways in which myths and legends are alike and the ways in which they are different.
4. Read to the class several explanations that man has held concerning the beginning of the world.
5. Read to the class several beliefs held by early man to explain the changes of the seasons.
6. Read to the class the story of Proserpina (38).
7. Read to the class the story of Baldur (13, 55).
8. Tell the class some of the highlights from the *Iliad* (46) and the *Odyssey* (47).
9. Make a list of the words that Hans Christian Andersen used to give vigor and strength to his stories.
10. Read excerpts to the class from *The Story of My Life* (2) by Hans Christian Andersen.
11. Analyze two of Hans Christian Andersen's first four stories (1): "The Tinder Box," "Big Claus and Little Claus," "The Princess and the Pea," and "Little Ida's Flowers." Compare the story line in the two that you choose to read.
12. Read one or two folk tales by each of the following: the Brothers Grimm (35–37), Peter Christen Asbjornsen (6), and Joseph Jacobs (51). How do they compare in story line, characterizations, and style?
13. Select one of Hans Christian Andersen's popular stories. Find two or three different translations of the same story. Which one do you like the most? Give your reasons. Read the different translations to the class. Observe and record their reaction. Do they show a preference for one story more than another?
14. Make a list of arguments for and against the use of fairy tales with young children.
15. Read to the class one story from each of the following groups:
    a. Märchen
    b. Accumulative stories
    c. Beast tales
    d. Droll stories
    e. Pourquoi stories
16. Read the "Three Billy Goats Gruff" (6) to the class.
17. Read a droll story to illustrate a plot built around the youngest of three sons who is considered to be a simpleton.

18. Read three beast stories to the class. Discuss with the class the differences in these beast tales.
19. Read "Why the Bear Is Stumpy Tailed" (20) to the class.

Extending Experiences for Children

1. Select a Norse god and his counterpart in Greek mythology. List the characteristics that are similar and those that are different.
2. Read one of the following myths and share it with the class: Phaëton, Baucis and Philemon, Jason.
3. Collect advertisements that show a relationship to mythology, for example, Vulcan tires, Venus pencils, Ajax powder. Find others to share with the class.
4. List some of the everyday expressions that have come down to us from mythology, for example, "Achilles' heel," "by Jove," "like a Trojan." Find others and use them in sentences.
5. Write brief descriptions of these supernatural creatures: unicorn, phoenix, Gorgon, dryads, satyrs, nymphs.
6. Find out how the origins of the following words are related to mythology: "music," "calliope," "terpsichore," "echo," "hyacinth," "narcissus." Use these words in sentences and share them with the class.
7. Plan a dialogue among three or four children impersonating folk characters such as William F. Cody, Wild Bill Hickok, Annie Oakley, and Buffalo Bill.
8. On individual maps of the United States color the areas in which legendary characters lived and became famous. Explain what they were noted for.

References

1. ANDERSEN, HANS CHRISTIAN. *Andersen's Fairy Tales.* New York: Macmillan, 1963. Grades 1–5.
2. ———. *The Story of My Life.* New York: Hurd & Houghton, 1872. Reprinted, Detroit, Mich.: Gale.
3. ANDERSON, ROBERT L., AND JOHN BRADFORD. *The House That Jack Built and Other Favorite Jingles.* New York: Harlan Quist, 1964, 1967. n.g.l.
4. ARMSTRONG, GERRY, AND GEORGE ARMSTRONG. *The Fairy Thorn Tree.* Chicago: Albert Whitman, 1969. Grades 2–4.
5. ARNOLD, MATTHEW. *Sohrab and Rustum.* Boston: Houghton Mifflin, n.d. Paperback. Grades 7–12.
6. ASBJORNSEN, PETER CHRISTEN. *Popular Tales from the Norse.* G. W. Dasent (tr.). New York: Putnam, 1908.

7. BEALS, CARLETON. *Stories Told by the Aztecs: Before the Spaniards Came.* New York: Abelard-Schuman, 1970. Grade 7 and up.

8. BELLOWS, HENRY ADAMS (trans.). *Edda Saem Undar.* New York: The American Scandinavian Foundation, 1923.

9. BENSON, SALLY. *Stories of the Gods and Heroes.* New York: Dial, 1940. Grades 4–6.

10. BERTOL, ROLAND. *Sundiata: The Epic of the Lion King.* New York: T. Y. Crowell, 1970. Grade 5 and up.

11. BOGDANOVIC, TOMA. *The Fire Bird.* New York: Scroll, 1971. Grade 1 and up.

12. BOWMAN, JAMES CLOYD. *Pecos Bill.* Chicago: Whitman, 1937. Grades 5–8.

13. BULFINCH, THOMAS. "The Death of Baldur." *Mythology.* New York: Random House, n.d.

14. CHETIN, HELEN. *Tales from an African Drum.* New York: Harcourt Brace Jovanovich, 1970. Grades 4–6.

15. CLARKE, MOLLIE. *The Three Brothers.* Chicago: Follett, 1967. Preschool–grade 3.

16. COLUM, PADRAIC. *The Girl Who Sat by the Ashes.* New York: Macmillan, 1968.

17. COOLIDGE, OLIVIA. *Greek Myths.* Boston: Houghton Mifflin, 1964.

18. COOPER, JAMES FENIMORE. *Leatherstocking Saga.* New York: Pantheon, 1954. Grades 7–8.

19. DAMJAN, MISCHA. *Ivan and the Witch: A Russian Tale.* New York: McGraw-Hill, 1969. Preschool–grade 3.

20. DASENT, GEORGE W. *Popular Tales from the Norse.* New York: Appleton-Century-Crofts, 1859.

21. DE LA MARE, WALTER. *Tales Told Again.* New York: Knopf, 1959. Grades 4–6.

22. DE LEEUW, ADELE. *John Henry, Steel Drivin' Man.* Champaign, Ill.: Garrard, 1966.

23. DEUTSCH, BABETTE. *Heroes of the Kalevala.* New York: Messner, 1940. Grades 6–9.

24. DUMAS, ALEXANDER. *Robin Hood, Prince of Outlaws.* Lowell Blair (tr.). New York: Dell, n.d. Paperback.

25. *Edda. I. The Divine Mythology of the North. II. The Heroic Mythology of the North.* Lucy W. Faraday (comp.). New York: AMS Press, n.d.

26. FELTON, HAROLD W. (comp. and ed.). *Legends of Paul Bunyan.* New York: Knopf, 1947.

27. ______. *Pecos Bill: Texas Cow Puncher.* New York: Knopf, 1949.

28. FRANK, JOSETTE. *Your Child's Reading Today.* Rev. ed. Garden City, N. Y.: Doubleday, 1969.

29. FRASER, ANTONIA. *King Arthur and the Knights of the Round Table.* New York: Random House, 1971.

30. GINSBURG, MIRRA (reteller and tr.). *The Fox and the Hare.* New York: Crown, 1969. Preschool–grade 1.

31. GODDEN, RUMER. "Hans Christian Andersen," *Collier's Encyclopedia.* New York: Crowell-Collier Education Corp., 1971.

32. *The Golden Goose Book.* L. Leslie Brooke (ill.). New York: Frederick Warne, 1965. Grades 1–4.

33. GOLDSTON, ROBERT (reteller). *Song of Roland.* Indianapolis: Bobbs-Merrill, 1964. Grades 4–8.

34. GRAVES, ROBERT. *Greek Gods and Heroes.* Garden City, N. Y.: Doubleday, 1960.

35. GRIMM, BROTHERS. *Grimm's Fairy Tales.* Margaret Hunt (tr.). New York: Pantheon, 1944.

36. ———. *Household Stories from the Collection of the Brothers Grimm.* Lucy Crane (tr.). Walter Crane (ill.). New York: Macmillan, 1892. Reprinted: New York: Dover. Paperback. Grades 3–9.

37. ———. *Sleeping Beauty and Other Tales.* New York: Children's Press, 1969. Grade 4 and up.

38. GUERBER, H. A. "Demeter and Persephone," *Myths of Greece and Rome.* London: British Book Centre, 1963.

39. GUIRMA, FREDERIC. *Princess of the Full Moon.* John Garrett (tr.). New York: Macmillan, 1970. Grades 1–3.

40. HALEY, GAIL E. (reteller). *A Story, a Story.* New York: Atheneum, 1970. Kindergarten–grade 3.

41. HAMPDEN, JOHN. *The Gypsy Fiddle.* Cleveland: World Publishing, 1969. Grades 4–6.

42. HAVILAND, VIRGINIA. *Favorite Fairy Tales Told in Greece.* Boston: Little, Brown, 1970. Grade 3 and up.

43. HAZEN, BARBARA (reteller). *The Sorcerer's Apprentice.* Tomi Ungerer (ill.). New York: Lancelot Press, 1969. Grade 3 and up.

44. HOFFMANN, PEGGY, AND GYURI BIRO. *The Money Hat and Other Hungarian Folk Tales.* Philadelphia: Westminster, 1969. Grade 7 and up.

45. HOLLADAY, VIRGINIA. Louise Crane (ed.). *Bantu Tales.* New York: Viking, 1970. Grade 7 and up.

46. HOMER. *Iliad.* Alfred J. Church (ed.). New York: Macmillan, 1967. Grades 4–6.

47. ———. *Odyssey.* Alfred J. Church (ed.). New York: Macmillan, 1967. Grades 4–6.

48. HOPKINS, MARJORIE. *And the Jackal Played the Masinko.* Parents' Magazine Press, 1969. Kindergarten–grade 4.

49. HOSFORD, DOROTHY. *By His Own Might, the Battle of Beowulf.* New York: Holt, Rinehart & Winston, 1947.

50. HUTCHINSON, VERONICA (collector and reteller). *Chimney Corner Stories.* New York: Minton, Balch, 1925.

51. JACOBS, JOSEPH (collector). *English Fairy Tales.* New York: Putnam, n.d. Baltimore, Md.: Penguin, 1971. Paperback.

52. JOHNSON, EDNA, *et al.* *Anthology of Children's Literature.* Boston: Houghton Mifflin, 1959.

53. KEATS, EZRA JACK. *John Henry: An American Legend.* New York: Pantheon, 1965. Kindergarten–grade 6.

54. KIMISHIMA, HISAKO (reteller). *The Princess of the Rice Fields: An Indonesian Folk Tale.* New York: Weatherhill, 1970. Grades 4–6.

55. KING, CYNTHIA. *In the Morning of Time: The Story of the Norse God Baldur.* New York: Scholastic Book Services, 1970. Grade 8 and up.

56. KNOWLTON, WILLIAM. *The Boastful Fisherman.* New York: Knopf, 1970. Kindergarten–grade 3.
57. KREADY, LAURA F. *A Study of Fairy Tales.* Boston: Houghton Mifflin, 1916.
58. KRUEGER, KERMIT. *The Golden Swans: A Picture Story from Thailand.* Cleveland: World Publishing, 1969. Kindergarten–grade 3.
59. ———. *Serpent Prince: Folk Tales from Northeastern Thailand.* Cleveland: World Publishing, 1969. Grades 4–6.
60. LANIER, SIDNEY (ed.). *The Boy's King Arthur.* N. C. Wyeth (ill.). New York: Scribner, 1917.
61. LEATCH, MARIA. *The Rainbow Book of American Folk Tales and Legends.* Cleveland and New York: World Publishing, 1959.
62. LELAND, CHARLES GODFREY. *The Algonquin Legends of New England.* Boston: Houghton Mifflin, 1888. Reprinted: Detroit Mich.: Singing Tree, 1968.
63. LITTLEDALE, FREYA (ed.). *Ghosts and Spirits of Many Lands.* Garden City, N. Y.: Doubleday, 1970. Grade 10 and up.
64. LOWE, PATRICIA TRACY (reteller). *The Little Horse of Seven Colors and Other Portuguese Folk Tales.* Cleveland: World Publishing, 1970. Grades 4–6.
65. MC HARGUE, GEORGESS. *The Baker and the Basilisk.* Indianapolis: Bobbs-Merrill, 1970. Grades 2–4.
66. MALORY, SIR THOMAS. *King Arthur and His Knights.* Rev. and enlarged ed. E. Vinaver (ed.). Boston: Houghton Mifflin. Grade 9 and up.
67. MATSUTANI, MIYOKO. *Gengoroh and the Thunder God.* New York: Parents' Magazine Press, 1970. Kindergarten–grade 3.
68. ———. *The Witch's Magic Cloth.* New York: Parents' Magazine Press, 1969. Kindergarten–grade 4.
69. MEIGS, CORNELIA, *et al.* *Critical History of Children's Literature.* Rev. ed. New York: Macmillan, 1969.
70. NEWELL, EDYTHE W. *The Rescue of the Sun and Other Tales from the Far North.* Chicago: Albert Whitman, 1970. Grade 2 and up.
71. *Nibelungenlied.* D. G. Mowatt (tr.). New York: Dutton, n.d.
72. NIELSON, KAY, AND JON NIELSON. *The Wishing Pearl and Other Tales of Vietnam.* Lam C. Quam (tr.). Irvington-on-Hudson, N. Y.: Harvey House, 1969. Grades 3–6.
73. OVID. *Ovid's Metamorphoses.* Rolfe Humphries (tr.). Bloomington, Ind.: Indiana University Press, 1955. Paperback.
74. PERRAULT, CHARLES. *Puss in Boots.* Marcia Brown (tr.). New York: Scribner, 1952. Kindergarten–grade 4.
75. ———. *Tales of Mother Goose.* Charles Welsh (tr.). Boston: D. C. Heath, 1901.
76. *Poem of the Cid.* William S. Merwin (tr.). New York: New American Library, n.d.
77. POWER, RHODA (reteller). *The Big Book of Stories from Many Lands.* New York: Watts, 1970. Grades 4–6.
78. PREUSSLER, OTFRIED. *The Adventures of Strong Vanya.* New York: Abelard-Schuman, 1970. Grade 3 and up.
79. PENELOPE PRODDOW (trans.). *Demeter and Persephone.* Garden City, N. Y.: Doubleday, 1972.

80. PYLE, HOWARD. *The Merry Adventures of Robin Hood.* New York: Scribner, 1946. Grades 4–10.
81. ——. *The Story of King Arthur and His Knights.* New York: Scribner, 1954.
82. *The Random House Dictionary of the English Language.* College ed. New York: Random House, 1968.
83. SERRAILIER, IAN. *Havelok the Dane.* New York: Walck.
84. SLEATOR, WILLIAM (reteller). *The Angry Moon.* Boston: Little, Brown, 1970. Kindergarten–grade 3.
85. SMITH, LILLIAN H. *The Unreluctant Years.* Chicago: American Library Association, 1953.
86. STOUTENBURG, ADRIEN. *Fee, Fi, Fo, Fum.* New York: Viking, 1969. Grades 4–6.
87. TENNYSON, ALFRED LORD. *Idylls of the King.*
88. THOMPSON, STITH. *The Folktale.* New York: Dryden Press, n.d.
89. ——. *Tales of the North American Indians.* Cambridge: Harvard University Press, 1969.
90. THOMPSON, VIVIAN L. *Hawaiian Legends of Tricksters and Riddlers.* New York: Holiday House, 1969. Grades 4–6.
91. TURSKA, KRYSTYNA (reteller). *Pegasus.* New York: Watts, 1970. Kindergarten–grade 3.
92. TWAIN, MARK. *Jumping Frog.* New York: Dover, 1971. Paperback.
93. VARGA, JUDY. *Janko's Wish.* New York: Morrow, 1969. Kindergarten–grade 3.
94. —— (adapter). *The Magic Wall.* New York: Morrow, 1970. Kindergarten–grade 3.
95. WADSWORTH, W. C. *Paul Bunyon and His Great Blue Coat.* Garden City, N. Y.: Doubleday, 1964. Grades 6–9.
96. WALKER, BARBARA. *Korolu, the Singing Bandit.* New York: T. Y. Crowell, 1970. Grades 4–7.
97. WESTWOOD, JENNIFER. *Gilgamesh and Other Babylonian Tales.* New York: Coward-McCann, 1970. Grades 3–7.
98. WHITNEY, THOMAS P. *Vasilisa the Beautiful.* New York: Macmillan, 1970. Kindergarten–grade 3.
99. WIESNER, WILLIAM. *Happy-Go-Lucky.* New York: Seabury, 1970. Preschool–grade 3.
100. WILDE, OSCAR. *Little Hans: The Devoted Friend.* Indianapolis: Bobbs-Merill, 1969. Grades 2–6.

More Myths and Legends

BELTING, NATALIA M. *Calendar Moon.* Bernarda Bryson (ill.). New York: Holt, Rinehart & Winston, 1964. Myths related to the months of the year.

BIRCH, CYRIL. *Chinese Myths and Fantasies.* New York: Walck, 1961.

COLUM, PADRAIC. *The Adventures of Odysseus and the Tale of Troy.* New York: Macmillan, 1964.

FEAGLES, ANITA (reteller). *Thor and the Giants; An Old Norse Legend.* Gertrude Barrer-Russell (ill.). New York: Young Scott Books, 1968.

GARFIELD, LEON, AND EDWARD BLISHEN. *The God Beneath the Sea.* New York: Pantheon, 1971. Grades 9 and up. The complex dramas of the Greek legends have been combined into one long narration, in the manner of a novel.

HAMPDEN, JOHN. *Endless Treasure: Unfamiliar Tales from the Arabian Nights.* Fifteen little-known stories from the *Arabian Nights* are short, well told, and as full of magic and adventure as are the more familiar tales.

HAWKINS, QUAIL (reteller). *Androcles and the Lion.* New York: Coward-McCann, 1970. Kindergarten–grade 3. A retelling of the old tale of the slave boy and the lion, illustrated with excellent black, yellow, and red woodcuts.

HAWTHORNE, NATHANIEL. *Pandora's Box; The Paradise of Children.* Paul Galdone (ill.). New York: McGraw-Hill, 1967.

HELFMAN, ELIZABETH S. *The Bushmen and Their Stories.* New York: Seabury, 1971. Grades 3–6. Seventeen stories from the culture of the Bushmen of the Kalahari Desert include the Bushmen versions of the creation of the sun and the moon and many dramatic and amusing tales about their god Mantis.

ISH-KISHOR, SULAMETH. *The Master of Miracles.* New York: Harper & Row, 1971. Grades 3–7. The legend of Golen of Prague, a fictitious character who helped to abolish anti-Semitism in sixteenth-century Prague, is re-created by the author.

LEWIS, NAOMI (reteller). *The Story of Aladdin.* New York: Walck, 1971. Grades 1–4. A brilliant retelling of the familar story of Aladdin and his wonderful lamp. Well illustrated with bright blue-and-white drawings.

STOUTENBURG, ADRIEN. *American Tall Tales.* New York: Viking, 1966.

SERRAILLIER, DAN. *A Fall from the Sky; The Story of Daedalus.* William Dobbs (ill.). New York: Walck, 1966.

More Fairy and Folk Tales

ANDERSEN, HANS CHRISTIAN. *The Little Mermaid.* Eva Le Gallienne (tr.). New York: Harper & Row, 1971. Grade 7 and up. The beloved story of a mermaid princess who longs for an immortal soul and tries to win it through self-sacrifice.

______. *The Steadfast Tin Soldier.* New York: Atheneum, 1971. Preschool–grade 2. One of Andersen's favorite tales, this rendition about the one-legged tin soldier who loves a paper dancing doll is beautifully illustrated with water color paintings.

APPIAH, PEGGY. *Ananse the Spider: Tales from an Ashanti Village.* New York: Pantheon, 1966. Grades 4–7. Lively, humorous how-and-why stories:

"How the Pig Got His Snout," "Why the Lizard Stretches His Neck," and "Why Kwaku Ananse Stays on the Ceiling," among others.

AUNG, MAUNG HTIN, AND HELEN TRAGER G. *A Kingdom Lost for a Drop of Honey.* Pan Oothet (ill.). New York: Parents' Magazine Press, 1968. Grades 1–5. A simply told story of a poor traveler who sits near a merchant who is frying fish. When the merchant demands payment from the traveler for the smell of his cooking fish, the answer is given by The Princess Learned-in-the-Law, whose wisdom only Solomon excels!

EMRICH, DUNCAN (comp.). *The Nonsense Book.* New York: Scholastic Book Service, 1970. Grades 4–6. This interesting, comprehensive collection of American folklore including riddles, puzzles, tongue twisters, and rhymes of all kinds includes notes on the different forms of folk literature and an extensive bibliography.

GRAHAM, GAIL B. *The Beggar in the Blanket and Other Vietnamese Tales.* New York: Dial Press, 1970. Grades 1–5. An ambitious young man thinks himself too good to keep company with his lazy brother, but he soon finds that his fine friends will not help him in trouble. Through the cleverness of his wife he learns the value of a brother.

GRIMM, JAKOB LUDWIG KARL, AND WILHELM KARL GRIMM. *Hansel and Gretel.* Arnold Lobel (ill.). New York: Delacorte, 1971. n.g.l. With wash drawings in earth colors, Arnold Lobel retells the Hansel and Gretel story.

HAUFF, WILHELM. *The Big Book of Stories by Hauff.* New York: Watts, 1971. Grades 4–6. This collection of Wilhelm Hauff's best-known fables and fairy tales from around the world has been newly illustrated by the distinguished artist Jausz Grabianski.

HOGROGIAN, NONNY. *One Fine Day.* New York: Macmillan, 1971. Kindergarten–grade 3. Impressed by an Armenian folk tale, well-known illustrator Nonny Hogrogian has written her first book and illustrated it with full-color pictures.

KENT, JACK. *The Fat Cat, a Danish Folktale.* New York: Parents' Magazine Press, 1971. Kindergarten–grade 2. A folk tale from Denmark about a cat whose insatiable appetite leads him to eat everything in sight, including his owner.

MAHOOD, KENNETH. *The Laughing Dragon.* New York: Scribner, 1971. Kindergarten–grade 3. A tale about the Japanese Emperor's pet dragon, whose fiery breath causes a variety of complications until a wise turtle shows him how to turn a problem into an asset.

MANNING-SANDERS, RUTH. *Gianni and the Ogre.* New York: Dutton, 1971. n.g.l. A collection of 18 tales from the lands that touch the Mediterranean. There are stories of knights and princesses, witches and wolves, robbers and golden eagles to read about.

MATSUTANI, MIYOKO. *How the Withered Trees Blossomed.* Philadelphia: Lippincott, 1971. n.g.l. A well-known Japanese folk tale is retold in a picture-story book designed in Japanese style. The book reads from back to front in Japanese with English translation added.

MOSEL, ARLENE. *Tikki Tikki Tembo.* Blair Lent (ill.). New York: Holt, Rinehart, & Winston, 1968. Kindergarten–grade 2. A humorous folk tale with lively and colorful picture book format tells of the custom in China of giving long names to all sons until Tikki Tikki Tembo-no sa Rembo Chari Bari Ruchip Peri Pembo falls into a well. The time needed to tell what has happened to a small boy with such a long name results in Tikki Tikki Tembo's being very blue before he is finally rescued. From then on all sons are given much shorter names.

PROVENSEN, ALICE, AND MARTIN PROVENSEN (comps.). *The Provensen Book of Fairy Tales.* New York: Random House, 1971. n.g.l. Twelve stories, some well-known oldies, others more recent, are illustrated by the Provensens.

SHERLOCK, PHILIP (reteller). *West Indian Folk-Tales.* New York: Walck, 1966. Grades 4–6. "The Caribs were the first people. There were no other people before them. Their first home was the moon. They knew light and dark, day and night, and they obeyed the ancient one, Kabo. This appears to be an attempt to explain the beginnings of things and natural phenomenon" (p. 7).

SINGER, ISAAC BASHEVIS. *Alone in the Wild Forest.* New York: Farrar, Straus & Giroux, 1971. n.g.l. Joseph, the hero of the story, wins the hand of the princess, but he needs the help of an angel as he incurs the jealousy of a rival.

TASHJIAN, VIRGINIA (reteller). *Once There Was and Was Not.* Boston: Little, Brown, 1966. Grades 2–6. Seven tales based on stories by Hovannes Toumanian. Folklore flavor permeates both illustrations and text of these attractive retellings. The style and length make them appropriate for storytelling.

TAYLOR, MARK. *The Fisherman and the Goblet.* San Carlos, Cal.: Golden Gate, 1971. Grade 3 and up. An old Vietnamese folktale about a beautiful princess who loves a poor fisherman because of his singing but rejects him because of his ugly face.

WALKER, BARBARA. *Watermelons, Walnuts and the Wisdom of Allah and Other Tales of the Hoca.* New York: Parents' Magazine Press, 1967. Grades 1–5. "There is a hoca tale to fit almost any human situation, and the Hoca's wit and wisdom do indeed illuminate the problems and perplexities of everyday life. The wisdom includes such gems as 'Any man who sits on the outside end of a branch he is chopping is certain to fall'" (p. 10).

WILLIAMS, JAY. *The Silver Whistle.* New York: Parents' Magazine Press, 1971. Kindergarten–grade 3. A fairy tale about a homely girl with a merry heart whose lively mind and silver whistle enable her to outwit everybody else.

WYNDHAM, ROBERT. *Tales the People Tell in China.* New York: Messner, 1971. Grade 3 and up. A collection of tales Robert Wyndham has culled from China's ancient myths, legends, folk tales, and anecdotes.

YOLEN, JANE (ed.). *The Emperor and the Kite.* Ed Young (ill.). Cleveland: World Publishing, 1967. Kindergarten–grade 3. The fourth and last princess in this story is so little that she is often forgotten and amuses herself by kiteflying. When her father the Emperor is seized by wicked men, the very small princess sends food to him by kite. Finally with an ingeniously conceived kite she even rescues him. The rainbow-colored illustrations appear to be cut-out designs from watercolor washes.

———. *Silent Bianca.* Cleveland: World Publishing, 1971. Kindergarten–grade 5. The story of a maiden whose words make no sound but immediately crystallize into ice. When the ice melts, her voice can be heard without her being present.

The Wind in the Willows by Kenneth Grahame, illustrated by Arthur Rackham.

11

Fantasy and Science Fiction

Fantasy and science fiction have always appealed to children. They provide vehicles by which the reader may travel to strange places and new worlds, meet fascinating people and creatures, and use science and imagination for enjoyable reading. Both genres have the power to launch children into unknown worlds.

Favorite Classics of Fantasy

The literary critic Lillian Smith (70) says that fantasy like poetry uses the metaphorical approach to the perception of universal truth. The word "fantasy" comes from the Greek and, literally translated, means "a making visible" (p. 150).

The dictionary defines fantasy as "1. imagination, especially when extravagant and unrestrained. 2. the forming of grotesque mental images. 3. a mental image, esp. when grotesque. 4. *psychol.*—an imaginative sequence, esp. one in which desires are fulfilled; day-dreams. 5. a hallucination. 6. a supposition based on no solid foundation. 7. caprice, whim. 8. an ingenious or fanciful thought or creation" (*The Random House Dictionary of the English Language*, College Edition, p. 478). These definitions offer limitless possibilities for writers and readers.

Fantasy enjoys a unique place in literature. It takes a creative mind to produce it and it draws upon the imaginative powers of the reader to enjoy it. Fantasy prompts the reader to leave the printed page and follow Alice down the rabbit hole and through the looking glass; to ride with Åse under the magic of Peer Gynt's spell; or to come in on the East Wind and to leave on the West Wind with Mary Poppins.

These fantasies have delighted one generation after another by capturing and stirring their imagination. A part of their appeal is the introduction of unusual characters who have the privilege of magically moving back and forth from the possible to the impossible, from the serious to the absurd. The authors are artists in the use of words as they create imaginary characters, settings, and situations.

Alice in Wonderland

Alice's Adventures in Wonderland (29) holds its place today, as it did when it was first published in 1865, as one of the most popular books in children's literature. It has a wonderful combination of nonsense and magic that young children as well as adults appreciate and enjoy. The imagination of the young is not yet curtailed by the demands of their culture. They can create their own fantasies, in which magic is taken for granted. If a person is too big to go down the rabbit hole, just make him small! If he is too short, make him tall! Such is the logic of fantasy.

Alice in Wonderland was written by Reverend Charles L. Dodgson, a learned English mathematician, who used the pen name of Lewis Carroll. The story of Alice took shape in an interesting manner. Reverend Dodgson was shy with adults but very fond of children. He loved to make up stories to tell them. The daughters of a friend and colleague were among his particular favorites. When he told them the story of *Alice in Wonderland,* Alice Liddell, whose name he had chosen for the girl in his tale, begged him to write down the story for the enjoyment of other children. He not only wrote it but also illustrated it and presented it to her as "a Christmas gift to a dear child in memory of a summer's day" (p. 211). The story was passed around and read by Dodgson's friends, who encouraged him to have it published. Six years later he published a second part to the story, *Through the Looking Glass* (29).

Much of the fascination in the Alice stories is in the dialogue, such as the conversation between Alice and the Cheshire-Cat. Walking through the woods, Alice:

> . . . was a little startled by seeing the Cheshire-Cat sitting on a bough of a tree a few yards off.
>
> The Cat only grinned when it saw Alice. It looked good-natured, she thought: still it had very long claws and a great many teeth, so that she felt that it ought to be treated with respect.
>
> "Cheshire-Puss," she began, rather timidly, as she did not at all know whether it would like the name: however, it only grinned a little wider. "Come, it's pleased so far," thought Alice, and she went on. "Would you

The Complete Works of Lewis Carroll by Lewis Carroll, illustrated by Sir John Tenniel.

tell me, please, which way I ought to go from here?"

"That depends a good deal on where you want to get to," said the Cat.

"I don't much care where—" said Alice.

"Then it doesn't much matter which way you go," said the Cat.

"—so long as I get *somewhere*," Alice added as an explanation.

"Oh, you're sure to do that," said the Cat, "If you only walk long enough."

Alice felt that this could not be denied, so she tried another question. "What sort of people live about here?"

"In *that* direction," the Cat said, waving its right paw round, "lives a Hatter: and in that direction," waving the other paw, "lives a March Hare. Visit either you like: they're both mad." [Pp. 80–81]

One of the most nonsensical dialogues to be found in literature is that carried on at the Mad Tea Party. Uninvited, Alice has seated herself at the table.

The table was a large one, but the March Hare, the Hatter, and the Dormouse were all crowded together at one corner of it. "No room! No room!" they cried out when they saw Alice coming. "There's *plenty* of room!" said Alice indignantly, and she sat down in a large arm-chair at one end of the table.

"Have some wine," the March Hare said in an encouraging tone.

Alice looked all round the table, but there was nothing on it but tea. "I don't see any wine," she remarked.

"There isn't any," said the March Hare.

"Then it wasn't very civil of you to offer it," said Alice angrily.

"It wasn't very civil of you to sit down without being invited," said the March Hare.

"I didn't know that it was *your* table," said Alice: "It's laid for a great many more than three."

"Your hair wants cutting," said the Hatter. He had been looking at Alice for some time with great curiosity, and this was his first speech.

"You should learn not to make personal remarks," Alice said with some severity: "it's very rude." [Pp. 84–85]

The reader finds such quips and philosophies as:

"Now, here you see it takes all the running you can do, to keep in the same place. If you want to get somewhere else you must run at least twice as fast as that!" [P. 189]

and:

". . . I suppose you don't want to lose your name?"
"No, indeed," Alice said, a little anxiously.
"And yet I don't know," the Gnat went on in a careless tone: "Only think how convenient it would be if you could manage to go home without it! For instance, if the governess wanted to call you to your lessons, she would call out 'Come here —'; and there she would have to leave off, because there wouldn't be any name for her to call, and of course you wouldn't have to go, you know." [Pp. 200, 201]

Few authors have equaled the grave nonsense, absurd puns, mock logic, and fantastic happenings that occur in these two books.

The Wind in the Willows

In 1908 Kenneth Grahame's *The Wind in the Willows* (37) arrived on the literary scene.

Grahame had the enjoyable habit of telling stories in nightly installments to his little son Alastair, who had the nickname Mouse. Fortunately for the reading world, when one summer Alastair was to leave for the seaside, he refused to go because he did not want to miss the adventures of Toad, Badger, Rat, and Mole. His father sent him the future installments in writing. Alastair's governess, sensitive to their unusual quality, mailed them back to Mrs. Grahame.

The Wind in the Willows by Kenneth Grahame, illustrated by Arthur Rackham.

Grahame had enjoyed considerable success in the literary world with his two books *The Golden Age* (36), written in 1895, and *Dream Days* (36), written in 1898. When an agent called on Grahame and asked him to write on any subject of his choosing, Mrs. Grahame remembered the manuscript of the bedtime stories, and she gave it to him. Much to the publisher's later regret, he turned down the manuscript. In 1908 the book, with the title *The Wind in the Willows,* was published in both London and New York. It was not long before Toad, Badger, Rat, and Mole had worked their way into the hearts of children and adults around the world.

The fantastic happenings in *The Wind in the Willows* follow a logical course of action. Toad, Badger, Rat, and Mole arouse the reader's interest and concern to such a degree that they appear as human beings rather than as animals. The author reveals human experiences through the lives of the animals.

As *The Wind in the Willows* opens, Mole is busy spring-cleaning his little house. One can't blame him for giving up the cleaning. "Spring was moving in the air above and the earth below and around him, penetrating even his dark and lowly little house in its spirit of divine discontent and longing" (p. 1). Readers go along with Mole to take in Spring through all their senses.

The lyrical quality of Grahame's style continues throughout the story and often turns prose to poetry. There is a whirling playful rhythm in the prose, as in Mole's description of the river: ". . . This sleek sinuous, full-bodied animal, chasing and chuckling, gripping things with a gurgle and leaving them with a laugh, to fling itself on fresh playmates that shook themselves free, and were caught and held again. All was a-shake and a-shiver—glints and gleams and sparkles, rustle and swirl, chatter and bubble" (pp. 3–4).

Grahame quickly expresses his own joy of living as he develops the friendship and tenderness between Mole and Rat. Mole and Rat are returning from a long day's outing with Otter. As they pass through a little village at dark, they peer through the lighted windows along the way and see intimate, cozy scenes of home life.

A longing for home, with its comforts of warmth, food, and friendship, comes over Mole and Rat as they hurry along. Following behind Rat, Mole suddenly smells his old home. Rat is far ahead and doesn't hear Mole's calling to him. Mole finally catches up with Rat and tearfully tells him how he had smelled his old home but that they have long since passed it. Rat, sensitive to Mole's feelings, insists they retrace their steps and they arrive at Mole's home, which has Mole End printed in Gothic lettering on the door. In spite of evidences of lack of housekeeping and Mole's insistence that his home is shabby, Rat declares that it is the jolliest little place he has ever visited. Turning the day into a happy homecoming for Mole, the field mice arrive to sing Christmas carols. One of the happiest Christmas parties to be found in children's literature follows.

Touches of fantasy prevail throughout the story—in the descriptions of the seasons, in the comfortable living of Toad, Rat, Badger, and Mole, and in the mutual understanding and appreciation among the characters. Even the beautiful word pictures hold the reader's anticipation.

Mary Poppins

Mary Poppins (74) by Pamela L. Travers is a delightful story for young readers with its light-hearted nonsense, whimsy, and magic.

The fantasy in Mary Poppins operates in a framework of reality. The story moves so cleverly back and forth from reality to fantasy that the reader is inclined to accept the fantasy as the truth. For example, in the Banks' home, the stairs have a banister. Mrs. Banks walks up the stairs, but as Jane and Michael, the children, watch from the landing, Mary Poppins with her large carpetbag in her hands slides gracefully *up* the banister. According to Mary Poppins, "everybody's got a Fairyland of their own" (p. 28).

The Borrowers

Fantasy reached one of its high points in children's literature with the arrival of Mary Norton's *The Borrowers* (60) in 1953. The "Borrowers" —Pod, Homily, and Arrietty—hold an honored place with characters from *Alice in Wonderland, The Wind in the Willows,* and *Mary Poppins.*

Mary Poppins and Mary Poppins Comes Back by P. L. Travers, illustrated by Mary Shepard.

The Borrowers by Mary Norton, illustrated by Beth and Joe Krush.

People often put things away carefully and remember exactly where they put them. Why do they mysteriously disappear and where have they gone? In *The Borrowers* Mary Norton gives the answer to this puzzle.

The Borrowers are little creatures who live in a world of their own under the floorboards, along the pipes, under the clocks, and on the mantels of homes. They furnish their cozy quarters with all the things that the human beings of the house have put away and then cannot find. The history of these interesting folk has a considerable amount of traditional fairy-tale wisdom worked into it. The reader lives in a world where safety pins become giant tools, and spools of thread become stools.

Arrietty, her father Pod, and her mother Homily enjoy luxurious living, as is evident by the description of their living quarters:

Arrietty wandered through the open door into the sitting room. Ah, the fire had been lighted and the room looked bright and cozy. Homily was proud of her sitting room: the walls had been papered with scraps of old letters out of waste-paper baskets, and Homily had arranged the handwriting sideways in vertical stripes which ran across from floor to ceiling. On the walls, repeated in various colors, hung several portraits of Queen Victoria as a girl; these were postage stamps, borrowed by Pod some years ago from the stamp box on the desk in the morning room. There was a lacquer trinket box, padded inside and with the lid open, which they used as a settle; and that useful stand-by—a chest of drawers made of match boxes. There was a round table with a red velvet cloth, which Pod had made from the wooden bottom of a pill box supported on the carved pedestal of a knight from the chess set . . . The knight itself—its bust, so to speak—stood on a column in the corner, where it looked very fine, and lent that air to the room which only statuary can give. [Pp. 15–16]

The Borrowers come to life again in the stories that followed Mary Norton's first book. Pod, Homily, and Arrietty continue to meet their difficulties fortified with a wise inner philosophy. They never lose their personalities or their individuality as they move to the other stories in the series. The titles give the reader an idea of the whereabouts of the Borrowers and the kinds of experiences one might expect them to have. *The Borrowers* was followed first by *The Borrowers Afield* (61) and then by *The Borrowers Afloat* (62); the fourth book in the adventures of the Borrowers is *The Borrowers Aloft* (63). *Poor Stainless: A New Story About the Borrowers* (64) is the most recent addition to the Borrowers' series. The story revolves around Stainless, one of Homily's cousins.

Other Favorite Fantasies

Lloyd Alexander has written a series of books called the "Prydain Cycle," which tell the story of Taran, an apprentice pig keeper who wants to be a hero. These fantasy tales, based on the Welsh legend *The Maginogion*, record the clash between good and evil in the mythical land of Prydain. Suggestive of the Arthurian legend, the series introduces the orphan Taran and relates his adventures in the first four books: *The Book of Three* (2), *The Black Cauldron* (1), *The Castle of Llyr* (3), and *Taran Wanderer* (5). *The High King* (4) brings Taran to manhood and the series to a satisfying end.

Older boys and girls have particularly enjoyed this series, as it is filled with both conflict and magic. It portrays the desire of a boy to be a hero and traces his slowly acquired realization of the nature of heroism. Woven into this majestic theme are the many values of civilized tradition—courage, comradeship, and love. The cycle has an epic quality that has earned it an outstanding place in children's literature. *The High King* received the Newbery Award in 1969.

Robert Lawson's fantasy *Rabbit Hill* (46) has given pleasure to readers of all ages since its publication in 1944. The story is told in a superb style that reveals Lawson's love of nature and his deeply rooted reverence for all wildlife creatures. The beautiful descriptions and illustrations give each animal a distinct personality. *Rabbit Hill* received the Newbery Award in 1945.

Stuart Little (80) by E. B. White is an unusual fantasy that is a delight to both the imagination and the emotions. When Mr. and Mrs. Frederick C. Little's second son is born, everyone is amazed that he is much smaller than a mouse! The Littles accept the situation calmly, name the new arrival Stuart, and begin to make all the necessary adjustments to his size. White has written a lively, tender story. The text is complemented by Garth Williams' numerous illustrations.

Another fantasy by E. B. White is *Charlotte's Web* (79), the story of ten-year-old Fern; Charlotte, a large, gray spider; Wilbur, a runt in a litter of pigs; and Templeton, a rat. When a litter of pigs is born on the Arable farm, Fern's father lets her keep the runt. Fern names the pig Wilbur and cares for him as she would a baby brother. Even after Fern is persuaded to sell Wilbur to her uncle, she spends much of her spare time keeping Wilbur company and quietly observing the other animals. Wilbur is lonely when Fern doesn't come to visit, until Charlotte offers to be his friend. In spite of the warm friendship that develops between them, Wilbur is depressed when one of the sheep tells him that he will be killed at slaughtering time. Charlotte promises Wilbur that she will save him. This tender story moves back and forth between reality and fantasy.

E. B. White has blended true birdlore and fanciful adventure in a witty fashion in *The Trumpet of the Swan* (81). Louis is a trumpeter swan without a voice. Sam, a boy who appreciates birds, teaches Louis to read and write, making it possible for him to communicate with people. To help him communicate with birds, Louis' father steals a trumpet from a music store, and Louis learns to play so well that he wins a lovely swan mate. At the end of the moving story, Louis and his mate return to a natural life in the wilds of Canada.

The Ghosts (8) by Antonia Barber is a fantasy in which four children move through time. Two of the children, whose mother is the caretaker of a remote English country house, come upon the ghosts said to haunt the house. This is a happy tale filled with surprises and cleverly resolved mysteries.

From the moment young Egan arrives in Instep, he senses the spell cast over the village by Megrimum, the mysterious Something that lives on the mountain in *Kneeknock Rise* (7) by Natalie Babbitt. Soon

Charlotte's Web by E. B. White, illustrated by Garth Williams.

Egan decides to climb the Rise to find a practical explanation for the strange phenomenon.

In *The Giant Under the Snow* (35), a story of suspense by John Gordon, Jonquil Winters and her classmates Bill Smith and Arthur Minnett are unintentionally caught up in the final act of a struggle between the ancient forces of good and evil. For a time, the three young people have the ability to fly by the magic of a remarkable, ageless woman, and they are able to combat the evil menace of a savage warlord who continues to arise again. The fantasy is full of weird suspenseful adventure.

Realism and fantasy are combined to give strength and humor to *The Smallest Monster in the World* (53) by William MacKellar. In the quiet Scottish village of Abermuir young Wullie learns from a 250-year-old kelpie about the monster Maggie, who lives in Loch Moyne. From a visiting paleontologist, he discovers the possibility of living fossils. The descriptions of the villagers are convincing and add local color to the story.

Exotic settings and names add a touch of glamour to the fantasy *Zeki and the Talking Cat, Shukra* (45) by Laszlo Kubinyi. A wise, talking cat, a cruel czar, a maiden, and an evil boar combined with the right amounts of good, evil, adventure, and humor make a lively tale.

The Happiness Flower (85) by Eva-Lis Wuoris concerns the friendship between a lonely, unhappy girl and Peikko, a Finnish troll. While collecting wild flowers, Maia helps to break a spell for the peikko, who uses his magic to bring Maia's father back to his family. Descriptions of the Finnish landscape add to the pleasure of the reading.

The Little Indian and the Angel (33) by Mildred Feague tells the story of a little Navajo boy and his special angel friend as they move along through the seasons of Icy-Thin-Sheet and Young-Eagles-Are-Born to December-Star-Makes-Big-Wind-Blow. The story is illustrated with delicate watercolor illustrations.

A highly original fantasy, *The King of the Copper Mountains* (9), by Paul Biegel, was awarded the 1965 Dutch children's book prize. A series of stories are related by a group of animals to keep their king alive and to entertain him while they wait for the doctor.

The Daybreakers (23) by Jane L. Curry is an intriguing fantasy in which the evils of the present mesh with those of the past. Callie and her brother, who are Black, and Liss, who is white, travel back and forth through time from their mill town in West Virginia to the ancient Indian village of Abaloc, which formerly stood on the same site.

In *Mindy's Mysterious Miniature* (24), also by Jane L. Curry, Mindy buys a wonderful old doll house at an auction. When a mysterious stranger makes off with it, Mindy and a neighbor are caught inside. Mindy finally figures a way out. Miss Curry has also written *Change Child* (22).

Two little girls, Tee and Puffin, enter fairyland through their green closet and have many exciting adventures in *The Gruesome Green Witch* (19) by Patricia Coffin. Puffin incurs the enmity of the gruesome witch, who is eventually conquered by a magic brew. The humorous text is highlighted by a green design.

Narrated in an Irish brogue, *Brogeen and the Bronze Lizard* (51) by Patricia Lynch features a leprechaun named Brogeen, a young girl with a strange lizard bracelet, and a circus that has seen better days.

Lions Backward (11) by Burke Boyce is a fantastic spoof set in New York City. While writing rhymes, George says "snoil" (lions backward), and three lions instantly appear. That they walk backward and are not interested in eating people make them even more fascinating. One can imagine the consternation they cause when they walk along Fifth Avenue past the Central Park Zoo to the Public Library, where the great carved lions turn on their pedestals. How George maneuvers the lions and how he manages to get rid of them make a good story. Amusing illustrations add to the fun.

Freshness and delight radiate from *Lisa and the Grompet* (20) by Patricia Coombs. Unhappy because she is always being ordered around by her family, Lisa goes into the woods to mope. She meets a grompet, a tiny, little, furry, winged creature who is unhappy because no one has ever ordered him to do anything. The grompet falls in love with Lisa as soon as she gives him a command. He goes home to live with her, happy to be taking orders from her, and Lisa becomes happy taking orders from the rest of her family.

Humor and tenderness abound in *Sylvester and the Magic Pebble* (71) by William Steig. The donkey Sylvester finds an unusual pebble with wish-fulfilling magic power. Suddenly confronted by a hungry lion, Sylvester wishes the lion were a rock, and presto he becomes one! The outcome of that particular wish develops into a hilarious situation.

In the humorous fantasy *Mooncoin Castle* (75) by Brinton Turkle the combined efforts of a restless ghost, a professor, a second-rate witch, and a large community of jackdaws save an historic Irish castle. The happy ending features a ghost who finds some peace and a witch and a jackdaw who watch western movies together.

Suspense and surprise await the readers of *Pipkin* (34) by S. Forst. Pipkin is the lone survivor of a flooded-out underground kingdom of gnomes. He is discovered by an old widow who is believed to be a descendant of the knights of the castle in the forest. Pipkin makes his home in a decorated Easter egg in the old widow's comfortable cottage. One near disaster follows another until a ladybug finds him and persuades him to visit the Ladybug Kingdom. Here he meets a little girl gnome, also a survivor of the flood.

Scientific fact is woven into *Danny Dunn and the Smallifying Machine* (84) by Jay Williams and Raymond Abrashkin. Danny's Professor, Bulfinch, working for the government, has invented a miniaturizer that by accident reduces almost everyone to insect size until a colleague arrives and turns off the machine. Fantasy enthusiasts will enjoy the final twist to the story.

Three kings find that it is quite a trick to outwit the sun and make it conform to their wishes in *The Three Kings* (54) by Marcello Mariotti. Bold color illustrations give a royal touch to the story.

Walk Out of the World (57) by Ruth Nichols is a gripping fantasy about Tobit and Judith, a devoted brother and sister who walk into another world. There they are chosen to lead the people of the Wanderer on the march to regain their ancient capital city, which had been taken from them 500 years before.

In *The Grandma in the Apple Tree* (50) by Mira Lobe eight-year-old Andi has a favorite thinking spot in an apple tree. He is the only child on the block who doesn't have a grandmother. One day, while in the apple tree, he is joined by an imaginary grandma who takes him on tiger hunts and journeys to pirate-infested seas. His imaginary grandma serves him only on Sundays until old Mrs. Finch, a new neighbor, introduces him to the pleasures that a real everyday grandma can bring.

Lots of candy before bedtime provokes the imagination of a small boy in *Rockabye to Monsterland* (52) by Frances McKee. A colorful circus of dragons, giraffes, bewigged pigs, and snorting crows illustrated in three colors combine to produce a multidimensioned fantasy.

Science Fiction

There is a marked relationship between fantasy and science fiction. Science fiction has been called the fiction of prophecy—a fiction of things to come based on things at hand. Science fiction deals with fantasy—the fantasy of the possible. Writers of science fiction are the explorers of the twenty-first century, embarking on voyages to new worlds.

"Science fiction" is a rather pervasive term applied to stories of a speculative nature that prophesy new worlds to come, new discoveries in science, future inventions, and man's further control and extension of his environment. As children progress through the grades they become more and more questioning. They find science fiction rich with material for questions as well as with material for building dreams. The stories challenge their imagination and stimulate them to wonder about the present world and about other possible worlds waiting to be explored.

Lois and Stephen Rose, authors of *The Sheltered Ring: Science Fiction and the Quest for Meaning* (67) and widely recognized as authorities in the field of science fiction, say:

> There are numerous definitions of science fiction. It is sometimes seen as literature which has come inevitably into being as the fate of the world is seen to hang on the interaction of man and science. It is said to differ from fantasy because its scientific explanations make it seem plausible. Or it differs from straight fiction because it presupposes something—operative space travel, advanced cybernetics, a galactic political situation, or an environment not drawn from anyone's life experience—that is not yet, or may never be, visibly operative in our every day life. Perhaps science fiction is best defined, however, by an enumeration of its themes. These can be grouped into the following categories: Technological gimmickry, space travel, future scenarios, and finally, the exploration of inner space and ultimate meaning. [P. 19]

The science fiction writer M. Jean Greenlaw (38) says:

> Science fiction is the genre of literature that imaginatively depicts plausible events that are logical extrapolations of known facts and are descriptive of the social impacts of science and technology. Though the plots may seem impossible to man in his present condition, they do reflect the possibilities of the future. [P. 196]

Isaac Asimov (6), an outstanding authority in the field of science fiction, offers the following brief definition: "Science fiction is that branch of literature which is concerned with the impact of scientific advance upon human beings" (p. 158).

Although there are numerous definitions of science fiction, each stresses that the genre is prophetic, descriptive of the social impacts of science, and set in novel, imaginative, and possibly fantastic situations.

Early Science Fiction

Some early science fiction stories, if they can be so labeled, were Sir Thomas More's *Utopia* (56) and François Rabelais's *Gargantua and Pantagruel* (66) in the sixteenth century, and Defoe's *Robinson Crusoe* (26) and Swift's *Gulliver's Travels* (73) in the eighteenth century.

One of the most colorful and exciting authors of the nineteenth century was Jules Verne (1828–1905). A prolific writer, he left a rich heritage of imaginative writing that has yet to be surpassed. Verne admitted that it was his intense admiration for Defoe's *Robinson Crusoe* that started him writing in the vein in which he was destined to make a significant contribution to literature for both young and adult readers around the world.

Although Verne probably never held a test tube in his hand, his writings became an inspiration to scientists and discoverers throughout the world. Before radio had been invented, he had conceived of television. He imagined helicopters a half century before the Wright brothers flew, and dirigibles before Zeppelin. Other twentieth-century wonders foreseen by this wizard of the nineteenth century were neon lights, escalators, skyscrapers, air conditioning, guided missiles, tanks, electrically operated submarines, and airplanes. He wrote about the wonders of tomorrow with such precision and indisputable detail that he was taken seriously by learned societies and mathematicians who spent weeks checking his figures. It was reported that when his book about going to the moon, *From the Earth to the Moon and a Trip Around It* (77), was published, 500 people volunteered for the next expedition. Verne lived to see many of his predictions and fantasies come true.

After numerous unsuccessful attempts to get a publisher, Jules Verne finally succeeded in publishing his first book, *Five Weeks in a Balloon* (76). He signed a contract with the publisher binding him to the production of two novels a year. The result was some hundred novels during his lifetime, most of them in the field of science fiction.

Twenty Thousand Leagues Under the Sea (78) continues its popularity with both children and adults. Written in 1869, it is a story of scientific speculation in which the author introduces the submarine in science fiction years before it made its appearance in reality.

Motifs of Science Fiction

Among the popular science fiction stories are those that deal with space travel to and from other planets, solar systems, and galaxies. These stories are built around the discovery, exploration, and settlement of new worlds inhabited by unearthly life forms. This is the motif in *Dimension A* (25) by L. P. Davies, a story based on the supposition that an infinity of worlds exists in the same space. A professor, his nephew, and a friend are drawn by magnetic force into another dimension, a threatening world where alien inhabitants fight among themselves in a struggle to invade Earth.

Twenty Thousand Leagues Under the Sea by Jules Verne, illustrated by Hildebrand.

Many science fiction stories feature characters who move back and forth in both time and space. *Who Has Poisoned the Sea?* (21) by Audrey Coppard relates how Tim Dunwoodie was daydreaming in his hideout overlooking the sea when Percy, a boy from the twenty-fifth century, appears before him. Tim learns from the boy that a poison released in the twentieth century has contaminated nearly all the oceans of the world.

Changes in both mind and matter occur in many science fiction stories. In Sybil Leek's story *Tree That Conquered the World* (47), Julian, the son of a scientist and nephew of a member of a team of astronauts lost on a flight to Mars, is interested in science, especially plant life. He discovers a strange plant that grows overnight into a talking tree almost ten feet high. With his friends, Julian establishes "Operation Treetop" to propagate the tree and reduce the smog and air pollution.

A large number of science fiction stories are built around the supernatural talents and powers of the characters in the stories. These talents and powers are sometimes brought about through technological discoveries and sometimes through advances in the sciences. Among such characters in television and comic strips are Superman and Batman. Some characters retain their popularity over long periods of time, others come and go. Although their names may change, their behavior and exploits remain pretty much the same.

Some of the most interesting of the science fiction stories are those in which advances in the social sciences are applied directly to changes in human behavior. In *Exiled from Earth* (10) by Ben Bova a group of scientists in the twenty-first century are condemned to exile from earth because their accomplishments are threatening world stability. Likewise, *Weathermonger* (27) by Peter Dickinson relates a future time when a strange force opposed to all machines and technology has taken control of the Middle Ages. *Storm over Warlock* (59) by André Norton relates how beautiful women overpower men by thought control.

Robert A. Heinlein, an outstanding writer of science fiction for children, relates the search for justice and personal identity of the boy Thorby in *Citizen of the Galaxy* (41). At an early age Thorby becomes the property of a crippled beggar, "Pop" Baslim, after he is auctioned off in the slave market of Jubbulpore, capital of a group of outer planets known as the Nine Worlds. After living with Pop for several years, Thorby learns that Baslim is active in a spy network that is plotting against the cruel Sargon, dictator of the Nine Worlds. Rather than face the questioning of Sargon's police, Baslim commits suicide. Following Baslim's death, Thorby moves in and out of a number of difficult and exciting situations.

A prolific writer, Heinlein has given quality to science fiction for children. Although the settings for his stories are in the far future, they deal with universal problems that have always concerned man. Among his early books that are still popular with young readers are *Space Cadet* (43), *Between Planets* (40), and *Have Space Suit—Will Travel* (42).

Modern Science Fiction

In her Foreword to *Enchantress from the Stars* (31) Sylvia L. Engdahl says, "The locale of this story can be fixed neither in space nor in time. Perhaps it is the planet Earth—but then again, perhaps not, for whether this is a tale of the past or of the future is anybody's guess." Most of the action of the story related by the heroine, Elana, takes place on the planet Andrecia. Elana, her father, and her fiancé are on their way to a family reunion when a group of colonizers from another culture land on Andrecia. They return to Andrecia where they become involved in one harrowing escapade after another. *Enchantress from the Stars* was a runner-up for the Newbery Medal in 1971.

Elana relates further experiences as a specially trained agent of the Interplanetary Federation in *The Far Side of Evil* (32). She is sent as an observer to a planet whose inhabitants unknowingly face a choice of using their technology either for space exploration or for nuclear war. The intervening of a fellow agent in local affairs increases the danger of war. Elana's reactions to the activities of the fellow agent offer a series of suspenseful situations.

Dread Companion (58) by André Norton is a fantastic blending of folklore, spacelore, sorcery, and science used as the background for a story with its setting on another planet in the year 2422. Kilda c'Rhyn is a house aide in charge of two children in the Zobak family. Kilda and the two children penetrate another space-time continuum where their strange experiences make a good science fiction story.

The setting of *Journey to Untor* (83) by Leonard Wibberly is the many-dimensioned world of Untor to which the characters in the story are transmitted by a pinpoint of light called a Noen. The characters are the four children of Wibberly's *Encounter Near Venus* (82), their two younger siblings, and their Uncle Bill. Three of the children who slip into time past live in a fourteenth-century castle. The action of the story moves rapidly when the seven are reunited and under hazardous conditions cross the Mountains of Untor.

Lord of the Stars (72) by Jean and Jeff Sutton relates the experiences of an Earth boy, Danny, who is stranded on the planet of an emerald sun. Danny's loneliness ends when he discovers telepathic communication with the planet creature Zandro and the Earth girl Arla. Danny and Arla struggle with Zandro for supremacy. Through mental processes Zandro is defeated, and the story ends with the triumph of good over evil.

Spacepaw (28) by Gordon Dickson is a science fiction story with many exciting plot elements. An early twist in the plot finds astronaut Bill Waltham, the hero of the story, facing a bewildering situation on the planet Dilbia. Nine-foot gorilla-like inhabitants confront the astronaut as he solves a major crisis that turns out to be amusing.

The Prince in Waiting (17) is the first book in a new science fiction trilogy by John Christopher, England's outstanding author of science fiction for older children. A view of life in a machineless medieval society that developed following the destruction of world civilization by violent earthquakes is presented.

Christopher's earlier science fiction trilogy has its setting in the future in an age controlled by the Tripods, described as machines made by men which revolt against them and enslave them. *The White Mountains* (18), the first in the trilogy, revolves around the teen-ager Will and his companions, who struggle against difficulties to keep a free and challenging mind. Through their determination the three boys escape to the Alps. In *The City of Gold and Lead* (13), Will and one of the other escapees face further hardships. In the third story, *The Pool of Fire* (16), a fascinating invention offers the boys a means to conquer the Tripods' cities and to free the earth.

Other compelling books by Christopher are *The Lotus Caves* and *The Guardians.* With its setting in the twenty-first century *The Lotus Caves* (15) is a story of adventure on the moon. While on an unofficial exploratory trip across the moon's surface, fourteen-year-old Marty and his friend Steve fall into a series of strange caves that prove to be the home of an intelligent plant.

Set in England, *The Guardians* (14) also takes place in the twenty-first century. Thirteen-year-old Rob Randall lives in a rigidly controlled society comprised of two parts: the masses and the upper classes. Rob makes his home in a state boarding school until life becomes unbearable. He defies custom and crosses the barrier that separates the two classes. He is befriended by Mike Gifford and adopted into the Gifford family. When revolution and rebellion strike the country, Rob learns of the Guardians, who comprise a ruthless oligarchy who control people's lives.

A Wrinkle in Time (48) by Madeleine L'Engle relates the stirring experiences of an unusual family. The Wallaces are scientists who have reared their children in an unconventional manner. The father has disappeared mysteriously while on a secret space mission. His daughter, twelve-year-old Meg, and her five-year-old brother Charles make the acquaintance of Mrs. Whatsit and her two companions, Mrs. Who and Mrs. Which, three ladies who appear to have supernatural powers. They agree to help Meg, Charles, and their friend Calvin find Meg's father. The children must travel in space by the fifth dimension, a tesseract that has the power to reduce the distance between two points by creating a wrinkle in time. By means of the tesseract the children move from one suspenseful situation to another. The story encompasses such serious themes as the need for individuality, respect for the differences of others, the power of love, and the nature of good and evil. *A Wrinkle in Time* received the Newbery Medal in 1963.

The Day of the Drones (49) by A. M. Lightner revolves around N'Gobi of Africa, who is an outcast because of his light skin in a land of Black people. An expedition is organized to explore the dangerous lands around Africa. Because N'Gobi is skilled in the operation of machinery, he is allowed to go as pilot of the worn-out helicopter left by the ancient ones. With four others he travels north to ancient lands that were once populated. There they discover the Bee people, dwarfed descendants of predisaster white people.

Reality, fantasy, and science fiction are the ingredients of *Ride a Wild Horse* (12) by Ruth Carlsen. In her search for a "transmuter" that will enable her to return to her other worldly home, Julie involves twelve-year-old Barne in a series of exciting adventures.

Ecology in Fantasy and Science Fiction

The current awareness of the problems man has caused to his environment, including overuse and pollution of natural resources, has found expression even in literature for children. Many well-known authors of children's books, for example, Dr. Seuss, Edith Hurd, and Alvin Tresselt, have written stories encouraging children to respect and to improve their environment. Many of the stories have imaginary characters or settings and lie within the realm of fantasy or science fiction.

In Edith Thatcher Hurd's *Wilson's World* (44), a young boy paints himself a bright, beautiful world. But as it fills up with people, it also fills up with cars, buildings, and smog. So Wilson paints himself a better world, in which the people want to keep it clean and beautiful.

Wonder-Fish from the Sea (39) is a nature fantasy written by Josef Guggenmos and translated by Alvin Tresselt. Falling leaves follow the wind and become fish when they fall into the water.

Colorful illustrations together with a bit of ecological teaching contribute to *The Monstrous Glisson Glop* (55) by Diane R. Massie. In this rhymed fantasy a sea monster can't say no to a diet of lantern fish and electric eels until he is left in the dark.

In *Clean Air, Sparkling Water* (68) by Dorothy Shuttlework parallel accounts describe the experiences of two hypothetical towns situated on opposite sides of a river. The story makes a dramatic plea for clean air, pure water, and conservation of natural resourses.

The Wumps—simple, grass-eating animals who live in a small world of meadows, trees, and flowing streams—are suddenly invaded by Pollutions and their spaceships. *The Wump World* (65) by Bill Peet relates how the invaders build cities that fill the air with noise and smoke and the land with trash. The pollution becomes so bad that the Pollutions themselves must move on to find another world to pollute.

In *Beaver Valley* (30) Walter D. Edmonds relates what happens to a valley and all the living creatures inhabiting the valley when the beavers move in and begin to apply their ideas of engineering and land development. Readers can easily see the parallel between the beavers' destruction and human ecological destruction.

Extending Experiences for the Reader

1. List the ingredients in *Alice in Wonderland* (29) that have enabled it to hold an esteemed position in children's literature throughout the years.
2. Select to read to the class a number of dialogues that abound in nonsense.
3. List the qualities that differentiate the characters in *The Wind in the Willows* (37) from characters in other fantasies.
4. Select to read to the class dialogues between different characters in *The Wind in the Willows.*
5. Select to read to the class word pictures of places from *The Wind in the Willows*—for example, descriptions of the River and of the Mole's home.
6. With the class develop guidelines for evaluating science fiction stories.
7. Prepare a bibliography of science fiction stories for the class.
8. Prepare a bulletin board using both book jackets and original drawings to arouse interest in science fiction.

Extending Experiences for Children

1. With clay model Mole, Rat, Badger, and Toad from *The Wind in the Willows.*
2. Make a Mary Poppins puppet. Prepare a skit based on *Mary Poppins* (74) to present before the class.
3. Collect pictures of moon landings by astronauts to make into a class scrapbook.
4. Plan a parade of fantasy characters. Dress as a character from your favorite book.

Chapter References

1. ALEXANDER, LLOYD. *The Black Cauldron.* New York: Dell, 1969. Paperback. Grades 5–9.
2. ———. *The Book of Three.* New York: Dell, 1969. Paperback. Grades 5–9.

3. ______. *The Castle of Llyr.* New York: Dell, 1969. Paperback. Grades 2–8.
4. ______. *The High King.* New York: Dell, 1969. Paperback. Grades 5–9.
5. ______. *Taran Wanderer.* New York: Dell, 1969. Paperback. Grades 2–8.
6. ASIMOV, ISAAC (ed.). *Tomorrow's Children.* Garden City, N. Y.: Doubleday, 1966. Grades 7–9.
7. BABBITT, NATALIE. *Kneeknock Rise.* New York: Farrar, Straus & Giroux, 1970. Grade 3 and up.
8. BARBER, ANTONIA. *The Ghosts.* New York: Farrar, Straus & Giroux, 1969. Grades 6–9.
9. BIEGEL, PAUL. *The King of the Copper Mountains.* Gillian Hugh (tr.). New York: Watts, 1969. Grades 4–6.
10. BOVA, BEN. *Exiled from Earth.* New York: Dutton, 1971. n.g.l.
11. BOYCE, BURKE. *Lions Backward.* Garden City, N. Y.: Doubleday, 1970. Grade 10 and up.
12. CARLSEN, RUTH. *Ride a Wild Horse.* Boston: Houghton Mifflin, 1970.
13. CHRISTOPHER, JOHN. *The City of Gold and Lead.* New York: Macmillan, 1970. Paperback. Grade 5 and up.
14. ______. *The Guardians.* New York: Macmillan, 1970. Grade 6 and up.
15. ______. *The Lotus Caves.* New York: Macmillan, 1971. Paperback. Grades 5–7.
16. ______. *The Pool of Fire.* New York: Macmillan, 1970. Paperback. Grade 5 and up.
17. ______. *The Prince in Waiting.* New York: Macmillan, 1970. Grades 5–9.
18. ______. *The White Mountains.* New York: Macmillan, 1970. Paperback. Grade 5 and up.
19. COFFIN, PATRICIA. *The Gruesome Green Witch.* New York: Walker & Co., n.d. Grades 5–7.
20. COOMBS, PATRICIA. *Lisa and the Grompet.* New York: Lothrop, Lee, & Shepard, 1970. Kindergarten–grade 3.
21. COPPARD, AUDREY. *Who Has Poisoned the Sea?* New York: S. G. Phillips, 1970. n.g.l.
22. CURRY, JANE L. *Change Child.* New York: Harcourt Brace Jovanovich, 1969. Grades 3–9.
23. ______. *The Daybreakers.* New York: Harcourt Brace Jovanovich, 1970. Grades 4–6.
24. ______. *Mindy's Mysterious Miniature.* New York: Harcourt Brace Jovanovich, 1970. Grades 4–6.
25. DAVIES, L. P. *Dimension A.* Garden City, N. Y.: Doubleday, 1969. Grades 7–9.
26. DEFOE, DANIEL. Angus Ross (ed.). *Robinson Crusoe.* Baltimore, Md.: Penguin, 1965. Paperback. Grade 9 and up.
27. DICKINSON, PETER. *Weathermonger.* Boston: Atlantic Monthly Press, 1969. Grade 7 and up.
28. DICKSON, GORDON. *Spacepaw.* New York: Putnam, 1969. Grades 6–8.

29. DODGSON, REVEREND CHARLES L. (Lewis Carroll). *Alice's Adventures in Wonderland and Through the Looking Glass.* Sir John Tenniel (ill.). Cleveland and New York: World Publishing, 1946. Grades 4–9.
30. EDMONDS, WALTER D. *Beaver Valley.* Boston: Little, Brown, 1971.
31. ENGDAHL, SYLVIA L. *Enchantress from the Stars.* New York: Atheneum, 1970. Grade 6 and up.
32. ———. *The Far Side of Evil.* New York: Atheneum, 1971. Grades 7–9.
33. FEAGUE, MILDRED. *The Little Indian and the Angel.* Chicago: Children's Press, 1970. Kindergarten–grade 3.
34. FORST, S. *Pipkin.* New York: Delacorte, 1970. Grades 3–6.
35. GORDON, JOHN. *The Giant Under the Snow.* New York: Harper & Row, 1970. Grade 5 and up.
36. GRAHAME, KENNETH. *Golden Age; Dream Days.* New York: New American Library, 1964. Paperback. Grades 4–6.
37. ———. *The Wind in the Willows.* Ernest H. Shepard (ill.). New York: Scribner, 1908, 1968. Grades 7–12.
38. GREENLAW, M. JEAN. "Science Fiction: Impossible! Improbable! or Prophetic?" *Elementary English, National Council of Teachers of English,* 48 (April 1971), 196–202.
39. GUGGENMOS, JOSEF. *Wonder-Fish from the Sea.* Alvin Tresselt (tr.). New York: Parents' Magazine Press, 1971. Grades 3–6.
40. HEINLEIN, ROBERT A. *Between Planets.* New York: Scribner, 1957. Grades 5–11.
41. ———. *Citizen of the Galaxy.* New York: Scribner, 1957. Grades 5–11.
42. ———. *Have Space Suit—Will Travel.* New York: Scribner, 1958. Grades 5–11.
43. ———. *Space Cadet.* New York: Scribner, 1948. Grades 5–11.
44. HURD, EDITH THATCHER. *Wilson's World.* New York: Harper & Row, 1971. Grades 1–3.
45. KUBINYI, LASZLO. *Zeki and the Talking Cat, Shukra.* New York: Simon & Schuster, 1970. n.g.l.
46. LAWSON, ROBERT. *Rabbit Hill.* New York: Dial, 1968. Paperback. Grades 2–8.
47. LEEK, SYBIL. *Tree That Conquered the World.* Englewood Cliffs, N. J.: Prentice-Hall, 1969. Grades 3–7.
48. L'ENGLE, MADELEINE. *A Wrinkle in Time.* New York: Farrar, Straus & Giroux, 1962. Grade 6 and up.
49. LIGHTNER, A.M. *The Day of the Drones.* New York: Bantam, 1970. Paperback. n.g.l.
50. LOBE, MIRA. *The Grandma in the Apple Tree.* Doris Orgel (ill.). New York: McGraw-Hill, 1970. Grades 2–6.
51. LYNCH, PATRICIA. *Brogeen and the Bronze Lizard.* New York: Macmillan, 1970. Grades 4–6.
52. MC KEE, FRANCES. *Rockabye to Monsterland.* New York: Putnam, 1970. n.g.l.
53. MAC KELLAR, WILLIAM. *The Smallest Monster in the World.* New York: David McKay, 1969. Grades 4–6.
54. MARIOTTI, MARCELLO. *The Three Kings.* New York: Knopf, 1970. Kindergarten–grade 3.

55. MASSIE, DIANE R. *The Monstrous Glisson Glop.* New York: Parents' Magazine Press, 1970. n.g.l.
56. MORE, SIR THOMAS. *Utopia.* Paul Turner (tr.). Baltimore, Md.: Penguin, n.d. Paperback.
57. NICHOLS, RUTH. *Walk Out of the World.* New York: Harcourt Brace Jovanovich, 1969. Grades 4–6.
58. NORTON, ANDRÉ. *Dread Companion.* New York: Harcourt Brace Jovanovich, 1970. Grades 10–12.
59. ———. *Storm over Warlock.* Cleveland: World Publishing, 1960. Grades 7–9.
60. NORTON, MARY. *The Borrowers.* Beth Krush and Joe Krush (ills.). New York: Harcourt Brace Jovanovich, 1953. Paperback. Grade 3 and up.
61. ———. *The Borrowers Afield.* New York: Harcourt Brace Jovanovich, 1970. Paperback. Grade 4 and up.
62. ———. *The Borrowers Afloat.* New York: Harcourt Brace Jovanovich, 1959. Grade 3 and up.
63. ———. *The Borrowers Aloft.* New York: Harcourt Brace Jovanovich, 1961. Grade 3 and up.
64. ———. *Poor Stainless: A New Story About the Borrowers.* New York: Harcourt Brace Jovanovich, 1971. Grade 3 and up.
65. PEET, BILL. *The Wump World.* Boston: Houghton Mifflin, 1970.
66. RABELAIS, FRANÇOIS. *Gargantua and Pantagruel.* John M. Cohen (tr.). Baltimore, Md.: Penguin, n.d. Paperback.
67. ROSE, LOIS, AND STEPHEN ROSE. *The Sheltered Ring: Science Fiction and the Quest for Meaning.* Richmond, Va.: John Knox Press, 1970.
68. SHUTTLEWORK, DOROTHY. *Clean Air, Sparkling Water.* New York: Doubleday, 1968.
69. SILVERBERG, ROBERT. *Starman's Quest.* New York: Hawthorne, 1969. Grades 7–10.
70. SMITH, LILLIAN. *The Unreluctant Years: A Critical Approach to Children's Literature.* Chicago: American Library Association, 1953.
71. STEIG, WILLIAM. *Sylvester and the Magic Pebble.* New York: Simon & Schuster, 1969. Preschool–grade 3.
72. SUTTON, JEAN, AND JEFF SUTTON. *Lord of the Stars.* New York: Putnam, 1969. Grades 6–10.
73. SWIFT, JONATHAN. Donald Greene (ed.). *Gulliver's Travels.* New York: Bantam, 1971. Paperback. n.g.l.
74. TRAVERS, PAMELA L. *Mary Poppins.* New York: Harcourt Brace Jovanovich, 1934; 1962. Grades 4–6.
75. TURKLE, BRINTON. *Mooncoin Castle.* New York: Viking, 1970. Grades 4–6.
76. VERNE, JULES. *Five Weeks in a Balloon; Around the World in Eighty Days.* Arthur Chambers and P. Oesages (trs.). New York: Dutton, n.d. Paperback.
77. ———. *From the Earth to the Moon and a Trip Around It.* New York: Dutton, 1970.
78. ———. Harry Shefter *et al.* (eds.). *Twenty Thousand Leagues Under the Sea.* J. Walter Miller (tr.). New York: Simon & Schuster, n.d. Paperback.

79. WHITE, E.B. *Charlotte's Web.* New York: Dell, 1967. Paperback. Grades 3–7.
80. ______. *Stuart Little.* Garth Williams (ill.). New York: Dell, 1967. Paperback. Grades 3–7.
81. ______. *The Trumpet of the Swan.* New York: Harper & Row, 1970. n.g.l.
82. WIBBERLY, LEONARD. *Encounter Near Venus.* New York: Farrar, Straus & Giroux, n.d. Grade 5 and up.
83. ______. *Journey to Untor.* New York: Farrar, Straus & Giroux, 1970. Grade 5 and up.
84. WILLIAMS, JAY, AND RAYMOND ABRASHKIN. *Danny Dunn and the Smallifying Machine.* New York: Simon & Schuster, 1971. Paperback. Grades 3–6.
85. WUORIS, EVA-LIS. *The Happiness Flower.* Cleveland: World Publishing, 1969. Grade 6 and up.

More Fantasy for Children

Kindergarten–Grade 3

ASTURIAS, MIGUEL ANGEL. *The Talking Machine.* Garden City, N. Y.: Doubleday, 1971. A frog and a talking machine are the heroes of a fantasy by a winner of the Nobel Prize, Guatemalan Miguel Angel Asturias.

COLMAN, HILA. *Watch That Watch.* New York: Morrow, 1962. The humorous adventures of a most unusual gold watch and what happens to the owners when it is lost are related in this story.

COOPER, MARGARET. *The Ice Palace.* New York: Macmillan, 1966. The Queen Mother has an ice palace built to cool off her extra-warm little princess in this humorous fantasy about a very cold winter in St. Petersburg in 1740.

CUTLER, IVOR. *Meal One.* New York: Watts, 1971. A little boy awakes with a plum seed in his mouth which his mother helps him plant under his bed.

DARLING, LOIS. *The Sea Serpents Around Us.* Boston: Little, Brown, 1965. This book describes sea serpents in various parts of the world, including the legend about the Loch Ness Monster of Scotland.

DELESSERT, ETIENNE. *How the Mouse Was Hit on the Head by a Stone and Discovered the World.* Garden City, N. Y.: Doubleday, 1971. Under the guidance of a leading specialist, a noted author/artist has worked with a group of children and a team of psychologists to create this story.

DIETMEIER, MEL. *Felicia and Mimi.* Boston: Addison-Wesley, 1971. Two friends have a cat named Noodle and a mouse that shrugs its shoulders.

EHMCKE, SUSANNE. *Necklace for Laurie.* New York: Harcourt Brace Jovanovich, 1971. A little girl thinks a necklace of precious stones will make her a princess.

GWYNNE, FRED. *The Story of Ick.* New York: Windmill Books, 1971. All ages. Walking along a polluted beach, a small boy meets a strange creature named Ick.

HERMANN, FRANK. *The Giant Alexander.* New York: McGraw-Hill, 1965. A modern-day English helper of those in distress whether it be poor farmers or the lord mayor of London is sixty-three feet high.

HOLL, ADELAIDE. *The Man Who Had No Dream.* New York: Random House, 1969. Although he was rich, Mr. Oliver could neither sleep nor dream. Mr. Oliver needed to be needed.

JANOSCH, BOLLERBAM. *Just One Apple.* New York: Walck, 1966. Walter's fantastic-size apple is the highlight of this story.

MCCREA, JAMES, AND RUTH MCCREA. *The Magic Tree.* New York: Atheneum, 1965. A discontented princess becomes contented as she tends her rose garden.

MCHARGUE, GEORGESS. *The Wonderful Wings of Harold Harrabescu.* New York: Delacorte, 1971. Harold uses strange materials to build a pair of huge wings in his cellar. Then one day both Harold and the wings are gone.

MADDEN, DON. *Lemonade Serenade.* Chicago: Whitman, 1966. An elf playing a boombamaphone disrupts the afternoon lemonade in an enchanted garden.

MAHY, MARGARET. *The Boy with Two Shadows.* New York: Watts, 1971. A witch entrusts a little boy with her shadow in exchange for some powers the little boy has.

MASSIE, DIANE R. *A Birthday for Bird.* New York: Parents' Magazine, 1966. A bird celebrates his birthday with his friends.

MINARIK, ELSE. *The Little Giant Girl and the Elf Boy.* New York: Harper & Row, 1963. A small giant girl picking flowers for the table also picks up a tiny elf boy who had been sent by his mother to find a bud and a leaf.

PEET, BILL. *How Droofus the Dragon Lost His Head.* Boston: Houghton Mifflin, 1971. A good dragon hides from the king's knights until he is befriended by a small boy and finds his true vocation as an overgrown farm hand.

———. *Kermit the Hermit.* Boston: Houghton Mifflin, 1965. A kind boy saves a greedy hermit crab and is rewarded by having gold pieces dropped into the chimney by the crab helper, a pelican.

RICE, INEZ. *A Long, Long Time.* New York: Lothrop, Lee & Shepard, 1964. A little boy decides to be a tree when a leaf falls on his head, but he is finally released from his make-believe by a puff of wind.

STORM, THEODOR. Doris Orgel (reteller). *Little John.* New York: Farrar, Straus & Giroux, 1971. In this modern English version of a nineteenth-century German story, Little John in his trundle bed goes flying past the moon to the sun and finally ends in the dawn.

TREZ, DENISE, AND ALAIN TREZ. *The Royal Hiccups.* New York: Viking, 1965. An Indian prince cures his case of hiccups.

VALENS, EVANS G., JR. *Wingfin and Topple.* Cleveland: World Publishing, 1962. This imaginative story is about one flying fish who does not know that his long fins are really wings and another who has felt the excitement of flying.

UNGERER, TOMI. *The Beast of Monsieur Racine.* New York: Farrar, Straus & Giroux, 1971. Monsieur Racine's life motto, "No selling, no sharing" is undermined by his unexpected friendship with a strange and deceiving beast.

WAHL, JAN. *The Muffletumps: A Story of Four Dolls.* New York: Holt, Reinhart & Winston, 1966. Victorian dolls take a breather from the attic trunk each summer.

WONDRISKA, WILLIAM. *John John Twillinger.* New York: Holt, Reinhart & Winston, 1966. Reforms in Merryall town are accomplished by a red-haired boy, his red-haired dog, and a red-haired machine-gun man.

Grades 4–6

BRELIS, NANCY. *The Mummy Market.* New York: Harper & Row, 1966. Three children go to the Mummy Market to find a new mother.

BRENNER, PETER. *King for One Day.* New York: Scroll Press, 1971. A woodcutter is allowed to pretend he is king for one day, but he takes his imaginary role too seriously.

CUNNINGHAM, JULIA. *Viollet.* New York: Pantheon, 1966. A loyal dog and the singing thrush Viollet defend a gentle old count from the vicious foreman of his estate, who is trying to steal the estate and then kill the count.

CURRY, JANE L. *Beneath the Hill.* New York: Harcourt Brace Jovanovich, 1967. The Strip Mining Company unleashes an evil that has lain undisturbed under the mountain.

DODGSON, J. H. *Little Murphy.* New York: Dodd, Mead, 1971. This fantasy is about a mischievous monkey named Murphy who often exasperates a little girl with his comments and adventures.

FARALLA, DANA. *The Wonderful Flying-Go-Round.* Cleveland: World Publishing, 1965. This humorous fantasy about two boys features a dump yard and the amazing Florabella who has a special kind of magic.

FUJITA, TAMAO. *The North Star Man.* New York: Watts, 1971. Two children meet a mysterious man who actually lives on the North Star.

HARVEY, JAMES C. *Beyond the Gorge of Shadows.* New York: Lothrop, Lee & Shepard, 1965. This fantastic tale, set in North America 10,000 years ago, is about three sixteen-year-old boys who leave their tribe and go on a journey to find other men.

HOLMAN, FELICE. *Professor Diggins' Dragons.* New York: Macmillan, 1967. Five children hunt dragons at the seashore with a lovable old professor, whom Mr. Pym, a trillionaire, makes dean of a college of dragon hunting.

IRVING, WASHINGTON. *Rip Van Winkle.* New York: Watts, 1966. Shiftless Rip, his nagging wife, and the twenty-year sleep are described in this story.

JACOBS, FRANCINE. *The Legs of the Moon.* New York: Coward-McCann, 1971. Paka, the littlest of the menehumes, volunteers to hold the legs of the moon to delay the coming of night so that the rest of the menehumes may leave the island in safety.

JANSSON, TOVE. *Moominsummer Madness.* New York: Walck, 1961. This story relates the odd adventures of make-believe characters in the strangest house imaginable.

JOHNSON, ELIZABETH. *No Magic, Thank you.* Boston: Little, Brown, 1964. A boy and girl encounter a group of little people, the Rublucks, and fun follows.

KOSHLAND, ELLEN. *The Magic Lollipop.* New York: Knopf, 1971. Black-and-white photographs by the author tell a story about a lively little boy with a magic lollipop.

LEWIS, C. S. *The Lion, the Witch and the Wardrobe.* New York: Macmillan, 1970. Three children find their way into a magic land through the back door of a wardrobe.

LIFTON, BETTY JEAN. *The Silver Crane.* New York: Seabury, 1971. A ghostly silver crane suddenly appears on a moonlit pond.

LINDGREN, ASTRID. *Karlsson-on-the-Roof.* New York: Viking, 1971. This is the story of a little boy and his friend Karlsson, who is very clever, is extremely conceited, and best of all, can fly.

MENDOZA, GEORGES. *The Hunter, the Tick and the Gumberoo.* New York: Cowles, 1971. Hunting an evil creature, a hunter himself becomes the hunted in this eerie fantasy in the tradition of the Brothers Grimm.

NICKLESS, WILL. *Owlglass.* New York: John Day, 1966. This witty satire concerns a group of small woods animals who form a typically English fellowship club featuring storytelling by one member at each club meeting.

PHILLIPS, LOUIS. *The Man Who Stole the Atlantic Ocean.* Englewood Cliffs, N. J.: Prentice-Hall, 1971. Six-year-old Harry Frogfoot III is the hero of this fantasy in which the Atlantic Ocean is missing.

TAYLOR, THEODORE. *The Children's War.* Garden City, N. Y.: Doubleday, 1971. A fantasy of what might have happened if the Japanese had landed a strike force in Alaska in June 1942, this story revolves around a twelve-year-old boy.

TRESSELT, ALVIN. *The Beaver Pond.* Roger Duvoisin (ill.). This poetic story relates what happens to the beavers' pond and the part the pond plays in the lives of the many creatures of the woods and water.

WILLIAMS, JAY. *Philbert the Fearful.* New York: Norton, 1966. A fearful knight is the hero when his fellow knights rescue the emperor's daughter.

Grades 7–9

BACON, MARTHA. *The Third Road.* Boston: Little, Brown, 1971. A fantasy adventure begins when the Craven children are transported on the back of their grandmother's unicorn to the court of a Spanish *infanta.*

DE TREVINO, ELIZABETH BORTON. *Beyond the Gates of Hercules: A Tale of the Lost Atlantis.* New York: Farrar, Straus & Giroux, 1971. On one of the islands of the lost Atlantis, a girl with her mystical powers saves her people before their land sinks beneath the sea.

DRURY, ROGER. *The Finches' Fabulous Furnace.* Boston: Little, Brown, 1971. Complications harass the Finch family when they discover that their new house has a small but active volcano in its cellar.

More Science Fiction for Children

Kindergarten–Grade 3

SLOBODKIN, LOUIS. *The Three-Seated Space Ship.* New York: Macmillan, 1964. A nonsense explanation of the incredible speed that a spaceship is able to attain and the excitement of a one-hour tour of London are included in this story.

UNGERER, TOMI. *Moon Man.* New York: Harper & Row, 1967. Moon Man flies down to join the fun on earth.

WALTERS, HUGH. *Mission to Mercury.* New York: Criterion, 1965. When the wrong female twin stays on earth, tense situations develop among the five male astronauts going to Mercury.

WASSERMANN, SELMA, AND JACK WASSERMANN. *Moonbeam and Dan Starr.* Chicago: Benefic, 1966. Moonbeam the Chimpanzee takes a rocket flight.

Grades 4–6

ASIMOV, ISAAC. *The Best New Thing.* Cleveland: World Publishing, 1971. Isaac Asimov's first science fiction for young children introduces the concepts of space and gravity in story form.

BEATTY, JEROME. *Matthew Looney in the Outback.* Reading, Mass.: William R. Scott, 1969. Moonman Matthew Looney combines ingenuity and charm as he faces protestors from home and patriots from abroad.

BOVA, BEN. *The Many Worlds of Science Fiction.* New York: Dutton, 1971. This collection of stories ranges from the adventures of star travel to happenings on a college campus at the turn of the next century.

ERWIN, BETTY K. *The Summer Sleigh Ride.* Boston: Little, Brown, 1966. This story involves a time machine and the disappearance of one of four girl friends.

HUGHES, TED. *The Iron Giant.* New York: Harper & Row, 1968. An iron giant who eats metal is challenged by a horrifying monster from outer space.

LEE, ROBERT C. *The Day It Rained Forever.* Boston: Little, Brown, 1968. Mike and his friends stop the rainfall by destroying the professor's rain machine.

LESSER, MILTON. *Spacemen Go Home.* New York: Holt, Rinehart & Winston, 1961. A dangerous ex-spacepilot attempts to use force to retrieve earth's place among the worlds.

LORD, BEMAN. *The Day the Spaceship Landed.* New York: Walck, 1967. The encounter of a ten-year-old boy with visitors from outer space.

SILVERBERG, ROBERT (ed.). *Mind to Mind.* New York: Nelson, 1971. This is a collection of short stories by masters in the science fiction field.

______ (ed.). *The Science Fiction Bestiary: Nine Stories of Science Fiction.* New

York: Nelson, 1971. This collection of science fiction stories features animals such as gnurrs, hurkles, hokas, back bugs, and even a blue giraffe.

SUTTON, JEFF, AND JEAN SUTTON. *The Boy Who Had the Power.* New York: Putnam, 1971. A young boy finds a stone that launches him into space adventure.

WAHL, JAN. *The Furious Flycycle.* New York: Dell, 1968. A great inventor gives Melvin a mysterious pellet that turns his bike into a flying machine.

WALTERS, HUGH. *Journey to Jupiter.* New York: Criterion, 1966. Difficulties arise during a space probe to the planet Jupiter, and one of the astronauts maneuvers the rocket to avoid a collision.

WHITE, DALE. *Is Something Up There?* Garden City, N. Y.: Doubleday, 1968. This is a story of flying saucers and reported encounters with creatures from outer space.

WILLIAMS, JAY, AND R. ABRASHKIN. *Danny Dunn and the Automatic House.* New York: McGraw-Hill, 1965. The annual science and industry fair's major exhibit is Danny's idea.

———. *Danny Dunn and the Voice from Space.* New York: McGraw-Hill, 1967. Danny Dunn travels to England to investigate the beings from outer space.

WILSON, HAZEL. *Herbert's Space Trip.* New York: Knopf, 1965. Herbert convinces the beings on another planet that he does have intelligence.

Grades 7–9

BALLOU, ARTHUR. *Bound for Mars.* Boston: Little, Brown, 1970. Misfit George Foran conspires to stop the landing on Mars but the ship's commander handles the trouble expertly.

———. *Marooned in Orbit.* Boston: Little, Brown, 1968. An oxygen leak endangers the lives of the two men in a spaceship orbiting the moon.

BOVA, BEN. *Out of the Sun.* New York: Holt, Rinehart & Winston, 1968. A fighter bomber disintegrates on approaching an unknown bomb, and a scientist-detective is appointed to find out why.

KNIGHT, DAMON (ed.). *Worlds to Come.* New York: Harper & Row, 1967. These short stories are about man's exploration of outer space.

MANLEY, SEAN, AND GOGO LEWIS. *Ladies of Horror.* New York: Lothrop, Lee & Shepard, 1971. Fourteen stories of the occult and science fiction demonstrate how well women writers have contributed to the literature of the supernatural.

NORTON, ANDRÉ. *The Zero Stone.* New York: Viking, 1968. A mysterious stone from a long extinct world leads to space-age adventure.

SUTTON, JEAN, AND JEFF SUTTON. *The Programmed Man.* New York: Putnam, 1968. An agent of the galactic secret service races to a crashed spaceship destroyed in an effort to keep the secret of the N-bomb from the enemy.

WALTERS, HUGH. *Terror by Satellite.* New York: Criterion, 1964. An engineer with a secret transmitter controls an unbalanced scientist in command of a satellite observatory.

Further Reading for Teachers, Librarians, and Parents

BEREIT, VIRGINIA. "The Genre of Science Fiction," *Elementary English*, 46 (November 1969).

BRETNOR, REGINALD (ed.). *Modern Science Fiction. Its Meaning and Its Future.* New York: Coward-McCann, 1953.

GREEN, ROGER LANCELYN. *Into Other Worlds.* New York: Abelard-Schuman, 1958.

GREENLAW, M. JEAN. "A Study of the Impact of Technology on Human Value as Reflected in Modern Science Fiction for Children." Unpublished Ph.D. dissertation, Michigan State University, 1970.

HEINLEIN, ROBERT A. "Ray Guns and Rocket Ships," *Reading About Children's Literature.* E. R. Robinson (ed.). New York: David McKay, 1966.

HELSON, RAVENNA. "Fantasy and Self-Discovery," *The Horn Book*, 46, 2 (April 1970), 121–134.

MOSKOWITZ, SAMUEL. *Explorers of the Infinite: Shapers of Science Fiction.* Cleveland and New York: World Publishing, 1963.

———. *Seekers of Tomorrow: Masters of Modern Science Fiction.* Cleveland and New York: World Publishing, 1966.

Ghosts and More Ghosts by Robert Arthur, illustrated by Irv Docktor.

12 Adventure and Mystery

The Appeal of Adventure

Children of every age are ready at almost any time for an adventure story. Today, the very young child, by viewing television, can have adventures that take him back in time to the olden days or ahead in time to a wonderful world of make-believe. He can also find excitement in his world of today. Strange places across town as well as frontiers on land, in the air, or at the bottom of the ocean are ideal settings for adventure. Tales of Indians, pirates, pioneers, and explorers describe hair-raising exploits. Characters who get lost in the mountains, on the desert, in a cave, or at sea share their adventures through modern media.

The ingredients that make good adventure stories make exciting reading. The first demand that young readers make is that the story has action—the more action the better the story. The characters need to be real, and they must be true to their roles once they are established. They must get into one predicament after another—predicaments that come about either by the characters' own doing or through situations over which they have no control.

Outstanding authors have sensed the hold that adventure stories have on children and have put together the ingredients that make a good adventure story in various ways. Many of these adventure stories have become the favorites of several generations.

Early Writers of Adventure

Daniel Defoe (1660–1731) and Jonathan Swift (1667–1745) were two great writers who wrote deliberately for adults. It is an interesting facet of the history of children's literature that Defoe's *Robinson Crusoe* (1719) and Jonathan Swift's *Gulliver's Travels* (1726) were usurped by young readers as if these stories had been written solely for them.

If we consider the ponderously written didactic material that had been the literary diet of young readers for years, it becomes obvious why children welcomed these two literary masterpieces as wonderful adventure stories. These stories have lived through the centuries and have been translated into almost every known language. They have been adapted, edited, shortened, cut into scenes, and made into dramatic episodes. The acquaintance that most children have with these two great books is through the adaptations and excerpts in their school readers.

Robinson Crusoe

How Defoe came to write *Robinson Crusoe* (25) makes an interesting story. An account had been published of the sojourn of a sailor, Alexander Selkirk, who had run away to sea and joined a privateering expedition to the island of Juan Fernandez off the coast of Chile. A ship deserter, Fernandez had lived alone for five years from 1704 to 1709 until he was rescued by privateers and taken back to England. How he had survived for five years was the question of the day.

The story of Juan Fernandez struck Defoe's fancy and sparked his imagination. He must have kept Juan Fernandez' story in mind, embroidering it until finally ten years later it emerged as *Robinson Crusoe.* How Robinson Crusoe survived is spelled out in one loosely joined episode after another. Shipwrecked and stranded alone on an island, Crusoe describes how he was faced with man's age-old problems of providing himself with shelter, food, and clothing. How he copes with these problems is woven into an interesting, exciting, and suspenseful story.

Gulliver's Travels

Jonathan Swift, one of the great English satirists, wrote *Gulliver's Travels* (70) for adults as a satire of the human race. Published in 1726, the original title was *Travels into Several Remote Nations of the World in Four Parts by Lemuel Gulliver.*

The first-person narrator gives this imaginative story a ring of authenticity for young readers. The authenticity is furthered by Gulliver's giving the exact time of day and date of happenings as well as exact locations in terms of latitude.

At the beginning of Part I, Gulliver swims ashore after a shipwreck

Gulliver's Travels retold by Padraic Colum, illustrated by Willy Pogany.

and finds himself in the land of the Lilliputians, where one situation after another charges the imagination and brings humor to the story. Gulliver's second journey in Part II takes him to Brobdingnag. In contrast to the little people of Lilliput, the inhabitants of Brobdingnag are giants. Not all of Gulliver's experiences with the people of Brobdingnag are as pleasant as his experiences with the people of Lilliput, but young readers thoroughly enjoy the elaborate exaggerations about the giants. The last two parts of the book continue with surprises, adventure, and humor, taking Gulliver to the flying island of Laputa and the country of the Houyhnhnms, the wise, talking horses. Very often the editions for young readers are limited to Gulliver's voyages to Lilliput and Brobdingnag.

Robinsonades

The popularity of Defoe's *Robinson Crusoe* was the impetus for a flood of Crusoe stories. The pattern of the stories was always much the same: The setting was the sea, a shipwreck, and a deserted island, where pitted against nature, savages, and wild beasts man fended for himself and still survived. Of course, there were variations to the pattern. The motif of man against nature fit well into the philosophy of the times. Crusoe stories sprang up in Germany and France as well as in England and North America. The French literati gave these stories the label *Robinsonades.*

One of the most popular *Robinsonades* was *The Swiss Family Robinson* (81) by Johann Wyss, pastor and almoner of the Swiss troops. The book was published by Zürich in two parts in 1812 and 1813. The full title of Wyss' book was *The Swiss Family Robinson or Adventures on a Desert Island.* It was originally written in German and was translated into French and afterward into English. Wyss wrote the tale for the entertainment of young readers after the style of Defoe, to whom he was indebted for many of his ideas.

The story is built around the experiences of a shipwrecked family who are deserted by the captain and the crew of the vessel on which they were passengers. They finally reach land in safety and are extremely inventive in the use they make of everything that comes to hand. The family thrives and prospers for several years until, finally, a ship arrives at the island, and they are able to communicate with the mainland. By this time they have become so happy with their island home that they decide not to leave it. Wyss left the book unfinished, which prompted a number of sequels giving varying accounts of the continued existence of the family.

Two other early writers of adventure stories were Captain Frederick Marryat (1792–1848) and James Fenimore Cooper (1789–1851). Marryat wrote to amuse his children, whereas Cooper wrote for adults. However, as in the case of the writings of Defoe and Swift, young readers took over Cooper's writings and still enjoy them as if they had been written especially for children. Both Marryat and Cooper wrote from experience.

Captain Frederick Marryat

Frederick Marryat entered sea service as a midshipman at the age of fourteen, an age at which boys of that time often went to sea. He used his experiences with the sea as the background for his stories. When he realized that young readers were enjoying his writing, he began to write directly for them. He was a keen observer of human behavior. Written in a lively style, his stories move rapidly and his characters are well portrayed. His stories are interspersed with humorous incidents.

Marryat's first story, *Masterman Ready, or the Wreck of the Pacific* (1841), like Johann Wyss' *Swiss Family Robinson,* showed the influence of Defoe's *Robinson Crusoe.* The plot moves rapidly in an interesting and amusing manner. The many experiences of Tommy Seagrave, an incorrigible rascal, enliven the story.

Masterman Ready was followed by *The Children of the New Forest* (49) and *The Little Savage.* These stories were also popular with young readers.

James Fenimore Cooper

James Fenimore Cooper, an American writer, grew up in Cooperstown, New York, a town founded by his father, where Indians were the Coopers' next-door neighbors. After several years at Yale College, Cooper went to sea, where he served as a cabin boy, and later joined the navy. Retiring from the navy, he settled down with his family in Cooperstown and devoted his time to writing. A prolific writer, he turned out fifty books, many of them as popular today as when they were first published.

His *Leatherstocking Saga* (20) is still widely read by precocious children. The tales include *The Pioneers* (1823), *The Last of the Mohicans* (1826), *The Prairie* (1827), *The Pathfinder* (1840), and *The Deerslayer* (1841). They tell the story of Leather stocking, a frontiersman, and his Indian friend Chingachgook, a Mohican chief.

Of the *Leatherstocking Saga, The Last of the Mohicans* is probably the most widely read in this country and abroad. The story is built around Natty Bumppo and Chingachgook; the action takes place in upper New York State during the French and Indian War. The emphasis is on plot, and the suspense is convincingly maintained. It is a fresh, virile plot full of vigor that appeals to both adults and young readers. Cooper is generous in his use of words and details in describing situations and portraying characters in a way that fascinates

The Deerslayer by J. F. Cooper, illustrated by Reginald Marsh.

the reader. Where there is tragedy, it is convincing because of its inevitability. Through his writing Cooper re-created the history of our country as it related to European powers, Indians, and settlers during the eighteenth century.

Robert Michael Ballantyne

Born in Edinburgh, Scotland, Robert Michael Ballantyne (1823–1894) started writing adventure stories at the age of thirty. At sixteen years of age he served as a clerk with the Hudson's Bay Company in Canada; his experiences in Canada and his travels to Norway and Africa provided rich material for him to use later in his stories. A productive writer, Ballantyne wrote about eighty books. *The Young Fur Traders* (1856), Ballantyne's first book, and *Ungava Bob, A Tale of Eskimo Land* (1857), both dealing with the Hudson's Bay Company, were very successful; the latter book is still being read. Perhaps Ballantyne's best-known and most liked story is *Coral Island* (6), written in 1857.

William Henry Kingston

Another writer of adventure stories is William Henry Kingston (1814–1880). Kingston spent most of his youth in Portugal where his father was in business. An extremely prolific writer, Kingston wrote 150 books for children in addition to the novels and travel books that he produced. He is best remembered for his children's books, such as *Rival Crusoes.*

Richard Henry Dana, Jr.

After his second year at Harvard, Richard Henry Dana, Jr. (1815–1882) suffered eyesight damage from an attack of measles, and he was forced to give up his studies. In an effort to improve his health, Dana went to sea as an ordinary seaman on the brig *Pilgrim,* which went around Cape Horn to California, and in two years returned aboard the *Alert.* Four years later he was graduated from Harvard Law School.

While doing service at sea, Dana kept a diary. In 1840 the diary was published as *Two Years Before the Mast* (23). No aspect of a sailor's life was omitted. Dana presented a realistic account of the monotony, cruelty, hardships, and daily experiences of men in the merchant marine. His writing was in such a sympathetic style that it aroused a great deal of public interest in the lot of the sailor. First published more than one hundred years ago, *Two Years Before the Mast* is still popular with older children.

Robert Louis Stevenson

A great writer who became famous for his adventure stories is Robert Louis Stevenson (1850–1894). He wrote for his own enjoyment as well as for the enjoyment of others. He believed that if a story is good, it should appeal to all ages. However, he was most interested in reaching young readers, particularly with a story like *Treasure Island.* Stevenson seemed to revel in breaking the pall of didacticism that still weighed heavily on children's literature and in giving boys and girls a story that would satisfy their interests and encourage them to ask for more.

Stevenson was born in Edinburgh, Scotland, and later lived and died in Apia, Western Samoa. The Samoans called him *Tusitala,* which means "Teller of Tales."

An Island Adventure, published in 1878, describes his first trip to Europe. There he met Mrs. Fanny Osbourne, an American woman whom he followed to California and married in 1880. They lived for a time in a mining town. Before returning to Scotland, Stevenson wrote *Silverado Squatters,* based upon his experiences in the town.

Although Stevenson is still remembered for many of his works including *An Inland Voyage* (65), *Dr. Jekyll and Mr. Hyde* (64), *Kidnapped* (66), the *Master of Ballantrae: A Winter's Tale* (67), and *A Child's Garden of Verses* (63), it was with *Treasure Island* that he found his way into the hearts of children and adults.

Treasure Island (69) had an interesting beginning. One day, hoping to amuse his stepson, Lloyd Osbourne, Stevenson idly drew a rough,

Treasure Island by R. L. Stevenson, illustrated by S. van Abbé.

water-color map of an island. Out of this accidental beginning, the story *Treasure Island* came into being. It was first published serially in the magazine *Young Folks,* from October 1, 1881, to January 28, 1882, under the title of *The Sea Cook.* The editor changed the title from *The Sea Cook* to *Treasure Island.* It had little success when run serially, but when it appeared in book form in 1883 its success was phenomenal with adults as well as with young readers.

It is interesting to look at the ingredients of this story, which has not only held its own for ninety years, but has also gained in popularity. Stevenson states what effect he thinks an adventure should have on the reader (68):

> In anything fit to be called by the name of reading, the process itself should be absorbing and voluptuous; we should gloat over a book, be rapt clean out of ourselves, and rise from the perusal, our minds filled with the busiest, kaleidoscopic dance of images, incapable of sleep . . . , and the story, if it be a story, repeat itself in a thousand coloured pictures to the eye. It was for this pleasure that we read so closely, and loved our books . . . in the bright troubled period of boyhood. [P. 247]

In his inimitable style Stevenson tells how the ingredients for a story should be put together (68):

> The great creative writer shows us the realization and the apotheosis of the day-dreams of common men. His stories may be nourished with the realities of life, but their true mark is to satisfy the nameless longings of the reader, and to obey the ideal laws of the day-dream. . . . Crusoe recoiling from the footprint, Achilles shouting over against the Trojans, Ulysses bending the great bow, Christian running with his fingers in his ears, these are each culminating moments in the legend, and each has been printed on the mind's eye forever. [Pp. 255–256]

Stevenson's word portraits of his characters are memorable. One of the most outstanding in *Treasure Island* (69) is that of the Captain's arrival at the Admiral Ben Bow Inn. Jim Hawkins, son of the innkeeper, is speaking:

> I remember him as if it were yesterday, as he came plodding to the inn door, his sea chest following behind him in a handbarrow; a tall, strong, heavy, nut-brown man; his tarry pigtail falling over the shoulders of his soiled blue coat; his hands ragged and scarred, with black broken nails; and the sabre cut across one cheek, a dirty, livid white.
>
> . . .
>
> His stories [the Captain's] were what frightened people worst of all. Dreadful stories they were; about hanging, and walking the plank, and storms at sea, and the Dry Tortugas, and wild deeds and places on the Spanish Main. [Pp. 17–18]

Treasure Island by R. L. Stevenson, illustrated by S. van Abbé.

It is only natural that Jim Hawkins, a central figure in the tale, should become involved in the mystery to be woven through the story. The suspense is sustained by such disclosures as:

> Every day when he [the Captain] came back from his stroll, he would ask if any seafaring men had gone by along the road. . . .
>
> . . .
>
> He [the Captain] had taken me aside one day, and promised me a silver fourpenny on the first of every month if I would only keep my "weather eye open for a seafaring man with one leg" and let him know the minute he appeared. [Pp. 19–20]

One senses the alliance Stevenson builds between nature and action immediately. After failing to get help from the townspeople following the sudden death of the Captain, Jim Hawkins and his mother start back to the inn. Stevenson creates an eerie atmosphere with fog, the moon, and darkness.

> My heart was beating finely when we two set forth in the cold night upon this dangerous venture. A full moon was beginning to rise and peered redly through the upper edges of the fog, and this increased our haste, for it was plain, before we came forth again, that all would be as bright as day, and our departure exposed to the eyes of many watchers. [P. 44]

It would be difficult to find a young reader or an old one who fails to be captured by the buried treasure, pirates, strange noises, seafaring, the resourceful and likable young hero, and a villain designed to outdo all villains in Stevenson's *Treasure Island.*

Rudyard Kipling

Shortly after Robert Louis Stevenson's success in the field of literature, Rudyard Kipling (1865–1936) arrived on the literary scene. Born in Bombay, India, the son of the director of an art school, Kipling became renowned throughout the world as a writer of prose and poetry. He received the Nobel Prize for Literature in 1907.

Kipling left one of the most beautiful autobiographies (43) to be found in literature. As the heading to the first chapter, he wrote, "Give me the first six years of a child's life and you can have the rest" (p. 3). His belief that the first six years of a child's life are the most important colored both his later years and his writings. His autobiography reveals a man who was extremely sensitive to the sounds, colors, and sights that made up his world and who had keen perceptiveness to the ways of man and beast. No richer heritage was there than India's for a storyteller interested in legends and folk tales. Throughout his life Kipling kept his love of imagery and metaphor.

Plain Tales from the Hills, a collection of stories, was Kipling's first contribution to literature. The stories were praised by some critics and damned by others, but all recognized something in his writing that was out of the ordinary.

Kipling told his stories both in prose and in poetry. The story of *Gunga Din,* an Indian boy who is shot while carrying water to British soldiers in the thick of battle, is expressed through poetry. The degradation and hanging of a British soldier is told in one of the *Barrack Room Ballads* (40) titled "Danny Deever." Countless other poems by Kipling also tell a story. Young readers enjoy the lively, swinging, robust rhythm of his poetry.

Kim (42), one of Kipling's best novels, deals with the adventures of an Irish orphan who grows up in the native quarters of Lahore. He meets a Tibetan lama and joins him in his search through India for the River of Immortality. Later, Kim is sent to a college in Lucknow, where he is groomed for the British Secret Service. The atmosphere of India—its bazaars and its crowded millions—flavors the story. The characterization of Kim builds an outstanding adventure story.

Another adventure by Kipling, equally popular with boys and girls, is *Captains Courageous* (41), the author's contribution to the outstanding sea stories in children's literature. The tale is set on the Grand Banks of Newfoundland and is built around the son of an American millionaire, Harvey Cheyne, who is rescued by a fishing schooner. From being a petted boy leading an idle, selfish life, Harvey changes into a physically fit, self-disciplined, self-reliant young man.

Modern Adventure Stories

Furious Moose of the Wilderness (44) by Jim Kjelgaard is an exciting story of the North Woods. Pete, a young trapper, vows to kill a monstrous moose that kept him in a tree all night. In killing the moose, he thereby saves the life of Hailey Zulski, a young Polish refugee.

The adventures of the Deane children as they learn to accept their island home where they have been sent to live with their cantankerous old grandfather are what make *Home on Star Island* (75) by Christina M. Welch an enjoyable story. The beauty of the remote Isles of Shoals and the adventures of the children are well described.

Soon after his arrival in Yorkshire, Tom's father is killed, and Tom's only choice is to agree to apprentice himself to a local clothier in Phyllis Bentley's *The Adventures of Tom Leigh* (10). The author has woven into this fast-moving story a great deal of information about the process of weaving and about the life and social customs of the times.

The Year of the Big Cat (26) by Lew Dietz is a fast-moving North Woods adventure set around 1900. Fifteen-year-old Ben and his dog Old Nick search for an aging renegade cougar.

Danger on Shadow Mountain (59) by Marian Rumsey is a fast-paced story with its setting in the Northwest. It relates how Pete visits his brother in a wilderness area and finds himself involved in an abduction and exciting rescue operation.

Based on fact, *Flight Toward Home* (27) by Wolfgang Ecke is a tense novel that tells the story of a twelve-year-old boy who tries to flee to West Germany, having run away from an orphanage in the Russian zone.

Storms, sea engagements, murder, and hidden treasure provide exciting reading in *Under the Pirate Flag* (38) by Laurence Hyde. There is adventure in store for Stephen Corruthers, a Nova Scotia lad of fifteen, when he stows away on a pirate frigate. After many exciting adventures, Stephen returns home a hero.

The organization of a ship's crew, the description of their duties, and the refreshingly human qualities of the first mate are skillfully used to support the action in the story *Trial Trip* (3) by Richard Armstrong. A sixteen-year-old, lonely orphan, who goes to sea as a galley boy, meets an old schoolmate who with determination succeeds in restoring the orphan's morale and ambition.

The real feeling for the prairie country of Nebraska is portrayed in *Growing Up in the Wild West* (17) by Allen P. Clark (Charles van Doren). The story is an account of life in the days of the cattle ranchers and early homesteaders and the competition between the white men and the Indians for the buffalo and prairie land. The story is told by Jackie who lives in a sod house and by the Indian boy Little Dog. The friendship of the two boys ripens into appreciation and understanding as they grow to manhood.

Salvage Diver (8), an adventure story by Zachary Bell, is about two young Seminoles whose charter cruiser is hired by a salvage outfit to hunt for sunken ships. The story is set off the Florida Keys in the undersea world of reefs and marine life.

Pioneering in Michigan during the period following the Civil War is portrayed in *The Time of the Wolves* (24) by Verne T. Davis. Two brothers twelve and fourteen years old winter the cattle on swamp grass two day's distance from the farm. The winter brings dangers—blizzards, panthers, and a pack of wolves—climaxed when the boys' father and neighbors meet the defenseless boys and the herd just as the wolves are attacking.

Robert Silverberg's vivid descriptions of Egypt, archaeological operations, and Egyptian art and history make *The Mask of Akhnaten* (62) a fascinating story in which historical facts and fiction are interwoven. Fifteen-year-old Tom Lloyd and his newspaper-reporter uncle join an archaeological expedition in the upper Nile Valley. The dig begins as a routine excavation of an ancient trading post, but events take an unexpected twist.

Dive to Danger (37) by Oyvind Holmvik and Hans Faye-Lund is a tale of courage and danger translated from the Norwegian. A group of young friends are exposed to an intensive course in skin diving and become involved in a hunt for pirate treasure and a scheme of international espionage.

Adventure and mystery involve the teen-agers in a South Seas tale, *Road Under the Sea* (56), by Ruth Park. Polynesian legends are woven into the story to help the reader better understand some of the ways and attitudes of the natives. Discovery of the underwater ruins of some ancient civilization, including valuable artifacts, becomes public knowledge through the efforts of Nancy, an Australian who grew up in the islands; Phoebe and Cass, an English girl and her younger brother; and Pussy, a native boy who has been Nancy's lifelong friend.

Torpedo Run (79) by Robb White is a well-written, fast-moving adventure story of a PT boat in World War II. The characters are well drawn, and the crew emerges as a tight-knit fighting group. Mature readers interested in the navy and war stories will enjoy this exciting adventure.

Oliver Finch, a twelve-year-old, is kidnapped and taken aboard a pirate ship because of a supernatural power he is supposed to possess in *The Ghost in the Noonday Sun* (31) by Sid Fleischman. Because Oliver was born on the stroke of midnight, Captain Scratch believes that he can see ghosts and can help locate a buried treasure on a tropical island. Oliver has many adventures and learns about storms, treasures, ghosts, and pirates. He finally returns safely to his New England home after having turned the tables on Captain Scratch. It all adds up to a tongue-in-cheek, robust pirate story.

Teen-age Pete and his younger brother sign on as crew to bring a forty-foot ketch from Hawaii to California. When the captain has an accident, Pete assumes command. The story, *Seawind from Hawaii* (55) by Patrick O'Connor, is filled with suspense as man struggles against the forces of nature.

The Woolacombe Bird (74) by Ann Welch is a thrilling story about a thirteen-year-old boy and his twelve-year-old sister living in a village in 1588 and assisting a youthful inventor as he secretly builds a mysterious wood and canvas bird, patterned after Leonardo da Vinci's design. Their adventures and experiences in gliding off the cliffs of Woolacombe Sands and the distrust and resentment of the superstitious witch-hunting villagers make an exciting tale.

The Secret of Rocky Ridge (13) by Gladys B. Bond and F. B. Bertram relates the adventures of Alison Reed, who spends her summers in a logging camp in northern Idaho. The story carries the flavor of the out of doors.

Contemporary New Mexico is the setting for the fast-moving adventure story *Please Stand Clear of the Apache Arrows* (77) by Budd Westreich. While visiting an anthropologist and his daughter, teen-age Derek gets mixed up in an exciting mystery that involves caves, buried treasure, and a seventeenth-century diary. The descriptions of the New Mexico landscape are vivid and the historical facts are accurate.

The Saga of Shorty Gone (76) by Bob Wells is an entertaining basketball story starring little Shorty Gone and big Slats Thayer. Shorty, Slats, their teammates, and the computer, Chester, have the hilarious kinds of adventures that appeal to sports fans.

An involved adventure story for more mature readers, *No Man's Land* (78) by Robb White involves Garth, young marine toxicologist, who is engaged in researching lethal poisons produced by certain species of sea life off an island in the South Pacific. Garth becomes involved in a search for lost jewels and is urged to leave the island because of native taboos.

Richard Armstrong has selected and edited twelve stories about buried treasure by the authors of seafaring books for boys, *Treasures and Treasure Hunters* (4). Included in the collection are excerpts from tales by such outstanding writers as Edgar Allan Poe, H. G. Wells, Victor Hugo, and Robert Louis Stevenson.

Finders Keepers: Stories of Treasure Seekers (30) by Phyllis Fenner is a selection of amusing adventure and suspense stories about treasure hunts written by such outstanding writers as Stephen Vincent Benét, Ellery Queen, Dorothy Cottrell, and Elizabeth D. de Trevino. Each story provides exciting reading for young addicts of adventure stories.

Neil and Swede at first think of the machine as a trick gadget, as something to use for fun in Keith Robertson's *The Money Machine* (58), until one of the people they have fooled calls the Secret Service and the boys learn that a counterfeiter is actually at work in the area. By following a series of clues the two boys find that an elderly friend is being used as a dupe by innocently printing copies of rare stamps for a not-so-innocent nephew.

An unusual and well-written medieval adventure story, *Merlin's Mistake* (54) by Robert Newman revolves around sixteen-year-old Brian, son of a knight supposedly killed while fighting in the Holy Land. Brian goes on a quest with Tertius, a young page endowed by Merlin with only future knowledge.

Albatross (2) by Richard Armstrong is a stark, realistic story about four boys who face danger because of their inability to trust any adult. Seventeen-year-old Arthur Judd is picked up on a life raft after a devastating experience with three of his friends in a hijacked ketch, the *Albatross.* The boys have discovered a hoard of pirate treasure buried on the island of San Salvadore hundreds of years ago. Excitement runs high as the boys desert their ship.

Adventure, suspense, and danger travel along with two teen-age boys in *A Long Way to Whiskey Creek* (7) by Patricia Beatty. The setting of the story is Texas in the year 1879. Parker Quiney, his dog J. E. B. Stewart, and his companion Nate Graber travel from Cottonwood, Texas, to Whiskey Creek, a distance of over four hundred miles. They must perform the grim mission of bringing home for proper burial the body of Parker's older brother, who was killed in a gun battle. Frequently at odds with each other, the two boys together face and overcome many obstacles. They meet all kinds of people on the journey: some kind, some cruel. The delineation of the characters is excellent. The plot shows extensive research and the use of accurate dialect and terminology on the part of the author.

Mystery

Some of the ingredients that make good adventure are to be found in a good mystery story. A haunted house from which strange sounds emerge, where objects move around without help from humans, and where things mysteriously disappear is always a good setting for a mystery story. A lost or stolen deed to a mine or a treasure can provide motivation for a search. False clues that lead to nowhere add to the suspense, and an eccentric, mysterious, or villainous character also contributes to the building of a good mystery. A mystery story most often presents a problem to be solved and a hunt for clues to solve the problem.

Older boys and girls like to have a bit of romance flavoring their adventure and mystery stories. As they move toward adolescence, they begin to show interest in the opposite sex. This interest is just awakening in some; in others it is an all-consuming passion. Most, however, like to meet in the books they read boys and girls their age or a little older who are interested in each other. Authors of children's stories are sensitive to this interest and have written a wealth of stories filled with adventure and mystery with a sprinkling of romance.

Three children and a dog join forces in a mystery story by Mary C. Jane, *Mystery in Longfellow Square* (39). The children unravel the mystery of an intruder in Miss Goddard's library as well as another one in the old church belfry. The setting for the story is the famous Longfellow Square in Portland, Maine.

A villain, a lost treasure, and young boys intent on finding the treasure combine to make a bang-up mystery story, *The Mystery of Arroyo Seco* (60) by Jessica Ryan. An eccentric old lady has the key to the lost treasure. Only through a series of exciting incidents do the boys succeed in rescuing her and the lost treasure.

The Deer-Jackers (29) by Alf Evers is a story of deer-jacking in the Catskill Mountains of New York and of a young amateur detective, his cousin, and his dog who all help to solve the mystery of deer carcasses, the hideout, the masks, phony reporters, the scientist, and the strange actions of an uncle and his son who disappeared. Suspense is maintained until the end when the case is finally solved.

Two eleven- and twelve-year-old boys and their families have exciting experiences while living at Ship's Cove, Nova Scotia, a location of many ancient shipwrecks, in *Hurricane Treasure* (12) by Clare Bice. It was believed that treasure had been buried just offshore of Gull Island. Hurricanes and many adventures lend excitement to this mystery story.

Trail to Lone Canyon (71) by Gus Tavo is an exciting story for middle-grade children. A city boy and his cousin, who has grown up on a cattle ranch, become close friends through their discovery of mountain gold that leads them on a trail of mystery, adventure, and near-disaster.

Trail to Lone Canyon by Gus Tavo, illustrated by Gil Walker.

The Riddle of the Ring (1) by Karin Anckarsvard is a mystery for teenagers. Tommi, aged fourteen, and her boyfriend Henrik search for a lost ring and stumble across some stolen jewels, all of which leads to the arrest of the thief. The lost ring comes to light in a most unexpected way during a get-together of classmates and a game of charades. The emphasis is placed on the relationships among individual students, attitudes of children, and classroom scenes.

The mysterious appearance of a huge, half-starved, odd-looking dog in the little town of Aberfyne, Scotland, is the basis for William MacKellar's *A Dog Like No Other* (45). The dog brings luck to his young owner, Robbie Duncan, in helping to solve the mystery of the famous lost sword of Bonnie Prince Charlie.

The Mystery of the Buried Indian Mask (18) by Margaret Goff Clark centers around an archaeological dig on a farm in New York State. Into the story is woven information about Indian artifacts and archaeology.

Built around the theme "judge not until the facts are known" is the story of young Pete who becomes friendly with Ivan, the houseboat boy, in Lois Trimble Benedict's story *Canalboat Mystery* (9). Canalers mean trouble to Pete's parents and to the townspeople, and, as a result, Pete's faith and confidence in his friend are hard to defend. The human relationships are well portrayed in this setting on the Erie Canal during the time when boats were drawn by horses.

Malcolm Nelson's eagerness for adventure is more than satisfied when he and his friend Debbie discover a tunnel that leads to a hidden cave, complete with waterfalls and an underground lake. The setting provides the perfect situation for Mabel Sears Meaker's mystery *The Secret of Hollow Hill* (50). With a maximum of action, each chapter ends on a note of suspense.

Fourteen-year-old Eben Hall, a Texan by birth, is nevertheless very proud of his New England seafaring ancestors. When Eben is sent to live with his Uncle Silas, an expert lobster fisherman, he discovers to his dismay that he is subject to seasickness. He cannot help with the fishing but is able to make himself useful in other ways and, best of all, he solves the mystery of the lobster thief in *The Threatening Fog* (73) by Leon Ware.

In Jean Bothwell's story *The Mystery Clock* (15) time is something Benny cannot seem to use properly, so he decides to make a clock. Benny becomes so proficient that he is called on to solve the mystery concerning the grandfather clock that had stopped running about the time its owner's father died.

A nine-year-old girl goes to live with two maiden aunts in a spooky house on San Francisco Bay. A pipe-smoking ghost plays a mysterious role in *The Mystery of the Swan Ballet* (35) by Shyrle Hacker.

Danger on the Ski Trails (80) by Zita L. Wright is about a group of high-school students belonging to a ski club. Mystery abounds: Skis are stolen, a towrope is cut, the clubhouse is ransacked, and trails are tampered with. All evidence points to a club caretaker. Pat, one of the girls, and three other members of the ski club do some sleuthing and discover the real culprit.

In *Broom Adelaide* (33) by Barbara C. Freeman the young Grand Duchess Adelaide discovers a small red fox on her window sill. Adelaide is sure she is dreaming when the fox tells her that he flew up to her window sill on a broom. It turns out that it is not a dream but the beginning of a series of amazing adventures that reveal the evil power of Adelaide's feared and hated governess. It also explains the disappearance of the gold from the royal treasury.

A restless ghost, a painter in Holland during the time of Rembrandt, and a tricky embezzler who encourages crimes appear in three very separate spooky stories in *The Restless Ghost: Three Stories by Leon Garfield* (34) by Leon Garfield. The intrigue in each of the stories makes suspenseful reading.

Detective story fans will enjoy *The Mystery of the Talking Skull* (5) by Robert Arthur. Jupiter, one of the Investigators, buys a talking skull at an auction. The three young Investigators have an exciting time solving its secrets.

Nothing Said (14) by Lucy Maria Boston is a short, beautifully written story with an air of mystery and magic. A week's visit to the home of her mother's friend in an isolated old cottage by the side of a rock-strewn river turns out to be quite an experience for a little Londoner.

The Restless Ghost by Leon Garfield, illustrated by Saul Lambert.

An old Confederate fort half submerged in a swamp near New Orleans is the perfect setting for John Foster's mystery *Marco and the Sleuth Hound* (32). Marco and his friend Sally start out on a vacation adventure that becomes a contest of wits with criminals and ends when the children retrieve a fortune in Confederate gold.

A teen-age reporter exposes some unsavory secrets in a typical small town when he begins investigating an old mystery that had led to the supposed suicide of his predecessor in Ernie Rydberg's well-told *The Yellow Line* (61).

The Mystery Man (22) by Scott Corbett is a fast-moving story full of suspense. Recuperating from a broken leg, young Tod Emmet visits his uncle's resort inn. Tod encounters an unexpected guest and the arrival of a strange package leads to a treasure hunt.

On his way to deliver money that he and his friends have collected for charity, Geoffrey is robbed by a supposed blind man in Paul Berna's story *A Truckload of Rice* (11). With the help of Commissioner Sinet and a goldfish clue, the pickpocket is apprehended.

The seven or eight families who live on Dove Square in London are the heroes of *Battle of St. George Without* (46) by Janet McNeill. The once elegant homes are slated for demolition. The old church, no longer being used, is boarded up. The children discover that the church is being vandalized by a bunch of crooks. Excitement runs high as the children help to discover the crooks.

Janet McNeill added a sequel to the *Battle of St. George Without* in another exciting mystery tale, *Goodbye, Dove Square* (47). It relates how some of the characters who have moved out of Dove Square return for a visit to find themselves threatened by a mysterious, unpleasant salesman.

The eight members of the Evans family decide to move to the city of Seattle, in order to find a house big enough for all of them, in Betty K. Erwin's story *Go to the Room of the Eyes* (28). Suspense begins when they find that their new home had been used as the setting for a treasure hunt by an earlier family. Every member of the Evans family becomes involved in the mysteries that surround his new home.

Joanne, a Mariner Scout, and a sister scout find adventure and mystery when they visit an island in the Bahamas in *The Secret of the Sunken Treasure* (72) by Marcella Thum. They unexpectedly find themselves involved in a search for a sunken treasure.

Diamonds Are More Trouble (21), also by Scott Corbett, is a lively mystery story about a young lawyer and his rich aunt. Action begins when the aunt commissions her nephew to bring a diamond necklace from the bank to her private island. The young lawyer becomes involved in escapades with a renegade uncle-by-marriage, a couple of escaped convicts, and a pretty girl.

The Mystery of the Giant Giraffe (19) by Ruth P. Collins has its setting in an oasis in the Sahara Desert where Sandy and his amateur archaeologist father are investigating an ancient rock painting. The natives are unfriendly and try to get them to leave, but Zora, an old chief's daughter, helps Sandy to discover the explanation of the mystery.

The Haunted Night (57) by Joan Phipson is a frightening story of four girls who encounter a mystery when they have to spend an apprehensive night alone in a haunted country house.

The Sandy Shoes Mystery (53) by Elizabeth Mooney is a fast-moving story set on a Caribbean island. Emily and her brother solve the mystery of some disappearing jewels.

The plot of *The Ghost of Crabtree Hall* (52) by Evelyn Minshull proves again that haunted houses make good settings for mystery stories. The book features the twins Jimmer and Jill, whose family moves into a rambling, run-down country home that was once an inn. The house may be haunted by the ghost of Senator Crabtree, the former owner, who disappeared mysteriously along with a priceless coin collection.

The Mysterious Bender Bones (51) by Susan Meyers is a light-hearted story about a boy's efforts to earn $200 quickly in order to buy a boxer pup. His efforts involve digging up some old bones, a deep mystery, and lots of detective work that all lead up to a hilarious climax.

In *The Inway Investigators or the Mystery at MacCracken's Place* (82) by Jane Yolen ten-year-old David and his friends use an old house as a meeting place. When someone buys the house and builds a concrete wall around it, the "Investigators" decide to find out what's going on behind the wall. The disappearance of David's dog sends the Investigators into action. The result is that they not only rescue David's dog but also break up a criminal ring involved in stolen pets.

Alfred Hitchcock has edited a collection of eleven stories that stress detection rather than violence or horror in *Alfred Hitchcock's Daring Detectives* (36). Among the authors whose stories are featured are Agatha Christie, Erle Stanley Gardner, Ellery Queen, and McKinley Cantor.

The setting of *Spice Island Mystery* (16) by Betty Cavanna is an island in the Caribbean Sea. Following her high school education in New England, Marcy returns to her island home where she unravels a mystery involving smugglers.

New Tenants (48) by Margaret M. MacPherson is set on the Isle of Skye. Liz Shearer's father is the only member of his family who is optimistic about their move from a slum in Glasgow to a croft (a small farm) that his uncle has willed him. Although Liz begins to enjoy life on the croft, she mistrusts a neighbor, Danny Ross. Liz goes through a frightening experience as she exposes Danny's scheme to defraud the Shearers.

Extending Experiences for the Reader

1. Select several of Robert Louis Stevenson's word portraits in *Treasure Island* (69) to read to a group.
2. Select an adventure story and analyze the steps in the plot.
3. Read a *Robinsonade* and compare it with Defoe's *Robinson Crusoe* (25).
4. Read from Kipling's *Barrack Room Ballads* (40) to the class.
5. Review one story from James Fenimore Cooper's *Leatherstocking Saga* (20) for the class.
6. Play a recording of Rudyard Kipling's stories to the class.
7. Discuss the ingredients of an adventure story.
8. Select a mystery story and analyze the steps in the plot.
9. Read the beginnings of a mystery story to the class and have members predict the steps in the plot and the solution of the mystery.

Extending Experiences for Children

1. List the ingredients that make a good adventure story.
2. Review your favorite adventure story for the class.
3. Select an adventure story and diagram the plot.
4. Write a sketch of Robert Louis Stevenson's life.
5. Make a model in clay of one of the characters in Stevenson's *Treasure Island* (69).
6. Dress as characters from Stevenson's *Treasure Island.* Plan and present, in costume, skits dramatizing a number of particularly exciting situations in the story.
7. Select passages that set the mood for the action in *Treasure Island* and share them with the class.
8. Share with the class a list of colorful words Stevenson used to describe his characters in *Treasure Island,* for example, "the horrible, soft-spoken, eyeless creature" (p. 38); "a voice so cruel, and cold, and ugly" (p. 39); and "a tall, strong, heavy, nut-brown man" (p. 17).
9. Select passages in which nature contributes to the mood of the story, for example, "a bitter, foggy, frosty afternoon" (p. 37); "There was no usual sound—nothing but the low wash of the ripple and the croaking of the crows in the woods" (p. 43); and "On stormy nights when the wind shook the four corners of the house and the surf roared along the cove and cliffs, I would see him in a thousand forms and with a thousand diabolical expressions" (p. 20).
10. Plan a mural depicting events in *Robinson Crusoe* (25).
11. Write a story with the title "How I Survived Alone in the Mountains for a Week Following the Crash of My Plane."
12. Make a large map of North and South America. Chart the course followed in *Two Years Before the Mast* (23).
13. Read a mystery story, then read the first chapter aloud to the class and have members of the class tell how they think the plot will unravel.

Chapter References

1. ANCKARSVARD, KARIN. *The Riddle of the Ring.* Annabelle MacMillan (tr.). New York: Harcourt Brace Jovanovich, 1966. Grades 5–7.
2. ARMSTRONG, RICHARD. *Albatross.* New York: David McKay, 1970. Grade 9 and up.
3. ______. *Trial Trip.* Eau Claire, Wis.: Hale, 1963. Grades 6–10.
4. ______ (ed.). *Treasures and Treasure Hunters.* New York: David McKay, 1969. Grade 7 and up.

5. ARTHUR, ROBERT. Alfred Hitchcock (ed.). *The Mystery of the Talking Skull.* New York: Random House, 1969. Grades 4–7.
6. BALLANTYNE, ROBERT M. *Coral Island.* New York: William Collins, n.d.
7. BEATTY, PATRICIA. *A Long Way to Whiskey Creek.* New York: Morrow, 1971. Grades 7–9.
8. BELL, ZACHARY. *Salvage Diver.* New York: Holiday House, 1961.
9. BENEDICT, LOIS TRIMBLE. *Canalboat Mystery.* New York: Atheneum, 1963. Grades 3–7.
10. BENTLEY, PHYLLIS. *The Adventures of Tom Leigh.* Garden City, N. Y.: Doubleday, 1964. Grades 5–7.
11. BERNA, PAUL. *A Truckload of Rice.* New York: Pantheon, 1970. Grade 5 and up.
12. BICE, CLARE. *Hurricane Treasure.* New York: Viking, 1965. Grades 4–8.
13. BOND, GLADYS B., AND F. B. BERTRAM. *The Secret of Rocky Ridge.* New York: Abelard-Schuman, 1965.
14. BOSTON, LUCY MARIA. *Nothing Said.* New York: Harcourt Brace Jovanovich, 1971. Grades 2–5.
15. BOTHWELL, JEAN. *The Mystery Clock.* New York: Dial Press, 1966. Grades 4–9.
16. CAVANNA, BETTY. *Spice Island Mystery.* New York: Morrow, 1969. Grades 7–9.
17. CLARK, ALLEN P. [Charles Van Doren]. *Growing Up in the Wild West.* New York: Hill & Wang, 1966. Grades 3–7.
18. CLARK, MARGARET GOFF. *The Mystery of the Buried Indian Mask.* New York: Watts, 1962. Grades 4–6.
19. COLLINS, RUTH P. *The Mystery of the Giant Giraffe.* New York: Walck, 1969. Grades 4–6.
20. COOPER, JAMES FENIMORE. *Leatherstocking Saga.* New York: Pantheon, 1954. Grades 7–8.
21. CORBETT, SCOTT. *Diamonds Are More Trouble.* New York: Holt, Rinehart & Winston, 1969. Grades 7–11.
22. ———. *The Mystery Man.* Boston: Little, Brown, 1970. Grades 4–6.
23. DANA, RICHARD HENRY. Harry Shefter *et al.* (eds.). *Two Years Before the Mast.* New York: Simon & Schuster, 1968. Paperback. Grade 9 and up.
24. DAVIS, VERNE T. *The Time of the Wolves.* New York: Morrow, 1962. Grades 3–6.
25. DEFOE, DANIEL. *Robinson Crusoe.* Boston: Houghton Mifflin, 1968. Paperback. Grade 7 and up.
26. DIETZ, LEW. *The Year of the Big Cat.* Boston: Little, Brown, 1970. Grade 7 and up.
27. ECKE, WOLFGANG. *Flight Toward Home.* Anthony Knight (tr.). New York: Macmillan, 1970. Grade 5 and up.
28. ERWIN, BETTY K. *Go to the Room of the Eyes.* Boston: Little, Brown, 1969. Grades 5–7.
29. EVERS, ALF. *The Deer-Jackers.* New York: Macmillan, 1965. Grades 3–7.
30. FENNER, PHYLLIS R. (ed.). *Finders Keepers: Stories of Treasure Seekers.* New York: Morrow, 1969. Grades 7–9.

31. FLEISCHMAN, SID. *The Ghost in the Noonday Sun.* Boston: Atlantic Monthly Press, 1965. Grades 5–7.
32. FOSTER, JOHN. *Marco and the Sleuth Hound.* New York: Dodd, Mead, 1969. Grades 3–7.
33. FREEMAN, BARBARA C. *Broom Adelaide.* Boston: Atlantic Monthly Press, 1965. Grades 5–9.
34. GARFIELD, LEON. *The Restless Ghost: Three Stories by Leon Garfield.* New York: Pantheon, 1969. Grade 6 and up.
35. HACKER, SHYRLE. *The Mystery of the Swan Ballet.* New York: Watts, 1965. Grades 3–5.
36. HITCHCOCK, ALFRED (ed.). *Alfred Hitchcock's Daring Detectives.* New York: Random House, 1969. Grade 5 and up.
37. HOLMVIK, OYVIND, AND HANS FAYE-LUND. *Dive to Danger.* Evelyn Ramsden (tr.). New York: Harcourt Brace Jovanovich, 1964. Grades 7–11.
38. HYDE, LAURENCE. *Under the Pirate Flag.* Boston: Houghton Mifflin, 1965. Grades 4–6.
39. JANE, MARY C. *Mystery in Longfellow Square.* Philadelphia: Lippincott, 1964. Grades 4–6.
40. KIPLING, RUDYARD. *Barrack Room Ballads.* Mount Vernon, N. Y.: Peter Pauper Press, n.d. Paperback.
41. ———. *Captains Courageous.* New York: Dell, n.d. Paperback. Grades 5–9.
42. ———. *Kim.* New York: Macmillan, 1962. Paperback.
43. ———. *Something of Myself.* Garden City, N. Y.: Doubleday, 1937.
44. KJELGAARD, JIM. *Furious Moose of the Wilderness.* New York: Dodd, Mead, 1965. Grade 8 and up.
45. MAC KELLAR, WILLIAM. *A Dog Like No Other.* New York: David McKay, 1965. Grades 4–6.
46. MC NEILL, JANET. *Battle of St. George Without.* Boston: Little, Brown, 1969. Grades 3–7.
47. ———. *Goodbye, Dove Square.* Boston: Little, Brown, 1969. Grades 5–9.
48. MAC PHERSON, MARGARET M. *New Tenants.* New York: Harcourt Brace Jovanovich. Grade 7 and up.
49. MARRYAT, CAPTAIN FREDERICK. *The Children of the New Forest.* New York: Dutton, 1955. Grades 7–11.
50. MEAKER, MABEL SEARS. *The Secret of Hollow Hill.* New York: Watts, 1961. n.g.l.
51. MEYERS, SUSAN. *The Mysterious Bender Bones.* Garden City, N. Y.: Doubleday, 1970. Grade 10 and up.
52. MINSHULL, EVELYN. *The Ghost of Crabtree Hall.* Philadelphia: Westminster, 1970. Grades 4–7.
53. MOONEY, ELIZABETH. *The Sandy Shoes Mystery.* Philadelphia: Lippincott, 1970. Grades 4–6.
54. NEWMAN, ROBERT. *Merlin's Mistake.* New York: Atheneum, 1970. Grades 4–8.
55. O'CONNOR, PATRICK. *Seawind from Hawaii.* New York: Washburn, 1965. Grades 6–8.

56. PARK, RUTH. *Road Under the Sea.* Garden City, N. Y.: Doubleday, 1966. Grades 5–6.
57. PHIPSON, JOAN. *The Haunted Night.* New York: Harcourt Brace Jovanovich, 1970. Grades 7–9.
58. ROBERTSON, KEITH. *The Money Machine.* New York: Viking, 1969. Grades 4–6.
59. RUMSEY, MARIAN. *Danger on Shadow Mountain.* New York: Morrow, 1970. Grades 4–6.
60. RYAN, JESSICA. *The Mystery of Arroyo Seco.* Indianapolis: Bobbs-Merrill, 1962. Grades 2–6.
61. RYDBERG, ERNIE. *The Yellow Line.* New York: Meredith, 1969. Grades 6–8.
62. SILVERBERG, ROBERT. *The Mask of Akhnaten.* New York: Macmillan, 1965. Grades 5–9.
63. STEVENSON, ROBERT LOUIS. *A Child's Garden of Verses.* Baltimore, Md.: Penguin Books, n.d. Paperback. Grades 3–5.
64. ______. *Dr. Jekyll and Mr. Hyde.* New York: Simon & Schuster, 1968. Paperback.
65. ______. R. E. C. Houghton (ed.). *An Inland Voyage.* New York: St. Martin's Press, n.d.
66. ______. *Kidnapped.* New York: Macmillan, 1962. Paperback.
67. ______. *Master of Ballantrae: A Winter's Tale.* New York: Oxford University Press, n.d.
68. ______. *Memories and Portraits.* New York: Scribner, 1887, 1895; St. Clair Shores, Mich.: Scholarly Press, 1969.
69. ______. *Treasure Island.* Chicago: Childrens Press, 1968. Grade 5 and up.
70. SWIFT, JONATHAN. *Gulliver's Travels.* New York: Bantam Books, 1971. Paperback.
71. TAVO, GUS. *Trail to Lone Canyon.* New York: Knopf, 1963. Grade 5 and up.
72. THUM, MARCELLA. *The Secret of the Sunken Treasure.* New York: Dodd, Mead, 1969. Grade 8 and up.
73. WARE, LEON. *The Threatening Fog.* Philadelphia: Westminster, 1962. Grades 5–9.
74. WELCH, ANN. *The Woolacombe Bird.* Cleveland: World, 1965.
75. WELCH, CHRISTINA M. *Home on Star Island.* Boston: Little, Brown, 1962.
76. WELLS, BOB. *The Saga of Shorty Gone.* New York: Putnam, 1969. Grades 6–8.
77. WESTREICH, BUDD. *Please Stand Clear of the Apache Arrows.* New York: David McKay, 1969. Grades 7–9.
78. WHITE, ROBB. *No Man's Land.* Garden City, N. Y. Doubleday, 1962. Grade 9 and up.
79. ______. *Torpedo Run.* Garden City, N. Y.: Doubleday, 1962. Grades 8–10.
80. WRIGHT, ZITA L. *Danger on the Ski Trails.* New York: Lothrop, Lee & Shepard, 1965. Grade 7 and up.

81. WYSS, JOHANN. *The Swiss Family Robinson.* New York: Dell, n.d. Paperback. Grades 5–9.
82. YOLEN, JANE. *The Inway Investigators or the Mystery at MacCracken's Place.* New York: Simon & Schuster, 1970. Paperback. Grades 3–5.

More Adventure for Children

Kindergarten–Grade 3

EASTMAN, P. D. *Sam and the Firefly.* New York: Beginner Books, 1958. An owl named Sam and a firefly named Gus become acquainted. Sam is amused by Gus' nighttime skywriting and the tricks he plays.

HOUSTON, JAMES A. *Tikta'liktak: An Eskimo Legend.* New York: Harcourt Brace Jovanovich, 1965. The simple and extremely rugged life of the Eskimo is told through the experiences of one adrift on an ice floe.

Grades 4–6

BAMMAN, HENRY, AND ROBERT WHITEHEAD. *The Lost Uranium Mine.* Chicago, Ill.: Benefic, 1964. Two young men find a mine in the Rocky Mountains.

BROWN, MICHAEL. *Shackleton's Epic Voyage.* New York: Coward-McCann, 1969. Ernest Shackleton and five of his crew cross 800 miles of the stormy Antarctic Ocean in a small boat in order to save the lives of 27 men waiting on Elephant Island.

BURGESS, ROBERT F. *Where Condors Fly.* Cleveland: World Publishing, 1969. Impassable jungles, treacherous Indians, and live volcanoes combine to make an exciting story. Professor Gannon searches for a fabulous Inca treasure he believes is hidden in an active volcano in the Andes.

CATHERALL, ARTHUR. *Duel in the High Hills.* New York: Lothrop, Lee & Shepard, 1969. The setting of this story is the Himalaya Mountains. A thirteen-year-old son of a Himalayan trader struggles to survive after his father is clawed by a starving snow leopard.

———. *Kidnapped by Accident.* New York: Lothrop, Lee & Shepard. A fourteen-year-old boy and his thirteen-year-old sister go to the aid of a man on a yacht in the Baltic Sea.

FAIRMAN, JOAN. *A Penny Saved.* New York: Lantern Press, 1971. Three boys save the life of their pet dog.

FLEISCHMAN, SID. *Chancy and the Grand Rascal.* Boston: Little, Brown, 1966. A boy and his uncle travel on the Ohio River and across the Midwest.

FRANCIS, FRANK. *Timimoto's Great Adventure.* New York: Holiday House, 1969. A Japanese boy goes out into the world to seek adventure. Beautiful double-spread illustrations in soft colors add atmosphere to the theme of courage.

FREWER, GLYN. *Adventure in the Barren Lands.* New York: Putnam, 1966. A helicopter crashes in this story of two families who must live off the land in the Arctic, make contact with Eskimos, and are finally rescued.

GRIFFITH, VALERIA. *A Ride for Jenny.* Philadelphia: Lippincott, 1964. Exciting adventures result from the money-raising projects taken by Jenny and her friends to finance a visit to a ranch.

HALL, DANIEL W. *Arctic Rovings.* Jerome Beatty (ed.). New York: W. R. Scott, 1968. An edited version of a true-life adventure of a teen-age boy, first, aboard a whaler and, later, as a deserter in Siberia.

HALLARD, PETER. *Boy on a White Giraffe.* New York: Seabury, 1969. The setting of this action-packed story is East Africa. Martin, alone in camp with a sprained ankle, relies on a wild albino giraffe to escape when a sudden storm starts a flash fire.

HAYS, WILMA P. *Cape Cod Adventure.* New York: Coward-McCann, 1964. A city family's summer adventures on Cape Cod lead to their decision not to sell Grandfather's old house.

HAZELTON, ELIZABETH. *Tides of Danger.* New York: Scribner, 1967. This rapid-moving adventure story of Mexican life involves pearl fishing and an encounter with greedy pearl fishers.

JOHNSON, CROCKETT. *Gordy and the Pirate.* New York: Putnam, 1965. Adventures on the way home from school are told through the humor of a child.

NEVIN, EVELYN C. *The Triumphant Adventures of Chee Chee Monerney.* New York: Four Winds Press, 1971. Many hardships are faced by a fourteen-year-old half-Indian girl and her three traveling companions as they make their way to the Yukon to seek gold.

PICCARD, JOAN RUSSELL. *Adventure on the Wind.* Los Angeles: Nash, 1971. A girl navigates her father's gas balloon to help gather information for Union forces during Civil War times.

ROLERSON, DARRELL A. *Mister Big Britches.* New York: Dodd, Mead, 1971. The story of a boy's adventure into independence as he runs away to keep the fox cub he has secretly adopted.

STANLEY, JEAN. *Danger on Pine Hill.* Philadelphia: Westminster, 1963. A summer boarder on a Tennessee timber farm betrays his friends. Conservation and engineering procedures and principles are involved in the construction of a dam.

STREATFEILD, NOEL. *Thursday's Child.* New York: Random House, 1971. An English girl escapes from a cruel orphanage and has a series of adventures among canal-boat people and the eccentric cast of a traveling theatrical company.

WECHTER, NELL WISE. *Swamp Girl.* Winston Salem, N. C.: John F. Blair, n.d. In this story a young North Carolina girl and her grandmother search for treasure once hidden from the Yankees on the family plantation.

WEIR, ROSEMARY. *The Heirs of Ashton Manor.* New York: Dial, 1966. Two Australian children move to an elaborate family estate in England and with a cousin live there on limited means.

WILLIAMS, JAY. *Danny Dunn and the Swamp Monster.* New York: McGraw-Hill, 1971. A new adventure in the Danny Dunn series in which Danny tries to trap a monster with a supermagnet.

Grades 7–9

AMERMAN, LOCKHART. *The Sly One.* New York: Harcourt Brace Jovanovich, 1966. Teen-agers and their elderly uncle and dog foil the plot of an international crook.

ANNIXTER, JANE, AND ANNIXTER, PAUL. *Wagon Scout.* New York: Holiday House, 1965. This adventure story is set in the rugged West in the post-Civil War period.

ATWATER, MONTGOMERY. *Snow Rangers of the Andes.* New York: Random House, 1967. A forest service avalanche-control specialist discovers the maneuverings of great powers operating behind a veil of secrecy to gain control of a valuable mine.

BAWDEN, NINA. *The Runaway Summer.* Philadelphia: Lippincott, 1969. Mary is staying with her grandfather in an English seaside resort. She involves herself in an embarrassing web of lies and engages in some illegal activities. Fortunately for her everything turns out well.

BENCHLEY, NATHANIEL. *Gone and Back.* New York: Harper & Row, 1971. In this pioneer adventure story a young boy reaches maturity on the long road from New England through Kansas to Oklahoma during the Great Land Rush.

BOSWORTH, J. ALLEN. *A Wind Named Anne.* Garden City, N. Y.: Doubleday, 1970. The affection of a teen-ager for a half-grown killer whale and the way in which he saves its life are described in this exciting adventure story.

BOTHWELL, JEAN. *Ride, Zarina, Ride.* New York: Harcourt Brace Jovanovich, 1966. This colorful cloak-and-dagger story has its setting on an estate in sixteenth-century Mogul India.

CORCORAN, BARBARA. *The Long Journey.* New York: Atheneum, 1970. In a tense adventure story set in Montana, thirteen-year-old Laurie rides her horse across country to get help for her ailing grandfather.

DAVIES, L. P. *Adventure Holidays, Ltd.* Garden City, N. Y.: Doubleday, 1970. Pete Cullimore gets more adventure on his visit to Wales than he bargains for but he is determined to find out why attempts are made to kill him.

HAUGAARD, ERIK. *A Slave's Tale.* Boston: Houghton Mifflin, 1965. This adventure story is told by a slave girl.

LEIGHTON, MARGARET. *The Canyon Castaways.* New York: Farrar, Straus & Giroux, 1966. A flash flood in a canyon in the Southwest isolates a young girl babysitting. However, when eighteen-year-old Greg arrives, there is a bit of romance.

MC DANIEL, RUEL. *Deep Water Boy.* San Carlos, Calif.: Golden Gate Jr. Books, 1964. Adventure takes place aboard a shrimp boat at sea.

MARTINI, TERI. *The Lucky Ghost Shirt.* Philadelphia: Westminster, 1971. Contemporary Indian life is well described in this story set on a South Dakota Sioux reservation. A young Indian boy is accused of horse stealing by a racist rancher. Ethnic problems are forcefully treated.

MASON, HERBERT. *Duel for the Sky.* New York: Grossett & Dunlap, 1970. This book describes the fighter pilots of World War II in their bitter struggle to win the war. Excellent photographs help to make it an exciting story.

MOREY, WALT. *Angry Waters.* New York: Dutton, 1969. After taking part in a supermarket robbery, Don Malloy is paroled to an Oregon dairy farm.

MURPHY, ROBERT. *The Haunted Journey.* New York: Farrar, Straus & Giroux, 1969. This account of the expeditions of Vitus Bering to Kamchatka, 1725–1729, and to Alaska, 1733–1743, was adapted from the 1961 adult version of the book.

O'DELL, SCOTT. *The Black Pearl.* Boston: Houghton Mifflin, 1967. The son of a pearl dealer has a life-and-death struggle with a sea monster larger than the largest ship in the harbor of La Paz, in Baja California.

REESE, JOHN. *Dinky.* New York: David McKay, 1964. A retired miniature steam locomotive is put back into running order by a sixteen-year-old boy summer vacationing in the Mother Lode country of California.

SCOTT, J. M. *Michael Anonymous.* Philadelphia: Chilton, 1971. Adventure at sea is mixed with the story of growth, change, and personal interaction between two college friends as they face crises together.

WHITEHOUSE, ARCH. *The Laughing Falcon.* New York: Putnam, 1969. The third book by Arch Whitehouse about the Lafayette Escadrille, a group of American volunteers, flying with the French Aviation Service in World War I.

WILLIAMS, SUSAN. *Elephant Boy.* New York: David McKay, 1964. This action and adventure story is set in Burma prior to and during World War II. An elephant boy is given the elephant Po Sein, early in its infancy.

More Mystery for Children

Kindergarten–Grade 3

DU BOIS, WILLIAM PENE. *Elisabeth the Cow Ghost.* New York: Viking, 1964. The adventures of Leo, a young boy who lives in the countryside of Normandy, France, and his cow Elisabeth are described in this exciting story.

Grades 4–6

ADRIAN, MARY. *The Indian Horse Mystery.* New York: Hastings House, 1966. An eleven-year-old Yakima Indian boy and his friend, whose father owns a cattle ranch on the Yakima Indian Reservation in Washington State, discover a cattle thief.

ARTHUR, ROBERT. *The Mystery of the Green Ghost.* New York: Random House, 1965. The mystery of a haunted house and a green ghost is solved by three young investigators.

BABBITT, NATALIE. *Goody Hall.* New York: Farrar, Straus & Giroux, 1971. A tutor and his pupil, a troubled family, a mysterious house, a seance, a fortune in jewels, and a descent into the family tomb combine to make a bang-up mystery story.

BONHAM, FRANK. *Mystery in Little Tokyo.* New York: Dutton, 1966. In the Japanese section of Los Angeles, a boy and girl visiting their grandparents help solve the mystery of the missing sword and end a neighborhood feud.

BOWEN, IRENE. *The Mystery of the Talking Well.* Philadelphia: Lippincott, 1966. A deserted house and a haunted well both make a good mystery story.

BRINK, CAROL R. *The Pink Motel.* New York: Macmillan, 1959. A normal family from the northern United States inherits a motel in Florida whose tenants seem very unusual. The mystery involves coded messages and some unusual characters who stir up much nonsense.

GEER, CHARLES. *Dexter and the Deer Lake Mystery.* New York: Norton, 1965. A boy and a girl on a month's holiday, interested in being amateur detectives, help apprehend culprits responsible for several robberies.

GEORGE, JEAN CRAIGHEAD. *Who Really Killed Cock Robin?: An Ecological Mystery.* New York: Dutton, 1971. A group of children in an ecology-conscious community carry on an investigation in an effort to determine what killed one of the robins nesting on the mayor's porch.

HICKS, CLIFFORD B. *Alvin's Secret Code.* New York: Holt, Rinehart & Winston, 1963. Alvin becomes interested in codes and learns much about cryptography from a former spy. A detailed explanation of some codes and ciphers should interest puzzle fans.

HILDICK, E. W. *The Prisoners of Gridling Gap.* Garden City, N. Y.: Doubleday, 1971. Set in a small New England town the story follows the adventures of two sets of brothers and sisters through a variety of intrigues that lead them to a subterranean city.

JACKSON, JACQUELINE. *Missing Melinda.* Boston: Little, Brown, 1967. Twin daughters of a literary scholar solve the theft of a valuable antique doll.

JOSLIN, SESYLE. *The Spy Lady and the Muffin Man.* New York: Harcourt Brace Jovanovich, 1971. A mystery story about four children who spend their summer on Cape Cod uncovering the identity of the beautiful lady whom they believe to be a spy.

LAUGHLIN, FLORENCE. *The Seventh Cousin.* New York: Macmillan, 1966. This mystery story involves seven cousins who are trying to kidnap an heiress.

MAC KENZIE, JEANETTE. *The Hawkness House Mystery.* New York: Washburn, 1966. The setting is Massachusetts with an exciting background of summer sports. The characters are involved in providing authentic proof of the age of a seventeenth-century house.

MALONE, MARY. *Young Miss Josie Delaney, Detective.* New York: Dodd, Mead, 1966. The search for a missing rocking horse that may be a museum piece adds to the excitement and fun of a summer vacation for two girls.

MARTIN, FREDERIC. *The Mystery at Monkey Run.* Boston: Little, Brown, 1966. Two boys are intrigued by mysterious happenings. A thief is captured with a case of stolen coins for which there is a reward of $250.

RASKIN, ELLEN. *The Mysterious Disappearance of Leon (I Mean Noel).* New York: Dutton, 1971. The disappearance of Leon (I mean Noel) Carillon, heir to the huge Pomato soup fortune, is only one of the puzzling things that happens in this suspense-packed mystery.

REID, EUGENIE C. *Mystery of the Carrowell Necklace.* New York: Lothrop, Lee & Shepard, 1965. A diamond necklace, hidden fifty years ago on a family estate in Florida, is located by combined efforts of the great-grandchildren.

RYDBERG, ERNIE. *The Dark of the Cave.* New York: David McKay, 1965. This is an unusual mystery story of real courage and friendship between a blind boy and his friend.

ST. JOHN, WYLLY FOLK. *The Mystery of the Other Girl.* New York: Viking, 1971. Relates an odd mystery that haunts a young boy's life and finally reaches a climax involving other people on the night of a historical festival.

TRASK, MARGARET P. *At the Sign of the Rocking Horse.* New York: T. Y. Crowell, 1964. This mystery story about two, young, would-be detectives presents an attractive picture of the loyalties and pleasures of a small town.

WAHL, JANE. *Crabapple Night.* New York: Holt, Rinehart & Winston, 1971. A mystery story about the adventures that follow when Elmer Fink disappears and his wife becomes the meanest lady in town.

WINTERFIELD, HENRY. *Mystery of the Roman Ransom.* Edith McCormick (tr.). New York: Harcourt Brace Jovanovich, 1971. Events are related with zest and humor in a mystery set in ancient Rome.

Grades 7–9

AIKEN, JOAN. *Night Fall.* New York: Holt, Rinehart & Winston, 1971. The setting of this weird suspense story is first a gloomy London house and then the coast of Cornwall. A young girl is terror-stricken by a nightmare that continues to recur. She finally finds herself the missing link in the solution of an old murder.

GUILLOT, RENE. *Mountain with a Secret.* Princeton, N. J.: Van Nostrand, 1965. A boy living on his uncle's isolated farm in New Guinea solves the mystery of the former owner's missing son.

MEYERS, SUSAN. *Melissa Finds a Mystery.* New York: Dodd, Mead, 1966. Clues from the past save a great-aunt's home from foreclosure and unravel a mystery.

NELSON, MARGARET. *Mystery of the Missing Cannon.* New York: Farrar, Straus & Giroux, 1966. This enjoyable story takes place in a run-down fishing village in the state of Washington.

NORTH, JOAN. *The Cloud Forest.* New York: Farrar, Straus & Giroux, 1966. A twelve-year-old boy unravels a mystery and exposes his fraudulent mother.

ROBERTSON, KEITH. *Three Stuffed Owls.* New York: Viking, 1954. Two teenage boys start a detective agency with offices in a garage. The wealth acquired carries them straight to a carnival.

WISSMANN, RUTH H. *The Scuba Divers Mystery.* New York: Dodd, Mead, 1966. Facts about scuba diving and a good mystery are combined in this book.

A Hound, a Bay Horse, and a Turtle-Dove by James Playsted Wood, illustrated by Douglas Gorsline.

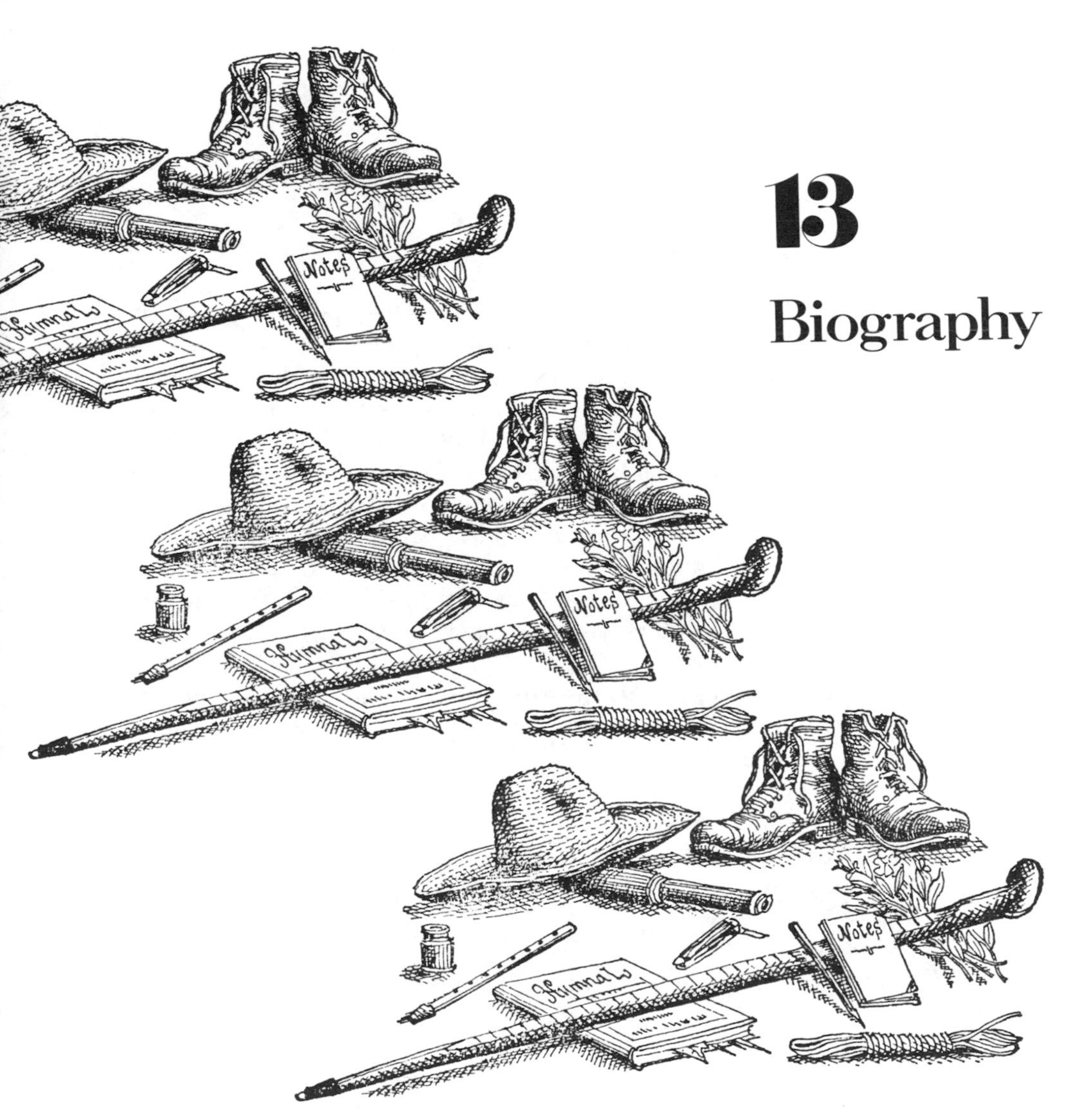

13 Biography

Boys and girls have always been interested in people who were successful in their lines of endeavor and in the effect their achievements have had upon the lives of other people. They are interested in the past and in the men and women who have contributed to the improvement of living in our country and in other parts of the world.

Biographies not only satisfy these interests, but they also instill an appreciation of man's efforts to improve his environment through new knowledge in such areas as statesmanship, the physical and social sciences, and human relations. Children in the middle and upper grades begin to value the courage and bravery of men and women who in many cases have sacrificed their lives for the causes in which they believed.

Biography should meet the same criteria established for fiction and historical fiction. In addition it should have authenticity without obtrusive presentation of facts. The author should be so thoroughly familiar with the milieu and historical background of his subject that the story can be told naturally, accurately, and with an eye for the details that characterize a particular time and place. In presenting a biography from the vast mass of detail available on a subject, the author should form some framework, some motif, that gives unity to the work.

Thus the major ingredients of a biography are as follows:

The facts given are authentic.

The author's interpretation of the events included is sound.

The author provides authentic documentation for the hero's words and actions.

The hero's deeds speak for themselves, without the author's making personal judgments.

The purpose for writing the biography is made clear.

Sources of information are acknowledged.

Stereotypes are avoided.

The heroes of the biographies are presented in such a way that they do not appear as idols.

Biographies for young children do not always include all of these ingredients. Most of them are fictionalized. They are sometimes not documented, and they may not be a complete account of a person's life. They often omit sorrowful or unsavory events that beset the person who is the subject of the biography. Today, however, more and more biographies include even tragic realities. To add suspense and drama to the biography, many biographers relate known facts in dialogue and interpret the thoughts of their characters. These are ways of bringing the characters to life. As children gain experience with biographies, they begin to evaluate them according to the criteria given above. Not only do they look for the ingredients peculiar to biographies, but they also expect biographies to have the ingredients that make a good story (see page 408).

History of Biography for Children

Biographies for children were slow to take their place in literature. One of the first significant biographies was Carl Sandburg's *Abe Lincoln Grows Up* (79), which was adapted from Sandburg's *Prairie Years* (80) and was published in separate form for children.

A particular quality of Sandburg's style makes it seem as if he is visiting in an intimate, easy-going way with the reader. He writes as though he knows Abraham Lincoln well and is eager to share his knowledge with others. The biography is pervaded by an air of loneliness that is relieved by episodes of humor and the spirit of Lincoln's greatness that is caught in the telling.

Another pacesetter in children's biographies published in the early 1930s is Cornelia Meigs' *Invincible Louisa* (61), a sympathetic account of the life of Louisa May Alcott. In addition to telling the story of Louisa May Alcott's life, which includes the Alcott family and their friends and relatives, it portrays the times in which she lived. Places and people are described in an intimate style. Miss Meigs' description of the Boston Common is a classic in word work:

> Here Louisa played upon the grass, made friends with passers-by, or plumping down to rest, would sit looking up at the tall elms with their high trunks, and enormously long branches, so different from the round leafy beeches of the woods at her birthplace. The tall elderly houses of Beacon Hill looked

Daniel Boone by James Daugherty.

down upon her out of their many-paned windows, where the blue and purple glass was a sign of exceedingly aristocratic old age. Along Beacon Street there toiled by, on the rough pavement, an endless procession of market carts, of creaking wagons, and those shiny, low-hung carriages which, a little later, were to be named Victorias. In them sat beautiful ladies, overflowing the seats with billowing skirts and carrying the most minute of parasols to protect their complexions from the sun. Sellers of fruit, of pies, of strawberries went by, calling their street cries to attract customers. . . . It was all wonderful and exciting to the little girl, so extraordinarily different from the still rose-bowered garden in Germantown, and the view over green rolling hills. [Pp. 23–24]

Cornelia Meigs' attention to details gives the reader the impression that the author knew the people and lived in the places about which she wrote.

Just as Cornelia Meigs opened the 1930s with a significant contribution to the field of biographies, James Daugherty closed them with his powerful biography *Daniel Boone* (19). The places described in *Daniel Boone* have a ring of truth to them, and the spirit of the times pervades the entire biography, which reads like an exciting story. There is an earthiness about Daugherty's descriptions. Of Boone he says:

So Boone grew lean and strong with his toes in the good black dirt, with the ring of the anvil in his ears, strong and sure-handed with tools and guns, and his head clear and cool as the spring above his cabin door. (P. 14)

Daugherty's rugged, powerful, and poetic style re-creates with vigor the rough, exacting, and severe life of the pioneers and makes Daniel Boone one of the most convincing pioneer heroes in the history of our country.

In the 1940s Daugherty authored two other outstanding biographies: *Poor Richard* (21) and *Abraham Lincoln* (18). *Poor Richard* emphasizes Benjamin Franklin's contribution to the political and diplomatic life of our country in its early days rather than his inventions. *Abraham Lincoln* is a beautiful biographical portrait that brings out Lincoln's spiritual strength. Daugherty uses quotes from Lincoln's well-known speeches and letters and includes many of the legendary incidents for which Lincoln is famous.

Jeanette Eaton also contributed excellent biographies. *Narcissa Whitman: Pioneer of Oregon* (26) is an inspiring story based on the letters and memoirs of a brave woman who set out from New York for the Oregon Territory in 1836. In *Lone Journey: The Life of Roger Williams* (25) Miss Eaton presents the biography of a man of strong convictions who left Europe to fight for freedom of speech and worship in colonial America. In *That Lively Man, Ben Franklin* (27) Miss Eaton relates details of Benjamin Franklin's life from the time of his apprenticeship in Boston through his activities in Philadelphia as a printer, civic leader, and patriot. Included are his experiences abroad. Interesting anecdotes portray him as a genial man full of fun and always ready for a good joke. The biography also presents a good picture of colonial life.

Another interesting biography of the 1940s was *The Story of Clara Barton of the Red Cross* (69) by Jeannette Covert Nolan. It is an intimate portrayal of one of America's outstanding women. It relates how Clara Barton spent her life in service to humanity as a teacher, a nurse, and founder of the American Red Cross.

The Subjects of Biographies

Biographers in the 1950s and the 1960s continued to choose pioneers, statesmen, scientists, inventors, musicians, and artists about whom to write. Some writers dipped back into history for their subjects; others wrote about individuals who were outstanding in various fields of endeavor at the time the biography was written. A number of the early biographers have continued to contribute to the literature in this field, and many new writers have added to the list. It is interesting that many biographers have chosen the same person about whom to write.

Explorers

Explorers cut their way through virgin forests, raft down strange rivers, find passages through forbidding mountains, blaze trails across parched desert lands, and fathom the ocean's depths. They seek out places to explore where man has not yet been. The stories of their exploits as they search for new worlds to discover and to conquer are packed with courage and daring. What young reader, or old one for that matter, can resist the excitement of discovering and exploring new worlds with fearless men like Leif Ericson, Christopher Columbus, Marco Polo, Magellan, and Sir Francis Drake; conquering rivers, forests, and mountains with Lewis and Clark; or unfurling the United States flag at the top of the world with Commodore Peary?

Marco Polo deserves particular notice among explorers. His travels with his father and uncle from Venice to China in the thirteenth century excited the minds of European travelers and explorers and aroused an intense interest in the Far East. Charles P. Graves gives a simplified but interesting account of Marco Polo's travels in *Marco Polo* (34).

Christopher Columbus, perhaps more than any other discoverer or explorer, holds a place of high esteem in the minds of young readers. There is more authenticated information about him than about others who might have preceded him. *The Voyages of Christopher Columbus* (95) by Guido Waldman portrays Columbus as a man who, though many of the learned men of Spain laughed at his ideas, stubbornly refused to give up his dream and after many disappointments and failures was successful in making it come true.

Columbus' daring adventure and discovery had an atomic effect upon the lives of many adventurers, navigators, explorers, and noblemen of the early part of the sixteenth century. A desire to discover new lands spurred them to action. Their daring and exploits make fascinating reading.

Young readers will enjoy Faith Y. Knoop's *Amerigo Vespucci* (48). Following the discoveries of Columbus, Vespucci made voyages to the Indies and found that they were not part of Asia but were instead a whole new world.

Written in an interesting yet simple style, Ronald Syme's biography *Vasco Da Gama: Sailor Toward the Sunrise* (92) follows the explorer's voyage to India and is filled with little-told details. The activities of the Arabs in trade and exploration are described.

Ponce De Leon (6) by Wyatt Blassingame is a biography rich in historical background. Ponce De Leon is pictured not only as an adventurer

Amerigo Vespucci by Nina Brown Baker, illustrated by Paul Valentino.

but also as a family man eager to settle with his wife and children in an exciting new land.

Walter Buehr's *The Portuguese Explorers* (8) is a short, well-written account of the Portuguese explorers of the fifteenth and sixteenth centuries who helped to build the far-flung Portuguese Empire. The author concentrates on Henry the Navigator but also covers other explorers from Bartholomeu Dias to Vasco Da Gama. Half-tone illustrations by the author supplement the text.

Word of the wonders of the New World spread through Europe and brought forth a rash of explorers particularly from France and England. The purposes of later explorers were quite different from the purpose of most of the previous ones. They did not expect to find fabulous cities with streets of gold, but rather to claim land for their crowns and to build settlements in the new land that would extend their empires. The stories of their adventures in the new land provide exciting reading.

In *Solomon Juneau, Voyageur* (53) Marion Lawson relates the adventures of Solomon Juneau, who had lived in a village near Montreal, and became one of the famous voyagers to leave the Province of Quebec. After life as a trader and ruler over Indians, he became a United States citizen and founded a town that is known today as Milwaukee, Wisconsin.

It was not long before adventurers began to look beyond the limits of continents and to move out to make the entire world their own. Not all their ventures were successful, but the records they made provide adventurous reading that is even more exciting than fiction.

One of the first navigators to change the map of the world was Magellan. His voyage around the world is vividly described in *Five Ships West: The Story of Magellan* (42) by Charles E. Israel.

Sir Francis Drake's life was so full of adventure that his story as told by Will Holwood in *The True Story of Sir Francis Drake, Privateer* (41) reads like the most imaginative of fiction. Born to seafaring as a way of life, he utilized well his boundless enthusiasm for the sea and ships.

George Rogers Clark: Frontier Fighter (63) by Helen M. Miller relates how through bravery, vision, and frontier experience George Rogers Clark led a small band of poorly equipped soldiers to success in capturing British outposts and claiming the lands north to the Great Lakes and west to the Mississippi.

The wide sea and the rolling ocean from the southeast Mediterranean to the Caribbean is the stage upon which Nelson plays his role as the dauntless sailor, dedicating his activities to England's advancement. His exploits as recounted by Oliver Warner and Chester W. Nimitz in *Nelson and the Age of Fighting Sail* (97) are set among the power struggles of France, Spain, Denmark, and England including her American colonies.

Of Courage Undaunted: Across the Continent with Lewis and Clark (20) by James Daugherty reports the Lewis and Clark expedition of 1804–1806 into the Northwest as recorded in the journals kept by the leaders. The parts played by Charbonneau, the Shoshone Indian who served as interpreter for the party, and his wife Sacajawea are described.

Journey into Ice: John Franklin and the Northwest Passage (91) by Ann and Myron Sutton is an impressive biography of Sir John Franklin. It details his exploits with Nelson, his exploration of Australia, and his attempts to find the Northwest Passage. Maps and photographs illustrate the text.

Frémont made five expeditions to the west coast of America to map the area. He played important though controversial parts in the Mexican and Civil wars and suffered changing financial and political fortunes. An excellent portrayal of this courageous explorer appears in *Frémont: Soldier, Explorer, Statesman* (85) by Fredrika S. Smith.

Robert Peary's struggle and determination to reach the North Pole are described in an interesting adventure story by Erick Berry titled *Robert E. Peary: North Pole Conqueror* (5). This account of history is enlivened by incidents of family life.

Adele De Leeuw wrote a thrilling story of Richard E. Byrd, the first man to fly over both the North and South Poles. His career in the United States Navy and his numerous explorations are vividly described in *Richard E. Byrd: Adventurer to the Poles* (22).

Mature readers will enjoy *Captain Edward L. Beach: Around the World Under Water* (1) by Beril Becker. It is the story of Captain Beach's historic around-the-world underwater trip—a top-secret mission—in the atomic-powered submarine *Triton.*

Advanced readers will take pleasure in a well-written biography of Sir Austen Henry Layard, the nineteenth-century British diplomat and archaeologist whose love of travel and adventure took him to the East and led to the discovery and excavation of the ancient city of Nineveh. Without fictionalizing, Robert Silverberg's *The Man Who Found Nineveh* (84) colorfully describes Layard's travels, explorations, and discoveries and makes clear his contributions to Assyriology and archaeology.

The story of Arthur Evans' life—his boyhood, his dream of finding lost civilizations, and the final realization of his dream on the Mediterranean island of Crete—is told by George Selden in *Sir Arthur Evans: Discoverer of Knossos* (81). Although few details are given, the uncovering of the palace of King Minos is accurately described. The story provides for young readers a good introduction to archaeology and biography.

Frontiersmen

Frontiersmen follow explorers into the various areas of man's endeavors. There is a restlessness in the make-up of a frontiersman that urges him to leave the old and try the new, regardless of the hardships that often accompany such adventures. To the frontiersman there are always new worlds to conquer and new lands to settle. The exciting adventures and hardships of frontiersmen are told in many thrilling stories.

Historical events in England, France, The Netherlands, and the English colonies in America provide a broad stage for a well-written biography of William Penn. Leader of the colony of Pennsylvania, Penn is presented as humane in his treatment of the natives and people of other faiths and as a strong advocate of democracy in Hildegarde Dolson's story *William Penn* (23).

In *Negroes in the Early West* (9) Olive W. Burt presents brief biographies of the brave Black men and women who went west as cooks, messengers, or mule drivers. These slaves or newly freed men and women took part in every undertaking that helped to win and develop the United States.

I Elizabeth: A Biography of the Girl Who Married General George Armstrong Custer (74) by Ruth P. Randall is a biography of Libbie Bacon, wife of General George Custer, who led the United States soldiers in

William Penn by Hildegarde Dolson, illustrated by Leon Fisher.

the disaster at Little Big Horn. A picture of life on the prairies as that area was being settled enhances this biography.

The many interests and activities of a brilliant writer and a pioneer aviator are related in *Antoine De Saint-Exupéry* (11) by Curtis Cate. The philosophy expressed in Saint-Exupéry's writings will assure their popularity for years to come.

Scientists and Inventors

Significant advances in man's ways of living have been made as the result of scientific experiments. Uncertainty of outcome seems to intrigue experimenters and to keep them working toward their goals in spite of the strenuous work frequently involved. As man finds a way to build a bridge, to construct a skyscraper, or to wipe out a disease, he creates ways of controlling his environment and helps people in all parts of the world. The difficult tasks and persistence of scientists, their successes and failures, and the contributions they have made to the improvement of living are told in many biographies written especially for children.

The biographies of Euclid, Archimedes, Aryabhata, Descartes, Newton, Von Neumann, and other outstanding mathematicians through the centuries are included in *Famous Mathematicians* (88) by Frances B. Stonaker.

More mature readers will find *Aristotle, Dean of Early Science* (24) by Glanville Downey an interesting biography of this Greek philosopher and naturalist.

The Quest of Johannes Kepler (50) by Barbara Land brings to life an era of scientific investigations in Germany. Kepler was the earliest well-known astronomer to uphold openly the theories of Copernicus.

The contribution of Samuel Morse to communication in our country and around the world is well treated in *Samuel Morse and the Electronic Age* (38) by Wilma P. Hays.

The emphasis in *Louis Pasteur, the Germ Killer* (58) by John H. Mann is on Pasteur's scientific career rather than on his personal life. This simply written biography describes his experiments and clearly explains the theories behind his research in bacteriology. The accounts of his research into the causes of silkworm disease, chicken cholera, anthrax, and rabies are particularly well described.

Russell Freedman has written a dynamic and illuminating biography of Jules Verne. In *Jules Verne: Portrait of a Prophet* (32) the author suggests the motivating influences and keenness of mind that led to the science-fiction writer's outstanding accomplishments.

Sam and Beryl Epstein's *George Washington Carver* (29) is a simply written account of Carver's life from babyhood to his death. The theme of his tremendous drive to succeed is carried throughout the book.

Joanne L. Henry wrote a story about Marie Curie in which concepts of physics are simply presented for young readers—*Marie Curie: Discoverer of Radium* (39). *She Lived for Science: Irene Joliot-Curie* (56) by Robin McKown is an excellent biography of Irene Curie, daughter of Marie and Pierre Curie. The discovery of artificial radioactivity won for Irene Curie and her husband Frederic Joliot the Nobel Prize in Chemistry in 1935.

The advances made in nuclear science during the life of Austrian physicist Lise Meitner (1878–1968) are well presented in *Lise Meitner, Atomic Pioneer* (17) by Deborah Crawford.

In *Incredible Man of Science* (99) Virginia V. Westervelt narrates the biography of the electrical wizard Irving Langmuir, Nobel Prize winner for his studies in surface chemistry and his pioneer research of the atom.

Inventions in the various fields of endeavor have made it possible for man to increase his control over his environment. The world has been made smaller, and men have been brought closer together through the achievements of inventors. Biographies of inventors stress their hard work and determination to turn their ideas into realities.

Eli Whitney's life from the time he took his father's watch apart and put it together again at ten years of age until he was finally acclaimed as the inventor of the cotton gin thirty-two years later is told in a simple and dramatic manner in Jean Lee Latham's *Eli Whitney: Great Inventor* (51).

Trail Blazers of Technology (57) by Harland Manchester consists of biographical sketches of nine men of the nineteenth and twentieth centuries who made tremendous contributions to the world through their inventions.

Elizabeth Rider Montgomery has written a fast-moving story of the life and works of Alexander Graham Bell. *Alexander Graham Bell: Man of Sound* (64) is the story not only of Bell's invention of the telephone but also of his contribution to the teaching of deaf children.

The experiences of Thomas A. Edison from the time of early childhood until his golden jubilee celebration eighty-two years later are related in *Thomas Alva Edison: Miracle Maker* (45) by Mervyn D. Kaufmann. Edison's steady determination, despite the many failures he encountered, led to the success of more than 1000 inventions.

Sea and Earth: The Life of Rachel Carson (87) by Philip Sterling penetrates deeply into the personality of Rachel Carson and reveals her sympathy for all living things and her feeling of responsibility for the future of the Earth. The biography is rich with many details about Miss Carson's life.

Wernher Von Braun: Rocket Engineer (96) by Helen B. Walters is a biography that emphasizes Von Braun's scientific career and also provides a simple history of liquid-fuel rocketry.

Statesmen and Civic Leaders

Statesmen are well versed in the art of government and they show wisdom in directing public matters. They occupy themselves with affairs of government and are influential in shaping legislation. Statesmen past and present have been and are a rich resource in the countries of the world. Beginning with the founding fathers through the present times, statesmen in America have risen to the challenges that were the dreams of our forefathers. This is particularly true today. In the last few years, as social, economic, and political problems have surfaced in the world, leadership has evolved. Leaders have come particularly from minority groups—Indians, Blacks, and Mexicans in our country—and through their leadership have pushed further out the boundaries of democratic living.

Presidents of the United States are thought of as statesmen of the highest order serving both our country and the world. Numerous biographies have been written, both in fictional and factual styles, to inform young readers and to help them appreciate the statesmanship of our Presidents.

Maude and Miska Petersham present brief biographical sketches of the Presidents of the United States up to Lyndon B. Johnson in *Story of the Presidents of the United States* (73).

Thomas Jefferson was a man of many accomplishments. He was a naturalist, scientist, musician, archaeologist, inventor, and statesman. This many-sided man who served as ambassador to England, Vice-president, and finally President of the United States is fittingly described in *Thomas Jefferson, His Many Talents* (43) by Johanna Johnston.

The character and accomplishments of John Quincy Adams as seen through the eyes of his wife, Louisa, are told by Laura Kerr in *Louisa: The Life of Mrs. John Quincy Adams* (47). Louisa's life as a young girl, a wife, and a mother is interestingly portrayed.

Frontier President: The Life of James K. Polk (82) by Bill Severn is the biography of a little-known President. The beginning is partly fictionalized, but this does not interfere with the portrayal.

In Lincoln's Footsteps: The Story of Andrew Johnson (83), also by Bill Severn, is the life story of the statesman who succeeded Lincoln as the seventeenth President of the United States. Severn portrays Johnson as one who strove against tremendous opposition and political intrigue to carry out Lincoln's plans for fair treatment of the South following the Civil War—a man whose faith in the people and in the Constitution never wavered.

Catherine O. Peare has written a perceptive full-length biography of Herbert Hoover titled *The Herbert Hoover Story* (72). From boyhood to death, Mr. Hoover is presented as a dedicated man with an unsatiable desire to perform outstanding service to his country.

Ralph G. Martin's biography *President from Missouri: Harry S Truman* (59) captures the personality of the man and describes his early life and his accomplishments as President: the Truman Doctrine, the Marshall Plan, NATO, and the Point Four program. The historical world events influenced by his decisions are realistically presented.

Alfred Steinberg has written an interesting biography about Dwight D. Eisenhower. *Dwight David Eisenhower* (86) starts with Eisenhower's childhood and relates the events in his life as a cadet at West Point, as commander of the United States invasion forces in Europe during World War II, and as President of the United States.

I. E. Levine's biography *Young Man in the White House: John Fitzgerald Kennedy* (55) describes Kennedy's early childhood, his family life, his relations with his older brother, his father's ambitions for his sons, his college and war years, and his public career as senator and President. The book is not merely a recital of facts: The author presents a warm and sympathetic portrayal, devoid of sentimentality, of the emerging character of a young man.

With simple text and photographs Ann Campbell presents excerpts from the life of Richard Milhous Nixon. *The Picture Life of Richard Milhous Nixon* (10) relates events of his growing years, education, political achievements, travels, and service to his nation.

An objective, smoothly flowing biography, *Harriet Beecher Stowe: Woman with a Cause* (100) by Winifred E. Wise, is well supported by facts, quotations, and events. The emphasis is on Mrs. Stowe's flexibility, common sense, and courage.

Written in a lively style and illustrated with many drawings, *Women of Courage* (66) by Dorothy Nathan presents profiles of five American women who had the courage to venture into new areas of endeavor: Susan B. Anthony, suffragette; Jane Addams, social worker; Mary Mcleod Bethune, black educator; Amelia Earhart, aviatrix; and Margaret Mead, anthropologist.

John Muir's dedication to our national parks is well told in *Trails of His Own: The Story of John Muir and His Fight to Save Our National Parks* (36) by Adrienne Grossman and Valerie Beardwood. The biography portrays Muir's deep love of nature. The virgin territories of the West, where Muir did most of his tramping and exploring, are beautifully described.

In *Oliver Cromwell* (54) by I. E. Levine, Cromwell is described as a man dedicated to his own religious principles who, in his burning desire to see justice triumph over the divine right of kings, established a free commonwealth of England and became its lord protector,

Women of Courage by Dorothy Nathan, illustrated by Carolyn Cather.

thereby launching a golden age of progress in education, science, and trade.

In Hendrik Willem Van Loon's inimitable style, the personalities, habits, and social contributions of Thomas Jefferson and Simón Bolívar are presented in *Fighters for Freedom: Jefferson and Bolívar* (94). The social, economic, and political world of each subject is sketched with ease and clarity. As the title suggests, Van Loon spotlights the work for freedom that was a vital part of each man's career.

A biography of Napoleon that mature readers will enjoy is *The True Story of Napoleon, Emperor of France* (14) by Anthony Corley. The important events in Napoleon's life are related.

The long struggle of the Indians to keep their hunting grounds and home territory is the subject of Cecile Pepin Edwards' story *King Philip* (28). The Indian hero Pometacom was sent to Plymouth to obtain a white man's education. The book relates the life of Pometacom (renamed Philip) and his desire to settle the differences between the white men and the Indians through understanding, rather than through war.

The story of Osceola and his fight to resist the compulsory emigration of the Seminoles from their homeland in Florida to Oklahoma is dramatically told by Gordon L. Hall in *Osceola* (37).

Another Indian chief who served his people and struggled to provide the leadership needed was Crazy Horse, the last of the Sioux Indian chiefs. *Crazy Horse: Sioux Warrior* (60) by Enid L. Meadowcroft contains easy-to-read material.

An inspiring book with vocational overtones is the full-length biography of a pioneer in American medicine in the field of pathology, *Prophet with Honor: Dr. William Henry Welch* (16) by William D. Crane. The work done by Dr. Welch at Johns Hopkins University helped to revolutionize the entire structure of American medical research.

A survey of women of achievement in the field of nursing is told through the life stories of ten outstanding nurses in *American Women of Nursing* (104) by Edna Yost. Coming from all walks of life and from a variety of backgrounds, these women opened new paths of service in their profession.

The Story of Winston Churchill (62) by Earl Schenck Miers features the important phases of Churchill's career and highlights his indomitable character. The text is enhanced with photographs—some in color—from various new sources.

Frances Perkins: First Lady of the Cabinet (52) by Don Lawson begins with Miss Perkins' attempts to improve working conditions for women and children and traces her growing interest in social reform, her early work with Franklin Delano Roosevelt, and her later position as Secretary of Labor during the Roosevelt administration.

Leaders of Our Time (98) by Robert N. Webb presents capsule biographies of Queen Elizabeth II, Ludwig Erhard, Emperor Hirohito, Lyndon B. Johnson, Martin Luther King, Robert Gordon Menzies, Pope Paul VI, Hyman G. Rickover, Sargent Shriver, Achmed Sukarno, Josip Broz Tito, Earl Warren, and Harold Wilson. The accounts cover highlights of each person's career and each one's significant impact on the course of the world in the twentieth century.

In a fast-moving biography Fred J. Cook presents Walter Reuther's involvement in problems of labor and the incidents leading up to the union strikes and skirmishes of the 1920s and the 1930s. *Walter Reuther: Building the House of Labor* (13) will interest mature readers.

Leslie A. Lacy has written in *Cheer the Lonesome Traveller* (49) a sympathetic biography of W. E. B. Du Bois, sociologist, historian, and civil rights leader.

The highlights of Dag Hammarskjold's life are presented in *Dag Hammarskjold: A Biography* (46) by Emery Kelen. The effective leadership displayed by the Secretary General during United Nations crises is emphasized.

Robert F. Kennedy: Man Who Dared to Dream (35) by Charles P. Graves presents a sympathetic picture of both the man and the things he stood for. The book describes him from childhood days to the fateful presidential campaign in 1968.

Mighty Hard Road: The Story of Cesar Chavez (93) by James Terzian and Kathryn Cramer is the timely biography of a Mexican-American who has successfully fought against the plight of the migrant workers in California. Today he continues his struggle to better conditions for workers in the farming industry.

Musicians, Artists, and Writers

As individuals are aroused emotionally, they seek a channel through which they can express themselves and release their feelings. The medium of expression they choose to impose upon their experience may take many artistic forms. It may be in such areas as music, painting, sculpture, dance, carpentry, cooking, or designing clothes. Each person tends to use the medium most satisfying to him.

Mozart (102) by Peggy Woodford is an interesting portrayal of Mozart that concentrates on the composer in relation not only to his art but also to the time in which he lived. Mozart's life from birth until death is described, with numerous quotes from letters written by him and by others.

Chopin (12) by Joan Chissell is a well-written account of the life of Chopin based on letters and other biographical writings. For further enjoyment, thirteen piano pieces of moderate difficulty are included, the first composed when Chopin was seven and the last in the year of his death.

Joseph Haydn's kindness and helpfulness to young composers and his love for his friends and country are depicted in a thoughtful biography told in story form, *The Story of Haydn* (44) by Helen L. Kaufmann.

The Waltz King: Johann Strauss, Jr. (70) by Kurt Pahlen is a carefully researched full-length biography that brings out the conflict between young Johann and his famous father.

Gilbert and Sullivan (103) by Norman Wymer is a well-written story of the partnership of Gilbert and Sullivan in the English theater and world of music. The author not only draws definitive pictures of the two main characters, but also recreates the customs and people of the Victorian era. The plots of some of Gilbert and Sullivan's operas are outlined, and a few song lyrics are quoted.

Louis Armstrong (76) by Kenneth G. Richards is the biography of a musician who entertained the world. He relates the events in Armstrong's life from boyhood to his place at the top of the musical world. Photographs accompany the text.

A perceptive and warm story of the life of a great cellist is found in *Pablo Casals: Cellist for Freedom* (31) by Aylesa Forsee. Not only is Casals one of the world's great musicians, but he also is a humanitarian—a man who has held fast to his ideals and is a champion of freedom everywhere. Casals emerges as a warmly human personality against the violent backdrop of the Spanish Civil War.

Leonard Bernstein (75) by John Reidy tells how the sickly son of Russian-born Jewish immigrants developed into a many-faceted musical genius.

The life of Leonardo Da Vinci and a picture of Italy during his lifetime are well woven together in Iris Noble's *Leonardo Da Vinci: The Universal Genius* (67). The personality of Da Vinci is emphasized as are the people around him. The present locations of some of Da Vinci's paintings are given.

The Great Adventure of Michelangelo (89) by Irving Stone is an edition of his *The Agony and the Ecstasy* that has been especially edited and illustrated for young readers. Retaining the feeling of the original version, the author portrays the life and turbulent times of Michelangelo with special emphasis on Florence and Rome.

Velazquez (78) by Elizabeth Ripley is a brief biography of the seventeenth-century Spanish artist which shows his gradual development as a great artist and his importance and status in the Spanish court of his day. The book is enriched by excellent black-and-white reproductions of Velazquez's paintings that are arranged chronologically on pages facing the text that describes them.

Elizabeth Ripley's *Gainsborough* (77) brings to life the admirable character of this talented English painter. Black-and-white reproductions of Gainsborough's paintings are included.

In *The Boyhood of Diego Rivera* (7) Leah Brenner presents five stories about Diego Rivera's boyhood that give insight into the developing personality of the artist. The characters in these tales show strength and simplicity as do the illustrations by Rivera.

The five artists in Clide Hollmann's *Five Artists of the Old West* (40) were adventurous men who preserved eyewitness records of the old West. The artists—Catlin, Bodner, Miller, Remington, and Russell—were different in many ways. These swiftly paced biographies illustrate each artist's devotion to his art, to the people of the West, and to the West itself.

Episodes and details for *Robert Frost: America's Poet* (30) by Doris Faber were selected especially for young readers. The authentic, continuous story is not too complex and yet gives a first acquaintance with Frost that may lead to further reading.

Elisabeth P. Myers' *Langston Hughes: Poet of His People* (65) portrays Langston Hughes with warmth and sympathy. His unsettled childhood, his young adulthood when he gained self-confidence and pride in his race, and his years of productive writing are described.

The Gay Poet: The Story of Eugene Field (68) by Jeannette Covert Nolan relates the life of Eugene Field, who is best known today for his poetry. Field was also a famous journalist and the first newspaper columnist of note. Some of his poems are included in the book. The author has captured the amusing personality of a famous American.

Laura Benet presents brief biographical sketches of twenty-six American and British poets who have contributed to children's literature in *Famous Poets for Young People* (2). A well-known poem of each poet is included in her biography.

The life story of Francis Scott Key is simply told in Lillie Patterson's *Francis Scott Key: Poet and Patriot* (71). Important events in his life from childhood until later years are reported. The description of the battle at Fort McHenry and the writing of "The Star-Spangled Banner" after the battle give insight into Key's background of courage and patriotism.

More mature readers will enjoy *The Story of John Keats* (33) by Robert Gittings and Jo Manton. The inspiration for many of his poems is woven into his life story, and poetry is included. Keats' friends—Wordsworth, Lamb, and others—also have a part in the book.

The place of John Milton in the struggle for personal freedom that took place in England during the century following the departure of the *Mayflower* is presented in *John Milton* (90) by Flora Strousse. This well-written story of Milton's life includes his role as a public figure, his writing on education and freedom of the press, and his genius as a poet.

One of the first writers to create a literature of our country is well portrayed by Laura Benet in *Washington Irving: Explorer of American Legend* (3). This biography recounts some of the happenings in Irving's life from childhood to early manhood. His life in New York during the early part of the nineteenth century when the Dutch customs still abounded and his later travels on the Continent and in England are interestingly described.

The biography *Young Edgar Allan Poe* (4) by Laura Benet concerns itself with Poe's early childhood up to the height of his literary career. The incidents in Poe's life are striking in their contrasts.

A carefully detailed, well-written biography of Henry David Thoreau is found in *A Hound, a Bay Horse and a Turtle-Dove* (101) by James P. Wood. Included are illuminating sidelights on Thoreau's contemporaries and the early nineteenth-century New England world in which he lived. Emphasized is Thoreau's independent, nonconformist character and the beliefs and attitudes embodied in his work. Numerous quotations from Thoreau's own writing enhance the biography.

Children find satisfaction in biographies of men and women who have achieved fame in the various areas of living. They are particularly interested in the biographies of people who are making an impact upon living today. The explosion of knowledge in recent years has defined old problems and brought new ones to the surface. Every area of living is being affected by this new knowledge. The present emphasis is largely upon social values and the effect of the economy, politics, and civic responsibility upon these values. An

A Hound, a Bay Horse, and a Turtle-Dove
by James Playsted Wood,
illustrated by Douglas Gorsline.

awakening of social sensitivity in adults is being reflected in the behavior of children in the middle and upper grades. As more people become involved in current affairs and work to find solutions to present-day problems, more biographies of contemporary leaders, particularly leaders from minority groups, will emerge.

Extending Experiences for the Reader

1. Read *Abe Lincoln Grows Up* (79) by Carl Sandburg. In what ways does it meet the criteria of a good biography?
2. Read *Abraham Lincoln* (18) by James Daugherty. Compare Daugherty's biography of Lincoln with the one written by Carl Sandburg. In what ways are they alike and different? Do they achieve the same purpose?
3. Read excerpts from the above biographies to the class. What are the outstanding features of their literary style?
4. Read *Invincible Louisa* (61) by Cornelia Meigs. Read some of the descriptions of places in *Invincible Louisa* to the class, for example, the Pennsylvania countryside (p. 4) and early days at Fruitland (pp. 53–58).
5. Make a list of the qualities attributed to the different members of the Alcott family.
6. Prepare exercises as suggested below. Adapt them to the group with whom you are working, making sure that the books used have been available to the boys and girls.

   Directions: Match the sentence beginnings in the first column with the sentence endings in the second column.

1. Carl Sandburg	is known as the Father of our National Parks.
2. John Muir	is known as Poor Richard.
3. Benjamin Franklin	was a pioneer in the field of pathology.
4. Austen Henry Layard	wrote a biography of Abraham Lincoln.
5. William Henry Welch	discovered and excavated the ancient city of Nineveh.

Extending Experiences for Children

1. Prepare a scrapbook with original drawings of events in the life of a person whose biography you have read.
2. Four or five pupils who have read *Daniel Boone* (19) by James Daugherty

may relate for the class the most exciting events in the life of Daniel Boone.

3. Four or five pupils who have read the same biography may prepare and present a series of skits based on the book they have read.
4. Choose one of the following about whom to write a biography: your father, mother, grandfather, grandmother, aunt, uncle, or neighbor. Share your biography with the class.
5. Write your autobiography. Include your birthplace, family life, school experiences, interests, and plans for the future.
6. Plan a series of skits for dramatizing important events in the life of Abraham Lincoln. Present the skits in an assembly program.
7. Narrate an incident in the life of a person whose biography you have read as if you were that person.
8. Keep a personal record of the biographies you read, including author, title, publisher, date, and a brief written reaction.
9. Prepare a chronology chart of important events in the life of a person whose biography you have read.

Chapter References

1. BECKER, BERIL. *Captain Edward L. Beach: Around the World Under Water.* Chicago: Encyclopaedia Britannica Press, 1962. Grades 4–6.
2. BENET, LAURA. *Famous Poets for Young People.* New York: Dodd, Mead, 1964. Grades 7–9.
3. ______. *Washington Irving: Explorer of American Legend.* New York: Dodd, Mead, 1944. Grades 7–9.
4. ______. *Young Edgar Allan Poe.* New York: Dodd, Mead, 1941. Grades 7–9.
5. BERRY, ERICK. *Robert E. Peary: North Pole Conqueror.* Champaign, Ill.: Garrard, 1963. Grades 4–6.
6. BLASSINGAME, WYATT. *Ponce De Leon.* Champaign, Ill.: Garrard, 1965. Grades 4–6.
7. BRENNER, LEAH. *The Boyhood of Diego Rivera.* Cranberry, N. J.: Barnes, 1964. Grades 4–6.
8. BUEHR, WALTER. *The Portuguese Explorers.* New York: Putnam, 1966. Grades 4–6.
9. BURT, OLIVE W. *Negroes in the Early West.* New York: Messner, 1969. Grades 4–6.
10. CAMPBELL, ANN. *The Picture Life of Richard Milhous Nixon.* New York: Watts, 1969. Kindergarten–grade 2.
11. CATE, CURTIS. *Antoine De Saint-Exupéry.* New York: Putnam, 1971. n.g.l.
12. CHISSELL, JOAN. *Chopin.* New York: T. Y. Crowell, 1965. Grades 4–6.
13. COOK, FRED J. *Walter Reuther: Building the House of Labor.* Boston: Little, Brown, 1969. n.g.l.

14. CORLEY, ANTHONY. *The True Story of Napoleon, Emperor of France.* Chicago: Childrens Press, 1964. Grades 4–6.
15. CAVANAH, FRANCES, AND ELIZABETH L. CRANDALL. *Meet the Presidents.* Rev. ed. Philadelphia, Pa.: Macrae Smith, 1965. Grades 7–9.
16. CRANE, WILLIAM D. *Prophet with Honor: Dr. William Henry Welch.* New York: Messner, 1966. Grades 7–9.
17. CRAWFORD, DEBORAH. *Lise Meitner, Atomic Pioneer.* New York: Crown, 1969. Grades 7–9.
18. DAUGHERTY, JAMES. *Abraham Lincoln.* New York: Viking, 1943. Grades 7–9.
19. ______. *Daniel Boone.* New York: Viking, 1939. Grades 7–9.
20. ______. *Of Courage Undaunted: Across the Continent with Lewis and Clark.* New York: Viking, 1951. Grades 7–9.
21. ______. *Poor Richard.* New York: Viking, 1941. Grades 7–9.
22. DE LEEUW, ADELE. *Richard E. Byrd: Adventurer to the Poles.* Champaign, Ill.: Garrard, 1963. Grades 4–6.
23. DOLSON, HILDEGARDE. *William Penn.* New York: Random House, 1961. Grades 4–6.
24. DOWNEY, GLANVILLE. *Aristotle, Dean of Early Science.* New York: Watts, 1962. Grades 7–9.
25. EATON, JEANETTE. *Lone Journey: The Life of Roger Williams.* W. Ishmael (ill.). New York: Harcourt Brace Jovanovich, 1944. Paperback. Grades 7–9.
26. ______. *Narcissa Whitman: Pioneer of Oregon.* New York: Harcourt Brace Jovanovich, 1941. Grades 7–9.
27. ______. *That Lively Man, Ben Franklin.* New York: Morrow, 1948. Grades 7–9.
28. EDWARDS, CECILE PEPIN. *King Philip.* Boston: Houghton Mifflin, 1962. Grades 4–6.
29. EPSTEIN, SAM, AND BERYL EPSTEIN. *George Washington Carver.* New York: Dell, 1968. Paperback. Grades 4–6.
30. FABER, DORIS. *Robert Frost: America's Poet.* Englewood Cliffs, N. J.: Prentice-Hall, 1964. Grades 4–6.
31. FORSEE, AYLESA. *Pablo Casals: Cellist for Freedom.* New York: T. Y. Crowell, 1965. Grades 7–9.
32. FREEDMAN, RUSSELL. *Jules Verne: Portrait of a Prophet.* New York: Holiday House, 1965. Grades 7–9.
33. GITTINGS, ROBERT, AND JO MANTON. *The Story of John Keats.* New York: Dutton, 1963. Grades 7–9.
34. GRAVES, CHARLES P. *Marco Polo.* Champaign, Ill.: Garrard, 1963. Grades 4–6.
35. ______. *Robert F. Kennedy: Man Who Dared to Dream.* Champaign, Ill.: Garrard, 1970. Grades 4–9.
36. GROSSMAN, ADRIENNE, AND VALERIE BEARDWOOD. *Trails of His Own: The Story of John Muir and His Fight to Save Our National Parks.* New York: David McKay, 1961. Grades 7–9.
37. HALL, GORDON L. *Osceola.* New York: Holt, Rinehart & Winston, 1964. Grades 4–6.

38. HAYS, WILMA P. *Samuel Morse and the Electronic Age.* New York: Watts, 1966. Grades 7–9.
39. HENRY, JOANNE L. *Marie Curie: Discoverer of Radium.* New York: Macmillan, 1966. Grades 4–6.
40. HOLLMANN, CLIDE. *Five Artists of the Old West.* New York: Hastings House, 1965. Grades 7–9.
41. HOLWOOD, WILL. *The True Story of Sir Francis Drake, Privateer.* Chicago: Childrens Press, 1964. Grades 4–6.
42. ISRAEL, CHARLES E. *Five Ships West: The Story of Magellan.* New York: Macmillan, 1966. Grades 4–6.
43. JOHNSTON, JOHANNA. *Thomas Jefferson, His Many Talents.* New York: Dodd, Mead, 1961. Grades 7–9.
44. KAUFMANN, HELEN L. *The Story of Haydn.* New York: Grosset & Dunlap, n.d. Grades 4–6.
45. KAUFMANN, MERVYN D. *Thomas Alva Edison: Miracle Maker.* Champaign, Ill.: Garrard, 1962. Grades 4–6.
46. KELEN, EMERY. *Dag Hammarskjold: A Biography.* New York: Hawthorn, 1969. Grades 7–9.
47. KERR, LAURA. *Louisa: The Life of Mrs. John Quincy Adams.* New York: Funk & Wagnalls, 1964. Grades 7–9.
48. KNOOP, FAITH Y. *Amerigo Vespucci.* Champaign, Ill.: Garrard, 1966. Grades 4–6.
49. LACY, LESLIE A. *Cheer the Lonesome Traveller.* New York: Dial Press, 1970. n.g.l.
50. LAND, BARBARA. *The Quest of Johannes Kepler.* Garden City, N. Y.: Doubleday, 1963. Grades 4–6.
51. LATHAM, JEAN LEE. *Eli Whitney: Great Inventor.* Champaign, Ill.: Garrard, 1963. Grades 4–6.
52. LAWSON, DON. *Frances Perkins: First Lady of the Cabinet.* New York: Abelard-Schuman, 1967. Grades 7–9.
53. LAWSON, MARION. *Solomon Juneau, Voyageur.* New York: T. Y. Crowell, n.d. Grades 7–9.
54. LEVINE, I. E. *Oliver Cromwell.* New York: Messner, 1966. Grades 7–9.
55. ———. *Young Man in the White House: John Fitzgerald Kennedy.* New York: Simon & Schuster, 1969. Paperback. Grades 7–9.
56. MCKOWN, ROBIN. *She Lived for Science: Irene Joliot-Curie.* New York: Messner, 1961. Grades 7–9.
57. MANCHESTER, HARLAND. *Trail Blazers of Technology.* New York: Scribner, 1962. Grades 7–9.
58. MANN, JOHN H. *Louis Pasteur, the Germ Killer.* New York: Macmillan, 1967. Grades 4–6.
59. MARTIN, RALPH G. *President from Missouri: Harry S Truman.* New York: Messner, 1964. Grades 7–9.
60. MEADOWCROFT, ENID L. *Crazy Horse: Sioux Warrior.* Champaign, Ill.: Garrard, 1965. Grades 4–6.
61. MEIGS, CORNELIA. *Invincible Louisa.* Boston: Little, Brown, 1968. Grades 7–9.

62. MIERS, EARL SCHENCK. *The Story of Winston Churchill.* New York: Grosset & Dunlap, 1957. Grades 4–6.

63. MILLER, HELEN M. *George Rogers Clark: Frontier Fighter.* New York: Putnam, 1968. Grades 4–6.

64. MONTGOMERY, ELIZABETH RIDER. *Alexander Graham Bell: Man of Sound.* Champaign, Ill.: Garrard, 1963. Grades 4–6.

65. MYERS, ELISABETH P. *Langston Hughes: Poet of His People.* Champaign, Ill.: Garrard, 1970. Grades 7–9.

66. NATHAN, DOROTHY. *Women of Courage.* New York: Random House, 1964. Paperback. Grades 7–9.

67. NOBLE, IRIS. *Leonardo Da Vinci: The Universal Genius.* New York: Grosset & Dunlap, 1965. Grades 4–6.

68. NOLAN, JEANNETTE COVERT. *The Gay Poet: The Story of Eugene Field.* New York: Messner, 1941. Grades 7–9.

69. ———. *The Story of Clara Barton of the Red Cross.* New York: Messner, 1941. Grades 7–9.

70. PAHLEN, KURT. *The Waltz King: Johann Strauss, Jr.* T. McClintock (tr.). Chicago: Rand McNally, 1965. Grades 7–9.

71. PATTERSON, LILLIE. *Francis Scott Key: Poet and Patriot.* Champaign, Ill.: Garrard, 1963. Grades 4–6.

72. PEARE, CATHERINE O. *The Herbert Hoover Story.* New York: T. Y. Crowell, 1965. Grades 7–9.

73. PETERSHAM, MAUDE, AND MISKA PETERSHAM. *Story of the Presidents of the United States.* Rev. ed. New York: Macmillan, 1966. Grades 4–6.

74. RANDALL, RUTH P. *I Elizabeth: A Biography of the Girl Who Married General George Armstrong Custer.* Boston: Little, Brown, 1966. Grades 7–9.

75. REIDY, JOHN. *Leonard Bernstein.* New York: Childrens Press, 1967. n.g.l.

76. RICHARDS, KENNETH G. *Louis Armstrong.* Chicago: Childrens Press, 1967. Grades 4–6.

77. RIPLEY, ELIZABETH. *Gainsborough.* Philadelphia: Lippincott, 1964. Grades 7–9.

78. ———. *Velazquez.* Philadelphia: Lippincott, 1965. Grades 7–9.

79. SANDBURG, CARL. *Abe Lincoln Grows Up.* New York: Harcourt Brace Jovanovich, 1931. Grades 7–9.

80. ———. *The Prairie Years.* New York: Dell, n.d. Vol. I. Paperback. n.g.l.

81. SELDEN, GEORGE. *Sir Arthur Evans: Discoverer of Knossos.* New York: Macmillan, 1964. Grades 2–6.

82. SEVERN, BILL. *Frontier President: The Life of James K. Polk.* New York: Washburn, 1965. Grades 7–9.

83. ———. *In Lincoln's Footsteps: The Story of Andrew Johnson.* New York: Washburn, 1965. Grades 7–9.

84. SILVERBERG, ROBERT. *The Man Who Found Nineveh.* New York: Holt, Rinehart & Winston, 1964. Grades 7–9.

85. SMITH, FREDRIKA S. *Frémont: Soldier, Explorer, Statesman.* Chicago: Rand McNally, 1966. Grades 7–9.

86. STEINBERG, ALFRED. *Dwight David Eisenhower.* New York: Putnam, 1968. Grades 7–9.

87. STERLING, PHILIP. *Sea and Earth: The Life of Rachel Carson.* New York: T. Y. Crowell, 1970. Grades 5–8.
88. STONAKER, FRANCES B. *Famous Mathematicians.* Philadelphia: Lippincott, 1966. Grades 7–9.
89. STONE, IRVING. *The Great Adventure of Michelangelo.* Abr. ed. Garden City, N. Y.: Doubleday, 1965. Grades 7–9.
90. STROUSSE, FLORA. *John Milton.* New York: Vanguard, 1960. Grades 7–9.
91. SUTTON, ANN, AND MYRON SUTTON. *Journey into Ice: John Franklin and the Northwest Passage.* Chicago: Rand McNally, 1965. Grades 7–9.
92. SYME, RONALD. *Vasco Da Gama: Sailor Toward the Sunrise.* New York: Morrow, 1959. Grades 4–6.
93. TERZIAN, JAMES, AND KATHRYN CRAMER. *Mighty Hard Road: The Story of Cesar Chavez.* Garden City, N. Y.: Doubleday, 1970. Paperback. Grades 4–6.
94. VAN LOON, HENDRIK WILLEM. *Fighters for Freedom: Jefferson and Bolívar.* Crowell, 1962. Paperback. Grades 4–8.
95. WALDMAN, GUIDO. *The Voyages of Christopher Columbus.* New York: Golden Press, 1966. Grades 4–6.
96. WALTERS, HELEN B. *Wernher Von Braun: Rocket Engineer.* New York: Macmillan, 1964. Grades 7–9.
97. WARNER, OLIVER, AND CHESTER W. NIMITZ. *Nelson and the Age of Fighting Sail.* New York: Harper & Row, 1963. Grades 7–9.
98. WEBB, ROBERT N. *Leaders of Our Time.* New York: Watts, 1969. Vol. IV. Grades 7–9.
99. WESTERVELT, VIRGINIA V. *Incredible Man of Science.* New York: Messner, 1968. Grades 7–9.
100. WISE, WINIFRED E. *Harriet Beecher Stowe: Woman with a Cause.* New York: Putnam, 1965. Grades 4–6.
101. WOOD, JAMES P. *A Hound, a Bay Horse, and a Turtle-Dove.* New York: Pantheon, 1963. Grades 7–9.
102. WOODFORD, PEGGY. *Mozart.* New York: Walck, 1966. Grades 4–6.
103. WYMER, NORMAN. *Gilbert and Sullivan.* New York: Dutton, 1963. Grades 7–9.
104. YOST, EDNA. *American Women of Nursing.* Rev. ed. Philadelphia: Lippincott, 1955. Grades 7–9.

More Biographies for Children

Kindergarten–Grade 2

BOONE-JONES, MARGARET. *Martin Luther King, Jr.* Chicago: Childrens Press, 1968. Dr. King's achievements in helping his people are related.

FRIEDMAN, ESTELLE. *Ben Franklin.* New York: Putnam, 1961. The facts about Franklin's boyhood days in Boston, his avid reading interests, and two trips to France are offered in short, simplified form.

GRAVES, CHARLES. *Frederick Douglass.* New York: Putnam, 1970. This book is a simply written biography of Frederick Douglass, an American slave who fought against the living conditions to which he was subjected.

YOUNG, MARGARET B. *The Picture Life of Ralph J. Bunche.* New York: Watts, 1968. Ralph Bunche, a man from a poor midwestern Black family, made significant contributions to the social life of the nation. He became Under-Secretary for Special Political Affairs at the United Nations and was awarded the Nobel Peace Prize in 1950.

Grades 4–6

ALLEN, LEE. *Babe Ruth.* New York: Putnam, 1966. This biography of Babe Ruth highlights his interest in and support of young people's activities.

BACON, MARGARET H. *Lamb's Warrior.* New York: T. Y. Crowell, 1970. This book is an informative biography of Isaac Hopper, a Quaker, zealous abolitionist, and crusader for human rights.

BERTOL, ROLAND. *Charles Drew.* New York: T. Y. Crowell, 1970. Charles Drew pioneered blood preservation and plasma transfusions in the United States. Because he was Black, Dr. Drew faced and overcame many obstacles to obtain an education as he worked to make his contribution to American society.

BLASSINGAME, WYATT. *Eleanor Roosevelt.* New York: Putnam, 1967. This First Lady traveled around the country meeting people and finding out how the government could make their lives better.

BROWNMILLER, SUSAN. *Shirley Chisholm.* Garden City, N. Y.: Doubleday, 1970. A narrative biography of Shirley Chisholm is unfolded. The able, first Black Congresswoman represents Brooklyn's newly created 12th Congressional District.

DE KAY, JAMES T. *Meet Martin Luther King, Jr.* New York: Random House, 1969. This book tells the story of Martin Luther King, Jr., who brought Black people together in a great and peaceful struggle for freedom.

EPSTEIN, SAM, AND BERYL EPSTEIN. *Harriet Tubman.* Chicago: Garrard, 1968. This great Black woman dedicated her life to helping her people gain freedom.

FABER, DORIS. *Enrico Fermi, Atomic Pioneer.* Englewood Cliffs, N. J.: Prentice-Hall, 1966. The brilliant scientist's personal life, his work, and his contribution in the development of the atomic bomb are told.

FALL, THOMAS. *Jim Thorpe.* New York: T. Y. Crowell, 1970. This biography about the famous American Indian athlete includes highlights of the outstanding events of his career.

FELTON, HAROLD W. *Mumbet: The Story of Elizabeth Freeman.* New York: Dodd, Mead, 1970. This is a true story of a brave, determined Black woman who was the first slave to gain legal freedom in the Massachusetts courts in 1781.

———. *Nat Love, Negro Cowboy.* New York: Dodd, Mead, 1969. An interesting account is given of the life and exploits of Nat Love, the most famous of Black cowboys. Born in Tennessee in 1854, Nat Love traveled west when he was fifteen years old to seek his fortune as a cowboy.

FENDERSON, LEWIS. *Thurgood Marshall, Fighter for Justice.* New York: Mc-

Graw-Hill, 1969. Important events in Marshall's private life and public career are highlighted from his boyhood to his appointment as a Justice of the United States Supreme Court.

FRANCHERE, RUTH. *Cesar Chavez.* New York: T. Y. Crowell, 1970. This book tells in simple style the life story of Cesar Chavez, the most prominent figure in the struggle to improve the working and living conditions of migrant workers in the United States.

GRIFFIN, JUDITH B. *Nat Turner.* New York: Coward-McCann, 1970. Simply written, this biography of Nat Turner relates the events that resulted in the famous rebellion that the famous Black leader led in 1831. The struggle between his deeply religious nature and his will to be free is movingly told.

HAYS, WILMA P. *Patrick of Ireland.* New York: Coward-McCann, 1970. This fictionalized account of the early life of St. Patrick of Ireland is based, according to the author's notes, on material from Patrick's *Confessions.*

HEILBRONER, JOAN. *Meet George Washington.* New York: Random House, 1965. The major phases of Washington's career are told without exaggeration. He is shown as gentleman farmer, soldier, statesman, and Virginia aristocrat.

KELLY, REGINA Z. *James Madison, Statesman & President.* Boston: Houghton Mifflin, 1966. The fourth President of the United States is portrayed from age eight until the time of his death.

MALICK, ARDEN D. *Dolley Madison.* New York: Putnam, 1970. A biography of Dolley Madison gives a brief sketch of the political events of her time.

MARTIN, PATRICIA M. *Zachary Taylor.* New York: Putnam, 1969. The life of Zachary Taylor is traced from his childhood days on the Kentucky frontier to the time when he became a soldier in the war with Mexico and finally President of the United States.

MOOS, MALCOLM. *Dwight D. Eisenhower.* New York: Random House, 1964. The story of the General from childhood to retirement includes a description of his two terms as President of the United States.

OLDS, HELEN D. *Richard E. Byrd.* New York: Putnam, 1969. An easy-to-read biography about the great explorer of the South Pole.

REYNOLDS, MACK. *Puerto Rican Patriot.* New York: Macmillan, 1969. This biography tells the story of how Luis Muñoz Revera battled first against Spain and then against the United States in order to achieve "home rule" for Puerto Rico.

SADIE, STANLEY. *Beethoven.* New York: T. Y. Crowell, 1967. This story of Beethoven will appeal to the student interested in classical music.

SKREBITSKI, G. A. *Forest Echo.* New York: Braziller, 1967. This Russian naturalist-author's autobiography, with many wildlife encounters, is illustrated in two colors and written in the first person.

SNOW, DOROTHEA J. *Benjamin West: Gifted Young Painter.* Indianapolis: Bobbs-Merrill, 1967. The feelings, hopes, difficulties, and accomplishments of the "Father of American Painting" are expressed realistically in this biography.

STEVENSON, JANET. *Spokesman for Freedom.* New York: Macmillan, 1969. Archibald Grimke, son of a white plantation owner and a slave girl, rose from slavery to be a graduate of Harvard Law School, a writer, editor, defender of civil rights, organizer of the NAACP, and United States Consul to Santo Domingo.

SYME, RONALD. *Benedict Arnold.* New York: Morrow, 1970. An objective biography presents both the strengths and the weaknesses of this Revolutionary War traitor.

———. *Bolívar the Liberator.* New York: Morrow, 1968. This outstanding biography details Bolívar's life and the South American revolution. Quotations from Bolívar's letters and speeches are included.

WESTCOTT, FREDERIC. *Bach.* New York: Walck, 1967. Bach is seen not only through his art but also in relation to his fellow men.

WINDERS, GERTRUDE H. *George M. Cohan.* Indianapolis: Bobbs-Merrill, 1968. This biography of George M. Cohan recounts his life in show business. Through the years Cohan began to compose songs and musical plays and finally became one of the great composers and directors in America.

WISE, WILLIAM. *Aaron Burr.* New York: Putnam, 1968. The early decades of the Republic are vividly portrayed as a background for a story that describes Burr's life as a Revolutionary hero, as Vice-President under Thomas Jefferson, and as an opponent of Alexander Hamilton.

Grades 7–9

ABODAHER, DAVID. *Freedom Fighter.* New York: Messner, 1969. This carefully researched biography tells of the Polish cavalry officer Casimir Pulaski, who came to America to help in the colonists' cause.

ALLEN, LEE. *Dizzy Dean.* New York: Putnam, 1967. This biographical sketch of Jay Hanna Dean, who became known by baseball fans as Dizzy Dean, relates how, through his determination, he moved from pitching for an army team to a career as a colorful pitcher for the St. Louis Cardinals.

ANDERSON, JEAN. *Henry the Navigator.* Philadelphia: Westminster, 1969. This biography of Portugal's national hero, Henry the Navigator, tells how he brought together men of science during the Middle Ages.

ARCHER, JULES. *Angry Abolitionist.* New York: Messner, 1969. The author describes the life of William Lloyd Garrison, the early nineteenth-century abolitionist who published the *Liberator,* a newspaper that was instrumental in the growing movement for the emancipation of slaves.

———. *Fighting Journalist: Horace Greeley.* New York: Messner, 1966. Greeley's rise to prominence and his influence on national, political, and social life, as well as his role in mid-nineteenth-century journalism, are portrayed in this biography.

———. *World Citizen.* New York: Messner, 1969. This biography portrays Woodrow Wilson's character and covers the negotiations and controversies produced by the Mexican War and the Versailles Treaty. Pro and con opinions by Wilson's critics and defenders are presented.

BAKER, NINA BROWN. *Next Year in Jerusalem.* New York: Harcourt Brace Jovanovich, 1950. This biography of Theodore Herzl, the Zionist leader, provides a good background for understanding the establishment of Israel.

BERGER, PHIL. *Joe Namath.* New York: Cowles, 1969. This well-written biography relates Joe Namath's growing years, college performance, professional activities, and colorful personal life.

BIGLAND, EILEEN. *Queen Elizabeth First.* New York: Criterion, 1965. This biography of a shrewd and impressive monarch makes Elizabeth's motives and reactions more understandable.

BUCHMAN, DIAN P. *The Sherlock Holmes of Medicine.* New York: Messner, 1969. Highlights are described in the career of Dr. Joseph Goldberger, whose research helped to control and prevent epidemics of diseases.

CAVANAH, FRANCES, AND ELIZABETH L. CRANDALL. *Meet the Presidents.* Rev. ed. Philadelphia: Smith Macrae, 1965. Including brief biographical sketches of the Presidents, this book describes a dramatic event in the life of each of our Presidents.

COMAY, JOAN. *Ben-Gurion & the Birth of Israel.* New York: Random House, 1967. A well-written account of Ben-Gurion's role in the establishment of a national homeland for Jews in Palestine is presented.

COOLIDGE, OLIVIA. *Gandhi.* Boston: Houghton Mifflin, 1971. An interesting portrait of Gandhi is compiled from photographs, newspaper articles, pamphlets, and personal letters.

DOBLER, LAVINIA, AND WILLIAM R. BROWN. *Great Rulers of the African Past.* Garden City, N. Y.: Doubleday, 1965. Africa from the thirteenth to the seventeenth centuries—shifting borders, religious conflict, and foreign domination—is portrayed through the lives of its leaders.

GILBERT, MARTIN. *Winston Churchill.* New York: Dial Press, 1967. This is a short biography of one of England's greatest statesmen.

GRAHAM, FRANK. *Lou Gehrig: A Quiet Hero.* New York: Putnam, 1942. After being stricken with multiple sclerosis, Lou Gehrig worked on the New York City Parole Board where he gave boys an understanding based on his own boyhood needs.

GRAY, ELIZABETH. *Penn.* New York: Viking, 1938. William Penn's beliefs and his practice of them in the New World are portrayed in this biography.

GREEN, MARGARET. *Paul Revere: The Man Behind the Legend.* New York: Messner, 1964. Paul Revere is portrayed as a famous silversmith, a courageous member of the Sons of Liberty and the Committee of Correspondence, a courier for the Massachusetts Provincial Assembly, and the designer and engraver of the first seal of the United Colonies.

JAKES, JOHN. *Mohawk.* New York: Macmillan, 1969. This story of an outstanding Indian chief, Joseph Brant, relates his efforts to save his people by means of a powerful Indian league.

KAMM, JOSEPHINE. *The Story of Emmeline Pankhurst.* New York: Meredith, 1968. This biography of Emmeline Pankhurst describes militant suffragism in England and the years of abuse that followers suffered until their goal was won in 1928.

KEATING, LAWRENCE. *Fleet Admiral: The Story of William F. Halsey.* Philadelphia: Westminster, 1965. This biography of Admiral Halsey follows his early training and further preparation for command of the forces in the South Pacific area and his role in the progress of World War II.

KYLE, ELIZABETH. *Song of the Waterfall.* New York: Holt, Reinhart & Winston, 1970. This biography gives a lively account of Edvard Grieg's life and his interest in creating music that reflected Norwegian characteristics and that brought about an appreciation of Scandinavian music.

LEWIS, CLAUDE. *Benjamin Banneker.* New York: McGraw-Hill, 1970. In a carefully researched narrative biography, the author brings to life an eighteenth-century Afro-American scientist who played an important role in the planning and surveying of the nation's capital city.

LOMASK, MILTON. *Odd Destiny.* New York: Farrar, Straus & Giroux, 1969. The life of Alexander Hamilton is described in this outstanding biography of the Revolutionary leader, Federalist, and promoter of the idea of a strong central government.

LUCKOCK, ELIZABETH. *William the Conqueror.* New York: Putnam, 1966. The history and the struggle for power and the alliances that were formed during the era of the Battle of Hastings in 1066, when Harold the King was defeated by William, are related in this biography.

MELTZER, MILTON. *Tongue of Flame: The Life of Lydia Marie Child.* New York: T. Y. Crowell, 1965. Primarily an abolitionist, but not a militant one, Lydia Child wrote many books and articles dealing with the problems of slavery. Descriptions of Boston and New York during the mid-nineteenth century are excellent.

MEYER, HOWARD N. *Let Us Have Peace: The Life of Ulysses S. Grant.* New York: Macmillan, 1966. This biography of Ulysses S. Grant shows the unrest in the United States over slavery and includes the Civil War and postwar periods.

NEIMARK, ANNE E. *Touch of Light.* New York: Harcourt Brace Jovanovich, 1970. In this biography Louis Braille's childhood and youth are emphasized—the horrible accident that took his sight at age three, his desire to do something that would help the blind, and finally his success in developing the Braille system.

NOBLE, IRIS. *Great Lady of the Theatre: Sarah Bernhardt.* New York: Messner, 1960. One of the most courageous and accomplished women of the theater is described in this book.

NORRIS, MARIANNA. *Dona Felissa.* New York: Dodd, Mead, 1969. This book relates the life of Felissa Rincon de Gautier, who in spite of a traditional, strict Spanish background rose to become the successful, well-loved mayor of San Juan, Puerto Rico.

NORTH, STERLING. *Mark Twain and the River.* Boston: Houghton Mifflin, 1961. This biography follows Mark Twain from the anecdotes and adventures of his boyhood, through his golden years of maturity and love and to his final days.

ORMONT, ARTHUR. *Fighter Against Slavery.* New York: Messner, 1966. The unsung hero of human rights during the early 1880s, Jehudi Ashmun, an American missionary, dedicated his life to reestablishing American Black slaves in Liberia and eliminating the slave trade in West Africa.

PHILIPSON, MORRIS. *Count Who Wished He Were a Peasant: A Life of Leo Tolstoy.*

New York: Pantheon, 1967. This is a balanced, colorful biography of the Russian writer Leo Tolstoy.

ROBINSON, JACKIE, AND ALFRED DUCKETT. *Break Through to the Big League.* New York: Harper & Row, 1965. This is the story of how Jackie Robinson was elected to the Baseball Hall of Fame.

ROBINSON, LOUIE. *Arthur Ashe, Tennis Champion.* Garden City, N. Y.: Doubleday, 1970. This biography tells the dramatic story of a tennis champion of national and international stature who has made his way to the top in the "white" world of tennis.

ROLL, WINIFRED. *The Pomegranate and the Rose: The Story of Katherine of Aragon.* Englewood Cliffs, N. J.: Prentice-Hall, 1970. This daring biography tells of the controversial queen Katherine of Aragon. The author presents a scholarly, documented study—based on contemporary or near contemporary sources—that reveals a tragic but not a pathetic woman determined to save her good name and her soul.

ROLLINS, CHARLEMAE HILL. *Black Troubadour: Langston Hughes.* Chicago: Rand McNally, 1971. Rollins traces the poet's life from boyhood; discusses his stories, novels, plays, and poems; and emphasizes his distinctive qualities as an interpreter of both the Black and universal human experience.

SEVERN, BILL. *John Marshall.* New York: David McKay, 1969. The post-Revolutionary War years provide a vivid background for this biography of John Marshall that explores his role as a statesman particularly in establishing the power of the Supreme Court.

______. *William Howard Taft.* New York: David McKay, 1970. The only man to serve the United States as both President and Chief Justice of the U. S. Supreme Court is portrayed in an objective, well-written biography.

SIMON, CHARLIE M. *Andrew Carnegie Story.* New York: Dutton, 1965. This sympathetic biography relates how Andrew Carnegie made the American dream of the successful poor boy come true.

STEINBERG, ALFRED. *The Kennedy Brothers.* New York: Putnam, 1969. A social and political sketch of the Kennedy brothers traces the clan since first settling in the United States. Much emphasis is placed on the patriarch father, Joseph Kennedy, and his efforts to educate his sons for the presidency of the United States.

STERLING, DOROTHY. *Lucretia Mott.* Garden City, N. Y.: Doubleday, 1964. A happy wife, mother, and crusader, Lucretia Mott was a pioneer together with Elizabeth Cady Stanton, in organizing protests for the rights of women.

SYME, RONALD. *Nigerian Pioneer: The Story of Mary Slessor.* New York: Morrow, 1964. This excellent biography portrays the daring Mary Slessor, who left Scotland for a Presbyterian mission in Nigeria in 1876.

WERSTEIN, IRVING. *Labor's Defiant Lady.* New York: T. Y. Crowell, 1969. This book relates the colorful and dramatic account of the life and career of Irish-born Mary Harris Jones, a militant trade union organizer in the American labor movement from the 1870s to the 1920s.

WOOD, JAMES PLAYSTEAD. *Lantern Bearer: A Life of Robert Louis Stevenson.*

New York: Pantheon, 1965. This well-documented biography of Robert Louis Stevenson's life contains much adventure.

———. *The Unpardonable Sin: A Life of Nathaniel Hawthorne.* New York: Pantheon, 1971. This biography of Nathaniel Hawthorne relates the contradictions in his life.

WYNDHAM, LEE. *Florence Nightingale.* Cleveland: World Publishing, 1969. Born into wealth and social position, Florence Nightingale was aware of the differences in the living conditions of people around her. She had compassion for the poor and the sick and decided to devote her life to them. Her organizing and administrative ability led her to the battlefield in the Crimean War as head of a small group of nurses. Miss Nightingale never ceased working to improve hospital conditions.

Biographies in Collections

Grades 4–6

FINLAYSON, ANN. *Stars of the Modern Olympics.* Champaign, Ill.: Garrard, 1967. Brief biographies of Bob Garrett, Ray Ewry, Felix Caravajal, Jim Thorpe, Duke Kahanamoku, and Paavo Nurmi are included.

Grades 7–9

COOLIDGE, OLIVIA. *Lives of Famous Romans.* Boston: Houghton Mifflin, 1965. Portraits of twelve famous Romans of the period 86 B.C. to the death of Constantine in A.D. 337 are included in this collection.

FLEMING, ALICE. *Great Women Teachers.* Philadelphia: Lippincott, 1965. A number of the lesser-known women teachers who achieved success are included in this collection of ten short, well-written biographies.

HOLLANDER, ZANDER (ed.). *Great American Athletes of the Twentieth Century.* New York: Random House, 1966. This collection contains colorful profiles of forty-nine great sports heroes who starred in a number of sports.

PETERS, ALEXANDER. *Heroes of the Major Leagues.* New York: Random House, 1967. This collection gives excellent informative reports on ten outstanding baseball players of the present time.

RITTENHOUSE, MIGNON. *Seven Women Explorers.* Philadelphia: Lippincott, 1964. The explorations of seven women and their contributions, along with brief reference to the other important aspects of their lives, are described in this book.

ROLLINS, CHARLEMAE. *Famous Negro Entertainers of Stage, Screen, & TV.* New York: Dodd, Mead, 1967. Biographical sketches of sixteen Black entertainers in various fields of the performing arts are included in this collection.

Drusilla by Sulamith Ish-Kishor, illustrated by Thomas Morley.

14 Historical Fiction

Historical fiction holds an important place in children's literature. Children in the middle and upper grades have a strong penchant for the intrigue, suspense, and bravery that it offers, and through it they can vicariously experience life in, say, the Bronze Age in Denmark with Heather and Wolf Stone in the *Faraway Lurs* (10) or in England with Drem in *Warrior Scarlet* (81). They can live in the thirteenth century with young Adam Quartermayne as he sets out from St. Albans Abbey to London to find his father in *Adam of the Road* (45), follow the phantom stag of Hun legends into the promised land with Attila in *The White Stag* (78), or relive with the Charnetski family the excitement of the fifteenth century in Poland in *The Trumpeter of Krakow* (60). They may be fascinated by life in Chungking as young Fu goes about the city learning the urban mores and meeting the impact of modern ideas in *Young Fu of the Upper Yangtze* (63). They can meet a brave girl in *The Courage of Sarah Noble* (25) and travel with her into the Connecticut wilderness, and join Kit Tyler in rebelling against the strictures of a Puritan community in 1687 in *The Witch of Blackbird Pond* (79). Readers share excitement and danger with John Sager as he faces the hardships of the Oregon Trail in *On to Oregon* (69). Through historical fiction children can transcend all barriers of space and time.

Background for Historical Fiction

Nations throughout the world have moved from early primitive beginnings to their present ways of life. History records man's struggle to defend his property from invasion, to build a nation, and to be free from oppression and tyranny. Man's efforts to realize these goals have frequently led to crises out of which have emerged heroes who have led their people through the difficulties facing them.

It is only natural that these difficulties became the subjects of folk tales and later of written records. The people involved in the events became heroes who were praised in songs and stories down through the ages. In addition to the historical events to be remembered and the heroes to be venerated in the nation as a whole, the subcultures within a nation have particular persons and events that they wish to remember and honor. This is especially true in our nation, where people coming from many different countries bring with them their own holidays, festivals, and celebrations.

Our country has a rich heritage of historical events that have been the subjects of countless books, both nonfiction and fiction. Outstanding authors have told the story of our country—the events that shaped the destiny of our nation, the people who suffered hardships and often risked their lives to make the dreams of our forefathers come true, the scientific discoveries that have made possible advances in medicine and technology, and the social movements in the interest of people's welfare that have contributed to the improvement of living conditions throughout the world. These books help adults and children to appreciate the past and to see the relation of the past to the present and the future.

History Textbooks and Historical Fiction

The function of history textbooks is to report as accurately as possible. They are planned to inform the reader rather than to arouse his emotions. Historical fiction adds more excitement or glamour to the factual accounts of events recorded in history books. It is interesting to compare the way a particular event is treated in a history book with the way it is handled in historical fiction.

In the textbook *Land of the Free* (67) the opening of the Revolutionary War is described as follows:

> The break came on April 19, 1775, in Massachusetts. The British commander, hearing alarming reports that the colonists were stockpiling arms and ammunition, ordered out a detachment of troops to find out what had been going on at Concord.
>
> The troops could move out toward Concord by boat across Boston's Back Bay, or they could go by land around the Bayshore. Colonists were keeping watch on these soldiers. From the belfry of Boston's Old North Church, they were to give a signal if the soldiers moved. One lantern would be shown if the soldiers went by land, two if they went by sea. At midnight, as they waited on the other side of the Bay, Paul Revere and William Dawes saw two

lanterns flare at the church. Dashing along the roads, they called out to their countrymen that the British were coming.

On their march the British were surprised to see many colonists with arms in hand. At Lexington they found a group of men who refused to put down their guns. Firing began. After killing eight and wounding ten, the redcoats marched on to Concord. They found and destroyed the military stores there but the aroused Americans rallied against them and turned them back. [Pp. 132–133]

Johnny Tremain (33) by Esther Forbes is a marvelous illustration of how historical fiction can bring historical facts to life. Interested in the period preceding the Revolutionary War, Miss Forbes had done much research related to this period for her book *Paul Revere and the World He Lived In* (34), an adult biography that was awarded the Pulitzer Prize in 1942. While doing this research, Miss Forbes became interested in the trade apprentices and the role they played during the early history of our country. The more fascinated she became, the more determined she was to write a historical novel about apprentices. The result was *Johnny Tremain,* which received the Newbery Medal in 1944. Johnny's experiences as the apprentice to a silversmith and later as a dispatcher for the *Boston Observer* bring to life the hectic days preceding the Revolutionary War.

Whereas the textbook *Land of the Free* states in brief terms the necessary facts in reporting what happened at Lexington and Concord, the people involved in the facts come alive in *Johnny Tremain* (33). News of the fighting at Lexington and Concord and the retreat of the British to Charlestown have reached Boston. Disguised as a British foot soldier, Johnny watches the wounded British being

Johnny Tremain by Esther Forbes, illustrated by Lynd Ward.

brought by boat from Charlestown to Boston. By careful maneuvering, Johnny succeeds in getting to Charlestown. His job is to find Dr. Warren and report everything he has seen and heard.

Although past midnight, lights showed in all the abandoned houses. The people of Charlestown were in a panic. They dared not go to bed with over a thousand British soldiers suddenly camped upon them—defeated soldiers whose mood might turn ugly. These soldiers only wanted to be let alone, allowed to sleep, but the inhabitants thought they might butcher them all.

Johnny glanced in at two or three taverns. British officers were sleeping in chairs, on benches, on the floors, but he remembered that one of the tavern-keepers was a prominent Son of Liberty. There he tiptoed in among the sleeping guests, found a nine-year-old girl servant hidden behind a flour barrel in the pantry and got her to lead him to the summer house where the tavern-keeper and his wife had moved for the night.

From the tavern-keeper he learned for the first time what had happened after the skirmish at Lexington. Colonel Smith had indeed marched on to Concord, possessed the town, destroyed such military stores as had not yet been hidden. And there had been another skirmish. You might even call it a battle, at North Bridge. But from everywhere, all about, had come the Minute Men. Obviously Smith had been a little afraid of leaving the safety of the village. He would wait where he was for the reinforcements he had sent for, even before Lexington.

But Percy did not come and did not come. Every moment more and more Minute Men were arriving, surrounding the village. At noon, Smith had decided to try to take his men back. He dared wait no longer. Then the shooting began. The Minute Men, from behind stone walls and barns, trees, bushes, had opened fire. Beaten and bloody, almost in a panic, Colonel Smith's troops struggled through to Lexington. Not until then did Percy's reserves arrive. If they had not come, every one of Smith's command would have been killed.

And from Lexington, the British had drawn back to Menotomy. And from there the wounded scarlet dragon had crawled over Charlestown Common, crossed into safety at Charlestown Neck, and were covered by the Somerset's guns. And here they were. They had been badly beaten. [P. 243]

Evaluating Historical Fiction

Well-written historical fiction holds a unique place in literature because of certain discernible ingredients. A well-constructed plot is the most important of these. To hold the interest of young readers, the plot should be intriguing enough to keep them reading in order to find out what happens next, and the solution of one problem should give rise to more complications. It is also important that the narrative be believable and the final climax be convincing.

A story that qualifies as good historical fiction for children should have the following characteristics:

1. The story should have its setting at a particular time in history either by date or by approximate period.
2. The story should be located in a definite locality, and the physical environment should be described with a high degree of authenticity without obtrusive use of historical facts. Historical facts should be free from distortion.
3. A person, an event, or a known social, political, or economic movement should be the agent for carrying the plot to a conclusion.
4. The hero or heroine's behavior should be portrayed in ways that are understandable to the reader, but stereotypes should be avoided.

Early Historical Fiction in America

In the late eighteenth and early nineteenth centuries, literature for children was of a didactic nature. Our forefathers were concerned more with winning their freedom from England and carving out a strong new nation capable of taking its place with the nations of the world than with writing children's books. It was not until the middle of the nineteenth century that literature for children moved away from the didactic and concentrated on the glories of the past—largely the victorious naval and land battles fought by our forefathers. One of the writers at that time was Charles C. Coffin, whose *The Boys of 1776* (1877) became popular with both young and old. Earlier, in 1826, James Fenimore Cooper presented a widely read romanticized story of the American Indian in *The Last of the Mohicans* (24) (see also page 380).

A milestone in children's literature came in the middle of the nineteenth century with the publication of Francis Parkman's *The California and the Oregon Trail* (72). In 1846, Parkman, a cultured young Bostonian, journeyed with four companions from St. Louis, Missouri, to Fort Laramie, Wyoming, over the Oregon Trail. He was particularly interested in the customs of the Indians he met along the trail. In order to know them better he lived for several weeks with the Sioux. His recounting of his experiences with the Indians and the hardships he encountered on the trail add up to a good adventure story. In spite of its heavy style, *The California and the Oregon Trail* was popular reading for years after it was published.

In addition to the stories related to the naval and land exploits, some writers turned to the opening of the West for stories of adventure and romanticism that emphasized the courage and bravery of the pioneers and added glory to the achievements of the young nation. Just following the turn of the century, Joseph Altsheler wrote stories with Civil War settings as well as tales of Indian warfare. Such robust stories as *The Young Trailers* (6) and *The Horsemen of the Plains* (5) were great favorites of young readers in the early twentieth century.

Modern American Historical Fiction for Children

A number of outstanding writers of stories for children have turned to events in history for their subjects. Stories are built around expeditions, discoveries, achievements, political upheavals, and war. Of these events, wars provide the background for the majority of historical stories for both children and adults. By choosing a war for the subject, the author need not exert himself to develop the conflict: It is already there with the antagonists and protagonists usually clearly defined. The plot is built upon the events leading to a confrontation; the characters are a combination of historical figures and people created by the author; the suspense is maintained through risks, intrigue, and diplomacy, and the outcome is based on historical fact. Popular themes are dauntless courage, bravery in the face of danger, commitments to convictions, the prevalence of good over evil, the weaknesses and strengths in human nature, and the futility of war.

Colonial Times

Children find excitement and satisfaction in the stories about people who have the courage it takes to leave their homelands, to face hardships, and to make their homes in a new nation.

Kate and the Devil (51) by Ruth L. Holberg, a story of colonial times, is filled with everyday details of log houses, cornhusk beds, and herb gathering, as well as the religious beliefs that played such an important part in the lives of early settlers. The story centers around twelve-year-old Kate, who sang and danced even though she knew that people in Massachusetts Bay Colony thought that these activities were inspired by the devil. Kate is sent away from home when she encourages other Puritan children to follow her example.

The familiar story of the first Thanksgiving is told with dignity by

Alice Dalgliesh in *The Thanksgiving Story* (26). The story, which revolves around the Hopkins family whose daughter, Oceanus, is born on the *Mayflower,* has a simple style strengthened by Helen Sewell's illustrations.

Flight to Jewell Island (48) by Lyn Harmon is a story of adventure and bravery based on an actual happening. The story centers around the Potts family and their neighbors, who were forced to leave their cabins in northern Maine and flee to Jewell Island during the Indian raids in 1676.

The Revolutionary War

The Revolutionary War has provided source material for much of the best juvenile fiction written and published in the past 30 years. Scholarly research, adherence to authenticity, vivid imagination, and superb writing style on the part of authors have re-created the hectic days leading to the conflict, the war itself, and the exciting days that followed. As Josette Frank (41) has said, "Such stories, when they are well authenticated, not only offer the young reader a reflection of the attitudes and ways of life of an earlier day but fill in for him the homely details of day-to-day living which give him a feeling of orientation in time and place" (p. 93).

Most young children of American parentage are on familiar terms with the midnight ride of Paul Revere. Leonard Everett Fisher in *Two if by Sea* (32) describes the roles played by four men whose actions on the evening of April 18, 1775, started the midnight ride that sparked the opening of the Revolution. An air of suspense pervades the story as the actions of Dr. Joseph Warren, leader of the Sons of Liberty, Paul Revere, active member of the Committee of Safety, Robert Newman, sexton at Christ Church, Boston, and General Thomas Gage, Royal Governor of Massachusetts and Commander-in-Chief of all the King's forces in America are related in a convincing manner. The bold illustrations on every page of the book further the excitement of the story.

Accurate historical detail related to colonial life is woven into *Patriots' Gold* (87) by Virginia F. Voight. Fourteen-year-old Sam, apprentice to a Philadelphia printer for the Continental Congress, becomes involved in the revolutionary events from July 4, 1776, until the Valley Forge winter of 1777. Excitement and suspense fill this story.

Set on Long Island during the American Revolution, *The Cow Neck Rebels* (36) by James Forman presents a realistic picture of the emotional upheavals of people, their strained loyalties, and the suffering that is war. The story is told by sixteen-year-old Bruce Cameron, who with his bold brother Malcolm and his plucky, Scots grandfather fights against the British at the Battle of Long Island—a battle that costs the life of Malcolm. The strong character portrayals give depth to the story.

The historical background is sound and the characterizations are well drawn in a Revolutionary War story *The Hornet's Nest* (88) by Sally Watson. To escape British oppression Lauchlin McLeod and her brother leave the Isle of Skye to visit distant English cousins in Williamsburg. Much of the story is concerned with the feud between the Scots and their Tory cousins.

Told against the background of the Revolutionary War, *A Spy in Old Philadelphia* (30) by Anne Emery is a suspense-filled story in which a fervently patriotic boy helps the cause by delivering supplies.

Genevieve Foster has written *Year of Independence, 1776* (39) to present to young readers a broad view of world events in 1776. The style used is the same horizontal approach to history as *Year of Columbus, Fourteen Ninety-Two* (38) and *Year of the Pilgrims, Sixteen Twenty* (40). Incidents and personalities connected with significant happenings in the world in 1776 are introduced with brief text. The many two-color illustrations add to the book.

An outstanding piece of historical fiction, *Early Thunder* (42) by Jean Fritz, has its setting in Salem, Massachusetts, in 1775. Young Daniel West is faced with making the decision whether he should

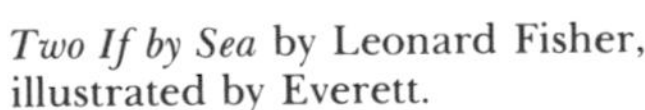
Two If by Sea by Leonard Fisher, illustrated by Everett.

remain a Tory with his family or become a Whig and take an active part in the Revolutionary War.

Much of the activity within the colonies in Revolutionary days is revealed in *Winter Patriot* (77) by Benjamin Schneider. Seth Kimble returns to the colonial cause when his father is killed by a Hessian soldier. Seth joins the army and aids the cause of liberty in the climactic battle of Trenton. George Washington rewards Seth for exceptional bravery.

The Girl in the Witch House (50) by Ruth L. Holberg is an inviting bit of historical fiction about the everyday life of the Revolutionary period. The story centers around the Rowe family, who go about their daily routines—the men farm, the women cook the meals in the fireplace, make soap, and gather wild berries and catnip—while the son and uncle are fighting the British.

Pioneers and Indians

Pioneer stories of life in any country hold a fascination for young readers—particularly stories that relate the suffering and bravery of the men and women whose determination in the face of hardships built a new nation according to their ideals. Young adolescents often find in these stories characters they wish to emulate.

Wolf Hunt (29) by Walter D. Edmonds is an exciting story of a man, a boy, and the American frontier of the late 1700s. The pioneers in Delaware are no longer worrying about Indian raids. Their worry is over a stump-toed wolf that is raiding their flocks of sheep. Danny Gallagher and his uncle Hocty set out to kill the marauder. They travel for several days through storms and bitter cold. While on the hunt Danny does some growing up and Hocty proves to the lady he hopes to marry that he is a special man.

A compelling story of pioneer life, *The Matchlock Gun* (28) also by Walter D. Edmonds is based upon fact. It tells of the bravery of a pioneer family, particularly that of a ten-year-old boy who fires a musket twice his size to stop an Indian massacre. The make-up of the book has a beauty that softens some of the horror of the story. Paul Lantz's brightly colored, double-page illustrations, as well as those done in shades of black and gray, help relieve the tenseness and foreboding of the story. *The Matchlock Gun* received the Newbery Medal in 1942.

William O. Steele has written a number of fascinating stories that dip back into the past of our country for their settings and characters. The action-filled plots, much to the satisfaction of young readers, frequently involve hardships, danger, and Indian warfare. *The Year*

The Matchlock Gun by Walter D. Edmunds, illustrated by Paul Lentz.

of the Bloody Sevens (80) is a realistic story about an eleven-year-old boy, Kelsey Bond, who journeys from Virginia to Kentucky through dangerous Indian territory to reach his father.

Sing Down the Moon (70) by Scott O'Dell relates the forced migration of the Navahos in the mid-1860s from their homeland, Canyon de Chelly in Arizona, to Fort Sumner in New Mexico. The story of the 300-mile journey is poignantly told from the Indian point of view by Bright Morning, a Navaho girl who is stolen from her tribe by Spaniards and sold as a servant. Bright Morning escapes with the aid of Tall Boy, a young Navaho warrior, to whom she is engaged. The Navahos fail to escape from the white soldiers and are forced to walk to Fort Sumner. The story reaches dramatic heights as the Navahos are freed and start for their new home, "A Wilderness located in the Four Corners country, a lonely, wind-swept desert of little rain" (p. 136). In the postscript O'Dell says, "This 300-mile journey of the Navahos is known as the Long Walk. To this day, Navaho men and women speak of it with bitterness. And if you talk to a Navaho child for more than a few minutes he will tell you the story. He has heard it in the cradle and learned it at his mother's knee" (p. 136).

Laura Ingalls Wilder grew up and spent the major portion of her life in a number of frontier towns of the Middle West. Life for the close-knit Ingalls family was filled with all the hardships that accompany pioneer living, but they accepted these hardships as challenges and made the most of the discomforts, dangers, and disappointments. They relied upon their inner resources and built a happy life worth remembering. Laura Ingalls Wilder has told the story of pioneering in one part of our country with charm and distinction.

In *Little House in the Big Woods* (92), the first book in what has come to be known as the "Wilder Series," the reader meets the members of the Wilder family and lives through a winter with them in their home in Wisconsin.

This book was followed by *Little House on the Prairie* (93), in which the Ingalls family travels farther West in a covered wagon and builds a cabin on the Kansas prairie. In *On the Banks of Plum Creek* (96) the Ingalls family travels on into the Minnesota wheat country where they experience fire, floods, grasshopper invasions, and a three-day blizzard.

The next three stories portray life in the Dakota Territory. In *By the Shores of Silver Lake* (90) a railroad-building camp is seen through the eyes of Laura, who is thirteen years old at the time. In *Long Winter* (95) the Ingalls family and the Wilder family, who had been introduced in an earlier story, *Farmer Boy* (91), are brought together. The plucky Ingalls family moves from their claim on the prairie into their store in town to escape the severe weather. *Little Town on the Prairie* (94) is another picture of life in the Dakota Territory—summers spent on the homestead and winters in the prairie town. Laura's adolescent ambitions and interests are revealed. Descriptions of church suppers, spelling bees, religious revivals, and literary societies re-create the social and cultural life of the frontier.

These Happy Golden Years (97) completes Laura Ingalls Wilder's simple, homey saga of pioneer days in our country. In this final episode Laura, not yet sixteen, becomes a teacher. When the school term is over, she marries Almanzo Wilder, the young man whom she first met in an earlier story.

Garth Williams' illustrations for the anniversary edition of the Wilder stories are a rare bit of Americana which portray the intimacy and pleasures of family life.

The Meeker Massacre (73) by Lewis B. Patten and Wayne D. Overholser is a historical novel about the 1879 Meeker Massacre at White River, Colorado. Nathan Meeker, a well-meaning Indian agent, tries to make farmers out of Ute hunters and horsemen. He is violently rejected by the tribe. The exciting and realistic characterizations add up to a good western.

Forged in Silver: The Story of the Comstock Lode (98) by Bob and Jan Young, an adventure story filled with the excitement of the old West, tells of the Comstock Lode and the men who fought for its riches. With its setting in wide-open Virginia City, it is an interesting record of Nevada around 1859, a time when incredible fortunes were quickly made and lost.

Rebecca Caudill's *Tree of Freedom* (19) has been popular for the past twenty years and has a good chance of continuing its popularity in the future. It is a story of pioneer homesteading in Kentucky told with imagination and unusually fine characterization. In the year 1780 Joseph Venable and his five children make the long trek from North Carolina to Kentucky where they have a tract of land waiting for them. Thirteen-year-old Stephanie and her capable, hard-working brother Noel are determined to bring beauty with them into their new home in spite of Indians, war rumors, and the strenuous daily battle against the wilderness.

Do Not Annoy the Indians (7) by Betty Baker is a humorous, down-to-earth picture of life in the Far West in 1858. The setting is Arizona City where thirteen-year-old Jeff Barnes, taking over his father's duties as stationmaster for the Butterfield Overland Mail Company, has to put up with the rules and regulations of the stage line, a spoiled younger brother, a bossy older sister, and a crowd of friendly, interfering Indians.

Based on an actual incident, *The Courage of Sarah Nobel* (25) by Alice Dalgliesh tells of a little girl who overcomes her timidity and endures the hard life of a pioneer as she participates in the founding of New Milford in the Connecticut wilderness. This book gives a clear picture of the relations of the pioneers and the Indians.

One story that has stood the test of time and that seems destined for many more years of popularity is *Away Goes Sally* (21) by Elizabeth Coatsworth. In a little house built on a sled Sally, her family, three hired men, a little cub, and all their worldly goods travel all the way from their comfortable farm in Massachusetts to a new home on the Penobscot River in Maine. The story is told with such integrity that one senses the atmosphere of the period in the history of our country when the New England states were being settled and developed. The moods and colors of the seasons are vividly described, and there is just enough of the vernacular to give the story a "Down East" flavor. The illustrations by Helen Sewell look like embroidered samplers, in perfect harmony with the atmosphere of the story.

1776–1861

The Open Gate: New Year's Eighteen Fifteen (49) by Wilma P. Hayes is an easy-to-read story of New Orleans in 1815, the year Jackson saved it from the British. The story is told as seen through the eyes of a ten-year-old girl from a French family.

John Jewitt, a blacksmith on the brig *Boston,* and a companion, the only survivors of a disaster, sail into Nootka Sound on Vancouver Island in 1803, where they live for two years with the Indians. *Nootka: Being the Adventures of John Jewitt, Seaman* (56) by Michael Hyde is a fictionalized account of the two men's experiences based on the actual journal of John Jewitt.

The Civil War

The Civil War, like the Revolutionary War, has been a source of material for countless stories of literary significance. In *Across Five Aprils* (53) Irene Hunt contributed a Civil War story of quality. The story revolves around the Creighton family: Ellen and Matt Creighton, their sons John, Bill, Tom, and Jethro, and their daughter Ellen. They are a hard-working, peace-loving, pioneer family living in southern Illinois when the war breaks out. During the war the Creighton family is torn apart by divided loyalties, and Jethro, who at the beginning of the war is a child of ten, emerges at the end of the story a man of fourteen. He is one of the most convincing and admirable characters in children's literature. The other members of the Creighton family and their relations with the other characters in the story are treated with sensitivity and sympathy by the author. The beauty of the countryside, a family's love of life and of each other, and their concern for people everywhere point up the futility and waste of war. *Across Five Aprils* received the Follett Award in 1964 and was a runner-up for the Newbery Award in 1965.

Harold Keith has written a vivid Civil War story that emphasizes the ugliness and tragedy of war. Following the pattern of most war stories, *Rifles for Watie* (59) is packed with danger, intrigue, and heroism. In the spring of 1861, violence breaks out on the Kansas-Missouri border. Frequent raiding parties of proslavery Missourians terrorize the farmers on the Kansas side. Following one of these raids, sixteen-year-old Jeff Bussey volunteers for service in the Union Army. During the war, Jeff makes both friends and enemies, earns the Congressional Medal of Honor, is stricken by malaria, and serves as a spy behind enemy lines. When the war ends, he returns home much more mature than when he left four years earlier. Older children should enjoy this story, which portrays the individual courage, the results of divided loyalties, and the human tragedy of the Civil War. *Rifles for Watie* received the Newbery Medal in 1958.

Johnny Reb (1) by Merritt Parmelee Allen depicts the Civil War from the Southern point of view. Seventeen-year-old Ezra Todd is the hero of the story. Ezra's parents, both Northerners, die when he is ten years old, and he goes to live with a cruel man named Jed Sears and his son, Bert. Ezra is clawed by a bear that was wounded by Wade Hampton, a wealthy Southern landowner who lives nearby. The Hamptons take Ezra into their mansion to recuperate and he becomes very fond of them. When he returns to the Sears, he is taunted and ridiculed for his feelings toward the Southerners. He leaves the Sears and hikes to Columbia, South Carolina, to join the cavalry unit Colonel Hampton has formed. From then on his life is a series of daring raids, bloody battles, and narrow escapes. All the horrors of war and the heartaches of defeat are portrayed in stark realism as the story moves to its conclusion. This book is outstanding in the fairness with which it treats both sides in the conflict. It reveals great personal heroism and sacrifice and testifies to the dignity that man can maintain in the face of defeat.

High Spy (4) by Robert E. Alter is a fast-paced story based on the lives of two actual Union Army officers who escaped from Confederate prisons. Their adventures are combined in this story about William Thaxton, an aerial observer in the Union Army's balloon corps, who was captured, escaped from prison, and then managed to steal a balloon to get secret rebel strategy back to the Union troops. Accurate historical references serve as a framework for the story.

Slavery in America is described in personal details that are vivid and tragic in *To Be a Slave* (62) by Julius Lester. Most of the text is based on the memories of Black men and women who themselves have been slaves. The author contributes a commentary that is both sympathetic and relevant. The material, arranged in historical sequence, begins in Africa and culminates with the Civil War and Emancipation. *To Be a Slave* was a runner-up for the 1969 Newbery Award.

The Great Depression

In *No Promises in the Wind* (54) Irene Hunt shows the same sensitivity to the intimate feelings of people that made her previous stories significant contributions to children's literature. *No Promises in the Wind* is a drama of hatred and affection, hope and despair played against the tragic days of the Depression. Just as the Civil War tore apart the Creighton family in *Across Five Aprils,* the Depression of the 1930s has the same effect on the family in *No Promises in the Wind.* Resentful of his defeated father's nagging, Josh runs away from home expecting to make his way by playing the piano. He is followed by

Joey, his younger brother, who insists on going with him in spite of Josh's protests. Together they experience the suffering that became a part of the lives of so many people during the difficult 1930s.

Two World Wars

Today, children are close to war because of situations in their homes and in the world. Some of them have fathers and grandfathers who served in one of the World Wars or fathers and brothers who have fought in Korea or Vietnam. They have listened to the war experiences of their relatives and friends. Television, radio, and newspapers emphasize war news. Many books have been written to emphasize to children the horror and futility of war.

Lawrence and His Desert Raiders (8) by James Barbary is the story of the Arab campaign against Aquaba during World War I, which relates how Lawrence of Arabia led fifty Arab fighters across the desert to capture from the Turks that important Red Sea port, gateway to the Suez Canal.

Many boys and girls have enjoyed the action-packed sports stories by John R. Tunis. In *Silence over Dunkerque* (84), Mr. Tunis chose World War II as the background for his grimly realistic picture of warfare and its effect on both soldiers and civilians. The story is set in France at the time of the invasion by the Nazis which led to the evacuation of the Allied troops from Dunkerque in May 1940.

A small Bavarian town does not escape the heartaches that accompany war. *The Traitors* (37) by James Forman relates the anguish of Pastor Eichorn as he sees his congregation, and then his son, adopt the Nazi cause.

The House of the Four Winds (86) by Colette Vivier portrays the everyday school and family-life activities in France as they continued throughout the German occupation and Allied deliverance of World War II. Drawn with unusual integrity, some of the characters fail in their pursuits, while Michel, around whom much of the story revolves, grows into a mature young man.

Ceremony of Innocence (35), one of the several books James Forman has written with World War II as the background, relates the effect of the Nazi philosophy on the lives of individuals. Through a series of flashbacks Forman tells the events leading to the arrest by the Gestapo of Hans Scholl and his sister Sophie. Their opposition to the Nazi regime and the values they hold are clearly portrayed in this powerful story.

When Mother Was Young (61) by Maxine W. Kumin offers glimpses into the past showing young readers what life was like during World War II. Victory gardens, rationing, blackouts, and defense stamps are some of the subjects treated in well-written style with colorful illustrations.

Historical Fiction Around the World

Estevan, a wealthy Spanish boy, finds that he and his former Indian slave must give up old beliefs and hatreds to survive when the Pueblo Indians unite with other tribes and stage a full-scale rebellion to drive out the Spanish conquerors of New Mexico during the late 1600s. *Prisoner of Taos* (64) by Helen B. Lobdell is a suspenseful story based on accurate historical events.

For Glory and the King (65) by Lucile McDonald and Zola H. Ross relates the experiences of a boy who is shanghaied aboard a small schooner that is setting out to explore the California coast before the Russians can claim it. The story is based on a log kept by the boy, who is one of three survivors of the voyage.

Sixth-century England is the setting for George Finkel's *Watch Fires to the North* (31), an exciting novel of the wars between the Roman Christians and Saxons as related by a young king of a northern province. This story presents an unusual version of the Arthurian legend that casts Arthur as a general protecting the last of Roman Britain and building the Anglo-Saxon England that would survive until the Battle of Hastings. This is an entertaining and thoughtful story for more advanced readers.

English medieval life is portrayed in Clyde Bulla's well-told story *The Sword in the Tree* (15). The story centers around Shan, a young boy who frees his father from a dungeon with the help of King Arthur.

Tales of the Crusades (23) by Olivia Coolidge is a collection of twelve well-told tales about the Crusades from 1094 to 1464. The stories are woven around the personal experiences of crusading priests, kings, knights, peasants, and children who participated in these historic events. The exciting narratives convey the atmosphere of the times.

Rosemary Sutcliff is one of the more prolific writers of historical stories of England. Her latest is *The Witch's Brat* (82). At the age of twelve Lovel is stoned away from West Sussex because his grandmother had the wisdom of healing and was believed to have been a witch. When he hides in a monastery his own wisdom with herbs and healing are discovered. Later the boy's skills are thought miraculous and he learns about himself and his fellow man. Twelfth-century England provides a background.

Bows Against the Baron (83) by Geoffrey Trease recalls the romantic days of Robin Hood in a story that is heavy with intrigue and action. To his horror, Dickon discovers that he has killed a deer belonging to the King. There is nothing left for him to do but disappear and join Robin Hood's band. The light-hearted air of the story makes it happy reading.

Men of Iron (75) by Howard Pyle presents a realistic picture of the feudal system and of political intrigue in England in the 1400s. The story revolves around Myles Falworth, a boy who is trained to become a knight and then proves himself by a deed of valor.

The Door in the Wall (27) by Marguerite De Angeli, with its setting in colorful fourteenth-century England, is a story of a young lad's victory over a physical handicap through perseverance and willpower.

The Spaniards Are Coming (76) by Ruth Manning Sanders is a well-written short story with Elizabethan England as its background. Twelve-year-old Simon and his younger sister, Beth, are left on their own after their father is pressed into the service of the Queen's navy. Together they start out for their uncle's home in Plymouth. They work their way performing as jugglers. The concern of everyone they meet—thieves, peddlers, and kindly peasants—is the threatening approach of the Spanish Armada.

I Will Adventure (46) by Elizabeth Janet Gray is a believable story of life in Elizabethan times that centers around young Andrew Talbot, who comes to London to be a page in his uncle's home. The life and the theater of Shakespeare add interest to the story.

Hester Burton's *Castors Away* (16) is an exciting story of an English family in the early 1800s. The family becomes involved in a series of events related to Lord Nelson's coming encounter with the French at Trafalgar. The younger son is sent to join his uncle's ship and the older boy goes to London to be apprenticed to a doctor. The story is based on fact although many of the characters are fictional.

A Sheltering Tree (71) by Richard Parker is a well-written historical story with its setting in the early years of the Industrial Revolution when many people were displaced from previously secure jobs in England. After Stephen's father loses his position as a teacher, Stephen joins his uncle in the profitable, but dangerous, smuggling trade. His adventures and those of his friend, David, who becomes unwillingly involved in the smuggling, make a fast-moving exciting plot.

Oath of Silence (11) by Phyllis Bentley is a gripping adventure based on the Yorkshire textile industry in the early nineteenth century when machines were first introduced in the manufacture of cloth. A hand-cropper and a thirteen-year-old boy become involved in the activities of the Luddites, an outlawed secret organization of hand-craftsmen determined to destroy the new machines that are putting them out of work. The historical background, local color, and believable characters provide fascinating reading.

English life and the English countryside of the 1880s are the background for *Journey to England* (85) by Edith Unnerstad. Brosus and his sister Margita set out from Sweden for England to find their mother, who has gone to London in search of work. The trail leads from London into the Cotswold countryside and at last to Malvern, where they meet the famous singer Jenny Lind and also find their mother.

Piper to the Clan (20) by Mary S. Clarke is a colorful novel of seventeenth-century Scotland, told through the eyes of a young descendant of a long line of Highland Clan pipers. The story relates the tragic episode in which the Scots were defeated by Cromwell's English soldiers at Dunbar in 1650 and the death march of the prisoners from Dunbar to Durham Castle. The survivors of the march are shipped to Lynn, Massachusetts, to work in the iron works for seven years. The grimness of the situation is convincingly told and the characters are vividly portrayed.

Rich with the good humor and the hardiness of the Irish peasant, *Beware of Moonlight* (47) by Aylmer Hall moves without a letdown from beginning to end. Part of the story revolves around the age-old conflict between the Irish peasants and the English landlords. The more endearing part of the story revolves around half-Irish Larry O'Driscoll, whose mother is dead and whose father has joined the French army. Larry lives in Corcalee Castle, the home of his late uncle. Romance enters the picture and loyalties are challenged when Larry's first cousin, young Lord Corcalee, coming from England to visit, brings his beautiful young sister Charlotte with him. Larry forgets the loyalty to the poverty-stricken tenant farmers with whom he was identified in his infatuation over Charlotte and for some time he wrestles with his conscience. A convincing picture of Ireland around the middle of the eighteenth century is presented.

Madeleine Polland has written a love story set in Granada in the fifteenth century. *Alhambra* (74) tells of a young Spanish boy and his sister who are captured by the Moors and grow up in the Alhambra. Their way of life is beautifully described.

During his training Idrun, a youth who lived in eighth-century France before it became a nation, meets many challenges before he wins his father's approval in *A Candle at Dusk* (2) by E. M. Almedingen. The spirit and rigors of the time are conveyed as Idrun faces a wild boar, rescues a maiden, overcomes hunger, battles with the Moors, and exposes a crafty tax collector before his training is completed.

A Boy of Old Prague (57) by Sulamith Ish-Kishor is a moving story, told in the first person, about Tomas, a young Jewish boy in the Prague ghetto of the sixteenth century. Tomas relates his reaction to being treated with kindness and respect for the first time. The sad, drab existence of the ghetto pervades the story.

William Tell and His Son (55) by Bettina Hurlimann is the story of William Tell's rebellion against the tryanny of Gessler, who was sent by the Austrian emperor to control the Swiss 600 years ago. The handsome black-and-white illustrations emphasize the drama of the people's struggle to keep democracy alive.

Burke Boyce's *The Emperor's Arrow* (13) is a well-written story based on the legend of Charlemagne's search for a cure for the dreaded Black Plague. A young serf discovers a cure for the disease in a plant that he brings to the king. The strong black-and-white illustrations supplement the excellent information about social changes in the Middle Ages.

A Song for Young King Wenceslas (66) by Cecil Maiden brings to life

A Boy of Old Prague by Sulamith Ish-Kishor, illustrated by Ben Shahn.

fourteen-year-old Prince Wenceslas, who later as a king is commemorated in the well-known Christmas carol. The story relates the conflict between the young prince, a devout Christian, and his mother's and brother's adherence to paganism. When Prince Wenceslas seizes power from his mother, who has been appointed Regent upon the death of his father, the young King Wenceslas gives her land to the south of the country. The story is full of intrigue and the struggles for power that surround court life.

Cecelia Holland's *Ghost on the Steppe* (52) is an interesting portrayal of nomadic Mongol life and customs in the Middle Ages. The story concerns Djela, grandson of the ruling Khan of the Merkit tribe, and his inner struggles and difficulties in assuming the responsibilities of growing up.

Young Mark (3) by E. M. Almedingen is set in eighteenth-century czarist Russia. This powerful novel relates the adventurous journey of a young boy who leaves his Ukrainian home and travels to the great city of St. Petersburg determined to fulfill his ambition to become a singer.

With its setting in Russia early in the nineteenth-century *Masha* (58) by Mara Kay is based on authentic information about the Smolni Institute for noble girls, which was founded by Catherine the Great. Masha attended the school for nine years and following graduation received an appointment as lady-in-waiting to the Grand Duchess.

Hunters of Siberia (9) by Barbara Bartos-Hoppner is the strange story of exiles in Siberia during the czarist regime. Its setting is an isolated community in Siberia where the youth Nikolai, his father, Ibrahem, and his mother live happily in spite of the rugged living conditions. Ibrahem is a hunter who has earned a prominent position in the community. A commissioner is sent to the small town to regulate the hunting. One suspense-filled situation follows another in this well-written story.

Five centuries in the history of the Viking peoples and their ocean voyages are traced by Walter Buehr in *The Viking Explorers* (14). From the surprise raids the Vikings made in their small boats along European coasts in the early ninth century, the reader is taken to the British Isles, France, Russia, Iceland, Greenland, and finally to the continent of North America, where these explorers made inland expeditions.

The Land Seekers (12) by Alan Boucher is a thrilling story of the Norse migrations to Iceland in the ninth century. The action-packed story is built around the daring undertaking of fourteen-year-old Olaf and twelve-year-old Jarp.

The Journey of the Eldest Son (44) by Jennifer G. Fyson is an exciting tale of ancient times with its setting in the Babylonian city of Ur.

The story revolves around Shamashazir, the fourteen-year-old son of a rich caravan merchant who travels on his first caravan journey to the distant White Mountains. He returns—a man filled with new ideas—to his home city of Ur where he becomes a leader of his people.

East to Cathay: The Silk Trade (22) by Robert Collins is an account of the main trade route between China and the Western world from ancient times to the middle of the fourteenth century. Descriptions of life in ancient times are combined with interesting details about early silk making and trade in the stories of merchants, monks, and conquerors.

A good supplement to American history collections is a reissue of a 1945 title, *Wildcat Furs to China: The Cruise of the Sloop* Experiments (17), by Carl Carmer. This book is a factual account of the voyage of the second trading ship to sail from the United States to China as seen through the eyes of two young deck hands.

Exiles in the Sahara (43) by Kelman Frost is an exciting, suspenseful tale of survival in the desert. The Ibadite tribe is forced to flee their peaceful eleventh-century oasis home because of the threat of invasion and death at the hands of the hostile Melchites. The plot revolves around the orphan Hassoun, his blind friend Yusuf, and his goat Jimm. Hassoun and Yusuf overcome a number of difficulties and are honored as heroes when the goat leads them to water and the site for their new village.

Betty Morrow's *A Great Miracle: The Story of Hanukkah* (68) is a fast-moving story centering around the five sons of Mattathias who fight against the armies invading the land of Israel. How the modern Jewish holiday of Hanukkah came to be is interestingly explained.

A newly established Israeli Kibbutz near an Arab village is the setting for *The Mukhtar's Children* (89) by Sally Watson. The timely and timeless conflict between cultures old and new makes an exciting introduction to the complex Middle Eastern situation.

Extending Experiences for the Reader

1. Read excerpts from several stories that describe different aspects of colonial living, for example, work, schools, hardships, and recreation.
2. Read excerpts to the class that describe the character and work of Paul Revere from *Paul Revere and the World He Lived In* (34) by Esther Forbes.
3. Read the description of Boston from the first chapter in *Johnny Tremaine* (33) by Esther Forbes. Read to the class other excerpts that describe Johnny's character.
4. Prepare a time line showing historical events from the time the Pilgrims landed at Plymouth Rock to the end of the Revolutionary War.

5. Plan a Hall of Fame by having the group vote for individuals who made outstanding contributions to early American life.
6. Read at least three stories for children in which the futility of war is stressed.
7. Read excerpts from *My Antonia* (18) by Willa Cather to the class.
8. Prepare a bibliography of stories related to World War II.

Extending Experiences for Children

1. Make a scrapbook with pictures of colonial homes and furnishings.
2. Plan an exhibit of dolls in colonial dress.
3. Make mobiles using cut-out characters in a historical fiction story that you have read.
4. Select a leader in one of the colonies and list his contributions to the life of the colony.
5. Write a character sketch of Johnny Tremaine.
6. Organize into two groups of four or five. Plan a discussion with one group giving arguments for the Revolutionary War and the other group giving arguments against.
7. Prepare and present dramatic skits based on the meetings of the Continental Congress.
8. Select humorous episodes from war stories to share with the class.
9. Illustrate scenes from several of the stories mentioned in "Historical Fiction Around the World."
10. From your reading make two lists of the machinery of war used in (1) the Revolutionary War and (2) the present time.
11. After four or five children have read *When Mother Was Young* (61) by Maxine W. Kumin, compare the war-related activities of people today with those in the story.
12. Write a biographical sketch of a revolutionary leader in the world today.
13. Write a description of John Sager's behavior at the beginning of the story *On to Oregon* (69) by Honoré Willsie Morrow and a description of his behavior at the end of the book.
14. Write slogans that could be used to entice people to move westward following the Revolutionary War.
15. Impersonate a homesteader and tell about your life on the homestead.

Chapter References

1. ALLEN, MERRITT PARMELEE. *Johnny Reb.* New York: David McKay, 1952. Grades 7–9.
2. ALMEDINGEN, E. M. *A Candle at Dusk.* New York: Farrar, Straus & Giroux, 1969. Grade 7 and up.

3. ———. *Young Mark.* New York: Farrar, Straus & Giroux, 1968. Grades 7–10.
4. ALTER, ROBERT E. *High Spy.* New York: Putnam, 1967. Grade 5 and up.
5. ALTSHELER, JOSEPH A. *The Horsemen of the Plains.* New York: Macmillan, 1967. Grade 7 and up.
6. ———. *The Young Trailers.* New York: Hawthorn, 1950.
7. BAKER, BETTY. *Do Not Annoy the Indians.* New York: Macmillan, 1968. Grades 4–6.
8. BARBARY, JAMES. *Lawrence and His Desert Raiders.* New York: Meredith, 1968. Grades 4–7.
9. BARTOS-HOPPNER, BARBARA. *Hunters of Siberia.* New York: Walck, 1970. Grades 7–9.
10. BEHN, HARRY. *The Faraway Lurs.* Cleveland: World, 1963, 1971. Grades 7–11.
11. BENTLEY, PHYLLIS. *Oath of Silence.* Garden City, N. Y.: Doubleday, 1967. Grades 7–9.
12. BOUCHER, ALAN. *The Land Seekers.* New York: Farrar, Straus & Giroux, 1968. Grades 7–9.
13. BOYCE, BURKE. *The Emperor's Arrow.* Philadelphia: Lippincott, 1967. Grades 3–5.
14. BUEHR, WALTER. *The Viking Explorers.* New York: Putnam, 1967. Grades 3–7.
15. BULLA, CLYDE ROBERT. *The Sword in the Tree.* New York: T. Y. Crowell, 1956. Grades 2–5.
16. BURTON, HESTER. *Castors Away.* New York: Dell, 1971. Paperback. Grades 10–12.
17. CARMER, CARL. *Wildcat Furs to China: The Cruise of the Sloop* Experiments. New York: David McKay, 1969. Grades 4–6.
18. CATHER, WILLA. *My Antonia.* Boston: Houghton Mifflin, n.d. Paperback. Grade 7 and up.
19. CAUDILL, REBECCA. *Tree of Freedom.* New York: Viking, 1949. Grade 7 and up.
20. CLARKE, MARY S. *Piper to the Clan.* New York: Viking, 1970. Grade 7 and up.
21. COATSWORTH, ELIZABETH. *Away Goes Sally.* New York: Macmillan, 1934. Grades 4–6.
22. COLLINS, ROBERT. Edward Sammis (ed.). *East to Cathay: The Silk Trade.* New York: McGraw-Hill, 1968. Grade 5 and up.
23. COOLIDGE, OLIVIA. *Tales of the Crusades.* Boston: Houghton Mifflin, 1970. Grades 9–12.
24. COOPER, JAMES FENIMORE. *The Last of the Mohicans.* W. Charvat (ed.). Boston: Houghton Mifflin, n.d. Paperback.
25. DALGLIESH, ALICE. *The Courage of Sarah Noble.* Illustrated by Leonard Weisgard. New York: Scribner, 1954. Grades 1–4.
26. ———. *The Thanksgiving Story.* Illustrated by Helen Sewell. New York: Scribner, 1954. Kindergarten–grade 3.
27. DE ANGELI, MARGUERITE. *The Door in the Wall.* Garden City, N. Y.: Doubleday, 1949. Grades 3–6.

28. EDMONDS, WALTER D. *The Matchlock Gun.* New York: Dodd, Mead, 1941. Grades 4–6.
29. ______. *Wolf Hunt.* Boston: Little, Brown, 1970. Grade 7 and up.
30. EMERY, ANNE. *A Spy in Old Philadelphia.* Chicago: Rand McNally, 1958. Grades 3–6.
31. FINKEL, GEORGE. *Watch Fires to the North.* New York: Viking, 1967. Grade 7 and up.
32. FISHER, LEONARD EVERETT. *Two If by Sea.* New York: Random House, 1970. Grades 5–9.
33. FORBES, ESTHER. *Johnny Tremain.* Boston: Houghton Mifflin, 1943. New York: Dell, 1969. Paperback. Grades 7–9.
34. ______. *Paul Revere and the World He Lived In.* Boston: Houghton Mifflin, n.d. Paperback. Grades 9–12.
35. FORMAN, JAMES. *Ceremony of Innocence.* New York: Hawthorn, 1970. n.g.l.
36. ______. *The Cow Neck Rebels.* New York: Farrar, Straus & Giroux, 1969. Grade 7 and up.
37. ______. *The Traitors.* New York: Farrar, Straus & Giroux, 1968. Grade 7 and up.
38. FOSTER, GENEVIEVE. *Year of Columbus, Fourteen Ninety-Two.* New York: Scribner, 1969. Grades 2–6.
39. ______. *Year of Independence, 1776.* New York: Scribner, 1970. Grades 2–6.
40. ______. *Year of the Pilgrims, Sixteen Twenty.* New York: Scribner, 1969. Grades 2–6.
41. FRANK, JOSETTE. *Your Child's Reading Today.* Rev. ed. Garden City, N. Y.: Doubleday, 1969.
42. FRITZ, JEAN. *Early Thunder.* New York: Coward-McCann, 1967. Grades 7–11.
43. FROST, KELMAN. *Exiles in the Sahara.* New York: Abelard-Schuman, 1964. Grades 5–9.
44. FYSON, JENNIFER G. *The Journey of the Eldest Son.* New York: Coward-McCann, 1966. Grades 5–9.
45. GRAY, ELIZABETH JANET. *Adam of the Road.* New York: Viking, 1942. Grades 4–8.
46. ______. *I Will Adventure.* New York: Viking, 1962. Grades 5–9.
47. HALL, AYLMER. *Beware of Moonlight.* New York: Nelson, 1970. Grade 6 and up.
48. HARMON, LYN. *Flight to Jewell Island.* Philadelphia: Lippincott, 1967. Grades 4–6.
49. HAYES, WILMA P. *The Open Gate: New Year's Eighteen Fifteen.* New York: Coward-McCann, 1970. Grades 4–7.
50. HOLBERG, RUTH L. *The Girl in the Witch House.* New York: Hastings House, 1966. Grades 4–6.
51. ______. *Kate and the Devil.* New York: Hastings House, 1968. Grades 4–6.
52. HOLLAND, CECELIA. *Ghost on the Steppe.* New York: Atheneum, 1969. Grades 3–7.

53. HUNT, IRENE. *Across Five Aprils.* New York: Grosset & Dunlap, 1965. Grade 7 and up.
54. ———. *No Promises in the Wind.* Chicago: Follett, 1970. Grade 5 and up.
55. HURLIMANN, BETTINA. *William Tell and His Son.* Elizabeth D. Crawford (tr.). New York: Harcourt Brace Jovanovich, 1967. Grades 3–6.
56. HYDE, MICHAEL. *Nootka: Being the Adventures of John Jewitt, Seaman.* New York: Walck, 1969. Grades 7–9.
57. ISH-KISHOR, SULAMITH. *A Boy of Old Prague.* New York: Pantheon, 1963. Grade 7 and up.
58. KAY, MARA. *Masha.* New York: Lothrop, Lee & Shepard, 1968. Grade 7 and up.
59. KEITH, HAROLD. *Rifles for Watie.* New York: T. Y. Crowell, 1957. Grade 7 and up.
60. KELLY, ERIC P. *The Trumpeter of Krakow.* Rev. ed. New York: Macmillan.
61. KUMIN, MAXINE W. *When Mother Was Young.* New York: Putnam, 1970. Grades 2–4.
62. LESTER, JULIUS. *To Be a Slave.* New York: Dell, 1970. Paperback. Grade 7 and up.
63. LEWIS, ELIZABETH F. *Young Fu of the Upper Yangtze.* New York: Holt, Rinehart & Winston, 1932.
64. LOBDELL, HELEN B. *Prisoner of Taos.* New York: Abelard-Schuman, 1970. Grade 7 and up.
65. MCDONALD, LUCILE, AND ZOLA H. ROSS. *For Glory and the King.* New York: Hawthorn, 1969. Grade 5 and up.
66. MAIDEN, CECIL. *A Song for Young King Wenceslas.* Reading, Mass.: Addison-Wesley, 1969. Grades 6–8.
67. MEADOWCROFT, LA MONTE E. *Land of the Free.* New York: T. Y. Crowell, 1961. Grades 2–5.
68. MORROW, BETTY. *A Great Miracle: The Story of Hanukkah.* Irvington-on-Hudson, N. Y.: Harvey House, 1968. Grades 3–6.
69. MORROW, HONORÉ WILLSIE. *On to Oregon.* New York: Morrow, 1926. Grades 2–6.
70. O'DELL, SCOTT. *Sing Down the Moon.* Boston: Houghton Mifflin, 1970. Grade 5 and up.
71. PARKER, RICHARD. *A Sheltering Tree.* New York: Hawthorn, 1969. Grades 6–8.
72. PARKMAN, FRANCIS. *The California and the Oregon Trail.* New York: Holt, Rinehart & Winston, 1931. Grade 9 and up.
73. PATTEN, LEWIS B., AND WAYNE D. OVERHOLSER. *The Meeker Massacre.* New York: Cowles, 1969. Grades 5–9.
74. POLLAND, MADELEINE. *Alhambra.* Garden City, N. Y.: Doubleday, 1970. Grades 7–9.
75. PYLE, HOWARD. *Men of Iron.* New York: Harper & Row. Grade 6 and up.
76. SANDERS, RUTH MANNING. *The Spaniards Are Coming.* New York: Watts, 1970.
77. SCHNEIDER, BENJAMIN. *Winter Patriot.* Philadelphia: Chilton, 1967. Grades 4–6.

78. SEREDY, KATE. *The White Stag.* New York: Viking, 1937. Grade 7 and up.
79. SPEARE, ELIZABETH G. *The Witch of Blackbird Pond.* New York: Dell, 1971. Paperback. Grade 7 and up.
80. STEELE, WILLIAM O. *The Year of the Bloody Sevens.* New York: Harcourt Brace Jovanovich, 1963. Grades 4–6.
81. SUTCLIFF, ROSEMARY. *Warrior Scarlet.* New York: Walck, 1958. Grades 7–9.
82. ______. *The Witch's Brat.* New York: Walck, 1970. Grades 7–9.
83. TREASE, GEOFFREY. *Bows Against the Baron.* New York: Meredith, 1967. Grades 4–8.
84. TUNIS, JOHN R. *Silence over Dunkerque.* New York: Morrow, 1962. Grades 7–9.
85. UNNERSTAD, EDITH. *Journey to England.* New York: Macmillan, 1961.
86. VIVIER, COLETTE. *The House of the Four Winds.* Miriam Morton (tr.). Garden City, N. Y.: Doubleday, 1969. Grades 7–9.
87. VOIGHT, VIRGINIA F. *Patriots' Gold.* Philadelphia: Macrae, 1969. Grade 5 and up.
88. WATSON, SALLY. *The Hornet's Nest.* New York: Holt, Rinehart & Winston, 1968. Grades 5–8.
89. ______. *The Mukhtar's Children.* New York: Holt, Rinehart & Winston, 1968. Grades 5–8.
90. WILDER, LAURA INGALLS. *By the Shores of Silver Lake.* New York: Harper & Row, 1971. Paperback. Grades 4–7.
91. ______. *Farmer Boy.* New York: Harper & Row, 1953.
92. ______. *Little House in the Big Woods.* New York: Harper & Row, 1971. Paperback. Grades 1–5.
93. ______. *Little House on the Prairie.* New York: Harper & Row, 1971. Paperback. Grades 1–5.
94. ______. *Little Town on the Prairie.* New York: Harper & Row, 1971. Paperback. Grades 4–8.
95. ______. *Long Winter.* Rev. ed. New York: Harper & Row, 1953. Grades 4–7.
96. ______. *On the Banks of Plum Creek.* New York: Harper & Row, 1971. Paperback. Grades 2–7.
97. ______. *These Happy Golden Years.* New York: Harper & Row, 1971. Paperback. Grade 5 and up.
98. YOUNG, BOB, AND JAN YOUNG. *Forged in Silver: The Story of the Comstock Lode.* New York: Messner, 1968. Grade 7 and up.

More Stories for Children

Colonial Times

CHESSMAN, RUTH. *Bound for Freedom.* New York: Abelard-Schuman, 1965. Grades 3–7. Historical details of a New England settler's family are presented through an account of the adventures and experiences of two London waifs who have been sold into bondage.

GIBBS, ALONZO. *The Fields Breathe Sweet.* New York: Lothrop, Lee & Shepard, 1963. Grade 7 and up. The story of eighteen-year-old Gretje Harmensen, oldest daughter of a hard-working Dutch farmer living on Long Island, New York, offers a vivid picture of life in the late 1600s with particular emphasis on the early struggle for religious toleration.

HOLBERG, RUTH L. *At The Sign of the Golden Anchor.* Garden City, N. Y.: Doubleday, 1947. Grades 3–7. How the New Englanders endured the Embargo Acts is interestingly related.

LATHAM, JEAN LEE. *This Dear-Bought Land.* New York: Harper & Row, 1957. Grade 6 and up. Authentic and colorful historical backgrounds are portrayed in this story of the Jamestown settlement.

PILKINGTON, ROGER. *I Sailed on the* Mayflower: *A Boy's Discovery of the New World.* New York: St. Martin's Press, 1966. Grades 4–6. Love Brewster, ten-year-old son of William Brewster, narrates the events of the Pilgrims' last months in Holland, their crossing on the *Mayflower,* and their first year in America.

STEPHENS, PETER J. *Towappu: Puritan Renegade.* New York: Atheneum, 1966. Grades 4–8. An honest account is given of conditions that existed between the members of the early Plymouth settlements and the Indians.

Revolutionary War

ALTER, ROBERT E. *Rabble on a Hill.* New York: Putnam, 1964. Grades 5–9. Adventures of a young man in Boston, his work as a spy, his involvement with the British patrol, and his participation in the battle of Breed's Hill make this an exciting story.

CLAGETT, JOHN. *Gunpowder for Boonesborough.* Indianapolis: Bobbs-Merrill, 1965. Grades 6–9. The tense world of the American Revolution and the courageous men who fought against the Tories and their Indian allies are interestingly portrayed.

MANTEL, S. G. *Tallmadge's Terry.* New York: David McKay, 1965. Grade 7 and up. A fifteen-year-old boy and his friend Joshua, a runaway slave, are involved in a fictional account of espionage during the Revolutionary War.

RUSKIN, ARIANE. *Spy for Liberty: The Adventurous Life of Beaumarchais.* New York: Pantheon, 1965. Grade 6 and up. A French watchmaker-nobleman-spy-author instigates French aid for the American colonists at the time of the American Revolution.

TAYLOR, ALLAN. *Morgan's Long Rifles.* New York: Putnam, 1965. Grades 5–9. A seventeen-year-old boy joins the volunteer riflemen in the Revolutionary War, is captured, imprisoned, and escapes to rejoin the army.

TOMERLIN, JOHN. *Prisoner of the Iroquois.* New York: Dutton, 1965. Grades 4–7. This exciting historical novel is based on actual events of the relations between the Indians and the settlers in the Mohawk Valley immediately following the news of the Declaration of Independence.

Pioneer

BARBARY, JAMES. *The Fort in the Wilderness.* New York: Norton, 1965. Grades 5–9. Children will enjoy reading about Ensign Dick Christie's capture and later escape from the Indians.

BEATTY, PATRICIA. *Bonanza Girl.* New York: Morrow, 1962. Grades 5–9. Frontier life in the Idaho Territory vividly portrayed.

DRURY, MAXINE. *George and the Long Rifle.* New York: David McKay, 1957. n.g.l. The westward expansion into Ohio is convincingly re-created.

EVERNDEN, MARGERY. *The Golden Trail.* New York: Random House, 1952. Grades 5–7. This is the story of the role of Captain Anza's expedition in the founding of San Francisco.

FIELD, RACHEL. *Hitty: Her First Hundred Years.* New York: Macmillan, 1937. Grades 4–6. Hitty is a doll, carved of mountain-ash wood, whose adventures give a vivid picture of nineteenth-century life in America. This is a Newbery Award book.

FRAZIER, NETA L. *One Long Picnic.* New York: David McKay, 1962. Grades 4–6. This spirited, realistic book tells of the westward movement along the Oregon Trail in 1850.

HARRIS, CHRISTIE. *West with the White Chiefs.* New York: Atheneum, 1965. Grade 5 and up. An Assiniboin Indian youth guides two young Englishmen over seldom traveled terrain from Fort Pitt to the Canadian gold fields.

HUNT, MABEL LEIGH. *Better Known As Johnny Appleseed.* Philadelphia: Lippincott, 1950. Grades 7–9. A colorful picture is painted of the Ohio-Indian region over which Johnny Appleseed wandered, generously planting his apple trees.

KROEBER, THEODORA. *Ishi, Last of His Tribe.* Berkeley, Calif.: Parnassus Press, 1964. Grades 4–10. This exciting account is based on true experiences of the last surviving member of the Yahi Tribe, a people of peace who lived in northern California.

ROBINSON, BARBARA. *Trace Through the Forest.* New York: Lothrop, Lee & Shepard, 1965. Grade 7 and up. This historical novel is told through the eyes of a fourteen-year-old boy who accompanies Colonel Zan and his eleven men to blaze a trail to Ohio. The story is full of adventure.

ROWLAND, FLORENCE W. *Pasquala of Santa Ynez Mission.* New York: Walck, 1961. Grades 4–6. This is a story of an Indian girl whose family dares to leave the tribe for a Christian life in a mission in California in the 1800s.

SMITH, FREDERIKA S. *The Sound of Axes.* Chicago: Rand McNally, 1965. Grades 3–6. This book portrays the early lumbering industry of eastern Wisconsin.

STEELE, WILLIAM O. *The Lone Hunt.* New York: Harcourt Brace Jovanovich, 1956. Grades 4–6. A lively picture of Cumberland Plateau backwoodsmen in 1810 is portrayed in this story.

VOIGHT, VIRGINIA FRANCES. *The Girl from Johnnycake Hill.* Englewood Cliffs, N. J.: Prentice-Hall, 1961. n.g.l. This excellent story is set in Connecticut in 1870.

War of 1812

ANDREWS, MARY EVANS. *Lanterns Aloft.* New York: David McKay, 1955. Grades 5–8. The setting of the story is the summer of 1813 when the British fleet threatened the eastern shore of Maryland.

BEYER, AUDREY W. *Capture at Sea.* New York: Knopf, 1959. Grade 7 and up. Two Yankee boys impressed by the British are taken aboard a British man-of-war.

DERLETH, AUGUST. *The Captive Island.* New York: Duell, Sloane, 1952. n.g.l. The siege of Mackinac Island during the War of 1812 is excitingly portrayed.

FINGER, CHARLES J. *Cape Horn Snorter.* Boston: Houghton Mifflin, 1939. n.g.l. The story of the frigate *Essex* in the battle of Valparaiso, March 1813, is convincingly told in this book.

HOWARD, ELIZABETH. *Candle in the Night.* New York: Morrow, 1952. Grade 7 and up. A vivid picture of Detroit at the time of its capture by the British in 1812 is portrayed in this story.

MAYS, VICTOR. *Action Starboard.* Boston: Houghton Mifflin, 1956. Grades 6–9. This exciting story relates the adventures of a cabin boy on an American brig that attempts to run the British blockade in 1813.

PRUDDEN, T. M. *The Frigate Philadelphia.* Princeton, N. J.: Van Nostrand, 1966. Grade 7 and up. Fifteen-year-old Jonas Herring ships aboard the frigate *Philadelphia* and has many exciting adventures, giving us a dramatic picture of American Naval Service in the early days of the Republic.

REEDER, COLONEL RED. *Attack at Fort Lookout.* New York: Duell, Sloane & Pearce, 1959. Grades 7–10. A Lake Huron frontier outpost during the lull before the Indian attack at Tippecanoe in 1811 is the setting for this story.

SPERRY, ARMSTRONG. *Black Falcon.* New York: Holt, Rinehart & Winston, 1949. Grades 7–9. The story of the son of a New Orleans planter and Jean Laffite during the privateering raids by the pirate against the English in 1814.

———. *Storm Canvas.* New York: Holt, Rinehart & Winston, 1944. Grades 7–9. Sea battles, duels, and characters like King Christophe of the West Indies are featured in this story of the War of 1812.

SWANSON, ANNE S., AND NEIL H. SWANSON. *The Star-Spangled Banner.* New York: Holt, Rinehart & Winston, 1958. Grades 4–6. The siege of Fort McHenry during the War of 1812 is described in this story.

Civil War

FISHER, AILEEN. *A Lantern in the Window.* Eau Claire, Wis.: Hale, 1957. Grades 4–7. A station where Negro slaves escaping from the South can stop and be helped on their way to Canada is the setting for this remarkable story.

HAVIGHURST, MARION B. *The Sycamore Tree.* Cleveland: World Publishing, 1960. Grades 7–9. A teen-age, Southern belle is torn between loyalty to two brothers, one of whom is fighting in the Union Army, the other in the Army of the Confederacy.

HODGES, CARL G. *Baxie Randall and the Blue Raiders.* Indianapolis: Bobbs-Merrill, 1962. Grades 5–9. A twelve-year-old orphan boy becomes a hero during General Grierson's raid through the South to Baton Rouge during the Civil War.

MC NICOL, JACQUELINE. *Ride for Old Glory.* New York: David McKay, 1964. Grades 3–7. Johnny Linn, who became a courier for General James Wilson of the Union Army, narrates the battle of Nashville, one of the last major engagements of the War.

MEADER, STEPHEN W. *The Muddy Road to Glory.* New York: Harcourt Brace Jovanovich, 1963. Grades 7–9. A boy of sixteen from Maine enlists in the army, is taken prisoner, escapes, and rejoins the army until the end of the Civil War.

SPRATT, BARNETT. *Miss Betty of Bonnet Rock School.* New York: Hastings House, 1965. Grade 7 and up. The diary of a young girl teaching in a rural school during the Civil War makes an interesting story.

Pre-World War I

TAYLOR, SYDNEY. *All-of-a-Kind Family.* Chicago: Follett, 1951. Grades 4–6. An engaging period story about a family living in New York at the turn of the century—rich in atmosphere and family relations. *All-of-a-Kind Family Uptown* follows, 1958.

World War II

LEVIN, JANE W. *Star of Danger.* New York: Harcourt Brace Jovanovich, 1966. Grade 7 and up. This story reveals the courage of two Jewish boys and those who risked their lives to help them when they escaped from the Nazis via the Danish underground to neutral Copenhagen.

WERSTEIN, IRVING. *The Long Escape.* New York: Scribner, 1964. Grades 7–11. In this exciting story of World War II, the children living in a convalescent home escape from the Germans, reach Dunkerque, and embark for England.

WHITE, ROBB. *Surrender.* Garden City, N. Y.: Doubleday, 1966. Grades 8–10. A boy and girl, survivors of the Japanese invasion of the Philippines, search for the leader of the Philippine guerrillas and a way to safety. The fall of Corregidor and the Bataan Death March are included in the realistic World War II setting.

World History

BARTOS-HOPPNER, BARBARA. *Save the Khan.* S. Humphries (tr.). New York: Walck, 1964. Grades 7–9. In this adventure story with a colorful historical background, a young Tartar prince fights against a Russian invasion.

BEATTY, JOHN, AND PATRICIA BEATTY. *Campion Towers.* New York: Macmillan, 1965. Grade 7 and up. A panoramic view of life in England under the Protectorate is presented in this book.

BERRY, ERICK. *Honey of the Nile.* New York: Viking, 1963. Grade 7 and up. This story, with its setting during the time of King Tutankhamen, has strong period details and historical background.

BURLEIGH, DAVID ROBERT. *Messenger from K'itai.* Chicago: Follett, 1964. Grades 4–6. This book relates the adventures of fourteen-year-old Dashan in the year 1246, as he trains to be a messenger to his queen, the Khanate of Tuli of Mongolia.

CAPON, PAUL. *Kingdom of the Bulls.* New York: Norton, 1962. Grades 5–9. Life in ancient Britain and Crete is portrayed in this story.

COATSWORTH, ELIZABETH JANE. *Door to the North.* New York: Holt, Rinehart & Winston, 1950. Grades 7–9. This is a fictionalized telling of the Viking voyage to the New World and into Minnesota in the fourteenth century.

DREWERY, MARY. *Devil in Print.* New York: David McKay, 1966. Grades 8–12. This historical novel is set in England, Germany, and Holland around 1525 during the period of the Reformation.

GREEN, ROBERT JAMES. *The Whistling Sword.* New York: St. Martin's Press, 1962. n.g.l. This is a story about the fierce and cruel Mongol tribes and their leader Genghis Khan, who ruled during one of the most dramatic periods in history.

HAUGAARD, ERIK CHRISTIAN. *Hakon of Rogen's Saga.* Boston: Houghton Mifflin, 1963. Grade 7 and up. This action-packed story portrays a power struggle on a Viking island.

HAVIGHURST, MARION B. *Strange Island.* Cleveland: World Publishing, 1957. Grades 7–9. Blennerhassett Island is the setting of this story about Burr's conspiracy.

HERRMANN, RALPH. *Children of the North Pole.* Annabelle MacMillan (tr.). New York: Harcourt Brace Jovanovich, 1964. Grades 2–5. This suspense-filled story describes two Eskimo children living in Greenland.

HODGES, CYRIL WALTER. *The Namesake: A Story of King Alfred.* New York: Coward-McCann, 1964. Grades 5–7. This exciting adventure story is set in England during the reign of King Alfred.

JEWETT, ELEANORE MYERS. *Big John's Secret.* New York: Viking, 1962. Grades 7–10. Feudal background is portrayed in this story of thirteenth-century England.

JONES, RUTH FOSDICK. *Boy of the Pyramids.* New York: Random House, 1952. Grades 4–6. Interesting and authentic details are related at the time of the building of the pyramids in Egypt.

KALISH, BETTY. *Eleven! Time to Think of Marriage, Farhut.* New York: Atheneum, 1970. Grades 7–9. This story describes the life of a Moslem family in Bengal during the first part of the twentieth century.

KAUFMANN, HERBERT. *Adventure in the Desert.* New York: Astor-Honor, 1961. Grade 7 and up. This stirring story of a wandering singer gives a vivid picture of the life of the Tuareg tribes of North Africa.

KIRTLAND, G. B. *One Day in Ancient Rome.* New York: Harcourt Brace

Jovanovich, 1961. Grades 4–6. This humorous story describes a day in the life of two Roman children living in A.D. 75.

KOTZWINKLE, WILLIAM. *Elephant Boy.* New York: Farrar, Straus & Giroux, 1970. Grades 1–3. This story about a Stone Age boy and his father describes primitive man's feelings toward his environment.

LAURING, PALLE. *The Stone Daggers.* New York: Macmillan, 1964. n.g.l. This story of the Bronze Age is set in a Danish village.

LEIGHTON, MARGARET. *Voyage to Coromandel.* New York: Farrar, Straus & Giroux, 1965. Grades 6–10. Two brothers who are Viking hostages serve as pages at the Court of King Alfred.

LOCKE, ELSIE. *The Runaway Settlers.* New York: Dutton, 1966. Grades 5–8. An Australian family overcomes untold obstacles in order to stay together.

MC GRAW, ELOISE J. *The Golden Goblet.* New York: Coward-McCann, 1961. Grades 5–8. This lively adventure story is set in ancient Egypt.

MALORY, SIR THOMAS. Sidney Lainer (ed.). *The Boy's King Arthur.* New York: Scribner, 1917. Grades 7–11. This is one of the most enduring and acceptable adaptations of Malory's text *History of King Arthur and His Knights of the Round Table.*

NURENBERG, THELMA. *My Cousin, the Arab.* New York: Abelard-Schuman, 1965. This story conveys a realistic picture of people living in a world of hate and fear at the kibbutz outside Haifa in the early days in Israel.

O'DELL, SCOTT. *The King's Fifth.* Boston: Houghton Mifflin, 1966. Grades 7–10. The crimes committed and the extreme suffering endured by members of Coronado's expedition in search of the golden cities of Cibola are told by Esteban de Sandoval, the mapmaker.

OSBORNE, CHESTER G. *The Wind and the Fire.* Englewood Cliffs, N. J.: Prentice-Hall, 1959. n.g.l. A fast-paced story in a convincing setting tells of two boys living in the Stone Age in the region that is now Ireland.

PYLE, HOWARD. *Otto of the Silver Hand.* Rev. ed. New York: Scribner, 1954. Grades 4–10. This robust adventure story of the Middle Ages is set in Germany.

RAY, MARY. *The Voice of Apollo.* New York: Farrar, Straus & Giroux, 1965. Grade 10 and up. This colorful story of ancient Greece is set in Delphi.

RENAULT, MARY. *The Lion in the Gateway.* New York: Harper & Row, 1964. Grade 5 and up. The Greeks, supported by their fundamental belief in freedom, are able to turn back the Persians, who although stronger in numbers are dependent on the single, often unreasoning will of a despotic ruler.

SCHWEITZER, BYRD B. *One Small Blue Bead.* New York: Macmillan, 1965. Kindergarten–grade 3. With rhyming text and beautiful illustrations, this picture story about a small boy who wonders about a blue bead introduces readers to the culture of primitive man.

SPEARE, ELIZABETH G. *The Bronze Bow.* Boston: Houghton Mifflin, 1961. Grade 7 and up. In this moving story of early Christian times, a young Jewish rebel learns from Jesus to love rather than to hate.

SUTCLIFF, ROSEMARY. *The Eagle of the Ninth.* New York: Walck, 1954. Grades 7–9. In rich style with authentic historical details this story tells how a young Roman finds in Britain the last eagle of his father's command.

TREASE, GEOFFREY. *Web of Traitors.* New York: Vanguard, 1952. Grade 6 and up. This exciting story is set in Athens during the time of Socrates.

TREECE, HENRY. *The Horned Helmet.* New York: Criterion Books, 1963. Grades 6–10. This is a vivid, convincing story of a Viking voyage set in the early part of the eleventh century.

WEIR, ROSEMARY. *The Star and the Flame.* New York: Farrar, Straus & Giroux, 1964. Grade 10 and up. This historical novel is based on Restoration England at the time of the plague and the great fire.

WILSON, BARBARA KER. *In the Shadow of Vesuvius.* Cleveland: World Publishing, 1965. n.g.l. This is a dramatic story of life in Pompeii and the eruption of Vesuvius in A.D. 79.

WISE, WILLIAM. *The Two Reigns of Tutankhamen.* New York: Putnam, 1964. Grades 6–10. This informative book describes the discovery of King Tutankhamen's tomb.

WOJCIECHOWSKA, MAIA. *Odyssey of Courage: The Story of Cabeza Da Vaca.* New York: Atheneum, 1965. Grade 5 and up. Vividly written descriptions enliven this dramatic story of Cabeza da Vaca's two long visits to the New World in the sixteenth century.

Further Reading for Teachers, Parents, and Librarians

BILLINGTON, MONROE. *The American South: A Brief History.* New York: Scribner, 1971. A review of the history of the South from precolonial times through Reconstruction, with a comprehensive examination of the dominant features of regions in the past and present.

BROWN, DEE ALEXANDER. *Bury My Heart at Wounded Knee: An Indian History of the American West.* New York: Holt, Rinehart & Winston, 1971. Relates the happenings from 1860 to 1890, when the Indians fought for—but lost—their ancestral lands. Based on diaries, pictographic records, autobiographies, and other primary sources.

BROWN, WALLACE. *The Americans: The Loyalists in the American Revolution.* New York: Morrow, 1969. A well-documented account of the eighteenth-century Americans who opposed the Revolution and remained loyal to the crown.

CARSWELL, JOHN. *The Descent on England: A Study of the English Revolution of 1688 and Its European Background.* New York: John Day, 1969. A vivid description of the foreign elements that influenced the various aspects of life in seventeenth-century England.

ECCLES, WILLIAM JOHN. *The Canadian Frontier, 1534–1760.* Histories of the American Frontier Series. New York: Holt, Rinehart & Winston, 1969. A vivid picture of the harsh realities of daily life on the French Canadian frontier.

GAXOTTE, PIERRE. *The Age of Louis XIV.* Michael Shaw (trans.). New York: Macmillan, 1970. A French historian depicts a great French king, his reign, and his accomplishments.

HARRIMAN, WILLIAM AVERELL. *America and Russia in a Changing World.* New York: Doubleday, 1971. Intro. by Arthur M. Schlesinger. Critical impressions, observations, and thoughts on the past, present, and future of Soviet-U. S. relations that are relative to war and peace in Europe and Vietnam. Based on Harriman's experiences and conversations in his various official and unofficial diplomatic capacities.

LOCKRIDGE, KENNETH A. *New England Town: The First Hundred Years.* Essays in American History Series. New York: Norton, 1970. The evolution of a New England town from its beginnings in the wilderness to one hundred years later, when it had become a thriving community.

MARCH, TONY. *Darkness over Europe: First Person Accounts of Life in Europe During the War Years 1939–1945.* New York: Rand, 1969.

O'CONNOR, RICHARD. *The Cactus Throne: The Tragedy of Maximilian and Charlotte.* New York: Putnam, 1971. An intriguing narrative of Archduke Maximilian of Austria and Princess Charlotte of Belgium and their roles as rulers of Mexico.

TOLAND, JOHN. *The Rising Sun.* New York: Random House, 1970.

WEINSTEIN, DONALD. *Savonarola and Florence: Prophecy and Patriotism in the Renaissance.* Princeton, N. J.: Princeton Press, 1971. An insightful study that reflects life in Florence during the time of monk Savonarola.

WILSON, THEODORE A. *The First Summit: Roosevelt and Churchill at Placentia Bay 1941.* Boston: Houghton Mifflin, 1969. A brilliant doctoral dissertation based on the meeting of Roosevelt and Churchill, out of which came the Atlantic Declaration in 1941.

The Smallest Elephant in the World by Alvin Tresselt, illustrated by Milton Glaser.

15

Organizing and Evaluating the Literature Program

With the wealth of beautiful books for children of all ages flooding the market and with outstanding authors, artists, and publishers working together to produce books for home, school, and community libraries, children should be enjoying the satisfaction and pleasures that can come from experiences in literature. Literature programs in most elementary schools today have advanced considerably since the days of the McGuffey readers, but many programs still have far to go.

The Changing Structure of the Curriculum

For a long time literature in the elementary school was limited to the stories that teachers read or told and to those found in readers, which were usually adaptations of well-known stories. More literature experiences were provided as the social studies programs became organized around such settings or studies as colonial life or the westward movement. Literature programs were then geared to these settings or studies and the stories read were those related to a particular study. As more related books were published, extensive bibliographies were prepared to accompany the studies.

The Individualized Program

A move was started in the 1950s to broaden the literature program by having children read freely regardless of whether or not the stories were related to the studies in progress. The 1950s also saw a significant move toward individualized self-instruction programs in literature, based largely upon the theory that all learning is really a process of self-selection. A further trend has been the integration of literature and other areas of the curriculum including art, music, composition, and the sciences.

Among the outstanding early research related to different aspects of individualized reading programs were those by Dayton Rothrock (20), Patrick Groff (10), and Miriam Aronow (2). Rothrock found that self-selection brought an immediate and marked improvement in attitude toward reading. Groff's study showed that under a self-selection program the amount of reading considerably increased. And in Aronow's research the children showed significant gains in reading skill.

The limited amount of research related to literature in the elementary school is concerned with the content of children's literature with emphasis on the disadvantaged, the atypical, and the child in a problem situation. Hal Thompson contributed a comprehensive review of research in the publication of the Association for Supervision and Curriculum Development, *Interpreting Language Arts Research for the Teacher.*

Hal Bishop (3) states that the data compiled since 1920 to determine the effects of free reading as distinct from prescribed reading have consistently favored extensive free reading over intensive reading: Harry W. Sartain (21) studied free reading with elementary pupils and found that pupils read more widely when there is self selection. Hoyle D. Lawson's (15) research compared various mixes of free reading time and systematic skill instruction with sixth graders. He found that the highest reading achievement resulted from use of a combination of 30 minutes of skill instruction and 15 minutes of free reading.

Two recent researches follow that were not reported in the Bishop synopsis.

A study by Claire Elizabeth Morris involved forty sixth graders of three mental maturity levels—low, middle, and high—who were randomly assigned to classes using either the Preplanned Sequentially Structured Approach or the Incidental Unstructured Approach to determine the differential effectiveness of these two approaches in the teaching of literature appreciation. The effect of literature study upon writing ability was also explored. In forty prose and twenty poetry periods, the Preplanned Sequentially Structured Group followed literature lessons that provided for oral reading, discussion, and related language activities designed by the investigator to foster appreciation. The Incidental Unstructured Group did not follow any previously planned lessons but through pupil-teacher interaction evolved a program that included oral reading, discussion, and individual or small group activities. The effectiveness of the two treatments upon the appreciation of literature was determined by comparing the performance of the two groups in understanding, interpretation, and attitudes toward prose and poetry. Differences in writing ability were measured by nine sets of writing examples. The author concluded that pupils of high intelligence interpret literature on a significantly higher level and evidence greater writing proficiency than pupils of middle or low intelligence regardless of the teaching method.

In a paper presented at the conference of the American Educational Research Association in 1971, Anna Elizabeth Teigland and coworkers compared the effectiveness of the individualized approach with the basal reader approach using a criterion based on vocabulary, comprehension, and attitude toward reading as well as the number, type, and difficulty of books voluntarily read during the second grade. Near the end of kindergarten, children in three schools were randomly assigned to one of the two approaches. At the end of second grade there were sixty-five basal pupils and sixty-nine individualized approach pupils for whom data were available. When the California Reading Test was administered at the end of second grade, the individualized reading group had significantly higher scores on comprehension than had the basal group; the vocabulary scores favored the individualized group but were not significant. No significant differences were found in attitude toward reading from the San Diego County Inventory of Reading Attitudes. The quantity, variety, and difficulty of books read overwhelmingly favored the individualized approach.

The Structured Program

Today, structure is playing a prominent role in curriculum development. Some educators hold that children are ready to discover the structure of a discipline at a far earlier age than was formerly expected and that, therefore, the study of literature as a discipline need not be delayed until high school. In many primary schools an individualized reading program has been offered as both an alternate and a supplement to the basal reading program. However, in cases where the children differ widely in experiential backgrounds, interests, and maturity, this theory would not apply. All the children in a group may not be ready for the same experience at the same time. In such instances, rather than handing down concepts and generalizations to the entire group, the educator should provide abundant experiences that will make it possible for individuals to build meanings into concepts and arrive at sound generalizations on their own.

In some situations plans are made for all the children to read the same story and then to spend a period of time each day for three or four days in a discussion group directed toward purposes that the teacher has in mind. Such a limiting procedure has turned many children away from literature. Listening to a lengthy discussion of the *Story of the Three Bears*, a little boy is said to have uttered, "That's a lot of fuss to make over a bowl of porridge!"

Although the curriculum may be structured in a number of different patterns, usually similar areas exist in each. Most programs include folk tales, fantasy, animal stories, adventure stories, myths and legends, fables, stories of other lands, historical fiction, and biography. However, various programs may differ somewhat in nomenclature and breakdown of the broader content areas.

Although a structured curriculum has the advantages of securing an important place for literature in all the grades of the elementary school and providing guidelines for persons responsible for the preparation of courses of study, it may have the disadvantage of restricting both the teacher and the students. In many situations the materials that follow the content framework do not take into account the range of differences in reading ability and interests in a group. They tend to dictate the procedures to follow, as far down as first grade, leaving little encouragement for creative teaching. Stories are listed for study in each of the content areas for each of the elementary grades, and materials provided for the teachers include aids for analyzing the stories to be used. The procedures are very much like those recommended in teachers' manuals accompanying basal readers. One wonders what is left of such treasured characters as Peter Rabbit, Cinderella, and Winnie the Pooh for children to enjoy after the analysis is over.

Essentials of a Good Program

There are certain essentials in planning and organizing a good literature program for children. An adequate supply of books is obviously one essential. No matter how large and varied the supply may be, there must be time for both listening and reading. In addition, children must have time to share their reading experiences with others.

Securing an Adequate Supply of Books

The standard number of books recommended for schools of 250 students or more by the American Library Association and the National Education Association (8) is at least 6,000–10,000 titles representing a total of 10,000 volumes or 20 volumes per student, whichever is greater (excluding professional materials for the faculty, dictionaries, encyclopedias, magazines, newspapers that are required for classroom use, and textbook collections).

The usual resources for the supply of books are the instructional media centers in the school building, in the central school administration center, and in the office of the county superintendent of schools. In some states the county instructional media center is the chief resource for the supply of books. In other states the relation of the local school districts to the county instructional media center is limited or nonexistent. In most school systems instructional media are made available through the cooperative arrangements of the different levels of school organization; bibliographies and other materials prepared at the different levels are shared. Community libraries also serve as excellent resources.

Selecting Books

Various procedures exist at the local and county levels for the selection of books and other media of communication. A common practice at both levels is the use of evaluation committees, usually made up of teachers, curriculum workers, librarians, and occasionally school-board members and parents. Publishers interested in having their materials adopted for use in the schools supply copies of their books for review. Various practices for reviewing are followed. In some situations the members of evaluation committees, which vary in size, read the books and make their recommendations for adoption. Another procedure has teachers try out the book with their pupils. The reactions of the pupils are then noted, and the teachers make recommendations to the evaluation committee.

The American Library Association and the National Education Association in *Standards for School Media Programs* (8) include five basic policies that should shape the selection of materials for the media center:

1. The school and the school system have a written statement of selection policy, formulated and endorsed by the school administration, the media specialists, and faculty, and adopted by the school board. This statement

indicates the general objectives and procedures of selection, and affirms such American freedoms as described in the *Library Bill of Rights* [7], the *School Library Bill of Rights* [1], and *The Students' Right to Read* [17].

2. The collection meets the requirements of the various curriculum areas and provides for the diverse learning skills of individuals representing all levels and types of ability. Materials are also included that inspire and meet the independent interests and research needs of students. Therefore, the media collection is rich in breadth and depth in the subjects covered, the types of material included, and the forms of expression represented.

3. Media selection, distribution, and use reflect current trends in education and communications. Such developments as the multimedia approach to materials, the widespread use of paperbacks, and the emergence of information systems, instructional design, and computerized programs of learning and instruction have had a marked influence on the scope and use of materials in the school and in the media center. The findings of research in learning development, the increased sophistication of youth, the rising expectations of deprived young people, the crisis of the central city, and the curricular innovations influence the selection of materials.

4. The selection of materials by a process of competent evaluation is the responsibility of qualified specialists [including teachers—au.] at the local, state, regional, or national levels. The process of selection is expedited by consulting reviews, recommended lists, standard bibliographical tools, and special releases.

5. Sufficient duplicate copies of materials are available to meet the needs of students and teachers . . . This is not identical with the provision of copying services. The latter necessitates adherence to the copyright law on the part of school administrators and media specialists in reproducing and making facsimile copies of copyrighted materials, both print and nonprint. [Pp. 20–21]

The teacher is confronted with a seemingly endless array of interests to be satisfied. He must realize that there are books available to satisfy not only such fiction interests as adventure, mystery, science fiction, and animal stories, but also such nonfiction interests as photography, embroidery, and scuba diving.

Interests change constantly as children move from one phase of development to another. The teacher should be aware that although most children go through the same phases of reading interests, each progresses at a rate peculiar to himself. The important precept is that the books available for a particular group are those that will satisfy their prevailing interests. The teacher has a significant role to play in helping children develop new interests as well as in satisfying present ones.

Motivation

Teachers use numerous methods for motivating children to read. Many of them fall short of the expected outcomes because they emphasize extrinsic rewards, such as stars on a chart, rather than intrinsic rewards. Reading many books is certainly not as important as comprehending what is read. Too often motivational devices are single purposed—they aim only to increase the number of books read. They are often lengthy and tedious. Emphasis is placed on competition rather than on cooperation. Students are encouraged to read more books than do their peers rather than to share their reading experiences with each other.

Numerous ways exist for motivating reading through multipurposed group activities. For example, if a class decides to have a puppet play, it will read with the purpose of selecting a story applicable for a play. Groups are organized to write the play, to design the sets, and to make the costumes. The processes involved are as important as the production itself, for the cooperative enterprise provides opportunity in which children assume responsibility, increase their skill in planning, and work with one another.

Activities such as round-table discussions and story-book pageants are other group activities related to literature that have in them the potential for motivating reading as well as providing both individual and group growth.

The best motivation comes from the kind of climate that pervades the classroom. When a friendly relationship exists between the teacher and the pupils, the children feel secure and free to communicate with the teacher and with each other. Enthusiasm for something on the part of one person can start a chain reaction that will generate interest on the part of others. The teacher who is sensitive to the intrinsic values in literature will project her feelings in such a manner that the majority of the class will catch the spark and begin to enjoy the pleasures waiting for them.

The Role of the Home

One test as to whether or not reading for pleasure has caught on is the amount of reading a child does outside the school in the community library or at home. Test data regarding a child's reading skills are important only in relation to their application in the individual's personal reading situation. Some children are avid readers, some are only browsers, and others want nothing to do with reading if they can avoid it.

Many factors influence the amount of time that children spend reading outside the school. One factor is the availability of reading materials. Not all school libraries are operated on a loan basis. Another factor is the variety of environments in which children grow up. Some are in close proximity to public libraries; others live in remote areas where library facilities are extremely limited. Thousands of children live in substandard housing in rural or urban slums, where there is little or no chance for the quiet and privacy that encourage reading.

Wherever the conditions are favorable for reading, enthusiasm can be vitalized. Parents can make the home environment one that will encourage children to read. If there are books and magazines around the house and children see their parents reading, they will naturally imitate them. They will begin to recognize that reading is part of a pleasant way of living. Books can provide a point of communication between parents and children.

In many instances parents put so much emphasis on reading that their children develop emotional blocks toward it. Today's children encounter tremendous pressures to attain higher education; the home environment should provide a buffer for these pressures, not accentuate them. Parents help most when they set an example by reading, by sharing their reading, and by encouraging their children to build a personal library.

Time for Reading

Too often children are not allowed enough school time for reading of literature. Most of the reading during the school day is done for the purpose of acquiring and practicing reading skills, finding the answers to questions, and securing information. Classes still exist in which reading for pleasure is limited to a one-hour library period or a "free" reading period, usually on Friday afternoon.

Fortunately, in many schools literature is an integral part of the daily program, which provides a specific time to read for enjoyment and to discuss and to share reading experiences. Usually the stories are selected on the basis of individual interest.

Children should be introduced to the school and community libraries as early as kindergarten. A visit to the community library exposes children to the happy times available there: stories to hear and to read, records to play, movies to see, television programs to view, skits to take part in, games to play. Teachers and parents can help children start the library habit early. Both should encourage children to own and use their library cards.

A reading center or library corner is a must in every classroom. The floorplan of the room and the arrangement of the furniture determine the best location for the center. The areas selected should be properly lighted, close to the book supply, and as attractive as possible. Art objects, flowers and plants, and posters add to the related atmosphere and attractiveness of the center.

A bulletin board related solely to reading and literature should have a prominent place in the center. Book jackets, dolls and puppets representing story characters, background murals depicting scenes from stories, painting of dramatic scenes from stories, and models or figurines of story characters can all be used to add color to the displays as well as to acquaint the children with books both old and new.

Time for Listening

Most teachers enjoy reading stories to their classes, and the children usually like listening. For countless children this may be their first introduction to written stories. Knowing the interests of a particular group of children, the teacher can select a story that most of the boys and girls will enjoy. The story may be read for a short period of time either at the opening or at the end of the school day. There are often times before and after recesses when reading a story aloud may quiet a class as well as provide entertainment.

By listening to stories read, children can have their reading range broadened and their reading horizons extended. They can become accustomed to living as easily in the realm of make-believe as in the world of reality. Teachers themselves should read certain stories or parts of stories to the class. It would be unfortunate for any child to fail to make the acquaintance of such literary masterpieces as *Alice's Adventures in Wonderland* (6) by Lewis Carroll, *The Wind in the Willows* (9) by Kenneth Grahame, or *Rabbit Hill* (16) by Robert Lawson. The subtle humor and elaborate nonsense in *Alice* are often lost unless children hear parts of the story read. Similarly the delightful characterizations in *The Wind in the Willows* and the friendly relationships that man establishes with animals in *Rabbit Hill* are often better grasped by children if the stories are read aloud.

The teacher's enthusiasm for the story he is reading is contagious, and a love of literature can be developed in boys and girls through the attitude the teacher shows toward it. The stories the teacher selects to read to the class can improve the literary understanding and tastes of the pupils. Both Ruth Sawyer in *The Way of the Story Teller* (22) and Marie L. Shedlock in *The Art of the Storyteller* (24) emphasize the importance of the spoken word in the introduction of literature to children.

Many stories fill the criterion of being able to hold the attention of a listener. In *The Incredible Journey* (5) by Sheila Burnford a Labrador retriever, a bull terrier, and a Siamese cat take a 250-mile journey through the Canadian wilderness to the place and people who mean home to them. Marguerite Henry has written a number of outstanding stories that have storytelling qualities. *King of the Wind* (12) relates the hardships that are the lot of a great Arabian stallion sent as a gift to the King of France. Recognition finally comes to King of the Wind when he sires a famous line of horses of which Man o' War will be a descendant. Children in the preschool and primary grades enjoy listening to *Nobody Listens to Andrew* (11) by Elizabeth Guilfoile. Andrew vainly tries to get the attention of his family and a neighbor until his screams bring about a humorous conclusion.

A listening center in a classroom may serve a number of purposes. The teacher may use the center for telling stories to small groups of children, individuals may use the center to read stories to each other, and groups may gather there to listen to records of stories and songs. The center should be well equipped with a listening post, a projector, and a screen or wall space that can serve as a screen. A single tape recorder or phonograph may be equipped with a listening post or distribution box containing several jacks into which earphones can be plugged. With this arrangement, one or more persons may listen without disturbing those engaged in other listening activities in the center. Using a projector and screen, the teacher can show illustrations from books and children's drawings while the group listens to a narration. As teachers work with small groups, they will find more and more uses for the listening post.

A story well told is a stimulant to the child's imagination. He hears the words, and in his mind he has to create the setting and imagine the characters. As he listens to stories, he begins to build a favorable attitude toward literature. Through a love of literature he will increase his span of attention and improve his powers of concentration and listening habits.

Time for Sharing

Sharing is an integral part of the literature program. Reading a story or listening to a story may be either an individual or a group experience. The many ways of sharing tie together and bring to fruition the various aspects of the literature program. The teacher plays an important role in stimulating children to share their reading in creative ways. He enthusiastically shares his own reading, and he makes available a variety of materials through which children can share their reading experiences with others.

Sharing may be done through the use of different art media such as crayons, watercolors, oil, charcoal, pen and ink, papier-mâché, clay, wood, cloth, and plastics. The different materials can be used for such activities as the following:

- Illustrating dramatic incidents in a story
- Drawing original book jackets for a bulletin board display
- Painting murals depicting the sequences in the plot of a story
- Painting stage sets for skits, plays, or puppet shows
- Drawing scenes described in stories to show with an overhead projector
- Making a movie of a book by:
  - Drawing a series of pictures on a long sheet of paper, the ends being fastened to rollers that are turned to move the pictures into view
  - Making a double frame so that while one picture is being shown in one frame, a second one can be fed into the other frame
  - Actually using a motion-picture camera
- Drawing backdrops for peep shows in a shoe box
- Painting pictures of characters from stories to use in a mobile
- Making wood carvings of characters in a story
- Modeling characters out of clay
- Making clothing and dressing dolls and puppets as characters in stories

Children may also use the language arts as vehicles for sharing their experiences in literature. They enjoy engaging in such activities as:

- Giving oral reviews of stories read to the class
- Giving oral descriptions of characters and places in a story read to the class
- Engaging in a round-table discussion on a subject related to literature
- Telling stories using a flannel board
- Reading to the class a humorous incident from a story
- Writing reviews of stories
- Writing skits, plays, and puppet shows utilizing scenes from favorite stories

One of the major values of literature is the pleasure it gives people. Too often, children have had the fun of reading diminished and often spoiled by having to produce evidence that they read a book. A popular practice for years was the requirement of a written book report that amounted to a test as to whether the individual had read the story. The report gave little evidence of what the book had done for the reader. Today children are encouraged to extend the experience they have enjoyed by sharing it with others. Numerous ways of sharing give pleasure to both the producers and the consumers and also contribute to a deeper appreciation of the story. Teachers need to guard against letting these experiences deteriorate into requirements. Not every child is interested in sharing a book he reads. In too many situations, the premium is placed upon the uniqueness of the sharing experience as if it were more important than the reading of the story.

Using Other Media for Enrichment

In addition to books, the teacher has many other media of communication with which to enrich the literature program. Television and radio programs; films, film strips, and slides; recordings, tapes, and cassettes; and magazines and newspapers may be used in close correlation with books. The teacher determines the medium that will best motivate and enrich the reading of a particular story.

Television

Children of today accept television without question. It has been a part of their daily lives since they were born. Few homes in our country do not have television, and in many homes family life is built around television programs.

The rapid increase in the use of television in American life has become the concern of many educators and parents. Some educators have favored television from its beginning for its educational possibilities; others have been concerned with the inferior quality of the programs. Parents express their concern over the addiction of their children to televiewing; teachers claim that they have had greater difficulty in interesting children in school subjects. In contrast, some parents feel that television has improved family relationships and has brought the family closer together. Many teachers express the viewpoint that television serves to motivate children in their school work.

In spite of many poor programs, particularly those steeped in crime and violence, a number of worthwhile programs have the potential for enriching the literature program. What better homework could be assigned than having children view a good television program and then discuss it in class? Frequently, stories dramatized on television are changed considerably from the book with which the children are familiar, and children enjoy pointing out the changes that have been made. Through such experiences they learn that a book is one medium of expression, whereas television is another.

Films

In the past few years there has been a significant increase in the production of films for use as enrichment material in the elementary school curriculum. The materials are available from the producers as well as from the multimedia centers that have been established at the district, county, and state levels. Colleges and universities also serve as suppliers. Most materials are on loan from multimedia centers but can also be rented or purchased from producers and distributors. Materials should be previewed before purchase: Catalogs are available from most sources, which usually also provide film strips, slides, and art reproductions.

Children particularly enjoy viewing films. They satisfy their interest in animals in such delightful films as *Smallest Elephant in the World,* an animated version of Alvin Tresselt's adventure story about an undersized elephant. In *Walter the Lazy Mouse* a mouse learns to provide for himself when he loses his family. Children of all ages delight in *One Wide River to Cross,* an adaptation of the old folk song which shows animals entering Noah's ark.

Films provide many experiences for children—aesthetic, psychological, sociological, scientific. *Gilbert and the Wind* tells the story of a boy who finds the wind both a pleasurable and an exasperating companion. Two children take a walk in *We Explore Field and Meadow*

The Smallest Elephant in the World by Alvin Tresselt, illustrated by Milton Glaser.

and see plants and animals that live there. They learn how these living things depend upon each other for their needs. *Haiku—Introduction to Poetry* shows the visual impressions of the sensations of life that create poetry. Among the many advantages that films provide is the opportunity for children to meet people living under different conditions and in different places from themselves. *Kevin* is the story of a blind boy and his awareness of the dark world in which he lives. *Legend of the Parano* portrays the cultural life of the Colombian people through the fantasy of a twelve-year-old boy. The experiences of a teen-age boy living in the Bayou country of Louisiana are related in *River Boy.*

Sheila Schwartz (23) states: "Short art films have rarely been used in the elementary and junior high classroom." Her article in *Elementary English* "is a plea for their use for," she writes, "they serve a threefold purpose: (1) They involve and interest students, (2) they begin to familiarize students with the world of film, and (3) they can be studied and evaluated in ways which are closely related to literary study and therefore illustrate and illuminate basic literary concepts with directness and clarity." Miss Schwartz pursues Jerome S. Bruner's (4) idea, expressed in *The Process of Education,* that the structure of a subject can be taught to students at any grade level, depending on how it is taught.

Hannah Miller expresses an idea similar to that of Sheila Schwartz. After stating that "children's films have been neglected in the United states for a variety of reasons and in a variety of ways," she attributes this neglect to the lack of support of the big money markets and the limited support from public libraries and the networks as well as the unwillingness of American producers to take a chance on a financial investment.

In her article Miss Schwartz selects certain films and illustrates how they may be used to enrich the literature program. Miss Miller presents a sampling of what is available to teachers and librarians interested in including films in their curriculum.

Films may spur creative expression through the use of various art media. They may motivate the child who is yet unawakened to the joys of reading. Films have tremendous potential that is just beginning to be utilized in enriching the literature experiences of children.

Comics

Comic strips and comic books are an institution in American life. In the United States more than 100 million people read the comic strips every day. According to George Perry and Alan Aldridge (19),

"There are 160 weekly strips available for the special Sunday supplements and more than 250 daily strips produced by the syndicates" (p. 10).

The strips originally produced were meant to provoke laughter and were therefore called "comic strips" or "funnies." Through the years there has been a shift from humor to human interest, adventure, and wish fulfillment. It is evident that children read comic books to satisfy their desire for action, excitement, and adventure. The characters' predicament is immediately apparent. The story line is built on suspense and the conclusion is quickly reached. Comics are easy to read: Even if the words are difficult, the pictures carry the story; the dialogue is limited and to the point. The "good" guys and the "bad" guys are easily identified.

Although television has cut into the comic-book market, most children, particularly boys in the middle and upper years of the elementary school, read comics, which seem to be a phase of growing up. Slow learners enjoy them as much as do bright children.

In planning an approach to the problem of comic-book addiction, the teacher should realize that both the comic strips and comic books vary widely in content, style, and format. The teacher's aim should be to provide balanced reading fare rather than to eliminate the comics entirely. The resourceful teacher looks for positive ways to use them.

If a few children in the group read nothing voluntarily, the comics may be the first step in establishing the habit of reading for enjoyment. Once children have begun reading comics, the teachers may transfer their interest from poorer to better ones. Materials from the comics may even be used in related lessons. Discussion of word meanings, individual and class evaluations of comic books, location of parallel stories in literature or current events, and dramatization of the stories may all grow out of reading the comics. Facts in geography, history, and science that appear in the comics may be checked for accuracy. Since there are only a few plots for stories and countless variations of one plot, the teacher can often refer the child who is reading a comic book to a short story or book that contains the same kind of plot, characters, or setting.

Paperbacks

The deluge of paperbound books has been one of the most interesting developments in the book publishing industry in recent years. Among the thousands of titles published each year, the overwhelming majority are either titles that have stood the test of time or reprints of books that were well received when they appeared a few years previously.

Paperbacks can be found at newsstands, supermarkets, discount stores, travel terminals, and drugstores as well as in the long-established bookstores and specialty paperback bookstores. This abundant distribution is evidence of increased reading on the part of children as well as of adults. Close to 30,000 paperback titles are published each year and the number of young readers is increasing. Such well-known favorites as *Across Five Aprils* (13) by Irene Hunt, *Flowers for Algernon* (14) by Daniel Keyes, and *Rascal* (18) by Sterling North can be found in paperback editions.

The astonishing popularity of paperbacks can be accounted for, in large measure, by the simple fact that paperbacks cost much less than clothbound books. The low cost is frequently incentive for children to build personal libraries. They can have the pleasure of bringing their own books from home to the classroom. Low cost makes it possible for school districts to buy a number of paperbacks of the same title and plan follow-up activities for the groups that have read the same story.

An outgrowth of the publication of paperbacks in the 1950s was the organization of book clubs for young readers. Book clubs often allow pupils to get books at very low prices. Selections often include excellent classic sources that some children might not be able to own at hard-cover prices. However, care should be taken that the books meet the same literary standard used for the original works. In some instances the books are not only low in price but also low in quality. Perhaps teachers should select only those titles with which they are already acquainted. Since children make and pay for their choices, this may be difficult.

Objectives of the Literature Program

The important objectives of the literature program are thought of and stated in such intangibles as attitudes, appreciation, values, and interests. Growth in these areas is difficult to measure. It is unlikely that the reading of one book will cause an individual to change radically his attitudes, appreciations, values, and interests. However, an accumulation of similar experiences, firsthand and vicarious, might make its imprint on one's personality development. It is growth in these intangibles inherent in the literature program that is so difficult to evaluate. Nevertheless, the teacher needs to know what effect, in general, the literature program is making on the individuals whose reading he is guiding. Is growth taking place in desirable directions? What are some of the signs of growth that can be observed?

There are three dimensions to consider in evaluating the literature program: the teacher, the content of the program, and the pupil.

Evaluating the Teacher

The teacher is an integral part of the evaluating process. His attitude toward literature is extremely important. The teacher with an appreciation for literature transmits this feeling to his class. He talks with enthusiasm about a story. He expresses an intimacy with the characters in the stories that brings them to life. He feels with them as they struggle to overcome difficulties and rejoices with them in their successes. He shows his satisfactions with the outcomes of stories and is eager to share his reading with others.

If the teacher is to be effective in guiding children toward the objectives of a good literature program, he must know them as individuals—their needs, their interests, and the level of their reading skills. He uses observations, conferences with individuals, and interest inventories to become acquainted with them. He familiarizes himself with the research related to the reading interests, in general, of different age groups, and engages in classroom research to find the reading interests of particular individuals. Using diagnostic tests, he gets information related to the reading skills of the children with whom he is working.

As well as knowing the individuals in the group, the teacher needs to be acquainted with books. Reviews and annotations are valuable aids to teachers. However, it is most important for the teacher to know the stories well enough to make comments and ask questions indicating that he has read the story. Furthermore, knowing the story makes it possible for him to share it with an individual or with the class.

Evaluating the Program

In addition to knowing the children in the class as individuals and knowing books, the teacher can engage in numerous activities to give direction to the program. The following questions may be used by the teacher as guidelines for children to experience literature:

Are reading and listening centers arranged in the room?

What bulletin boards have been prepared to interest the class in certain titles and subjects?

What bibliographies have been prepared on different subjects—sports, mystery, fantasy, and so forth?

What displays of books are set up?

What stories and poems have been read to the class?

What motion pictures, film strips, slides, and records have been used?

What stories and poems have been read to the class to motivate creative writing?

What persons have been used as resources—librarians, local authors, local bookstore personnel?

How is literature integrated with the other areas of curriculum?

Are books relevant to the needs, interests, and abilities of the different age groups available?

What art materials are available for illustrating situations and incidents in stories read?

How are stories used to motivate dramatization?

Has time been scheduled for listening to stories told, read, or shared?

Has time been scheduled for children to read on the basis of their own interests?

How have children been helped to acquire the skills involved in interpretive reading?

How have the pupils been helped to develop criteria for judging the quality of what is read?

Evaluating the Pupil

The pupil, in the final analysis, is the most important dimension to consider in evaluating the literature program. The teacher needs to rely heavily on his day-to-day observations of the group and of individuals to get a good idea of how the group and individuals in the group are reacting to experiences in literature.

The following questions will give a fairly accurate picture of the group's interests and enjoyments:

Does the group look forward to the time for literature?

Does the group avoid wasting time getting the period started?

Does the group enter into the activities with enthusiasm?

Is the attention of the group held during activities?

Is there a high degree of group interaction and involvement?

Do ideas for planning activities flow freely from the children?

The questions that follow will give a fairly accurate picture of each pupil's growth toward the objectives of the literature program:

Does the pupil read widely in different fields—travel, biography, adventure, myths and legends, folk and fairy tales, fantasy, tall tales, animal stories?

Does he like to share his pleasure in reading by talking about stories, reading sections of stories and poems to his classmates, or recommending what he has read to others?

Does he express the ideas he has gained from stories in creative writing?

Does he use a variety of art media to illustrate situations and incidents in the stories he has read?

Does he use new words in his speaking vocabulary that he has met in the stories he has read?

Does he use the words in the stories he reads in the compositions he writes?

Has he read stories related to his personal interests?

Has his reading helped him with his personal problems?

Does he patronize the public library?

Is he starting a library of his own?

Do his comments indicate that he is building a personal philosophy that appears to be influenced by his reading?

Traditionally, the achievements of pupils have been evaluated by means of tests. Testmakers recognize the difficulty in measuring growth in such tangibles as those that constitute the goals of a literature program, since many of the things that really count in the reading process cannot be evaluated quantitatively. Many of the tests purported to indicate growth in perception are memory exercises. Most of the test questions are built on the premise that all the children in a certain grade have read the same book. However, the book may never have been available for particular children to read; even if it had been, any number of them might not have been interested in reading it.

Teachers are in a position to prepare tests, if they feel they are necessary, that will be aimed at finding out what children know about a certain aspect of literature. The following illustrates such a test for middle- and upper-grade pupils. The results will not only reveal certain knowledge that individuals have acquired, but they should also reveal the extent to which the pupils have experienced a balanced program.

Name School Grade

Write your meaning for each of the following words—some words have a number of different meanings. Give the meaning for each of the words in the list as they relate to the stories you have read or are reading.

Literature	Picture Books
Situation	Fiction
Characters	Historical Fiction
Plot	Fables
Subject	Comic Books
Title	Poetry
Climax	Prose
ABC Books	Folktales
Nursery Rhymes	Fairy Tales
Mother Goose	Series

Exercises such as the following give some indication of the depth of the reader's identification with the characters in a story. Such an exercise may also reveal the type of character the reader is inclined to emulate. Sharing nominations and deciding how to handle them can be great fun for pupils. Some groups may decide to nominate one boy and one girl for their Literary Hall of Fame once a month. Others may decide to do their selecting more often.

OUR LITERARY HALL OF FAME

Name School Grade

You are invited to nominate a boy and a girl for the *Children's Literature Hall of Fame.* Name the boy and girl you liked best in stories you have read. In two or three sentences give the reasons for your nominations.

I nominate ______________________ as my favorite boy in ______________________ by ______________________ ________ because

I nominate ______________________ as my favorite girl in ______________________ by ______________________ ________ because

One of the major purposes of literature is entertainment. Instead of making a test threatening, teachers can transplant some of the fun in literature into a test such as the following:

1. Who earned her living by washing cups and saucers and brushing crumbs away?
2. What small boy lived with his grandmother by the shores of Gitchee Gumee?
3. What famous fife player charmed children and animals and caused them to leave their homes to follow him?
4. In what book did a small offering laid on the altar at Christmas cause the church bells to ring out?
5. What small bull preferred to sit in the meadow and smell the flowers rather than to fight in the bull ring?
6. In what story do the March Hare and the Mad Hatter have tea together?
7. What animal appears in the famous fable about some grapes just out of reach?

8. In whose garden did silver bells and cockle shells grow?
9. To what little boy did Winnie the Pooh belong?
10. Where can you find an account of the way in which the camel got his hump?

Extending Experiences for the Reader

1. Read at least two of the following books on curriculum:

   Bruner, Jerome S. *The Process of Education.* Cambridge, Mass.: Harvard University Press, 1960.

   Fleming, Robert S. (ed.). *Curriculum for Today's Boys and Girls.* Columbus, Ohio: Merrill, 1963.

   Manolakes, George. *The Elementary School We Need.* Washington, D. C.: Association for Supervision and Curriculum Development, N.E.A., 1965.

   Taba, Hilda. *Curriculum Development, Theory and Practice.* New York: Harcourt Brace Jovanovich, 1962.

2. Keep a record of your teaching activities by the hour for a period of from two to five days in order to determine what percentage of your day or week is spent working with children in the field of literature.
3. Participate in district- and county-wide book selection committees.
4. Work with your group to prepare a form to use as a basis for selecting books.
5. Involve the group in reading and evaluating new books.
6. Plan a visit to the community library. Observe and record the library skills that individuals in the group are using. Discuss with the group the skills necessary to effectively use the library. Plan several more trips to the community library to practice library skills.
7. Prepare bibliographies of stories to tell to children in preschool, kindergarten, the primary grades, the middle grades, and the upper grades.
8. If possible, invite authors of juvenile stories and storytellers from the community to tell stories to your class.
9. Monitor television series to recommend for viewing. Prepare a bibliography of books to read to accompany the viewing.
10. Prepare a form on which the family can monitor and rate television programs.
11. Using the criteria developed for selecting books, make a list of twenty books to recommend for an elementary school library or for a home library.
12. Make a list of the things you can do to encourage children to take proper care of their books.
13. Collect copies of early comic strips. Use the strips in a bulletin board display.

14. Prepare a form on which parents and children can evaluate comic strips.
15. Show several films and film strips related to children's literature.
16. Have the group listen to several recordings of children's books.
17. Have the group listen to recordings of stories told by well-known storytellers.

Extending Experiences for Children

1. Participate with others in the class in evaluating new books.
2. Visit the community library. Make a list of the skills one needs to get the most from the facilities of the library.
3. Describe three ways in which you like to share your reading with your friends.
4. Describe your favorite television program and tell why it is your favorite.
5. Participate in a round-table discussion of the values of television viewing.
6. Draw an original comic strip.
7. Describe your favorite comic strip and tell why it is your favorite.

References

1. AMERICAN ASSOCIATION OF SCHOOL LIBRARIANS. *The School Library Bill of Rights.* Chicago, 1955.
2. ARONOW, MIRIAM S. "Study of the Effect of Individualized Reading on Children's Reading Test Scores," *The Reading Teacher,* November 1961, pp. 86–91.
3. BISHOP, HAL. "Research in the Realm of Literature," *Interpreting Language Arts for the Teacher.* Washington, D. C.: Association for Supervision and Curriculum Development, N.E.A., 1971, pp. 98–105.
4. BRUNER, JEROME S. *The Process of Education.* Cambridge, Mass.: Harvard University Press, 1960.
5. BURNFORD, SHEILA. *The Incredible Journey.* Boston: Little, Brown, 1961.
6. CARROLL, LEWIS. *Alice's Adventures in Wonderland and Through the Looking Glass.* Cleveland: World Publishing, 1946.
7. COUNCIL OF AMERICAN LIBRARY ASSOCIATION. *Library Bill of Rights.* Rev. ed. Chicago, 1967.
8. ———, and the NATIONAL EDUCATION ASSOCIATION. *Standards for School Media Programs.* Chicago and Washington, D. C., 1969.
9. GRAHAME, KENNETH. *The Wind in the Willows.* New York: Scribner, 1953. Paperback.
10. GROFF, PATRICK. "Comparisons of Individualized and Ability-Grouping Approaches as to Reading Achievement," *Elementary English,* 40 (March 1963), 258–264.

11. GUILFOILE, ELIZABETH. *Nobody Listens to Andrew.* Chicago: Follett, 1957.
12. HENRY, MARGUERITE. *King of the Wind.* Chicago: Rand McNally, 1948.
13. HUNT, IRENE. *Across Five Aprils.* New York: Grossett & Dunlap, 1965. Paperback.
14. KEYES, DANIEL. *Flowers for Algernon.* New York: Bantam, 1967. Paperback.
15. LAWSON, HOYLE D. "Effects of Free Reading on Reading Achievement of Sixth-Grade Pupils." Nashville, Tenn.: George Peabody College for Teachers, *Dissertation Abstracts*, 25, 11 (May 1965), 6340–6341.
16. LAWSON, ROBERT. *Rabbit Hill.* New York: Dell, 1968. Paperback. Grades 2–8.
17. National Council of Teachers of English. *The Students' Right to Read.* Champaign, Ill., 1962.
18. NORTH, STERLING. *Rascal.* New York: Avon, 1964. Paperback.
19. PERRY, GEORGE, AND ALAN ALDRIDGE. *The Penguin Book of Comics.* Norwich, England: Jarraold & Sons, 1967.
20. ROTHROCK, DAYTON. "A Comparative Study of Basal Reading, Homogeneous Grouping, and Individualized Reading." Unpublished dissertation, University of Nebraska, 1959.
21. SARTAIN, HARRY W. "Research on Individualized Reading," *Education*, 81, 9 (May 1961), 515–520.
22. SAWYER, RUTH. *The Way of the Story Teller.* New York: Viking, 1962.
23. SCHWARTZ, SHEILA. "Introducing Literature Through Film," *Elementary English*, 48, 3 (March 1971).
24. SHEDLOCK, MARIE L. *The Art of the Storyteller.* New York: Dover, 1951.

Further Reading for Parents, Teachers, and Librarians

ANDERSON, VERNON. *Curriculum Guidelines in an Era of Change.* New York: Ronald, 1969.

______. *Principles and Procedures of Curriculum Improvement.* 2nd ed. New York: Ronald, 1965.

ARDLEY, ROSE. "Independent Reading for First Grades: A Listing," *Elementary English*, 46, 4 (April 1969).

BABBITT, NATALIE. "How Can We Write Children's Books If We Don't Know Anything About Children?" *Publishers' Weekly*, July 19, 1971, pp. 64–66.

BAKER, AUGUSTA (selector). *The Black Experience in Children's Books.* New York: The New York Public Library, n.d.

BEATTY, WALCOTT H. (ed.). *Improving Educational Assessment and an Inventory of Measure of Affective Behavior.* Washington, D. C.: Association of Supervision and Curriculum Development, N.E.A., 1969.

CARNEGIE CORPORATION OF NEW YORK. "The Gross Educational Product: How Much Are Students Learning?" *Carnegie Quarterly,* 14, 2 (Spring 1966).

CHAMBERS, DEWEY W. "Children's Literature and the Allied Arts," *Elementary English,* 48, 6 (October 1972).

CHUKOVSKY, KORNEI. "Confessions of an Old Story Teller." Lauren G. Leighton (trans.). *The Horn Book Magazine,* 46, 6 (December 1970).

COHEN, DAVID. *Recommended Paperbacks for Elementary Schools.* Jamaica, N. Y.: Book Mail Services.

EBEL, ROBERT L. *Measuring Educational Achievement.* Englewood Cliffs, N. J.: Prentice-Hall, 1965.

EGOFF, SHEILA. "Children's Books: A Canadian's View of the Current American Scene," *The Horn Book Magazine,* 46, 2 (April 1970), 142–150.

FELDMAN, MARTIN, AND ELI SEIFMAN (eds.). *The Social Studies: Structure, Models, and Strategies.* Englewood Cliffs, N. J.: Prentice-Hall, 1969.

FENNIMORE, FLORA. "Creative Ways to Extend Children's Literature," *Elementary English,* 47, 4 (April 1971).

FENWICK, SARA INNIS (ed.). *A Critical Approach to Children's Literature.* Conference of the Graduate Library School, August 1–3, 1966. Chicago: University of Chicago Press, 1967.

FRAZIER, ALEXANDER (ed.). *The New Elementary School.* Washington, D. C.: Association for Supervision and Curriculum Development and Department of Elementary School Principals, N.E.A., 1968.

GLASSER, WILLIAM. *Schools Without Failure.* New York: Harper & Row, 1969.

GOODLAD, JOHN I., *et al. The Changing School Curriculum.* New York: The Fund for the Advancement of Education, 1966.

HEFFERNAN, HELEN, AND VIVIAN E. TODD. *The Kindergarten Teacher.* Boston: D. C. Heath, 1960. Chap. 12.

HOFFMAN, BANESH. *The Tyranny of Testing.* New York: Crowell-Collier-Macmillan, 1962.

LEE, DORIS M., AND R. VAN ALLEN. *Learning to Read Through Experience.* New York: Appleton-Century-Crofts, 1964.

LEEPER, ROBERT R. (ed.). *Curriculum Change: Direction and Process.* Washington, D. C.: Association for Supervision and Curriculum Development, 1966.

LOBAN, WALTER. "Balancing the Literature Program," *Elementary English,* 43 (November 1966), 746–751.

MACDONALD, JAMES B., *et al. Strategies of Curriculum Development.* Columbus, Ohio: Merrill, 1965.

MCDONALD, FREDERICK J. *Educational Psychology.* 2nd ed. Belmont, Cal.: Wadsworth, 1969.

MIEL, ALICE. "In-Service Education Reexamined," *National Elementary Principal,* 41 (February 1962), 464–476.

MONSON, DIANNE L. "Evaluation: Quantity and Quality," *Elementary English*, 47, 5 (May 1971).

ODLAND, NORINE. "New Approaches to Literature in the Elementary School: Validity of the Criterion of Newness," *Elementary English*, 48, 5 (May 1971), 452–545.

PERKINS, HUGH V. *Human Development and Learning*. Belmont, Cal.: Wadsworth, 1969.

PITCHER, EVELYN GOODENOUGH. "Values and Issues in Young Children's Literature," *Elementary English*, 46, 3 (March 1969), 287–294.

POSTMAN, NEIL, AND CHARLES WEINGARTNER. *Teaching as a Subversive Activity*. New York: Delacorte, 1969.

REUTER, ALEX. "Listening Experiences: Instructional Materials Center, Dial-A-Tape System Advances Learning," *Elementary English*, 46 (November 1969).

ROSENTHAL, ROBERT, AND LENORE JACOBSON. *Pygmalion in the Classroom: Teacher Expectation and Pupils' Intellectual Development*. New York: Holt, Rinehart & Winston, 1968.

TABA, HILDA. "Techniques of In-Service Training," *Social Education*, 29 (November 1965), 464–476.

TORRENCE, E. P. *Guiding Creative Talent*. Englewood Cliffs, N. J.: Prentice-Hall, 1963.

TYLER, RALPH W. "Assessing the Progress of Education," *Phi Delta Kappan*, 47 (September 1965), 13–16.

UNRUH, GLENYS G. (ed.). *New Curriculum Developments*. Washington, D. C.: Association for Supervision and Curriculum Development, N.E.A., 1967.

VAN STOCKUM, HILDA. "Storytelling in the Family," *Horn Book Reflections*. Boston: The Horn Book. Pp. 332–337.

VEATCH, JEANNETTE. "Let's Put the Joy Back in Reading," *Library Journal*, May 15, 1970, pp. 1899 ff.

WILHELMS, FRED T. (ed.). *Evaluation as Feedback and Guide*. Washington, D. C.: Association for Supervision and Curriculum Development, N.E.A., 1967.

Treasure Island by R. L. Stevenson,
illustrated by S. van Abbé.

Appendix A
Sources for Selecting Literature

Guide to Choosing Books

Adventuring with Books: A Book List for Elementary Schools. Elizabeth Guilfoile and Jeannette Veatch. National Council of Teachers of English, 508 South Sixth Street, Champaign, Illinois 61820. Rev. ed. 1966. A classified bibliography of over 1250 titles.

A Basic Book Collection for Elementary Grades. Miriam Snow Mathes, *et al.* American Library Association, 50 East Huron Street, Chicago, Illinois 60611. 3rd ed. 1960. An annotated bibliography of about 1000 books and magazines for kindergarten–grade 8, arranged by Dewey classification with author, title, and subject index.

A Basic Book Collection for Junior High Schools. Margaret V. Spengler, *et al.* American Library Association, 50 East Huron Street, Chicago, Illinois 60611. 3rd ed. 1960. An annotated bibliography of about 1000 books and magazines for grades 7–9, arranged by Dewey classification with author, title, and subject index.

Best Books for Children. Jean Sragow. R. R. Bowker Company, 1180 Avenue of the Americas, New York, New York 10036. Annual. An annotated bibliography for kindergarten–grade 12, arranged by grades and subjects.

A Bibliography of Books for Children. Association for Childhood Education International, 3615 Wisconsin Avenue, N. W., Washington, D. C. 20016. Rev. ed. 1968. An annotated bibliography of over 1500 books for ages 2–12. Author and title index and reference books section.

Books for Children, 1960–1965. American Library Association, 50 East Huron Street, Chicago, Illinois 60611. 1966. A compilation of 3068 books with detailed annotations, recommended in the *Booklist and Subscription Books Bulletin* and arranged according to a modified Dewey classification with subject, author, and short title index.

CLA Booklist. Sister Mary Girolama. Catholic Library Association, 461 West Lancaster Avenue, Haverford, Pennsylvania 19041. Annual. A graded annotated bibliography for kindergarten–grade 8.

Caldecott Medal Books. American Library Association, 50 East Huron Street, Chicago, Illinois 60611. Annual. Annotated brochure of award-winning picture books.

Children's Booklist for Small Public Libraries. New York Library Association Committee. New York State Library, Division of Library Extension, Albany, New York 12224. Rev. ed. 1964. An annotated bibliography of about 750 books for preschool–grade 8 arranged by subject.

Children's Books. Virginia Haviland and Lois Watt (compilers). Superintendent of Documents, Government Printing Office, Washington, D. C. 20402. Annual. An annotated bibliography arranged by subject and age group with reading level indication.

Children's Books for Holiday Giving and Year 'Round Reading. Children's Department, Cleveland Public Library, Cleveland, Ohio. Annual. An annotated list of books arranged by age level.

Children's Books for Schools and Libraries: 1968–1969. R. R. Bowker Company, 1180 Avenue of the Americas, New York, New York 10036. 24,000 in-print juvenile books arranged by author and title. Many are on the recommended lists and are so coded.

Children's Books of the Year. Book Committee of Child Study Association of America, 9 East 89th Street, New York, New York 10028. Annual. A classified annotated bibliography of about 500 selected children's books arranged by ages and subject areas.

Children's Books Suggested as Holiday Gifts. New York Public Library Committee, Library Sales Office, 5th Avenue and·42nd Street, New York, New York 10018. 1968. (Back issues available.) An annotated bibliography of books of the year arranged by subject areas.

Children's Books Too Good to Miss. May Hill Arbuthnot, *et al.* Western Reserve University Press, 2029 Adelbert Road, Cleveland, Ohio 44106. 5th ed. 1966. An annotated bibliography for kindergarten–grade 8.

Children's Catalog. Rachel Shor and Estelle A. Fidell. H. W. Wilson Company, 950 University Avenue, Bronx, New York 10452. 11th ed. 1966. A classified annotated guide to 4274 books for kindergarten–grade 6.

Elementary School Library Collection. Mary V. Gaver. Bro-Dart Foundation, 113 Frelinghuysen Avenue, Newark, New Jersey 07114. 4th ed. 1968. 7420 titles, plus professional and audiovisual materials arranged by Dewey classification and indexed by subject, author, and title.

Fanfare . . . 1961–1968. Horn Book Committee. The Horn Book, Inc., 585 Boylston Street, Boston, Massachusetts 02116. 1968. A classified list of books for preschool–grade 12, selected from the Horn Book reviews.

Good Books for Children. Mary K. Eakin. University of Chicago Press, 5750 Ellis Avenue, Chicago, Illinois 60637. 3rd ed. 1966. A selection of over 1400 books for kindergarten–grade 12 from 1950–1965.

Good Reading for Youth. Siri Andrews and the American Library Committee. Library Services Company, 553 Carroll Street, Akron, Ohio 44303.

1968. An annotated listing of over 300 books arranged by grade and age groups.

Junior High School Library Catalog. Rachel Shor and Estelle Fidell. H. W. Wilson Company, 950 University Avenue, Bronx, New York 10452. 1965. A classified annotated guide to 3310 books for junior high schools.

Let's Read Together: Books for Family Enjoyment. Committee of the National Congress of Parents and Teachers, and Children's Services Division, American Library Association, 50 East Huron Street, Chicago, Illinois 60611. 2d ed., 1964. An annotated bibliography of about 750 titles, grouped by reader interest and age level.

Newbery Medal Books. American Library Association Committee, 50 East Huron Street, Chicago, Illinois 60611. Annual. A brochure listing Newbery Award books with occasional annotations.

Notable Children's Books 1940–1959. American Library Association Committee, 50 East Huron Street, Chicago, Illinois 60611. 1966. A reappraisal of twenty years of notable books.

Notable Children's Books 1971. American Library Association Committee, 50 East Huron Street, Chicago, Illinois 60611. Annual. Folder listing the past year's titles alphabetically by author with brief annotations.

A Parent's Guide to Children's Reading. Nancy Larrick. Doubleday, Garden City, New York 11530. 3rd rev. ed. 1969. A handbook for parents with an extensive, annotated bibliography.

Selections for a Classroom Library. Mary Harbage. Association for Childhood Education International, 3615 Wisconsin Avenue, N. W., Washington, D. C. 20016. A beginning list for primary schools, arranged by author with occasional brief annotations.

Studying Africa in Elementary and Secondary Schools. Leonard S. Kenworthy. Teachers College Press, 525 West 120th Street, New York, New York 10027. Rev. ed. 1965. Lists of books for grades 1–12, arranged primarily according to country.

Subject Index to Books for Primary Grades. Mary K. Eakin and Eleanor Merrit. American Library Association, 50 East Huron Street, Chicago, Illinois 60611. 3rd. ed. 1967. A bibliography of about 1000 trade and text books, arranged by subject with independent reading level indication.

Subject Index to Books for Intermediate Grades. Mary K. Eakin. American Library Association, 50 East Huron Street, Chicago, Illinois 60611. 3rd ed. 1963. A bibliography of about 1800 books for grades 4–6, arranged by subject.

A Teacher's Guide to Children's Books. Nancy Larrick. Charles E. Merrill Books, Inc., 1300 Alum Creek Drive, Columbus, Ohio 43216. 1960. A book on children's literature with annotated bibliographies.

Sources for Stories to Listen to

ANDERSEN, HANS CHRISTIAN. *It's Perfectly True and Other Stories.* New York: Harcourt Brace Jovanovich, 1938.

BABBITT, ELLEN (reteller). *Jakata Tales.* New York: Appleton, 1965.

BAKER, AUGUSTA (selector). *The Golden Lynx and Other Tales.* Philadelphia: Lippincott, 1960.

——— (selector). *The Talking Tree and Other Stories.* Philadelphia: Lippincott, 1955.

BALDWIN, JAMES. *The Story of Roland.* New York: Scribner, 1930.

BLEECHER, MARY NOEL. *Big Music.* New York: Viking, 1946.

BOGGS, RALPH STEELE, AND MARY GOULD DAVIS. *The Three Golden Oranges.* New York: David McKay, 1940.

BOWMAN, JAMES CLOYD, AND MARGERY BIANCO. *Tales from a Finnish Tupa.* Chicago: Whitman, 1936.

CARLSON, NATALIE SAVAGE (reteller). *The Talking Cat and Other Stories of French Canada.* New York: Harper & Row, 1952.

CARPENTER, FRANCES. *Tales of a Chinese Grandmother.* Garden City, N. Y.: Doubleday, 1937.

CHASE, RICHARD. *Grandfather Tales.* Boston: Houghton Mifflin, 1948.

COURLANDER, HAROLD, AND GEORGE HERZOG. *Cow-Tail Switch and Other West African Stories.* New York: Holt, Rinehart & Winston, 1947.

CRANE, LUCY (tr.). *Household Stories.* New York: McGraw-Hill, 1968.

CURRY, JANE LOUISE. *Down from the Lonely Mountain.* New York: Harcourt Brace Jovanovich, 1965.

DALGLIESH, ALICE. *The Enchanted Book.* New York: Scribner, 1958.

DAVIS, MARY GOULD. *A Baker's Dozen.* New York: Harcourt Brace Jovanovich, 1930.

DE LA MARE, WALTER. *Animal Stories.* New York: Scribner, 1940.

———. *Tales Told Again.* New York: Knopf, 1927.

DOBBS, ROSE. *Once Upon a Time.* New York: Random House, 1950.

EATON, ANNE THAXTER. *The Animal's Christmas.* New York: Viking, 1944.

FENNER, PHYLLIS. *Giants and Witches and a Dragon or Two.* New York: Knopf, 1943.

———. *Magic Hoofs.* New York: Knopf, 1951.

FILLMORE, PARKER. *The Shepherd's Nosegay.* Katherine Love (ed.). New York: Harcourt Brace Jovanovich, 1958.

FINGER, CHARLES J. *Tales from Silver Lands.* Garden City, N. Y.: Doubleday, 1924.

GAER, JOSEPH. *The Fables of India.* Boston: Little, Brown, 1955.

HAMILTON, EDITH. *Mythology.* Boston: Little, Brown, 1942.

HARPER, WILHELMINA. *Ghosts and Goblins.* New York: Dutton, 1965.

HARRIS, JOEL CHANDLER. *The Favorite Uncle Remus.* Boston: Houghton Mifflin, 1948.

JAGENDORF, M. A., AND R. S. BOGGS. *The King of the Mountains.* New York: Vanguard, 1960.

JEWETT, ELEANOR M. *Which Was Witch?* New York: Viking, 1943.

LANG, ANDREW. *Arabian Nights.* New York: David McKay, 1946.

LEODHAS, NIC SORCHE. *Gaelic Ghosts.* New York: Holt, Rinehart & Winston, 1964.

LIPKIND, WILLIAM. *Boy of the Islands.* New York: Harcourt Brace Jovanovich, 1955.

RACKHAM, ARTHUR. *Arthur Rackham's Fairy Book.* Philadelphia: Lippincott, 1950.

RANSOME, ARTHUR. *Old Peter's Russian Tales.* New York: Nelson, 1967.

UCHIDA, YOSHIKO. *The Dancing Kettle and Other Japanese Folk Tales.* New York: Harcourt Brace Jovanovich, 1949.

UNDSET, SIGRID. *True and Untrue and Other Norse Tales.* New York: Knopf, 1945.

WHITE, ANNE TERRY (reteller). *Aesop's Fables.* New York: Random House, 1964.

WIGGIN, KATE DOUGLAS, AND NORA A. SMITH. *The Fairy Ring.* Garden City, N. Y.: Doubleday, 1967.

Sources for Films

American Library Association, 50 East Huron St., Chicago, Illinois 60611.

Bailey-Film Associates, 11559 Santa Monica Boulevard, Los Angeles, California 90025.

Churchill Films, 662 North Robertson Boulevard, Los Angeles, California 90069.

Classroom Film Distributors, Inc., 5620 Hollywood Boulevard, Los Angeles, California 90028.

Coronet Films, Coronet Building, 65 East Water Street, Chicago, Illinois 60601.

Encyclopaedia Britannica Films, 425 North Michigan Avenue, Chicago, Illinois 60611

Grover-Jennings Productions, PO Box 303, Monterey, California 93940.

Holt, Rinehart & Winston, 383 Madison Avenue, New York, New York 10017.

International Film Bureau, 332 South Michigan Avenue, Chicago, Illinois 60604.

Jam Handy Organization, 2821 East Grand Boulevard, Detroit, Michigan 48211.

Library of Congress, *Library of Congress Catalogue: Motion Pictures and Film Strips,* Washington, D. C. 20025.

McGraw-Hill Text Films, 330 West 42nd Street, New York, New York 10018.

National Educational Television, Film Library, Indiana University, Bloomington, Indiana 47401.

National Film Board of Canada, 680 Fifth Avenue, New York, New York 10019.

Scott Foresman & Co., 1900 East Lake Avenue, Chicago, Illinois.

Society for Visual Education, Inc., 1345 Diversey Parkway, Chicago, Illinois 60614.

Sterling Educational Films (A Division of Walter Reade Organization, Inc.), 241 East 34th Street, New York, New York 10016.

Syracuse University, Film Library, Syracuse, New York 13210.

Teaching Film Custodians, 25 West 43rd Street, New York, New York 10036.

University of Michigan, Audio-Visual Education Center, Ann Arbor, Michigan 48103.

Weston Woods Studios, Inc., Weston, Connecticut 06880.

Sources for Recordings

American Library Association, 50 East Huron Street, Chicago, Illinois 60611.
Caedmon Records, 461 Eighth Avenue, New York, New York 10001.
Children's Reading Circle, 1078 St. John's Place, Brooklyn, New York 11213.
CMS Records, Inc., 14 Warren Street, New York, New York 10007.
Droll Yankees, Inc., 14 Warren Street, New York, New York 10007.
Elektra Records, 51 West 51st Street, New York, New York 10019.
Enrichment Teaching Materials, Inc., 246 Fifth Avenue, New York, New York 10001.
Folkways Records, 121 West 47th Street, New York, New York 10036.
London Records, Inc., 539 West 25th Street, New York, New York 10001.
National Council of Teachers of English, 508 South Sixth Street, Champaign, Illinois 61922.
Pathways of Sound, Inc., 102 Mount Auburn Street, Cambridge, Massachusetts 02188.
Riverside Records, 235 West 46th Street, New York, New York 10036. (Also distributes Washington and Wonderland Records.)
Spoken Arts Records, 1150 Wilmette Avenue, Wilmette, Illinois 60091.
Weston Woods Studios, Inc., Weston, Connecticut 06880.

Literature for Children—Media Other than Books

Chapters 1–3

Motion Picture

Story of a Book. Churchill, 1962. 11 min., color. Author Holling C. Holling is shown writing, illustrating, and making final preparations for printing *Pagoo,* the story of a hermit crab.

Chapter 4

Motion Pictures

Indian Boy of the Southwest. Film Associates, 1966. 15 min., color. A Hopi Indian boy tells of his life and home.
Joshua. ACI Films, Inc., 35 West 45 Street, New York, New York 10032. 16 min., black and white. The interpersonal relations of a Black teen-

ager are described on the day before he leaves for college on a track scholarship.

Mexico: The Land and the People. Encyclopaedia Britannica Films (EBF), 1964. 20 min., color. This film portrays the social changes that have taken place in modern Mexico, including the growth of a middle-class society developing as a result of education and industrial progress.

African Continent: An Introduction. Coronet, 1962. 16 min., color. A geographical, historical, and cultural overview of the world's second largest continent.

Africa in Change: East Africa. EBF, 1965. 21 min., color. The variety of natural beauty in Kenya, Tanganyika, and Uganda is explored.

Africa in Change: West Africa. EBF, 1964. 22 min., color. The three different regions of Nigeria and its people are presented.

China, the Land and the People. Coronet, 1955. 15 min., color. The similarities and differences in climate, in topography, and in crops of Northern and Southern China are shown.

Boy of Japan: Ho and His Kite. Coronet, 1964. 11 min., color. Through the simple story of a boy and his kite, the people of Japan and their customs are introduced.

Film Strips

American Indians of the Southwest. 35 mm, color. Five phonodiscs and guide for use with manual or automatic projector. 1970. A comprehensive and informative examination of the American Indian tribes of the Navaho, Apache, Pima, Ute, and Pueblo, who now live in the "four corners" areas of the Southwest where Arizona, New Mexico, Colorado, and Utah meet. "Who They Are." 52 frames. "Their History." 54 frames. "Their Homes." 51 frames. "Their Handicrafts." 52 frames. "Their Religions." 53 frames. "Their Life Today." 51 frames.

If You Were Born in Canada. Written by Helen Allen, ill. by Larissa Lawreynenko. Troll Associates, 1969. 44 frames, color. Full-color drawings showing the people and land of Canada.

Lucille of Jamaica. 1969. 61 frames, color. 12-in., 33-rpm phonodisc including teacher's guide. Photographer follows Lucille as she and her family prepare for her big brother's visit from school.

The Cow Who Fell in the Canal. Weston Woods, 1969. 41 frames, color. 12-in., 33-rpm phonodisc coordinated with book by Phyllis Krasilovsky. The story of Hendrika the cow.

African Art and Culture. 1968. 3 film strips, about 65 frames each, color. Three 12-in., 33-rpm phonodiscs, including teacher's manual. Three-dimensional art from both ancient and modern Africa. Also traditions, religions, livelihoods, and tribal customs are presented.

Israel: Urban and Industrial Development. McGraw-Hill, Middle East geography series, Set 1, 1968. 41 frames, color. Photographs describe major cities, important and developing industries, and trade and transportation of Israel. Series also includes: *Iran: Farmers and Nomads; Iran: Cities and Industries; Turkey: The Village and the Land; Turkey: Its Cities and Industrial Future.*

Afghanistan, Nepal, and Pakistan. Eye Gate House, 1965. 9 film strips, color. Includes teacher's manual. The people, land, and industries of these three areas are introduced in general terms.

Chapter 5

Motion Pictures

Mark Twain Gives an Interview. Coronet Films. $1^1/_4$ reels, $13^1/_2$ min., color. Mark Twain is impersonated by Hal Holbrook as he is interviewed about his writings.

Mark Twain: Background for His Works. Coronet Films. $1^1/_4$ reels, $13^1/_2$ min., color. Events from Mark Twain's life are enriched by the use of quotes from his works.

How the Elephant Got His Trunk. Produced by Stephen Bosustow and distributed by Learning Corporation of America, 711 Fifth Avenue, New York, New York 10022. 16 mm, 10 min., color. A film version of the humorous Kipling tale from *Just So Stories.*

Film Strips

Bear Party. By William Pene Du Bois. Viking, 1970. 46 frames, color. 7-in., 33-rpm phonodisc. Film strip based on the book by the same title.

Little Bear's Visit. By Else Holmelund Minarik. 1967. 59 frames, color. 7-in., 33-rpm phonodisc. Correlated with cassette. Based on the book by the same title, illustrated by Maurice Sendak.

Recordings

Happy Birthday to You! and Other Stories. By Dr. Seuss. Caedmon. 12-in., 33-rpm phonodisc, or cassette. A reading of some of the most popular Dr. Seuss stories.

Mark Twain. Spoken Arts (SA) 778. 12-in., 33-rpm phonodisc. Stories and essays read by Hiram Sherman.

Tom Sawyer. Caedmon. 12-in., 33-rpm phonodisc. 7-in., 2-track tape, $3^3/_4$ m. A number of the hilarious adventures of Tom Sawyer are read by Ed Begley.

Chapter 6

Motion Pictures

Charlie Squash Goes to Town. Produced by the National Film Board of Canada, distributed by the Learning Corporation of America. 16 mm, 5 min., color. Includes guide. Cree Indian Duke Redbird wrote and designed this short film that describes the plight of the modern North American Indian.

Incident on Wilson Street. NBC News Production. McGraw-Hill. Parts I and

II. 51 min., black and white. Individual and group reactions to an in-school incident in which a student suddenly strikes out at her teacher.

. . . and Now Miguel. Parts I and II. U. S. Office of Education, 1953. 63 min., black and white. Story of a Spanish-American family of the Southwest steeped in the tradition of sheep raising. The fulfillment of young Miguel's dreams is his being accepted as the equal of his father and his brothers.

Film Strip

Thy Friend Obadiah. Produced and distributed by Viking Press, 1971. 35 mm, 28 frames, color. With phonodisc and guide for use with manual. A seagull follows Obadiah wherever he goes. Obadiah shuns him for a time but later changes his mind.

Chapter 7

Recordings

Just So Stories. By Rudyard Kipling. Vol. I. Caedmon JC 1038. 12-in., 33-rpm phonodisc. A reading of several of the animal dialogue stories by Boris Karloff. Vol. II. Caedmon JC 1088. 12-in., 33-rpm phonodisc. More readings of tales about the animal kingdom.

Mowgli's Brothers. By Rudyard Kipling. Caedmon Children's Classic. 12-in., 33-rpm phonodisc. One of the *Jungle Book* stories about the wilderness boy who is a brother to the animals. Read by Boris Karloff.

Art Portfolio

Caxton and the Early Printers; A Collection of Contemporary Documents. By Sylvia Nickels. Kit 655.1. Grossman Publishers, 1968. A comprehensive history of printing. Portfolio includes illustrations of early printing.

Chapter 9

Motion Pictures

Ezra Jack Keats. Produced and distributed by Weston Woods Studios, 1971. 16 mm, 17 min., color. Well-known author-illustrator Ezra Jack Keats tells about his work.

A Letter to Amy. 16 mm, 7 min., color. Produced and distributed by Weston Woods Studios, 1970. From the book by Ezra Jack Keats. The story of Amy's invitation to Peter's birthday party.

The Little Drummer Boy. Produced and distributed by Weston Woods Studios, 1970. 7 min., 16 mm, color. From the book by Katherine Davis, illustrated by Ezra Jack Keats.

Rosie's Walk. Produced and distributed by Weston Woods Studios, 1970.

From the book by Pat Hutchins. Rosie the hen walks across the barnyard, around the pond, under the beehives, and is back home in time for dinner.

Film Strips

Hush Little Baby. Produced and distributed by Weston Woods Studios, 1970. 16 frames, 35 mm, color. From the book by Aliki. A lullaby brought from England that has become popular in the Appalachian region.

Let's Be Enemies. Produced and distributed by Weston Woods Studios, 1970. 30 frames, 35 mm, color. From the book by Janice May Udry, illustrated by Maurice Sendak. The story about two boys who try to be enemies but find it more fun to be friends.

Let's Tell Picture Stories. Coronet Films, 1970. 35 mm, color. Four film strips with two phonodiscs and guide, manual or automatic projector. Describes the picture stories done by young students in an art class at Martin Luther King, Jr., Laboratory School, Evanston, Illionis. Series includes "My Home," "My Family," "My Neighborhood," and "My Favorite Fun."

A Letter to Amy. Produced and distributed by Weston Woods Studios, 1970. 36 frames, 35 mm, color. From the book by Ezra Jack Keats.

Stone Soup. By Marcia Brown. Produced and distributed by Weston Woods Studios. 46 frames, color. Correlated with 7-in., 33-rpm phonodisc. Original illustrations from the book by the same title. Includes picture-cued text booklet.

What Do You Do, Dear? Produced and distributed by Weston Woods Studios, 1970. 35 mm, 5 min., color. From the book by Sesyle Joslin, illustrated by Maurice Sendak. The strip dramatizes the proper way to behave in many unusual situations.

Where the Wild Things Are. By Maurice Sendak. 34 frames, color. Correlated with 1⅞-ips cassette. Based on the Caldecott Medal book by the same title.

Cassettes

Animals. Produced and distributed by Bowmar, 622 Rodier Drive, Glendale, California 91201. Includes *The Happy Lion, Anatole, Timothy Turtle, Dinny and Danny, I Like Animals,* and *I Am a Mouse.*

The World of Nature. Produced and distributed by Bowmar. Includes *inch by inch, Swimmy, Tim Tadpole and the Great Bullfrog, Under the Trees and Through the Grass, Seeds and More Seeds,* and *The Attic of the Wind.*

Chapter 10

Film Strip

The North Wind and the Sun. Produced and distributed by Weston Woods Studios, 1970. 35 mm, 34 frames, color. From the book by Brian Wildsmith. A retelling of La Fontaine's fable about the sun's warmth.

Recording

Cinderella and Other Fairy Tales. Produced and distributed by Caedmon. Read by Claire Bloom. Walter de la Mare's versions of "Cinderella," "The Musicians of Bremen," and "Bluebeard."

Cassettes

Folk Tales Retold. Produced and distributed by the American Library Association. 9 tapes. A collection of stories of both European and American folklore and mythology, narrated by well-known storytellers. Among the nine cassettes are *Baldur,* the Norse myth, told by Gundrun Thorne-Thomsen; *Frog,* a Spanish folktale told by Ruth Sawyer; and a Paul Bunyan tale told by Jack Lester.

Chapter 11

Recordings

Gulliver's Travels. Spoken Arts (SA) 858. 12-in., 33-rpm phonodisc. Chapters 1–3 and 5 of the Swift classic are read by Denis Johnston.

How to Tell Corn Fairies and Other Rootebaga Stories. Caedmon TC 1159. 12-in., 33-rpm phonodisc. Carl Sandburg tells eight of his own stories.

Mary Poppins. Caedmon. 12-in., 33-rpm phonodisc. The first of a series of recordings of the Travers' classics. Other recordings include *Mary Poppins Comes Back* and *Mary Poppins and the Banks Family.*

Walt Disney's Mary Poppins. Buena Vista S-4026. 12-in., 33-rpm phonodisc. Songs from the motion picture version recorded from the sound track.

The Mouse That Roared. CMS Records, Inc., 1970. 12-in., 33-rpm phonodisc. Leonard Wibberley reads excerpts from his satirical novel.

Pinocchio. Caedmon, 1970. 12-in., 33-rpm phonodisc. Condensed account of the adventures of the puppet are read by Cyril Richard.

Rootebaga Stories. Caedmon TC 1089. 12-in., 33-rpm phonodisc. Carl Sandburg tells twelve tales from his Rootebaga Country.

Chapters 13 and 14

Motion Pictures

Black Man and Iron Horse. Association of Industrial Materials, 600 Madison Avenue, New York, New York 10022, 1970. 17 min., color. Relates the contribution of Black men toward the development of American railroads.

Children of the Wagon Train. McGraw-Hill, 1960. 18 min., color. Re-creates the life of a family as they accompany a wagon train over the Oregon Trail in 1849.

Colonial Life in the Middle Colonies. Coronet. 11 min., color. Portrays life in the Middle Colonies prior to the Revolutionary War through the enactment of a postrider's trip from Philadelphia to New York.

Colonial America in the 1760's. Cahill, 1968. 17 min., color. Actors at Colonial Williamsburg portray the circumstances that led to the American Revolution.

Dawn of the American Revolution: A Lexington Family. Coronet. 16 min., color. Authentic enactment of the events that led to the American Revolution as seen through the eyes of a young boy.

Folksongs of America's History. Coronet. 13½ min., color.

Folksongs of the Westward Movement (1787–1853). Coronet. 13½ min., color.

Folksongs of the Western Settlement (1865–1900). Coronet. 13½ min., color.

Gold Rush Days. Coronet. 13½ min., color. Young David Whitcomb travels overland from Vermont to California to take part in the Gold Rush.

Jamestown: The First English Settlement. Encyclopaedia Britannica Educational Corporation. 22 min., color. Narrator John Rolfe describes the first landing, the building of a fort, trade with the Indians, and the growth of the colony.

Lexington, Concord, and Independence. Cahill, 1957. 17 min., color. Handsomely made models and live-action scenes dramatize the ride of Paul Revere and the gradual uniting of colonial America.

Life in Ancient Greece: Home and Education. Coronet. 13½ min., color. The story of an Athenian boy and a vase provide the structure for finding out about life in Athens in 440 B.C.

Life in Ancient Rome: The Family. Coronet. 11 min., color. The activities of Marcus and his family during a typical day in ancient Rome. Filmed in Rome and other authentic settings.

Life in a Medieval Town. Coronet. 16 min., color. The detailed picture of daily life in a medieval town.

New England. Coronet. 11 min., color. How the physical and social background of New England is reflected in the literature of the nineteenth century.

Paul Revere's Ride. Society for Visual Education, 1957. 11 min., black and white. The people and events surrounding Revere's famous ride to alert the colonists.

Film Strip

Ola. 1970. 35 mm, 53 frames, color. Relates the adventures of a Norwegian boy in the legendary North.

Recordings

Black Boy. By Richard Wright. Caedmon, 1970. 33-rpm phonodisc. Also available on cassette. An abridged version of Richard Wright's famous autobiography.

Invincible Louisa. Newbery Award Records NAR 3009. 12-in., 33-rpm phonodisc.

Literature of Revolutionary America. Educational Record Sales, 157 Chambers

Street, New York, New York 10007. 12-in., 33-rpm phonodiscs. Recordings include excerpts from speeches, documents, letters, and so forth, of the Revolutionary period.

Literature of World Wars I and II. Educational Record Sales. 12-in., 33-rpm phonodiscs. Readings from speeches, documents, letters, and newspaper reports of the period.

Matchlock Gun. Newbery Award Records (NAR) 3005. 12-in., 33-rpm phonodisc. A dramatization based on the book of the same name.

Robert E. Lee and the Road to Honor. Enrichment Records. 12-in., 33-rpm phonodisc. Dramatization of the life of the Southern general, who did not favor the Civil War. Based on the book of the same name by Hodding Carter.

Study Prints

Negroes in Our History. Afro-American Publishing Company, 1969. 24 prints, 11 × 14 in., color. 3 Portfolios. Includes important contributors to America's progress from Crispus Attucks to Mary McLeod Bethune with short biographical sketches.

Chapter 15

Motion Pictures

Helping Teachers Understand Children. Audio-Visual Center, Indiana University, Bloomington, Indiana. 16 mm, black and white. Part I, 21 min.; Part II, 25 min. Part I presents a case study of one child and illustrates sources of information. Part II shows a summer workshop in child study.

Learning to Understand Children. Audio-Visual Center, Indiana University, Bloomington, Indiana. 16 mm, black and white. Part I, 22 min.; Part II, 25 min. Part I presents the case of an emotionally and socially maladjusted child of fifteen. Part II continues the case study.

Film Strip

Personal Development: Growing Up and Knowing What To Do. Troll Associates, 320 Route 17, Mahwah, New Jersey 07430, 1970. 35 mm, color. Three film strips present a guide to the behavior of young children.

Magazines and Newspapers for Children

American Girl, The. Published monthly by Girl Scouts of the U.S.A., 830 Third Avenue, New York, New York. Girls, ages 10–15.

Boys' Life. Published monthly by the Boy Scouts of America. New Brunswick, New Jersey. Boys, ages 10–16.

Calling All Girls. Published monthly except June to August by Parents' Institute, Inc., 52 Vanderbilt Avenue, New York, New York. Girls, ages 7–14.

Child Life. Published monthly at 30 Federal Street, Boston, Massachusetts. Ages 3–9.

Children's Digest. Published monthly except July and August by Parents' Magazine Press, Inc., 52 Vanderbilt Avenue, New York, New York. Ages 6–12.

Humpty Dumpty's Magazine. Published monthly except July and August by Parents' Magazine Press, Inc., 52 Vanderbilt Avenue, New York, New York. Ages 3–7.

Jack and Jill. Published monthly by Curtis Publishing Co., Independence Square, Philadelphia, Pennsylvania. Ages 3–10.

Junior Natural History. Published ten times a year by the American Museum of Natural History, Central Park West at 79th Street, New York, New York. Ages 8–12.

Junior Scholastic. Published weekly except June to August by Scholastic Magazines, 33 West 42 Street, New York, New York. Published five times during the summer months. Grades 6–8.

My Weekly Reader. Published weekly except June to September by American Education Publications, Education Center, Columbus, Ohio. *Surprise News Pilot,* kindergarten–grade 1; *News Ranger,* grade 2; *News Trail,* grade 3; *Explorer,* grade 4; *Newstime,* grades 5–6.

Young Americans. Published monthly except July and August by Strong Publications, Inc., Box 1399, Grand Central P. O., New York, New York. Ages 10–14.

Book Clubs for Children

Arrow Book Club. Scholastic Book Services, 33 West 42 Street, New York, New York. Grades 4–6. Five book offers are made during each year, each offer consisting of eighteen paperbound books. Books are reviewed by an editorial advisory board and each offer includes books for slow, average, and accelerated readers. Books include adventure stories, animal stories, children's classics, historical fiction, sports, humor, mysteries, and how-to-do books. *Memo: to Teachers* is sent to each teacher-sponser.

Catholic Children's Book Club. 260 Summit Avenue, St. Paul, Minnesota. A club for five levels ages 6–16. Monthly (or every other month) offerings September to June. Selections show preference for Catholic background or theme; emphasis is on building character, moral values, and family relationships.

Catholic Youth Book Club. Garden City, New York. Monthly offers for ages 9–16. Biographical books on great Catholic figures in history.

Junior Literary Guild. Garden City, New York. Monthly offerings for five groups ages 5–16.

Parents' Magazine's Book Club for Children. Bergenfield, New Jersey. Monthly offerings for ages 7–12.

Teen-Age Book Club. Scholastic Book Services, 33 West 42 Street, New York, New York. Grades 7–10. Eight monthly offerings are made during the year, each offering consisting of eighteen paperbound books. Selections include adventure, horse and dog stories, personal growth stories, biography, sports, mystery, classics, and science. *Memo: to Teachers* is supplied to each teacher-sponser.

The Weekly Reader Children's Book Club. Education Center, Columbus, Ohio. Two levels offering books to children ages 5–8 and ages 8–12. Members get six books a year, including one free bonus book. Selections include animal tales, folklore, fairy tales, science, fantasy, humor, adventure, biography, and stories about people from other lands and other times.

Young Readers of America (Division of the Book-of-the-Month Club). 345 Hudson Street, New York, New York. Monthly offerings for children ages 9–14. Selections include books on history, science, and nature.

Hawaiian Legends of Tricksters and Riddlers by Vivian L. Thompson.

Appendix B
Awards and Prizes

Among the most coveted awards in our country in the field of children's books are the Newbery and Caldecott medals awarded annually by the Children's Services Division of the American Library Association.

At the 1921 American Library Association meeting of the Section for Library Work with Children, Frederic G. Melcher, the American John Newbery, made the proposal of an annual medal for the most distinguished children's book of the year. He suggested that the medal be named the John Newbery Medal in honor of the revered eighteenth-century bookseller. Melcher stated the purpose of the medal as:

> . . . to encourage original and creative work in the field of books for children. To emphasize to the public that contributions to the literature for children deserve recognition as do poetry, plays, and novels. To give those librarians who make it their life work to serve children's reading interests an opportunity to encourage good writing in this field.

The Newbery Medal is:

> . . . awarded annually to the author of the most distinguished contribution to American literature for children, the award being made to cover books whose publication in book form falls in the calendar year last elapsed. The award is restricted to authors who are citizens or residents of the United States. Reprints and compilations are not eligible for consideration. There are no limitations to the character of the book except that it be original work. It need not be written solely for children; the judgment of the librarians voting shall decide whether the book be "a contribution to the literature for children." The award considers only the books of one calendar year and does not pass judgment on the author's previous work or other work during that year outside the volume that may be named.

There have been only slight changes in the terms of eligibility for the Newbery Medal since 1922.

In 1937 Melcher suggested a second medal be given annually to the artist who has created the most distinguished picture book of the year. He proposed that it be called the Caldecott Medal in honor of Randolph J. Caldecott, the outstanding nineteenth-century English illustrator. The second proposal also met with an enthusiastic response from the members of the Section for Library Work with Children. Melcher had the Caldecott Medal designed by René Paul Chamellan, who had also designed the Newbery Medal.

The original terms of eligibility for the Caldecott Medal state that:

> The Caldecott Medal shall be awarded to the artist of the most distinguished American picture-book for children published in the United States during the preceding year. The award shall go to the artist, who must be a citizen or resident of the United States, whether or not he is the author of the text. Members of the Newbery Medal Committee will serve as judge. If a book of the year is nominated for both the Newbery and Caldecott awards the committee shall decide under which heading it shall be voted upon, so that the same title shall not be considered on both ballots.

As in the case of the original terms of eligibility for the Newbery Medal there have been slight changes in the original terms of eligibility for the Caldecott Medal.

Winners of the Newbery Award

1922 *The Story of Mankind.* Hendrik Willem van Loon. London: Liveright.
1923 *The Voyages of Doctor Dolittle.* Hugh Lofting. New York: Lippincott.
1924 *The Dark Frigate.* Charles Hawes. Boston: Little, Brown.
1925 *Tales from Silver Lands.* Charles Finger. New York: Doubleday.
1926 *Shen of the Sea.* Arthur Bowie Chrisman. New York: Dutton.
1927 *Smoky, the Cowhorse.* Will James. New York: Scribner.
1928 *Gayneck, the Story of a Pigeon.* Dhan Gopal Mukerji. New York: Dutton.
1929 *The Trumpeter of Krakow.* Eric P. Kelly. New York: Macmillan.
1930 *Hitty, Her First Hundred Years.* Rachael Field. New York: Macmillan.
1931 *The Cat Who Went to Heaven.* Elizabeth Coatsworth. New York: Macmillan.
1932 *Waterless Mountain.* Laura Adams Armer. Longmans Green.
1933 *Young Fu of the Upper Yangtze.* Elizabeth Lewis. New York: Holt, Rinehart & Winston.
1934 *Invincible Louisa.* Cornelia Meigs. Boston: Little, Brown.

1935 *Dobry.* Monica Shannon. New York: Viking.
1936 *Caddie Woodlawn.* Carol Brink. New York: Macmillan.
1937 *Roller Skates.* Ruth Sawyer. New York: Viking.
1938 *The White Stag.* Kate Seredy. New York: Viking.
1939 *Thimble Summer.* Elizabeth Enright. Holt, Rinehart & Winston.
1940 *Daniel Boone.* James Daugherty. New York: Viking.
1941 *Call It Courage.* Armstrong Sperry. New York: Macmillan.
1942 *The Matchlock Gun.* Walter D. Edmonds. New York: Dodd, Mead.
1943 *Adam of the Road.* Elizabeth Janet Gray. New York: Viking.
1944 *Johnny Tremaine.* Esther Forbes. Boston: Houghton Mifflin.
1945 *Rabbit Hill.* Robert Lawson. New York: Viking.
1946 *Strawberry Girl.* Lois Lenski. Philadelphia: Lippincott.
1947 *Miss Hickory.* Carolyn Sherwin Bailey. New York: Viking.
1948 *The Twenty-One Balloons.* William Pene du Bois. New York: Viking.
1949 *King of the Wind.* Marguerite Henry. Chicago: Rand McNally.
1950 *The Door in the Wall.* Marguerite de Angeli. Garden City, N. Y.: Doubleday.
1951 *Amos Fortune, Free Man.* Elizabeth Yates. Aladdin.
1952 *Ginger Pye.* Eleanor Estes. New York: Harcourt Brace Jovanovich.
1953 *Secret of the Andes.* Ann Nolan Clark. New York: Viking.
1954 *. . . And Now Miguel.* Joseph Krumgold. New York: T. Y. Crowell.
1955 *The Wheel on the School.* Meindert De Jong. New York: Harper & Row.
1956 *Carry On, Mr. Bowditch.* Jean Lee Latham. Boston: Houghton Mifflin.
1957 *Miracles on Maple Hill.* Virginia Sorensen. New York: Harcourt Brace Jovanovich.
1958 *Rifles for Watie.* Harold Keith. New York: T. Y. Crowell.
1959 *The Witch of Blackbird Pond.* Elizabeth George Speare. Boston: Houghton Mifflin.
1960 *Onion John.* Joseph Krumgold. New York: T. Y. Crowell.
1961 *Island of the Blue Dolphins.* Scott O'Dell. Boston: Houghton Mifflin.
1962 *The Bronze Bow.* Elizabeth George Speare. Boston: Houghton Mifflin.
1963 *A Wrinkle in Time.* Madeleine L'Engle. New York: Farrar, Straus & Giroux.
1964 *It's Like This Cat.* Emily Neville. New York: Harper & Row.
1965 *Shadow of a Bull.* Maia Wojciechowska. New York: Atheneum.
1966 *I, Juan de Pareja.* Elizabeth (Borten) de Trevino. New York: Farrar, Straus & Giroux.
1967 *Up a Road Slowly.* Irene Hunt. Chicago: Follett.
1968 *From the Mixed-Up Files of Mrs. Basil E. Frankweiler.* E. L. Konigsburg. New York: Atheneum.
1969 *The High King.* Lloyd Alexander. New York: Holt, Rinehart & Winston.
1970 *Sounder.* William Armstrong. New York: Harper & Row.
1971 *The Summer of the Swans.* Betsy Byars. New York: Viking.
1972 *Mrs. Frisby and the Rats of Mimh.* Robert O'Brien. New York: Atheneum.

Caldecott Awards

1938 *Animals of the Bible, a Picture Book.* Illustrated by Dorothy P. Lathrop. Text selected by Helen Dean Fish. Philadelphia: Lippincott.

1939 *Mei Li.* Illustrated and written by Thomas Handforth. Garden City, N. Y.: Doubleday.

1940 *Abraham Lincoln.* Written and illustrated by Ingri and Edgar d'Aulaire. Garden City, N. Y.: Doubleday.

1941 *They Were Strong and Good.* Written and illustrated by Robert Lawson. New York: Viking.

1942 *Make Way for Ducklings.* Written and illustrated by Robert McCloskey. New York: Viking.

1943 *The Little House.* Written and illustrated by Virginia Lee Burton. Boston: Houghton Mifflin.

1944 *Many Moons.* Illustrated by Louis Slobodkin. Written by James Thurber.

1945 *Prayers for a Child.* Illustrated by Elizabeth Orton Jones. Written by Rachael Field. New York: Macmillan.

1946 *The Rooster Crows . . .* Illustrated by Maud and Miska Petersham. New York: Macmillan.

1947 *The Little Island.* Illustrated by Leonard Weisgard. Written by Golden MacDonald (Margaret Wise Brown). Garden City, N. Y.: Doubleday.

1948 *White Snow, Bright Snow.* Illustrated by Roger Duvoisin. Written by Alvin Tresselt. New York: Lothrop, Lee & Shepard.

1949 *The Big Snow.* Written and illustrated by Berta and Elmer Hader. New York: Macmillan.

1950 *Song of the Swallows.* Written and illustrated by Leo Politi. New York: Scribner.

1951 *The Egg Tree.* Written and illustrated by Katherine Milhous. New York: Scribner.

1952 *Finders Keepers.* Illustrated by Nicolas (Nicolas Mordvinoff).

1953 *The Biggest Bear.* Written and illustrated by Lynd Ward. Boston: Houghton Mifflin.

1954 *Madeline's Rescue.* Written and illustrated by Ludwig Bemelmans.

1955 *Cinderella, or the Little Glass Slipper.* Illustrated and translated from Perrault by Marcia Brown. New York: Scribner.

1956 *Frog Went A-Courtin'.* Illustrated by Feodor Rojankovsky. New York: Harcourt Brace Jovanovich.

1957 *A Tree Is Nice.* Illustrated by Marc Simont. Written by Janice May Udry. New York: Harper & Row.

1958 *Time of Wonder.* Written and illustrated by Robert McCloskey. New York: Viking.

1959 *Chanticleer and the Fox.* Adapted from Chaucer's *The Canterbury Tales* and illustrated by Barbara Cooney. New York: T. Y. Crowell.
1960 *Nine Days to Christmas.* Illustrated by Marie Hall Ets. Written by Marie Hall Ets and Aurora Labastida. New York: Viking.
1961 *Baroushka and the Three Kings.* Illustrated by Nicolas Sidjakov. Written by Ruth Robbins. Berkeley, Calif.: Parnassus.
1962 *Once upon a Mouse.* Retold and illustrated by Marcia Brown. New York: Scribner.
1963 *The Snowy Day.* Written and illustrated by Ezra Jack Keats. New York: Viking.
1964 *Where the Wild Things Are.* Written and illustrated by Maurice Sendak. New York: Harper & Row.
1965 *May I Bring a Friend?* Illustrated by Beni Montresor. Written by Beatrice Schenk de Regniers. New York: Atheneum.
1966 *Always Room for One More.* Illustrated by Nonny Hogrogian. Written by Sorche Nic Leodhas. New York: Holt, Rinehart & Winston.
1967 *Sam, Bangs, and Moonshine.* Written and illustrated by Evaline Ness. New York: Holt, Rinehart & Winston.
1968 *Drummer Hoff.* Written and illustrated by Ed Emberly. New York: Prentice-Hall.
1969 *The Fool of the World and the Flying Ship.* Arthur Ransome. New York: Farrar, Straus & Giroux.
1970 *Sylvester and the Magic Pebble.* William Steig. New York: Simon & Schuster.
1971 *A Story, A Story.* Gail E. Haley. New York: Atheneum.
1972 *One Fine Day.* Nonny Hogrogrian. New York: Macmillan.

Laura Ingalls Wilder Award

The Laura Ingalls Wilder Award was first presented in 1954. The award is given every five years to an author or illustrator whose books, published in the United States, have over a period of time made a significant contribution to literature for children. When the award was introduced in 1954 it went to Laura Ingalls Wilder. Recipients since then have been:

1960 Clara Ingram Judson
1965 Ruth Sawyer
1970 E. B. White

National Book Awards

At its annual meeting in 1969 the National Book Awards included for the first time in its twenty-year history a prize for children's literature. The award is contributed by the Children's Book Council and administered by the National Book Committee. The award is presented annually to a juvenile title that a panel of judges considers the most distinguished written by an American citizen and published in the United States in the preceding year.

1969 *Journey from Peppermint Street.* Meindert De Jong. New York: Harper & Row.
1970 *A Day of Pleasure.* Isaac B. Singer. New York: Farrar, Straus & Giroux.
1971 *The Marvelous Misadventures of Sebastian.* Lloyd Alexander. New York: E. P. Dutton.
1972 *The Slightly Irregular Fire Engine, or the Hithering Thithering Djins.* Donald Barthelme. New York: Farrar, Straus & Giroux.

Index